FAMILIES, SCHOOLS, AND COMMUNITIES
Building Partnerships for Educating Children

Third Edition

CHANDLER BARBOUR
Towson University, Emeritus

NITA H. BARBOUR
University of Maryland, Baltimore County, Emerita

PATRICIA A. SCULLY
University of Maryland, Baltimore County

PEARSON

Merrill
Prentice Hall

Upper Saddle River, New Jersey
Columbus, Ohio

Library of Congress Cataloging-in-Publication Data

Barbour, Chandler.
 Families, schools and communities : building partnerships for educating children /
Chandler Barbour, Nita H. Barbour, Patricia A. Scully.—3rd ed.
  p. cm.
 Includes bibliographical references and index.
 ISBN 0-13-112800-0
  1. Home and school—United States. 2. Community and school—United States. 3. School environment—United
States. 4. Students—United States—Social conditions. 5.
Education—Curricula—United States. 6. Child development—United States. I. Barbour,
Nita. II. Scully, Patricia A., 1949–III. Title.

LC225.3.B27 2005
371.19´0973—dc22   2004005210

Vice President and Executive Publisher: Jeffery W. Johnston	**Photo Coordinator:** Kathy Kirtland
Publisher: Kevin M. Davis	**Cover Design:** Ali Mohrman
Editor: Julie Peters	**Cover Image:** SuperStock
Editorial Assistant: Amanda King	**Production Manager:** Laura Messerly
Production Editor: Sheryl Glicker Langener	**Director of Marketing:** Ann Castel Davis
Production Coordination: Wendy Druck, The GTS Companies/York, PA Campus	**Marketing Manager:** Autumn Purdy
	Marketing Coordinator: Tyra Poole
Design Coordinator: Diane C. Lorenzo	

This book was set in Melior by *The GTS Companies*/York, PA Campus. It was printed and bound by R. R. Donnelley & Sons Company. The cover was printed by Coral Graphic Services, Inc.

Photo Credits: Steven Barbour, pp. 12, 54, 108, 117, 125, 127, 138, 180, 189, 198, 273, 315; Keith Brofsky/Getty Images, Inc.–Photodisc, p. 323; Corbis/Bettmann, pp. 27, 35, 41, 49; Scott Cunnigham/Merrill, pp. 46, 69, 135, 214, 277, 291, 307, 341, 352; Laima Druskis/PH College, p. 347; Dan Floss/Merrill, p. 283; Marian Fowler, pp. 57, 145, 169; Tony Freeman/PhotoEdit, p. 24; Jose Galvez/PhotoEdit, p. 98; Getty Images, Inc.—Photodisc, p. 122; Scott Haskell/Bangor Daily News, p. 311; Brenda Haynes, pp. 16, 295; Ken Karp/PH College, p. 113; Belle Kuhn, pp. 6, 285; courtesy of the Library of Congress, p. 36; Anthony Magnacca/Merrill, pp. 185, 254, 266, 320, 339; Valerie Mekras, pp. 1, 193, 203; Lawrence Migdale/Pix, p. 87; Linda Coan O'Kresik/Bangor Daily News, pp. 141, 221; Pearson Learning, p. 261; Mary Jane Porterfield, p. 225; Barbara Schwartz/Merrill, pp. 157, 164, 229, 329; Patricia Scully, pp. 10, 80, 93, 104, 152, 176, 233; Ian Shaw/Getty Images, Inc.—Stone Allstock, p. 22; U.S. Department of the Interior, p. 243; Anne Vega/Merrill, pp. 63, 78, 131, 160, 238, 247, 251, 300; Tom Watson/Merrill, p. 333; Todd Yarrington/Merrill, p. 74; Yellow Dog Productions/Getty Images, Inc.—Image Bank, p. 209.

Pearson Education Ltd.
Pearson Education Singapore Pte. Ltd.
Pearson Education Canada, Ltd.
Pearson Education–Japan

Pearson Education Australia Pty. Limited
Pearson Education North Asia Ltd.
Pearson Educación de Mexico, S.A. de C.V.
Pearson Education Malaysia Pte. Ltd.

10 9 8 7 6 5 4 3 2 1
ISBN: 0-13-112800-0

We dedicate this text edition to our children, our grandchild, and our nieces and nephews who have given us wonderful help and support in our writing efforts and lots of love along the way.—CB & NHB

I dedicate this text edition to my children, Catherine and Jack, who have added delight in my life and new meaning to my work.—PAS

EDUCATOR LEARNING CENTER: AN INVALUABLE ONLINE RESOURCE

Merrill Education and the Association for Supervision and Curriculum Development (ASCD) invite you to take advantage of a new online resource, one that provides access to the top research and proven strategies associated with ASCD and Merrill—the Educator Learning Center. At *www.Educator Learning Center.com* you will find resources that will enhance your students' understanding of course topics and of current educational issues, in addition to being invaluable for further research.

How the Educator Learning Center will help your students become better teachers

With the combined resources of Merrill Education and ASCD, you and your students will find a wealth of tools and materials to better prepare them for the classroom.

Research
- More than 600 articles from the ASCD journal *Educational Leadership* discuss everyday issues faced by practicing teachers.
- A direct link on the site to Research Navigator gives students access to many of the leading education journals, as well as extensive content detailing the research process.
- Excerpts from Merrill Education texts give your students insights on important topics of instructional methods, diverse populations, assessment, classroom management, technology, and refining classroom practice.

Classroom Practice
- Hundreds of lesson plans and teaching strategies are categorized by content area and age range.
- Case studies and classroom video footage provide virtual field experience for student reflection.
- Computer simulations and other electronic tools keep your students abreast of today's classrooms and current technologies.

Look into the value of Educator Learning Center yourself

A four-month subscription to Educator Learning Center is $25 but is **FREE** when used in conjunction with this text. To obtain free passcodes for your students, simply contact your Merrill/Prentice Hall sales representative, and your representative will give you a special ISBN to give your bookstore when ordering your textbooks. To preview the value of this website to you and your students, please go to **www.EducatorLearningCenter.com** and click on "Demo."

Preface

Over 55 million children attend American public and private schools today. In addition, another 20 million preschoolers are growing rapidly in homes, care centers, and communities across our nation. Teachers, social services providers, and administrators, as well as family members, community members, and caregivers of all kinds, have a tremendous responsibility to ensure the most productive education possible for this huge section of the American public, which will be the mainstay of our society in the future. The responsibility is staggering, and, as many know, our success rate in meeting the responsibility is questioned by numerous critics.

Education reform and renewal has surfaced periodically for generations in America, and in recent decades it has been debated by political leaders. Renewal, repair, or reconsideration seems to be on everyone's mind. All candidates for major offices now have an education plan or outline, and while this highlights the urgency in education matters, it also contributes to a zigzag in frequent changes in state and national proposals.

In the 8 years since the first edition of this text, a number of events have unfolded, and all have implications for how we nurture, protect, and educate our children. The face of our world can never be the same again, and most people realize that the requirements for citizens in the 21st century are very different from those of a generation ago. Consider the following developments:

- The dazzling economic picture of the 1990s has dimmed, and financial woes now beset many states and municipalities. The national welfare reform plan of the late 1990s has experienced some successes, but recently, less fortunate results are associated with that reform effort. For one thing, almost one fifth of our children to live in poverty—this figure duplicates statistics for the late 1980s. The denial of adequate health care for this population is even more alarming.

- Globalization in our attitudes as well as our economic base continues to rush forward, even while a significant part of the world is wrapped in warlike conditions. But a number of investigators show that we have more isolation in our society in spite of the growing population and enhanced communication devices. People are keeping more to themselves and social networks are thinner. One disturbing outgrowth of new media is its effect on socialization and human connections to others. Ironically, a society that has encouraged citizens to communicate instanteously with almost anyone on the planet has the sobering quality of removing those same persons from many family and collegial relationships. Social and emotional isolation is on the rise.

- An extraordinary projection of growing isolation comes to us in current literature. In his futuristic novel *Feed*, M. T. Anderson presents us with a sobering view of life in the 22nd century, where schools have become anachronisms because all education, communication, and even motivations are fed to individuals via the microchip implanted in their brains at birth. This scary Orwellian world of the future makes us ponder both the means of achieving a technology to arrive there—and more interestingly, the sacrifices in social and emotional domains required to tolerate that existence. Perhaps this scenario provides an extra incentive for people in the helping professions to study very carefully what makes us human and how we value the social dimensions of our life spaces now.

- Brain research and genetic experiments are providing more answers to nagging questions about development, educational processes, and even parent roles. Marital statistics have changed considerably too. Divorces are less frequent, but so are marriages, and more than 25% of American children are raised in single-parent homes. Definitions for an American family are steadily changing.

- Mass media and electronic communication have created vast new opportunities and challenges for all citizens. The rapid rise of the Internet in the past few years has outdistanced all estimates, and it signals changes in the way Americans will communicate, purchase materials, and access information in the future. Features of our new high-tech world have seized a great deal of time and attention from all young Americans. While a boon for motivation, the virtual worlds now open to youth must be associated in some way to our mainstream society.

- Our federal government, as well as most state governments, is displaying more interest in education and seeks to play a more influential role. The effect of this governmental interest and role is perceived differently by educators, parents, and community leaders.

In addition to all the new and sobering challenges, old demands are still evident in our postindustrial society. Cultural and ethnic diversity is expanding rapidly in the United States, and efforts to address the needs of exceptional children grow each year. Many authorities see good strides in adjusting societal expectations for the greater diversity of America; others point out the need to do more.

All these concerns point to a need to develop education agendas aimed at blending interests, using cooperation to the fullest, and identifying all resources possible for addressing children's educational needs. And most authorities agree that major changes in the procedures and formats of many U.S. schools are needed as never before. For many, the greatest changes focus on drawing more partners into the management of children's formal education. A number of educational collaborations and partnership designs have spread across the United States, and they have served as effective bridges in many school districts. This text moves in a similar direction, and the authors support the designs that emphasize the benefits of collaboration among the many agencies and persons working with our children.

A basic tenet of *Families, Schools, and Communities: Building Partnerships for Educating Children* is that schools will always be a primary venue for educating the young child, and educators must be in the forefront of any endeavor to bring about change. However, the authors stress that to accomplish the tasks at hand, all school districts must develop vibrant partnerships—uniting parents and community members with teachers in educating tomorrow's citizens. Schools are where the action will bloom, but respectful collaboration is the key to success.

Significant steps for improving children's education through collaboration are already being made in schools and communities across the United States. A growing number of research studies, controlled assessments, and personal accounts support new partnership approaches. The authors salute all these efforts. We maintain that most schools do not need to reconceptualize curricula or most of their current teaching practices. The big job now is to study and adapt the amazing examples that already exist.

NEW TO THE THIRD EDITION

New and Expanded Topics. Building on the success of the second edition, we have re-arranged some material and topics to give the text more coherence and usefulness. Users of this text and objective reviewers of our second edition have pointed out areas for amplification. We have increased coverage of the following topics:

- Family diversity (e.g., gay/lesbian parents, biracial families) in America
- Political and governmental involvement in schools
- Effects of media on learning
- Expansion of educational models and programs (Reggio Emilia, charter schools, partnership schools)

Diversity. We have inserted more information on special education, although we realize that the scope for this text serves only as a beginning step for this important area of educational experience. We have added more information on protection of children and included a new section on the grandparent curriculum. We have included more material on diversity in the racial and ethnic makeup of America and the exciting contributions that flow from our country's varied cultural makeup.

Updated References, Resources, and Figures. Because research studies and findings are frequently expanded or replicated, we have also updated a large number of references. We have updated the Resources section in each chapter to include new publications, other media, and websites that we believe will have staying power. New and updated figures and tables in each chapter synthesize information for the reader.

A New Author. Dr. Patricia A. Scully, joined the Barbour and Barbour team in revising the third edition. Dr. Scully, who currently directs the program for preservice early childhood teachers at the University of Maryland, Baltimore County (UMBC), brings a new perspective to the text topics as well as 30 years experience working with early education programs.

ORGANIZATION OF THIS TEXT

We feel it vital for pre-service and in-service teachers as well as other social services providers to acknowledge the numerous influences on children's lives and how the structures of homes and communities affect children's learning in schools. The authors believe that by studying and analyzing this broader scope of curriculum, teachers in training and other young professionals will recognize the crucial educative forces of family, peer group, and community.

The vignettes about children's experiences in all the chapters, plus the model programs outlined in Chapter 12, serve to bring the text messages closer to reality.

We begin this text with an overview of the powerful influences surrounding all young children. Along with this, we identify the three primary social settings of home life, school life, and community life and discuss how these settings interplay to affect children's lives. Society does change, of course, and some forces influencing children have intensified in recent years. We categorize these influence patterns so that readers will gain a better perspective of what exists in the United States today.

Chapter 2 focuses on (a) how responsibilities for children's education emerged over time, (b) the range of philosophies and perspectives that have appeared in American education, and (c) how different ethnic groups in the United States have been affected educationally for more than three centuries. We look particularly at the uneven progress of collaborations associated with schoolwork.

Chapters 3 and 4 present information on U.S. family life, and the authors review various family patterns and clarify the different ways in which families function. The information there will help prospective teachers grasp the range of situations that professionals encounter as they work with children in a diverse society. Our hope is that readers will appreciate our urging of more collaborations in light of this diversity.

Chapter 5 is devoted to the expanding out-of-home care programs for the millions of preschool-aged children as well as young school-aged children. Far more mothers have joined the American workforce and must now find adequate care for their preschool-aged children and their in-school children who need care during after-school hours. We discuss the various child care arrangements and practices as well as the agency-directed preschool programs that a growing number of young children encounter.

Chapter 6 examines the responsibilities of parents and professionals in each of the three social settings. In this section we point out the various educational assignments and expectations that each setting places on the others.

Chapters 7, 8, and 9 deal with curriculum in the three social settings. Curriculum surrounds children, and though we do not always take notice of it, much of what children learn comes from the world outside the classroom. The reader must recognize that all citizens are educators and that when teachers acknowledge this, an even greater potential for learning exists.

Users will note that the authors have merged two chapters at the end of the text. Both dealt with examples and models of collaborative ventures, and we feel that combining them strengthens the organization of the book.

The last three chapters focus on the possibilities for collaboration among the three social settings. Chapter 10 highlights effective social settings and extends ideas about the ingredients for developing partnerships. In Chapter 11, we discuss traditional as well as new ways for teachers, parents, and others to work together. Chapter 12 examines the demanding and often difficult process of merging the efforts of people interested in collaboration. In this final chapter we present five successful models that demonstrate collaboration. The authors believe that these time-tested programs can provide a good template for agencies and communities seeking to marshall efforts to arrive at healthy partnerhsips.

Appendix I for the third edition is an extensive bibliography of children's books to help make the family, school, and community diversity presented in this text more pertinent and meaningful.

Appendix II presents the Code of Ethical Conduct that the NAEYC (National Association for the Education of Young Children) promulgates. The authors consider this a foundation for the text thesis.

SPECIAL FEATURES

To assist instructors and students using this text, we have included several pedagogical aids.

Chapter Objectives, Implications, and Summaries. Concise statements of each chapter's main ideas serve as advance organizers for the content that follows. In addition, we have placed a brief section near the end of each chapter that urges the reader to reflect on and personalize the chapter information. This "Implications for Professionals" section is designed to increase understanding by relating text to self. A chapter summary reviews the highlights of the content in each chapter.

Vignettes. Depictions of real-life events that the authors have encountered clarify many concepts throughout the text chapters. The children in the vignettes represent a wide range of ethnic and socioeconomic families, and they live in a variety of geographic areas. These personal stories are all from the authors' experiences (except the names used) and give a human connection to the chapter information and purpose.

Suggested Activities and Questions. Each chapter ends with questions and activities that give instructors another means to make the text applicable to their course outlines and to students' lives. For students, the activities will help apply concepts presented and will stimulate reflection and discussion on the reading as well as their own experiences. In addition, an instructor's manual extends the activities and questions for processing the chapter information and concepts.

Resources. No text can give comprehensive coverage to the diverse topics included here, for community workers or teacher candidates. All instructors will supplement this content with their specialized knowledge, particular readings, and projects. The authors present a framework that points to ways that material can be organized and processed. To underscore this point, we give a number of resources in each chapter.

In addition to citing extensive references within the text and featuring tables and figures that encapsulate text content, we list particular titles at the end of each chapter to allow for a more thorough examination of text content. We also have extended the third edition chapters with other resources: (a) up-to-date films and videos to provide another medium for the chapter concepts, (b) lists of key organizations and agencies that relate to the profession, and (c) several Web sites that will give current status reports for our chapter features.

Bibliography of Children's Literature. The selections in the children's book section (Appendix I) depict valuable examples of children in different family arrangements learning in a variety of settings. This updated bibliography provides instructors as well as in-service teachers and other professionals with curriculum material to illuminate the chapter content. It will be particularly valuable for Chapters 3, 4, 5, 7, 8, and 9.

Glossary. Because the text draws from sociology, psychology, human development, and anthropology as well as from pedagogy and curriculum content, we include a glossary to help readers with specialized terms.

ACKNOWLEDGMENTS

Many people assisted in providing content and in assembling this text. We would like to acknowledge particularly the following individuals: Janel Hino for unflagging support and encouragement; Valerie Mekras for supplying background material and references on special-needs programs and photos for several sections; UMBC colleagues, Mary Rivkin and Barbara Bourne, for good counsel; Audrey Jewett for providing research on materials and retrieval of children's literature topics; and Steven Barbour for supplying numerous photos plus suggestions for illuminating several text sections.

Many thanks go to our professional colleagues, several classroom teachers, and several parents who willingly supplied photos to illustrate our text. Library personnel at the University of Maine and at the University of Maryland, Baltimore County, have been patient, helpful, and supportive in filling numerous requests and supplying materials in a timely fashion.

We wish to thank Julie Peters, our associate editor at Merrill/Prentice Hall, for her guidance for this text. We also thank Anne Mattson and Wendy Druck, our production editors at The GTS Companies/York, and Christopher Thornton, our copyeditor, for their many valuable contributions. Several individuals reviewed the second edition of this text and made valuable comments and suggestions to improve this third edition. We thank them here: Susan Matoba Adler, University of Illinois, Urbana–Champaign; Rena Hallam, University of Kentucky; Linda Koehler, Central Missouri State University; Anne Raybin, State University of New York, Stony Brook; and Sharon Rosenkoetter, Oregon State University.

Discover the Companion Website Accompanying This Book

THE PRENTICE HALL COMPANION WEBSITE: A VIRTUAL LEARNING ENVIRONMENT

Technology is a constantly growing and changing aspect of our field that is creating a need for content and resources. To address this emerging need, Prentice Hall has developed an online learning environment for students and professors alike—Companion Websites—to support our textbooks.

In creating a Companion Website, our goal is to build on and enhance what the textbook already offers. For this reason, the content for each user-friendly website is organized by topic and provides the professor and student with a variety of meaningful resources. Common features of a Companion Website include:

For the Professor—

Every Companion Website integrates **Syllabus Manager**™, an online syllabus creation and management utility.

- **Syllabus Manager**™ provides you, the instructor, with an easy, step-by-step process to create and revise syllabi, with direct links into Companion Website and other online content without having to learn HTML.

- Students may logon to your syllabus during any study session. All they need to know is the web address for the Companion Website and the password you've assigned to your syllabus.

- After you have created a syllabus using **Syllabus Manager**™, students may enter the syllabus for their course section from any point in the Companion Website.

- Clicking on a date, the student is shown the list of activities for the assignment. The activities for each assignment are linked directly to actual content, saving time for students.

- Adding assignments consists of clicking on the desired due date, then filling in the details of the assignment—name of the assignment, instructions, and whether or not it is a one-time or repeating assignment.

- In addition, links to other activities can be created easily. If the activity is online, a URL can be entered in the space provided, and it will be linked automatically in the final syllabus.

- Your completed syllabus is hosted on our servers, allowing convenient updates from any computer on the Internet. Changes you make to your syllabus are immediately available to your students at their next logon.

For the Student—

- **Introduction**—General information about the topic and how it will be covered in the website.
- **Web Links**—A variety of websites related to topic areas.
- **Timely Articles**—Links to online articles that enable you to become more aware of important issues in early childhood.

- **Learn by Doing**—Put concepts into action, participate in activities, examine strategies, and more.
- **Visit a School**—Visit a school's website to see concepts, theories, and strategies in action.
- **For Teachers/Practitioners**—Access information you will need to know as an educator, including information on materials, activities, and lessons.
- **Observation Tools**—A collection of checklists and forms to print and use when observing and assessing children's development.
- **Current Policies and Standards**—Find out the latest early childhood policies from the government and various organizations, and view state, federal, and curriculum standards.
- **Resources and Organizations**—Discover tools to help you plan your classroom or center and organizations to provide current information and standards for each topic.
- **Electronic Bluebook**—Paperless method of completing homework or essays assigned by a professor. Finished work can be sent to the professor via email.
- **Message Board**—Virtual bulletin board to post and respond to questions and comments from a national audience.

To take advantage of these and other resources, please visit the *Families, Schools and Communities: Building Partnerships for Educating Children* Third Edition, Companion Website at
www.prenhall.com/barbour

Brief Contents

CHAPTER 1
Home, School, and Community
Influences on Children's Lives   1

CHAPTER 2
Historical and Philosophical
Perspectives   27

CHAPTER 3
Viewing Family Diversity   57

CHAPTER 4
Parenting the Child   87

CHAPTER 5
Meeting Child Care Needs From
Infancy Through School Age   117

CHAPTER 6
Responsibility for Educating
and Protecting Children   141

CHAPTER 7
Curriculum of the Home   169

CHAPTER 8
Curriculum of the School   203

CHAPTER 9
Curriculum of the Community   233

CHAPTER 10
Effective Social and Cultural
Settings for Learning   261

CHAPTER 11
Traditional and Innovative Strategies
for Working Together   291

CHAPTER 12
Models for Parent–School–Community
Partnerships   323

APPENDIX I   359
Bibliography of Children's Books   359

APPENDIX II   365
NAEYC Code of Ethical Conduct   365

GLOSSARY   373

REFERENCES   383

INDEX   409

Contents

CHAPTER 1
Home, School, and Community
Influences on Children's Lives   **1**

Children's Perceptions and Attitudes   4
 Home Influence on Attitudes
  and Perceptions   5
 School Influence on Attitudes
  and Perceptions   6
 Community Influence on Attitudes and
  Perceptions   8
Age Levels and Influence   9
 The Early Years—Strong
  Home Influence   9
 Preschool and Kindergarten
  Years—Increasing School Influence   13
 Primary Years—Growing
  Community Influence   14
 Peer Group Influence   15
Media Influence   16
 Print Materials   18
 Television   19
 The Entertainment Industry   21
Special-Interest-Group Influence   22
Implications for Professionals   24

CHAPTER 2
Historical and Philosophical
Perspectives   **27**

Overview of Philosophical Viewpoints   28
Historical Patterns   32
Family as a Significant Educational Force   34
Community as a Significant
 Educational Force   36
School as a Significant Educational Force   38
 Parent Involvement in Schools   39
 Federal Government Involvement   41
 Goals 2000 and New Federal Directions   42
 Partnerships and Collaborations   43

Children with Specific Needs   44
 Children in Poverty   44
 Children with Disabilities   45
 Minority Populations   47
Multicultural Emphasis   51
 Attitude Change   52
 Staffing Patterns   52
 Curriculum and Teaching Materials   52
 Interaction Patterns   53
Implications for Professionals   53

CHAPTER 3
Viewing Family Diversity   **57**

Different Types of Families   61
 Nuclear Families   61
 Extended Families   61
 Single-Parent Families   62
 Blended Families   64
 Adoptive Families   64
 Subfamilies   64
 Foster Families   64
 Gay and Lesbian Families   65
 Other Family Groupings   65
Social Factors Relating to Families   66
 Racial, Ethnic, and Cultural Factors   66
 Minority Status   67
 Limited-English-Proficiency Families   68
 Biracial and Interethnic Families   69
Socioeconomic Status of Families   70
 Historic Class Descriptions   70
 The Underclass—A New Dimension   71
 Economics and American Families   72
 Effects of Economics   76
Families with Children with Special
 Needs   77
Religious Orientation   77
 Applications of Religion   79
Changes in Contemporary Families   80
Implications for the Professional   83

CHAPTER 4
Parenting the Child   87

Nurturance in Families   88
   Range of Child Rearing   88
   Features of Positive Nurturance   89
Family Roles   91
   Economic Support   91
   Emotional Support   92
   Socialization   92
   Educational Underpinnings   95
   Changes in Functions for the
     21st Century   96
Cultural Patterns and Family Functions   96
   Parenting Features in Various
     Cultures   97
Interaction Styles Within Families   100
   Baumrind's Classification   100
   White's Study   101
   Bernstein's Work   101
   Hart and Risley Studies   103
Experiences of Families   104
   Skill Levels and Experience   105
   Mobility of Families   106
Other Influences on Parenting   107
   Child Care Arrangements   107
   Stress in Families   108
Competent Families   113
Implications for Professionals   114

CHAPTER 5
Meeting Child Care Needs from Infancy
Through School Age   117

History of Child Care   119
   Government Remedies   120
   State Standards   121
Child Care Needs in the United States
   Today   121
   Trends in Child Care   122
   Concerns About Child Care   123
Child Care Arrangements   124
   In-Home Child Care   125
   Family Child Care   126
   Child Care Centers   126
   Other Programs   129

Child Care Regulations and Voluntary
   Accreditation   129
Features of Quality Child Care   130
   Structural Elements   131
   Process Elements   132
   Characteristics of Quality Child Care   134
   Effects of Quality Child Care   136
Quality, Affordability, and Other Issues   136
   Questions About Quality   136
   Financial Considerations   136
   Other Issues   137
   Implications for Professionals   139

CHAPTER 6
Responsibility for Educating and
Protecting Children   141

Young Children's Learning   143
   Components of Home Responsibility   144
   Components of School Responsibility   147
   Components of Community
     Responsibility   148
   Linking Responsibilities   154
Nurturing Educational Opportunity   155
   Families and Nurturance   155
   Schools and Nurturance   158
   Communities and Nurturance   159
Governance of Education   160
   Legal Requirements   161
   Home Governance   162
   School Governance   163
   Community Governance   164
Implications for Professionals   165

CHAPTER 7
Curriculum of the Home   169

Learning Roles and Responsibilities   171
   Parents Foster Roles and
     Responsibilities   171
   Extended Family Fosters Roles and
     Rituals   174
   Siblings Aid in Role and Gender
     Identification   175
Physical Environments of the Home   177
   Space Influences Emotional Growth   177

*Space Influences Intellectual
    Development   177*
*Space Influences Physical and Creative
    Development   178*
Home Learning   179
    Daily Routines   179
    Rituals and Traditions   184
    Sharing Interests and Skills   184
    Family Outreach   187
Grandparents Provide a Curriculum   190
    *Grandparents Influence Children's
        Development   191*
    *Advantages of Grandparent
        Curriculum   194*
Home Schooling   195
    History of Home Schooling   195
    Motives for Home Schooling   196
    Who Does Home Schooling?   196
    *Teaching Methods in Home
        Schooling   197*
    Legal Aspects of Home Schooling   199
    *Criticisms and Successes of Home
        Schools   199*
Implications for Professionals   200

CHAPTER 8
Curriculum of the School   203

Overall Program of the School   205
Preschool and Child Care Programs   206
Curriculum Orientations   207
    Traditional   208
    Constructivist   211
    Personal Relevance   212
Organizing Schools   213
    Staffing Plans   214
    Physical Organization   218
Curriculum Forms   218
    Formal Curriculum   220
    Informal Curriculum   224
    *Hidden Curriculum in Homes,
        Schools, and Communities   225*
    *Special Education and
        Curriculum   227*
Results of School Educative Processes   229
Implications for Professionals   230

CHAPTER 9
Curriculum of the Community   233

Community Structure Affects Curriculum   235
    Service Agencies   237
    Transportation Services   238
    Political Agencies   239
    Social and Cultural Agencies   241
    *Business and Commercial
        Enterprises   244*
    Media Forms and Configurations   245
Physical, Social, and Emotional
    Environments in a Community   248
    Social Networks   248
    Ethnic Community Contributions   252
    Natural Environments   253
Interactions Among Community
    Agencies, Families, and Schools   255
Implications for Professionals   257

CHAPTER 10
Effective Social and Cultural
Settings for Learning   261

Competent Families   263
    Organization and Management   264
    Beliefs and Value Structures   265
    Literary and Intellectual Stimuli   265
    *Parental Knowledge of Child
        Development   268*
    Health and Nutrition   268
    *Consistent Social and Emotional
        Environments   270*
Effective Schools   271
    Student Achievement   271
    Values and Beliefs   273
    *Provision for Individual Differences
        and Inclusion   274*
    Positive School Features   275
    Barriers for Effective Schools   276
    Changes in Schools   278
    National Goals and Standards   278
    Evaluating Schools   279
Effective Communities   281
    Community Organization   281
    Social Networks   284

Effective Partnerships   286
    Schools as Brokers for Social Settings   286
    Programs for Teacher Preparation   287
Implications for Professionals   287

CHAPTER 11
Traditional and Innovative Strategies
for Working Together   291

Establishing Relationships with Families   293
    Tools for Early Contacts   293
    Formal and Informal Classroom Visits   294
    Home Visits   295
Establishing Ongoing Communication
    with Parents   296
    Informal Contacts   297
    Written Communication   297
    Parent–Teacher Conferences   299
    Keys to Effective Communication   303
Parents in the Schools   304
    School Visitation   304
    Parents as Aides or Volunteers   306
    Parents and Community Members
        as School Resources   308
    Parents as Advocates   309
    Parent Education   309
Community Involvement   311
    Trips Into the Community   311
    Community as the Resource for
        Materials   312
    Involving the Business Community   313
Working with Selected Families   313
    Children with Disabilities   314
    Ethnic Diversity   315
    Homeless and Migrant Families   316
    Children of Gay and Lesbian Parents   317
Handling Collaborative Relationships   317
    Conditions for Positive Relationships   317
    Barriers to Good Relationships   318
Implications for Professionals   320

CHAPTER 12
Models for Parent–School–Community
Partnerships   323

Levels of Involvement in Collaborations   325
    Understanding Involvement   326

Components of Successful Change   328
    Planning   329
    Implementation   329
    Assessment   330
    Communication   330
    Features of Successful Collaboration   330
Program Models   331
    Head Start   331
    Comer's School Development
        Program   335
    Reggio Emilia   340
    National Network of Partnership
        Schools   345
    Guiding Principles   347
    Charter Schools   350
    Critical Features of Partnerships   354
Achieving Partnerships   354
    Individual Responsibility   354
Implications for Professionals   355

APPENDIX I   359
Bibliography of Children's Books   359

Different Cultures   359
Divorced Families   360
Blended Families   361
Single-Parent Household and Special
    Relationship with One Parent or
    with Grandparents   361
Adoptive Families   362
Foster Care, Orphanages, and Shelters   362
Multigenerational Households
    and Extended Families   362
Homeless Families   363
Migrant Workers and Immigrants   363
Gay and Lesbian Families   363
Children, Family Members, and Friends with
    Special Needs   364
Defining Families   364

APPENDIX II   365
NAEYC Code of Ethical Conduct   365

Core Values   365
Conceptual Framework   365
Ethical Dilemmas Always Exist   366
Ethical Responsibilities to Children   366

Contents

Ethical Responsibilities to Families   367
Ethical Responsibilities to Colleagues   368
 A—Responsibilities to co-workers   *368*
 B—Responsibilities to employers   *369*
 C—Responsibilities to employees   *369*
Ethical Responsibilities to Community
 and Society   370
Statement of Commitment   371
 To the best of my ability I will   *371*

GLOSSARY   **373**

REFERENCES   **383**

INDEX   **409**

NOTE: Every effort has been made to provide accurate and current Internet information in this book. However, the Internet and information posted on it are constantly changing, and it is inevitable that some of the Internet addresses listed in this textbook will change.

Home, School, and Community Influences on Children's Lives

There was a child went forth every day, And the first object he looked upon and received with wonder or pity or love or dread, that object he became, And that object became part of him for the day or a certain part of the day . . . or for many years or stretching cycles of years.

(Whitman, 1855, p. 90)

This beginning chapter highlights the many ways in which young children's learning, behaviors, and viewpoints are affected by family members, school personnel, and members of the immediate community and forces in the larger community. In reading this chapter you will learn the following:

1. How the three social settings—home, school, and community, including children's peer groups—affect children's perceptions and attitudes about learning and success in their schooling.

2. How these three **social settings** have greater or lesser impact depending on the child's age, stage of development, and the social context.

3. How various forms of media, including the entertainment industry, exert enormous influence on children and how that influence affects children's attitudes, learning, and behavior.

4. What the impact of special interest groups can be on children's perception of their world and on their behavior.

Zach was waiting impatiently at the child care center for his mother to pick him up. He looked in his "cubbie" for the big green fists—a gift from his father during last week's visit. Zach picked up the vibrating Incredible Hulk Hands from his backpack, where he had left them on arriving at the center and approached Kelsey, also waiting for her mother. He grinned, and in his deepest voice, he said, "I'm warning you, if you don't tell me where you
planted the bomb, I'm going to clobber you," and he lunged at Kelsey. "No, I won't tell. We'll all blow up," giggled Kelsey, entering into the play and holding up her fists to Zach. The children jabbed at each other, growling and hissing until Zach accidentally struck Kelsey's head, and Kelsey began to cry. At that moment, Zach's mother and the teacher entered the room. The teacher, calming Kelsey, said to Zach's mother, "We don't allow aggressive play here at the center. I really wish you wouldn't let Zach bring toys like that."*

In spite of Zach's attempt to explain what had happened, his tired mother, while she got ready to go out, informed him that he couldn't watch television. When they reached home, she let Zach select Three Billy Goats Gruff and Max's Dragon Shirt to read while he waited for his father to pick him up. When Tom, Zach's mother's boyfriend, arrived, Zach asked him to read. As Tom got to the first little goat crossing the bridge, Zach exclaimed, "Oh, let me read the troll part," and pulling the book closer, asked, "Is this where the troll speaks?"

"Yeah, how did you know?" Tom exclaimed.

Zach replied, "Dad told me," and then, in a gruff, "pretend read" voice, demanded, "Who's that tramping on my bridge?" At each goat's passing, his voice got gruffer, and he clenched his fist as he told the goats he was going to eat them up. When the third goat passed, Tom, in character, gave Zach a gentle push, hugging and tickling him as the "goat" pushed the troll into the river. Zach giggled and said, "Let's read it again, and I'll be the goats this time." When Zach got to the third goat part, he butted Tom, who pulled Zach off the couch with him, "falling into the river." A bit of horseplay ensued. Zach then got up and said, "Now, let's read Max's Dragon Shirt. *You know, I'm gonna ask my dad to buy me a dragon shirt like that. Isn't it wild?"*

All children are constantly developing, and their development is a result of both genetic and environmental factors. Throughout the 20th century, researchers debated the importance of each factor and attempted to determine which aspect exerted the greatest influence. Up through the 1980s, most authorities credited social and environmental factors as exerting the most influence, but we find far more appreciation of a **bidirectional process** since that time (Maccoby, 2002).

One feature often ignored in these development studies was the role children played in their own growth. The important role children play in their own development has been underscored by **interactionist–constructionist theories** of development and even extended by **cultural–context theories**. Bronfenbrenner's **bioecological theory** maintains that there are multiple contexts (physical, mental, social, and historical) affecting a child's growth and development. The interactions between the child, other people, objects, and symbols in these contexts unleashes the child's genetic potential to produce many and varied changes (Ceci & Hembrooke, 1995). Current brain research further supports this **transactional process of development** (Bruer, 1998). In the preceding vignette, you can see that Zach's development is being influenced by the ways in which he interacts with the experiences and episodes in his life.

Experiences of one kind or another bombard the **perceptual field** of any child, constantly influencing learning and development (Sameroff, 1993), for better or worse. Zach's feelings and attitudes toward aggressive behavior, as well as his reading habits, are influenced by his interactions at school, at home, and in his community and by what he witnesses through the media.

The messages children receive from their surroundings aren't always consistent, but all still influence attitudes and values. One can't be sure, for example, exactly what Zach is internalizing. It appears that his attitude toward reading is positive and that he is getting similar messages from those close to him. Reading appears to be fun; people answer his questions about the text and respond to his reactions to the story. Though his mother denied him television that day, she allowed him to select books to entertain himself.

The messages Zach receives about aggression, though, may not be as consistent. Zach's father buys him toys that represent aggression, but the **child care** center bans them. In spite of the ban, his friend Kelsey seems to share in his "aggressive-acting behavior," at least until she is hurt. The mother attempts to reinforce the school's nonaggressive policy by forbidding television temporarily and by suggesting a more passive activity. Still, Zach finds acceptance of his need to express aggression by reenacting a story with his mother's friend and engaging in horseplay.

As a teacher or community worker, you cannot ensure that all the influences impacting children are positive, so you must be sensitive to the idea that children's learning will be affected both positively and negatively by many factors beyond your control. You must also be attuned to your own feelings and reactions, as these, too, affect children's growth.

As you identify the strengths of **family,** media, and community influences, you should strive to build on these qualities. When outside influences or your own disposition adversely affects children's learning, attempt to counter some of the dissonance and the negative effects. Figure 1–1 shows the relative

Figure 1–1   Social setting influences according to age.
Note: Percentages show the waking-hours experience of composite American children. The increasing influence of school and community relates to other factors in addition to age, for example, stage of development, location, family socioeconomic status, and extent of contact.
Source: Adapted from Berns, 2000; Douville-Watson & Watson, 2002; Woolfolk, 2000.

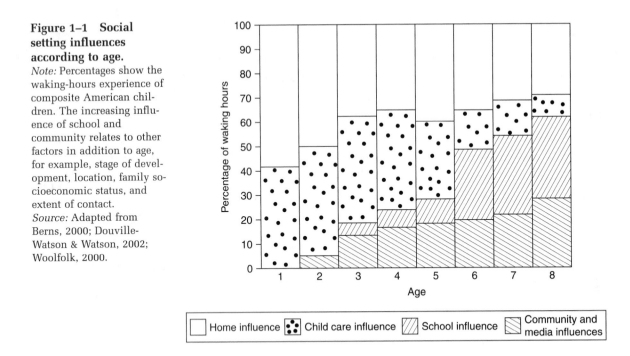

influence on children of their home, school, and community experiences.

CHILDREN'S PERCEPTIONS AND ATTITUDES

Attitudes determine what individuals attend to in a situation, how they perceive the situation, and even their response to the event. Children acquire certain attitudes by hearing words, observing actions, and surmising the feelings of significant others in their environment. These attitudes then become more firm when children are encouraged to express such beliefs. Adult attitudes result from perceptions sustained over years.

Attitudes change, of course, but those demonstrated at any one time affect those children exposed to them. How parents or teachers view their roles will affect the socialization and learning of children under their supervision (Ecksel, 1992). For example, at early ages, children are aware of their fam-

ily's and community's attitudes regarding education, other cultures, racial or religious groups, and roles that males and females play in society (Coleman, 1996; Sadker & Sadker, 1995).

The impact of parental behaviors and attitudes is not linear with regard to children's development. In fact, children are actively involved in their own development. As they change over time, there is a dynamic and continuous process between children and their parents and environment (Deiner, 1997). During the child's infancy, parents respond to the child's perceived need level. As babies respond and develop trust, they begin to sense control over self, and thus interaction patterns are established (Bornstein, 2002). Over time, both parent and child attitudes and behaviors change, and these influences and interactions affect the child's intellectual ability. Clearly, children's early experiences form a foundation for helping them cope with change (Bornstein, 2002).

Home Influence on Attitudes and Perceptions

Children's attitudes from home influences develop early. Family members communicate to even very young children how they feel about themselves and their neighbors and about their schools and community.

Mrs. Kohl was astonished when her 3-year-old, Brittany, spat at Mrs. Foster, an older woman. Mrs. Kohl didn't remember that the day before, when Mrs. Foster knocked at the apartment door, she had told her husband not to answer, saying, "I'm tired of the old hag coming around, nosing in our business, and always borrowing something. I feel like spitting, she annoys me so." When Brittany's mother took her to her room as punishment, the child said defiantly, "I spit. She old hag."

At this point, it may be just Mrs. Foster that Brittany has antipathy for, but continued negative attitudes expressed by her parents and others toward older persons will affect the child's acceptance and attitude toward older persons' presence, interactions, and authority.

Parental attitudes and feelings will influence their children's feelings about school in similar ways. The annual Gallup–Phi Delta Kappa polls (Rose & Gallup, 2002) over the past quarter century show that on the whole, Americans value their local schools and have confidence in them. But we find vast differences throughout the country in the faith that individuals have for schooling in general. Parents communicate this faith, or lack thereof, to their children and thus influence how their children react to their teachers, to their learning experiences, and even to attending school.

A few years later, Mrs. Kohl and her neighbor Mrs. Reed received letters stating that their daughters would be in Mrs. Owens's kindergarten. Reactions in the two households differed, and each affected the children's feelings about school. Mrs. Reed was delighted. Turning to her daughter, she said. "Oh, Sammie, you're going to love school! Mrs. Owens was my teacher, and you'll just love all the fun things you'll do in class."

Mrs. Kohl, on the other hand, felt quite different. She expressed her thoughts to her husband in her daughter's presence, "Rats, Brittany has that old Mrs. Owens. I was hoping she'd get the new young teacher." It was no wonder the two children reacted differently when they met at the bus stop on the first day of school. Samantha jumped up and down and grabbed Brittany's hand as she ran toward the stopped bus, saying, "Oh, we're going to have so much fun." But Brittany pushed her away and refused to get on the bus. No amount of cajoling from the adults could convince her that she should get on. Mrs. Kohl was forced to drive Brittany to school for several days before the child would take the bus with her friend.

Initially, both children appear to be responding to their parental attitudes as they viewed and responded to schooling. It is also difficult to determine what caused the change in Brittany. School may have been fun, and she may have started to enjoy her teacher. Or, perhaps her peers influenced her thinking on "how one ought to go to school."

Parental attitudes, interests, and involvement regarding such things as home organization, disposition toward work, or attitudes toward reading provide models for children's interests and involvement. Because young children learn by manipulating their environment, we can see that how parents and caregivers organize their surroundings affects children's intellectual development. Researchers (Sigel, Dreyev, & McGillicuddy-DeLisi,

Even very young children respond positively to books when significant adults engage them in literacy interactions

1984) have found strong positive correlations between higher IQ scores and child interaction in environments rich with appropriate materials and space. Coleman (1991) pointed out that children whose parents stress the importance of good work habits, punctuality, and task completion carry these traits over into their schoolwork and have greater academic success.

Since Durkin's (1966) classic study of the commonality of influences on early readers, other studies relating to the effect of home environment and parental perceptions of literacy development indicate that parental attitudes and modeling regarding reading with young children are critical factors in children's development. Adults engage in literacy events with their children in nearly all homes (Heath, 1983; Teale, 1986), but considerable differences exist in adults' attitudes toward the importance of books and in the ways in which adults interact around literacy events (Bus & Van Ijzendoorn, 1995; Paratore, 2001). Children respond more positively to books when they engage in a greater amount of literacy in-

teraction with adults and when the adults believe in the importance of these interactions (Clay, 1991; Leland & Kasten, 2002). Readers will find a fuller examination of parenting skills and practices in Chapter 4.

School Influence on Attitudes and Perceptions

Even though the thesis is questioned by some (Harris, 2002; Rowe, 1994) most developmentalists agree that parental attitudes have been a major effect on children's learning and acceptance of school (Borkowski, Ramey, & Stile, 2002). In turn, school personnel attitudes affect how children learn. Research by the Institute for Responsive Education regarding educators' attitudes toward low-income parents shows that many didn't expect low-income parents to be productive participants in their children's education and, in turn, that those parents felt that their participation wouldn't have much effect and therefore often had negative attitudes toward the schools (Heleen, 1990). Children internalize these attitudes of mutual disrespect. Children's self-worth is diminished or enhanced as the children sense how school personnel view the lifestyle and culture of their families, and these attitudes can breed tolerance or intolerance for others.

In the following vignette, Camille and Helen reacted differently to a bus driver's careless words, but both were distressed.

Camille and Helen arrived at their homes upset over a comment their bus driver had made. There were empty cans on the bus, and the driver said, "Don't touch them cans. I just drove a bunch of Black kids on a trip, and they aren't clean." Camille exclaimed to her mother, "But I ride the bus everyday. Does he think I'm not clean 'cause I'm Black?"

Helen's distress was similar, but from a different perspective. "We had to ride the bus after a bunch of Black kids today, and they left it dirty. Ugh!" Both Camille and Helen could have misinterpreted the bus driver's words, but their attitudes about self and others were affected by the driver's careless speech.

Teachers can't prevent what happened to Camille or Helen. They can only be alert to problems and provide an emotional climate that accepts all children regardless of their ethnic or social class standing. They must be cognizant of how their own words and actions can bring to pass the self-fulfilling prophecies noted long ago by Rosenthal and Jacobson (1968).

Rosenthal and Jacobson advance the notion that teachers' expectations of children result in self-fulfilling prophecies and that children who teachers perceive as capable and intelligent will do much better than those children whom teachers do not perceive to be capable. In this classic study, first and second graders appeared to be most subjected to their teachers' attitudes. Studies conducted in the 1970s, 1980s, and 1990s continue to show that children are affected by their teachers' perceptions of them and react both behaviorally and academically according to their teachers' expectations (Gallego & Cole, 2001; Proctor, 1984).

In grade school, girls are likely to do better academically than boys (Tittle, 1986), but by the time students graduate from high school, boys score higher on **SAT** tests (Sadker & Sadker, 1995). Some researchers suggest that the reason for this is that teachers treat boys and girls differently. Researchers have noted that as early as preschool, girls are inclined to select activities with more rules, guidelines, and suggestions for accomplishing the task, while boys tend to select activities allowing for more open-ended behavior. Being rewarded for such behavior, girls tend to become more compliant and boys become more assertive (Eccles, Wigfield, Harold, & Blumenfeld, 1993). As children progress through school, these reinforced behaviors get boys more attention, more opportunities for classroom discussion, and more specific guidelines as to the correctness of their responses. Girls are called on less often than are boys, are asked to raise their hands, are given less feedback on their responses, and are encouraged to listen rather than to participate. Girls tend to be praised for their neatness, while boys receive praise for academic contributions. Consequently, girls get the message that their academic responses are not important (Sadker & Sadker, 2003). Because in elementary school achievement is often measured on tasks that require skill mastery, girls, reinforced for obeying the rules, can be expected to do better than boys, but as children progress and school success depends more on problem solving and assertiveness, boys, having been reinforced for more aggressive behavior, can be expected to outperform girls (Sadker & Sadker, 1995; Tittle, 1986).

Teachers also may discriminate against children of different ethnic and ability groups by treating them differently, as a result of their expectations for different children's performance (Bartoleme & Macedo, 1997; Ogbu, 1994). Teachers are likely to give high achievers and majority-culture children more opportunities to respond, more praise, and more time to formulate a response. Teachers who perceive minority children to be low achievers do not expect them to know answers and do not give them as many opportunities or as much encouragement to respond. Such differential treatment over time lowers children's involvement in school and may prevent their developing confidence in their abilities (Dilworth & Brown, 2001; Hrabowski, Maton, & Greif, 1998).

Community Influence on Attitudes and Perceptions

Community influence on children's attitudes varies because of the different perspectives held by the organizations within a community as well as the interactions of individual citizens. Bronfenbrenner (1986, 1993) points out that a community's influence on children's growth and development will be from both **formal** and **informal community structures.** Influence from formal structures comes from political and social systems, health and recreational services, business enterprises, entertainment, and educational services. The informal structures are the social networks that each family establishes with people outside the home. Members of many communities hold common attitudes toward their local schools, as evidenced by communitywide political support for various activities, in linkages established with other community organizations, and in news coverage by local media.

It is difficult to measure the actual effect of community attitudes on student achievement, but we know that children quickly assimilate attitudes expressed by adults around them. Research suggests that a community's

social climate and the personal relationships that children form within the community influence their attitudes about learning (Hoffer & Coleman, 1990). For example, if school sports activities are highlighted in the media coverage and the teams get money for trips but the school librarian can't buy children's literature for the library, children soon get the message that being a good athlete is more important than being a good reader. When a community paper publishes the poems, stories, and artwork of local primary school children, children understand that the community values their academic achievements. Primary-school children are less likely to make such direct connections to community attitudes toward their schools, but they get excited about winning a pizza for reading a certain number of books. Eventually, they get a message that reading is important.

Businesspeople often provide support for various school programs. Sometimes children witness that support and learn that important people value learning. When children hear the local grocer, businessperson, or politician comment on the positive qualities of teachers, they learn that others value the learning experiences these teachers provide.

As a teacher or community worker acting alone, you have minimal opportunity to change the attitudes, feelings, and biases of others that impinge on local classrooms. You can, however, become alert to your own attitudes and how they affect the children with whom you work. You can listen to and work with parents who feel that the school is "discriminating against" their child and assist in a reevaluation of the child's progress. And while you cannot change all of the negative aspects of a child's environment, you can as a teacher provide a supportive school or child care environment. When businesses or other community agencies offer support, you can write letters of thanks. You can also encourage your students (or take them on a field trip) to visit the bank, post office, or other establishment where children's work is on display. Observe and encourage your students and families to note how the grocery store has posted the thank you letters that schools have written to them. By providing curricula and activities that take into account the attitudes and feelings of children's families and community, you help create coherent learning experiences for your students.

AGE LEVELS AND INFLUENCE

Community, home, and school exert a greater or lesser influence on children's learning, depending on the age of the children concerned (note again Figure 1–1). Many theorists have described the stages in children's development from dependency to independence and have theorized how children learn. (See Table 2–1 in the following chapter for a review of selected theories.) In practice, parents, teachers, and community people rarely subscribe to one particular theory, but the decisions they make about children's learning will reflect a stronger belief in one viewpoint. As you develop strategies to promote **partnerships** for children's education, it is helpful to keep in mind that others may have a different perspective on development from your own.

The Early Years—Strong Home Influence

Early researchers such as Maslow (1970), Erikson (1963), and Piaget (1967) all emphasize the strong need for attachment and environmental support of infants and toddlers. Developing children require a physically and emotionally supportive environment in which their basic needs can be met. Infants must first develop trust in others so that they can explore their surroundings. According to Piaget, it is this exploration that enables them to construct knowledge about themselves and their world (Piaget, 1967).

Neuroscientists have discovered links between brain structure and brain activity, and recent brain research substantiates the notion that a child's knowledge develops because of an interactive process, beginning even as the brain develops before birth. Heredity may determine the framework of a developing child's brain, but researchers point out the many ways in which genes, environment, and infant responses interact to develop the connections between the brain cells that account for learning (Education Commission of the States, 1996; Pinker, 2002). Nash (1997) explained that "experts now agree that a baby does not come into the world as a genetically programmed automaton or a blank slate at the mercy of the environment" (p. 52). However, this process is complex, and though the early years are important, the brain is highly plastic and able to reorganize itself (even in adulthood) as a result of enriched environments (Bruer, 1998). Such evidence confirms that both "nature" and "nurture" are not only crucial to development but depend on each other for its direction (D'Arcangelo, 2003).

Because of this brain–environment interactive development, we can see that myriad events will affect growth, some positively and some negatively. The type of housing, the presence of caregivers, and the lifestyles associated with different homes influence children's lives in profound and dramatic ways. Some environments are extremely supportive and nurturing, while others are dominating, negligent, and even dysfunctional. For example, affectionate interactions, consistent practices, organized schedules, and high-quality nourishment bring support and security to young children (Carnegie Corporation, 1994). Such nurturing environments have secure caregivers who respond to their children by touching, cuddling, talking to, and reading with them. Most authorities agree that emotional support and interactions with the child provide building blocks for intellectual competence and language comprehension.

Affectionate interactions between adults and children in everyday events of play/work brings security to young children

On the other hand, the trials of homelessness, highly mobile families, absentee parents, and poverty often mean that parents are unable to provide positive and secure environments. This lack of a responsive environment that stems from the parents' own life experience will affect a child's intellectual, social, and emotional competence. However, the young brain is quite resilient, and later stimulation or strong emotional bonds can help many children overcome some of the negative results of early deprivation (Bruer, 2002; Newberger, 1997).

Regardless of family configuration, American society expects all families to perform certain functions: economic support, psychological support, socialization skills, and **role expectations,** plus emotional support and intimacy. Nurturing families are those that sustain their infants and toddlers in these major areas. In contrast, negligent or dysfunctional families rarely provide the help in these areas that is crucial for children's positive development.

Other variables will also have a large effect on home influence. All American cultural and ethnic groups have fewer extended families now, and all have busier parents. Fewer people live close to their relatives, and everyone moves more frequently. As Mary Pipher (1996) put it, "We are separating more from our kin." All these factors present bigger challenges for optimal child care, nurturance, and family focus.

Economic Support.   The dependent infant relies on its mother and significant others for food, clothing, and shelter, all of which require a basic economic foundation. Inadequate nutrition, prenatally and in the early years, certainly affects children physically, emotionally, and cognitively. In many cases, an ill-nourished child becomes unresponsive to adults. When this happens, the mother may become detached in her disposition toward her child, and the vital interactions for healthy emotional and intellectual growth become impaired (Owens, 1993). Many families are unable to provide adequate housing, or they may live in unsafe neighborhoods. Separation and divorce has a considerable impact on children's physical and emotional needs (Hetherington & Kelly, 2002; Wallerstein, Lewis, & Blakeslee, 2000), and statistics show that separated parents suffer economically.

The results of poverty almost always cause a family great stress, and children then can become the victims of poor health, maltreatment, and inadequate parenting, all of which place children at risk of not developing normally. Erikson (1963) summarized the primary features of economic support, stating that when basic needs are met, children develop a sense of trust that enables them to venture forth and explore their environment. When basic needs are not met, exploration is hampered, and the child's development is jeopardized.

Psychological and Socialization Support.
Infants and toddlers begin their socialization process in a family structure when they begin

to communicate their needs and respond to their primary caregiver. As their actions are reinforced or rejected, infants and toddlers come to understand what is appropriate social behavior in dealing with others. Infants coo, cry, and gurgle, and nearby adults respond to these sounds as if the baby is trying to communicate (Meadows, 1996). As adults respond and babies' needs are satisfied, babies begin to differentiate the sounds they make based both on intent and on expected response. As they do so, their caregivers adjust their own responses to the sounds they hear, conforming them to what they both understand and desire them to mean.

℮

Sarah was very confident in dealing with her new baby. She maintained she could tell exactly what Aaron needed when he cried because he cried differently when he was hungry, was wet, or was bored and wanted company. Not only did she inform anyone present of her knowledge, but she also told her infant that she provided whatever "he was asking for." Whether the infant really understood may be debatable, but Sarah and Aaron were establishing attachment and communication links.

This early infant–mother attachment is an important factor in how children develop the socialization and intellectual skills that enable them to function effectively later on with peers and in school.

Family Status and Role Expectations.
Because infants and toddlers are extremely dependent on all aspects of their environment, their status and role within the family and community are not clearly defined. They gradually begin to understand that an important relationship exists between themselves and other members of the family. This developing

understanding will later enable them to function in the larger society. In the following vignette, Susan has incomplete information about roles in her family but has formed some notions.

❧

Susan, 18 months old, was accustomed to her mother's feeding her juice each morning. Sometimes, when her mother wasn't available, she would accept help from her older sister, calling her "li-ul mamma." The first time Susan was left with her aunt's family, she expected similar treatment, referring to her aunt as "aunt mamma." But when her uncle tried to feed her juice, she balked at the idea, asking for "aunt mamma." When that strategy didn't work, Susan looked about in vain, searching for her "li-ul mamma."

Susan, even by 18 months, has some defined role expectations for members of her fam-

ily and transfers this information in a new situation. She clearly becomes upset when her role expectations are challenged in her new environment. As she interacts in new situations, she will begin to recognize the various roles she and others play in other family units. Parents and significant others are laying the foundation for Susan's understanding of how to behave in socially accepted ways in more than one setting.

Emotional Support and Sense of Intimacy. Infants and toddlers require emotional support and a sense of intimacy. When significant adults in a baby's environment express joy and delight in the baby as a social being, the baby develops a sense of well-being and responds (Leach, 1994). As the baby grows older, this basic emotional security leads to a desire to share its feelings and emotions with loved ones. Ecksel (1992), summarizing several studies, stated that infants who formed secure attachments to their mothers were more socially competent later in school than were children

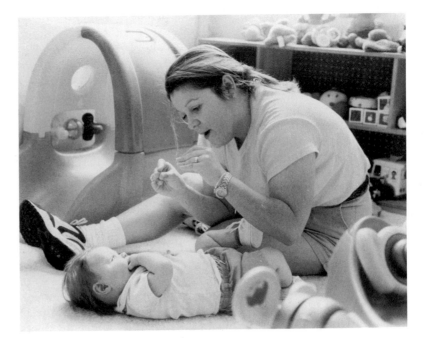

Infants and toddlers require emotional support and a sense of intimacy from a primary caregiver whether it is in the home or in a quality child care center

whose mothers were unable to give their infants warm, supportive surroundings.

Some families lack the emotional or social ability to provide adequate emotional nurturance. Divorce, illness, and other upheavals in a family will almost always produce a negative impact on emotional support and intimacy (Hetherington & Kelly, 2002). We find some households with problems so great that adults lack the inner resources to manage an infant's many needs. Other families with deficits, however, have social support systems to rely on or may know how to use community support systems, such as child care and health and human services, to supplement their own meager resources. Schools and **child care providers** should always assist needy parents by informing them of available services and reinforcing parents' attempts to meet their children's basic needs, and families with children with special needs may require additional support and services. See Chapter 4 for a fuller examination of parenting skills.

Influence of Out-of-Home Care. Since the 1940s, changes in American lifestyles have been altering the early influences of the home. Today, with 62% of women with preschool children in the labor force (as opposed to 25% in 1940; U.S. Bureau of the Census, 2002b), we find a steady increase in the need for some type of **out-of-home care** for many children. Many are cared for by relatives or by nonrelatives in a home environment, but increasing numbers are in a **family child care** group or in **center-based care**. This change is a concern for today's society, since it means that the development of infants and toddlers is being affected by other social settings at a much earlier age (Bornstein, 2002).

Since the early Spitz (1945) studies examining whether infants were better cared for by their mothers or in an orphanage, the American public has been concerned that children may not develop emotionally, socially, or intellectually if they have multiple caregivers. However, new research indicates that infants in quality **child care centers** are able to form strong maternal attachments as well as secondary attachments to consistent caregivers (Clarke-Stewart, Allhusen, & Clements, 1995; Honig, 1993). Most studies indicate that though there may be some differences in social development, children who regularly attend child care centers show development patterns similar to children raised at home. Other issues such as economic factors, parenting styles, time away from mother, and quality of care do, of course, influence children's development, whether it be in a home or in a child care setting (Berns, 2001). We consider out-of-home care more fully in Chapter 5.

Preschool and Kindergarten Years— Increasing School Influence

Children developing a sense of autonomy need to learn the boundaries they can operate within and must learn to identify new ones they will encounter as they separate from home. Bronfenbrenner's (1979, 1993) bioecological model accurately explains the transitions from the intimate **microsystem** of home to the **mesosystem** of outer linkages that come to bear on the developing child's perceptions and behavior. As parents give their children necessary support, they must also give them freedom to try things on their own.

As we noted, one's sense of self first develops in the home and then extends into the neighborhood, child care center, and larger community. At school, the teacher and the children's peers begin to alter or reinforce this sense. Children modify their behavior in school in response to different rules and regulations and to perceived teacher and peer expectations. But remember, the significant others in the home setting continue to influence development as the early schoolers move from basic trust to autonomy and independence.

Many children have school-like experiences in their preschool years. For other children, school as a culture first comes into focus when they enter formal public or private schooling. In the preschool years, children may encounter several different types of school-like experiences. Head Start programs, child care centers, nursery schools, and **play schools** all demonstrate somewhat different philosophical orientations. Some programs provide rich experiences for children; others provide only custodial care. It is difficult to conduct rigorous studies to determine the influence different programs have on developing children, and such research is always confounded by **socioeconomic factors,** community support systems, types of curricula, and parental interaction styles. However, we have evidence that quality preschool programs do have lasting positive effect on children's academic growth and on subsequent life skill development (Campbell & Ramey, 1995; Schweinhart & Weikart, 1997).

Primary Years—Growing Community Influence

Community influence appears early in children's lives and progresses steadily as children mature; refer again to Figure 1–1 to see that by age 8 community impact is high. However, the effect of community depends on how families use neighborhood resources. The nature of that effect is not simple but derives from the many subsystems within the community (Bronfenbrenner, Moen, & Garbarino, 1984). For example, the family may live in a neighborhood that provides positive social and physical support or in a neighborhood where parents are afraid to take their children out. Early intervention for children with disabilities also helps to ensure their optimal development.

Positive interactions between community and family give a sense of security and well-being to all. And this situation helps families to provide the better nurturing that children need. Children raised in communities where considerable violence exists can be affected adversely as a result of the stress the violence causes. Inattentiveness to schoolwork and **hyperactivity** are but two effects that stress has on academic achievement (Groves, Zuckerman, & Marans, 1993).

As children expand their horizons, the living conditions of the neighborhood and community give them experiences on which to build their linguistic, kinesthetic, artistic, spatial, and interpersonal skills. Children who can visit zoos, museums, libraries, business establishments, parks, and other natural settings are better equipped (than children who can't) to deal with the many mathematical, scientific, social, and language concepts discussed in schools. Recent decades have produced a rich mix of cultural and ethnic diversity in many American communities—which contrasts starkly with the mid-20th century. Inclusive schools, ethnically diverse neighborhoods, and **transcultural** events in most vicinities all produce a positive effect on young children.

Primary-school children are becoming independent and are moving from the preoperational to the concrete operational stage of intellectual development. Traditions, cultural values, community mores, opportunities for recreation, and other social and cultural activities all play a part in children's development. Experiences interacting with adults in clubs, sports, and art and music activities open up children to differences in communication styles and offer them a range of experiences. Coleman (1991) called this type of involvement with adults a child's **social capital** and stresses that this capital is as important as financial capital in determining school performance. Heath and MacLaughlin (1989) pointed out how these interactive incidents with different adults give participating children greater opportunities to practice their negotiating, problem-solving, and intellectual skills. Steven, in the following vignette, begins to learn some of these important lessons.

‿

Steven, in second grade, had joined a riding club but was unhappy because the instructor was "always criticizing" what he did. "I don't even know what I do wrong," he told his mother.

"And what do you do when he tells you something?" she asked.

"Oh, I get so mad, I just glare and ride away."

"Are you sure he never compliments you?"

"Uh, uh, hardly ever," pouted Steven.

"Well, want to try an experiment?" his mother suggested.

"The next time he even suggests something is good, smile at him and say, 'Oh, that really helps me know what I should be doing,' and just ignore the criticisms." Steven reluctantly agreed to give it a try.

Two weeks later, a jubilant Steven returned from riding club saying, "Hey Mom, he really does tell me lots about what I'm doing right!" Whether Steven or the riding instructor changed behavior patterns isn't clear, but certainly Steven was learning new ways of working with adults so that he could profit from their instruction.

‿

Regrettably, not all communities provide healthy conditions for children. Community tolerance for gangs, illicit activities, or establishments with erotic content will have unhealthy and negative influences on the experiences as well as the growth of children. Violence in the streets limits everyone's sense of security. Any opportunity for positive interactions or for the use of community resources to expand children's skills is lessened in disruptive communities.

Peer Group Influence

In ways similar to the community, the peer group becomes an agency of **enculturation** and learning. Even very young children develop a sense of self from their perceptions of important people in their surroundings, including relatives, teachers, and peers. Socioeconomic status, ethnic identity, and parents' occupations affect how families view themselves and the process by which they socialize their children (Bornstein, 2002). Later, as children leave the home setting, their self-perception and socializing skills become influenced by how their peers view them.

Peer groups begin to form early or late, depending on a child's experiences and availability of playmates and on his or her personality and sociability (Harris, 1998; Parke, 1990). When children move out from family to child care centers, school, and the community at large, they begin to form attachments, and friendships emerge later through their play. These relationships influence behavior. Even infants and toddlers are observed reacting to other infants by touching them, by crying when others cry, and later by offering nurturance or comfort. By around age 3 early friendships begin to form and children's peers begin to have a more lasting influence (Parke, 1990).

Peer influence on behavior gradually becomes more dominant. Harris (1998, 2002) and Rowe (1994) maintained that peer groups have an even stronger influence than that of parents. Gradually children discover that others can share their feelings or attitudes or have quite different ones. The perspectives of others will affect how children feel about their own families. Children usually have a "family" view of their own and of other cultures. So, when confronted with other perspectives, they often need to rethink their own viewpoints. It is often difficult for children to adjust to the idea that other families can function radically differently from their own and yet hold many of the same attitudes and beliefs and be equally nurturing and secure. The peer group serves as a barometer for children examining themselves and their feelings about self and family.

The peer group also influences development of children's socializing skills. These early friendships help children learn how to negotiate and relate to others, including their siblings and other family members. They learn from peers how to cooperate and socialize according to **group norms** and group-sanctioned modes of behavior. The peer group can influence what the child values, knows, wears, eats, and learns. The extent of this influence, however, depends on other situational constraints, such as the age and personality of children and the nature of the group (Harris, 1998; Hartup, 1983). This socialization is particularly important for children with special needs, and it is the reason many programs have typically developing peers in special education programs or include children with disabilities in regular education classrooms.

In its most acceptable form, the peer group is a healthy coming-of-age arbiter where children grasp negotiating skills, learn to deal with hostility, and learn to solve problems in a social context. In its most destructive mode, the peer group can demand blind obedience to a group norm, which can result in socially alienated gangs with pathological outlooks (Perry, 1987).

MEDIA INFLUENCE

Today, all members of our society are influenced both directly and indirectly by powerful media vehicles, including printed materials, television, sound recordings, and the Internet. Publicists, promoters, and sales personnel have at some point used all of these media to advocate what people should wear, what they should eat, and what values they should hold. Vivid colors and language tell us both what is happening in the world and how to react to the events shown. While much of our society's media vehicles seem dominated by superficial chitchat, hyped news events, and depictions of

Television and Internet have the greatest impact on children in terms of memory recall

violence, they are also sources of education, humor, and nonviolent entertainment. Just remember that the effect of media will vary with a child's age and stage of development.

While most realize that the different media forms can be used elegantly for mediated learning, their major objectives are entertainment and product promotion. In the following section we discuss what we broadly term the entertainment industry in its role as a general, society-wide influence on young children. We first discuss two of its primary forms, print and television, and then treat other current media under the rubric of the industry in general.

Print media—such as books, magazines, and newspapers—present content using words and static images. Though both pictures and language convey a message, printed materials do require greater reliance on a reader's language development and life experiences to be understood. As children decode words from the printed page, thoughts generated by these words serve to create images, thus requiring children to rely on their imagination and interpretations (Newman & Roskos, 1993; Singer &

Singer, 1992). As spoken language is developed, print becomes an important stimulus for nurturing the child's mind. And when children are exposed to print, they begin to make the vital connections between print and oral language.

Of all media forms, television and the Internet appear to have the greatest impact in terms of memory recall. Input is presented using both sound and moving pictures, and the active images assist children in remembering familiar content (Desmond, 2001). Programs that children have easy access to are not always appropriate for young children and often do little to stimulate children's thinking and imagination. Families can control what children see by selecting programs, but most homes exert far less control over television and Internet access than over printed media (Thornburgh & Lin, 2002; Van Evra, 1998).

When Meringoff (1980) compared children's reactions to stories presented through television, books, and radio, children seemed to view television events as something not directly associated with themselves, but they appeared to personalize the events in books. Berns (2001) and Singer and Singer (2001) surmised that because the reader is more intimately involved in the book, it is a stronger socializing agent. However, the stronger personal influence of printed materials over television or the Internet also could reflect the manner in which the two are presented to children (Neuman, 1995). Young children first know about books because someone reads to them and interacts with them about the story, whereas more often than not children are left to watch television or to use computer games by themselves. We know that children are socialized on how to react to books, thus getting more personal meaning from them as they become readers themselves. Some researchers (Desmond, 2001; Neuman, 1997) suggest that when parents or other adults interact with children viewing television or using the computer, those children develop better interactive and processing skills.

The entertainment industry, a powerful influence on life in the United States, engulfs society through print, television, radio, sound recordings, computer networks, and live performances (Figure 1–2). These media influence the actions, dress codes, and values of many adults and capture and hold children's interests for a large part of each day. As a teacher or community worker, you must understand that the entertainment industry's influence on children both enhances and inhibits children's growth as human beings. You should not underestimate the effect of this influence, but rather try to incorporate it into your teaching or advising so that children assimilate it in a healthy context with the rest of their education. For example, knowledge that children pick up from TV can be startling but relevant. Depending on the program children watch, a great deal of learning is acquired through TV and the Internet. And schools, communities and families may reinforce the unexpected learning in positive ways.

❧

The teacher in Amanda's kindergarten class was introducing the letter–sound relationship of "J." When soliciting words children could recall, Mrs. Pineo got judge *from Juan. So she asked if anyone knew what* judge *meant. Children responded, "it's someone who would send you to jail if you did something wrong . . . especially if you murdered someone, he'd be sure to send you to jail!" When asked how they knew this, the class as a whole replied, "It was on television!" That evening during dinner, Amanda announced to her family, "a judge would put you in jail if you did something really bad—like murder." The give and take of the subsequent table conversation between Amanda and her parents provided further clarification on how Amanda was assimilating information from school, the media, and from home.*

⤳

One desirable outcome of our highly mediated world is that all people see and sense the diversity of individuals we have in modern American communities. As we view televised images of children playing in the streets of Guatemala, Iraq, or Kazahkstan, we see them delighting in the same things that children in Seattle or Pittsburgh find desirable. Cultures across the world are borrowing steadily from each other and far more rapidly than previous generations. In *American Skin* (Wynter, 2002), a hopeful thesis on diversity is advanced for the **transracial** effect now found throughout the United States. Wynter makes a persuasive case for most Americans no longer reacting to racial and ethnic differences but adopting wholeheartedly the interesting and beneficial features of other cultural groups. This appears to be a positive departure from our society's background of **ethnocentrism**.

Print Materials

Print materials reach the child indirectly, through parents and other caregivers, and directly, such as when children participate in a presentation or select particular publications. Newspapers, magazines, books, and other print media portray many different ideas, actions, and activities, and naturally they elicit reactions and outcomes. The printed material available implies the values of the community and certainly influences all areas of education.

Physical Development. Print media affect children's physical, emotional, and intellectual development indirectly through the publications their parents read. Books and magazines inform adults how to lead healthy and productive lives and proclaim the dangers of unhealthy practices. Mothers whose reading persuades them to quit smoking, acquire healthy eating habits, and avoid alcohol and other drugs during pregnancy produce for the most part healthier babies. In contrast,

parents who believe that early involvement in sports gives their children a head start in athletic prowess may exert pressure too early. This expectation pushes their children to learn tasks for which they may be physically unprepared.

Social Development. Advertising from both print media and television affects the type of clothes, food, and, especially, toys bought for children. Some toys engage children's imagination and are designed for groups of children playing together. Other toys are more suitable for children playing alone. Children's potential for social development is affected by which type of toy adults are influenced to buy. Both Piagetian theory of development and brain research studies report that children construct knowledge about their world by interacting with materials, adults, and peers in their surroundings (Bruer, 1998; Piaget, 1952). A flexible environment that has opportunities for imaginative play and group interaction enhances children's potential for social development. Environments with fewer opportunities inhibit such development.

Intellectual Development. The toys and games children acquire affect their intellectual as well as their social development. Some toys have multiple uses and engage children's imagination; other toys have only one use, resulting in less creative play. Thus, adults' choice of toys and games may enhance or inhibit children's intellectual development.

Print media also affect children's literacy development. Studies on early literacy indicate that the amount and types of printed materials that adults have in the home, as well as how adults interact with these materials around children, affect the children's interest and literacy achievement (Desmond, 2001). From the books that adults read to children, children internalize attitudes, feelings, and biases about their own and other cultures. Zach, in the chapter's opening vignette, had a chance

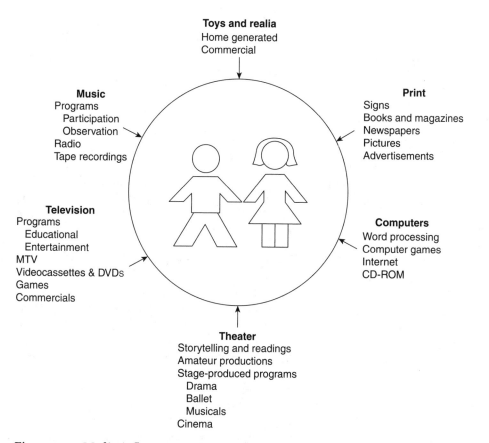

Toys and realia
Home generated
Commercial

Music
Programs
  Participation
  Observation
Radio
Tape recordings

Print
Signs
Books and magazines
Newspapers
Pictures
Advertisements

Television
Programs
  Educational
  Entertainment
MTV
Videocassettes & DVDs
Games
Commercials

Computers
Word processing
Computer games
Internet
CD-ROM

Theater
Storytelling and readings
Amateur productions
Stage-produced programs
  Drama
  Ballet
  Musicals
  Cinema

Figure 1–2   Media influence on children's lives.

to express aggression in acceptable ways through *Three Billy Goats Gruff.* He was influenced in the kind of clothes he wanted by the story *Max's Dragon Shirt.*

The kind of books that children read and have read to them influences and supports their emotional, social, and intellectual development both directly and indirectly. Sutherland (1996) pointed out that "to function successfully in society, children must learn to know themselves, to achieve self identity, . . . [to] learn about social interaction and recognize ways in which they are alike as well as different from others" (p. 20). Books, like peers, provide children with a vision of their world that sometimes reaffirms their own lives and sometimes challenges their perspectives.

Television

Television's substantial impact on all growing children began in the 1950s with the proliferation of TV sets. Three generations of children have been raised with TV, and very different role models, interaction modes, and experiences are now visited on American youth. Today, over 99% of American households contain at least one television set, and children start the viewing process early, as young as 2 years of age. Conservative estimates are that preschool children watch nearly 3 hours of TV per day (Gunter & McAleer, 1997), and this average continues through age 18 (Singer & Singer, 2001).

Most readers will recall the statistic: By the time a young person reaches 18, he or she will have watched more TV than total time spent in school. This becomes more sobering when we find that the typical elementary school child now has 3 hours of TV, 1 hour of recorded music, 1 hour of computer games and other computer usage; 39 minutes of radio, and just 44 minutes of reading (Singer & Singer, 2001).

In our new century, television viewing is becoming somewhat diminished because of increased use of computer games and the Internet, and also because children now spend more time in child care, school, and after-school care programs.

Television influences children in direct proportion to both time spent viewing and the overall effect of what is viewed (American Academy of Pediatrics, 1990). Certainly, eating habits, family interactions, and use of leisure time are considerably influenced by television (Arendell, 1997; Winn, 2002). Commercials take up 12 to 14 minutes of every hour of television, and in that time, advertisers try to influence viewers about all types of consumerism. Notar (1989) pointed out how advertisers use the power of imagery to hook both children and adults to their products. "Advertisers view training of children's imagery as all important. Once children are trained to view life in terms of commodities, they have many more years of productive consumption" (p. 67). Schools and parents are far behind advertisers in finding the most impactful ways of using media.

Children are especially susceptible to electronic media, and televised advertising has a huge effect. Heavy viewers are drawn to the advertised products, including unhealthy food products, and they tend to eat more snack foods and be overweight. Social interactions are also affected: Heavy viewers hold more traditional sex-role attitudes, behave more aggressively, are less socially competent, and perform less well in school (Arendell, 1997; Desmond, 2001).

Not all TV advertising is negative, of course. There have been efforts through TV to

modify behaviors such as smoking, drunken driving, and poor nutritional habits (Van Evra, 1998). How children are affected by both positive and negative advertisements also depends on such factors as parent–child interactions, how children are disciplined, and even to some degree on social–economic factors (Gunter & McAleer, 1997).

Advertising, of course, is not the only way in which television influences viewers. Two major concerns about the effects of television are the amount of violence, in both commercials and programs, and the amount of time children's television watching takes away from more creative and intellectual pursuits.

A large body of research shows that media violence contributes to aggression in our society and that the greatest impact is on young children (Bushman & Huesman, 2001). Concern over the effect of television violence resulted in the passage of the Children's Television Act of 1990. In 1995, the Federal Communications Commission (FCC) put more teeth into the act by requiring broadcasters to air 3 hours of educational programming for children each week. Fortunately, producers and advertisers have started to recognize the serious impact of television on children and the necessity of sharing responsibility for lessening the negative impact of advertising and violence (Bushman & Huesman, 2001; Murray, 1997).

Of course, not all television programming is violent, and we have some evidence of TV's positive effects. Some researchers indicate that programs depicting positive and altruistic actions also influence children. As a result, children prize such behavior and act in more positive ways toward their peers and family members (Arendell, 1997; Mares & Woodward, 2001). Public television has a long record of quality programs for children, for example, *Sesame Street* and *Barney and Friends.* Nickelodeon and Disney in recent years have produced a number of satisfying shows for preschoolers: *Blue's Clues* and *Dora the Explorer* are examples.

Research on the impact of television viewing on academic achievement indicates that such influence is complex in nature. Television viewing takes time away from important social interactions, such as conversation, storytelling, imaginative play, and for primary-school children, the leisure reading that promotes literacy. But we must remember that the amount of viewing, the kind of programs watched, IQ, and socioeconomic status are all factors that affect children's achievement (Winn, 2002; Wright & Huston, 1995).

The Entertainment Industry

Almost all young children in the United States are exposed on a daily basis to entertainment and education delivered through other media besides print and television. Films (in theaters and on cassette or DVD), radio, sound recordings on compact disc and audiocassette, computer games and CD-ROMs, plus access to the Internet are the main sources.

The entire entertainment industry now has a tremendous influence on American society. Whereas a few movie stars, musicians, and sports figures were the entertainment models for generations earlier in the 20th century, the visual and auditory stimuli of the new media bombard most homes and communities today. Some of this exposure is educational, positive, and directed at an appropriate level for young children. But a considerable amount of current fare is violent in nature, is provocative, and is presented in ways unsuitable for children's level of maturity (Van Evra, 1998). With the rapid expansion of electronic transmission devices, young people are exposed more than ever to both good and bad influences.

Producers and advertisers expand successful films and television shows by flooding sales counters with associated toys, clothing, and DVDs. Similar marketing comes from developers of video and computer games. These new forms influence individuals' values, compete for children's attention, and certainly reduce the amount of reflection and interaction time children have with both adults and peers (Singer & Singer, 2001). While some maintain that such games are opportunities for children to let off steam, others insist that there are better ways of achieving this goal.

In 2000 the U.S. Census Bureau (2001) found that 73% of married couples with children had a home computer and that 83% of those maintained Internet access. In addition, almost 90% of American elementary schools have Internet access. This means that the wonders, information, and dangers of global electronic communication are available to a large majority of American children.

The Internet is now the world's largest source of information and completely dwarfs even the world's renowned libraries. This is an extraordinary amount of information and resources for today's young people; it also carries great potential for misuse. For example, many primary-school children regularly surf the Net and tell about their findings. Pornography is widely available to any child willing to misrepresent his or her age. Even more alarming are the steadily expanding hate-group Web sites, and some are designed for children. Some help arrived with the Children's Online Privacy Act in 2000, and Web filtering software continues to expand.

Filtering systems for Internet use are a must for schools and homes to make Internet use more safe. WebBlocker is installed in many schools, and a 2003 Supreme Court decision permits the same for public libraries. Cyber Patrol and Net Nanny are examples of useful filters for home computers. This is a resource that must be harnessed successfully by families, school, and communities if its potential is to be productive (Hafner, 2002).

When adults work on the computer with children, the children benefit more

On the positive side, these media provide children with opportunities to practice skills, solve problems, create illustrations and graphs, and expand their knowledge base. For example, some primary-school children use the Internet for practicing chess, for e-mail, and for information from Net bulletin boards. Our best information for assessing the impact of these media on children's learning comes from observing how children use them.

When parents and other adults watch DVDs or television or use the computer with children, the children benefit more from the programs and the adults learn more about the children. Adults discover what children know and what interests or bores them and may act to enhance their learning. Adults may introduce children to the original stories

from which the TV programs were adapted, helping them to learn to make comparisons and develop better discrimination skills about stories and presentations. For children to be engaged in positive learning, it seems urgent that schools, parents, teachers, and other concerned individuals develop partnerships for interpreting and dealing with the products of both currently available media sources and those soon to appear in their communities (Murray, 1997; Paik, 2001). It is only when this begins to happen that the negative influences of the media industry can be reversed.

SPECIAL-INTEREST-GROUP INFLUENCE

In recent years, the United States has witnessed a steady increase in the number and potency of special-interest groups with agendas focused on political issues, environmental concerns, gender equity, or school curriculum issues. Groups such as the Family Research Council, Common Cause, Children's Defense Fund, Action for Children's Television, and the various prochoice and prolife groups are all organized to affect everything from legislative matters to informal controls on school procedures. These groups can have both direct and indirect influence on children's learning, depending on family, school, and community reactions to their efforts and objectives.

Though a number of special interest groups have a broadly conceived objective and have existed for many years, other citizen groups have a single objective and are ephemeral in nature. The single-issue group is frequently very successful in its endeavors because it focuses on an emotional issue that is newsworthy; an example is "Let's stop the building of more 'big box' stores in Newton." These groups die out quickly after a mission is accomplished.

Some groups have been formed by parents concerned about a particular educational issue affecting children. For instance, in 1968, Peggy Charren, concerned about the amount of violence in children's programs, organized a group of parents to form Action for Children's Television (ACT). This group lobbied for improved television programming and advertising during children's viewing time and worked to educate the public regarding television's positive and negative influences. This action resulted in the Children's Television Act of 1990.

Grassroots efforts by special interest groups resulted in the special education legislation of the 1960s for improving education for all children. As children with special needs were first mainstreamed into regular classrooms, curricula, classroom environments, and learning for all children expanded. Continued pressure by these special-interest groups has helped to examine the effects of the laws and to pass additional legislation to better serve children with special needs.

The influence of special interest groups is not always viewed as positive, though. Schott (1989) and Mahood (2000) noted that some conservative interest groups seek to effect legislation that would permit censoring of library books and dictating of particular elements in curricula. In many communities, both schools and libraries have been forced to remove certain books deemed quality literature by literary critics, because of the views of special-interest groups. One teacher was dismissed for focusing on Langston Hughes's poems, material that a special interest group found racially inflamatory (Kozol, 1991).

At the local level, some religious groups have succeeded in banning Halloween activities and even traditional fairy tales that include supernatural events and characters. Other groups have successfully changed units of study in schools about Christmas and Hanukkah and banned community displays of the Nativity. Special-interest groups have

positive influence when they act to initiate dialogue among parents and teachers as to the appropriateness of materials in schools. Their influence is negative when they seek to restrict children's access to humanity's best artistic, philosophical, and intellectual efforts and attempt to deny children's learning about different ethnic and cultural groups and other historical periods.

Federal Agencies as Special-Interest Groups

Though it is difficult to describe our federal government as a special-interest group, it does work that way at times. For over one and a half centuries, our national leaders left education entirely to the individual states, and only Supreme Court action on occasion visited the school arena. However, in recent times, political administrations have become increasingly concerned about educational policy and practice, because these have affected political goals and objectives.

In the 1960s, President Lyndon Johnson began the federal incursion with the very ambitious **War on Poverty** program, which carried many implications for schools. Since that time most administrations have deliberated about school problems, and they have seen fit to develop mandates and regulations and have used federal funding to stimulate action for one procedure or another. Enhancing legislation for science study is one example; promoting a voucher plan for selected groups is another; Goals 2000 was another; and a recent initiative is **No Child Left Behind (NCLB)**.

Federal mandates have expanded and are often fitted to different political agendas that bear little relationship to the needs, cultural expectations, and developmental levels of children in various parts of the country. The danger of such an approach is that the broad sweep of a mandate limits the diversity and uniqueness of individuals and groups. When schools reflect the political agendas of national

Federal government has provided support for special projects especially for science study

leaders rather than focus on teaching children to develop inquiring minds, our schools are in danger of becoming docile followers. **Standardized tests** have become commonplace in our schools, and in recent years we see even greater use of tests because officials worry that achievement is eroding in many American classrooms (Meier, 2002a). Overreliance on tests detracts from teacher oversight and opportunity to develop curricula keyed to the needs of particular children.

We need federal oversight and influence to promote certain programs that make life more productive and fair for children. Quality education is often cited as a dominant interest of the U.S. public, and most educators like to see our national government showing interest in schools, providing funds for programs, and being a partner in the huge task of educating young people. If these preferences are true, the

government has a reason to be involved in supporting our schools and community efforts. At times, though, the bureaucracy can be a burden.

IMPLICATIONS FOR PROFESSIONALS

Why is it important for you as beginning teachers, caregivers, or community workers to be knowledgeable of these influences that affect children's development? First, with an understanding of these influences, you will be able to recognize situations where children appear to be strongly affected. Then you can reinforce or give support for those events that exert positive influences on children. It is equally important to recognize and then offset the harmful influences. As suggested throughout this chapter and in remaining chapters, particular strategies do exist that teachers and community workers have used effectively to improve children's experiences.

As you work with children you will use various media, engage children in group processes, and take children into the community to learn important concepts. Often children will express very different responses to a learning situation that you provide. For example, Zach's teacher attempted to counter some of the influence of the home and peers by "not allowing" aggressive play in the school. This strategy may work well for this teacher, but there are other solutions, such as having a discussion with both children and parents, noting where electronic toys may be acceptable. Such a discussion might have been productive in this situation. Professionals try to be attuned to children's and parents' responses. If you follow such a course, you will become more sensitive and adept at responding to children's development and needs.

As children enter the primary school years, peers will exert greater influences on each other. When this influence is problematic and harmful, professionals will want to modify it. But counteracting negative peer influence is very difficult. Still, becoming aware of these influences gives you some background while you continue to show an accepting attitude and model positive interactions with all persons.

Your job is to provide the foundation for children's thinking skills, plus the development of competency in reading, writing, math, science, and social science concepts. Understanding the impact of both negative and positive influences on a child's learning makes your objectives and goals clearer as you plan for each student's learning.

SUMMARY AND REVIEW

Children become well or poorly educated, depending on many factors that both directly and indirectly influence what they learn and how they learn it. The attitudes, values, and interests that homes, schools, and communities have regarding children's learning can be in concert or in conflict. Young children are usually more strongly influenced by immediate or extended family attitudes, and primary-school children begin to be influenced by peer groups, media, and community mores and traditions. Teachers in many instances have no control over these factors and must study and be alert to their influence in order to provide appropriate education for children in their classrooms.

According to Coleman (1990), children need many types of support systems to grow into functioning adults. They need what he called human, financial, and social capital, which provide the nurturing and physical environment in which children learn to cope with their world. Children with little financial capital may still succeed if sufficient social and human resources are available to them. We find that families can compensate somewhat for lack of effective community and school influences on their children, and community and school personnel can exert influence and extend resources to compensate for missing family social resources. However, schools are far more effective in educating children when families, schools, and communities unite their efforts. When these three social settings recognize the influences on children's experience and work together in resolving conflicting issues undermining child development, the best possible circumstances result.

SUGGESTED ACTIVITIES AND QUESTIONS

1. List what you consider the major influences that guided your education. Are they different from those we have noted in this chapter? What influences did your classmates list? Discuss.

2. Watch a televised news program, a situation comedy, a soap opera, and a cartoon and chart the incidence of violence in each program. Identify what you believe could be the effect of such televised violence on primary-school children. Discuss your conclusions with your classmates.

3. Interview a teacher in a local primary school and determine whether any special interest groups influence the decisions this person makes with regard to curricula. Do some groups exert positive pressure? If so, how does the person view its benefiting children's learning? Do some exert negative pressures? If so, how does the person view these pressures as limitations on children's learning?

4. Discuss with a primary-school child a list of favorite books, movies, television shows, and entertainers. Find out what the child likes or finds important about these choices. Ask whether the child wants to be like any of the people or characters, and why. Attempt to determine how the media the child is exposed to has influenced these choices.

RESOURCES

Books

1. Beaty, J. J. (2002). *Observing development of the young child* (5th ed.). Upper Saddle River, NJ: Merrill/Prentice Hall.
2. Levin, D. E. (1998). *Remote control childhood? Combating the hazards of media culture.* Washington, DC: National Association for the Education of Young Children.
3. Ravitch, D. (2003). *The language police: how pressure groups restrict what students learn.* New York: Knopf.
4. Scully, P., Seefeldt, C., & Barbour, N. (2003). *Developmental continuity across preschool and primary grades* (2nd ed.). Olney, MD: Association of Childhood Education International.

Films and Videos

1. *Cooing, crying, cuddling: Infant brain development* and *laughing, learning and loving: Toddler brain development* [2 Videos, 28 min each]. (1998). Bloomington, IN: Indiana Public Broadcasting Stations with National Association for the Education of Young Children, Washington, DC.
2. *Space to grow: Creating a child care environment for infants and toddlers* [Video, 27 min]. (1998). Sacramento: California Department of Education.

Organizations

Action for Children's Television
46 Austin Street
Newtonville, MA 02160
(http://hugse1.harvard.edu/~library/act.htm)

American Library Association Booklist
50 E. Huron Street
Chicago, IL 60611
(http://als.lib.wi.us/ArrowheadBooklists.html)

National Center on Educational Media and Materials for Handicapped Children
Ohio State University
Columbus, OH 43202
www.csnp.ohio-state.edu

Websites

1. www.carnegie.org
   The Website entry to programs and reports supported by the Carnegie Organization.
2. www.newhorizons.org/blab.html
   New Horizons provides articles and resources on brain research.
3. www.superkids.com
   Reviews educational software for young children.
4. www.teacherzone.com
   A good one-stop resource for beginners on information about hardware, software, and the World Wide Web.

Chapter 2

Historical and Philosophical Perspectives

History is the witness of the times, the light of truth, the life of memory, the mistress of life.
(Cicero, *de Oratore*)

In this chapter the authors examine the evolution of roles played by persons in the home, in the school, and in the community for advancing children's education. In reading this chapter you will learn the following:

1. Beliefs about child development and modes of instruction all emanate from philosophical convictions that go back many generations.

2. Historically, the family and the community have always played significant roles in children's education, but at different periods each setting has had a more dominant position, with the school assuming leadership at the beginning of the 20th century.

3. Although *partnerships for educating children* is a relatively new term, parents, teachers, and community members have always worked together to some degree for children's benefit.

4. In recent decades, the federal government, in fostering better educational opportunities, has encouraged new procedures for parent involvement in children's education.

5. Since the 1960s, programs for poor children, children with special needs, and children of differing ethnic backgrounds have focused on the importance of parents as an educating force.

6. Although European American culture has dominated the shaping of American schools in the past, starting with the 1960s, other cultures have contributed to a **multicultural** emphasis for most present-day curricula, staffing patterns, and interaction patterns.

OVERVIEW OF PHILOSOPHICAL VIEWPOINTS

Historically, the philosophical ideas in society, along with political and sociological events, have influenced our underlying premises about children's educational development. And these ideas, which range from a conservative–academic approach to liberal progressivism, will influence the ways in which children are taught. As ideology and the political and social circumstances change, the type of relationship and dominant role that each of the three social settings has in the lives of children also changes. An overview of some major philosophical theories presents the forces that influence how families, schools, and communities understand their roles (see Table 2–1).

Some of the earliest theories tended to cluster around two contrasting views, known today as the nature–nurture controversy. With new scientific evidence, some theorists and researchers now propose that it is not an either—or viewpoint but an interactive—constructive perspective that more fully explains child development. And some psychologists maintain that indeed both environmental and biological factors influence development but that one can not understand the development of particular children without taking into account the cultural, historical, and ecological evidence around them.

John Locke (1632–1704) was an early advocate of the importance of environmental influences on children's behavior. He believed that a child's mind was a tabula rosa, or blank slate, and that stimuli from others and the environment was what controlled the child's development and learning. Following this, the behaviorists, such as John Watson (1878–1958) and B. F. Skinner (1904–1991), believed that children learned as a result of conditioning by adults who provided stimuli and then rewarded correct responses. Children learned because their needs were satisfied (or not satisfied) by another person or environmental factors.

In contrast, Jean-Jacques Rousseau (1712–1778) viewed children as unfolding and developing according to some innate plan. He held that people develop as a result of systematic and natural internal forces. In a related way, Arnold Gesell (1880–1961) documented children's growth, finding general developmental similarities and trends among children. He concluded that development is a result of laws and a sequence of maturation that is continuous and spiral. Gesell and his associates maintained that parents and teachers must follow the child's natural unfolding before learning can take place.

In the mid-1800's Charles Darwin's (1809–1882) work on evolution and natural selection provided enormous momentum for the scientific study of children, and his theory supports principles in both the nature and nurture positions. Darwin's studies of his own children as well as studies of different species in the Galapagos Islands challenged the idea of a fixed nature for species. Development, he insisted, unfolds in a natural, dynamic way and all species adapt to their particular environments in order to enhance their chance of survival (Thomas, 2001).

A third view, often labeled the interactionist–constructivist view, has emerged. Theorists with this orientation insist that both biological and environmental factors affect development in a reciprocal manner. As different theorists expanded this perspective over the 20th century, they focused on specific aspects of development. Jean Piaget (1896–1980), a cognitive theorist, proposed that children develop by assimilating and acting on stimuli, or information, from the environment and by accommodating new stimuli to already existing

structures. He held that children construct their own understanding and knowledge, which changes only as they find inconsistencies in their environment and incorporate the new information to produce new insights or knowledge.

Another view recognizing both internal and environmental influences was advanced by Sigmund Freud (1856–1939) and his followers. Freud was the first psychologist to view human nature as all encompassing. He formed his views by studying his dreams and recollections of his childhood experiences and that of his patients. His psychoanalytical theory was mainly concerned with human emotional, motivational, and personality development, even though he recognized the biological, social, and intellectual aspect of development. He believed both the positive and negative aspects of **sexual energy** are the driving forces of human behavior. He viewed sexual energy as biologically determined, but that environmental factors do determine how this energy is invested and thus how children grow. Followers of this view maintain that understanding this growth comes only by examining the dreams and recollections of childhood.

Erik Erikson (1902–1994), a follower of Freud, felt that sexual energy as the driving force of development was too limiting an explanation. Erikson identified eight **stages of development,** each with positive and negative attributes, and he insisted that cultural and social values affected how one progresses from one stage to another. For Erikson there are **critical periods of development**, and for a person to develop normal patterns of behavior the positive attributes at each stage need to be satisfied before the next stage can truly develop.

Social–cultural-context theorists, like Lev Vygotsky (1896–1934) and Urie Bronfenbrenner (1917–), also regard development as being influenced in a reciprocal manner

Table 2–1   Historical Perspectives of Major Theories of Child Development

Orientation	Nativism	Behaviorism	Interactionism
Basic premise	Based on Darwinian theory, *On the origin of Species* (1859), that all organisms seek to enhance their chances of survival. Genetics or internal mechanisms as primary focus in children's development.	Environment as primary force in children's development.	Both internal mechanisms and environment are forces for child development.
Major contributors	G. Stanley Hall (1844–1929) Arnold Gesell (1880–1961)	J. B. Watson (1878–1958) B. F. Skinner (1904–1991)	Jean Piaget (1896–1980)
Stages of development	Developed sequences of characteristic behavior. Maturational readiness means that a child must develop to an appropriate point before training or teaching has an effect.	No stages. Learning happens as a result of conditioning. Classical conditioning and unconditional stimuli result in reflex response, which later becomes a learned response. Operant conditioning means a child learns as a result of receiving positive reinforcers or rewards.	Children develop by assimilating external stimuli and accommodating new stimuli to already existing structures. Sensorimotor stage (birth–2 yr), use of senses. Preoperational stage (2–7 yr), use of mental imagery. Concrete operations stage (7–11 yr), logical thinking occurs.
Meaning for parents and educators	Adult supports development, observes outward behaviors that would indicate readiness of learning.	Adult determines desired behavior and sets up strategies for reinforcing children when behaviors occur.	Adults provide a rich and stimulating environment assisting children to interact with that environment as they construct their own knowledge.

(Continued)

by both biological and environmental factors. However, they believe that to understand development it is necessary to take into account the cultural and historical context in which development occurred. These theorists contend that there are a variety of social systems (e.g., family, school, neighborhood, community, and dominant beliefs in society) with which a child interacts, and it is a combination of these interactions that affects development. The social–cultural-context theorists have steered educators to an understanding and acceptance of the complexities of development.

Table 2–1   (*Continued*)

Psychoanalytical (Psychological)		Social–Cultural Context	Orientation
Sexual energy within humans as force for personality development		Environmental and biological factors affect human development, but cultural, sociological, and historical factors play an important part. Individual development depends on the relationship and interactions of all these elements	Major Premise
Sigmund Freud (1856–1939)	Erik Erikson (1902–1994)	Urie Bronfenbrenner (1917–) Lev Vygotsky (1896–1936)	Basic Contributors
Three structures: Id—instructive Ego—rational Superego—moral	Expanded on Freud's theories.	Multiple and distinct ecological systems affect development. The systems and all institutions within the systems interact and affect each other.	Stages of Development
Oral stage (birth–1 yr), need for gratification from mouth. Anal stage (2–3 yr), need for gratification from the anal area.	Basic trust (birth–1 yr), development of sense of inner goodness.	Microsystems: experiences and influences from school, family, peers, church, etc. Ecosystems: institutions that do not directly affect the child but indirectly affect the child's experiences—extended family,	
Phallic stage (4–5 yr), need for gratification from the genitals. Latency stage (middle years of repression of sexuality).	Autonomy (2–3 yr), development of sense of self and pride of achievement. Initiative (3–5 yr) takes charge of activities. Industry (6 yr to puberty), becomes producer and user of things.	neighbors, mass media, etc. Macrosystem: overarching values, laws, customs of a particular culture or society. Metrosystem: the interconnections between these systems.	
Adults provide the needed support so that children's instincts are satisfied, but not so much that children do not move appropriately from one stage to the next.		Adults are only one part of the influences that affect learning. Adults aware of influences can to some degree control these.	Meaning for Parents and Educators.

Vygotsky stressed the importance of recognizing both the biological–physiologic and cultural factors that influence a child's development. He insisted that it is the social interactions that children experience within their unique cultural and historical context that determines each child's unique developmental pattern.

In earliest development, Vygotosky believed the that biological and maturational factors do influence a child's physical and intellectual development to a large degree.

Later learning, he felt, was a result of children's independently acting on and interpreting their environment, and his theory shows that later in life the varying social factors better explain the physical and mental changes in children's development. For example, the Russian study (Vygotsky, 1978) shows that children interact in different ways with various adults. How these interactions progress over time will determine a particular child's learning.

As children's development approaches the problem-solving stage, Vygotsky believed that children have two spheres of operating. One is the ability to problem solve independently; the second is their problem-solving ability under the guidance of a more skilled person. The difference between these two levels was labeled the **Zone of Proximal Development** (Vygotsky, 1978).

In a similar fashion, Bronfenbrenner's theory examines the ecological systems that affect children's development. According to Bronfenbrenner, these social–ecological systems that are interacting and interdependent are the primary elements that differentiate and actualize the biological potential of children. (Bronfenbrenner, 1979) In other words, the interplay between biology and ecology causes changes in the child, which in turn produce other changes. In addition, the theory holds that these cascading changes have an ever increasing effect, both positively and negatively, on a child's development.

It should be clear that throughout history, theorists and researchers have stressed specific but different elements and aspects of development. All these theories, along with political and social events, have influenced how families, schools, and communities envision their roles in educating their children through out the generations. The authors believe that students should maintain a perspective of human development that recognizes the contributions of various theorists.

This provides a richer understanding of human growth and development.

HISTORICAL PATTERNS

Partnerships among homes, schools, and communities for children's education is a term of the 1980s, 1990s, and 2000s, yet throughout the history of the United States, we find connections among the functions of these three vital social settings. At different times, each, as an institution, has occupied a dominant role in children's education while acknowledging the others as important forces helping children to succeed in society (see Table 2–2).

In colonial times, the family was the major force for educating children, although the community exerted pressure on families not conforming to local codes of conduct. Later, as towns and villages developed, community leaders recognized that some families were not willing or able to educate their children successfully. Taking command in the later colonial period, community leaders gave needed support to families, started to develop laws concerning education, and eventually formed public schools to ensure that children met the community objectives.

In the late 1800s, as public schools developed into bureaucracies, professional educators moved to the forefront and took responsibility for overseeing schools and curricula. At the same time, the public mandated a more diverse curriculum, so teachers were required not only to teach academic skills but also to provide programs to help children develop socially, physically, morally, and emotionally. At this time, when blue-collar jobs increasingly required technical skills, schools became responsible for teaching vocational skills as well. In the later part of the 20th century, when only a part of the school population succeeded in these extended schools, questions began to arise. Parents and com-

Table 2–2 Events Affecting Family–Community–School Relationships

1600s		Families Responsible for Children's Education
	1642	Massachusetts Act requires all families to teach children to read Bible and laws of the land.
	1687	Old Deluder Satan Law requires every community of 100 or more to establish schools.
1700s		Community Responsibility for Children's Education (national influence—state responsibility).
	1779	South Carolina outlaws education for Negro children.
	1785–1787	Northwest Ordinances reserves land in the Midwest for the support of schools.
	1789	Constitution of the United States passed—no mention of education—assuming education was the states' responsibility.
1800s		Educational Establishment's Responsibility for Children's Education
	1815	First Parent Program established in Portland, Maine.
	1835	Massachusetts establishes first state board of education.
	1852	Massachusetts establishes compulsory education law.
	1867	U.S. Office of Education established.
	1873	First public school kindergarten founded in St. Louis.
	1888	Federation for Child Study founded.
	1889	G. Stanley Hall establishes first child study center at Clark University for studying children and disseminating information to parents about child-rearing practices.
	1896	*Plessy v. Ferguson* decision supports segregation.
	1897	National Congress of Mothers founded (later became Parent–Teacher Association).
1900s		Educational Establishment's Responsibility for Educating Parents as Well as Children
	1909	First White House conference on care of dependent children held.
	1912	Children's Bureau established in Washington, DC.
	1916	First parent cooperative founded at the University of Chicago.
	1920	Rehabilitation Act assists veterans of World War I to get job training.
Mid 1900s		Parent and Community Involvement in School Policies
	1954	*Brown v. Board of Education* opens the way for desegregation of schools.
	1956	Ford Foundation offers grant to New York City to train volunteers to work with teachers.
	1964	Civil Rights Act mandating desegregation of schools paves the way for compensatory education acts, which required parental involvement in schools.
	1965	Elementary and Secondary Education Act/Project Head Start; Title I/Chapter I.
	1965	First bilingual education act passed.
	1967	Economic Opportunity Act follow-through programs begun.
	1972	Home Start programs established.
	1975	Public Law 94-142, Education for All Handicapped Children Act (amended in 1990 to Individuals With Disabilities Act, IDEA)
	1975	Rehabilitation Act, Section 504, amended to prevent discrimination against persons with disabilities in programs using federal funds.
	1984	First national symposium on partnerships in education sponsored by the President's Advisory Council.
	1986	Federal Preschool and Early Intervention Program Act, Public Law 99-457, extends PL 94-142, mandating services for preschoolers.
	1986	Handicapped Children's Protection Act (PL 99-472) passed.

(Continued)

Table 2–2   *(Continued)*

Mid 1900s	Parent and Community Involvement in School Policies
1988	National Association of Partners in Education formed.
1988	Educational Partnerships Act, Title VI, passed.
1988	Family Support Act passed.
1990	American with Disabilities Act extends Section 504 of the Disabilities Act to prohibit discrimination against any person with disabilities in private or public employment.
1992	Head Start Improvement Act passed, extending services to infants and toddlers.
1994	Goals 2000: Educate America Act signed into law.
1996	Personal Responsibility and Work Opportunity Reconciliation Act (Welfare Reform Act) passed.
1997	IDEA reauthorized.
1999	Twenty-first Century Community Learning Act introduced as part of the Educational Excellence for All Children Act (Title X, Chapter 1—a reauthorization of the Elementary and Secondary Act).
2001	No Child Left Behind Act (Title I, Section A)—families in Title I schools have a right to select a "preferred" school if their child is in a "chronically underachieving school."

munities became perplexed and displeased about lower success rates, and alienation often set in.

Beginning in the 1990s, a new trend for developing collaborations (stimulated by researchers, professional educators, and more recently by federal agencies) became a focus for parents, community leaders, and teachers. In this way, many people came to appreciate the truth in the African proverb, "It takes an entire village to educate a child." As you review the following historical overview of relationships among parents, communities, and schools, consider what happens to children as society changes.

In this chapter, we trace the changes and forces that have shaped our present educational condition in the United States with respect to the roles played in childhood education by families, communities, and schools from the dominant culture. We also consider attitude changes over the 3 centuries toward children from minority cultures and other special populations. Naturally, all changes have affected the roles and responsibilities of the three institutions

for the education of all children. Table 2–2 lists major American events affecting family–community–school relationships.

FAMILY AS A SIGNIFICANT EDUCATIONAL FORCE

From prehistoric cultures to modern society, the family has been the most important social setting for educating the child. In all societies, children must learn skills of survival, the rules and regulations of the society in which they live, and the values by which their society functions (Sanderson, 1995). Children learn by following their elders' examples, through direct teaching of important skills by their elders, and by the oral communication of traditions, lore, attitudes, beliefs, and values (Bornstein, 2002).

In the original English colonies, the family was the prime educator, though the community exerted pressure on families to teach what society deemed important. The education that children received in the colonial period depended on economic status, ethnic background,

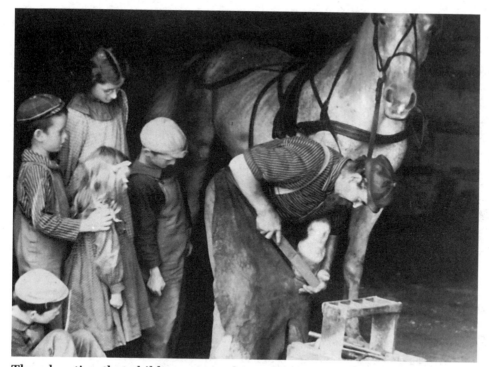

The education that children received in colonial times depended on their economic status and needed vocational skills.

child gender, and to some extent the section of the country the child lived in.

Early settlers for the most part were able to form cohesive family units, depending on each other for survival. Towns and villages, particularly in New England, were initially established around particular religious groups migrating from Europe. With their religious heritage, early colonists believed that children needed to learn not only the vocational skills necessary for survival but also particular codes of behavior and moral integrity. The more economically advantaged also valued reading and writing for their own children. It was a patriarchal society, and in most cases teaching was the responsibility of the home, with the father the dominant force. Parents, grandparents, and older siblings were the pri-

mary instructors. Fathers taught their sons skills needed to carry on the family vocation; mothers taught their daughters homemaking skills. In the intact homes, children had a profound appreciation and sense of family. They tended to understand who they were and how they were a part of the larger community (Zelizer, 1994).

Puritans in New England were adamant about the need to learn to read and write, and stressed the importance of reading the Bible. Parents assumed this responsibility. In addition, certain women who became more skilled in teaching gathered in their homes children whose parents were unable to teach reading and writing. This practice resulted in the creation of "dame schools," precursors of our current primary schools.

Puritans are credited with establishing the foundation of public education in the United States

In the southern colonies, wealthy settlers hired tutors to teach their children academic skills plus the behaviors befitting a plantation owner, while poor parents were responsible for educating their children as best they could. For the most part, African Americans were forbidden an education, and because of slavery, Black families were often torn apart, so that even parental teaching of basics was hampered (Berlin, 1998; Travers & Rebore, 2000).

When colonial children needed to learn skills the family was unable to provide, apprenticeships were sought, and boys as young as 7 years old were sent to live with a master craftsman. They could be apprenticed until age 21. Apprenticeships were the precursors of our later grammar schools, for in many colonies the masters were expected to teach reading and writing as well as the skills of their trade (Webb, Metha, & Jordan, 2003).

In the English colonies, basic formal education was available to established families, but children of slaves and Native Americans were considered unworthy of this basic education. There were, however, notable exceptions to this trend. The Church of England in the South and Quakers in the middle colonies provided educational opportunities for a few African Americans, some Native Americans, and some poor European colonists.

COMMUNITY AS A SIGNIFICANT EDUCATIONAL FORCE

As townships in the colonies became more established in the late 1600s and the 1700s, religious leaders became more dominant in determining the education of children within the community. Thus began the American heritage, extant today, that a community oversees its schools and determines school policy and curriculum.

The Puritans are credited with establishing the foundation of public education in this country because of their belief that all children, whatever their economic status, needed to be educated. They believed that every child in the land should learn the rigid codes of behavior for a religious society and the "meaning of salvation" from Bible reading. As early as 1642, a Massachusetts law required all parents and master craftsmen to teach reading and writing to children in their care to ensure that children attained "religious understanding and civic responsibility" (Travers & Rebore, 2000, p. 42). There was, however, difficulty in enforcing such a mandate because of widespread illiteracy in the adult population. Consequently, in 1647, the Old Deluder Satan Law was passed, requiring townships with 50 or more households to provide a teacher of reading and writing for young children in the community. Townships that had more than 100 households were also to provide a Latin grammar school to prepare boys for university study (Cohen, 1974).

Though these laws were not easy to enforce, they were important in establishing a precedent for education as the young nation expanded. First and foremost, the family had primary responsibility for educating a child, but the laws also laid a foundation for community responsibility in assisting families in educating the young. Since communities hired the teachers, they also taxed families on their property so as to have funds to pay teachers.

In the late 1700s and early 1800s, political and economic factors in the United States again affected the relationships of families and communities in educating children. The advent of the Industrial Revolution meant that families moved from an agrarian-based econ-

omy to one increasingly dependent on manufacturing. Now fathers, and sometimes mothers, left home to earn a living, and naturally there was little opportunity to teach children vocational skills or reading and writing in the home. As urban populations began to rise, many families became more isolated from their kin. Thus, the changed circumstances demanded a new response to the country's needs.

The republic came into being at the end of the 18th century, and as it unified, the strong influence of religious communities was replaced by the notion of nonsectarian education. Political leaders such as Benjamin Franklin and Thomas Jefferson believed that the new nation needed a literate populace and that it was not sufficient to educate only the wealthy and the strongly religious. Education, they felt, needed to be available to children from different social and economic classes and needed to be more functional. Merchants added their voice to that of politicians, for business interests realized that the nation needed workers with more than rudimentary literacy skills and more practical skills than those provided in Latin grammar schools (Sadker & Sadker, 2003).

If wider schooling opportunities were to be available, something needed to be done to help communities establish schools. The new government responded, and significant pieces of legislation, such as the Land Ordinance Act of 1785 and the Northwest Ordinance Act of 1787, were passed by the Continental Congress. These acts encouraged settlers to move to the Midwest and to set aside land to support schools. Such acts indicated the new nation's faith in education, even though in writing the Constitution the founding fathers did leave the responsibility for education to the individual states.

The ideas and practices of European philosophers and educators, such as John Comenius (1592–1670), Rousseau, Johann Pestalozzi (1746–1827), and Friedrich Froebel

(1782–1852), influenced educational thought in the United States. These new ideas, however, regarding who was to be educated and where and how did not immediately change American children's education. Community sentiment first had to endorse any practice. Even today, in a general sense, community standards, mores, and expectations are among the strongest determinants of social behavior and participation. We find that community validation continues to be necessary for any substantial change or redirection to take place in children's educational opportunities.

SCHOOL AS A SIGNIFICANT EDUCATIONAL FORCE

The mission of formal schools and support for public education have increased gradually over the more than 2 centuries of the United States as a nation. In spite of our founding fathers' expressing a need for universal, free, and secular education, it has taken a long time to achieve such a goal for all children.

Even in the early 1800s, the prevailing view was that education was a family responsibility; any education beyond a family's immediate capacity to give was a luxury. Some communities at that time maintained public schools for their children, and some charity schools existed for the poor. In addition, religious sects continued to provide schooling in some areas for all children, and, of course, there were private schools for the wealthy (Cremin, 1982). But universal education was not yet supported in the United States of the early 1800s.

It was the mid-1800s before the political and economic climate provided fertile ground for the establishment of free, open, secular schools in the United States. On one front, new immigrants were voicing dissatisfaction in not being a part of the political process. Trade unions were forming, and unionists believed that the path to success was by educating

their children. Also, humanists and educators, such as Horace Mann (1796–1859) and Henry Barnard (1811–1900), wrote and lectured about the benefits of universal and **secular education.** In addition, population movement from rural to urban areas meant that many families lacked the resources to educate children at home. The time for public education had arrived.

States at this time urged local communities to begin taxing themselves so as to provide public schools for their citizenry. States also started the practice of giving aid to communities needing support. In 1852, Massachusetts began to require compulsory attendance, but it wasn't until 1918 that the last state in the union—Mississippi—enacted legislation requiring children to attend school (Cremin, 1961). With such enactments, parents began to relinquish to schools the responsibilities for educating their children; however, home and community continued to influence many educational trends.

As schools became the major force in educating American children, a professional education establishment emerged that influenced parents as well as local and state government on curriculum. Some collaborations between schools and homes resulted, but often parents and communities were at odds regarding the specifics of children's education.

As compulsory education took hold in the late 1800s, it became apparent that many children in the United States were not being reared in the manner the dominant culture felt necessary. Poor children in urban communities were often viewed as neglected, and new immigrants from southern and eastern Europe, unable to speak English, had different values and views on child rearing. It became clear that schools with their prevalent Puritan ethic did not meet the needs of many children. Something needed to be done, and parent organizations with strong female advocates were formed to press for action on more comprehensive schools. Schools were urged to provide hot lunches for needy children, and immigrants were taught English so that they could be assimilated into American society (Kagan, 1993).

Philosophical swings in education, from conservative and academic to more liberal progressivism, have resulted from what the American public has perceived as needed in different periods. For example, with new immigrants and a growing urban, industrialized society, a movement emerged in the 1920s and 1930s for more openness in education, with schooling tailored to the needs, interests, and abilities of children. The methods used reflected the view that if children's innate abilities differed, then the type of teaching should differ, and the materials and time allowed for learning should also differ. Then, in the 1950s, as the space race captured people's imaginations, U.S. citizens became concerned about the lack of an academic focus, and a swing to a more rigorous **academic curriculum** followed, requiring all children to learn specific material or face failure.

Following the civil rights movement of the 1960s, social issues were of great concern, and again schools were pressured to change to a more responsive curriculum. Many recognized that a child's cultural setting had an influence on how he or she learned; therefore it was important to use techniques that accommodated these differences. In the 1980s and 1990s, globalization of economy and communications produced pressure from parent groups and communities to promote greater academic achievements.

As the 21st century begins, we find considerable interest in brain research, and this has implications for schools and curricula. Researchers emphasize the complexities of influences that effect how children grow and develop. Steven Pinker (2002) and others have pointed out that environmental, ecological, and contextual factors do make differences,

effect genetic development of the embryo, and extend through the prenatal stage. In spite of beliefs that the nature–nurture controversy would be resolved by now, political and social forces as well as genetic studies continue to challenge curriculum and how schools should operate. Families, schools, and communities are challenged to blend in these new perspectives to provide the best learning environment for each child.

Parent Involvement in Schools

At the turn of the 20th century, as society brought pressure on schools to change ways of operating, similar forces were directed at parents. No longer were parents viewed as knowing the best way to rear their children. Psychology as a science came into its own at this time, and young children quickly became a focus of study. A number of theories on child development and the best ways to rear children were advanced.

In 1815, the first parent education program was held in Portland, Maine, to instruct parents in proper child-rearing practices. Also, through the efforts of Elizabeth Peabody (1804–1894), a follower of Froebelian programs, kindergartens were established, first by church societies and settlement homes and later as part of public schools. Besides providing moral and religious training and a safe and healthy environment for children, the kindergarten was a subtle and indirect way to reach immigrant families and influence them in rearing children according to beliefs of mainstream society (Weber, 1969).

In the late 1800s and early 1900s, interest in the plight of children in urban settings became a focus for some early childhood educators. Armed with new knowledge of the importance of good nurturing and proper training in the early years, child care centers and family child care programs were established as extensions of kindergarten programs.

Many of these programs were directed at poor families in which mothers worked outside the home (Seefeldt & Barbour, 1998).

Early parent involvement meant educating parents as well as involving them in supporting school activities. The National Association of Parents and Teachers, later to become the Parent–Teacher Association (PTA), was established in 1897 for this very purpose. Community involvement in parent education came in the form of women's organizations, such as the Society for the Study of Child Nature (1888), the American Association of University Women (1882), and the National Association of Colored Women (1887). These organizations sponsored lectures and conferences and published magazines promoting parent education and stressing the importance of parents taking an active role in children's education (Schlossman, 1976).

Child study in the late 1800s became a focus at colleges and universities as a result of the work of G. Stanley Hall (1844–1929), one of the first psychologists to use a scientific method for studying children. Many universities established laboratory schools for preschool-age children, where educational theories and child-rearing practices could be tested. Supported by federal and private funds, these schools provided courses in child development and parent education and practice for teachers and researchers, and disseminated information on their research (Schlossman, 1976).

Perhaps the zenith of early parent involvement came with the founding of parent cooperatives at the University of Chicago in 1916. Founded by 12 faculty wives to provide quality care for their children and parent education for themselves, these programs were modeled after the British nursery school program, founded by Margaret McMillan (1860–1931). Though McMillan founded her school for the poor, **nursery schools** and the first **parent cooperatives** were adopted in the

United States by middle-class parents, and parent involvement became entrenched. An open, **play-oriented curriculum** was emphasized in both nursery schools and parent cooperative programs as they developed. However, not all the newer nursery school programs were committed to total parent involvement, as were the parent cooperative programs. Parents of children in cooperative programs were decision makers within the schools. They hired teachers, approved the type of program, served as assistants in classrooms, and planned the parent education programs (Taylor, 1981).

During the first half of the 1900s, parent education became viewed as vital to the welfare of society, and professional educators began to feel responsible for providing this service. Parents, even though no longer considered experts in child upbringing, were still viewed as essential components for children's success in school and later in life. Professionals felt that parents needed help in seeing how they could support their children's learning and thus benefit society (Taylor, 1981). A rather popular belief, at least among the middle class, was that the mother should be at home raising her children and learning how to raise them from the experts. But with urbanization, there have always been mothers working outside the home, and they needed child care services.

There have been periods in history when more emphasis has been placed on the need for society to help provide child care. In the 1930s, the Works Progress Administration (WPA) had a program providing full day care for families in poverty. Then, during World War II, **day care** centers were set up in factories so that mothers could help in the war effort. Great attention was paid to training teachers about child care development and in developing curricula. However, parents were seen not as collaborators, but rather as needing support and education.

The Works Progress Administration supported day care for families in poverty during the 1930s

In the late 1990s, with large numbers of mothers again in the workforce and welfare mothers required to return to work, quality child care services became very important as a buttress for all parents. National child care organizations like National Association of Education of Young Children established guidelines for quality care in the late 1980s, and the Welfare Reform Act of 1996, stressed the need for such care if mothers were to leave the welfare rolls.

Federal Government Involvement

Following the establishment of the U.S. Office of Education in 1867, the federal government took particular interest in families. The first White House Conference on Care of Dependent Children in 1909 sparked interest in child wel-

fare throughout the nation, and in 1912 the Children's Bureau was established as a follow-up. Following that period, educational opportunities abounded through university courses, lectures and conferences, school programs for parents, magazine articles, and books. Later, television programs were developed instructing parents on how to educate their children. Benjamin Spock's book *The Common Sense Book of Baby and Child Care* (first published in 1946) and Burton White's *The First Three Years of Life* became popular guides in child-rearing practices, especially for the middle class (Schlossman, 1976). A proliferation of such publications continued into the 21st century, with even more information available through Internet.

As society has become increasingly urban, decision making regarding children's education has become more complex. The federal government has become influential by granting monies for projects or by withholding the same from states not complying with federal mandates. State educational offices have also developed curricula and issued mandates regarding what should be taught in schools. Also, to qualify for state monies, local school authorities in recent years have begun to dictate certain educational requirements, and teachers have felt obligated to respond. The federal government has taken a somewhat different focus in recent years and now requires that the states take more responsibility. However, by establishing goals and then financially supporting schools by block grants and special funding for specific goals, the federal government continues to play an active role in influencing educational issues.

Goals 2000 and New Federal Directions

The Goals 2000: Educate America Act, signed into law in March 1994, signaled a change for federal involvement in educational practice. Goals 2000 was presented as a new face, where the federal role was to be one of support and facilitation to improve schools for all children. Provisions in the act established very general goals as incentives and then gave support to states and communities as they worked to meet those standards and objectives (Riley, 1995). The legislation, incorporating eight national education goals, which emerged from 1990 legislation by the first Bush administration (U.S.D.O.E., 1993b), is summarized as follows:

1. All children in the United States will start school ready to learn.

2. The high school graduation rate will increase to at least 90%.

3. U.S. students will leave Grades 4, 8, and 12 having demonstrated competency in challenging subject matter, including English,

mathematics, science, history, and geography; and every school in the United States will ensure that all students learn to use their minds well so that they may be prepared for responsible citizenship, further learning, and productive employment in the modern economy.

4. U.S. students will be first in the world in science and mathematics achievement.

5. Every adult American will be literate and will possess the knowledge and skills necessary to compete in a global economy and to exercise the rights and responsibilities of citizenship.

6. Every school in the United States will be free of drugs and violence and will offer a disciplined environment conducive to learning.

7. The nation's teaching force will have access to programs for the continued improvement of their professional skills and the opportunity to acquire the knowledge and skills needed to instruct and to prepare all American students for the next century.

8. Every school will promote partnerships that will increase parental involvement and participation in promoting the social, emotional, and academic growth of children.

Following establishment of Goals 2000, President Bill Clinton added the America Reads Challenge in 1996. Recognizing that reading is a skill developed not only in school but also in the home and community, the initiative called for schools to involve community organizations and homes to help ensure that all children would read by the end of third grade (Mitchell & Spencer, 1997).

In 2001, President George W. Bush signed the No Child Left Behind Act as part of Title I, Section A. Under this act, local, state and federal agencies assume certain responsibilities for ensuring that parents have better and expanded opportunities for their children in **Title I schools**. For example, if a child is in a chronically underachieving Title I school, parents have the right to select a preferred school and seek supplemental academic help from approved educational providers. Also under this law, "**faith-based organizations**" are eligible to apply for approval to provide supplemental educational services to low-income students, students with limited English proficiency, and students with disabilities. The approved organizations must provide help in language arts, reading, and math before or after school, on weekends and during the summer (U.S. Department of Education, 2003).

Partnerships and Collaborations

Partnerships in education is not a new concept, if we consider the various groups and interests that have worked with our schools over the years. As we have pointed out, families and community leaders have great input into the functioning of schools. The question arises as to how these would-be partners for the professional education establishment view their roles and how they assume responsibility and leadership.

In the 1950s and 1960s, the American public, for the most part, viewed all education as the responsibility of schools, and parents were expected to support teachers and their programs. However, the community school movement also developed at this time, and for those subscribing to the movement, the purpose of schools was more comprehensive. Community school advocates felt that schools, as well as serving young children, could serve the larger community by providing various resources for the public within the school facility (Kagan, 1993).

Educators took an active and strong role at this time, often advising parents on their roles and responsibilities. There was prosperity in

the United States and a belief that through education the United States could provide equal opportunities for all citizens.

Schools needed support to meet this goal, and volunteer programs sprang up as a result. In 1956, the Ford Foundation granted money to the Public Education Association in New York City to recruit and train volunteers to teach reading and to assist children who did not speak English fluently. In the beginning, these volunteers were primarily nonworking mothers, but as the programs expanded and spread to other areas, retirees, college students, and businesspeople also began providing volunteer services (Merenda, 1989).

A new impetus for collaboration came in the 1980s as businesses became concerned with the quality of education in the United States. Some government officials recognized that educational problems could not be solved by the public sector alone. Thus, an Educational Partnerships Program was established under the Educational Partnership Act of 1988. The purpose of the act was to encourage community organizations, including businesses, to form alliances to encourage excellence in education (Danzberger & Gruskin, 1993).

Partnerships no longer involved just the basics of establishing good relationships with parents and using the resources that a community provides. Businesses became involved in schools in a variety of ways. Partnership arrangements grew to include such supports as volunteers for the classroom, incentives for children to improve skills, internships for teachers, mentors and tutors for particular areas of study, visits to a business enterprise, special projects sponsored by businesses, provision of new technology for classrooms, and assistance in shaping school policy. The "business for education" movement grew from 17% involvement in 1983 to include around 40% of all schools by 1989 (Heaverside & Farris, 1989). The notion continued to prosper in the 1990s, when the 21st Century Community

Learning Centers Act was introduced as a part of Title 20. Under the act's provisions, communities acquired grants to establish safe places during after-school hours, homework centers, and tutorial services. In addition, special cultural, recreational, and nutritional opportunities were offered. Communities were encouraged to use public schools as a base for uniting the services within a community so as to deliver education and human resources for all members of the community.

CHILDREN WITH SPECIFIC NEEDS

Major social events in each generation result in social policy changes that affect persons with special needs. After World War I, Congress enacted the Rehabilitation Act to assist wounded veterans. This act enabled veterans to receive special training and therapy so they could return to work. In the 1930s, the Great Depression resulted in Franklin Roosevelt's New Deal programs. As education was being extended to persons with special needs, it soon became apparent that education alone was insufficient to provide opportunities for them to use these skills in the workplace. In 1975, the Rehabilitation Act was amended (Section 504). This amendment was intended to prevent discrimination against persons with disabilities; thus, a program receiving federal funding could not refuse employment to individuals solely on the basis of a disability. In 1990, the American's Disability Act extended these same rights to persons seeking employment in any public or private venue, whether or not these enterprises received public funds (Turnbull, Turnbull, Shank, Smith, & Leal, 2002).

In a similar vein, political movements in the 1960s resulted in sweeping changes for American education and in the corresponding roles of parents, schools, and communities. The civil rights movement resulted in the Civil Rights Act of 1964, which acknowledged that children in segregated schools received an inferior educa-

tion. Whereas middle-class White parents have generally felt themselves a part of their children's educational process, many parents in various minority and low-**socioeconomic** status groups felt disenfranchised prior to the landmark legislation of the 1960s. Parental involvement for all, regardless of heritage and economics, became highlighted in this era and continues to be an important issue.

Children in Poverty

In the 1930s, social welfare programs were seen as a way to help the poor. Aid to Families With Dependent Children was just such a program that existed at first primarily to assist unmarried mothers in providing for their children. Even with a rising economy after World War II, large numbers of children were still living in poverty. Such children entered school with many problems that affected their ability to learn. In 1965, President Lyndon Johnson launched the War on Poverty. Children raised in poverty were now to be given assistance before entering school and thus a greater chance at success in society. The Elementary and Secondary Education Act of 1965 (PL 89-10) was the largest grant ever made by the federal government to aid education. Educational programs such as Title I/Chapter I, **Head Start**, Home Start, and **Project Follow Through** were designed under this act to compensate for the lack of early education by children living in poverty. The Head Start project was perhaps the most comprehensive. In addition to receiving educational experiences, children and families were provided with health, nutritional, and psychological services. Parents also were to play important roles as volunteers, paid aides, and instructors in their children's education. Parents became a part of Head Start advisory boards, thus acquiring decision-making powers both in selecting teachers and in making curriculum decisions (Lazar, 1977). Teachers in these programs were expected to make home visits, and the curriculum used was expected to reflect both the experiences and the cultural heritage of the diverse children. By implementing the federal guidelines, these programs provided an early model for family–school–community involvement.

In the 1990s, Americans began to believe that though Head Start was ultimately deemed successful, the War on Poverty had somehow failed. In spite of many welfare programs, child poverty increased over 60% from the early 1970s to the 1990s (O'Hare, 1996). In an attempt to change this course of events, the Family Support Act of 1988 stressed education and job training for welfare recipients. Mothers on welfare who returned to work or enrolled in education programs were guaranteed child care assistance and coverage for health insurance through Medicaid.

After some degree of success, there were new proposals in the 1990s to modify the act considerably. The 1996 welfare reform bill replaced child care entitlement programs with a single federal Child Care and Development Block Grant (CCDBG) and gave more responsibility and decision making for administering and funding to the states. This bill required all child care funds to be administered from one lead agency, thus avoiding overlap of programs. Other aspects included the following: (a) a limit was placed on how long a family could receive welfare; (b) persons receiving welfare were required to get a part-time job or receive job training; and (c) mothers with a child under a year old were exempt, but only for one child (Blank, 1997). The funding stressed improving the quality of care for children and providing education for the parents, though child care was not guaranteed (Hagan, 1998). The welfare reform legislation is due for refunding in 2004.

Children with Disabilities

As the federally supported programs developed, parents realized they had power in determining their rights to educational opportunities for their children. A group of parents in Missouri, concerned about how their children with disabilities were being treated, united with a civil rights organization to focus on rights for children with disabilities. Thus, the Education for All Handicapped Children Act (PL 94-142) emerged in 1975. This act ensured a free and appropriate education to all children with disabilities, and in 1986, the Federal Preschool and Early Intervention Program Act (PL 99-457) extended rights and services to 3-year-olds. In the 1990 amendment, the title of the act was changed to the **Individuals with Disabilities Education Act (IDEA)**, and the term *handicapped* was changed to *disabled*. In keeping with this legislation, the Head Start Act was amended in 1992 by the Head Start Improvement Act, with services extended to infants and toddlers. In 1997, the act was reauthorized, with modifications in the delivery systems, requirements in placement of students with discipline problems, and provisions for professional development. IDEA became such a comprehensive law that it was divided into three parts: Part A describes the extent and policies of the law; Part B points to the rights and benefits for 3- to 21-year-olds; and Part C (formerly Part H) addresses infants and toddlers (Turnbull et al., 2002).

Under the preceding acts, parents are given rights of due process; they have the right to be involved in the entire process of their child's evaluation, placement, and educational objectives; and if there are differences of opinion, they have rights to the services of a mediator. Children placed in special education programs now must receive an **individualized education program (IEP)**, prepared by a school team, including the parents, and an **individualized family service plan (IFSP)**, for families with infants or toddlers with disabilities.

An important aspect of the law has been that children are to be placed in the **least restrictive environment** possible. Except for

An important aspect of
IDEA is that children with
disabilities are to be
included in the regular
classroom setting

extreme cases, this means that they are to be included in the regular classroom setting, with resource persons and support services available to assist the regular teacher. When a child's behavior is disruptive to others in the classroom, the child may be placed in alternative placement, but only if the behavior is a manifestation of the child's disability and not of the child's ability.

Over the years, interpretation of the law has often caused controversy. At one point, the term **mainstreamed** was used, and more recently the term **inclusion** has been used. Neither term has been used in the mandate that declares that school districts are obligated to provide an education for children with disabilities alongside typically developing children to the maximum extent possible. Removal is allowed only when the severity of the disability is such that even with special aides and services, the regular classroom cannot provide an appropriate education (Yell, 1998).

Parents have the right to accept or challenge any school decision and to examine all records the school keeps on their children. Parent involvement is assured in these procedures, and the acts have actually had the effect of forcing parents and educators into partnership relationships.

In many instances, parents and educators have collaborated successfully in educating children with special needs. They have also used the resources of the community in different ways, including having volunteers work one-on-one with children. However, not all school personnel and parents have agreed on the most appropriate education for particular children. Since the laws have been enacted, the number of children classified as having disabling conditions has risen steadily (Webb et al., 2003). Half of these identified children are now classified as learning disabled, and a disproportionate number are African American and Hispanic children. Concerns about inappropriate placement or the mislabeling of children have appeared as the number of children classified as learning disabled has risen. It is understandable that some parents have used their due process rights to sue schools for inappropriate placement. With such pressures, it becomes vital for schools to find new ways to work successfully with parents and to use community resources for improving education for all children.

Minority Populations

The history of parent–community–school involvement has taken a different course for many families. In the early years of immigration, many families saw their ethnic, cultural, religious, and social traditions blended into a homogenized "American ethic." Greater educational opportunities and material benefits were afforded to those immigrants living by the dominant code of values. For many families, however, assimilation was more difficult or less desirable. Poverty and race distinctions also caused many families to be denied opportunities for equal access to quality education or job opportunities. Today such access continues to be a problem, though in more subtle ways. In spite of antidiscrimination laws all over the United States, many families, though assimilated, still feel the sting of subtle discrimination. Poverty and race distinctions mean that certain persons have to work much harder to gain access to the rights and privileges assumed by White, middle-class Americans.

A poor immigrant child, whose father was a tenant farmer in a small midwestern community, was strongly advised to take technical and agricultural courses in high school instead of college courses. After all, his father was a tenant farmer, so any hope for attending college was slim. In spite of lack of school support, he persisted and surmounted many roadblocks. Today he is a college professor with a doctorate from one of America's outstanding universities. Though he achieved his goals, he had to overcome prejudice against poor tenant farmers in America. In more recent years, there has been progress toward more acceptance of other cultures.

In more open and supportive communities, some immigrant families have received support from local community groups and with persistence and hard work have been able to surmount difficulties. Some have even maintained their language and culture, succeeding in their attempt to operate in two cultures.

The history of the United States is a story of waves of immigration. In the 1600s and 1700s, western Europeans, bringing an Anglo-European culture and a Christian ethic, came to colonize different parts of the United States—crowding out Native Americans and bringing slaves from Africa. In the 1800s, more Roman Catholic groups moved to the United States as a result of the Irish famine and military acquisition of Mexican territories. Then, in the early 1900s, other groups from central and southern Europe and Asia came to the United States seeking new opportunity. In the later part of the 1900s, as other countries sustained internal strife, a large number of immigrants came from Latin America, Asia, the Caribbean, and Middle Eastern countries, seeking refuge from conflict and persecution. By the mid-1900s, three fourths of immigrants each year were from Asia and Latin America (DeVita, 1995). All of these immigrant groups have had an impact on American culture, values, and traditions. Still, at the beginning of this century, the dominant culture in America has remained European American, and the dominant religious traditions stem from Judeo-Christian religions (Gollnick & Chinn, 2002).

The early minority groups were assimilated in accordance with how much they were able or willing to adapt to the majority culture. This usually worked for Europeans but rarely with other ethnically different populations. Today, Native Americans, African Americans, and Hispanics are large ethnic groups in the United States and, in spite of civil rights legislation and affirmative action, have higher poverty rates than Whites (Lichter & Crowley, 2002). Throughout the history of the United States, these particular groups have been denied easy and equal access to quality education, which means that their chances of moving out of poverty are less than those of their White counterparts (Lichter & Crowley, 2002).

Minority Populations and Families. During the colonial period, the two major non-White ethnic groups were Native Americans and African Americans. For these two groups, the family, in conjunction with its ethnic community, was the primary means for educating children.

A communal ethic has always prevailed in Native American communities. Historically, community groups helped parents educate children and teach them economic skills, their cultural heritage, and spiritual awareness. The community expected all women to teach necessary homemaking skills, and boys as they matured were taught by various elders to hunt, survive, and fight. Through rituals, ceremonies, and oral traditions, the tribal elders passed on the religious beliefs and cultural heritage to young Native Americans (Szasz, 1988).

African Americans have lived in the United States since 1619, when the first individuals appeared as indentured servants at Jamestown. By the 1700s, most African Americans were slaves, and plantation owners exercised complete control over them. Though there were few opportunities for formal education in slavery, African Americans formed a distinct culture. It was the family and plantation that taught the children values, community behaviors, and as much of their native customs as possible. In some instances, the children learned reading and writing as they played with their owners' children (J. M. Rich, 1997). But during these early years, the sanctioned education for African American children was limited to the necessary skills for working and living within the plantation community.

Minorities and the Community. As the American expansion began, conflicts arose among the European American settlers regarding the education of non-Anglo persons. Some colonists believed that Native Americans should be annihilated and that African Americans should be kept from getting an education so as to avoid revolts (Berlin, 1998). Others, whether from religious zeal or from practical considerations, maintained it was necessary to acculturate minority children about European American culture through education. In different parts of the country, religious groups established schools and missions to educate and convert Native Americans. In the Southwest, priests and nuns taught Native Americans farming practices, vocational skills, and the Spanish language (Kidwell & Swift, 1976). Still, the major emphasis at that time was that all groups should accept the Caucasian conquerors' religious teachings and behavior codes.

In the South, despite laws forbidding education for African Americans, some plantation owners did teach the children of slaves to read and write so that they could become skilled workers and read the Bible. Owners introduced their own religion to their slaves, and thus a large number of African Americans adopted a form of Protestantism. Later, some African Americans formed their own clandestine schools (Weinberg, 1977). In the early part of the 20th century, a Black Muslim faith known as the Nation of Islam emerged to promote different views of Black history and culture (Gollnick & Chinn, 2002).

Despite these modest efforts to provide education, the majority community made no effort to work with Native American and African American children and their families. The European American community dictated the rules of conduct irrespective of the values and culture of other groups. For many minority groups, these early practices were the beginnings of alienation between schools and families. Such practices of disrespect have resulted

The aftermath of the Civil War offered greater chances for formal education for many African Americans

in serious alienation problems and further discrimination of minority-group members.

Minorities and the Schools.   In the 1800s, as schools became the major force for educating children of the dominant culture, schools were seen as the way of melding the increasing number of immigrants into a common cultural group for American society. But Mexican Americans and Asian Americans migrated to the United States in increasing numbers during the 1800s, and these groups created more variety in ethnic grouping and therefore more controversy. Differences that existed in earlier periods regarding how society provided schools for minority groups reappeared in the 1800s. The controversies continue in some areas today.

Native Americans.   To ensure better **acculturation** of Native Americans, boarding schools were established in the late 1800s, and children were removed from their families to attend them. Some schools were established on reservations, but the Bureau of Indian Affairs, not the tribe itself, was in charge of them. European American–style schools were established to teach Christianity, English, basic skills, and some vocational training to young Native Americans. No sense of partnership on education existed, and each Native American community was expected to submit to the type of education provided by the majority culture (Szasz, 1977).

African Americans.   The aftermath of the Civil War offered greater chances for formal education for many African Americans. "Freedman schools" were established in the South in which former slaves and their children, along with some impoverished White children, were taught the curriculum of the New England common schools. Reading, writing, math, geography, moral development, and industrial education became the curriculum so that these students would be ready for the labor force (Gutek, 2000). There was, however, so much resistance to literacy for African Americans from southern Whites after Reconstruction that until 1954, African American children were educated in segregated schools. The landmark case of *Brown v. Topeka Board of Education* (1954) precipitated action by African American leaders and many Whites that led to the Civil Rights Act of 1964, forcing school desegregation (Bullock, 1967).

Hispanic Americans.   For the Hispanic American population, family, school, and community attempts at partnerships have had a history more of alienation than of cooperation. When America gained possession of the northern half of Mexico in 1848, the Spanish–Mexican–Indian population was expected to become American. Attitudes of most Americans at that time were that Mexican Americans were inferior and could be denied their rights (J. M. Rich, 1997). However, in spite of negative attitudes and unequal treatment throughout the era, migration of Mexican Americans to the United States has continued to the present.

Large numbers of other Hispanic groups from Central America and the Caribbean have migrated to the United States, especially since the 1960s. Some new émigrés were affluent and had few economic and educational hardships, but this situation did not exist for the great majority. Presently, over 60% of Hispanic Americans in this country are Mexican American and, together with Puerto Ricans, experience the most discrimination (Sadker & Sadker, 2003). Hispanic Americans now number 37 million (U.S. Bureau of the Census, 2002), making them America's largest minority group.

From the beginning, the concept of assimilation in American public schools created

conflicts with Mexican American populations. English was the language of instruction, and newly enrolled children were expected to abandon Spanish as well as other aspects of their culture. Though no legal segregation existed for Hispanic Americans, de facto segregation did, and most Mexican Americans over the years attended separate and inferior schools or were placed in separate classes. They usually had fewer well-prepared teachers, and less money was spent on their education (Sadker & Sadker, 2003). Classrooms were **monocultural**—reflecting Anglo traditions, learning styles, and value systems.

These circumstances often alienated Hispanic parents, who saw no purpose in education that destroyed their family lifestyles (Weinberg, 1977), even though early political leaders in the Hispanic community urged assimilation to avoid trouble. During the civil rights movement of the 1960s, new leadership appeared for Mexican Americans. Parents and political leaders joined forces in making demands for better schools and more equal treatment. Some gains came in a curriculum more responsive to their cultural heritage, instruction in Spanish, and "culture-free" IQ tests (Weinberg, 1977). The Bilingual Act of 1968 and subsequent acts provided non-English-speaking children with instruction in both their native language and English, but much controversy regarding the best way to teach non-English speakers persists. In 1986, then Secretary of Education William Bennett changed the role of the federal government in bilingual education; states were given the responsibility of determining the type of language instruction for their students.

In states with large Hispanic populations, bilingual programs were popular. In these programs, children received at least some academic instruction in their native language. Many believed that these programs delayed Hispanic children's progress in English and denied them academic opportunities. In 1998,

California voters replaced their extensive bilingual programs with **structured English immersion** (SEI) programs. Children in these programs are immersed in English now, and get assistance as needed. Their own language is used only as it helps to clarify points (Baker, 1998). Shortly after the programs started, achievement scores went up, and opponents of bilingual education used this evidence as a reason to eliminate more programs. This has practically eliminated bilingual education in California. However, more recent studies (Gandra et al., 1999) challenge these findings and indicate factors other than SEI programs resulted in higher test scores. Most linguistic and sociocultural studies indicate that multilingual and multicultural experiences are important for the diverse population found in America today (Trawick-Smith (2003).

Asian Americans.   Asian Americans, an extremely varied group, are relatively late arrivals to this country. Chinese workers first came to the western United States in the 19th century in connection with railroad building. The first Japanese came at the beginning of the 20th century, and Southeast Asians immigrated in the 1970s and 1980s as they fled their war-torn countries. Korean immigrants have steadily moved to American cities over the last half century. As with all immigrants, the cultural and religious beliefs and practices vary, but Buddhism and Hinduism are two strong religious influences for Asians. Though Asians have been discriminated against and have experienced hardships adjusting to living in the United States, they have been, as a group, more academically and economically successful. However, like other émigrés, Asian Americans have been expected to put aside their languages, cultural mores, and customs and adjust to European American culture. Because there are many different Asian languages, schools struggle to find the best types of bilingual education programs for Asian children.

As with other minority groups, Asian American parents have often been alienated or confused by school expectations and by mainstream American culture. This problem often makes good parent–school–community relations in Asian communities difficult to maintain.

Arab Americans.   Immigrants of Middle Eastern and South Asian countries have come to the United States in relatively small numbers throughout American history. Many of them practice the Muslim faith, and individuals (though Caucasian in ancestry) have become a distinct minority community within the larger American culture. For a large number of Americans, an Islamic presence did not make an impact until the Al Qaeda attack on the World Trade Center in 2001. This brought the Muslim faith and Islamic culture into greater focus in America, and it highlighted the influence of minority religions in our country. The faiths are growing in numbers, and they are impacting traditional Judaic-Christian practices, for many European Americans are beginning to seek non-Christian spiritual guidance (Gollnick & Chinn, 2002).

MULTICULTURAL EMPHASIS

Adjustments for minority groups with regard to educational opportunity has changed dramatically in recent decades. As federal legislation has guaranteed educational opportunities for all children regardless of race, color, religious beliefs, ethnicity, ableness, class structure, sexual orientation, or intermarriage, a greater voice has been given to minority persons in spite of orientation. A change in attitude toward cultural diversity is slowly evolving. American schools and communities in general have moved in recent decades from an earlier **melting-pot thesis**, to a position of valuing multicultural education. As this type of education gains dominance, we find parent and community involvement more prominent in schools.

Multicultural education requires substantial change—in attitude, staffing patterns, curriculum and materials, and interaction patterns—from the techniques of the monocultural curriculum that has always dominated education in the United States.

Attitude Change

At the beginning of the 20th century, the prevailing attitude in the United States held that minority groups and new immigrants should be assimilated. The children from different groups were to learn the behavior codes, values, and cultural expectations of the majority culture. This attitude of assimilation continued into the 1950s and 1960s, making the tacit assumption that "something was wrong with the other culture" that assimilation could fix. **Cultural deprivation** was the term used during the 1960s War on Poverty and in the initial bilingual programs. Officials believed that children needed compensatory programs to make up for this deprivation (Stein, 1986). One healthy dimension in the legislation of this period was that parents became included as decision makers. This important step required teachers and parents to communicate and work together, thus affording all a chance to grow.

As parent–school–community partnerships became established in the 1980s and 1990s, attitudes toward ethnic groups and people of different heritages gradually changed. At first, recognition of different racial and ethnic groups was demonstrated, and steps were taken to incorporate and adjust to these differences. However, children of multicultural and multiracial families, as well as those in gay and lesbian families, also need respect for the values and codes of their particular family culture. As the 21st century unfolds, multicultural education is being implemented in many American schools. In schools adhering to principles of true cultural pluralism, attitudes will change so that children of diverse cultures, as well as their parents, are viewed as having strengths that contribute to and expand the education of all children. Acceptance of diverse cultural viewpoints and a sense of our pluralistic society are important goals for a multicultural curriculum.

Staffing Patterns

Historically, American thinking has been that if children were to be acculturated, it was important that teachers and administrators be from the majority culture so that children would have "proper" role models. In earlier periods, teachers who were recruited from minority groups were always sent to training schools that would educate them for the dominant culture (Gutek, 2000), thus continuing the ideas of monoculturalism.

As multicultural education gained ground, it became apparent that the staff in any school needed to have special training in cultural sensitivity, members working as a team, and representation from different cultures or orientations (Kagan & Neuman, 1997). Such diversity of staff is important, as it provides positive role models for children from different ethnic groups. All teachers can emphasize their own cultural heritage as they invite parents and members of diverse cultures and backgrounds to collaborate in providing richer classroom experiences. Using their own experiences, teachers from different minority groups can now help others understand different nonverbal behaviors and learning patterns, as well as acceptance of different beliefs.

Curriculum and Teaching Materials

Early publications and all curriculum materials were based on an European American worldview. Caucasian children were the main characters in stories where people lived in pleasant homes surrounded by nice lawns.

There were two parents, the father working hard, and the mother lovingly tended the children. Extended families were rarely depicted. Individuals with different lifestyles were often portrayed as somehow wrong, to be pitied, or quaint (Stein, 1986). Moral lessons, based on Puritan ethics, were often taught along with reading and writing. History and geography were taught from the Anglo-European viewpoint, and the contributions of other cultures to society's development were largely ignored (Sadker & Sadker, 2003)

Our newer multicultural curriculum presents materials from several perspectives. People of all cultures, religious beliefs, and those with differing degrees of disabilities and varied sexual orientations are viewed in a variety of situations, and children study the major contributions of numerous cultural groups. Customs, rituals, and traditions of different cultures are explored so that students may appreciate both similarities and differences. Teachers can now begin to view minority-group parents as a vital link in communicating aspects of culture to all children. However, textbook companies have, at times, yielded to "political correctness" pressure from ethnic groups and have at times distorted both history and cultures in an effort to "be fair" (Stille, 1998), and some school systems have banned textbooks or literary titles that expand on nonmainstream views. Teachers need to preview materials to be used with children for their accuracy and currency. When pressure groups exert so much influence that a skewed view of history, different cultural expectations, literary quality, and the makeup of American society hinder children's educational development, teachers must seek more appropriate materials (Elkind, 1995).

Interaction Patterns

When minority-group children were first educated in public schools, teachers assumed they learned in the same manner as children from the predominant culture. If they responded in an unfamiliar way, the teacher assumed they were being impolite or were not very bright (Stein, 1986). Official America had a correct way to rear children, and minority-group parents were expected to learn these ways or doom their children to failure. Competitive, individualistic, and aggressive learning styles have always been rewarded in traditional American schools, and cooperative learning, until recently, was seen as cheating.

Schools that now sponsor multicultural education recognize different learning styles and understand the need to employ different strategies to accommodate different children. In multicultural classrooms, children learn about these different patterns and learn to accept these differences. One can see that the family becomes an important part in providing a bridge from the family's cultural patterns to the more diverse patterns found in a multiethnic and multicultural society. With proper opportunities, we find that all children can learn to be conversant with more than one culture (Banks, 2002; Salend, 2001).

IMPLICATIONS FOR PROFESSIONALS

As you become immersed in the study of various aspects of teaching and children, the concerns of the present can cloud your thinking and objectivity. Every generation has its problems and successes in educating children. Understanding the major issues at different historical periods helps you view current events in a broader light. In studying this chapter, you have seen that home, schools, and communities have always affected how children learn, but recognition or use of this knowledge by educators has varied. In the 21st century, family structure and societal expectations are very different from those at the beginning of the 20th century. Because of these

In multicultural classrooms, children learn to accept differences

changes and the complexity of society, there are no easy solutions for how to work and deal with the families of today. But some things haven't changed, and how parents, families, and communities were viewed in the past can be beginning points of how to work with parents today.

Look at the first picture in the chapter text in which children are observing a process that was a part of their lives—shoeing a horse. Now look at a modern picture—the girls at the tidal pool, for example, in Chapter 7. The girls, too, are observing a process important to their lives. Adults in the two pictures realize the important educative process of the environment, but how each adult handles the learning will depend on the times and the culture.

Understanding how the relationships among parents, teachers, and community members has changed in different generations gives you a broader perspective as you learn the expectations of your particular community.

SUMMARY AND REVIEW

Parents, communities, and schools have always assumed significant roles and responsibilities for the education of children in any society. At different times in American history, each of the three social settings assumed greater leadership and responsibility than did the other two. And in most periods, we find some instances of parent–school–community cooperation and collaboration. At other times, conflicts appeared when one institution seemed to dominate the way children were educated.

In colonial times, the family was responsible for educating children. The Puritans of New England are credited with the notion that the community at large should oversee education, and early laws in that colony regulated the teaching of academics, behavior codes, and moral development. By the 1800s, communities became the strong voice in organizing schools, hiring teachers, and taxing themselves to support these schools. Professional educators gained dominance over curriculum decisions in the 20th century.

Parents, communities, and schools have, of course, collaborated from time to time. Not until recently, however, have we seen any significant joining of forces. By the 1980s, it became clear that strong parent–school–community relationships were necessary if schools were to be responsible for educating all children. Various partnerships for educating children have been formed since then.

Though free and compulsory education has been a tenet of American educational theory for many years, most communities still have not extended equal opportunity to all cultural groups. From the 1800s to the mid-1900s, most minority-group children attended segregated schools or de facto segregated classrooms with fewer educational opportunities. As desegregation became more prevalent in the 1950s and 1960s, the federal government provided special programs for children living in poverty. Initiators of these programs recognized that to be successful, they must involve parents and the leaders in the community where these children live. As a result, many minority-group parents acquired decision-making powers over their children's education—a situation that had been absent for generations.

In the 1980s, Americans began to realize the importance of multicultural education for all children. Attitudes continue to change, school staffs have become diverse, and curriculum materials now present topics from a multicultural viewpoint. Many educators have started to value differences and, in the process, include parents as valuable partners in the curriculum.

At the beginning of the 21st century, in spite of many federal programs, the numbers of children in poverty have remained quite constant for over 10 years. American children seemed to lag behind academically, and more mothers now need out-of-home care for their children. The federal initiatives to solve problems that arose from these changes have been varied but have included welfare reform, the establishment of national goals, and growing support for schools to develop home, school, and community partnerships.

SUGGESTED ACTIVITIES AND QUESTIONS

1. Interview a senior citizen and determine whether he or she thinks family influence patterns have changed since his or her childhood.

2. Identify a federal law affecting education in the United States. Interview a teacher, a parent, and a local businessperson to assess their feelings about the law and how it affects them personally. Compare your findings with other classmates. What laws did your associates dislike?

3. Visit a primary-school classroom in your area. Interview the teacher to determine the amount of parental involvement he or she has at present. Ask the teacher whether this level of involvement has changed over his or her career.

4. Examine a primary-grade curriculum guide (or textbook) from the 1950s. Compare the amount of multicultural material and the philosophical perspective you find with that found in a current guide (or textbook). Make two columns listing the differences.

RESOURCES

Books

1. Bronfenbrenner, U. (1979). *The ecology of human development.* Cambridge, MA: Harvard University Press.
2. Corsaro, W. A. (1997). *The sociology of childhood.* Thousand Oaks, CA: Sage.
3. Mills, K. (1998). *Something better for my children. The history and people of Head Start.* New York: Dutton.

Films and Videos

1. *Childhood* [Video, 40 min]. (2002). Focuses on 20th century developments in childhood education. Companion video for use with publication of same title. Olney, MD: ACEI Publications.
2. *First five years last forever* [Video, 29 min]. (2002). Overview of children's early development with insights from T. B. Brazelton, and Barbara Bowman. San Luis Obispo, CA: Davidson Films.
3. *Play: A Vygotskian Approach* [Video, 26 min]. (1996). Shows how play affects child's development following the Vygotskian philosophy. San Louis Obispo, CA: Davidson Films.

Organizations

American Anthropology Association
2200 Wilson Boulevard
Arlington, VA 22201
www.aaanet.org

Children's Defense Fund
25 East Street, NW
Washington, DC 20001
www.childrensdefense.org

Council for Exceptional Children
1920 Association Drive
Reston, VA 20191
www.cec.sped.org

Websites

1. www.doe.gov Site for U.S. Department of Education. Contains comprehensive outlines of federal legislation and initiatives, such as Goals 2000, IDEA, and Drug-free Schools.
2. www.intac.com/-washington/sped1.htm Contains essential information regarding special education for teachers, parents, and administrators.
3. www.nap.edu Site gives information on brain research from neurons to neighbors.
4. www.nclb.org Relates to No Child Left Behind legislation—discusses how government is actively involved in education.
5. www.negp.gov Gives information on the national education goals and what different states have accomplished in reaching them.

Chapter 3

Viewing Family Diversity

We have to know where we come from—to understand where we can go. ("Give to the Tortoise," a Zulu folk song)

Families have been an institution since Paleolithic times and are one main reason that humankind has evolved to the point where we are now. Humans are the only species with a complex code of family relationships stretching through generations. Other mammals form simple family structures for a much more limited time—a few weeks to a few years.

Since the American family is a basic building block in our society, readers need to consider first this primary element in the social setting partnership and the ways these family units work with others and for themselves. The more we understand how families function, endure, and connect, the better we are able to bring them into a positive connection with the other two settings.

American families vary immensely in makeup, and if you talk with several colleagues, most likely all will have somewhat different descriptions of what "family" means to them. Chapter 3 focuses on the demographics and the diverse nature of families we find in the United States today. In reading this chapter you will learn the following:

1. American children are reared in many different types of households and family groupings.

2. Many social and economic factors affect family life.

3. Racial, ethnic, and language differences, as well as marital status of parents, affect the structure and functioning of families.

4. Religious factors, cultural expectations, and conditions of disability have an impact on family life.

5. Families are always in a process of change from one stage or condition to another.

The following vignette points out some not so uncommon changes that unfolded in one American family as the members progressed through several years of life.

Five-year-old Jana had just entered Mrs. Thompson's multiage classroom. Mrs. Thompson found her a happy child who came from a "nice family." As did other neighborhood mothers, Jana's mother walked her to school and at noon, her mother met her, and they walked to Gramma's to talk about Jana's day at school. In the evening, Jana bubbled away at the dinner table, telling her father and older brother all about her day. Jana was secure and snug in her world, where love abounded. But Jana's world was about to change.

Her mother became very ill that winter and was often hospitalized. Gramma came to take Jana to school on most days, though the child sometimes was angry with her. But then Jana became worried that Gramma would not be close by.

Jana's mother died within the year, and the following year, Jana's life was filled with adjustments. Gramma and Grampa came to live at her house and take care of her, and that helped. Jana missed her mother taking her to school, for now she had to go to school with her older brother, who wanted to be with his friends, not with her. Her dad, always involved in his work, just didn't seem to be there every evening, as she would have liked. Jana, however, worked hard in school and enjoyed the consistent routine Mrs. Thompson provided over the 3 years Jana was in her class.

At age 8, Jana's world shifted again. Her father remarried, and now she had an extra older brother and an older sister. Her own older brother became a "pain" when he looked after her while her father and stepmother were out. Sometimes when that responsibility was shared by her brother and stepbrother, the two boys quarreled and the house got messy. When Jana tried to tell her side of the boys' squabbles, it seemed that her stepmother always became annoyed and then unresponsive. Jana's father tried to comfort her in her room after the quarrels, but he implied that Jana should cooperate more and help become a part of their new life. Gramma and Grandpa had moved away that year, and this seemed to delight Jana's stepmother, who felt they interfered.

When Jana was 10, a new baby was born into the family. At times Jana enjoyed the delightful baby, but she also became jealous when the baby got a lot of attention. Jana did begin to develop a more accepting, although shaky, relationship with her stepmother—they especially enjoyed cooking together and taking special packages to neighbors who were ill or in need.

What is a family? Family can mean different things at different times. Jana, in this opening vignette, was always part of a family, but the structure changed several times in her growing-up years.

The term *family* describes particular household groupings that occur in all human societies. Historically, the designation indicated a specific home grouping, but in today's world sociologists argue that "family" denotes a variety of clustered adults and children (Bianchi & Spain, 1996; Teachman, 2000). For some families, the cluster remains relatively constant; other families, like Jana's, evolve into different arrangements over the years. Whatever the cluster, the family is a dynamic and ever changing force in a child's life and well being.

Though family composition may not have actually changed a great deal over the years, cultural concepts of what constitutes a "proper" family and the percentages of different family clusters have altered considerably. In the late 19th century, Victorian society in Britain and the United States idealized the family as consisting of two doting and proper parents with several adoring and capable children at their knees. Of course, this was far from universal even then, but through literature and folklore, people accepted this picture of what ought to be the situation in their towns, cities, and neighborhoods.

Changes in family arrangement in the latter part of the 20th century certainly were dramatic, and we now find far more diversity in the structural aspects and processes of American families.

Family arrangements became a political issue in the 1990s and the decade since, and the notion of "family values" has received extensive media coverage during election campaigns. Actually, this attention has provoked much more study and analysis of American families, and our population appears more knowledgeable today about the social, economic, and political upheavals that precipitated much of the change.

Traditional and idealized American family forms are obviously diminishing in contemporary America as other arrangements grow more commonplace (Allen, Fine, & Demo, 2000; Bianchi & Casper, 2000). While the total number of households expanded 22% between 1980 and 2000, the nuclear family (with two parents plus their biological children) decreased from 31% of all household units to only 24%, and in the same time period, single-parent families increased more than one fourth (U.S. Bureau of the Census, 2002).

While there may be distinct advantages to the traditional nuclear family, labeling it as the only "good" or "positive" family form is risky, to say the least. Many other family arrangements have proved coherent and viable (Coontz, 1997; Hetherington & Kelly, 2002).

Human service professionals need to be aware of subtle and unsubtle prejudices toward nontraditional families. It is all too easy for teachers to value or feel comfortable with only those configurations that approximate their ideal family unit. The important thing to remember is that many arrangements work quite well, and over time most young children will experience changes in their own family structure. As you learn about interacting with families, be sensitive to differences and carefully search out ways to support, value, and work with all the differing types you encounter (Banks, 2002; Hildebrand, Phenice, Gray, & Hines, 1996).

The family is the organizational arrangement recognized by almost all societies as foremost in protecting, nurturing, supporting, and mediating for children in their growing years. The term *family* in Western culture frequently connotes heterosexual and married adults. Our definition in this text is broader, as we look beyond marriage and sexual orientation. Many stable and prospering family units involve unmarried adults, and while some partners have been married to others, they have reconstituted a family singly or with a new partner without the formality of marriage.

As the 21st century begins, recognized family groups in the United States are very different and vary more from traditional arrangements than ever before. However, it is important to remember that less than one half (40%) of all American households have children. Statistics on family makeup cited in this text are based on families with children in the household. See Figure 3–1 for the breakdown of household units and note that our categories include only the first two bars of that graph.

Most families, like Jana's in the chapter's opening vignette, are dynamic. Family structure is never permanent; members form a particular configuration for only a brief time and then change comes about. For example, when Jana was in eighth grade, her teacher asked her

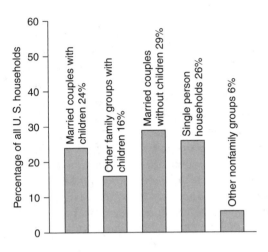

Figure 3–1   Types of American households in 2000.
Source: U.S. Census Bureau, Current Population Report P20-537, 2002.

to draw and label two pictures: one of her family when she was in kindergarten and another of her family now. Jana's explanation shows her grasp of family changes.

In her kindergarten picture, Jana drew and labeled, "my real mom, my dad, my brother, and me." In her eighth-grade picture she drew herself in the center with other people in clusters around her. Closest to her were figures labeled "dad and my older brother." On the other side but distanced from her were four people labeled "my stepsister, my stepmom, my stepbrother, and my little sister." In the right corner she had drawn a circle for four people and wrote, "my aunt, my uncle, me, and my cousin." When her teacher asked her to explain her pictures, she said, "This first picture is me and my family before Mom died. Dad remarried, so now I have a stepmom and a brother and sister and a little sister. These people," she added, pointing to the encircled, "aren't really my family, but I stay with them a lot, so sometimes they feel like my family."

Public schools in the United States must accept all children in a community, with whatever conditions, orientations and experiences they have. This means that any one classroom teacher relates to and interacts with representatives from several different family types. The backgrounds, values, and experiences vary from one child to the next, and teachers and other community workers must accept and value all families as they communicate and work to enhance programs. Sensitive and responsive interactions are the only base for healthy home–school–community relations.

In any description of family lifestyles it is impossible to include all configurations, but as a prospective teacher or community worker, you will want to ascertain the makeup of homes in your community and assess how they function. Chapter 4 discusses family functioning in depth.

DIFFERENT TYPES OF FAMILIES

Nuclear Families

From shortly after World War II through the early 1970s, media producers in the United States presented what they considered to be the typical American family. That image of the nuclear family with a father breadwinner and mother homemaker was viewed throughout the United States as the all-American, "Leave It to Beaver" model family. It appeared in film, on television, in books and magazines, and in advertisements of all types (Coontz, 1999).

This model, two-parent home with children usually was presented as stable, thrifty, economically secure, and very happy. Of course, individual situations varied with regard to health, social status, and problems encountered for the sake of plot or to meet current marketing needs. The archetype has been part of American and British (and, to a lesser degree, continental European) culture for generations. But the nuclear family, and particularly the version with the breadwinner father, is much less predominant today, and

Coontz (1997, 1999) stresses that it was widespread only in the 1940s, 1950s, and early 1960s.

A **nuclear family** is one in which the parents are first-time married, the children living with them are their biological children, and no other adults or children live in the home. This arrangement with breadwinning father and homemaker mother is true now for only 7% of U.S. households (U.S. Bureau of the Census, 2002). A minor variation is the home where the children are legally adopted rather than biological offspring.

Role redefinitions for males and females, social pressures, changing economics, relaxation of marriage mores, and reconsidered family functions have all affected the nuclear family's dominance. Census Bureau statistics show that in 2001, only 24% of children in the United States lived in a two-parent "Leave It to Beaver" family with a breadwinner and a homemaker. This significant demographic change for the nuclear family household implies concurrent changes for other types. Figure 3–2 shows this demographic distribution as of 2001. Children in nuclear families more often have the advantages of higher affluence, but there is no guarantee of less stress.

Extended Families

The multigenerational family unit resembles the nuclear family but with additions, usually adult relatives. The identifying feature of an **extended family** is that the reference person, head of household, or wage earner is the adult with young children. Older relatives or other adults are appended to this nucleus.

The extended family arrangement is typical for agrarian societies. Many farms have had three generations of a family living together. In the United States, many individuals who were born in the earlier part of the 20th century can remember living as part of an extended family. Intergenerational families have advantages

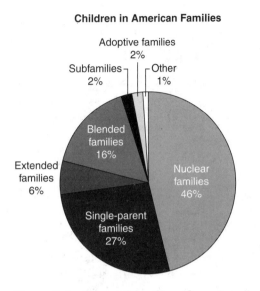

Children in American Families

Figure 3–2   Types of families where American children lived in 2001.
Note: Foster children are included in one or another of the categories.
Source: Adapted from 2001 census projections: U.S. Bureau of the Census, Current Population Reports P20-506 & P20-509, 2002.

over nuclear ones: The "extra" adults can provide care and nurturing for the young, to say nothing of helping with farm chores. The extended family was common in Europe in the 19th century, and immigrants to the United States brought the practice with them when resettling (Bailyn, Dalleck, Davis, Donald, Thomas, & Wood, 2000).

Extended families survived in urban areas for different reasons than they did in rural areas. The practice fit the need to economize, to bolster the cottage industries, and stabilize the social situations in which newcomers found themselves. Extended families became less common in American culture after industrialization, but the configuration has been retained in many minority-group homes (Webb, Metha, & Jordan, 2003) and sometimes temporarily in single-parent homes, as in the case of Jana in our vignette. Economics alone can

dictate a need for sharing a dwelling when families are pressed. Heritage, a need for security, reverence for elders, and the sharing of materials all combine to make the extended family a logical arrangement for many groups.

An **extended family** can occur in any of a number of combinations. Typical are the following:

1. Mother and father with children, plus one or more grandparents.

2. Mother and father with children, plus one or more unmarried siblings of the parents or other relatives.

3. A divorced or separated mother or father with children, plus grandparents or siblings or other relatives.

It is easy to see that extended families can be quite large, often including several related adults and children, but the decline in the number of extended families continues. Taylor (2000) indicated that only 6% of American children now live in this type of family. However, about 20% of African American children do.

Single-Parent Families

Single-parent families, in which one parent lives with her or his children, have always been present. The death of a spouse was not an uncommon disrupter in the lives of our ancestors. Surviving spouses in earlier periods often remarried soon after the death of a partner, creating stepfamilies. In recent years in the United States, divorce and separation, rather than death, have precipitated the increasingly large number of single-parent families. The rising number of out-of-wedlock births creates even more. The Kids Count Data Book (Annie E. Casey Foundation, 2002) noted that 22% of White babies born in 2000 were to unmarried mothers, while 40% of Hispanic babies were, and two thirds of Black children are in this category.

Heritage, a need for security, reverence for elders, sharing resources combine to make the extended family a logical arrangement

For a variety of reasons, the single-parent family is becoming one of the most common family groupings in the United States today. Census reports for 2002 show 27% of families with children are now single parent (Bianchi & Casper, 2000). This contrasts with 1970, when there were 11%. Projections also show that about 60% of all children born in the last 18 years will spend part of their minor years in a single-parent family (Annie E. Casey Foundation, 2002). Cohabitation of adults confounds some of these statistics, for some children are born (estimates range up to one third) into the homes of unmarried mothers and fathers. And same-sex couples do rear children but are not identified by the Census Bureau as two-parent "families." While many single parents achieve noteworthy results, a number of critical issues face the single parent family, and poverty is

foremost. The single-parent family has several structural variations:

1. Single mothers—divorced, widowed, or never married—living alone with their biological children

2. Single fathers—divorced, widowed, or never married—living alone with their biological children

3. Single parents (male or female) divorced, widowed or never married living alone with adopted children

4. Male or female parent living alone with children and spouse incarcerated, deserted, or moved away.

Single-mother families are by far the most common of one-parent families (87%), but fathers—1.8 million in 2000—raising their children alone are found much more often to-day than a few decades ago (U.S. Bureau of the Census, 2002).

Blended Families

Most divorced and widowed persons remarry, and **postnuclear family units** emerge from the remarriages. In some cases, a single adult joins an already existing single-parent family to form a stepfamily, and in others, an adult with his or her own children joins a partner with children to form a **blended or reconstituted family**. Each year about one-half million children in the United States experience a remarriage of their **custodial parents** (Hetherington & Stanley-Hagan, 2002). Several studies near the end of the 20th century (Bianchi & Casper, 2000; Mason, 1998) reported that this family form is destined to soon be the most common in America when we include cohabiting couples with children. The following are typical arrangements in blended families:

1. Parent with children remarries a single adult to produce a stepfamily for the new partner.
2. Two parents, each with children, remarry to produce stepchildren for each other and step siblings for the children. At least one half of such new marriages produce children who are half siblings for the existing children (Bianchi & Spain, 1996).
3. Cohabiting or common-law couples with children or with children from previous relationships live together but without marriage.

Not all parents seek marriages when re-aligning their living arrangements. Blended families can easily be formed without marriage, functioning exactly as married blends would. The Census Bureau in 2002 revealed that of 5 million couples sharing a household, over one third have children under 15 years of age (U.S.

Bureau of the Census, 2002). Figure 3–2 shows only blended families derived from marriages.

Adoptive Families

Most **adoptive families** function as nuclear ones, except that some of the family's children are not biological issue of either parent. Many families include both biological and adopted children, but almost one half of adoptions in the United States are **kinship adoptions** by a stepparent or a biological family member. Adoptive families can also be single-parent (divorce occurs in adoptive families too), and sometimes a single adult chooses to adopt children while foregoing marriage. In addition, some single-sex families (gay and lesbian partners) adopt children. About 3% of American children are adopted, and over 2% of "couples with children" fall into the adopted family category (Pavao, 1998).

Subfamilies

Though certainly not a new phenomenon, some family groupings, referred to as **subfamilies**, reside in other households for economic or protective reasons. The most common is the young single mother who takes up residence with her parents or other family members. The condition is much like the extended family, except that the parent with young children is appended to and is not the central family figure in the household. For tax purposes, these units do qualify for head-of-household status. We also find communal arrangements, in which two or more family groups choose to live together for economic and other support reasons (Edin & Lein, 1997).

Foster Families

Families with **foster children** have been in existence for centuries. Charles Dickens and other novelists have alluded (frequently in poignant terms) to foster home arrangements. The arrangements, both legal and informal, exist today in the United States and are increasing in many urban areas as social welfare agencies try to find suitable living quarters for orphaned, unwanted, abused, and neglected children. While sources vary in numbers of foster children, the Child Welfare League of America (2003) recorded 585,000 children, or about 1.3% of our children, in foster care. Two thirds of all foster children are children of color, and while one half of the total group are available for adoption, records show that only 18% are actually adopted.

At times, childless couples elect to become foster parents for children, but more frequently it is the nuclear family that extends itself to accommodate additional children. The Child Welfare League of America (2003) advanced the argument that kinship must be considered in any foster care arrangement to preserve a child's culture and family heritage. This gives rise to a new category of foster care: "**kinship care**"—care by close relatives. We also have to remember that children are frequently in foster care because of homelessness, abandonment, abusive situations, or medical involvement situations (AIDS and the like). This means that challenges are often present for foster care homes.

Arrangements for foster care are most often financial contracts by which a family agrees with a state agency to accept one or more state wards for a stated remuneration. Time elements vary from several weeks for newborns, who will be placed for adoption, up to 18 years for other children. In the 19th century, foster care was often without remuneration, and families accepted children for humanitarian reasons as well as economic objectives, such as for securing help for farms or households.

Gay and Lesbian Families

Gay and lesbian partnerships are becoming more mainstream in America, and this leads to greater acknowledgement of **gay and lesbian** family units. A child becomes part of a gay or lesbian family unit in several ways: a product of a previous heterosexual relationship, via adoption, through **alternative insemination**, or through a **surrogate parent program**.

While still a very small percentage of total family units, single-sex partnerships function much like other family units, have similar child care needs, and have similar numbers of separations. While a large percentage of employers provide medical and employee benefits to partners of either gender, no state at present recognizes same-sex marriages. This means that gay and lesbian families must work through the legal system to assure inheritance and other financial benefits for partners and children.

Other Family Groupings

As noted, the family types discussed here occur in many specific configurations. It is also true that some children, as Figure 3–2 shows, have no organized family, and are living in institutions or boarding facilities that serve as a family substitute. Other family groupings involve children living in homes not headed by a parent. Significant numbers of young children live with grandparents, aunts, uncles, cousins, and even nonrelated adults. Census Bureau reports show that in 2001, over 1% of American children were in such arrangements (U.S. Bureau of the Census, 2002). Other informal living arrangements involve runaways and abandoned children who have escaped social agency notice and have adapted to temporary homes that provide the basics. These arrangements are always fragile and extralegal.

The family types discussed in this chapter all exist to some degree across the United States, and while the quality of child rearing varies with individuals, all family structures can be viable. It is more than likely that you know people who fit into several of the previously noted patterns, as you do yourself. Economics and social pressures in our country ensure that diversity in family arrangements continues, and transformations from one type of family to another occur daily in thousands of homes, as happened in our opening vignette. One positive result of this continuing transformation is the acceptance now found in our society for a multiplicity of family forms. This attitude was not present a generation ago.

Diversity also is a challenge for professionals working with families. As a community worker or an educator, you must come prepared with knowledge, communication, and interaction skills, and an ability to accept differences. Think of how you will work for consensus with the myriad groupings as you help your community care for and educate its children.

SOCIAL FACTORS RELATING TO FAMILIES

Racial, Ethnic, and Cultural Factors

The U.S. Census Bureau has used four "racial" categories (plus "Other"), for a century, but in 1990, when respondents had an additional write-in blank for "race," they indicated nearly 300 different ethnic group labels (O'Hare, 1992). The 2000 census went one step further and provided citizens a place to indicate "more than one race." While only 1% of the population used the multiple categorization, demographers predict much higher use of the category in another census. **Biracial families** are emerging rapidly, and the public in general attaches less importance to race and ethnicity.

Physical characteristics, language, and cultural factors distinguish some families from mainstream culture in the United States and may give them a different identity. And it is important to remember that race, ethnicity, and culture are terms about human variation that are used constantly in discussions, publi-

cations, and research studies. All of this means that students of social action or education must ponder the uses of the terms and appropriateness of their use, since so much information is arbitrary and subjective.

Though racial awareness has a long history in our nation, "race" labels are often unproductive, inaccurate, and meaningless (Mukhopadhyay & Henze, 2003). The American Anthropological Association (AAA; 2002) has labeled race categories as political and social constructions with no basis in human biology. This clearly suggests that current labels provide inadequate information, but with continued reliance on census-based formulas for distributing aid, conducting demographic research, constructing election districts, and tracking racial discrimination, the United States seems destined to use them for some time yet.

In this text, the authors use the term **ethnic orientation** primarily to refer to the general complex of cultural and physical characteristics, and we use the term **cultural background** to refer specifically to that complex of created, linguistic, and societal—but nonphysical—characteristics that distinguish societies and groups. We do use *race* at times because it is a social reality and communicates generally used demographic data. In fact, we recommend that teachers teach about race; helpful materials are available from *AnthroNotes*, published by the Anthropology Outreach Office of the AAA (*anthroutreach@nmnh.si.edu*).

Ethnic identification does, however, more accurately represent the wide demographic palette in the United States. Table 3–1 gives statistics for the major racial and ethnic groups in the United States.

Until the 1970s, American schools and communities operated mostly on the basis of assimilating different cultural and ethnic minorities and language groups into the mainstream European American culture (Tiedt & Tiedt, 2001). Since the 1970s, the concept of

Table 3–1   U.S. Population by Race and Ethnicity in July 2003

Total U.S.	282,808,000
Non-Hispanic White	198,364,000
African American	34,657,000
Asian/Pacific Islander	11,738,000
Native American and Eskimo	2,131,000
Hispanic	35,919,000

Source: U.S. Bureau of the Census estimates. *www.census.gov/population*. Retrieved September 22, 2003.

cultural pluralism (discussed in Chapter 2) has taken root. A large number of schools and communities currently subscribe to the idea of recognizing the positive contributions and qualities of the numerous ethnic and cultural groups in the United States and use them to build a stronger society. Most professionals accept the notion that diversity does produce strength (Gonzalez-Mena, 2002; Hildebrand et al., 1996).

Applying this acceptance notion in communities and schools means emphasizing a multicultural curriculum that promotes positive multiethnic relationships among children, school personnel, parents, and community. As a teacher, you must be prepared to occasionally alter your curriculum to accommodate special cultural characteristics and qualities and to make adjustments in discussions and interactions with parents. Among these are minority versus majority ethnic–cultural status and the presence in your class of children belonging to bilingual and interethnic families.

Minority Status

The United States, whose population was once predominantly of western European, Caucasian (White) derivation, has expanded swiftly in the past century to include numerous ethnic and cultural groups. At the begin-

ning of the colonial era, the eastern seaboard colonists were mostly Europeans, with a tiny minority of African Americans. A large group of Native Americans, indigenous to the continent, existed as a separate and parallel cultural complex.

The minority population in the United States reached 20% in 1980; it was 27% in 1995, and in 2003 was about 30% (U.S. Bureau of the Census, 2002a). Projections show that the minority population in 2010 will be one third of the predicted total population of 300 million. Minority families are now common in all but a few of the 50 states. In Figure 3–3 you can see that African American, Asian, and Hispanic minorities will grow much faster than the Caucasian population in the decades ahead. Minority children currently account for almost 40% of our youth population (18 and under), and 22 of the 25 largest city school systems have over 50% minority students (U.S. Bureau of the Census, 2002b). Census projections indicate that by 2028, one half of our school-aged children will be minorities. We will soon need a descriptive term to replace *minority.*

Six states have arrived at or are nearing a 50% minority population (U.S. Bureau of the Census, 2002), which means that European Americans are approaching minority status in some parts of our country. These figures indicate a homogenizing of America, for whereas a few decades ago minorities were concentrated in the West and South, the dispersal of minorities throughout the continental United States has grown rapidly in the last 2 decades.

Educational orientations, expectations, and learning styles vary within all families, and many minority families have favored and even encouraged different learning strategies (Hrabowski, Maton, & Greif, 1998; Webb et al., 2003). Schools and communities must recognize that people have different ways of "knowing" and acknowledge that many differences can be beneficial. As a teacher, you will be

Figure 3–3   Growth of minority populations in the United States.
Source: U.S. Bureau of the Census, Current Population Report P25-1104 and projections, 1995.

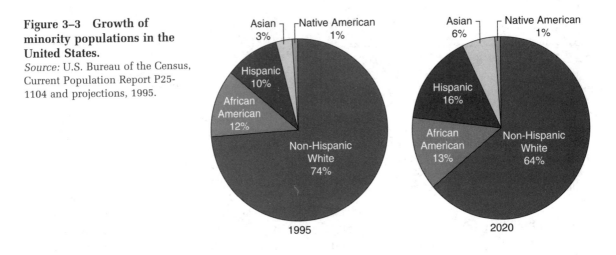

Limited-English-Proficiency Families

Linguistic differences are far more common for American children than is generally perceived. Eighteen percent of the American population over 5 years of age speaks a language other than English at home, and 11 million of these people do not speak English well or they speak no English (U.S. Bureau of the Census, 2002). For decades, bilingual school programs have been developed in response to the growing numbers of linguistically different children. In recent years, **bilingual education** has been most closely associated with teaching Hispanic minorities, but programs exist for over 90 other minority groups in U.S. schools (Population Reference Bureau, 2003). In recent years, large numbers of children with limited English have been assigned to special education classes, and this confounds the objectives of those classes.

Approximately 3.6 million students in the United States show a need for special linguistic assistance in order to participate in a public school curriculum. But less than 10% of that figure are now in bilingual programs (Webb et al., 2003). These statistics are significant for communities and schools where concentrations of non-English-speaking families live and work. Particular problems in communication and general acceptance do appear, and since English is the language of instruction in most schools, children with less than full fluency are in some ways handicapped.

During the 1990s, a backlash against bilingual instruction started, and funding for the programs has suffered (AmeriStat, 2003). For example, California in 1998 approved a referendum that virtually bans bilingual education in that state. **Immersion and submersion programs** of "all instruction in English," with some follow-up work in a child's native language, have moved beyond the pilot phase and are being adopted steadily in states with high Hispanic and Asian populations. Publications by the National Association for Bilingual Education (NABE) and English First show the various viewpoints on this continuing debate. One of your challenges in community and school programs will be to support children and families with different language backgrounds in seeking language instruction. This challenge forms another basis for school–home–community discussion and action.

Educational orientations, expectations, and learning styles vary within all families and children have different learning strategies

Biracial and Interethnic Families

Since **interethnic** and **interracial** marriages are becoming more common, more children with parents of different backgrounds attend American schools today. When given a chance in the 2000 census to indicate more than one race, over 4 million (one half were minors) indicated more than one race identity. Demographers predict that this figure will rise dramatically in the next census, since the actual numbers are much higher and sensitivity will be less.

In the popular press, one frequently finds descriptions of the changing racial diversity in the United States, and this indicates a gradual homogenizing of our population. The notion is supported when we find 5% of all births nationally as "mixed race" or having two or more racial heritages (U.S. Bureau of the Census, 2002a). Higher proportions of interracial and

interethnic marriages occur in Asian and Hispanic groups. One new magazine, *Interrace*, published in Atlanta, is aimed particularly at this increasing group of Americans with combined heritages. More than anyone else in recent years, Tiger Woods, the young golfing phenomenon, drew attention to multiracial backgrounds by labeling himself "Cablinasian."

Since different ethnic groups generally hold differing cultural expectations, interethnic families will have varying perceptions about culture and their child's participation in school and community. There is also the pressure that biracial children feel for acceptance. While there are advantages of living in two worlds, Root (1999) noted that some feel rejection by one parent's cultural group, or both.

Through adoptions, some families are rearing children from a culture different from that of the adoptive parents, and many of those parents are interested in preserving features of the adopted child's heritage. Other families will have a multiethnic makeup as a result of remarriage or combinations of parent and child ethnicity.

Race has been and continues to be an issue in America, and while great strides have been made in merging the interests, opportunities, and talents of all members on the racial palette, the job of educators, community leaders, and families themselves is to work to celebrate racial differences. Race should not be avoided but validated in our community lives.

❧

Annie is an adopted Asian child living in a totally European American small town. She brings no Asian culture to the community, as she would if her biological family resided there, but her race is evident and she constantly brings up the fact of her difference. Her fourth-grade teacher works hard in featuring photos of minority persons and particularly Chinese. The objective is to validate the accomplishments, heritage, and history of this particular ethnic group. One new project that has started well, and is exciting for all classmates, is the e-mail writing exchange with children in a Chinese sister city school.

Wynter (2002) expressed encouraging thoughts on racial acceptance. He indicated that America is moving into a "post-racial" period and that multiculturalism will soon be irrelevant. He uses the crossover phenomenon examples in the music, toy, sports, entertainment, and advertising businesses to show how the race of featured persons becomes irrelevant in mainstream America. Barbie's new playmate, Kayla, is typical of the new forms we find in toy manufacture to show ambiguous race. However, this acceptance is still far from total. For the next decade or two, race will undoubtedly be in focus in American schools and neighborhoods.

Culture and ethnicity are family characteristics. As the United States becomes more culturally and ethnically diverse, professionals need a stronger grasp of the range of different cultural interests. The history of race relations in the United States has seldom been positive, and most minority-group children have felt the stings of racism and ethnocentrism. If children from our various ethnic groups are to succeed, they need to know and feel that schools and communities want them to succeed. All educators must be sensitive, and a multicultural emphasis is probably required for at least another generation.

SOCIOECONOMIC STATUS OF FAMILIES

During the 1950s and 1960s, American writers, educators, and politicians tried to downplay social class, but class levels have become more obvious in recent decades and greater acknowledgement is now made (Coontz, 1999). One only has to look at the growing polarization of wealth in America to find the vast differences in buying power, access, and vocational opportunity for citizens at different levels on the economic ladder, and this is closely related to socioeconomic status (SES).

Social classes are not easily portrayed because there are overlaps, but in general, class standing is based on the occupation, income, education, and values of the parents in a family. Figure 3–4 diagrams the social classes generally used to show the organization of American society.

Historic Class Descriptions

The **upper class** in the United States parallels the aristocracy in other societies. These families have inherited wealth and a close-knit circle of friends, family, and colleagues. Children from upper class families normally attend exclusive private schools and prepare for careers

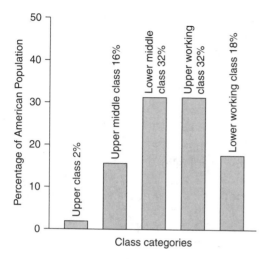

Figure 3–4   Social class in America.
Sources: Adapted from Levine, D. U. & Levine, R. (1995). *Society and education,* 9th ed. Boston: Allyn & Bacon; and Hess, A. (2001). *Concepts of social stratification: European and American models.* New York: Palgrave.

in a family enterprise or in public service, such as in politics or with social help organizations. Family heritage and "proper rearing" are very important in this class, and children are expected to conform to established standards of behavior, etiquette, and education.

Middle-class families have arrived at their status through vigorous pursuit of education and industry. Upper middle-class American families are affluent, hardworking, and achievement oriented. They are often the community's leaders, physicians, lawyers, and successful businesspersons. A defining quality for these families is the practice of delayed gratification; children are reared from an early age to exercise self-discipline, to avoid conflict, and to wait for rewards. Families are often nuclear and closely knit. Middle- and lower middle-class families are much the same as those of the upper middle class in expectations and desires. Less highly paid professionals are in this category, as are many successful

businesspersons. This is "middle America," which enjoys many social advantages and high-quality living standards.

Upper working-class families represent skilled tradespersons, factory workers, and other hourly wage earners. Members of this class emphasize hard work but hold education to be less important than do members of the middle and upper classes. Working-class children are encouraged to expect a life of wage earning. Economic ups and downs often affect working-class families, who are more likely to deplete their available resources for unexpected expenses like illness. Child raising is more direct, and parents often dominate their children and frequently use physical punishments. Archie Bunker in the 1970s television series *All in the Family* made the stereotypical behavior attributed to this class well-known to the viewing public.

The **lower working class** is made up generally of unskilled laborers, who are susceptible to layoffs and at times must depend on welfare for subsistence. Male and female roles are definitely shaped in this section of the scale, and males dominate most family decisions. Families in this class will often live in substandard housing, have poorer diets, and accept marginal health practices. Children of lower working-class parents are expected at an early age to develop responsibilities for taking care of their siblings and doing chores. Cramped living quarters is a trademark of those living in cities. Even though a large part of American wealth, capital, and general services come as a result of working class labor, people in this segment of society are most at risk in the emerging high-tech global labor market.

The Underclass—A New Dimension

Sociologists and demographers now recognize a subgroup (although not represented in the classic diagram), previously merged with the lower working class, that occupies the lower margin of our economic and social scales (Benson, 1997; Sugrue, 1999). The **underclass** comprises individuals and families locked into a debilitating cycle of poverty and despair from which they can find little escape. The combination of **welfare to work programs** plus economic boom times in the late 1990s reduced the numbers in this group, but by 2002, with recession and high unemployment figures, the numbers had expanded once again (Urban Institute, 2002).

Underclass families subsist primarily on welfare, other government assistance, and an underground economy. Members live in inferior housing or on the streets, and face lives frequently racked by crime, deprivation, chemical dependency, and abuse. Since most individuals in this class possess little education and limited work experience the culture of poverty spirals onward. This perpetuation of economic and social dislocation gives individuals and families little chance for working out of the chain of burdens. Renewed concern now appears for children in this group, because many underclass families have exhausted the social benefits of the welfare-to-work programs and must depend again on charitable institutions.

Many **at-risk children** are in the underclass, which means that nutrition and health care are minimal, and illness, disease, and neglect are common. Minority families are also highly represented in this once more expanding group (Goetz, 2003). The dilemma of how to help the underclass is perhaps the greatest challenge we face in our efforts to eradicate poverty (America's Children 2002, 2002).

We have considerable evidence that Americans move from one socioeconomic or social class group to another via education and successful personal improvement efforts. While upward movement for middle-class Americans seems almost assured, options for the underclass seem far less promising in the future. Education levels and minimal experiences as well as the neglect by mainstream America represent a fixed ceiling for this group. With welfare reform spreading across America since the mid-1990s, many families suffer even more hardship (Lichter & Crowley, 2002).

Economics and American Families

The economic base of a family is extremely important for its members. It determines the family's quality of life, health care, nutrition, and living conditions, as well as the level of self-worth and ability to function in a community. While a majority of U.S. families maintain a high standard of living compared with the rest of the world, we find increasing numbers of families in poverty. Industrial jobs are rapidly being eliminated in America and are being replaced with lower paying service employment. The effect is that real wages for most families fell 18% between 1973 and 2000 (Lichter & Crowley, 2002), and the buying power of a majority of households was even less throughout the 1990s (Morris & Western, 1999). Downward mobility, rather than upward movement, has become the pattern for more Americans in the present generation. Note in Figure 3–5 that the lowest 20% and the middle 60% of households receive only about one half of the total income distributed in our country. Discouraging as it appears, we seem destined for more bipolar economic situations in most U.S. regions.

In an attempt to ward off declining living standards, more nuclear families now have both parents working. This condition has negative implications for quality of life in these families, as well as for their participation in their schools and communities. Economics correlates with risk factors; almost always, the lower the income, the higher the risk. However, we do find "at-risk" children in middle- and upper income families, and teachers and other helping professionals must be alert to the frequently disguised risk factors.

Figure 3–5   Distribution of American Household Income, 1974–2001.
Source: U.S. Bureau of the Census, Current Population Report P60-213, 2002.

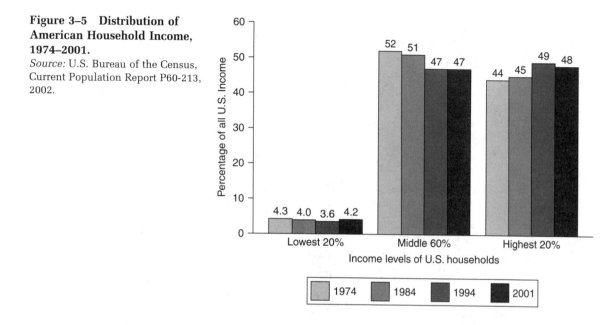

Middle-Income Families. The American dream has been to achieve a middle-class style of life. The middle class are supposed to enjoy full employment and the esteem that society places on the engine that propels the nation. For many, this scenario is true. In 1996, over 28 million families enjoyed an income above the median, one that permitted them to enjoy a better-than-average lifestyle (U.S. Bureau of the Census, 1998a). However, we must keep in mind that real earnings slipped badly in the 1970s and 1980s, so to remain in the middle class, many of these families have moved to the dual-income plan in order to maintain the features of suburban living, recreational opportunity, and college education for their children (Teachman, 2000).

Middle-income families often hold to traditional values. Child-rearing practices are in line with status, featuring reasoning with children in lieu of physical punishment. Communication is valued. Middle-income families are more easily involved in school and community activities, and the parents' educational level usually makes communication easier.

Parents' volunteer work can be considerable, and since their participation has a history, minimal instruction or organization is necessary. Members of this group can make valuable contributions to a school program in sharing talents, giving presentations, or managing projects. But time may be scarce with middle-income parents, and new demands—especially with dual-income families—does result in time constraints.

Working-Class Families. Values in working-class families often differ from those presented in schools. While we need to draw all families into school and community service, professionals need to be prepared for communicating and interacting with people who want productive lives for their children but do not always understand school and agency strategies or objectives.

Working-class families fit well into school and community programs where tasks are carefully defined and arranged. Family members here consider themselves as "doers" and normally are willing to work avidly on specific

Middle-income families are more easily involved in school activities, volunteering and making valuable contributions to the schools

projects or use other means to support a school or agency. Comer (1997) pointed out that many schools successfully arrange for participation by up to one half of their working-class family members.

Underclass Families. As discussed, the United States has for generations contained an underclass of families with limited education, limited employment, and a history of subsisting on government and institutional assistance. In addition, financial reversals and economic deterioration in some locations have resulted in poverty for previous working-class American families. In the beginning year of the 21st century, the number of families in the United States at or below the subsistence level was growing again. In 1994,

statistics (O'Hare, 1996) showed 15% of our population below poverty level, and in 2001 the rate was 12.5%, but the total number of people was more. These figures do not count the numbers in welfare-directed institutions. Lichter and Crowley (2002) noted that 20% of our children live in poverty. Minority children under the age of 6 have the highest rate of poverty, with figures ranging up to 40% (Burtless & Smeeding, 2001). Refer again to Figure 3–5.

Poverty is a risk factor associated with numerous negative outcomes—particularly for children. In the 1980s and 1990s, poverty became more permanent because of difficulties individuals have in breaking out of menial jobs. The United States appears to now have a permanent underclass (poverty figures have remained almost static for nearly 25 years), and two expanding groups at this level are **homeless and itinerant families**.

Homeless Families.   Some families suffering economic hardships surrender their homes; others have a history of wandering from state to state; and changes in mental health regulations in many states have resulted in previously institutionalized persons' being left to their own devices. These persons and their families make up our homeless population.

Because they have no permanent address, homeless families spend increasing amounts of time in shelters, in automobiles, or on the street. Welfare reform will undoubtedly push more families into homelessness when benefits expire in the near future (Goetz, 2003).

Whereas the typical media image of the homeless person is the unemployed male who abuses substances and wanders the streets, statistics show that over 25% of the homeless in 2001 were family persons, and 58% of the family members are children (Urban Institute, 2002). The numbers of homeless are difficult to ascertain, and estimates differ sharply. Conservative figures show that 200,000 American children are homeless in the course of a year (America's Children 2002, 2002). The Urban Institute (2002) presents estimates of 2.3 to over 3 million Americans experiencing homelessness at some point in a given year. This represents about 1% of our population.

Many of the parents in homeless situations are employed but work in low-end jobs that pay insufficiently for housing. In addition, homelessness is related to seasons and seasonal work. Winter figures for the homeless (in most states) are almost 50% higher than during summer and early fall.

Some children from homeless situations manage to attend school, although usually only part-time. Clearly, such circumstances offer a challenge to communities and schools working together to produce basic health and nutrition services for our neediest children (Swick, 1999). One positive example is the U.S. Office of Education's validating the efforts of Sandra McBrayer by naming her 1994 Teacher of the Year for her work with homeless students on the streets of San Diego. Another inspiring example is the B. F. Day Elementary School in Seattle, Washington, with special provisions for homeless children. See Chapter 7 for one unexpected benefit of shelter life for some children.

Migrant and Itinerant Families.   Some families are highly mobile because of erratic work availability and the unsettled lifestyles of the parents. Living conditions for families in this category are normally poor, and family members often suffer from serious health problems (DeVita & Mosher-Williams, 2001; Morse, 1997).

Migrant workers constitute a significant block of both U.S. citizens and resident aliens who move up and down the continent during harvesting seasons. The United States has over 1 million migrant workers in any one year (Waller & Crawford, 2001). Many families are without a permanent home—children are in one location for several weeks and then move to another. Life for these children has little security, health care, or stability, and this group has greater likelihood of infant mortality, disabilities, and chronic illness of any cohort in the nation (Culatta & Tompkins, 1999; Romanowski, 2001).

Migrant-worker families and itinerant families pose a particular problem for schools and teachers. Children are forced into new situations every few weeks and thus have little continuity in school or community experiences. The progress in cognitive growth for migrant children is often minimal, and such children frequently become socially alienated simply because they cannot feel a part of any school or community (National Commission on Migrant Children, 1992; Tao, Khan, & Arriola, 1997). **Even Start** programs are attempts to bolster educational opportunity for the young children of at-risk families, and 5% of Even Start funds are earmarked for migrant families (Dimidijian, 2001; Tao, Khan, & Arriola, 1997).

Low-SES families have been a constant in American society for generations. Large amounts of federal funds have been spent, but positive results come about infrequently. Community action teams, school program developers, and others need to continue to identify realistic educational initiatives that will produce better opportunities for the economically beset. On the positive side, we do have programs that work (see models outlined in Chapter 12). Selected plans across the country show that low-SES children need not follow the spiral of agony and misery so frequently associated with a disadvantaged life.

Ansel's parents are migrant farm workers following employment from Florida to Maine each year, harvesting crops. Their life is filled with needs for food, clothes, car repairs, and medical treatment. Still, 4-year-old Ansel has many happy days exploring farm life and playing with pet animals and other migrant children.

The parents work daily in the fields, with children helping on small tasks in the harvest. At one Georgia site, a child care worker visited the worker's quarters, and in spite of their exhausting day, Ansel's parents learned how to enroll him in the local Even Start program. It was a success, and after his first week, Ansel showed off his favorite picture books, an art project, and the three games he had learned. Now, in the few hours at the end of each day, Ansel shares material with his tired but willing parents.

In Maine a farmer's wife gave Ansel a box of paperback picture books, and Ansel enjoys "reading" the pictures to his parents. In another community in early fall, a child care worker started a portfolio of Ansel's artwork and his writings—from scribbles to forming numbers and letters. She encouraged Ansel and his parents to share these "recordings" at the next several stops when returning to Florida. Gradually the parents are learning to ask the right questions to find preschool programs in other communities.

Ansel will start kindergarten in the fall and will follow a similar intermittent pattern of schooling. But Ansel's parents are beginning to develop skills in reaching out to the community for help and in sharing his portfolio with others. Educating migrant children is never an easy task, but caring parents, community interest, and receptive schools provide great help for the resilient migrant child.

Effects of Economics

The economic foundation of a society governs in large part the socioeconomic status (SES) of individuals within that society. Financial resources for families become the most important variable in determining class status and opportunity; money governs diet, place of residence, access to health care, and chances for the future. Naturally, children's achievement in school is affected tremendously by these factors.

Early studies by Coleman (1966) showed a strong correlation between family SES and children's cognitive development and achievement. More recent studies qualify those findings. Mayer (1997) pointed out the importance of the home psychological environment for child learning. Hrabowski et al. (1998, Hrabowski, Maton, Greeve, & Greif, 2002) found a similar pattern, noting that parental behaviors toward children are more strongly predictive of cognitive growth than are SES variables. We may thus hope to keep alive the chance for upward mobility and improvement for economically disadvantaged populations if we can deliver to these families intervention in the form of educational programs. If parent attitudes and behaviors represent those characteristics that can be affected by education and training (Ramsey, 1998; Walberg, 1984), schools and communities have the best chance for engaging parents in the process of educating their children.

FAMILIES WITH CHILDREN WITH SPECIAL NEEDS

The special education of children with disabilities involves a large number of diverse families with children whose disabilities range from physical impairments to severe mental retardation. In spite of a generation living under regulations requiring the inclusion of persons with disabilities in all aspects of American schools, individuals and families frequently encounter conditions of discrimination and segregation. All professionals must seek to acknowledge all children according to their abilities rather than their disabilities.

During the 1997–1998 school year, 5.5 million children and youth from age 3 through age 21 were served under federal programs for children with disabilities (U.S. Department of Education, 1999). In addition, about 780,000 preschool children received **early intervention services** in that same year (Turnbull et al., 2002). This is a significant population (12% of children in that age bracket, according to U.S. Census Bureau statistics) and places considerable challenge and pressure on available assistive time and resources. When professionals work with schools and communities, they need to understand not only particular disabilities but also those problems and pressures that

affect both the family and the child. They must be both sensitive and supportive when working with families of children with disabilities. (Note the legacy recounted in Chapter 2.)

Families with special needs are a part of all communities, and since disabilities cut across all socioeconomic groups, affected children will be present in most schools. Diversity is always a challenge for education professionals, but often the special-needs families require more school–home–community planning to realize the most positive outcomes. While major physical disabilities are evenly distributed across SES groups, milder disabilities (called **school-identified disabilities**) occur much more frequently in poor and disadvantaged families (Lichter & Crowley, 2002). Poverty, lack of health care, and particularly lack of prenatal care are responsible in large part (America's Children 2002, 2002; M. Wagner, 1995) for the disproportionate number of disabilities in minority families. Programs for children with special need are thriving all over the United States. See Turnbull et al. (2002) for a series of life stories that feature youth with special needs prospering in carefully planned programs.

RELIGIOUS ORIENTATION

Ethnic origin, SES, and the presence of disabilities are demographically identifying family characteristics. The family's religious affiliation is another. In their attempt to follow the requirements of the constitutional indications for "separation of church and state" in the United States, schools often try to ignore or deliberately overlook the religious affiliation of children and their families. However, religious affiliation and commitment affect how children feel about school activities, rules, and the behavior of others.

Religious practices may affect interaction and participation, holiday observances, foods eaten, and gender roles. Remember that 90% of Americans indicate a religious preference (Hoge, 1996), so it is important that school and community professionals know and respect the tenets of the different religions represented in community families. A school's ability to accommodate different religious practices directly affects whether the school's work with children, their families, and particular communities will be successful.

You will find inquiry about America's religious groups highly educational, and the information will be valuable for groups and individuals. For all our ethnic and religious diversity, most American children and adults are ill informed about Judaism, Buddhism, and Islam, to say nothing of Native American religious practices. Good references in reflecting on religious practice are Melton's (2002) *Encyclopedia of American Religion* and the Gollnick and Chinn (2002) text on multicultural education.

The religious landscape in the United States is in constant flux, as one would expect in a country where religious tolerance abides. New faith traditions emerge frequently, and membership in established congregations moves up and down (Lindner, 2003). The major faiths represented in the United States are Christianity, which includes Protestants and Catholics; Judaism; and Islam. Much smaller representations of Hinduism, Buddhism, and other Eastern beliefs are found in major U.S. cities also. All major faiths are divided into smaller sects and denominations, which vary considerably. For example, within the Protestant Christian faith are dozens of denominations, ranging socially and politically from liberal to conservative. Catholic subgroups include Roman Catholic and Eastern Orthodox. Jewish groups range from conservative Hasidic sects to liberal Reform synagogues. The rapidly expanding Islamic affiliations in the United States include Black Muslim groups and Near

Religious affiliations may affect how children feel about school activities, rules and the behavior of others

Eastern aggregations, as well as immigrants from East Asia. Mosques are now becoming much more common in U.S. urban landscapes.

Religion helps many persons find purpose and meaning in their lives. While socioeconomic success does not seem to be linked with any particular faith, some researchers indicate a correlation between religious commitment and moral behavior (Gorsuch, 1976; Hoge, 1996). This statistic should be comforting, considering that 90% of Americans profess to having a religious attachment. However, attendance at religious services rarely exceeds 20% of the population in any one community.

The *Yearbook of American and Canadian Churches, 2002* (Lindner, 2003) catalogs the religious affiliation of approximately 248 million persons in the United States indicating a religious connection. Of that figure, the membership percentage for the predominant groups is as follows: Protestant Christians, 57%; Catholic Christians, 26%; Muslims, 3%; Jews, 3%; no religion, 9%; and other, 1%.

These figures affirm a dominant Protestant religious heritage in many areas of the United States. This stems from a strong Protestant affiliation during the colonial era of the country.

Religion directly influences how families rear children, as well as how they conduct their affairs and relate to a community (Hoge, 1996). Even though the federal and state court decisions (case law) have traditionally separated church work and state regulations, one finds a great deal in legal codes and the common law of the United States resting firmly on a Protestant ethic (Gollnick & Chinn, 2002; Melton, 2002). The administration of George W. Bush has supported more connections between religious institutions and government programs. Some of the faith-based social support groups and school **voucher plans** that include religious schools do take some new steps to involve federal and state governments in indirect support for religious organizations. Court decisions in 2003 upheld these new connections.

Applications of Religion

All religions deem sacred certain ideas, objects, or aspects of the natural world, and these dictates have implications for observance within those groups. Even though many children are only casually acquainted with the practice of their religion, it is still a background feature in their lives, and their behaviors and reactions will demonstrate that. The following are points to consider as you collaborate with parents and community members in educating children and directing programs.

Observance of Holidays. Most religions have selected, faith-specific holidays. Christians celebrate Easter and Christmas; Jews celebrate Passover, Yom Kippur, and other holidays; Muslims observe Ramadan, Bayrami, and other holidays.

Codes. Religious groups have codes relating to sexual behavior as well as to the observance of marriages, births, and deaths. Many religions have dietary laws, and children will seek or avoid specific foods at certain times or during particular occasions.

All religions have a moral code, and when we compare religious practices around the world, many aspects of the different codes resemble one another. Differences are in such features as locus of control. For example, Protestant groups hold that humans are individually responsible for determining their behavior, but other groups teach that it is loyalty to the group that counts and that individuals must adhere to acceptable practices as defined by the religion or its authorities.

Educators and other professional community workers must adhere to the following points regarding instruction about religion or comments and questions about religion (Gollnick & Chinn, 2002; Uphoff, 1993):

1. Be knowledgeable of the religious affiliations of associates, clients, schoolchildren, and community members.

2. The school should study what all people believe, but should not teach a student what to believe.

3. Learn to value all religious practices, and encourage people to share information about their faiths.

4. Learn about the larger community endeavors that focus on religion or feature religious holidays.

5. Learn how to use the various religious links in the school and community to educate children and to help them develop tolerance for others.

The key is for professionals to be knowledgeable and respectful and not underestimate the importance that Americans place on religion.

CHANGES IN CONTEMPORARY FAMILIES

Even though the concept of family has been with humanity since Paleolithic times, we still find gradual changes in form and function of this basic unit. In recent decades, America has seen new family forms and the public acceptance of one-parent households, cohabiting couples, gay families, as well as multiracial families. The focus of this text is on families in the United States at the beginning of the 21st century, but in this section we consider family evolution over the past 2 centuries. The comparisons will help explain how we arrived at our present situation.

From its inception to the mid-1800s, the United States was primarily an agrarian economy, and its population was mainly rural. This circumstance produced a typical farming family structure across the United States. This land-based family was often extended and often included three generations of members. Children were considered valuable assets to families at this time, since farm work involved numerous tasks calling for extra hands.

With the advent of the Industrial Revolution in the late 1700s and early 1800s, the American economy and social structure started to change. Urban centers expanded and whole new classes of jobs in manufacturing and commerce became available. Changes in the economic situation brought changes to families. A large working class emerged. A whole new ethic was injected into family life.

In recent decades there has been a greater acceptance of different family forms including multi racial and lesbian families

Roles in the home changed. The need for many hands in the home diminished, since children of factory workers did not participate in the work of parents. Homes changed from places where child rearing was linked with acquiring adult skills to environments where only child rearing took place. Education was no longer passed from older to younger family members but became something taught in "schools" as children's need for literacy and calculation skills moved beyond parental expertise.

By the end of the 19th century, the urbanization of the United States was well under way. Industrial and commercial development continued in rapid strides until World War II. Following the westward expansion in the 1880s and the general availability of railroad transport, relocation became relatively common for American families, especially after the early 1900s. Some families became more isolated from their relatives as they tried to establish roots in other communities and regions (Bailyn et al., 2000). It is during this period that the extended family diminished and the classic model of the nuclear family, typified by the smaller family of children living with their parents in an individual house with mother as homemaker and father as breadwinner became more prominent (Coontz, 1999). After World War II, mobility intensified as large groups moved to different parts of the country to find better living conditions. This activity and reorganization increased the prevalence of nuclear family features.

Of course there were many exceptions in early 20th-century households. Death often left single-parent families in its wake. Single parents clearly had a difficult task, so remarriages and, consequently, stepfamilies occurred frequently. Divorce was rare during this time, but foster care was not.

With World War II, new shifts in economics, a rise in minority populations, and changes in social habits had great impact on families in the United States. These changes included increasing numbers of women in the workforce, instability in marriages, a rise in divorce rates, increased mobility for families, and the rise of an influential peer group culture (Bailyn et al., 2000; Gollnick & Chinn, 2002).

Women joining the workforce became more independent, redefined family roles, and changed attitudes for both males and females. Many couples chose separation, remarriage, and different styles of living when they found they now held different expectations of family life. Female heads of households became more common, and there were fewer adults in a family unit. Figure 3–6 shows the dramatic changes for family support in the last part of the 20th century. (Remember that this is not the total work force, but only the workers supporting families.) The traditional breadwinning father and homemaking mother are now below 10%, and the dual-worker family members are now nearly up to 60%.

One drawback to this phenomenon is the loss of what Coleman (1991) called "social capital" in families—meaning adults' attention to and involvement with children's learning at home and in community life.

After a decade of legislation and social challenge from the civil rights movement, American social behavior took an even greater turn in the 1960s and 1970s. Younger Americans challenged an older order and experimented with different types of living arrangements. The more informal relationships, more flexible marriage and living arrangements, and new lifestyles since the 1980s are outgrowths from this period.

The postindustrial era arising in the United States at the beginning of the 21st century brings new directions and implications for families. The rise of massive service and communications industries shows that the importance of physical labor as known to previous generations has lessened considerably. In lieu of high-energy occupations, more U.S. workers now direct their attention to the service of equipment, the service

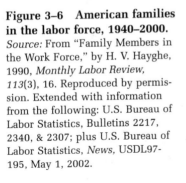

Figure 3–6 American families in the labor force, 1940–2000. *Source:* From "Family Members in the Work Force," by H. V. Hayghe, 1990, *Monthly Labor Review,* *113*(3), 16. Reproduced by permission. Extended with information from the following: U.S. Bureau of Labor Statistics, Bulletins 2217, 2340, & 2307; plus U.S. Bureau of Labor Statistics, *News,* USDL97-195, May 1, 2002.

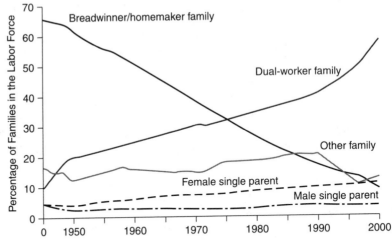

of living conditions, and the transmittal of information and processes. More and more employees work at home and in a variety of locations (Vosler, 1996). Thus, the notion of a constant skill for employment or an established workplace diminishes.

At the same time that the information age and the service industry blossom in the United States, we have a more noticeable differentiation in economic haves and have-nots. Blue-collar workers are finding physical labor less in demand. Automation and robotics increasingly replace manufacturing jobs, and large segments of our skilled labor force is witnessing the end of their vocations. Younger members of this force find themselves inheriting a decreasing number of available jobs, while others are moved to depend on welfare. While the information age has brought acceptance of different lifestyles, it has produced abrupt economic demands that leave Americans scurrying to find new ways to cope. Sociologists (DeVita & Mosher-Williams, 2001) have recently pointed out the need for recapturing viable communities and family traditions, for our new pace of life and new emphasis on individual work pushes all Americans toward isolation.

All of these changes have immense implications for family and home situations. These writers' recent experience underscores the rising problem of disconnected family members. We sat in a restaurant and observed a party of eight gathered for what appeared to be a Father's Day celebration. Conversation among the participants was intermittent but pleasant; however, it was frequently severed by the cell phone conversations that the senior male and one other male family member attended to. Family members seemingly accepted the interruptions, and the disjointed communications taking place.

As we move into the 21st century, new attitudes concerning sexual behavior have also emerged, and cohabitation without marriage has become socially acceptable. Interethnic marriages are more common, and out-of-wedlock births appear less controversial. Communal living arrangements are more accepted, as are same-sex partnerships and adoptions. Though flexibility and tolerance are key requirements for new lifestyles, educators must appreciate the need for a far more sophisticated education of all younger people. The demand on literacy, problem solving, and negotiating skills is higher for youngsters, who as adults will be very mobile and less constrained in living arrangements and will face frequent job changes and must constantly learn new methods for accomplishing things.

IMPLICATIONS FOR PROFESSIONALS

The familial landscape in America is ever changing socially, ethnically, and economically, and it will change more in decades to come. The reality is that children living in nontraditional families now represent a majority of the students in U.S. schools. It means that our schools and communities need a more sensitive and inclusive environment that supports children regardless of their family configuration.

Think of this as a challenging but interesting time for you to foster healthy change in educational opportunity as you go about school or community work. It means that you must figure out what the children and families in your district have to work with and where they come from. Benson (1997), in his ambitious book *All Kids Are Our Kids*, presents a fascinating "asset building" vision that helping professionals will want to consider for school and social service careers.

The information in this chapter forms a base of information for the strategies you use in working and interacting with the diverse families you will come in contact with. The essential element to grapple with is understanding and accepting the wide variety of family groupings in our towns and cities. The following chapters will extend your knowledge of strategies and resources for communicating and for making curriculum decisions. But before moving on, evaluate yourself on the major foci in this chapter.

1. *Language tolerance.* Your attitude about persons who speak a different language or use other forms of English is important. Develop a tolerant ear for the range of English forms spoken in the area where you work. If possible, identify persons who use the local language and arrange for them to help you with communication and cultural differences; this helps you to avoid misunderstandings.

2. *Lifestyles.* Your ability to value other lifestyles is another key item. Can you see quality in other than traditional relationships and how they work for the benefit of those individuals? Consider how you will extend the information you acquire in this chapter about different work styles, ways of earning a living, entertainment modes, and religious practices in your assigned community.

3. *Diversity.* Stretch yourself to see through different lenses and celebrate the diversity you find by joining the activities in a different community. For example, help plan a craft show for the neighborhood, attend different religious ceremonies, or volunteer in a classroom or on a farm. The main point is to adopt a multicultural ethic as soon as possible.

SUMMARY AND REVIEW

Family, though undergoing radical change in many communities, is still the primary social unit in the United States. Families vary in cultural, ethnic, religious, economic, and educational features, but all parents contribute in some way to their communities and to the schools where their children seek instruction and guidance.

The diversity of American families is said to be their strength. That fact can be generally interpreted as meaning that different heritages, values, work styles, and habits give a character to the American landscape that is both stimulating and an incentive for production. However, members of some of these diverse groups are in dire need of help and special support services.

Families have changed over the history of the United States and will continue to change.

Ethnic proportions are constantly changing, mobility will change, values will change, and even socioeconomic status will change. In the past, each generation has had its special problems and its particular successes. With this dynamic base, schools and communities must shape programs that can involve all participants fully and productively. Indeed, you will find in Chapters 10 and 12 that many such programs have already begun.

SUGGESTED ACTIVITIES AND QUESTIONS

1. Discuss the family structure in your own family of origin with several colleagues. Has it changed over time, or has it remained constant during your lifetime?

2. Survey the cultural and ethnic demographics in your school or neighborhood. How do your results compare with the overall U.S. population?

3. Have children in your group draw pictures of their families and then tell you about the persons portrayed. How much information do you receive about the types of families these children have?

4. Find out why children that you meet in your fieldwork are identified as disabled. Was a school or center involved in referrals? Did diagnosis come through a clinic, a family physician, or another source?

RESOURCES

Books

1. Banks, J. A., & McGee-Banks, C. A. (Eds.). (2002). *Multicultural education: Issues and perspectives* (4th ed.). New York: Wiley.

2. Huston, Perdita. (2001). *Families as we are: Conversations from around the world.* New York: Feminist Press.

3. Jones, G. W., & Moomaw, S. (2002). *Lessons from Turtle Island: Native curriculum in early childhood classroom.* St. Paul, MN: Redleaf.

4. Scully, J. L. (2002). *The power of social skills in character development: Helping diverse learners succeed.* Port Chester, NY: National Professional Resources.

5. Consult Appendix 1 for a sampling of many useful children's books that focus on family diversity.

Films and Videos

1. *Include us* [Video, 33 min]. (1997). Shows various children's disabilities with acceptance, independence, and friendship. Sioux City, IA: Tift Hill Productions.

2. *New faces on Main Street* [Video, 60 min]. (1998). Presents interviews with community members where new immigrants have settled. Focuses on problems, prejudice, and hopes as integration takes place. Green Bay: University of Wisconsin–Green Bay.

3. *Our families: Our future.* [Video, 58 min]. (1994). Visits to six family-support programs. Hosted by Walter Cronkite. New York: Filmmakers Library.

4. *That's a family!* [Video, 35 min]. (2001). Presents diverse families—gay, biracial and grandparent guardian—in a sensitive and educational way. San Francisco: Women's Educational Media.

5. *What rights has the child?* [16 mm film, 20 min]. (1990). Exploration of basic rights for children worldwide. New York: United Nations Publications.

Organizations

Council for Exceptional Children
1920 Association Dr.
Reston, VA 20191
(www.cec.sped.org)

National Council on Family Relations
3989 Central Ave., NE
Minneapolis, MN 55400
(http://lists.ncfr.org/)

Stepfamily Foundation
333 West End Ave.,
New York, NY 10023
(www.stepfamily.org)

Family Pride Coalition
P.O. Box 65327
Washington, DC 20035
(www.familypride.org).

Urban Institute
2100M Street NW
Washington, DC 20037
(www.urban.org)

Websites

1. www.adoptive parents.com   Comprehensive Website for general information on adoption, publications, adoption directories, statistics, laws, and other resources.

2. www.colage.org   A Website supporting young people with gay, lesbian, bisexual, and transgender parents.

3. www.prb.org   Population Reference Bureau entry Website for objective demographic statistics and analysis of U.S. and world population studies.

4. www.census.gov   The primary Web address for extensive information about your own state as well as national statistics.

Chapter 4

Parenting the Child

Competent parenting is both a protective factor that prevents social problems and a positive factor in promoting an individual's successful life course. (Westman, 2001, p. 69)

While differences in customs, modes of interaction, parenting styles, and outside influences affect the nurturing practices in all family situations, the importance of parenting in the lives of children is impossible to overestimate. This chapter discusses how these qualities and conditions affect the parent role and the outcomes of parent practices. In reading this chapter, you will learn the following:

1. Parents are key persons in providing the nurturance needs of young children.

2. Parents assume particular roles in children's upbringing, and these roles have changed in recent years.

3. Although there are commonalities in parenting practices, child rearing varies among different ethnic communities in the United States.

4. Researchers have determined that parents have different parenting styles and that these styles affect children's participation in school and community life.

5. Some forms of stress affect child-rearing practices, and in recent decades, new and intensified stressors have had a great impact on American families.

All families, irrespective of the ways they are constituted, share in community life and in school life, and most provide appropriate care for children. Although some household arrangements may be more vulnerable or sensitive, when considered against the dynamics of a particular community, each family can and does make positive contributions to children's development.

When we consider how families function, we find different customs, different priorities,

and even somewhat different values. Of course, the differences signal the uniqueness of our diverse society, but at the same time, those very different elements fuse in most families to provide coherence and stability for members in the household.

In spite of the differences, we find some constants that exist in all families with children. The first constant—the nurturance of children—precedes all others. Nurturance is followed by defined family roles, cultural patterns, interaction styles, and family experiences. Additional characteristics, such as child care arrangements, poverty, and divorce, can emerge as stressors that have an impact on the parenting quality of some family units.

NURTURANCE IN FAMILIES

Generally, nurturance means providing the basic necessities of life for children, but in a wider sense, it denotes general support, love, and cultivation for the growing child. In other words, nurturance is "parenting."

Few adults are actually trained for nurturing roles, but our society expects certain minimums of support and effectiveness from parents as they rear children. The assumption is that nurturance, in its general and wider sense, has been modeled by preceding generations and is refined by an individual's experience and participation in society. But the range of nurturing competence in U.S. homes is wide indeed.

Range of Child Rearing

The nurturer accepts responsibilities not only for giving children basic physiological care, guidance, and love, but also for stimulating a child's investigations of the world and monitoring of social relationships with others. The nurturing parent is one who is grounded in humane practice and who has a vision of what children can become.

While some aspects of parenting may be instinctual, the most effective nurturers have certain characteristics in common, such as motivation to be with children and knowledge about how to care for them. Health and a sense of well-being, empathy, predictability, responsiveness, and emotional availability have also been identified as traits that enhance parent effectiveness (Bornstein, 2001). On the other hand, certain traits like self-centeredness, depression, and drug or alcohol abuse can affect parenting adversely and may lead to abuse or neglect of children.

Abusive behavior in families moves parenting toward the antithesis of nurturing. While few parents are so disordered in outlook as to carry out destructive acts with children, a significant number suffer lapses in judgment and vision that result in psychological and physical abuse or indifferent care practices and neglect. But even families with less desirable child-rearing habits frequently have positive qualities, and through education, counseling, and support, they can learn to modify detrimental practices.

In spite of highly publicized accounts of dysfunctional family situations, the norm in all communities is that parents are nurturing and concerned for the welfare of their youngsters. Consequently, this text does not focus on the pathologies that accompany abuse and indifference; rather, we have chosen to consider the range of positive nurturance that is featured in the great majority of U.S. families.

Because of the cultural diversity that exists in the United States, communities and schools will serve children who have been reared with various nurturing practices. All families are linked with particular cultural groups, and each group will possess unique values and mores that individual families will follow to a greater or lesser extent. In a community with two or more cultural groups, we find somewhat different viewpoints and probably different practices. Just because a community contains different cultural groups, however, does not mean that antagonism is present. On the contrary, quite different child-raising patterns can easily coexist and interact positively. Cross-cultural exchange might even help families solve child-rearing problems.

Features of Positive Nurturance

Maslow (1970) provided a paradigm (Figure 4–1) that shows, in ascending fashion, the scale of human needs. When related to the lives of young children, the levels of the pyramid clearly imply the need for positive nurturance. It is easy to associate the early nurturing practices of parents—and these are almost universal—with the hierarchy developed by Maslow.

Addressing Physiological Needs. Food, warmth, and shelter are bare necessities for survival, and all parents provide them, except in rare cases when families are caught in physical distress, dislocation, or mental illness. In spite of positive intentions, some financially stressed families find difficulty in providing these basics. Cold or hungry children cannot respond to any educational program. At the same time, unhealthy living climates can lead to reduced functioning, and improper food choices can lead to obesity and other nutritional problems. Teachers and other service providers must be alert to problems and deficiencies, and arrange referrals for support.

Ensuring Physical Safety. The next level of Maslow's hierarchy involves safety. Ensuring a child's safety is almost instinctive with parents, and we expect this attention to be provided carefully and lovingly. While most

**Figure 4–1   Maslow's
hierarchy of needs**
Source: From *Psychology for
Teaching* (9th ed., p. 270), by G. R.
LeFrancois, 1996, Belmont, CA:
Wadsworth. Reprinted by permission.

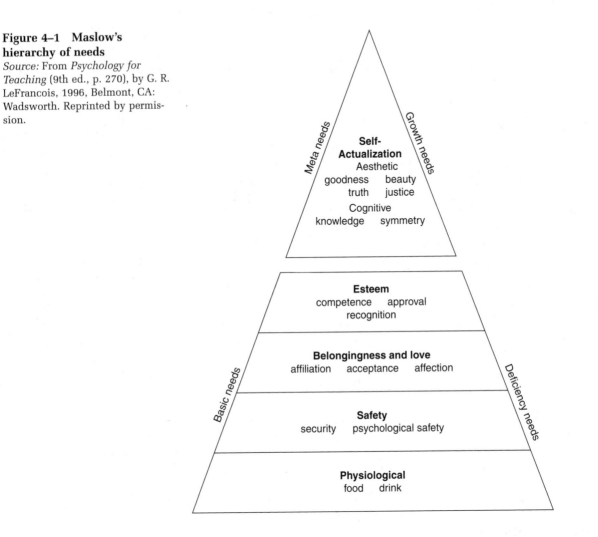

parents are alert to dangers from natural disasters (such as earthquakes and storms), it is all too easy to overlook hidden dangers such as lead paint, polluted areas, and unsafe objects and locations.

Providing Love.   Giving emotional support and providing love are features of nurturance that occur naturally in typical families. Families express these feelings in different ways. Expressions of love range from nonverbal signals and understated expressions to effusive expressions of affection. Differences in disci-

pline practices are linked with this area of nurturance as well. Some families use physical punishment, while others depend on verbal reprimand and discussion or explanation to rechannel behavior. All practices can be effective under particular circumstances. Occasionally, parents overdo their support role and encourage dependency and immaturity in their child. Overconcern and hovering often have undesirable consequences.

Promoting Esteem, Success, and Achievement.   Families vary greatly in how they foster esteem and support the achievements of their children. Some parents campaign vigorously with and for their children, while others gently encourage or deliberately withhold praise until the end of an activity or a task. Parents sometimes hold children to adult standards in playing games, conversing, or socializing. This expectation can be problematic if children do not succeed, for their aspirations may be deflated. Adult encouragement and delight in partial success normally provide a foundation for children to lift their levels of aspiration.

Self-actualization. The final level in Maslow's hierarchy is an adult level of competence, but families foster readiness for self-actualization by supporting children's growing independence and sense of responsibility and by encouraging problem solving and decision making at children's appropriate levels of growth.

FAMILY ROLES

The family at the beginning of the 21st century has crucial roles to perform. Because society evolves, these familial roles vary from those of a century ago. Lifestyles are different now, circumstances have changed, and new expectations have emerged. However, certain basics and constants of parent roles, such as providing economic and emotional support, socialization, and education for their children remain.

Fulfilling these functions varies from family to family, depending on circumstance. When parents are unable to carry out their responsibilities, other persons and agencies may assume parental capacities and duties. In all cases, the family roles are complemented by the efforts of teachers and various community agencies.

Economic Support

We recognized in Chapter 3 that some families in the United States live on a few thousand dollars per year while others enjoy extraordinarily high incomes. This variable determines the type of shelter and quality of food and clothing the family acquires, as well as other family living conditions.

Even though one or more family members are employed, some families are challenged to meet economic minimums and must depend on government assistance and private charities to supplement the basics. Since women in general make only 73% of men's annual earnings, and African American and Hispanic men earn 78% and 63% of White men's salaries (Haddock, Zimmerman, & Lyness, 2003), the families most likely to struggle economically are single-parent families headed by women and families of color. Although the United States is the wealthiest nation in the world, 18% of American children under the age of 6 live in families with incomes below the poverty line (Children's Defense Fund, 2001).

Almost all families do manage their economic responsibility, marginal as it may be at times. Although many U.S. families are subsidized, most do have adequate shelter, food, and clothing. Most families also have reasonable choices in how they allot their finances. But poverty is exacerbated for families struggling to make appropriate choices, and those with meager resources may need support and education to learn how to make sound financial decisions. A more desperate circumstance emerges for the underclass, where the basic levels of the Maslow hierarchy are often threatened.

Social agencies are established in communities to guarantee economic basics for all families. The success rate is reasonable, but communities must pursue even more aggressively the task of monitoring and guiding basic economic practices. While welfare reform measures have helped former recipients obtain jobs, adequate resources for housing, health care benefits, and child care are often not available (Boyd–Franklin, 2003). Extended training and education are needed to lift people out of poverty for good. Parent education that focuses on the economics of family life as well as parenting skills can be an important step in improving the lives of those living in difficult economic circumstances, and it is a focus that integrates well with collaborations among communities, schools, and families.

Emotional Support

Even though most parents have little training or instruction in psychological support roles, emotional nurturance for offspring appears to be a natural response. And although most new parents emulate the parenting skills they observed and experienced in their own childhood (Bornstein, 2001), others make a conscious decision to parent their children differently than they were raised.

The emotional bonds that form between parents and children provide the foundation for later loving relationships. Physical affection, appreciation of the child as an individual, and acknowledgement of a child's competence all contribute to the development of self-esteem in children, the basis of sound emotional health. Research on "strong families" (Westman, 2001) suggests that emotional development in children benefits from parenting practices that emphasize mutual respect for family members, open communication, and parental authority.

Parenting classes and clinics are available (and needed) for parents who are uncertain about ways to nurture their new children most effectively. A growing problem with our present generation is that smaller families, dual-income families, and, especially, single-parent families provide noticeably less modeling of parenting behavior (Casper & Bianchi, 2002). Again, community policies must ensure availability and use of resources to support parents who need guidance in providing emotional support for their children.

Socialization

While many agents, such as the school, the peer group, the church, and the media, are involved in socializing children, the family has the primary responsibility for beginning the process (Bigner, 2002). Socialization of young children involves learning to relate to a variety of people in varying circumstances and modifying behavior in different environments. Strong social skills, specifically the ability to get along with other children, are the best childhood predictors of adult competence (Henniger, 2002). Emotional and social development are closely linked, and children with high self-esteem are better able to face the challenges of social interaction.

As children enter school and community life today, other forces begin to exert increasing influence on their socialization (Berns, 2001). Parental impact on children's socialization was more significant in earlier periods of history. More isolated communities, less mobility, and the virtual dominance of parental figures ensured that values, beliefs, and attitudes were quickly inculcated in children through example and statement. In addition, communities in the early United States were highly idealistic in orientation, and role expectations were similar for everyone in the more restricted venues.

Patterns differ today. We have less general agreement in the United States on social mores as a result of the heterogeneous communities in which we live. Schools still have certain expectations for children, however, and those who enter without some of the rudimentary social skills of sharing, taking turns, cooperating, and respecting rules will find themselves at a disadvantage. Families must work harder to prepare their children for the social expectations of the school while maintaining their own values, beliefs, attitudes, family ethnic and religious identity, and gender roles.

Emotional bonds that form between parents and children provide the foundation for later loving relationships

Values, Beliefs, and Attitudes. Parents rarely plan to teach about values and beliefs. They do, however, model via their behavior what they value and prize and what they are willing to accept. This practice has both positive and negative aspects. If a parent rushes to help a stumbling neighbor, the idea is passed on to children; if a parent models lying, that habit is passed on. Recall that one part of Jana's story in the opening vignette in Chapter 3 was the way Jana's stepmother modeled "helping neighbors." Today, Jana is raising her own children and responds to neighborhood difficulties by preparing and donating food.

If we consider that children average nearly 30 hours a week watching TV or playing video games, many beliefs and values accrue to them from participating in these activities (Singer & Singer, 2001; Van Evra, 1998). Of particular concern is the increasing amount and level of violence in programming for children (Levin, 1998). The culture of violence created by the media teaches children lessons that do not fit into the value systems of most parents. Parents, of course, can monitor and watch programs to discuss actions and make comments, but the problem of media violence and other aspects of media culture is increasingly being viewed as a public health issue, and schools and community agencies are beginning to get involved in protecting children from unhealthy and undesirable images.

Gender Roles.   While both gender and parenting roles in today's society appear quite different from those for earlier generations and gender-related expectations are less rigid in many U.S. homes, most parents do seek to steer their children toward **gender-appropriate behaviors.**

The process of gender socialization often begins even before a child is born as parents use information about their coming child's gender in order to choose gender-appropriate names, clothing, and nursery decorations. Parents also tend to give children gender-stereotyped toys and to interact with their children differently depending on their gender (Haddock et al., 2003). While some gendering in family life is inevitable, rigid expectations perpetuate the inequities of power between men and women in our society.

In most U.S. families, fathers are still the primary economic mainstay, but that role is changing. Today, 65% of mothers with children under 6 are in the labor force (Children Defense Fund, 2001), and 75% of mothers with children between 6 and 17 are employed (Casper & Bianchi, 2002). In many dual-career homes, mothers and fathers now contribute equally to economic support. In addition, mothers are the breadwinners in most single-parent homes. Thus, the notion of associating economic support with one particular parent does not fit many children's life experiences.

Beyond economic dimensions is the changing character of family duties in the household. Historically, roles were that the mother was cook and general homemaker while the father was in the field or away at work. In the modern home, duties are not so clearly defined. It is still a small percentage, but some fathers now have major responsibilities for meal preparation and cleaning in addition to child monitoring. Fathers now attend childbirth and parenting classes along with their wives and take responsibility for infant care. The vast majority of married couples, however, still adhere to traditional family roles, and even women who are employed do about 80% of the household chores and child care (Haddock et al., 2003). Attempts to eliminate sexism in today's world are slowly recasting gender roles for U.S. society. Many quality children's books, noted in Appendix 1, now portray progressive gender roles.

Over the course of children's lives, they may live in various family configurations due to separation, divorce, death, remarriage, and other family changes. These reconfigured family structures will expose children to more flexible gender roles. Single-parent households and families led by gay or lesbian parents will also provide a less rigid idea of what roles men and women can play in family life and society (Ramsey, 1998).

Racial and Ethnic Identity. Defining race and ethnicity in the United States is a complex, and sometimes contested, endeavor. As our society has become more mixed physically (see Figure 4–2), it becomes increasingly difficult to categorize by race, as discussed in the previous chapter. In 1998, for example, 5% of Black Americans were foreign born (C. A. Banks, 2003). Many of these individuals are far more likely to identify with their ethnic her-

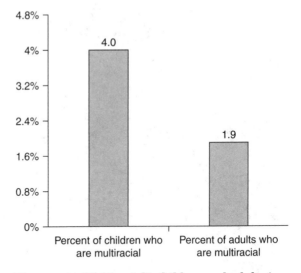

Figure 4–2   Multiracial* children and adults in the 2000 census
*Multiracial refers to people who chose more than one race on the 2000 census.
Source: Population Reference Bureau, analysis of data from U.S. Census Bureau, 2000 redistricting data (Tables PL1 and Pl2), 2003.

itage (Jamaican American, for example) than their racial identity. No matter how a family defines itself, however, most are interested in preserving their cultural heritage and teaching their children about their background (J. A. Banks, 1996).

While children begin to become aware of racial differences in skin color and other physical characteristics at around age 3 or 4 (Katz, 1976; Ramsey, 1987), their understanding of the social and political implications of race develops much later (Wright, 1998).

When Catherine, an African American 3-year-old adopted by a White family, asked what color her mother was, her mother replied, "Well, I am peach color, but most people would call me White." She went on to say that people would call Catherine Black, to which Catherine replied incredulously, "I'm not

Black, I'm silver!" By age 5, Catherine was coloring her skin brown in self-portraits and referring to herself as brown.

＞

Typically, Black children do become aware of their race at younger ages than White children (Wright, 1998), perhaps because of the continued salience of race as an issue for African Americans. Disparagement of a minority heritage typically is initiated by individuals in the dominant culture. Such disparagement leads, as in U.S. history, to many minority families' denigrating their own heritage. For example, Butler (1976), in reviewing ethnic preferences in literature, found that up through the 1960s, African American children across social and geographical settings preferred White dolls and White playmates. Since 1970, however, research findings have changed, and in most studies (Butler, 1976; Cross, 1987; Ramsey, 1987), African American children now show preference for Black characters. Ethnic identity and validation are clearly in the province of the family, and feelings about self depend on accurate information and sensitive guidance (Ramsey, 1998). Some minority homes provide support and foster pride in the family culture and give training on how to overcome derogatory messages. But responsibility for enhancing heritage goes beyond family efforts; it must be supported throughout the community.

Multicultural education is the term used for a concept that deals with reforms made in schools and other social institutions to respond to our diverse society (Sleeter & Grant, 2003). A positive outcome of multicultural education efforts is that racial and ethnic heritages are featured in schools, communities, museums, and the mass media. Families celebrate differences now, and few are opposed to sharing stories about their cultural background and traditions in schools or in community programs.

Much of a family's cultural history comes in the form of stories shared and passed down through generations. A fine example in adult literature is *Roots,* by Alex Haley (1976). Another is *Daughters of the Dust,* by Julie Dash (1992), a story of Gullah families in Georgia's outer islands. Children's literature (Corliss, 1998) has many examples as well (also see Appendix 1).

Educational Underpinnings

As we noted in Chapter 2, parents in previous centuries assumed a major role in all aspects of educating their children. Even in the 1800s, many families still attended to basic lessons for living and vocational preparation for their children. As the 1800s moved into the 1900s, however, schools expanded rapidly in scope and assumed most of the role for educating children in literary skills, calculation, and sciences. They even acquired the job of developing work habits; moral training and health education were added quickly thereafter. Today's school has expanded to include sex education, health and recreation training, vocational training, and other educational aspects formerly a family's responsibility. It appears that only the early educative tasks are retained by families in the modern United States.

One regrettable outcome of this transfer of educative roles is that many parents have become much less involved in teaching their children about essential responsibilities. While demands on today's homes are immense, parents are still answerable for 75% of their children's waking hours during the typical school week (Robinson & Godbey, 1999). This amount of parent supervision carries a responsibility for educating, in the broad sense that is too often overlooked.

Families can provide the support, critical demonstrations, and follow-up for a child's learning opportunities if they are mindful of (a) the parents' logical status as guide, (b) their intimate knowledge of the learner, (c) the influence parental status provides, and (d) the many chances for translating text material to everyday life. In fact, some parents are doing just that by home schooling their children. Chapter 7 provides more detail on home learning and on home schooling.

Changes in Functions for the 21st Century

As we have suggested, U.S. families are diverse and will continue to become more diverse for the foreseeable future. Roles for family members in the information age are still evolving, and certainly changes will continue to appear. One can only guess how different the typical family roles will be in another few decades.

Some changes in recent decades that show increased momentum are that fathers are more involved in early education, and this benefits children; mothers are more involved in sports and recreational activities, and this benefits children; but extended families continue to decrease in contact and impact, and this does not benefit children (Hoffer & Coleman, 1990). Single parenting, which can be less advantageous for children, is likely to continue at a similar pace. School responsibilities are still increasing, but efforts to share and exchange responsibilities are more in evidence (see Chapter 11 for particular models of cooperation).

Children of the 21st century face a very different socializing environment from previous generations. Less constancy is found in family matters, and more adults from outside the family are involved with children's experiences. Peer-group influences have expanded, to say nothing of the explosion in influence of the media and entertainment industries. All human service personnel must work for more joint efforts among homes, schools, and communities, where well-reasoned decisions about roles will enable families to provide quality experiences and opportunities for their children.

CULTURAL PATTERNS AND FAMILY FUNCTIONS

We are made up of increasingly different ethnic backgrounds in the United States, and we thus find differences in the ways groups perform tasks, establish values, and relate to one another (McGoldrick, 2003). Different ethnic groups frequently have varying cultural features, but we also find multiple cultures within the various groups (Bullivant, 1993; Hillis, 1996). Even among the same ethnic groups or culture, individuals vary enormously. This makes for an interesting cultural mix in our nation, and one that professionals must study and reflect on.

Ethnic background refers to the shared history and culture, common values, behaviors, and other characteristics that encompass a sense of identity among its members (C. A. Banks, 2003). While ethnic groups, such as African Americans, can have distinguishing racial characteristics, other ethnic groups, such as Puerto Ricans, include people who belong to several different racial groups. In the case of Jewish Americans, their shared religious and cultural background, rather than their racial identities, creates a common bond.

Culture refers to the attitudes, traditions, beliefs, symbols, and customs held by a group of people. In the United States, there is an overarching core culture shared to a greater or lesser extent by all individuals and groups within the nation. Ideas related to equality, individualism, and opportunity for social mobility are examples of the core ideals of the culture of the United States. Within our country, there are also many smaller subcultures that reflect the components important to particular groups.

Ethnicity and culture frequently overlap; for example, many Native Americans continue to identify themselves by ethnic background and hold cultural beliefs separate from mainstream U.S. culture. We also find groups of people with similar ethnic backgrounds who differ culturally. For example, in English-speaking regions, Appalachian Americans are very different from Oregonian ranchers or Connecticut commuters, even though they have similar roots. Their traditions, values, and attitudes place them in different cultural groups.

For simplification, we differentiate in this text between the European American (White), English-speaking majority and non–European American minorities in the United States, even though each of these contains more than one ethnic group. Table 4–1 presents the proportions of these primary minority groups as of 2001. While census charts include Hispanic Americans in other totals, our figure divides the population into Hispanic and non-Hispanic, and then calculates totals from those two categories to avoid counting Hispanic Americans twice.

Ethnic and cultural groups may have lifestyles, ways of communicating, and parenting practices that differ from the mainstream beliefs in the United States. Gender roles, social class, socioeconomic status, and parents' occupations are variables that may further impact a group's parenting style in unique ways, depending on the culture. With the increasing diversity and overlap of cultures, it is essential for professionals to examine their own behavior and increase their

Table 4–1 Major Ethnic Groups in the United States in 2000

Ethnic Group	Percentage of Population
African American	13 %
American Indian/Alaskan Native	1 %
Asian/Pacific Islanders	4 %
European Americans	69 %
Hispanic Americans	13 %

Note: Persons of Hispanic ancestry may be of any race but are separated from other groups for this table.
Source: U.S. Bureau of the Census, 121st Statistical Abstract of the United States, 2002.

awareness of other ways of living and communicating so that discussions with parents are carried out with respect. Professionals must keep in mind that individuals also vary greatly in their identification with their ethnic group and take care not to stereotype people on the basis of their ethnic background.

Despite the differences in parenting practices that families from various cultures may employ, it is important to be aware that most parents do have similar goals for their children. Families want their offspring to live healthy lives, achieve some economic stability, and adhere to certain cultural values (Greenfield & Suzuki, 2001). Parents from different cultures may, however, vary in their expectations about development of competencies at different ages (Bornstein, 2001).

The values of a culture are transmitted primarily through adult modeling, directions and instructions given to children, pressures from the cultural group, and reinforcements for certain serendipitous actions that each child displays. So while the goals for children's development are similar, various cultural groups may rear their children quite differently. However, you must also bear in mind that values and attitudes for many children are influenced more and more by the media, schools, and peers.

Parenting Features in Various Cultures

Child-raising practices in the United States changed considerably during the 20th century. We now find great variation from one cultural group to another within the society as a whole. The socioeconomic status (SES) of different families within one cultural group indicates that other differences exist as well.

For European American groups, behaviorism was valued in the early years of the 20th century, and many parents at that time valued the principles of reinforcement and extinction, popularized by psychologists. A child-centered phase bloomed in the middle years of the

Many Native Americans hold cultural beliefs separate from mainstream culture

century, but in recent decades, the swing has been toward a middle ground. Overall, contemporary European Americans are quite susceptible to current theories and depend less on folklore and tradition than did prior generations. Thus, cultural child-raising practices vary considerably over time. Although most minority cultures in the United States have retained their traditional child-raising practices much more than have European American families, the proliferation of ideas in the mass media has altered some of their practices as well.

Keeping all the complexity about approaches to parenting in mind, certain practices do tend to differ among various ethnic groups. It is essential to remember, however, that these are broad generalizations meant to suggest the range in approaches to caring for children. Although it is possible to find general characteristics of a group, individuals within the group may not conform to the generalizations. Further, socioeconomic level, education, and parental occupation are all important factors in determining an individual's child-rearing practices. The following behaviors are adapted from Berns, 2001; Greenfield and Suzuki, 2001; Janosik and Green, 1992; McDermott, 2001; McGoldrick, 1993; and Sadker and Sadker, 2003.

Infant Care. In the European American tradition, where the development of autonomy and separate individual existence is an important parental goal, babies tend to be held less than in many other cultures and to be left to cry after all obvious physical needs have been tended to. In Native American society, babies and mothers have traditionally had continuing contact, and other groups, such as African Americans, Hispanic Americans, and various Asian American cultures, tend to feed on demand and maintain very close physical connections between mothers and infants.

Cosleeping between parents and children is the norm in approximately two thirds of the world's cultures, and many minority and immigrant groups in the United States still hold on to cosleeping practices. Cosleeping of mother and infant are common in cultures that emphasize interdependence and family bonding above independence. Immigrants from many African countries, as well as Japanese Americans, Korean Americans, and other Asian groups, may cosleep or keep children in the same room with them through early childhood. Babies generally sleep alone in a room separate from their parents in the European American family.

The European American way of socializing children has been characterized as geared to the goal of technological intelligence, while other groups have a goal of social intelligence (Greenfield & Suzuki, 2001). The emphasis in European American families is on babies' manipulation and labeling of objects, while recent immigrants from Africa and Asian families seem to value positive interactions between babies and other people.

Physical Contact.   Different cultural groups vary greatly in the amount and kind of physical contact that exists between parents and their children. Affection is displayed in different ways, and physical punishment is used to a greater or lesser extent among various groups.

In many Asian American homes, the physical closeness common between infants and parents becomes more restrained as children grow, while in African American families, body contact is expected and encouraged throughout childhood. Less physical intimacy is found between parents and children in many European American homes, although playful interaction is encouraged. Physical punishment is accepted in Hispanic families, but these families also tend to be very physically affectionate with their children. African American families are more likely to use physical punishment than Native American families, who avoid its use.

Family Role.   In many cultures, the solidarity and importance of the family is primary, while in others, children are encouraged to be more independent. In some groups, the nuclear family is paramount, whereas in others the extended family and kinship network are essential aspects of child rearing. Patriarchal, matriarchal, and shared leadership can be found in different cultures.

Interaction styles within the family reflect the roles expected of children. In many Hispanic families, for example, children are encouraged and expected to play with siblings rather than peers, while European American families encourage their children to move beyond the family to establish other relationships. Asian American families expect their children to be family oriented and participate in working hard for the support of the family. Much value is placed on respect for elders within the family in most Asian cultures. African American families also place great emphasis on children being part of an extended family of relatives and other adults who function as part of a large kinship network, who all participate in raising the children.

Clearly, differences exist among ethnic groups in parenting practices, although we restate that these are general characteristics only. One can easily find homes displaying a few of the practices noted in the preceding sections. As you go forward in your professional preparation, remain open to parenting that may be very different than the way you were raised or intend to raise your children. Parenting practices generally make sense in the context of the culture the parent is trying to preserve. Becoming familiar with different cultural practices by speaking openly and listening respectfully to parents from varying backgrounds will help you to understand how parenting fits in with the larger cultural goals of different groups.

The numerous decisions parents must make regarding the conflicting forces that surround all homes in busy America—media, entertainment, peer culture, and other attractions—can make it very challenging for parents to meet their responsibilities. Parenting is complex, and often factors other than a family's culture or ethnic background can influence child-rearing behaviors. Birth order of children, the child's age, temperament or gender, parental experiences, and parent temperament will all have an impact on how a parent raises a particular child.

All parents, we find, use a mixture of child-rearing practices, and the impressions and the information from other sources will influence their behavior. Of course, how parents primarily interact with their children will have a significant impact on children's development. In the next section, we explore some of the variations in interaction styles within families that have been studied.

INTERACTION STYLES WITHIN FAMILIES

The child-rearing practices that parents employ influences children's behavior as we observe it in schools and communities, and researchers confirm the parent influence as well as the interactions between children and significant adults. The studies discussed in this section demonstrate connections between parenting and observed child behavior.

Baumrind's Classification

In Baumrind's (1968, 1971) classification, parenting styles are placed along a three-part continuum:

1. *Authoritative (democratic).* Controlling, demanding, but warm. Rational and receptive to child's communication.
2. *Permissive (child centered).* Noncontrolling, nondemanding, and relatively warm.
3. *Authoritarian (autocratic).* Detached, controlling, somewhat less warm.

In her classic study, Baumrind (1968) found that most children of authoritative parents showed independence and were socially responsible. These traits translated into competence and resistance to substance abuse during adolescence, according to a later study (Baumrind, 1995). Authoritative parents took into account their child's needs as well as their own before dealing with situations. The parents respected children's need to make their own decisions, yet they exerted control. They reasoned with their children and explained things more often than did other parents.

On the other hand, Baumrind found that those children of permissive parents frequently lacked social responsibility and often were not independent. She concluded that parents who looked at all behavior as natural and refreshing had unrealistic beliefs about young children's growth and socialization.

Baumrind found that children of authoritarian parents also showed little independence and were less socially responsible. Such parents feel that children need restraint and need to develop respect for authority, work, and traditional structure.

The following summary illustrates the adult behaviors that produce Baumrind's authoritative style. To foster socially responsible and independent behavior in children, parents

- Serve as responsible and self-assertive models
- Set standards where responsible behavior is rewarded and unacceptable behavior is punished
- Are committed to the child in a way that is neither overprotective nor rejecting
- Have high demands for achievement and conformity but are receptive to child's rational demands
- Provide secure but challenging and stimulating environments for creative and rational thinking.

Maccoby and Martin (1983) reviewed literature on parenting styles at a later point and in general supported the findings of Baumrind. Clark (1983) also produced similar findings. His "sponsored independence" style is consistent with Baumrind's authoritative style. Later studies measuring the long-term effects of the authoritative style produced more evidence that it engenders positive adolescent behavior (Holmbeck, Paikoff, & Brooks-Gunn, 1995; Steinberg, 1991).

One caveat is needed concerning this research. Baumrind used White, middle-class parents in her study, while later, in their replication studies, Maccoby and Martin (1983) found that Baumrind's conclusions did not always translate directly for poor, minority, and single-parent families. However, Clark (1983) found that the authoritative or sponsored independence behaviors in Mexican American and African American homes often made the difference between success and failure for minority children in schools.

White's Study

White (1971), in his Harvard preschool project, investigated the development of competence in children and then related his findings to their parents. White categorized the children in his study as A, B, or C, according to competence:

- A children knew how to hold adult attention, how to use adult resources, and how to express affection and hostility. They got along with others, were proud of achieving, and wanted to be grown up. They used language well and understood other points of view. They were able to concentrate on tasks and plan activities.
- Bs were less competent than As in all the skills.
- Cs were deficient in the social and work skills, and even lacked the ability to anticipate consequences.

When White and Watts (1973) looked at the homes of the participants, they found notable differences between the behaviors of the parents of the successful As and the less adequate Cs. White concluded that a parent's style of child rearing registered an effect on children as young as ages 1 and 2.

The main differences White and Watts (1973) found among parents were in interaction, attitudes, and attending to environment. The A mothers made themselves available to children, were eager and enthusiastic about helping children, and were tolerant of messes. They set limits and were firm and consistent. The C mothers were not as involved, even when they were in contact with their children. Some were disorganized and overwhelmed by home tasks, and most restricted their children by using playpens.

Bernstein's Work

Language is a primary avenue through which a child learns to understand and function in the world. Children tend to develop language on a predictable developmental scale, but different parental language styles and interactions affect children's socialization and literacy development. Bernstein's (1972) classic study of family language patterns produced two general linguistic codes used in many homes. He termed these very different patterns *restricted* and *elaborated*. The codes reflect two quite different styles: the **position-oriented family** and the **person-oriented family.**

Position-oriented families use a restricted code, and the family role system is positional, or object oriented and present oriented. In contrast, person-oriented families use an elaborated code, and the family role system is personal, or person oriented and future oriented. The following example will illustrate.

❧

In the space of 3 minutes, two attractive family groups approached a traffic-light-controlled crosswalk at a busy intersection. One mother and her preschool son approached hand in hand, talking freely. Within a few feet of the crosswalk, the mother leaned down toward her son and said, "See the light there? It's red, and we have to stop. See the cars still coming this way? We need to stay right back here, 'til we get the flashing walk light, OK? You watch and tell me when to go."

The second family, a mother, father, and little girl, approached the crosswalk and stopped. Suddenly, the mother noticed the child, who was slightly ahead, starting toward the crosswalk and yelled, "Stay here!" The girl continued to advance, and the mother screamed again, "Stay here, I said!" The father leaped and yanked the girl back beside him. "Just stand!" the mother said, and the family waited silently for the signal to change—bodies rigid, the parents holding tightly to the child.

The second family here is position oriented and has a prescribed role system. Members have little choice, and roles are assigned according to family position. According to Bernstein, their communication is object oriented and present oriented. Aspects of **restricted language code** appear, characterized by syntactically simple sentences and concrete meanings. The parents communicate one thing only to the daughter—to obey a single command. There is no explanation, and sentences are simple and direct.

The open quality of the mother and son in the person-oriented family, on the other hand, permits discretion in learner performance. Communication in the open system includes judgments and reasons, and children learn to cope with abstractions and ambiguity. The **elaborated language code** accommodates this type of content. The mother chats with her son about the crosswalk, explaining what is happening. She engages the child in the decision making.

Teachers must know that children from a closed or position-oriented family must depend on the school and the larger community to help them in acquiring elaborated language. As a teacher, you can become a vital communication model for children from families using restricted codes, as can other children. Older children may often help their teacher communicate with new children not familiar with school language and culture. We find this situation in the following vignette.

❧

Ms. Dansky, a White teacher, wasn't successful in getting Philip, an African American 5-year-old just entering school, to join other children in a circle. She had used a polite invitation to call all the children. When Philip didn't move, she gave a sterner and more specific command to Philip. Then Greg, a seasoned African American 8-year-old, raised his hand and asked quietly, "You want me to get him for you, Ms. D?" Upon receiving a polite "Yes, thank you," he yelled to Philip, "Boy, get yo'r butt over here, yu' hear!" When Philip came immediately to sit beside Greg, Greg leaned to him and continued, "When she say, 'Boys and girls join me,' she mean 'Come here.' And when she say, 'Philip, it's time for circle!'

she mean, 'Get yo'r butt here (pats a spot be-side himself) NOW!'"
(Seefeldt & Barbour, 1998, p. 340)

⁓

Greg had learned not only the correct language patterns of the school but also the politeness rules. He used language and tonal patterns familiar to Philip, and he skillfully switched between the two patterns to explain what their teacher's words meant. One can appreciate the advantages that elaborated codes have in the broadening requirements of the information age.

Hart and Risley Studies

Hart and Risley (1995) also concentrated on language development and demonstrated that quality of parenting and richness of linguistic environment are not necessarily bound with economic status or ethnicity. In their study of homes representing three SES levels, they discussed the linkages between young children's

language development and meaningful experiences. The longitudinal study convinces us that the type and amount of interaction between parents and children results in significant differences, irrespective of SES.

According to the study, the quality of interactions in everyday parenting will center on the following five variables:

1. *Amount and richness of vocabulary.* The parent deliberately uses various terms, labels, and expressions and models their use when talking. "Yes, these are all clothes—pants, shirts, socks."

2. *Sentence usage.* Parents make a connection between objects and events when responding to children. "Yes, it is a doll, and it's Cindy's, so you need to give it back."

3. *Discourse function.* Quality of utterances used is important when parents give choices or directions to prompt child behavior. "Did you remember to hang your coat?"

4. *Adjacency condition.* This variable centers on the relation between parent and child

Quality of interactions and richness of vocabulary in everyday parenting increases children's language development

behavior when the parent listens or initiates for child. Child: "Soup's good!" Parent models by: "Yes, it's delicious, isn't it?"

5. *Valence of communications.* The emotional tone given to interactions is important whether the parent tries to be pleasant or not. Simply smiling and repeating a child's word: "That's right, juice!" has positive valence.

The positive dimension of this study shows us that parenting behaviors leading to increased child performance can be learned and practiced. Hart and Risley assert that parents who purposely concentrate on the meaningful differences are being "social partners" with their children.

In a follow-up study, Hart and Risley (1999) suggested that the most important aspect of parent talk to young children is its amount. They learned from their study that parents who talk as they go about their daily activities expose their children to more than 1,000 words per hour. Even more important, however, is the way that conversation between parent and child during the first three years contributes to their relationship and builds a foundation of analytic and symbolic competencies that will serve them for a lifetime. Spending time talking together is the most important way parents can help their child learn to speak and listen. And, of course, speaking and listening are the foundations of literacy.

With parents' busy work schedules and the amount of television viewing by the entire family, substantive conversation—which does not include directions, commands, or reprimands—between parents and children is becoming rare in many homes. Some dramatic and startling figures command our attention. Schwartz (1995) pointed out that in far too many homes, fathers average only 8 minutes per weekday in meaningful conversation with their offspring, and working mothers only

11 minutes! Weekend interactions aren't much better (Richards & Duckett, 1994). Teachers and community workers alone cannot compensate for the shortage of meaningful parent–child interactions, but as you work to establish strong home and school partnerships, you can help parents become aware of the importance of conversation with young children.

No two families are exactly alike, and parents have diverse ways of managing. The various features of parenting make family behaviors very complex and difficult to understand. However, we can examine general patterns of parenting, and we can relate these patterns to children's behavior. The investigators previously noted, Baumrind, Clark, Maccoby, and Martin, found that neither extreme of the parenting pattern—referred to respectively as *permissive* and *dominative*—is ideal for children. In his Conditional Sequence Model, Larzelere (2001) reaffirmed the need for combining reason and discipline in effective parenting. Clearly, a combination of love and limits appears more beneficial.

Always remember that parenting styles are influenced by more than cultural background and interaction styles. As professionals, you must also be alert to the influence of family size, family SES, levels of stress in the home, and different community characteristics surrounding the children you work with.

EXPERIENCES OF FAMILIES

The life experiences of children within their families establish a background for their performance and their contributions in their school and community. What children see, hear, smell, taste, and do creates a foundation for their communication patterns, perceptual styles, and modes of thinking. Within the context of learning about life, children begin to comprehend messages and understand objects within the environment (Elgin, 1990; Ramsey, 1998). Likewise, children's understanding of encountered images frequently depends on explanations and connections made by nearby adults.

Culture and experiential background make a significant difference in how a child learns, communicates, and participates. In addition to basic nurturing, family histories of interactions, experiences, and practices will enhance or detract from children's development potential (Scarf, 1997). When stress or problems arise, some families are **resilient** and display an ability to deal with changes and modify problems; others are ill equipped and cannot cope (Werner & Smith, 1998). Some adults even lean on their own children for support (Garbarino, Dubrow, Kostelny, & Pardo, 1998). Such resilience or its absence derives from many aspects of family experience. The communication styles and parenting styles noted earlier have an effect, but we should also consider the skill levels of parents and the type and degree of family mobility.

Skill Levels and Experience

Most parents and caregivers have extensive knowledge of their world—how to operate within society and how to evaluate their surroundings. Adults in families always pass on some bits of this wisdom to their children, some in particularly beneficial ways.

Homemakers know their living quarters and what it takes to live in a particular home. Parents have experiences in food shopping, preparation, and serving, and some have added skills with nutrition and food presentation. Involving children in food management can be realized easily in all homes and contributes a basic foundation for healthy living.

Using tools to build or repair household objects is common in many homes. Some parents have woodworking or metal-finishing skills and perhaps have home workbenches. Almost all parents have interesting experiences involving tools, and many take pleasure in their use. Adults can easily transfer these skills to interested children through demonstration (Voss, 1993), home projects, or children's books, such as *The New How Things Work* (Macaulay, 1998).

Some families invest a great deal of time in gardening for relaxation or for summer vegetable acquisition. The growing of green things fascinates most youngsters, and it is the beginning of a basic science that children encounter during their school years. A child's home is a nice place to learn about gardening, and any growing project provides a healthy venue for discussion and interaction between adult and child. An example of "gardening" learning was demonstrated when our neighbor Melissa involved her 3-year-old son, in a very natural way, with her regular gardening, singing, and reading activities.

&

Having just received Inch by Inch *(Mallett, 1995) from the community's Growing Up Reading Project, Melissa and her son Adam immediately opened the new treasure and looked at the end pages, with pictures of vegetables. Adam saw a picture of a carrot and exclaimed, "That's a carrot." "Yes," said Melissa, "we've just gathered those from our garden, haven't we? See any more vegetables we have?" Adam thumbed through and found a huge beet. "Beet, yum, yum!" He turned to the end pages again and with a scooping motion began to "pick up" the imaginary vegetables, named them, and pretended to stuff them into his mouth. In the next few months, Melissa and Adam often played the "Garden Song" tape that accompanied this new book and sang the song together. It was a delight to see Melissa and Adam in the garden together the next spring, weeding. Adam trotted along the rows singing, "Inch by inch . . . make my garden grow . . . inch by inch, make my garden grow."*

Then he stopped to pull a "weed" and ex-claimed, "A carrot! No, a beet! Yum, yum."

Many games feature family interactions, and by using games as entertainment, parents can provide children with involvement in group activities, experience in strategy development and planning, positive use of aggressiveness, and practice in cooperative activities. Games are fundamentally simulations of life experiences, and children with extensive experience with various games internalize approaches for living and considerable amounts of strategy for facing interactive situations (Jones, 1988).

Storytelling plays an important part in children's growth. A large part of language development comes through stories. In families where stories are used for recreating family history, for entertainment, or as examples, listeners grow in appreciation of language and of their culture and of their family's experiences and identity. One very important manifestation is the story in book form. In a book, the story belongs to someone else, but it gives much the same satisfaction to the young child.

Parents' skill levels in these and other aspects of daily life can and should be passed on to children in the family. All community life and school programs must reinforce these practices. Given the right conditions, home management and repair, gardening projects, game playing, storytelling, and other family-oriented experiences represent important resources and a worthy heritage for parents to relay to their children. Most parents are not skilled instructors but can be very successful in teaching home activities and projects. When a caregiver is engaged with a single child on a topic of mutual interest, most classroom "teaching" demands are not present. Instructor and student can go directly to the task of transferring a particular skill to the

learner. Most parents are successful at this natural process, and most yearn to pass on their knowledge when an opportunity presents itself.

Mobility of Families

Another feature of experience that affect children's emotional and academic progress is the mobility that families have in and around their community and farther afield. Americans move more than people in other countries, and moves frequently place families further from their kin and other members of their social network. On the average, between 16% and 20% of our population moves in a year (McFalls, 1998), but a great deal of that relocating is for young adults moving out of the home for work, education, or marriage. However, we find that 23% of the persons who moved in 2000 were children under 5 (U.S. Bureau of the Census, 2002), and this has an impact. Studies of military families who move on the average of every 3 years indicated that many of the affected children gave up trying to form close friendships (Karpowitz, 2001).

High levels of residential mobility can foment social problems for adults as well as children—if the move is accompanied by significant change in the quality of home life. African American and Hispanic Americans move more often than Whites because their residences are often rented (McFalls, 1998). For most relocating families, mobility comes in two forms: forced and voluntary.

Forced mobility for families may be associated with migrant work, homelessness, coping with unemployment, gentrification and resulting higher rents, or escaping hostile actions or trouble. Many children also move after a divorce and go on to experience the difficulty of going back and forth between two homes. Forced mobility (apart from job-related transfers) is always a reaction to undesirable conditions and contributes to erratic lifestyles for parents and their children. Isolation is implied, for forced mobility signifies that a family lacks connections or community linkages that could provide help. Whatever the conditions, a family's forced move to a new environment presents different but rarely positive learning experiences for children. Little pleasure comes with a transfer from one area to another under duress.

On the other hand, voluntary travel and relocation, local or distant, frequently connotes an improved socioeconomic situation for the family or vacation time. Both local travel and long-distance travel involve the positive expectation of new encounters. Arranging for the travel is a learning experience. Getting to a destination involves a certain amount of investigation, map reading, negotiating bus schedules or checking driving requirements, and anticipating difficulties. Family members learn together, and these social and educational values are important. Transnational or international travel brings a family in touch with other cultures, as travelers need to adapt to new conditions, different foods, and a different sense of space. Such travel is expansive, and families gain psychic income and social capital.

The ways that families exploit surroundings, relationships, agencies, and even challenges show facets of their child-rearing practices and socializing acumen. Some families use their experience with great facility, while others do not. Such use of experience may be a function of SES, as economically privileged families have the means to provide the benefits of local and long-distance travel (Coleman, 1966; Jencks et al., 1972). However, we find instances of modestly endowed families enriching their children's lives through carefully developed experiences (Clark, 1983; Monroe, 1997), and some affluent families neglect the need for family interaction and experience (Metz, 1993).

OTHER INFLUENCES ON PARENTING

Parenting needs to be examined and analyzed in the context of culture and community. As noted earlier, numerous variables affect family life and may be external factors of community and environment as well as internal factors of cultural background, family demographics, and economics. Following is a brief discussion of some of these other dimensions.

Child Care Arrangements

With extended work schedules for most American families, a huge number of parents now must cope daily with requirements for temporary care of their children. At one time, when many mothers were homemakers, child care was merged with running the household. Mothers attended their preschool-age children, welcomed their older children home from school, and supervised most at-home activities.

At the present time, however, the situation is far different: Welfare reform has increased the number of parents in the workforce, single-parent and dual-income families grow every year, and fewer extended family members are available to care for children. Over 65% of mothers with children under 6 are in the workforce (Children's Defense Fund, 2001). This means that a huge number of young children are in some type of child care arrangement for part of every workday. These arrangements include center-based and family child care as well as less formal situations such as babysitters or care by slightly older siblings.

Infant, toddler, and preschool child care and after-school care for older children are now facts of life for most communities. As more families, formerly on welfare, enter the workforce, the demands for quality care for children will intensify. Many child care programs have waiting lists for children who need this service, and added requests will intensify the problem. While a number of schools now operate their own after-school care programs, the need for care outstrips the supply. Furthermore, the quality and costs of care are quite variable—adding another dimension to the problem for parents seeking care for their children. We consider the topic of child care more fully in Chapter 5.

Stress in Families

The circumstances of modern life have led to an increase in stress in children and their parents (Dahlberg, Moss, & Pence, 1999). Separation, divorce, chronic illness, and death of a parent can negatively affect children's feelings of security and subject them to new patterns of family life. Living within a blended family, a single parent household, or with parents who travel frequently also contributes to the stress level of all involved. While these circumstances are difficult for all families, children and parents who live in poverty face added challenges that can contribute to additional stress (Oehlberg, 1996).

Stressors resulting from changes in family life and economic difficulties can be challenging for every family, but some families, through coping skills and resources, are better able than others to handle problems. While a few stressors are self-inflicted, many are unavoidable or are developed through conflicts and economic pressures and through racist, elitist, and sexist practices.

Accumulated stressors lead to at-risk situations, and policy makers, educators, and others must be mindful of this possibility. The effects of risk on the intelligence measurements of preschool children (Sameroff, Seifer, Barocas, Zax, & Greenspan, 1987) are instructive (see Figure 4–3). As the figure shows, most children seem able to cope with low levels of risk, but an accumulation of more than two risk factors jeopardizes their mental development. The message is clear: We must either prevent or compensate for accumulated risk factors (Stanford & Yamamoto, 2001).

Before ending our discussion of family functioning, we review in the following paragraphs the concerns and risk factors that cause stress in families. But bear in mind, strategies

Demands for quality child care intensifies as more families enter the work force

exist to deflect or accommodate stress arising from these factors. Helping children and their parents cope with stress is becoming an increasingly important role for teachers and community-service providers (Scully, 2003).

Separation and Divorce.   As noted earlier, divorce has become common for U.S. families in recent decades, and while the divorce rate is no longer increasing, at the present time, first marriages in the United States have a 45% chance of breaking up, and second marriages a 60% chance (Wallerstein, Lewis, & Blakeslee, 2000). Consequently, over 40% of American children will experience a parental divorce, with nearly 90% placed in the physical custody of their mothers (although increasingly legal custody tends to be shared between parents). Of the children born in the 1990's, over half will spend some or all of their childhood in a single-parent household (Anderson, 2003), see Figure 4–4.

Liberalization of divorce laws in most states permits couples to separate more easily and more amicably, and while parents may adjust reasonably well to a divorce, many children of divorced parents tend to have long-term difficulties (Wallerstein, et al., 2000). Separation changes all roles in a family and alters the way a family functions. Responsi-bilities for the custodial parent increase dramatically, particularly with regard to child care arrangements. There are more household tasks to care for, and financial obligations are heavier than before. Complicating the situation for children is the likelihood of one or more of their parents remarrying (65% of divorced women and 75% of divorced men remarry within 4 years). Even more likely is one or more nonmarital short-lived cohabitations of either parent. One third of American children today will become part of a stepfamily (Greene, Anderson, Hetherington, Forgatch, & DeGarmo, 2003).

Financial Aspects of Divorce.   Mothers are most often given custody of children in a divorce, but

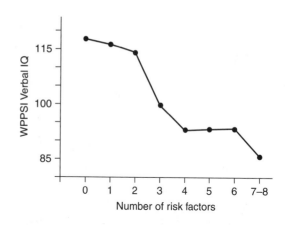

Figure 4–3   Effects of multiple risks on preschool intelligence
Source: From "Intelligence Quotient on Scores of 4-Year-Old Children: Social-Environmental Risk Factors," by A. Sameroff et al., 1987, *Pediatrics, 79,* 347. Copyright 1987 by the American Academy of Pediatrics. Reproduced by permission from *Pediatrics.*

this often has dire consequences for the resulting single-parent family. Casper and Bianchi (2002) reported that the poverty rate for single-mother households was 38.7%, compared to a rate of 6.9% in two-parent homes. It is a fact in the United States that women in the workforce earn less than men do, and even though child support judgments are made in divorce cases, fathers frequently do not pay, and mothers must assume full financial responsibility for their children. Casper and Bianchi (2002) stressed the financial inequities after divorce: Divorce improves the economic position of men but reduces that of women and children left with their mothers.

Other Consequences of Divorce.   Increased work hours for custodial parents are typical after divorce, and decreased social interaction with children results (Anderson, 2003). This means less parenting. Children in the home will face increased responsibilities and less time with either parent and less emotional support after separation. A serious long-range effect of divorce is the removal of marriage models for children affected.

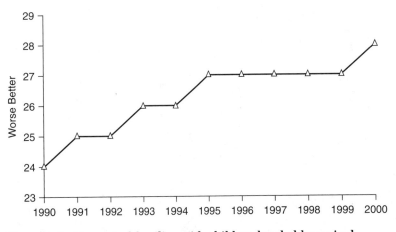

Figure 4–4   Percent of families with children headed by a single parent
Note: Percent of families with children headed by a single parent is the percentage of all families with own children under 18 living in the household, headed by a person—male or female—without a spouse present in the home. "Own children" include never-married persons under age 18 who are the sons or daughters of the householder's (head of the household). The householder's stepchildren and adopted children also are counted as "own children." *Source: Kids Count Data Book,* The Annie E. Casey Foundation (2003), *www.aecf.org; http://www.kidscount.org*

Behavioral changes for youngsters often result from divorce and separation. A considerable amount of research shows that the negative effects for children of divorce are sadness, anger, fear, aggressiveness, anxiety, and disobedience (Hetherington & Kelly, 2002; Schwartz & Kaslow, 1997; Wallerstein, 2001). But Olson and Haynes (1993) pointed out that many studies are slanted toward "what's wrong with single-parent families" (p. 260). They went on to demonstrate that single parenting can be successful and that strengths do exist in single-parent homes when compared to a predivorce situation: happier environments, better custodial parent–child relationships, more commitment to a wider community, and better-run households. Hetherington and Kelly (2002), in their review of hundreds of clients, found that most single-parent households do provide the nurturance that children need, despite the challenges.

Negative stereotypes continue to affect single parents and their children (Anderson, 2003; Greene et al., 2003), however. For example, teachers have a tendency to assume that problems in school are related to the single-parent home. In the foreseeable future, large numbers of young and school-age children will experience their parents' separation. Therefore, school personnel and community workers must find ways to accommodate the extra needs these individuals will have.

Support groups are available to help families after divorce through the initial period of adjustment, which is always one or more years. Children's literature, when sensitively read and discussed, can also help children who are caught in a family upheaval. See Appendix 1 for recommended titles.

Dual-Income Families.   Management of household life in the dual-income home produces stress at times (Fraenkel, 2003). While the double income enables a family to enjoy a higher standard of living, it has drawbacks, such as less time for family interaction, tighter schedules, increased dependence on child care, and fewer choices in recreation. Statistics show that 67% of children living with both parents have mothers and fathers in the workforce, and the trend increases each year (U.S. Bureau of the Census, 2001). In addition, over 7% of American working men and women hold two or more jobs (U.S. Bureau of the Census, 1998b), which could mean a total of four jobs for some dual-income families. Time for family interactions is, of course, minimal in such situations.

Poverty.   Poverty restricts many positive experiences for children and their families, because financial resources dictate quality of housing, diet, clothing, and amount of health care, to say nothing of entertainment and recreation. Most of all, poverty lays a veil of

despair on families, and aspirations and a sense of self-worth become hard to elevate. Of all the stressors present in U.S. families, poverty is perhaps the greatest, and it is expanding in the lower income brackets (refer again to Figure 3–5 in Chapter 3).

Children's Defense Fund (2001) findings show that in 1999 over 12 million, or almost 17%, of U.S. children under 18 were living below the poverty line. In addition, the record demonstrated little change in the amount of poverty in the United States during the 1990s—even with a robust economy. Although the rate dipped slightly by the end of 1999, economic downturns in the early 2000s suggests that the rate may again be on the rise. Poverty rates among minority groups are disproportionate to their populations. While the poverty rate for Whites was 11.2%, that for Hispanics was 27.8%, and for African American's 33% (U.S. Bureau of the Census, 2003). Figure 4–5 gives a picture of American children living in poverty.

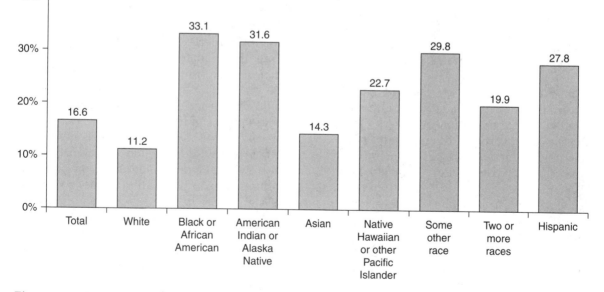

Figure 4–5   Percent of children below poverty by race and hispanic origin
Source: Population Reference Bureau, analysis of data from the U.S. Census Bureau, 2000 census summary, 2003.

Poor families are burdened with the need to survive, and their lives are punctuated with stress brought on by lack of money. Family members are frequently ill, they sustain injury more often, and they encounter hostility from numerous sources. Lives become saturated with despair, and each new plight adds to family discouragement (Benson, 1997; Dash, 1996; Polakow, 1993). The buildup of stress in poor families is extensive. Housing that is affordable to families below the poverty line tends to be in crime- and drug-ridden areas, where children and many adults lead lives of sheer terror (Garbarino, Kostelny, & Dubrow, 1998; Kotlowitz, 1991). Cramped living and meager diets result in illnesses that precipitate even more stress. Reversing the state of poverty in the United States requires strong community action and large investments in federal, state, and private aid to provide job training, child care, adequate housing, and health facilities to help rebuild families in besieged areas of society. Recommendations outlined in *The State of America's Children* (Children's Defense Fund, 2001) serve as a good starting point. Leach (1994), in *Children First,* reemphasized this challenging prescription, and Schorr (2001) suggested ways in which neighborhoods and communities can help families.

Abuse and Neglect.   Abuse and neglect of children can be associated with, although not limited to, the condition of poverty. Because families in poverty are in dire straits and services are meager, abuse rises in concert with the frustrations and anxieties of needy families (Bigner, 2002; Gersten, 1992; Pipher, 1996). Abuse also occurs at higher SES levels; it is not restricted to the poor. Neglect, and physical and sexual abuse occurs at all levels of society. The Children's Defense Fund (2001) stated that between 2 million and 3 million abuse cases are reported each year, with about one third of the cases substantiated. Neglect is the most prevalent form of child abuse, with more than

half the children mistreated suffering from neglect. Just over one third of the victims were physically or sexually abused, and one fourth of the children were mistreated in more than one way. Despite these large numbers, caseworkers assert that only a small fraction of abusive situations is ever reported (Osofsky, 1998).

Abuse is insidious and continues in the fabric of families for generations—too many abused children become abusive adults or victims of other abusers later in their lives (Scarf, 1997; Zeanah & Scheeringa, 1997). Abuse is an infection coloring the feelings and attitudes of families, and it destroys normal relationships for the entire family. Research has indicated that parent education can help to break the cycle of abuse and neglect. Interventions that help reduce parents' stress levels, increase their understanding of child development and their social coping skills, and assist them in developing supportive networks are most effective in reducing and preventing child maltreatment (Reppucci, Britner, & Woolard, 1997).

Illness.   Illness also is a stressor in families. When a family member becomes injured or ill, numerous interaction patterns must cease or be modified. The amount of family communication can be limited, and attention to those who are not ill becomes restricted. Realignment of the priorities in family functioning is a consequence of long-term illness. Illness of a wage earner has even greater consequences for the family. And if inadequate health care is the cause (which is the situation for one seventh of the nation's population), this particular stress gives rise to others. When a child in the family becomes seriously injured or is chronically ill, parents must develop coping skills to adjust to the needs for medical care and the other issues that arise. (Lee & Guck, 2001).

Children with Disabilities.   Caring for a child with a disability presents unique challenges to

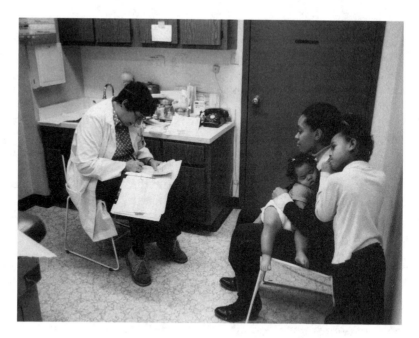

Illness is a stressor in families who must develop coping skills to adjust to the needs for medical care

families and often leads to an increase in the families' stress level (Lancaster, 2001). While some disabilities are evident from birth or early infancy, others, such as learning disabilities and emotional problems, may not show up until the child is in school. Not only do parents have to struggle with their own acceptance of the disability and the attendant shattered expectations, guilt, anger, and parental conflict, they must also expend great time and energy on the child. Just getting the child's disability identified can be a long process, and determining treatment, obtaining needed services, and following up on the child's progress are also time-consuming. Teachers and community service personnel play an important support role for families parenting children with disabilities.

Children and families all are resilient to some degree. We find situations that appear depressing and even disastrous, but children survive intact and view the traumatic events in their lives, such as death, divorce, and

hardship, with objectivity (Comer, 1988) and even with humor at later periods (Buchwald, 1994). This demonstrates that most children are not so fragile and impressionable that they must succumb to their problems. As a teacher or community service provider, you must be mindful that as long as reasonably positive experiences and interventions punctuate the lives of developing children, their outlook and perspective can be ultimately optimistic.

COMPETENT FAMILIES

Families function in a variety of ways and possess different attributes. If permitted to pursue their individual courses, most families, given reasonable conditions, develop along healthy lines and rear children who respect a home culture and get ready to meet the world. Though most are competent, many need the help and support of friends, community, and other services.

At times, stresses are too great, and a combination of cultural differences, poverty, and family problems causes family dysfunction. If this occurs, professional aid via the community is the first level of response. It may be possible that school professionals can help by advocating for the family, talking with family members, counseling the family, and listening to family members to show support. Recall the dramatic graph Sameroff et al. (1987, Figure 4–2) provided. We can demonstrate the likelihood that problems will emerge if risk factors continue unresolved.

Teachers need to know their students' families as well as their situations, for teachers are in a unique position to explain community to families, and vice versa. It is imperative for school personnel to take time to learn about family functioning to find out about values, ways of doing things, and methods of care that work for them. When you obtain this information, you may then find ways of integrating schoolwork with the home situation.

What is a competent family? The competent family does not require affluence, extensive education, or a particular setting. It will, however, provide for what Brazelton and Greenspan (2000) described as "the irreducible needs of children." In order to help their children grow and flourish, competent parents meet the following six needs:

1. Ongoing nurturing relationships
2. Physical protection, safety, and regulation
3. Experiences tailored to individual differences
4. Developmentally appropriate experiences
5. Limit setting, structure, and expectations
6. Stable, supportive communities and cultural continuity.

Children need unconditional love and affection from their parents. They also require the security that comes from a safe, familiar environment, a consistent daily routine, and the knowledge that adults expect certain behaviors from them. When planning experiences for their children, parents must consider their children's unique temperaments, learning styles, and interests. Further, parents who understand stages of child development are better able to plan experiences that are compatible with their child's level. Children also need parents who will guide their behavior in ways that will help them make responsible choices, cooperate with others, and develop self-confidence. Both parents and children need the support of the larger community for optimal development.

These needs will be met in different ways for different children, as good parenting varies from one family to another. As we have stressed throughout this chapter, there is no one best way to raise a child, and each family must find the ways that suit it best.

IMPLICATIONS FOR PROFESSIONALS

The parenting behaviors you have just read about are, of course, going to have an impact on the children you will work with. Since there is a broad spectrum of parenting behavior and competence, you are going to find yourself working with an equally wide range of child attitudes, behaviors, and skills coming from these diverse homes.

Understanding the different parenting styles and ways that families function will help to explain the situation of children you work with. You must also be prepared to understand your own attitudes toward parent dispositions and their modes of guiding and overseeing their children. This will help you adjust your own responses so that different children can feel a part of your classroom and adapt to expectations that may differ from what they experience in their home.

Remember that many family arrangements are possible and that most can be productive.

Understanding the positive aspects of different lifestyles can open your own views and prevent judgmental behavior. Stereotyping children because of the practices or behaviors of the family is not productive or solution oriented.

As you work with communities and families in any of several social settings, you will come face-to-face with the problems and stressors mentioned in this chapter that confront so many individuals. It is important to understand these and respond—though your responses may be expressions of empathy, guidance to community services, or even reports to authorities about abuse or illness. Teachers can refer persons to social agencies; community workers can refer clients to tutoring services, after-school programs, or other services that some children and families may need.

SUMMARY AND REVIEW

U.S. families are diverse. Rather than being a problem, diversity provides a richer society and produces numerous benefits. The United States is an unusual nation today, for nowhere else on the planet do such diverse racial, ethnic, and cultural groups work together so productively. Our acceptance of diversity, though far from perfect, continues to increase.

Different styles of interaction exist for all families. Research shows that the authoritative parent style usually produces better results for most parents and their children than does either a permissive or an authoritarian pattern.

Experience defines a family's quality of life, and some families show greater command over their environment than do others. All families pass on their culture and attempt to instruct children in profitable ways. Some families have natural gifts for instructing the young about tasks, thereby giving them added command of their lives. Mobility is one avenue for enhancing experience; another is manual work skills.

Handling stress is a mark of a family's ability to cope with surroundings. All families encounter stress, but processing and managing it are hallmarks of well-adjusted families.

Unified support and collaborations among homes, schools, and communities pay large dividends when cooperative spirits are willing to work together.

SUGGESTED ACTIVITIES AND QUESTIONS

1. Name three ways that families provide nurturance for their children. Speculate about how you see them manifested in one child with whom you work.

2. Consider the home environments of children appearing in the vignettes in the text to this point. Deduce the parenting style of each family and discuss with colleagues why you selected the styles.

3. Select two families represented in your classroom or community setting. What appear to be the social and cultural influences affecting them? Are there differences? What do you infer about the parenting practices in these families?

4. Observe a parent interacting with his or her child in a library. Observe a similar situation in a supermarket. What circumstances do you think account for any differences you see?

RESOURCES

Books

1. Bigner, J. J. (2002). *Parent–child relations: An introduction to parenting* (6th ed.). Columbus, OH: Merrill/Prentice Hall.
2. Smith, C. A. (Ed.). (1999). *The encyclopedia of parenting theory and research.* Westport, CT: Greenwood.
3. Westman, J. (Ed.). (2001). *Parenthood in America: Undervalued, underpaid, under siege.* Madison: University of Wisconsin Press.
4. Consult Appendix 1 for a sampling of useful children's books related to parenting.

Films and Videos

1. Developing Minds Video Library includes 22 videotapes with accompanying guides. The library is designed to help parents and teachers of elementary and middle school children explore differences in learning. Examples: *Language, Mastering the Challenge of Reading* (2002) and *Behavioral Complications* (2002). WGBH Boston Video in association with All Kinds of Minds.

2. *Learning before school: How adults can help* [Video, 19 min]. (2003). This video focuses on how parents can help children in the areas of communication, self-discipline, and curiosity. Crystal Lake, IL: Magna Systems Learning Seed Video.

3. *Shaping youngest minds* [Video, 24 min]. (1999). This video is about the day-to-day care of young children's brains and helps parents learn to talk, read, and sign to children and use loving touch. Crystal Lake, IL: Magna Systems, Learning Seed Video.

Organizations

American Association for Marriage and Family Therapy
112 S. Alfred Street
Alexandria, VA 22314
http://www.aamft.org

National Parenting Center
22801 Ventura Boulevard, Suite 110
Woodland Hills, CA 91367
http://tnpc.org

Zero to Three: The National Center for Infants, Toddlers, and Families
2000 M Street, NW, Suite 200
Washington, DC 20036
http://zerotothree.org

Websites

1. http://family.com The Family Network home page, connected with *Family Fun* magazine, has resources on many parent concerns.

2. http://npin.org The National Parent Information Network offers research-based information about the process of parenting and about family involvement in education. It has numerous links to other sites related to parenting.

3. http://lifematters.com Life Matters offers a compilation of articles from various authors that promote education, information, and support for those wishing to learn more about democratic styles of parenting.

Chapter 5

Meeting Child Care Needs From Infancy Through School Age

A "best fit" implies consideration of fit at many different points: child, parent, caregiver, neighborhood, community, beliefs, and values. . . . In most families, parents are the ultimate mediator of "best fit" in day care.

(Pence & Goelman, 1987, p. 117)

With over 65% of the mothers of children under 6 in the labor force and an even greater percentage of working mothers with older children (Children's Defense Fund, 2001), affordable, accessible, quality child care has become an increasingly important issue for families and communities. In reading this chapter, you will learn the following:

1. The need for quality child care from infancy through the school-age years has grown, reflecting societal changes in family structures and participation in the labor force by increasing numbers of women with children.

2. Quality child care allows family members to work and helps children to succeed.

3. Options in child care include **in-home care**, family child care, center-based care, and before- and after-school care, which is provided by individuals, private groups, nonprofit organizations, corporations, schools, and government agencies.

4. Considerable variation exists in the quality, cost, availability, and accessibility of child care across the United States.

5. Quality child care is the result of a combination of factors that include a healthy, safe environment, age appropriate staff–child ratios, and educational and social stimulation, plus warm, stable, well-trained caregivers.

6. Collaboration between parents, community, and caregivers is needed in order to develop social policies that will enhance the accessibility, cost, and quality of child care.

In about 3 weeks Renata and her partner Gregg anticipate the birth of their third child. They are excited about the prospect of having another child and have been preparing for their new arrival. Yet they are feeling anxious, too, because they wonder how they will cope with the additional financial burden. Renata currently works as office manager for a legal firm. When she is working, her 18-month-old daughter is cared for by a grandmotherly neighbor, Mrs. Carlson, at a cost of $75 per week. Their 4-year-old son Josh attends a nearby church-affiliated child care center at a cost of $80 per week. Neither facility is licensed, but both are in the neighborhood and are supervised by caring personnel.

Renata and Gregg have carefully considered their options. "If we have to pay out another $70 a week for child care," suggests Renata, it'll hardly be worth my while keeping my job. I'm not sure Mrs. Carlson will want to take both the new baby and Evelyn, and, you know, the center at church won't take Evelyn until she's potty trained," Renata said.

"Yeah, but we need the extra money, and you really like what you do," replied Gregg. Renata is unsure, though. She ponders for a while and thinks to herself. What with paying out over $200 a week for child care, we're going to have only a little bit left over! I may as well stay at home and look after the children myself. Finally she muses, "Boy, we really do have some tough decisions to make."

Renata and Gregg are part of the growing and changing child care dilemma that many

American families are facing. The number of children needing care outside the home in the United States has increased dramatically over the past 30 years. In 1973, about 30% of children under the age of 6 received care, and now approximately 65% of these children participate in some form of nonparental child care (Children's Defense Fund, 2001). Currently, about 59% of women with infants younger than 1 year are employed, compared to 31% in 1976. The percentage of children from ages 5 to 11 with working mothers is even greater than that for younger children. Clearly, the need for child care is a concern not only for families like Gregg and Renata's, but for many others as well.

In addition to increased dual-earner families, many low-income single mothers have recently entered the workforce due to welfare reforms. All of this puts more demands on communities and agencies to identify out-of-home care facilities. Affordable and accessible child care is increasingly seen as an issue not just for families but for society as a whole. Without child care, families can not work, and without quality care, children will not succeed.

Child care includes a wide array of arrangements that reflect the age of the child, the setting where care is provided, and the purpose for care, such as infant–toddler centers, family child care homes, and before- and after-school care. In this chapter, we will focus on the various child care arrangements that parents make who are working, in training, or unable to care for their children. Remember that all of these options have the potential to offer critical experiences that can positively support children's growth and development, but their primary purpose is to provide substitute care.

Increasingly, as parents become more aware of the importance of early learning, they are seeking care arrangements that offer appropriate cognitive stimulation and socializa-

tion experiences. For this reason, we find that there are more and more overlaps between the various programs. For example, nursery schools have started to offer extended day options, and child care centers are strengthening their instructional programs. It is difficult to describe these arrangements in neat categories, but child care programs that are defined primarily as educational will be addressed in Chapter 6.

In this chapter we trace the history of child care in the United States and provide an overview of the current state of affairs. Each type of child care arrangement will be described and issues related to quality will be discussed. Particular attention will be paid to the costs of care and how this relates to staff quality and turnover. Finally, we will address the effects of child care on children's development and the well-being of families, concluding with some of the policy issues that relate to raising the quantity, affordability, and quality of child care services.

HISTORY OF CHILD CARE

At earlier times in the United States, **extended families** tended to live together or near each other. When a mother found it necessary to work outside the home or a father lost his wife, the child was usually cared for by a female relative (Scarr, 1998). Since most of these caregivers were assumed to have some commitment to the well-being of their relative's child, quality of care was rarely a concern. The industrialization that started in the early part of the 19th century changed these informal family arrangements. As increasing numbers of families moved from rural areas to the cities and as immigrants entered the country, women found work in factories to help support their families. Child care centers were opened in Boston, New York, and Philadelphia at that time to provide care for children during the hours their parents worked (Seefeldt &

Barbour, 1998). Most of these centers provided custodial care to meet the basic needs of food, shelter, rest, and supervision, but some did provide instruction for both children and families. The care was in large part for reasons of social support, to help needy families (Berns, 2001) in those urban areas.

During World War II, large numbers of women, many with children, went to work in factories to support the war effort by taking the place of men who were fighting. Under the 1944 Lanham Act, the country intensified its mobilization on behalf of the defense industry and increased many services. Under provisions of the act, many communities were able to build excellent child care centers to serve the children whose mothers were working (Adams, 2001). When the war ended, however, and the men returned to the factories, many of the women lost their jobs and eventually most of the child care centers closed. The economic prosperity and sharp increase in births during the postwar years led to an arrangement in many families where the father worked outside the home and the mother cared for the children.

The economic boom of the 1950s, however, increased consumer demands for goods and services, and in turn opened up new opportunities for women to work. Gradually, more women became employed outside the home. As changing attitudes concerning the roles of women that began in the 1960s continued, women increasingly combined motherhood with working, whether from need or preference. Divorce became more common during this era, and often single mothers needed to contribute to their family's income. During the 1960s and 1970s, as more families sought care for their children, there was little support from either the government or the private sector to increase the availability of child care. Concerns began to be raised regarding the quality of the child care centers that did exist. The concerns focused on health and safety standards, plus the lack of training and the low

wages that led to high staff turnover. In the 1980s, additional concerns were raised regarding the consequences of child care on children's development (Casper & Bianchi, 2002).

Government Remedies

In the late 1980s, the Act for Better Child Care established what is known today as the Child Care Development Block Grant (CCDBG). Under this program, the federal government, in Fiscal year 2001, provided $4.5 billion for child care services for low-income families and other activities related to the provision of child care. States are required to spend at least 4% of the funds they receive from the CCDBG to improve the quality of care in their jurisdictions. Congress also set aside $173 million of the discretionary funds for additional quality building activities: $100 million for increasing and improving infant–toddler care programs; $10 million for child care research; and $18.1 million for school-age care and **resource and referral programs** (Children's Defense Fund, 2001).

Federal government support for child care also comes in the form of tax-based subsidies, which are designed to assist families in covering the costs of child care and encourage employers to address child care needs. The largest tax-based subsidy for child care is the Child and Dependent Care Tax Credit. This credit reduces the income tax liability of families at all income levels with work-related care expenses. However, since the credit is nonrefundable, its value to low-income families is limited, as the credit amount cannot exceed a family's tax liability. The maximum credit is $1,440 a year per family. In 2000, it provided $2.8 billion to working families and is considered the second largest source of federal child care assistance after the Child Care Development Block Grant.

The Personal Responsibility and Work Opportunity Reconciliation Act of 1996 (PL 104-93) is legislation that essentially eliminated the guarantee that child care help will be provided to families on or transitioning from welfare to participate in work or job training. While some support can be received from the Temporary Assistance for Needy Families (TANF) block grant funds, which repealed Aid to Families With Dependent Children (AFDC), individual states have enormous discretion on which families will be assisted and what services are provided. While these welfare reforms have resulted in dramatic increases in the number of working mothers, the lack of reliable child care and help paying for it may end up undermining efforts to lift families out of poverty.

The child care situation for low-income families varies greatly from state to state. Federal eligibility requirements allow states to provide child care assistance to families with annual incomes of up to 85% of the state's median income, but only four states do so (Hartman, 2003). In half the states, families with annual incomes above $25,000 are ineligible, and a large number are cutting assistance to families that are just above the poverty line but cannot afford the full cost of child care (Hartman, 2003). Actually, 40 states require copayments from families with incomes below the poverty level. Though Renata and Gregg are not at or below the poverty level, they are caught in a situation where their dual income is not enough to pay for the rising cost of child care, but it is above the $25,000 level. They are ineligible for any government subsidy or assistance.

State Standards

The standards for child care also vary greatly from state to state. The rates that states are willing to pay for child care for TANF families reflects the pressure to get as many children into child care at the lowest expenditure. In 2000, only 1.5 million of the 9.9 million eligible were receiving subsidized care. This is a reflection of the limited resources for care (particularly for school-age children), the inability to pay the

copayments, and being unaware of eligibility for assistance (Hartman, 2003). Consequently, many families among the working poor are patching together informal child care arrangements with relatives, friends, or neighbors.

Advocates for children are increasingly concerned about the outcomes for low-income children in the current climate of welfare reform. Substandard care, accidental injury or neglect, and an inadequate developmental environment can have devastating effects on children whose families lack adequate funds for quality child care.

For middle-class families, the emergence of a market-based system of child care services in the late 1980s and 1990s increased the visibility and availability of options for caring for their children (Uttal, 2002). During this time, a number of for-profit child care centers emerged to meet the needs of working families who could afford to pay for it. Resource and referral services made it easier to locate child care, which became more visible as centers sprang up in public places and family child care homes become more formally organized as small businesses.

CHILD CARE NEEDS IN THE UNITED STATES TODAY

While some form of informal, shared child care has always been practiced in the United States, the increased isolation and fragmentation of families, along with other changes in family structure and social expectations, have increased the need for more formal arrangements in recent decades. In many families today, both parents work outside the home in order to maintain or increase their standard of living. Also, welfare reform, which began in the late 20th century, requires many mothers of young children to work, and other women who have trained for a career choose to combine work and motherhood in order to maintain their professional opportunities.

The need for child care reflects the desire of women who have trained for a career to combine work and motherhood in order to maintain their professional careers

Fifty-five percent of working women in the United States contribute half or more of their family's total income (Bond et al., 1997). Consequently, the need for child care is a fact of life for many American families.

According to the most recent census reports (U.S. Bureau of the Census, 2001), 65% of mothers with children under age 6, and 78% of mothers with children age 6 to 13 are in the labor force, working, or actively seeking employment. Fifty-nine percent of mothers with infants (under age 1) are also employed. This places nearly 20.5 million children in non-parental care on a regular basis, according to an Urban Institute study (Sonenstein, Gates, Schmidt, & Bolshun, 2002).

Trends in Child Care

A significant trend in child care over the past 35 years has been the shift to center-based care.

In 1965, only 6% of U.S. preschool children were cared for in centers. By 1999, the percentage was 28%. Of the approximately 13 million children under 5 with employed parents, 14% were in family child care, 27% in relative care, 4% in babysitter or **nanny care,** 28% in center-based care, and the remaining 27% in parental care (Sonenstein, Gates, Schmidt, & Bolshun, 2002). Figure 5–1 shows the distribution as of 1999.

The situation for school-age children under 13 is quite different. Only about 15% are in before- and after-school centers, 23% in relative care, 7% in family child care, 10% in self care, and 45% in parent or other care. This last category includes parents who arrange their work schedules to care for their children, in enrichment activities not considered care, patchwork situations, and with parents who may not want to admit that children are in self care (Urban Institute, 2002). Figure 5–2 shows

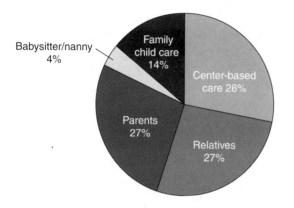

Figure 5–1   Primary child care arrangements for children under 5
Source: Sonnenstein et al. (2002).

the distribution of care arrangements for school-age children as of 2000. In highlighting the needs, one poll in 2000 (Afterschool Alliance, 2002) determined that 60% of voters felt that it was difficult to find after-school programs in their communities.

Families with two parents and higher incomes usually have more choice about the kind of child care arrangements they make. Higher income parents tend to use centers more than do low-income families, since this type of care is likely to be more expensive than family child care or informal arrangements with relatives and babysitters. Low-income families can be subsidized for child care expenses, but the availability of subsidies and the accessibility of programs who accept subsidized children can be major issues in limiting choices. Currently, no state serves all families eligible for child care assistance under federal regulations, and only 12% of eligible children nationally are receiving help (Children's Defense Fund, 2001). Full-day child care can cost between $4,000 to $10,000 yearly, a significant expense when one considers that one out of four families with young children earns less than $25,000 a year.

The numbers of family child care and center-based programs have increased over the past 20 years as the demand for services continues. The 2002 Family Child Care Licensing Study (Children's Foundation, 2003) reported that there were 306,802 regulated family child care homes in the 50 states, District of Columbia, Puerto Rico, and the Virgin Islands. Of these programs, 44,473 are considered group or large-family child care centers serving 7 to 12 children. The increase has more than doubled since 1984.

Concerns About Child Care

While there has been a significant increase in the numbers of family child care and center-based child care programs, concerns remain about the quality of these settings for young children. The Children's Defense Fund (2001), reporting on various studies on quality in child care centers, concluded that "much of the child care in the United States is poor to mediocre" (p. 2). In addition, a national study of family child care programs reported that over one third of the programs were rated as inadequate. These studies, of course, raise our

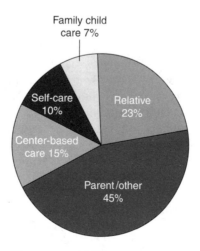

Figure 5–2   Child care arrangements for school-age children
Source: Urban Institute (2002).

concerns about children's safety as well as the harm to children's development.

We will now turn to the various types of child care arrangements and then proceed to a discussion of the characteristics of quality programs for infants, toddlers, and preschool and school-age children. A discussion of the effects of child care on children's development and the policy issues that will help to ensure available, affordable, quality care for all who need it will conclude the chapter.

CHILD CARE ARRANGEMENTS

Mr. McGee, Tina's father, is a bit surprised not to see Mrs. Holden in her office as he enters the child care center. The assistant smiles and says that Mrs. Holden is with the infants because an extra lap is needed. On the way to the 3-year-old room, Tina urges her father to stop and watch the fish in the tank. A mother watching the fish exclaims, "We've been stopping here lately, too. Just watching seems to help Janda relax before starting the day. Mrs. Holden did tell me what a boon this tank was, and I can see it."

Upon entering the classroom, Tina notices that Billy is crying loudly. Martha is holding him and saying, "Mama's coming to the phone, and she'll talk with you." Tina goes over to Billy, pats him, and says kindly, "It's okay!" She then puts her coat in her cubbie and hurries over to her friend Claire at the water table. Soon Billy's mother is on the phone, and her voice appears to be quieting Billy. As Mr. McGee waits to talk with Martha, he smiles at Felicity, who is seated on the floor with two other children reading. Several children are working at the table while Miranda pours juice. Martha turns to Mr. McGee, who asks if all is okay. "Oh, yes. Billy does take change hard. His dad brought him today for the first time, and now he seems uncertain about his mama. I got her on the phone, and she's reassuring him."

"Oh, that's good," replies Mr. McGee. "Well, I just need to remind someone that Tina's grandmother will pick her up this afternoon. Tina knows this, and I put it on her chart."

"OK. Just remember to let them know at the office on your way out."

Mr. McGee kisses Tina goodbye, saying, "Remember, Grandma will pick you up this afternoon, 'cause Mommy has to work late."

As Mr. McGee leaves the building, he greets the toddler teacher starting her first outing of the day. Five toddlers are happily seated in their cart for an excursion along the sidewalk to look in the shop windows. Mr. McGee thinks, "I remember how Tina enjoyed those cart rides. Boy, we were lucky to find such a great center so near home."

Quality child care makes a difference for families, and the McGees reflect the changes now taking place within American families. Tina's parents are both professional and believe it important that Mrs. McGee continue her career. They represent what Elkind (1995) called the postmodern family, in which most parenting for very young children is provided by the mother, sometimes with the father's assistance, and by other caregivers. Since Tina's arrival at this center, Tina's family has been blessed. Though the cost of care is high, this center has provided a consistency of caregivers and a safe environment. Many families use the center even into the school years, since it has extended-day programs.

Parents, like the McGees, seeking child care are faced with many issues in determining the appropriate arrangement for their children. Aside from issues of affordability, location, and availability, families also want to ensure that their children receive educational and social enrichment along with nurturing care. Resource and referral agencies have been established in many communities to support parents

Quality child care is reflected when children enjoy excursions to view shop windows

in locating child care centers and family child care homes, while other agencies can assist in locating nannies and au pairs. These various options for child care are described in the following sections.

In-Home Child Care

Care that takes place in the child's home is an unregulated arrangement. In the case of a babysitter, the family determines the necessary qualifications, screens applicants, and makes an agreement with the individual of their choice. The advantage of this type of care for parents with long work days or erratic schedules is its flexibility. The caregiver, who may even live in the child's home, becomes an employee of the family, who then assumes certain financial responsibilities in terms of taxes and Social Security deductions (and some decide not to report the income). Wage levels for these

positions are low, and the supply of babysitters is somewhat limited to persons who may have no training in child care and few options for other work. During the late 1990s, two high-profile cases of candidates for political appointment in the Clinton administration admitted hiring undocumented immigrants to provide child care and household help after experiencing difficulty in finding such assistance (Harrington, 2000).

Families can also hire a nanny to provide in-home care. Generally, nannies are registered with an agency and have had some training in the care of young children. Another option is an au pair, a young foreign-born person who exchanges child care and light housework for room and board and a small salary. The au pair system is organized by the U.S. Information Agency as a cultural exchange program to allow the young and usually well-educated participants to take courses and enjoy living and traveling in the United States. Generally, the au pair has minimum training and experience in child care. Other families make arrangements with a babysitter to provide care in the sitters own home. This is also unregulated care, that like the options for in-home care can have considerable variation in quality, depending on the individual caregiver.

Family Child Care

In this arrangement, children are cared for in the home of the provider. While care is usually limited to 6 children, regulations now allow providers with assistants to offer care for up to 12 children in what are called group or large family child care homes. Care is generally offered all day, five days a week, year-round, and can meet a family's needs for flexibility more easily than a center-based program with fixed hours of operation. While many providers begin this work as an extension of caring for their own children, some continue as an intentional career choice and may even become part of the movement to professionalize this type of care (National Association for Family Child Care, 2003). Many caregivers provide enriching educational and social experiences for the children in their care in the context of an appropriate daily schedule and an environment organized to support children's development.

Family child care is generally more affordable for families, since the fees are substantially lower than those charged in child care centers. Many families also prefer this type of arrangement, particularly for children under 2, due to its convenience, homelike environment, and unstructured play-oriented program. A family child care home can mirror a family, with children from infancy through school age served. While some caregivers will only accept particular age groups, others care

for the same children year after year as they grow older.

While all states have some type of licensing and regulation of family child care, the requirements and oversight are generally minimal. Unfortunately, with the pressing need for child care for mothers returning to work due to changes in the welfare regulations, beginning in 1996, regulations may become even less stringent.

Child Care Centers

Center-based child care can serve children from infancy through school age, although some programs limit themselves to a particular age group. Typically, child care centers, like the one the McGees selected, are open all day, 5 days per week, year-round, and close only for major holidays and extreme weather conditions. Many centers provide multiple programs, including half-day nurserylike classes for 3-, 4-, and even 5-year-olds, and many offer extended-day programs for children in kindergarten and up to 12 years old. Child care centers have long hours of operation, flexibility of hours, and the ability to serve children of various ages, which makes them a particularly convenient and appealing choice for many families.

As we noted before, the number of child care centers increased dramatically between 1977 and the present, with the largest growth area in for-profit programs. For-profit centers include independent programs or those that are part of local or national chains. Child care centers may also be run as nonprofit operations sponsored by organizations such as the Young Men's Christian Association (YMCA), churches, colleges, social service agencies, or local, state, or federal government agencies. Some **employer-sponsored child care** centers have opened over the last decades, although their numbers are still quite small. The U.S. Military Child Development Program has,

Child care centers, providing programs from infancy to school age, are convenient and appealing for different family lifestyles

however, created an extensive system of care centers and family child care to serve military personnel around the world. Some (Wardle, 2003) have suggested that these could serve as a model for other communities.

Child care centers are housed in a variety of locations, including community centers, church basements, former school buildings, store fronts, industrial parks, or in spaces built specifically for the center. Usually, a center will have multiple classrooms, each arranged for a particular age range. Increasingly, centers provide an educational curriculum appropriate for each age group. Although the requirements vary drastically from state to state, there are generally some educational requirements for staff and an expectation that staff participate in continued training activities.

Infant Toddler Programs.   While infant and toddler care in centers is a relatively recent

phenomenon, affluent parents are increasingly turning to this arrangement to meet their family's needs. Center care for children under 2 can be very expensive in those states that require a high teacher-to-child ratio. This ratio varies from one caregiver for three babies to as high as one to eight, depending on the state.

Infant and toddler programs require particular materials, equipment, and room arrangements. Many centers provide rooms designed for small groups of caregivers and infants in spaces comfortable for both. Rocking chairs, carpeting, mats, and duplicates of popular toys are basics. Ideally, a separate sleeping area is available with a designated crib for each child.

Center care for infants and toddlers should focus on several areas. The first area is the provision of their basic needs in terms of eating, sleeping, safety, cleanliness, and nurturance. Centers also provide educational support for infants through a developmentally and culturally appropriate curriculum (Bergen, Reid, & Torelli, 2001). Both planned and spontaneous experiences in the context of routine care and play are recognized as essential for optimal growth. As our knowledge of early brain development has increased, infant toddler programs have a great responsibility to contribute to the cognitive and social–emotional growth of the children in their care.

Preschool Programs.   Center-based care for 3- to 5-year-old children is the most popular option for American families. Young children cared for in centers can be there for up to 50 hours a week, so much of their basic needs must be met during that time. Centers make provisions for children to eat up to two meals and two snacks each day. Children also need opportunities to rest, play outdoors and inside, and interact with caring, consistent adults.

Providing for children's physical safety and basic needs, however, is only the beginning of what a preschool child care program should offer young children. Children need opportunities to participate in a program that enriches them emotionally, socially, and intellectually as well. While there are a number of approaches to early education programs for this age group, it is widely accepted that young children need to make choices and initiate their own activities for large blocks of time. While teacher-directed activities, such as stories, songs, and arts and crafts projects, should be part of the daily routine, play and child-initiated experiences should predominate (Bredekamp & Copple, 1997). Table 5–1 illustrates an appropriate schedule for preschool child care.

School-Age Child Care.   While some centers offer school-age care in addition to their serv-

Table 5–1   Sample Schedule for a Preschool Day

7:30–8:30	Arrival, breakfast, table toys, and transition to center
8:30–8:50	Opening circle/meeting
8:50–9:50	Activity period in centers/snack
9:50–10:00	Cleanup time
10:00–10:20	Circle: music, movement, or stories
10:20–10:30	Toileting
10:30–11:30	Outdoor play
11:30–12:00	Lunch
12:30–2:30	Rest and provisions for quiet play starting around 1:15 for nonsleepers
2:30–3:00	Toileting
3:00–3:45	Snack
3:45–4:45	Outdoor play
4:45–5:00	Story and songs
5:00–6:00	Free play, classroom cleanup, and transition to families

ices for younger children, other programs limit themselves to this age group. In some cases, centers rent space in the public schools, but increasingly school districts are offering care directly. No matter how they are administered, however, school-age child care programs provide a number of options for families who need care for the hours before and after school. In many programs, care is also available during weather emergencies, school holidays, and summer vacation.

School-age programs often provide breakfast for children who attend before school and offer a snack as children arrive at the end of the school day. Outdoor play is usually one of the first options for children as they transition from their academic program to the more relaxed setting of child care. Many programs offer time and support for children to do homework, and others facilitate children's involvement in extracurricular school activities such as scouting, sports, and other activities. See Table 5–2 for a sample schedule for before and after-school child care.

Table 5–2   Sample Schedule for Before- and After-School Child Care

7:00–8:00	Arrival, breakfast, quiet play, transition from home
8:00–8:30	Outdoor play
8:30–9:00	Quiet play and preparation for regular school
3:00–3:45	Choice of indoor or outdoor free play
3:45–4:15	Snack
4:15–4:45	Homework and quiet play
4:45–6:00	Self-selected activities, games, computers, clubs, and transition to home

Other Programs

To meet the needs of families for the kind of - informal and infrequent care that used to be provided by family, friends, or neighbors, other programs have emerged.

Mother's-Day-Out Programs. These programs are designed to offer a few hours of child care each week for stay-at-home parents who need time for activities like doctor's appointments, shopping, and respite from their children for a short period of time. Often sponsored by religious organizations or other community groups, these programs offer children a chance to play and socialize with other children.

Drop-In Child Care. Some child care programs provide child care services for parents with part-time jobs, flexible work schedules, and those who need a place to leave their children for short periods of time on occasion. Increasingly, centers designed only for **drop-in care** are being offered in shopping centers, gyms, movie theatres, and other conveniently located places. These are casual programs that provide safe supervision in a play environment.

CHILD CARE REGULATIONS AND VOLUNTARY ACCREDITATION

All 50 states and the District of Columbia have regulations concerning the operation of child care centers and family child care homes. In most cases, a child care center cannot operate unless it is licensed by the state. The regulations for family child care vary from registration to licensing, depending on particular state statutes.

Licensing regulations are minimum standards designed to protect the safety and well-being of children. Generally, the procedure for licensing includes regular inspections to ensure that programs are operating according to the guidelines. As you would expect, licensing regulations cover a multitude of issues, such as the ratio of adults to children, health, safety issues, building codes, and staff qualifications. The National Resource Center for Health and Safety in Child Care has a Web site with links to each individual state detailing the family child care and the center-based licensing regulations.

Some child care centers and family child care providers go beyond state licensing requirements by participating in voluntary accreditation programs. Accreditation is considered an indicator of child care quality and is the result of a process of collaboration between the program and other professionals to determine whether it meets nationally recognized standards of excellence.

The National Association of Family Child Care (NAFCC) is a national membership organization that works with more than 400 state and local family child care provider associations across the United States. It developed its first accreditation system in 1988, and by 1998 there were NAFCC-accredited family child care providers in 44 states and the District of Columbia. According to a study of accredited providers, accreditation increases providers' professionalism and self-esteem, improves quality of care, and develops leadership skills (Galinsky, Howes, & Kontos, 1995). In 1998, NAFCC piloted a new accreditation system for family child care. These quality standards were developed in conjunction with Wheelock College's Family Child Care Project in collaboration with providers, parents, and resource and referral staff, and are now in effect.

The National Association for the Education of Young Children's (NAEYC's) Academy for Early Childhood Program Accreditation administers the nation's largest voluntary accreditation system for all types of preschools, kindergartens, child care centers, and school-age child care programs. The process includes an extensive self-study by the program directors and a site visit by a team of trained volunteer valuators who verify the accuracy of the self-study. There are currently about 8,000 NAEYC-accredited programs, which can be located through www.naeyc.org. At the present time, the NAEYC is seeking input on the Suggested Program Standards for Early Childhood Programs Serving Children Birth Through Kindergarten as it works to increase the accreditation system's credibility and reliability (Goffin, 2003). See Appendix 2 for the complete NAEYC standards.

According to the NAEYC (1998), a high-quality early childhood program meets the physical, social, emotional, and cognitive needs of children. Such programs also meet the needs of the parents, staff, and administrator who are involved in the program. The following areas are studied in the current accreditation process:

- Interactions among staff and children
- Curriculum
- Staff qualifications and development
- Staffing patterns
- Physical environment

- Health and safety
- Nutrition and food service
- Program evaluation.

The accreditation process represents a professional judgment as to whether the center substantially complies with the accreditation criteria. Centers are usually granted accreditation for a period of 3 years, during which time annual reports are submitted to the NAEYC.

FEATURES OF QUALITY CHILD CARE

Although awareness and interest in accreditation as a hallmark of quality continues to grow, only about 10% of child care centers and an even smaller number of family child care providers have actually become accredited. Without the assurance of an accredited program, it is more difficult to determine the quality of a child care setting. Yet despite the great diversity in child care arrangements and the wide variations in state regulations governing center-based and family child care homes, there is much agreement among professionals concerning the characteristics of quality child care that provides the safe, healthy, and nurturing environments that parents want and children deserve.

High-quality care is the result of a combination of a healthy and safe environment along with educational and social stimulation appropriate to the age and development of the children being served (Fraenkel, 2003). These features of quality child care include both structural elements relating to the physical environment and staffing requirement and process elements relating to curricular practices, caregiver qualities, and parent involvement (Kontos, Howes, Shinn, & Galinsky, 1995). The McGee vignette suggests that the family has found a center that has both structural and process elements that assure quality.

High adult-to-child ratios are considered one of the strongest structural elements in supporting the intellectual and social development of children in child care

Structural Elements

The structural elements of a child care environment establish the foundation for optimal process conditions. Characteristics of the child care space, for example, are structural elements. The square footage required for each child, the amount and kind of outdoor space, the requirements for furniture, sinks, toilets, windows, flooring material, and myriad other details related to the classroom, kitchen facilities, bathrooms, and diaper-changing areas are included in this category. The adult–child ratio, amount of initial and continuing staff training required, plus the salaries, benefits, and working requirements for staff are all structural elements of child care.

The individual licensing requirements of each state sets minimum expectations for many of the structural elements, and a center or family child care home can get licensed by meeting these requirements. Unfortunately, these minimum standards do not necessarily lead to a quality program, and professional organizations and individuals have established optimal structural elements that can have a large impact on program quality. For example, while the state may only require one adult for every eight 2-year-olds and have no limit on the number in the total group, recommendations from the Center for Career Development in Early Care and Education at Wheelock College recommends a ratio of four children to one adult up to six children to one adult, with a maximum group size of 12 (Children's Defense Fund, 2001). High adult–child ratios are considered one of the strongest structural elements in supporting the intellectual and social development of children in child care and are important indicators of quality.

Quality programs also set up inviting environments with an abundance of appropriate resources in terms of furniture, equipment, materials, and toys, often far above the minimum requirements. The requirements for staff education and continued training are also above minimum requirements in quality centers.

Process Elements

Process quality refers to the experiences children have in child care and include such aspects as adult–child interactions, children's exposure to and involvement with learning materials, and parent–caregiver relationships. As you will deduce, these are critical components that directly affect children's behavior and learning experiences in the child care setting.

Qualities of Caregivers.   The most important process element in quality child care is the human relationships between the caregiver and the child and between the caregiver and the parent (Uttal, 2002). Caregivers who interact with children in a nurturing manner help to create attachments between themselves and the children, the foundation for further social development. Caregivers who engage children in conversation, ask questions, and respond to them when they speak are helping children acquire cognitive and language skills (National Institute for Child Health and Human Development [NICHD] Early Child Care Research Network, 1997). Not only do caregivers need to be knowledgeable about the developmental characteristics of the children they serve, understand how to provide enriching experiences for them, and be able to communicate effectively with the children's parents about their shared concerns, they must also be warm and nurturing people.

Ideally, those who care for young children will consider themselves professionals and have an educational background in child development and curriculum. Continuing professional education through attending conferences, participating in workshops, reading professional literature, and sharing ideas and information with colleagues are all indications of professional behavior. Partaking in activities like these builds commitment to the field, satisfaction with the work, and a greater sensitivity to the needs of children.

Unfortunately, the low wages associated with working with children in child care settings has had a very negative effect on the quality of caregivers (Harrington, 2000). Nonprofessional entry level salaries are rarely higher than minimum wage, particularly at national for-profit chains. Starting salaries for child care center teachers with college degrees was approximately $15,000 to $16,000 in the late 1990s, less than half of what many entry-level public school teachers receive. Low wages have kept the educational level of caregivers from rising and has spawned an annual turnover rate of about 30%. Those programs that manage to retain their caregivers are generally of higher quality than those that have a high turnover.

Curriculum.   Given the importance of the early years for children's physical, social, emotional, and cognitive development, another mark of a quality program is the curriculum. Curriculum in child care is generally understood as an approach toward learning that includes both planned and spontaneous educational experiences that occur within a predictable daily routine. Time is designated for outdoor and indoor play, large group gatherings for stories, music, movement, and more, and for routines like eating, toileting, and resting. A well-planned curriculum will meet the needs of the children enrolled by considering their age, developmental levels, interests, special needs, and cultural backgrounds.

A quality curriculum in a program serving infants and toddlers requires that caregivers be especially responsive to the rapid growth and change that is occurring during these years. Wortham (2002) summarized the characteristics of quality caregivers for this age group:

- Understand and appreciate children's unique temperaments and developmental stages
- Meet children's needs for care while encouraging increasing independence
- Frequently initiate physical, social, and verbal interactions
- Be responsive to children's physical, social, and verbal behavior most of the time
- Be consistent and predictable
- Plan experiences and interactions appropriate to the children's level of functioning.

This approach to curriculum has been termed "a dynamic interactive experience that builds on respect for and responsiveness to young children's interests, curiosity, and motives and to their families' goals and concerns" (Bergen, Reid, & Torelli, 2001, p. xiii). Play and routine caregiving activities are the fundamentals of the curriculum with this age group. A quality caregiver follows the lead of the children in determining when they sleep, eat, and need to be changed. Between these times, they interact with the infants and toddlers in an environment that has been set up to enhance their physical, cognitive, social, and emotional development.

As children reach age 2 and move into the preschool years, the curriculum changes to meet their developing needs. The daily schedule includes opportunities for children to work individually and in small groups most of the time, with some short periods of whole-group gatherings for stories and music. The classroom is arranged in activity areas, such as blocks, dramatic play, art, science, math, computer, language, and others. Each area is well stocked with interesting materials, which al-lows the children to make choices about what to do when they are there. Play is respected as the best way for children to learn and teachers facilitate their play to enhance the social, physical, and cognitive benefits for development (Wortham, 2002). Children's home cultures are represented in the classroom in various ways, and children with special needs can be included in the classroom to the benefit of all.

The curriculum in the quality before- and after-school age program tends to be more informal than those for younger children and will vary greatly depending on the needs and interests of the group. In a center, the room is set up in activity areas with space set aside for computer use and homework and other areas devoted to construction, games, music, art, and other interests. The best programs for this age group are seen by the children as clubs where individual interests can be pursued. Generally, the time before school is low-key, with breakfast available and time to participate in individual and small group projects. After-school usually begins with a period of vigorous outdoor play and is followed by snacks, some time for homework, and individual-choice activities. Allowing children as much choice as possible and providing lots of opportunity for socializing and pursuing interests are hallmarks of the most successful programs for school-age children.

Centers or family child care homes of high quality also offer extensive toys and materials appropriate to the children's ages and interests, and lots of free time for children to participate in self-directed activities. Full days in school-age care that occur during inclement weather, school holidays, and summers are characterized by a camplike atmosphere. School-age children are developing many interests, and the more the program can support the children's choices the more eagerly the children participate. In the highest quality programs, child care staff and the children's schoolteachers confer regularly and communicate issues of mutual concern.

While quality child care programs may have somewhat different philosophical orientations, all will offer a curriculum that extends the cognitive and socialization processes that have begun in the children's families. For many children, child care is where they first learn to interact with children and adults outside their families, and this marks the beginning of community socialization.

Parent Involvement.   Quality child care programs recognize the importance of parental involvement and the strong need that families feel to be fully informed about their child's progress. In a quality program, parents are asked to share detailed information about their child as they come into care so that caregivers can provide continuity with the home. Meeting prior to the child's beginning the program can help to build the rapport between parent and caregiver, which is essential to the success of the child care experience. Continuing collaboration between caregivers and parents facilitates the continuity of experiences for the child and enhances the potential for meeting the child's needs.

Collaboration relies on communication, and it is the provider's responsibility to establish many ways to keep families informed about their own child. Since most parents actually bring in and pick up their child at the child care setting, every day presents an opportunity to establish a relationship between the parent and the caregiver. Once such a relationship is established, the parent and caregiver can regularly and informally share information about what is going on with the child. In infant–toddler programs, parents and caregivers often record information about the child in a book that is passed back and forth between the child care setting and the home. Quality programs also schedule formal parent conferences throughout the year.

We find that parents want to be informed about what is going on in the child care program. In a small-family child care program this contact may be verbal, but larger programs will want to establish systems for passing information on to parents. Upcoming field trips, special events, requests for materials, and many other communications can be shared through notices on a parent bulletin board. Individual mailboxes are another way that information is shared in busy child care centers where a number of staff persons may work with a child over the course of the day.

Parents also welcome opportunities to become involved in the child care program. While some may have flexible work hours and be able to volunteer regularly in the classroom, others may have only one opportunity during the year to come in. Still, many parents would welcome the opportunity to assist the program in ways that don't interfere with their work schedules. Making phone calls to other parents, donating recyclables, sewing smocks, or washing the sheets used at nap time are all tasks parents may be willing to do. By becoming involved in these ways, parents feel more connected to the program and more committed to supporting it. Potluck dinners, family breakfasts, workshops on parenting, and other events can also build family involvement. Chapter 11 discusses both traditional and innovative strategies for establishing positive relationships between schools and child care programs and families.

Characteristics of Quality Child Care

Studies of child care quality in the United States suggest that there is room for improvement in both the structural and process aspects. Exemplary child care programs do share certain characteristics that can serve as a model for others seeking to improve the quality of care for children. According to Kinch

A quality center strengthens relationships with community by establishing a community advisory board

and Schweinhart (1999), a high-quality program includes the following features:

- *Financial resources.* Uses financial resources beyond parent fees, such as subsidies for low-income families and donations from individuals and foundations.

- *Creation of alliances.* Forges a variety of alliances with organizations to bring additional resources. For example, a center might collaborate with a community organization on fund-raising efforts.

- *Parent education.* Seeks ways to educate parents about the value of early childhood education. In doing so, parents become better consumers and are more likely to support programs.

- *Staff benefits.* Seeks additional salary and other benefits for their staff. In addition, they secure adequate planning time and

arrange opportunities for professional development.

- *Establishment of advisory committees.* Strengthens relationships with the community by establishing a board of directors or a community advisory board.

- *Recognition of needs.* Recognizes that family needs and stresses and working flexibly with families make a program viable for parents.

- *Institutional structures.* Plans for future existence through structures that promote quality, compensation, and affordability.

- *High standards.* Has established policies and clearly written standards on mission, philosophy, and educational approach.

Child care quality is essential in terms of children's everyday experiences and their later school achievement and social interactions.

When every child receives the highest quality care possible, the beneficial effects of child care will increase dramatically.

Effects of Quality Child Care

Research indicates that while the family remains the major influence on child outcomes, the quality and stability of the child care that young children receive have important effects as well. The most extensive investigation of non-maternal care in early childhood (NICHD Early Child Care Research Network, 1997) reported that the cognitive and language development of children and their social and emotional well-being are positively impacted by high-quality child care. Other research indicates that these positive effects on children's development are especially significant for low-income children and those at risk for school failure (Children's Defense Fund, 2001). Studies have also shown that quality school-age programs play an important role in children's school achievement and long-term success as well as their safety and well-being. As we have pointed out in other chapters, those who care for children make an important contribution to their lives.

QUALITY, AFFORDABILITY, AND OTHER ISSUES

Research has confirmed that quality programs are linked to positive outcomes for children (Mardell, 2002). Conversely, children in poor-quality care are at risk when they do not receive the attention, nurturance, and educational enrichment that will help them to succeed. Yet we find considerable variation in the quality of both centers and family child care homes.

Questions About Quality

The Cost, Quality, and Child Outcomes in Child Care Centers study examined over 400 child care centers and found that only 14% of programs provide high-quality care (Galinsky, Howes, Kontos, & Shinn, 1994; Helburn, 2002). The study also reported that 12% provided poor-quality child care arrangements, and the majority of programs were mediocre. The situation for infants and toddlers is even worse. Some studies suggest that only 1 out of 12 infants and toddlers are in a developmentally appropriate classroom, and 40% of classrooms are deemed potential threats to children's health and safety (Young, Marsland, & Zigler, 1997). Research on family child care programs and relative care is equally troubling. Only 9% of such care was of sufficient quality to positively influence children's development, 56% were considered adequate, and 35% were deemed of such poor quality that children's health and development were endangered (Galinsky et al., 1994; Hofferth, 1991). These are startling statistics for all families and professionals, and seemingly will not change soon (Greenspan & Salmon, 2001).

Financial Considerations

Most of the cost for out-of-home care is borne by individual families, and this can be prohibitive for many parents. While the average cost of child care for all families is around 8% of their income, low-income families spend approximately 23% and high-income families only 6% (Casper & Bianchi, 2002). As you can imagine, cost in relation to family income is a major factor influencing many families' child care arrangements. In the past, families on or transitioning off of welfare could receive subsidies for child care. As regulations have changed, these families may no longer receive assistance at the level or for the length of time needed. Middle- and low-income families are generally less able to afford high-quality child care than are high-income families. Consequently, a two-tier child care system has emerged, in which only certain families have access to the highest quality care (Cryer & Clifford, 2003; Scarr, 1998).

Carla, in the following vignette, provides an example of the benefits that subsidized care can offer low-income families. Later, however, she becomes a victim of a system that gives few options and produces a dilemma.

℮

Carla's sons Tommy and Cody both attended Head Start, and Carla became an active program participant. She gained skills and confidence in herself. As a result, 2 years ago, with Tommy in school and Cody in Head Start, she took a job as a part-time administrative assistant. Her employer was pleased with her work and urged her to continue her education and job training. With her salary added to her husband's part-time work, the family moved off welfare and even obtained medical insurance.

Suddenly things changed. This year, Carla's husband left and provides no financial support. Carla's employer wants her to get more training and become a full-time employee. But to continue her training, Carla must find partial child care for her boys. Such care is hard to find and expensive. Carla's salary increment is good, but it no longer covers her insurance payments and child care while still meeting basic needs.

Carla would be eligible for child care supplements, but when she applies, she is told that all new applicants are placed on a waiting list. As Carla seeks solutions, she is told she could go back on welfare since she hasn't used up all her allotted time. Presently working full-time, she makes too much money to receive any welfare support. If she works only part-time, she can get welfare benefits plus Medicaid, but her employer needs a full-time person. Her job, career training, and future employment are all in jeopardy. Carla is seriously considering going back on welfare until both children are a little older, but she's afraid that by then the skills she has gained plus her employer's goodwill will have vanished.

℮

One can see that those families whose income is above the poverty level but below $25,000 are less likely to be able to afford center-based care, as is the case with Carla in the preceding vignette. In short, these families have fewer options available to them when it come to selecting appropriate out-of-home care.

Other Issues

It is generally agreed that quality child care is directly related to the adults providing the care (Cohen, 2001). As noted earlier, however, the child care workforce which is 98% female and one third women of color, is inadequately compensated. The average center-based teacher earns about $7 per hour, and many receive only minimum wage. Teachers with a college degree and some experience earn on average barely $10 per hour. Family child care providers are even more poorly paid, and only one third of all child care staff has health benefits. Many must also contend with poor working conditions as well. Consequently, approximately one third of those who work in child care leave the field each year. The shortage of public school early childhood teachers—due to reductions in class size and increases in prekindergarten programs in elementary schools—has increased the job opportunities for well-trained early childhood teachers. Therefore, many are leaving the child care field to pursue better paid positions in the public schools.

The greatest concern in the 21st century is no longer that children will be cared for outside the home but that the quality of care they receive will be substandard (Greenspan & Salmon, 2001). Fortunately, numerous groups are working to resolve what has come to be seen as a real crisis for American families—finding affordable quality care for their children so they can work. The mission of the Center for the Child Care Workforce, which recently merged with the American Federation of Teachers Educational Foundation, has been to improve the

Some families are fortunate to have sufficient income to afford quality center-based care for their children

quality of child care services by upgrading the wages, benefits, training opportunities, and working conditions for child care teachers and family child care providers. The National Association of Child Care Resource and Referral Agencies works with communities to improve the supply and quality of child care through its research, ongoing professional development opportunities, parent education component, and support of accreditation. Many other national groups, such as the National Association for the Education of Young Children, Children's Defense Fund, National Association for Family Child Care, and the National Child Care Information Center, are committed to working to improve the quality of child care.

While child care policies in the United States lag behind most other modern industrialized countries (Cryer & Clifford, 2003), there are some indications that businesses are beginning to recognize the importance of supporting the family life of their workers. While the number of employer-sponsored child care centers is very small, a growing number of firms are providing child care assistance through referral services, partnerships with local child care programs, and the provision of **backup care** for the children of employees. Changes in benefit packages, including flexible spending accounts that allow employees to pay for child care in pretax dollars, offers some financial support as well.

In the political climate at the beginning of the 21st century, very few federal funds have been allotted to support quality child care (Hartman, 2003). Although welfare reform has successfully introduced many more women into the workforce, the provisions for quality child care have been less forthcoming. Extending tax credits, making parent's expenditures for child care refundable for poorer families, and other federal policies are needed. The reality of quality care is that providing the service can not be based solely on what parents can afford to pay. Families and programs need additional community and government support in order to make quality care available to every child (Lombardi, 2003).

IMPLICATIONS FOR PROFESSIONALS

As the need for quality care for infants through school-age children continues to increase, professionals in education and other social services have a responsibility to understand the issues related to child care. Early childhood educators and other professionals are in a unique position to assist and guide parents in finding the best care possible for their children.

Because of the lasting effects of the care children receive, implementing high standards for children in child care is essential. It is particularly important that you know what constitutes quality care for children at different ages. You can then use this knowledge to collaborate with parents and other advocates for children to work toward higher standards for child care. Supporting initiatives like the Worthy Wage Campaign, which is designed to improve child care through increased compensation and training for caregivers, is one example of a way professionals can be involved in national efforts to raise community awareness about the child care situation.

SUMMARY AND REVIEW

Child care is essential to family life today. National surveys confirm that an increasing number of children are being cared for outside the home so that parents can work. Increasingly, as families recognize the importance of early experiences on children's later development, they are seeking care that goes beyond custodial to that which has an educational component as well.

Child care arrangements include care that may be offered by a nanny, babysitter, or au pair in the child's home. Family child care occurs in the home of the provider and is offered for small groups of children, often of variable ages. Center-based child care can serve children from infancy through school age, generally in classrooms designed for children of a particular age range.

Considerable variation exists in the quality of child care services. While all states have regulations to govern family child care and center-based programs, very little oversight is provided for families who use in-home care. State regulations, however, only provide minimum guidelines, and being licensed does not guarantee that a program is of high quality. Nationally accredited centers and family child care homes, while still a small percentage of the total, serve as models of quality programs. Quality of care includes both process and structural components in the child care setting.

The most important indicator of quality is the caregiver. The 30% annual turnover rate of those working with children due to poor compensation, lack of benefits, and poor working conditions is a serious issue facing child care. The improvement of the quality, affordability, and accessibility of child care is one of the biggest challenges facing families, schools, and communities today.

SUGGESTED ACTIVITIES AND QUESTIONS

1. Interview several parents who use different kinds of child care arrangements. Determine how they feel about the care their child is receiving and the challenges they face navigating work and parenthood.

2. Obtain a copy of your state's child care regulations. What are the ratios of adults to children at various ages? What are the qualifications required of caregivers? How do these compare to national recommendations?

3. Visit a child care center and arrange to observe several of the classes. What elements of a quality curriculum can you see? What changes might you make?

4. In the McGee vignette, pick out the incidents that would indicate to Mr. and Mrs. McGee that the center probably has high structural and process qualities.

RESOURCES

Books

1. Bender, J., Flatter, C. H., & Sorrentino, J. M. (2000). *Half a childhood: Quality programs for out-of-school hours* (2nd ed.). Nashville, TN: School-Age NOTES.
2. Bergen, D., Reid, R., & Torelli, L. (2000). *Educating and caring for very young children: The infant/toddler curriculum.* New York: Teachers College Press.
3. Gonzalez-Mena, J. (1997). *Multicultural issues in child care.* Mountain View, CA: Mayfield.
4. Lombardi, J. (2003). *Time to care: Redesigning child care to promote education, support families, and build communities.* Philadelphia: Temple University Press.

Films and Videos

1. *Keys to quality infant and toddler care* [Video, 24 min]. (2002). This video helps parents recognize quality child care by focusing on relationships, responsiveness, and individualized care among the children, parents, and staff. Crystal Lake, IL: Magna Systems Video.
2. *Young children in action* [Video, 30 min]. (2001). This video illustrates an individualized, play-oriented curriculum for infants and toddlers at various stages of development. New York: Teachers College Press.
3. *Early child care and education* [Video, 29 min]. (2002). This video portrays different kinds of child care for children from infancy through school age and focuses on issues of quality appropriate for each level. Crystal Lake, IL: Magna Systems Video.

Organizations

Children's Foundation
725 Fifteenth Street, NW, Suite 505
Washington, DC 20005
www.childrensfoundation.net

National Association for the Education of Young Children
1509 Sixteenth Street, NW
Washington, DC 20036
www.naeyc.org

National Association for Family Child Care
5202 Pinemont Drive
Salt Lake City, Utah 84123
www.nafcc.org

School-Age NOTES
P.O. Box 40205
Nashville, TN 37204
www.schoolagenotes.com

Websites

1. www.afterschoolalliance.org The Afterschool Alliance provides information for establishing school-age programs as well as disseminating research to support after-school care.
2. www.ccw.org The Center for the Child Care Workforce is committed to quality of child care by upgrading wages, benefits, training opportunities, and working conditions for child care providers.
3. www.naccrra.net The National Association of Child Care Resource and Referral Agencies is a national network of community-based resource and referral agencies.
4. www.nccic.org The National Child Care Information Center provides linkages with other agencies interested in enhancing and promoting child care.

Chapter 6

Responsibility for Educating and Protecting Children

Families, neighbors, community members, and educators together create a web of support that contributes to the healthy and meaningful growth of children.

(Arce, 1999, p. 136)

Many have stated that our greatest resource is our nation's children, and more believe there is urgency in making certain that this resource is carefully and humanely developed. In this chapter, we consider the obligations for educating and protecting American children and the people and agencies that bear the responsibility for meeting these obligations. In reading this chapter, you will learn the following:

1. Societal traditions convey responsibilities to families, schools, and communities for educating and protecting the young.

2. Legal requirements exist for all social settings and hold families, schools, and communities accountable for providing different aspects of education and protection of children.

3. Society in general expects the informal or nonacademic curriculum to be arranged and fulfilled by homes and communities.

4. The formal academic curriculum, though overseen by the community, is largely the responsibility of school personnel.

5. Overlaps and even disagreements occur regarding responsibilities and obligations for some aspects of children's experience.

6. The impact of one social setting on children's education can at times run counter to the expectations of another.

7. Even with conflicts, partnerships among homes, schools, and communities are the best way to providing meaningful experiences for children.

Maria had been annoyed with her son's school for a month. From his second-grade class,

Tony kept bringing home paper after paper with instructions for Maria to go over and practice with him. Maria felt the teacher couldn't be doing her job, because Tony never seemed to understand what the assignments were all about. One day when Tony brought home a math paper, a reading paper, and a social studies assignment, Maria had had enough. She stopped working on the meal she was preparing for her six children and gathered up a basket of jeans and sweatshirts that needed laundering and mending. With the pile of laundry and Tony, she marched the three blocks to school. Maria entered Ms. Srichan's classroom and plunked the laundry basket on the teacher's table. "You expect me to do your work? I think you should help me with mine," she remarked angrily and then marched off with Tony in tow.

Whose responsibility is it to see that Tony learns his math, reading, and social studies concepts? In our opening vignette, the teacher and parent obviously are not in agreement and probably are not communicating at all.

In Chapter 1, we assert that young children become what their world provides and that they learn skills to the degree that surroundings guide, entice, or motivate them. The influences and forces affecting children at the beginning of the 21st century are numerous and constant. Children encounter them in all three of our fundamental social settings: family, school, and community. As you prepare for a career in teaching or community work, it is important for you to identify and understand where and how persons in each setting assume responsibility for children's learning and protection. You also need to understand that each institution can work in tandem or in conflict with the other two, as seems to be happening in Tony's case.

Societal expectations in the United States imply that families, schools, and communities have responsibilities for both formal and informal education and protection of children. Responsibilities range from instructing in basic social skills and hygiene practices to teaching the skilled manipulation of equipment to awakening children's aesthetic appreciation and reasoning ability. With the identification of the battered child syndrome in the 1960s and the eventual passage of child abuse reporting laws in all states, there has also been a recognition that society has a responsibility to step in when parents are unable or unwilling to care for their children adequately (Reppucci, Britner, & Woolard, 1997).

In the following sections, we examine the protection and educational responsibilities associated with each of the three social settings. We view these responsibilities both from a legal standpoint and as traditional and cultural practices found in communities in the United States. We discuss the following: (a) who determines appropriate content and experience for children's care and learning, (b) where we find nurturance and support for that care and learning, and (c) who governs, coordinates, and evaluates children's protection and education.

YOUNG CHILDREN'S LEARNING

An academic curriculum is provided for children enrolled in many different types of school environments: private and public schools, preschool, and child care. A formal school's academic curriculum is constantly affirmed by school professionals as well as by laypersons, and its purpose is, in general, to help children accumulate knowledge and skill. Much of what children learn, however, actually comes

from the experiences, associations, and interactions they have outside and beyond scheduled school activities. This is the unplanned, covert, or hidden curriculum that teachers and parents often don't recognize or overlook. This second curriculum is a dominant part of any child's life, and it must be related to the formal curriculum as prepared and implemented by schools (Apple, 1995; Dreeben, 1970; Giroux, 1978).

Children's interests and stage of development determine what is meaningful for them, and the stimuli and experiences that result in learning come from many forces within each child's life (Bronfenbrenner & Weiss, 1983). When we consider who is responsible for children's education, we must ascertain who has the most substantial and direct access to children's time, minds, and interests. We must take into account all of the forces bombarding children with information and experience. For example, a definite curriculum of the home exists, although we do not label it as such. It starts at birth and continues to be dominated by primary caregivers during children's earliest years. The community begins to affect children by the time they are toddlers. Children identified with special needs may begin receiving intervention services from community groups even earlier. School programs for these children may begin as early as age 3, and by age 5, almost all children are involved with school curricula. As Cowan and Cowan (2003) pointed out, even children with extensive preschool experiences are challenged to meet the rules and demands of elementary school which is a new and complex school environment.

While much of the informal curriculum is random and incidental, following daily living patterns in particular homes and communities, we find cases where some parents impose an almost academic curriculum, with definite ideas on what their children are to be exposed to and how. For instance, some parents obtain materials for teaching their children letter recognition at age 2 and arrange selected private lessons with specialists in the arts. Many families, while not going to those extremes, recognize that quality conversations, regular book-sharing sessions, and lots of hands-on experiences help to "prepare" their children for formal schooling.

On the other hand, some families, particularly those living in poverty, have been unable to adequately prepare their children for school. While low-income families and those linguistically and culturally different than the mainstream want their children to succeed in school just as much as their middle-class counterparts do, they often lack the necessary skills to prepare their children for schooling. Programs like Head Start and other publicly funded preschool and **family literacy programs** (Paratore, 2001) have been established to educate parents about school preparation and to help children make a more successful transition from home to formal schooling.

Some of the informal curriculum takes place within a community and may include children's playmates, neighborhood visits and activities, community agency activities, media involvement, and recreational areas. Specialists in urban schools underscore the case for teachers understanding communities as a bridge to more successful learning for children of poverty. As Woodruff (1999) noted, "Schools and curricula are most effective when rooted in children's needs and experiences. What goes on in a school, therefore, should be as much about a child's overall life as it is about academics" (p. 155).

In addition, the larger community creates an impression on all citizens, one that children feel and internalize. Communities control children's learning by (1) providing (or disallowing) opportunities in sports facilities, recreation arenas, libraries, museums and arts areas, and clinics and other health facilities, and (2) supporting or challenging particular attitudes, lifestyles, and mobility patterns. The "way of doing things here" is the community ethos and therefore part of children's informal curriculum. Children of color, for example, are still very young when they encounter the attitudes and mores, whether positive or negative, of the dominant racial group (Lightfoot, 1978).

Components of Home Responsibility

Parents and caregivers bear great responsibility for children's early learning and for the genesis of and support for the curriculum that children will use for their entire lives. Parents also have a significant role in nurturing the academic work children experience after entering school. In Chapter 7, we discuss the many opportunities for learning in the home.

No formal or legal demands exist that require parents to instruct their children. However, common cultural assumptions regarding child rearing imply that parents will guide and prepare children for life in a community. Also, statutes concerning abuse and neglect have emerged over the years, and parents parsimonious in nurturing and guiding their children risk citations of maltreatment and its consequences (Lazzara & Poland, 2001). Parents must also be vigilant in protecting their child from abuse from others entrusted with their care.

It is tradition, by and large, that encourages parents and homes to protect their children from harm and to provide the basics or beginnings of instruction. As we noted in Chapter 1, American society (considered in the abstract) has, through media, health, and medical advisements, and social service agencies, tried to influence families about educating, protecting, and rearing children since the 1800s.

Most societies do little to formally prepare parents for rearing children, and the United States is no exception. When extended families were more common, child raising was probably more coherent. Advice was more available, community standards were more constant, and families were far less mobile (Walsh, 2003). In today's society, with its matrix of ever increasing forces producing stress, mobility, and differing home styles, child-raising practice has become less consistent and more pressured (Elkind, 1988, 1994). Daily lives now are more frenetic, and some families come close to abandoning responsibilities for a home curriculum in favor of that offered by the media. Unfortunately, television, films, video games, CDs, and the Internet tend to offer role models that "emphasize commercialism, sexuality, substance abuse, and violence" (Bronfenbrenner, 2001, p. 199). Readers may wish to see Chapter 10 for more detail on mass media effects.

Nonetheless, expectations exist, and persons in other social settings anticipate that families will provide beginning experiences as children grow and move into the conventional school environment and the neighborhood. What are the responsibilities of homes and child care settings for looking after and educating children during the early years? We describe some representative areas in the following subsections.

Early Socialization Skills. Except in cases of severe neglect, parents and other family members automatically instill in children the basics of socialization. Children early and naturally learn to greet and respond to others, recognize acquaintances, play games with siblings, and mimic and follow one another. In addition, many parents recognize the importance of providing their children with educational toys and experiences with other children as part of the socialization process (Kieff & Casbergue, 2000). As noted in Chapter 5, over 65% of American preschool children are in some form of child care, and this means that socialization skills are affected considerably by events and people outside the home. Even though somewhat more aggression is noted in children who attend child care, research (Clarke-Stewart, 1993; Clarke-Stewart, Allhusen, & Clements, 1995) shows that most children mature much the same whether in or

Many parents recognize the importance of providing their children with educational toys and experiences with other children

out of child care. High-quality care in the center or family child care home is the most important criteria for the best outcomes for children (Cleveland & Krashinsky, 1998).

Language and Literacy. Babies are immersed in language from birth and begin to develop communication skills during the earliest months of life. Their skills expand rapidly because of planned and unplanned family interactions and experiences. Parents, echo their infant's vocalizations, name things, and direct their attention to the objects, people, and events around them. Parents, other family members, and caregivers often explain to the baby what they and the baby are doing, demonstrating with real objects accompanied by language. Increasingly, families are introducing babies to books during their first year. Talking about the pictures, turning the pages, and sharing the pleasure of snuggling together with a book become the foundation for later reading development. Writing emerges in much the same way. Toddlers, given paper and crayons, will scribble, draw, and make lists in imitation of their parents' writing. Later literacy development includes listening to, discussing, and making up stories, practicing reading and writing, and modeling more elaborate speech (Beaty, 2002). Literacy expands in quality preschool settings where caring adults support children's efforts with appropriate materials and activities (Christie, Enz, & Vukelich, 2003). As children find it necessary to communicate with different adults and with their peers and are given opportunities to practice their newfound skills, they develop language and literacy.

Exploration. Children's sensory play with toys, materials, and objects in the home lay important foundations for their cognitive growth. Beginning experiments with natural phenomena found outdoors were common family experiences in the past. Unfortunately, changes in modern life have restricted many children's access to the natural world as a regular part of daily life (Rivkin, 1995). As children spend more time in child care and schools, these settings will need to provide the opportunities for children to play vigorously outside and to freely explore the natural environment.

Interaction and Negotiating Skills. Imparting basic wisdom about human relationships must begin in the home. It is the family's responsibility to develop children's initial interaction and negotiating skills even though these are extended considerably in other groupings, for example, peer group, child care, and school situations. Teaching about sensitivity to others, the logic of cooperative action and taking turns, and the need to respect others and to share materials has its place in the social life of growing children (Black & Puckett, 2001).

Aesthetic Appreciation and Value Development. Children's earliest aesthetic development occurs within the home. Experimenting with music, graphic arts, and movement leads to pleasant associations with these art forms. Parents who validate these experiments, participate in the action, and demonstrate possibilities help young children form values and develop appreciation (Seefeldt & Barbour, 1998). Experiences with the arts also introduce children to their cultural heritage and the culture of others. Child care settings can also support children's aesthetic development when the arts are integrated into all areas of the curriculum. Althouse, Johnson, and Mitchell (2003) emphasized the importance of adults "listening to what children say about their artwork and of valuing their ideas and efforts. The more secure children feel in their environment, the better able they are to develop concepts through creative investigations" (p. 112)

Health Education and Sex Education.   Protecting and promoting the health of young children is an accepted part of the home
curriculum. Families are expected to provide
adequate and appropriate food for their children and to help them develop an interest in
nutritious food. Lifelong eating habits are
formed during the early years (Aronson,
2002), and families and child care providers
play an important role in introducing new
foods and establishing a relaxed eating environment. Hand washing, teeth brushing, and
caring for bodily functions are other expected aspects of the home curriculum and of
the child care settings where many young
children spend a large part of the regular
workweek.

Health education is always a part of a quality child care experience, but sex education
can be a controversial topic. Families have the
initial responsibility for children's sex education. At the minimum, families should focus
on attention to gender differences, names for
body parts, words for toileting, attention to privacy, and knowledge of "good touching" and
"bad touching." Chrisman and Couchenour
(2002) suggested that although there are different approaches to sex education among families, families who support healthy sexual
development "include respectful interactions
with one another, appropriate expressions of
affection among family members, and a sensitive awareness of both expected behaviors and
unacceptable behaviors" (p. 5). Essa and
Murray (1999) provided a brief but helpful
background on the sexual behavior of young
children and how parents and teachers can
cope with their concerns over what is normal
sexual play and what is deviant.

While some child care programs have a
planned curriculum of sexual education, most
take a more informal approach. Children will
ask questions or behave in certain ways that
will require a response by adults. Providing accurate information and positive guidance is

essential, but families must be aware of the
child care facility's policies in this area. Child
care programs can serve as a resource for families and support their role in children's sexual development.

Components of School Responsibility

A formal curriculum starts with "schooling"—
no matter how young the child. Schooling,
whether at nursery school, child care (including **infant–toddler programs**), or public or private school, will begin where some parts of the
formal and informal home curriculum have
paused or proven inadequate in preparing
children for their next educational step. Head
Start and **Early Head Start**, for example, are
comprehensive child development programs
that serve children from birth to age 5. The
overall goal of Head Start is to help the young
children in low-income families get ready for
school. Family literacy programs, while considerably narrower in focus, have a similar
goal of helping to boost the achievement of
poor and minority children through programs
that serve both children and their parents.

Educating Children in Schools.   The word
curriculum, used constantly in most schools,
serves as an organizer for all school programs.
Different conceptions of curriculum do exist,
and the philosophical orientation of a particular school's staff members will determine the
how and what of children's learning. (See
Chapter 8 for an overview of school curriculum.) In some schools, curriculum will be an
outline of content and the skills to be presented, while in others it will be a constantly
changing set of experiences that children and
teachers decide to pursue in satisfying their interests (Doll, 1995). All gradations between
these two are found in schools in the United
States. As a beginning professional, you should
anticipate the definition of *curriculum* as the
formal and informal content and processes

used by and for learners in gaining skills, knowledge, and appreciation (McNeil, 1996).

We discuss school curriculum more fully in Chapter 8, but for now, think of preschool and primary-school children extending the skills that were started in the home and expanded for many children in the child care center:

1. Language and Literacy skills: reading, writing, speaking, and listening competencies.

2. Math competencies: numeration skills, calculating, measuring, spatial relations, and problem solving.

3. Physical and natural science competencies: observing phenomena, representing observations, drawing conclusions, experimenting with plant growth, animal care, and everyday chemical combinations.

4. Social skills: those related to a variety of people in different circumstances—making friends, cooperating, respecting rules, the study of human relationships. These increase and intensify as children grow.

5. Health education, sex education, recreation skills: extension of skills and habits begun in the home.

6. Aesthetic education: participation in and appreciation of music, dance, graphic arts, crafts, and other fine arts.

7. Negotiating skills: procedures for planning activities, arranging teams, cooperative learning, and developing **assessments** (mostly in the informal curriculum).

8. Attitudes and values: social, ethical, and moral judgment, respect for and cooperation with others.

Protecting Children.　Besides tending to children's educational needs, school personnel must be aware of children who may be mistreated by their families or other adults and step in to assist them. Many factors contribute to the maltreatment of children, and a

complete discussion of this complex topic is beyond the scope of this text. It is essential, however, that educators and other community workers understand the types of abuse and neglect, and recognize the signs and symptoms of children who may be mistreated (Aronson, 2002). They must also be clear on the procedures for reporting their suspicions. Although the Child Abuse Prevention and Treatment Act of 1974 required all states to establish some mandatory reporting of suspected abuse or neglect, the agencies involved, definitions of abuse, and reporting procedures vary from state to state. School professionals are obligated to know the regulations in their state. Figure 6–1 offers a summary of commonly accepted definitions, symptoms, and signs of child maltreatment, which include intentional physical injury, neglect, sexual molestation, and emotional abuse. The Resources section at the end of this chapter provides additional sources of information.

By expanding and building on the curriculum started in the home, partnerships between school and home assure protection for children and continuity of their learning. Whenever one enhances the objectives of the other, the result is enriched experience for children.

Components of Community Responsibility

All communities have multiple facets, and the impact of different agencies and enterprises is pervasive in the lives of children. While it is true that the youngest children have limited contacts beyond their home or child care situation, primary-school children will experience, at some level, almost as much community conditioning, pressure, and influence as do adults.

Responsibility accrues to the community as an institution for supporting its citizens, families, and schools and for furnishing a "curriculum" of experiences and opportunities. No laws or mandates require this involvement, and few would enumerate the particular services of a

Maltreatment	Definition	Signs and Symptoms
Physical abuse	An intentional act affecting a child that produces tangible physical harm and can include shaking, beating, striking, or burning	Suspect physical abuse when a child has bruises, welts, burns, cuts, tears, scrapes or head injuries. The child may have repeated, unexplained injuries, complain of pain, report harsh treatment, show fear of adults, wear clothes to hide injuries, be frequently late or absent, or display withdrawn, anxious behavior or act out, especially if either is a change from usual behavior.
Emotional abuse	Psychologically damaging acts, such as verbal abuse, rejection, ignoring, terrorizing, isolating, or corrupting by parent or caregiver	Suspect emotional abuse when a child is generally unhappy, seldom smiles or laughs, is aggressive or disruptive or unusually shy and withdrawn, reacts without emotion to unpleasant situations, displays behaviors that are unusually adult or childish, exhibits delayed growth or delayed emotional and intellectual development, has low self-esteem, receives belittling or degrading comments from parents or guardians, or fears adults.
Sexual abuse	Any sexual act, such as rape, incest, fondling of the genitals, exhibitionism, or voyeurism, performed with a child by an adult who exerts control over the victim	Suspect sexual abuse when a child has physical indicators such as: difficulty walking or sitting; complaints of pain, itching, swelling of genitals; pain when urinating; vaginal discharge; bruises or bleeding in external genitalia; vagina, or anal areas, mouth, or throat. The child may also have behavioral indicators such as: unwillingness to have clothes changed or assistance with toileting, holding self, unwilling to participate in physical activities, withdrawn or infantile behaviors, unusual interest in or knowledge of sexual matters, or extremely aggressive or disruptive behavior.
Physical and emotional neglect	The failure to provide a child with the common necessities of food, shelter, a safe environment, education, and health care	Suspect neglect when a child is unwashed and wears dirty clothes inadequate for the weather, is left unattended at a young age or left in the care of other children, lacks dental and medical care, is chronically absent, complains of hunger or rummages for food, or lacks safe housing.

Figure 6–1 Definitions, signs, and symptoms of child maltreatment

Source: Adapted from Aronson, S. S. (2002). *Healthy young children: A manual for programs* (pp. 172–174.) Washington, DC: National Association for the Education of Young Children.

community as features of a curriculum. But in formal and informal ways, each community provides a way of life, bits of knowledge, chances for skill development, values and moral education, aesthetic validations, and an array of opportunities that will affect children's perceptions and promote attitudes (Haberman, 1992; Heath, 1983).

Formal and informal learning opportunities are found in various places maintained by the typical community. In terms of Bloom's classic taxonomy (Bloom, Englehart, Furst, Hill, & Krathwohl, 1956; Krathwohl, Bloom, & Masia, 1984), an influential organizational approach to curriculum design—a community's impact on its children—occurs primarily within the cognitive and affective domains. Three community elements with great influence on children are peer groups, entertainment facilities, and religious institutions.

Cognitive Impact.   Each community supplies news and information through publishing, television, and radio outlets that provide children with specific bits of knowledge. Religious centers have definite goals for developing understanding and practice. Recreation areas promote physical skills, exercise, and knowledge about sports and other activities. Libraries are increasingly improving their programs in support of literacy for even the youngest members of the community. Parks, zoos, museums, and theaters all provide information and aesthetic appreciation to benefit the growing child. Community service offices all have informational outlets to promote health, safety, and good parenting practices. These social organizations, religious institutions, and educational outlets interrelate with and expand the home and school curricula to promote skills, knowledge, and attitudes on various subjects. Figure 6–2 illustrates how the three social settings interrelate to develop and reinforce one cognitive area—mathematic ability.

Affective Impact.   In the affective domain, communities and neighborhoods provide children with a sense of security, well-being, and identity. The kinds of protective services available and the attitudes and values modeled by citizens and leaders send children clear messages about community values and concerns. For example, citizens can demonstrate and support fair play in games and sports. By playing fairly and rewarding all players, as opposed to emphasizing and rewarding only winners, sports directors and spectators communicate pride in striving and participating instead of in winning at any cost.

Community services and functions do not, of course, fall easily into categories of formal and informal learning, but they do in differing ways show children the range of human responses—from sensitive and reasonable to greedy and malicious. Lessons emerge as children sense their community at work and at play, when celebrating, and when struggling economically and politically or with natural disasters.

Peer Groups.   As we noted in Chapter 1, peer groups exert a strong influence in any community. **Peer groups** are social in nature and inculcate a curriculum of experience in those involved. Constructively, peer groups provide children's all-important coming-of-age experiences, where children encounter folklore and rituals, experience a sense of belonging, and begin developing competitive skills (Ladd & Pettit, 2002). Peer groups also provide early experience in social interaction and cooperation. Destructively, peer groups may evolve into alienated gangs that commit acts of violence and hostility.

Peer groups are ubiquitous—we find them everywhere clusters of children exist. They begin to form early in children's lives and reach a high point in middle childhood when children have far less contact with adults (Berndt

	HOME	SCHOOL	COMMUNITY
Age 1	Exploring nearby space		
Age 2	Rote counting, comparing objects for size		Sensing larger spaces
Age 3	Contrasting sizes More counting	Nursery rhymes of counting	Rote counting experiences
Age 4	Seriation, placing objects in sequence, acquiring number sense Grasp of time	Distinguishing geometric shapes Determining more and less, basics of addition and subtraction	Applying number sense to the larger world Counting games
Age 5	Ordering objects, grasp of money Sense of measurement in cooking and home projects	Making one-to-one correspondence Grasp of rational numbers Starting to understand time	Noting sizes of larger and less; noting geometric shapes
Age 6	Using knowledge of time; using concept of number in home to calculate	Addition algorithm, subtraction algorithm Measurement study Geometric study	Applying knowledge of money for purchases
Age 7	Application of measurement to projects and hobbies Estimating quantities, distances, etc.	Continuing practice of number facts Estimation problems	Figuring how far to throw a ball Sensing how long to walk to friends' homes
Age 8		Multiplication algorithm	Using math concepts to solve problems in play, etc.

Figure 6–2   Children's math development interrelated in three social settings

& Murphy, 2002; Harris, 1998). A community has a responsibility regarding the formation of peer groups and their assorted actions. Some parents assume responsibility for monitoring, evaluating, and imposing codes of acceptable behavior for the peer groups they encounter (Ladd & Pettit, 2002). This adult influence appears to have a positive effect. Consider the mother's positive monitoring in the following vignette.

Victoria and her mother walked next door to welcome to their southern California community the new family that had just arrived from Hawaii. The two new girls, Terry and Adrianne, came the next day to Victoria's yard to play. They taught Victoria a new version of hopscotch. But while the girls were playing, the neighborhood "gang" appeared and told Terry and Adrianne they had to leave because

Communities provide special events and parents communicate pride in participating instead of winning

"we don't play with Chinese kids." Victoria's mother, witnessing the scene, hurried out to the yard and asked the new neighbors to stay. "All children are welcome in this yard, as long as you play well together. Now, I saw the fun you two had showing Victoria that new hopscotch. Perhaps you'll teach these other children how to play it, too?" The mother tended her shrubs and observed for a while, but as all the children got involved in play, she left them to negotiate on their own.

⁓

Victoria's mother warded off hostility toward the new children in the neighborhood by suggesting and guiding a constructive experience. Teachers in schools as well as family members have a responsibility to monitor and guide children's peer interactions when conflict seems imminent.

Entertainment Facilities. The entertainment industry is a part of the greater community and is probably the most pervasive force in children's lives today (Strasburger & Wilson, 2002). From earliest times, societies have recognized a need for activities that lift spirits and entertain. A thriving community sanctions and supports entertainment for its citizens; few persons would disagree with that objective.

Communities have planned occasions and established recreational facilities that provide for entertainment—sports areas, natural areas, and parks. Also, parades, community fairs, and other celebrations are typical. In addition, an entire private industry has grown up in most communities for the purpose of entertainment on command, day or night. The following are typical entertainment formats that children and young people have ready access to:

- Radio and CDs
- Cable and broadcast television plus films on DVD
- Theaters, cinemas, malls, coffeehouses, and arcades
- Theme parks and sports facilities
- Computer games and Internet linkages.

While much of the entertainment industry's offerings are consonant with typical community endeavors, the time and expense allotted to them can intrude on families' and children's schedules, personal objectives, creativity, schoolwork, and socializing (Gunter & McAleer, 1997; Singer & Singer 2001). The challenge that parents and schools have is that entertainment may be overdone in proportion to other aspects of the home and school curriculum.

When is the community responsibility for expanding or limiting its entertainment opportunities? Communities have legal responsibility to protect children from inappropriate situations but assume little responsibility for children's overexposure to sanctioned entertainment forms (Van Evra, 1998). While the American Academy of Pediatrics officially recommended in 1999 that children under age 2 watch no television at all, responsibility in guiding television viewing at all ages rests primarily with families and primary caregivers; some cannot manage this well. Technology, including Web filters and the V-chip, is being developed to help parents control what comes in and out of the home, and other devices can actually control the time when the television is on and off.

When schools collaborate with parents and community leaders, it is possible to provide guidance to children regarding entertainment when parents need support in monitoring their children's exposure. Chapter 10 presents more information on entertainment guidelines. Some schools, communities, and families have successfully run programs in which children and their parents pledge to watch no television for a week. At the end of the week, sessions are planned to help the participants discuss the experience. The nonprofit organization TV-Turnoff Network provides an array of information and resources to encourage children and adults to watch much less television in order to promote healthier lives and communities. See the Resources section of this chapter for further information.

Religious Institutions.   Another private part of community learning experiences lies with organized religious groups and occurs in mosques, synagogues, churches, and other places of worship and study. The curriculum in religious locations is directed primarily toward participants' spiritual and moral growth but includes academic, philosophical, and theological knowledge, concepts, and interpretations. Many religious institutions also contribute to the larger community as well by sponsoring or providing space for nursery schools, Head Start programs, youth groups, and various other worthwhile endeavors. While endorsed on the whole by the larger community, religious establishments are selective in membership and orientation. In the past, community traditions gave religious institutions formal responsibility for moral training, expecting the inculcation of religious faith and the development in children of moral character and appropriate attitudes and practices. The situation today is much more ambiguous.

No state has statutes requiring religious practice, but all have laws insisting on religious freedom. In spite of mandates to prevent the establishment of a state-sanctioned church, cooperative action between some churches and local schools has resulted in appreciation of different religious practices and also for addressing social issues such as serving at-risk families and stemming violence in communities (American Association of School Administrators, 1986; Benson, 1997). Too often, educators, parents, and community agents are confused about laws regarding religion in and around public schools. All professionals in social and educational practice can benefit by obtaining a copy of the concise joint statement regarding religious practices recently developed by 35 organizations spanning the ideological, religious, and political spectrum (American Civil Liberties Union, 1995).

Linking Responsibilities

All communities have established schools (indeed, are legally required) within their boundaries to develop children's cognitive and affective skills. In recent years, however, increasingly heavy burdens have been placed on schools. Many present-day schools provide two meals per day plus handle before- and after-school care in addition to normal monitoring activity. Schools are assuming a large part of the parenting role. This increased load requires good communication, more understanding, and cooperation from families if the overload taking place in some schools is to be mitigated.

Some skills and attitudes are best enhanced through projects and activities under community sponsorship. We as educators must be alert for collaborations between community agencies and schools that promote children's education and welfare. The following vignette illustrates this point.

❧

Life in the small coastal community was quiet, but Josh and his friends were restless after a month of summer vacation. Returning from the ball field one day, they pedaled their bikes toward home, throwing rubbish from their lunches at poles and fences. They seemed intent on marring their community's quiet roadside beauty. At one lovely spot near the ocean, they noticed a painter setting up his easel and stopped to watch. The painter paused, then asked the boys if they would help him clean up debris near the shoreline so that he could paint the scene without distractions. The boys did, and then stayed to watch the man work. The boys became fascinated with the artist's rendering, and the painter became aware of how little experience these youngsters had in developing a sense of their surroundings.

A few days later, the artist and a colleague invited Josh, his friends, and their parents to their painting studio to talk about their art and its relationship to the world around them. This worked so well that the artists, with the help of a small group of parents, persuaded town officials to budget space and funds to open a modest gallery in the community. Classes in painting and art appreciation are now offered in the gallery, and the artists are helping teachers at the local elementary school to integrate the arts into its curriculum.

❧

No single agency—home, school, or community—felt a need or responsibility for developing the aesthetic senses of Josh and his friends, but an interested citizen was able to establish a link with this responsibility and provide a needed aspect of curriculum for the youth in that community.

NURTURING EDUCATIONAL OPPORTUNITY

At the beginning of the 21st century, we find more conflict regarding education. More ambiguity occurs, and we have more to accomplish with fewer resources. Critics are dissatisfied with children's skill levels and educational outcomes. Intensely involved parents challenge teachers and push for a greater voice in curriculum. Amid continued social turmoil, we have more homeless persons in all areas of the United States, including numerous children (Vissing, 1996), and more struggling family groups who have given up on schools.

Providing and arranging appropriate educational experiences for children require support, dedication, great interest, and commitment. All three social settings are involved in nurturing and supporting educational programs in some fashion, but less-than-uniform support exists throughout the United States.

New challenges reveal perplexing tasks for all who are concerned with American education. Are there ways to address the issues and restore both credibility in educational objectives and a commitment for moving ahead?

One person working alone seems inadequate. Chris Zajac, as recounted in *Among Schoolchildren*, tries hard to meet challenges in her classroom and despairs when one student loses out (Kidder, 1989). In the overall picture, does one individual's effort help that much? The well-focused family is usually successful, but without a follow-up program in school and community, its work can be sabotaged. Even in affluent families, nurturing educational opportunity can be accidental at best (Metz, 1993). Quality schools can do only so much to compensate for children who do not have supportive families. Sustained progress requires a united front.

As Epstein (2001) stated, "Everyone with an interest or investment in children is responsible for producing and maintaining good schools, productive partnerships, and successful students" (p. 563). These interested persons include parents, teachers, and administrators, of course, but also state and district leaders and members of the broader community. Child advocates (Benson, 1997; Children's Defense Fund, 1998; Leach, 1994) note that there is little question: Everyone in contact with children should nurture and support their educational experiences in society. Ideally, parents serve as their own child's advocate (Moriarty & Fine, 2001), but what about children whose parents are unable to assume this role alone? Who will help to determine what a child needs, what resources are available, and how to obtain them? This is where partnerships are essential. Cooperation among institutions in children's lives is required for full nurturance and will offer far better opportunities and more continuity of educational experience for children than will any of the alternatives.

Families and Nurturance

It seems natural for families to nurture and promote education and even seek enhanced opportunity for their offspring. Generations of humans have shown a disposition for nudging youngsters up the educational ladder. Only the most callous or indifferent families deny or prevent children from profitable gains in learning; some do better than others. Research with children involved in a family literacy project (Paratore, 2001) indicates that children who have parents who read to them, help with homework, monitor their performance in school by asking questions of them or their teacher, and who urged them to be on time and to behave courteously and respectfully achieved success in school.

Much has been written of educational opportunity and social class, which indicates that higher socioeconomic status (SES) groups provide and receive, in general, better quality education (Coleman, 1966). However, children who live in poverty or come from **linguistically diverse families** can succeed in school. Researchers involved with the Intergenerational Literacy Project (Paratore, Melzi, & Krol-Sinclair, 1999) noted "For these children, success in school was a complex process, dependent both on the actions of parents and teachers separately, and perhaps most importantly, on their interactions" (p. 107). Evidence exists to show that it is quality of interaction rather than socioeconomic group environment that makes the difference (Benson, 1997; Graue, Weinstein, & Walberg, 1983; Williams, 1997).

Natural Tendency to Nurture. If we accept a broad definition of **nurturance**, most families show evidence of this capability, at least in children's early years. It is almost natural for new parents to foster their child's growth. What parent does not express pleasure at a baby's beginning language? Parents reinforce almost any verbalization. What parent does not take an active interest in a baby's beginning steps or ability to manipulate toys and games? The active overseeing and encouragement of these basics and their deliberate arrangement all speak to the primal and natural nurturing tendencies of family members.

While nothing can replace the nurturing provided by the family, child care providers are assuming this role during the hours they care for young children. As Chapter 5 points out, infants are being cared for outside the home at a rapidly increasing rate. Obviously, the expectations of parents now are that other people will assume part of the responsibility for nurturing their small children. Continuing efforts must be made by parents and communities to ensure that this care is of the highest quality.

Parents and other family members normally show pleasure at later educational gains.

Opportunities for literary accomplishment, artistic endeavors, skill in crafts and sports, and social encounters are normally greeted with enthusiasm. Note that single parents as well as two-parent families are often successful in these endeavors (Anderson, 2003; Fraenkel, 2003). We should point out that affluence is not a guarantee that children will be well nurtured. Metz (1993) described the all too common cases of parental neglect and abuse in some socially prominent and affluent homes.

After children are in school, parental nurturance may be less evident. This is due to confusion about the family responsibility for directing educational experiences and to increased incursions in children's life by school, peers, and entertainment (Garbarino & Bedard, 2001). However, an underlying principle for most families is that the objective of supporting their child's growth and education is paramount. In general, nurturing adults in the family or child care setting share many of the following characteristics:

1. Monitor and provide for children's basic needs.
2. Interact with children in a consistent, kind and pleasant manner.
3. Provide reasonable problems and challenges for children to confront.
4. Model, extend, and enrich language.
5. Highlight successes and support self-esteem.
6. Help children acquire basic skills to function in the home, school, and community.
7. Plan recreational activities, games, and excursions.
8. Model productive work habits and organizing strategies.
9. Provide consistent guidelines and place limits for social behavior.
10. Support and extend aesthetic encounters.

Parents show pleasure in children's accomplishments such as artistic endeavors, skill in crafts and social encounters

Family nurturance and support are evidenced by accepting responsibility for "helping" children to integrate with community and school, whether preschool, Head Start, child care, or elementary school. Parents who learn about the program, assist the teachers as they are able, and attempt to follow regulations (even when they are confusing) are doing their part to support their children's success.

Inadequate Home Nurturance. Some families provide minimal support for their children's education, either through lack of background or uncertainty about how to help. Such families provide the basics of primary care—food, shelter, clothing, and safety—but do not grasp the basics of educational practice

or how learning comes about. **Parent education** (Moriarty & Fine, 2001) and family literacy programs (Paratore, 2001) can make a difference for minimally supportive families. Such programs help parents understand how to become more involved in their children's schooling and community life.

Marginalized families cannot or will not provide even basic family support. This special class of family has extensive need for social intervention and rehabilitation (Wagstaff & Gallagher, 1990). Some rehabilitation has been successful. When schools are able to bring marginalized families into planning sessions and management teams, there is substantial evidence that these families' self-concept and levels of achievement, and the motivations of at-risk children, are raised (Haberman, 1992; Maeroff, 1998).

❧

Peggy left the homeless shelter for the day with her two children, walking to the Head Start community center. She hopes the teachers there will keep her two children while she inquires about a job she'd heard about. She doesn't make it to the center, though, as the distance is far and the children start crying and are too heavy to carry. Dejectedly, she sits on the curb, then spends the rest of the day wandering in the open-air market looking for handouts.

Peggy has no immediate family and just moved to the shelter to get away from her abusive boyfriend. She has a history of moving in and out with her boyfriend, then living for short times with a friend and then her aunt—only to lose these places because of financial problems that lead to quarrels. Peggy has a brief work history, but she lacks the sense of well-being that would give her confidence in her abilities. She does not feel connected to the larger community, and she has little understanding of how her condition might change. The social worker at the shelter got her 3-year-old son enrolled in the community Head Start program. Head Start personnel and the social worker are trying to connect Peggy with the community's educational and child care projects, but Peggy's absenteeism from the projects she starts and the periodic appearance of her belligerent boyfriend make upward progress difficult.

Peggy's situation demonstrates the crying needs of marginalized families in America. The lack of skills, lack of options, and being locked into undesirable situations make progress difficult. Peggy has few connections to a social network for support and has difficulty keeping any commitment she makes and

little knowledge of how to get help. Aspiration is lacking—only the basics appear to be a concern, and those, at times, seem difficult to manage. What will her children become? The nurturance here must be considered minimal and will not change until intensive social reconstruction is arranged.

Schools and Nurturance

All schools provide a curriculum of experience. That is, of course, the main business of schools in the 21st century, as it was in earlier times. But nurturance goes beyond the basic curriculum to include the social and emotional enhancements for children's lives. If the school nurtures, it demonstrates a special concern for individual children, parents, and teachers.

Teachers choose to teach because they wish to facilitate children's educational attainment and growth. Nurturing teachers move beyond academics to find ways to link experience with children's learning styles and interests. We find such teachers in many preschools and primary schools today, although we find practices in some schools that appear to serve teachers more than children. Over 30 years ago, books such as *Death at an Early Age* (Kozol, 1967) and *How Children Fail* (Holt, 1964) detailed the unproductive and non-nurturing dimensions of some schools. Regrettably, while some improvements have been made (Kozol, 2000), many of these situations continue (Brooks, 2003).

Nurturing educational objectives means that teachers not only carefully plan, facilitate, and promote educational opportunity but also provide stimulation. In fact, some school personnel have assumed substitute parental roles in promoting the aspirations of particular children. As noted earlier, schools cannot do this alone. Haberman (1992) pleaded that "special attention must be given to schools that transcend traditional distinctions between learning in and out of school, between schooling as a traditional process limited in time and place to school buildings and education as a life process occurring in a variety of community contexts" (p. 35). A nurturing school displays the following characteristics:

1. It has a broad and up-to-date curriculum related to and guided by a philosophy that teachers and administrators support.

2. It is a welcoming place for children, parents, and others.

3. It thinks of children as individuals rather than as classes or groups.

4. It has a rich source of materials and supplies.

5. It is linked with parents, volunteers, and community agencies.

6. It works to heighten the self-esteem of all involved persons.

7. It provides a safe and healthy environment in which children develop diverse positive values and attitudes.

8. It is organized and serious about its mission.

9. It provides opportunities for children to develop concrete and abstract concepts and to use knowledge as a basis for reasoning.

10. It supports recreational and aesthetic encounters and includes them in its program.

Communities and Nurturance

Community commitment for enhancing children's educational opportunities undergirds family and school endeavors in nurturance. Children who live in an educationally nurturing community are indeed privileged.

In many communities, pride and care for schools are evident to visitors and newcomers. However, a groundswell of support for promoting education does not just happen; it means that committees, groups, and leaders have been active in establishing goals and lobbying for better conditions. We find that the electorate and the community decision makers are almost always motivated to lean over backward to support increased educational opportunities—particularly for young children. A community that is nurturing education is doing many things, including the following:

1. Planning new schools and community recreational centers

2. Producing scholarship money

3. Subsidizing programs in libraries, museums, and galleries for children as well as for adults and senior citizens

4. Supporting bond issues for educational plant and equipment

5. Funding grants for school or community educational experiments

6. Showing interest in participating as a partner in school activities

7. Displaying schoolwork and highlighting children's achievements throughout the community

8. Actively exploring new education programs

9. Supporting all school and club activities (scouting, 4-H, sports groups).

Interestingly enough, community leaders and agencies normally consider the larger context of curriculum when analyzing programs and raising support for schools. Arts programs, as well as sports and recreation, are often heralded first by community agencies, though it may begin with a strong initiative by an individual. This was the case of the artist in the vignette in this chapter. Community members often anticipate better than teachers the outcomes of particular educational projects for promoting healthier attitudes and better opportunities for children.

A nurturing community supports school and club activities

Regrettably, some communities do not facilitate and nurture children's education. Some references in this text portray conditions of despair and social crisis in too many U.S. communities (Coles, 2003; Garbarino, Kostelny, & Dubrow, 1998; Kotlowitz, 1991). Extensive social remediation is needed in all those locations. The community context affects and controls family and school settings to a large extent, and when economic, social, and political crises arise, community problems always detract from school programs and other educational objectives. Controversy often results in minimal nurturing, and too often it prevents the community from making changes that have been initiated in schools and the community at large, for example, after-school activities and recreational opportunities.

GOVERNANCE OF EDUCATION

Governance for educational opportunity is, like nurturance and curriculum, a shared responsibility for the institutions involved with children's welfare. Governance involves the management, coordination, and evaluation of children's educational opportunities, and frequently the factors are summed up by the word *administration*. Legal requirements as well as traditions relate to these responsibilities. While governance in education would seem in today's world to be a basic function of schools, some features of governance devolve to homes and the community setting.

The community at large must be the general overseer for educational practice, opportunity, and development. Direct administration and supervision are assumed by the local community school board.

Legal Requirements

Tradition, to some extent, and the large volume of local, state, and national statutes and regulations, to a major extent, are the means by which the several institutions focus on educational opportunity. All officials and administrators are aware of these requirements.

Most people believe that the United States, from the federal government to the local community, is laden with laws and requirements. In fact, the American legal system is conceptualized on the principle of "minimum restraint to be imposed on individuals to achieve an acceptable level of social orderliness" (O'Reilly & Green, 1992, p. 1). When we view this objectively, we find that U.S. citizens do make most decisions by themselves. This minimum restraint stems from centuries of precedent in Anglo-American social traditions and can be detected today in the way Americans operate businesses, schools, assemblies, and agencies. To protect citizens' rights, freedoms, and traditions to carry on life, pursue dreams, and educate children, legislatures and other authorities have, in general, enacted laws and regulations that permit people to live their lives with the least amount of interference and conflict. We are privileged, since this does not occur in many nations.

Our federal government, with the U.S. Constitution as a guide, has developed a number of significant education-related programs and laws. Head Start, for example, was established as a federally funded educational program for young children at risk for school failure. Public Law 94–142, the Education for All Handicapped Children Act of 1975, and its three later amendments established fundamental education rights for children with disabilities and their parents. The No Child Left Behind Act of 2001 is another recent example

of educational reform beginning at the national level.

The federal government was conceived as a minimal force in education, with the 10th Amendment to the Constitution relegating education (and many other responsibilities) to the individual states. Because of this, federal law is based on selected parts of the Constitution—those that invoke the government's role as protector of individual rights. The U.S. Supreme Court has done likewise in settling educational disputes referred to it. Most education court cases are heard at the state level, but the disputes over desegregation of schools in the 1950s are an important example of Supreme Court involvement in education law.

Legally, then, the bulk of school law comes from state constitutions, statutes, and regulations. These frequently change as a result of the shifting political processes and conditions extant in the United States today (Fuller & Olsen, 1998; O'Reilly & Green, 1992). Examples of state responsibility are to provide free public education to all children, to compel students to attend school, and to maintain the so-called separation of church and state, and to implement federal mandates such as those required by the No Child Left Behind Act. Each state has established a department of education to oversee matters within that state. One appendage of each state education department is the local education agency (LEA), often called the local school board. LEAs serve in individual communities to operate the state-required schools.

Local-Level Decisions.   At the local level, the school board (LEA) operates as an agent for the state but makes its own rules, regulations, and policies, which in turn serve the community involved. LEAs develop budgets, determine policies and oversee the schools in their jurisdiction, and hire administrators and teachers to carry out the day-to-day operation of the schools.

Court Decisions. One other agency involved is the judiciary—the courts. When adjudicating differences of opinion, courts may have much to say about education. Even though courts interpret rather than make laws, it is fair to say they became extensively involved in education matters in the late 20th century (Fuller & Olsen, 1998; Shoop & Dunklee, 1992). Some court decisions have pushed educational requirements in very different directions (Valente & Valente, 2001). Examples involve civil rights and free-speech issues, the so-called separation of church and state, and definitions of unreasonable search and seizure. In addition, claims of sexual and racial harassment connected to schools and communities have increased in recent years as growing awareness and diversity have brought these issues forward.

Home Governance

Various state laws specify parent or guardian responsibilities toward children in their care. These regulations reside in the general welfare statutes and are minimal. The laws are invoked when neglect is an issue and when local authorities or agencies find that families are not providing general safety and support for children in their care (Webb, Metha, & Jordon, 2003). In addition, all states have laws requiring home responsibility for supervising children and making sure they attend school (Valente & Valente, 2001).

The general requirements for home support have come down through the culture and are responsibilities that most families accept without question. It is the family that is in trouble where child maltreatment becomes an issue. If social welfare agencies are alerted by other parents, schools, or public safety officials, they may initiate legal proceedings to remove children. While child maltreatment is the exception to the rule in most families, abuse and neglect of children is a significant social problem in the United States. Neglect continues to be the predominant type of maltreatment, and about 80% of the perpetrators of child maltreatment are parents (Reppucci et al., 1997).

As children mature, home governance practices become more indirect, but laws and traditions still require basic support, parental guidance, and family monitoring through young adulthood. ("Do you know where your children are tonight?").

Other Family Governance. All families informally evaluate their schools, teachers, and communities. Without objective criteria for making these highly subjective and personal assessments, families use whatever they have at hand—their own experiences in school; what they have read, seen, or heard; and their own perceptions of what is right for education. Most schools do not have a process installed whereby outsiders may evaluate personnel, programs, or other school undertakings. As a result, feedback from families regrettably is often overlooked or neglected (de Carvalho, 2001).

While rare, there is provision in some school districts for direct family involvement in public school management and governance. We find family involvement most often in early childhood programs such as Head Start child care center boards and in **parent cooperative nursery schools**. One well-known international program that actively pursues parent involvement at the primary level is the Reggio Emilia plan in Italy (Edwards, Gandini, & Forman, 1998; Hendrick, 1997). A number of schools in the United States are now modeling their programs on this plan, in which parents and others are elected to hold advisory and even directory roles for school programs. (See Chapter 12 for a full description of the Reggio Emilia programs.)

Families are normally disenfranchised in governance of school curriculum, except in the role of follow-up for schoolwork (de Carvalho, 2001) and minor supporting roles as helpers in the school (Cutler, 2000; Henderson, Marburger, & Ooms, 1986). Actually, most families are quite willing for the school hierarchy—school board, administration, teachers, staff, and specialists—to continue with governance of the academic curriculum. The regrettable dimension here is that the close working relations with parents that could come about do not, and a potent resource is overlooked and underused. Schools lose chances to unite community members and develop better programs when they do not seek to involve parents.

School Governance

Schools are a highly visible feature in any society's structure. Although a few citizens in the United States contest the school's viability and purpose, most accept schools as necessary for the proper development of educational opportunity for young children. The Phi Delta Kappa/ Gallup survey (Rose & Gallup, 2003) finds year after year that Americans rate their own local schools highly.

Schools are established for the management, sequencing, and coordination of that formal curriculum we noted earlier, as well as to provide other educational services. In some cases, this responsibility has resulted in bureaucracies with all the trappings of large, multifaceted agencies (see Figure 6–3). Because of the structure and rigidity in many large school systems, some communities in recent years have argued for decentralization and **site-based management** for individual schools. Responsive school situations often result when decentralization is done carefully and with community involvement. The charter school movement (discussed in Chapter 12) is one recent example of decentralizing.

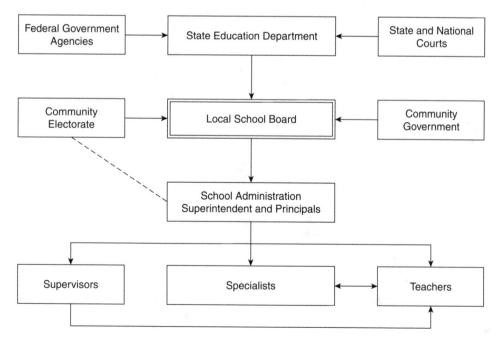

Figure 6–3   Governance of local schools

The preceding notwithstanding, we have probably no alternative to the school bureaucracy for supporting general education for the large numbers of school-age children in our highly technical and work-oriented society. The demands for literacy, scientific understanding, math and social science training, to say nothing of the socializing, recreational, and health needs of children are immense in the United States today. To accomplish this basic formal curriculum, our society needs carefully organized schools for the majority of the population. One has only to note situations where communities experience extended school strikes to see the confusion and exasperation that come with trying to fill in the gaps left by school closings.

As agents for the community school board (the LEA), administrators, and teachers exert the greatest influence and authority over what

happens in a community's schools regarding management and coordination of curriculum, time commitments, and assessments. This underscores the vast responsibilities that devolve to school personnel in all communities.

Community Governance

In theory, all educational governance starts with the community. All states delegate most responsibility to the local community for oversight of public safety, child welfare, and the development and operation of schools. That community may be a small municipality of a few hundred persons in Vermont or a huge metropolitan district like New York City or Dade County, Florida.

Deriving from state mandates, all initiatives in local school governance begin with the community school board (LEA) elected or

Teachers, administrators, and school board members exert the greatest influence over the curriculum

appointed to oversee schools. As noted, the LEA delegates authority for administration and implementation. Monies are raised from community taxes to support school programs the LEA has proposed. The school board's central office hires personnel to carry out these programs, and the board sets general directions for the curriculum and considers program evaluations. To a large extent, board members depend on their superintendent and their principals to give counsel for board actions and to carry out the day-to-day operation of schools. This means that most of the responsibility for operating or managing schools, interpreting curriculum, and conducting assessments is in the hands of school administrators and teachers.

Curriculum content for schools is also supposedly determined by the community served, but only in a general way does a community decide what is to be developed in its school programs. Community citizens most often surrender governance to the school board (whom they have elected) and its administrators, becoming involved in school matters only when a crisis surfaces in the curriculum or in response to political repercussions from nonaccomplishment, such as falling SAT scores.

A community's citizens do evaluate their schools, however. We find that most persons judge school performance by happiness of the children, tangible outcomes such as report cards, the later success of students, and how school is like or unlike what they experienced in their generation. These are valuable criteria and should be held as general guides. With the increased reliance on outcomes of standardized tests mandated by the No Child Left Behind Act, however, schools are being assessed by measures that may not connect with community aspirations for its schools.

Considering the anxiety about school programs in the United States and the burgeoning problems in many school districts, it may well be time for more direct community involvement in school life and governance. Shared decision making, more extensive exchange of information between school and community, and alliance among community representatives would produce more thoroughly understood programs, more successful outcomes, and a more supportive constituency.

IMPLICATIONS FOR PROFESSIONALS

It is important to see the overall responsibility of who speaks for children in our society. As Leach (1994) noted, children are the most subjected minority in our society. They are the weakest, most dependent, and vulnerable persons around us. Yet we do not have assigned advocates, and we assume the persons working with them—families, school professionals, and members of the community—will do the best job of protecting and educating children. We all know that that is sometimes far from true.

As a developing professional, you have an obligation to find the best opportunities for the children you encounter. In order to do this, you must be knowledgeable about the delegation of power, authority, and responsibility for children's lives and know how to initiate action if necessary.

Using the chapter's very general outline as a guide is a start for figuring out "Who is in charge here?" and, more important, "What should be happening for this child?" Once you have done that, you will have an idea of how you can be effective.

SUMMARY AND REVIEW

Many people, agencies, and organizations are responsible for and equipped to educate and protect children. Homes working with schools, which in turn work with communities, result in the best circumstances for enhancing educational opportunities for children and making certain they are receiving adequate care. The three social settings have a shared responsibility for making certain that optimal conditions and arrangements are in place and that model programs are publicized when implemented. Model programs exist today in selected areas (we discuss model programs in Chapter 12).

A curriculum of experience accrues to every child, but children have very different experiences, depending on circumstances in the three social settings. The curriculum is divided into two interactive parts: formal, or academic, and informal, or hidden. Tradition and law impose requirements on homes, schools, and communities to fulfill their share in presenting the curriculum, but overlap, disagreements, and redundancies are not unusual as children move from one setting to another. Education is most productive where strong cooperation and alliances exist among homes, schools, and communities.

The objective observer can see the unique and vital position of the school in any cooperative endeavor. Parents and communities, of course, have a vested interest in the education of their children. Public schools are delegated the responsibility of accepting all entrants, organizing a curriculum, executing that curriculum, and generally steering children through the educational process. Because educators are trained professionals with daily contact with children, they are in a unique position to monitor them in terms of possible maltreatment. Educators can also see the places where involvement from parents and the larger community will help. But if the school as an institution neglects to engender cooperative action among all social institutions, the interests and hopes of parents and communities are difficult to realize.

SUGGESTED ACTIVITIES AND QUESTIONS

1. Consider a new teaching situation in which you must figure out how to build support for several children from families recently arrived in the United States. You know that the families are struggling economically and trying to learn a new language and culture. Even though all three social settings bear responsibility, how can you best enhance educational opportunity for these youngsters?

2. Find a copy of your state's legal codes regarding child maltreatment. Discuss with colleagues your responsibility for reporting suspected abuse and neglect.

3. Construct a chart showing the areas of sex education that you think children normally encounter between ages 3 and 8. Indicate home, school, and community responsibilities at each age level.

4. Visit a local Head Start center and talk to the director and a teacher about the skills and understandings they feel responsible for developing with the children during the current month. Do they feel that the home and community should be involved in these learnings? What do they feel the balance should be?

RESOURCES

Books

1. Conley, D. T. (2003). *Who governs our schools? Changing roles and responsibilities.* New York: Teachers College Press.
2. Epstein, J. L. (2001). *School, family, and community partnerships: Preparing educators and improving schools.* Boulder, CO: Westview.
3. Consult Appendix 1 for a sampling of many useful children's books dealing with family and school situations.

Films and Videos

1. *Make a difference: Report child abuse and neglect* [Video, 28 min]. (1999). Discusses the indicators of abuse/neglect, what to do if maltreatment is suspected, and the impact on society. Washington, DC: National Association for the Education of Young Children.
2. *The role of parents and teachers* [Video, 29 min]. (2001). Examines how parents and teachers help

children develop literacy. Crystal Lake, IL: Magna Systems Video.

Organizations

Child Welfare League
440 First Street, NW Washington, DC 20001
www.cwla.org
National Clearinghouse on Child Abuse and Neglect Information
330 C Street, SW Washington, DC 20447
www.calib.com/nccanch

National Network of Partnership Schools
Johns Hopkins University
3003 N. Charles Street, Suite 200
Baltimore, MD 21218
www.nnps.csos.jhu.edu

TV-Turnoff Network
200 29th Street, NW,
Washington, DC 20007

Websites

1. www.cec.sped.org   The Council for Exceptional Children connects to training, events, professional standards, publications, and the ERIC Clearinghouse on Disabilities and Gifted Education.
2. www.childtrendsdatabank.org   The Child Trends Data Bank provides an extensive amount of information on children's well-being.
3. www.futureofchildren.org   The Future of Children promotes effective policies and programs for children by providing policy makers and service providers with timely, objective information based on the best available research.

Chapter 7

Curriculum of the Home

Every future leader for good or ill starts life with a mother, with a family. This primary experience leaves an imprint that sends ripples into the future of everyone who touches that life.

(Clawson, 1992, p. xix)

The home curriculum is all the experiences that children have while under the direction and influence of their families. And no single **home curriculum**, of course, is like any other.

Though it has always been true, 21st-century America is one of the most diverse nations in the world, with a mix of "cultures, races, old and new immigrants, exceptionalities and talents" (Futrell, Gomex, & Bedden, 2003, p. 381). This cascade effect of influence from the external cultural factors, plus the internal or home factors, becomes the home curriculum and leads children in their perceptions and interpretations of the world (Cloud, Landurand, & Wu, 1989).

In this chapter, the authors give examples of the many experiences children have at home, the implications of these experiences, and the resulting potential for their learning. In reading this chapter, you will learn the following:

1. Parents provide an organizational structure that teaches children their roles and responsibilities in society. The values, attitudes, and emotional qualities that parents exhibit will reinforce this learning.

2. Parental talents, the amount of space and freedom children have in using the home, and the ways families reach out into the community create a foundation for children's learning in the home.

3. The daily routines and rituals, plus traditions, religious practices, parental talents, and the ways families reach out to the community all create a foundation for children's learning in the home.

4. Extended family members—particularly grandparents—affect features in the home curriculum.

5. **Home schooling**, though not a new movement, has had a resurgence in the United States, and many families embrace this trend in assuming responsibility for the education of their children.

The educative processes of all homes are important ingredients for society in the United States, for, as social–cultural–context theorists indicate, how each person develops affects all who relate to that individual. Because of the diversity in U.S. families, we find not one single home curriculum but many variations. Too often, professional educators underestimate the power of the home curriculum and miscalculate the learning that children have acquired outside of school.

Research, over time, indicates that no matter what the ethnic or socioeconomic makeup of the family is, warm and responsive parenting styles, a structured environment, and stimulating activities support children's growth toward a productive lifestyle (Bronfenbrenner, 1979, 1986; Pierce, Alfonso, & Garrison, 1998; Sigel, McGillicuddy-DeLisi, & Goodnow, 1992). Conversely, in some family situations, parental styles and habits mitigate against children's natural pursuit of knowledge and positive development.

All families have an organizational structure that defines family members and their roles. This structure provides physical and emotional support as the child moves into the school and community, where all are expected

to adapt to the prevailing structure of obligations, rights, and labor divisions. The rewards
and punishments in the child's outside envi-
ronment-Bronfenbrenner (1995) labeled it the
mesosystem-are determined largely by the predominant culture (Coontz, 1999).

Whatever their environment, children
learn who they are, how to use the space, and
what kind of world they live in. No matter
what family structure exists, home learning
will be a consequence of family interactions
regarding the use of time and space, routines
of the day, sharing of interests and skills, family rituals, religious practices, traditions, and
family outreach to others.

Contrary to Harris's (1998, 2002) contention that parental influence is minimal, the
authors support the thesis that parents are
children's first and probably most influential
teachers. Further, we contend that despite vast
cultural and economic differences, there are
common elements in all families that educate
children; language is one of these. It is impossible to cover all the learning opportunities
that even one family provides and certainly
not the range of curricula that diverse families
contribute. However, in the following sections,
we illustrate some home activities and interactions that support children's growth and are
crucial to later education. The chapter con-
cludes with an examination of the home
schooling movement in the United States as an
indication that some parents choose to take
full responsibility for educating their children.

LEARNING ROLES
AND RESPONSIBILITIES

In Chapters 3 and 4, we discussed the diversity and functions of U.S. families and defined
a family unit as any two or more persons living together, sharing common goals, resources,
and commitment to each other. Children in
that household will have at least one adult (referred to in this text as a parent) who is re-

sponsible for them. Siblings, who play an important role in any child's learning, also may
be present. Many households have kinship
networks of extended family members and
friends who may or may not be living in the
home but who give added support and nurturance. The teaching in any family situation,
whether direct or indirect, intentional or accidental, will happen in a context and process
where several things are occurring simultane-
ously. In all situations, children's learning depends on their readiness for the tasks and
experiences they encounter, and this includes
child–parent interactions. Figure 7–1 shows
the range of children's learning at home and
the involvement of particular family members.

Parents Foster Roles and Responsibilities

An important part of the home curriculum is
for children to learn family values and ever
changing role expectations for themselves toward other members of the family or neighbors
and friends. Children also learn the role expectations of family members toward each
other and the extended family. All families
have commitments, values, and priorities.
Some of these sentiments are explicit and well
defined, but often many are only implied, and
this is especially true for **marginalized families** (Garbarino & Abramowitz, 1992). Some
family goals are more immediate and are often
expressed as wishes or as "what we are trying
to do." Some families have both long-range
goals and those planned for a limited period of
time. Other families are able only to function
from one day to the next.

Whatever the organizational structure
of the family, children absorb these goals
and their role in accomplishing them. As children grow older and other events happen to
families, such as the birth of a child with exceptionalities, what children learn about themselves can be vastly different and can be quite
contrary to school or the societal expectations

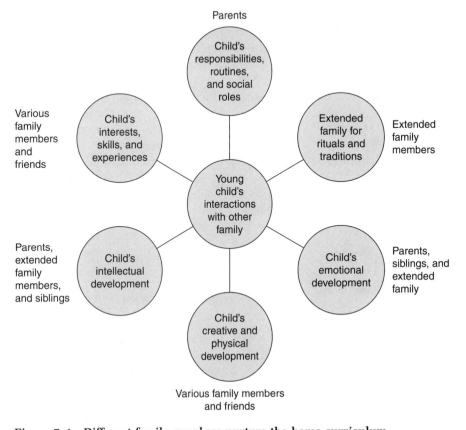

Figure 7–1 Different family members nurture the home curriculum
Note: Foundational skills, concepts, attitudes, and experiences are developed in the child's home environment. Some areas are influenced more strongly by particular family members and the child's peers.

of families. The following two vignettes show two different family approaches, but both are still strongly goal oriented by societal expectations. The third vignette demonstrates how a family adapted its expectations due to the birth of a child with Down syndrome.

☙

Every morning before her children left for school, Mrs. Martinez wished each child a good day in Spanish. In various ways she would remind each of a strongly held family principle: We are an honest and respected family, and what you do is important in main-taining such an honor. She then asked each child to make a small commitment for his or her conduct or learning for the day, frowning on a child who gave the same response each day or copied a sibling's statement. Studying hard, practicing the piano, or getting better at shooting baskets was an accepted goal. At dinner one evening when the family shared accomplishments and worries, José told his family he wasn't going to read with Louie (a child with Down's syndrome in his class) anymore because Louie was "just too hard to deal with." The older brothers and sisters sympathized with José, but they also reminded him of the ways they had read to him when he was little. Mrs. Martinez hugged José hard a few days later when he told her, "I'm going to read with Louie. I found out yesterday he can read lots of words if you start them out and whisper the real hard ones."

In the Martinez family, the mother was a strong and dominant influence. She believed in goal setting and certain family values and made them clear and explicit for her children.

On the other hand, Beth Clawson (1992), 1989 Michigan Mother of the Year, explains how she unconsciously set rules for her family and how important the rules were to the progress of her children.

"Long ago I put a list (titled 'A Cultured Home') on my kitchen bulletin board. It was a reminder to me of some elements that would be valuable in helping children. . . . One day I took it down. Before the day had ended, my children wanted to know why it was taken down. I had not realized that the list was a goal statement to them" (pp. xx–xxi).

Whether goals are stated each day, written down as reminders, or merely implied, notions of having purpose and direction in one's life are modeled and communicated to children. Such strong purposes can help a family adjust and adapt to an unexpected event as the Martinez family experienced.

At the end of José's third grade, Manuela, a child with Down's syndrome, was born. José was thankful for his earlier school experiences with Louie, for they helped him and his family as they weathered the many and dramatic effects of this event. The strong sense of unity in the family allowed them to adjust their lives so that all shared in the responsibilities for this child. José always came home on Tuesdays to help his mother. He was faithful to his task and found pleasure in Manuela as she developed. The following vignette demonstrates how one strong family helped the school to change its

policies while the family helped their child cope with conflicting expectations.

One Tuesday, José's teacher informed the class they would all have to stay after school because of their rowdiness. José, greatly dismayed, tried to explain to her why he couldn't, then walked out of school and went home. His mother was both pleased and dismayed, for she had received a phone call from the principal, telling her about the event. When José explained that he hadn't been rowdy and he couldn't let his mother down, the two of them began to work out plans for communicating their needs to the school personnel. Mrs. Martinez then called the school to make an early-morning appointment with the teacher and principal. At this meeting, many important changes between home and this family began to take shape. It was a step that enabled the teacher and principal to reevaluate how they worked with families' changing needs.

In Nick's family, there were multiple problems that often left Nick in the middle of conflicting situations. The following vignette demonstrates how one teacher resolved her dilemma in the conflict and hopefully helped Nick grow.

There were few routines or regular role expectations in Nick's family, except that the stepfather was to be obeyed. When Lucy, a beautiful child born with multiple disabilities, was 3 years old, Nick's stepfather suddenly decided that Nick had to come home every night to help his mother with Lucy. After a few weeks, Nick became disruptive in school and dropped out of soccer. One day he wrote some unsavory things on the classroom board and refused to respond to his teacher's counsel about the situation. In desperation, the teacher told Nick to stay after and clean the chalkboard. Nick, in a belligerent way, yelled that his father would surely get HER. When the teacher insisted that Nick stay until he talked with her or complied with the "punishment," Nick stayed but resisted cleaning the board, repeating that his stepfather would come to get her. True to his predications, the father arrived, yelling at the teacher. The teacher refused to budge. Looking the man in the eye, she told him to SIT DOWN. With a great deal of patience, the teacher finally got all three to tell their view of the situation. Then resolving the immediate problem, Nick and his father cleaned up the board while the teacher worked out conference times and other help for the family. Toward the end of the year, a proud set of parents brought Lucy to one of Nick's soccer games. Nick happily introduced them all to his teammates.

⟿

Most families have expectations that their children learn responsibilities that members living in the home are expected to undertake. Some of the responsibilities may be explicit, and others implicit. In some families, the responsibilities are fairly consistent with changes being negotiated, but in others they may be haphazard and even confusing to children. They may be communicated in dictatorial fashion, explained reasonably, or expected to be learned through observation. As with José and Nick in the vignettes above, changing family circumstance and changing expectations can affect children's behavior in schools.

At times, home expectations can be in conflict with school expectations. Children can't always express or explain conflicting values. When this happens, children become caught in the middle. In the two previous vignettes, parents were able to handle the situation and seek school support. In other families, negative attitudes can result in poor school and family relationships, and then both parents and schools must struggle. If you are to support the growth of all children in your community center or classroom, you must recognize that children and their families come with different skills and values. It is your responsibility to help them move comfortably into their "new" environment and to seek help and supportive services when needed. José's family was used to working with set rules and could take the leading role in working with the school to meet both sets of expectations. Nick's family knew only one way of handling the situation—a dictatorial manner. Fortunately, the teacher was skilled enough to facilitate the compromise to accommodate both sets of expectations.

Extended Family Fosters Roles and Rituals

In most families, parents garner emotional support from the extended family and in some cases receive economic support as well. Extended family members may live close by and be seen regularly, or they may live at some distance but still have strong ties. The extended family helps to educate children in many ways. Besides teaching about role expectations and hierarchical structures, the extended family helps children absorb the traditions and rituals of the larger group. An interesting example of such learning is told by Oladele (1999) as she explains how her mother, during the daily routines, taught her academics and spirituality and about her African heritage. Her grandparents also influenced and reinforced this learning, beginning with a ritual of listening to her Bible verse recitations.

Celebrations are often a time when children learn about who they are, as extended members share the rituals and customs of their particular culture. Children in bicultural homes often have very different experiences, especially when both sets of the extended family delight in sharing holidays with the nuclear family. Sila, in the vignette that follows, is the child of a European-American father, Dan, and a Turkish mother, Nara, whose own family members are practicing Muslims. Nara is no longer a practicing Muslim, but Sila is introduced to the Muslim faith through visits from extended family members.

~

Seven-year-old Sila is excited about the upcoming holidays since both Easter and Kurban Bayram are being celebrated close together. Greg, her father's brother, will be joining them for Easter week, and as he does every year, will help her dye Easter eggs, take her shopping, and on Easter Sunday will help her hunt for Easter eggs on the church lawn. Sila is only beginning to understand that Easter week is about Christ's crucifixion and has begun to ask questions such as "Why was Jesus killed? Did bad people kill him?" Though her father tries to explain, Sila is anxious for Uncle Greg's answer.

Then, at the end of the month, her mother's sister, Bilge, will join them to celebrate Kurban Bayram. Sila will not wear her new Easter hat or dress during this time, but instead will wear a special head scarf. The family will then go to the Muslim market to buy a lamb and have it killed in some special way, Sila believes, though isn't quite sure how. Last year her Aunt explained why they kept only a small part of the lamb for cooking. She will need to ask about the lamb again this year. Though they have no relatives in the Muslim community in the city, Aunt Bilge and her mother will take her to visit the mosque. She does remember Aunt Bilge telling her that Mohammad was a great prophet in the Muslim faith, as Jesus was in the Christian faith. She wondered if they were friends. She would certainly ask her Aunt Bilge this time.

In some families, both sets of extended family members have equal access to the

nuclear family, then the customs and habits children learn from these members are of equal importance. However, since family structures differ, what children learn from the extended family depends on the influence these relatives have on the nuclear family (Berns, 2001). The extended family expands the home curriculum by sharing its own values and interaction patterns. When both extended family members work out cultural differences and values of the other set, children like Sila will learn how to solve the problems or confusions that arise because of these differences.

Siblings Aid in Role and Gender Identification

When children grow up with other children, they experience changing role patterns not dependent on age. A new baby in a home will alter the roles that family members have. A child with special needs, as in José's and Nick's family, can affect children's school behavior. Nick became belligerent and José less communicative. When teachers (or parents) see behavior change, they need to communicate with families and work to resolve the situation. José's mother contacted the school and received support in resolving the conflict. Nick's father was belligerent, but the classroom teacher helped Nick resolve the different expectations.

When a new baby is born or when older siblings start school or leave home, circumstances within the family change for all members, and a different "curriculum" emerges. An older sibling who has been a playmate may suddenly become bossy after starting school, and younger children must learn new ways of interacting. Older children teach younger siblings "the ways of the world," but what is learned will depend on the younger children's interactions and emotional relationships with the older ones.

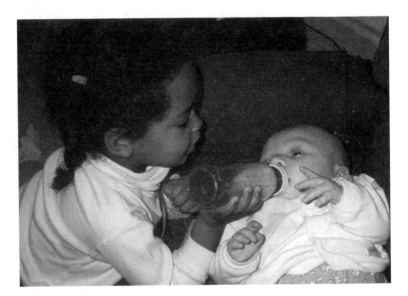

A new baby in a home will alter roles that family members have

The siblings in the following vignette react differently to their older sister, and this difference could partially account for their different rate of learning certain things.

❧

Much to her mother's surprise, Caitlin learned to spell some words when she was but 3 years old. Her older sister Jennifer, returning from second grade, often made Caitlin "her pupil" and insisted she "write her letters," giving her words and letters to do. Brad, closer in age to Jennifer, didn't know letter names until he entered first grade, even though Jennifer at times tried to be his teacher as well. As a baby, Caitlin often called Jennifer her "other" mama and thus apparently was more receptive to her teaching, whereas Brad and Jennifer were closer in age, and Brad resented Jennifer's bossiness.

❧

Academic learning is only part of the curriculum children learn from siblings. For example, children may learn physical skills

faster and at an earlier age by competing with a more skilled family member. Children learn strategies for convincing others of one's point of view as siblings squabble and solve their differences within the family unit. Even learning how to unite in family loyalty against the outside world gives children important social skills—although not always desirable ones.

All families experience changing circumstances that affect what and how children learn. Divorces and remarriages, geographical moves, and changing financial circumstances all put stresses on the family that change behavioral, educational, and emotional learning. The extended family may become more or less involved in a child's life during family changes, and siblings who were close playmates may become more distant. Due to the stress of these new roles, children can become more subdued or combative in school. Academic learning can be severely affected, as may physical and social development.

Children tend to overcome adversity and adapt best to changing circumstances where there has been positive sibling relationships, low conflict, and supportive extended families (Hetherington & Stanley-Hagan, 2002). Harris (1998) maintained that this learning from siblings and peers is even more potent than that from parents.

PHYSICAL ENVIRONMENTS OF THE HOME

Children's learning is greatly influenced by environmental factors. The amount of space, the kinds of materials found in the space, and the ways in which families allow children to use the space all affect what children learn in the home. Successful children from crowded conditions learn a great deal when the family is nurturing and supportive. If children are restricted in their movements or ignored in their environment, no matter the amount of space, learning is lessened. Before children can achieve intellectually, their basic physical and emotional needs have to be met. Clark (1983) found in his study of high and low achievers from poor families that, among other nurturing qualities, high achievers' parents carefully supervised their children's use of time and space.

Space Influences Emotional Growth

Great differences occur in the amount and kind of space that children have in their growing years. Of course, as family situations change, so can the amount of available space. Space can be a factor in the family's ability to support children's physical and mental health. Galle, Gove, and McPherson (1972) reported, from an early study on the amount of space families had per room, that the greater the density, the more the family was subjected to unhealthy conditions and stresses affecting children's development.

Children learn different things about themselves, depending on the amount and quality of space and how the adults respond to these conditions and their children. Hill (1967), in

Evan's Corner, created a poignant story of a child's desire for private space.

ᕤ

Evan lives with his family in a one-room flat. There is little sense of privacy; even the bathroom is shared with other families in the building. Evan longs for a little bit of space he can call his own. With the help of his mother, he clears a corner of the room which he barricades and furnishes with things he cherishes. Evan's sense of well-being is clearly portrayed, as he has the nurturing support of his mother for his own space. However, in the crowded space, Evan also has another lesson to learn. His younger brother wants to come into his space, and it is not without a struggle that Evan learns the joy of choosing to share.

ᕥ

Though not stated explicitly, Evan did learn his family's value of sharing what they had with others, even though theirs was a home with limited privacy.

Space Influences Intellectual Development

When rooms have different functions, children learn categorization skills for where household items belong and where people do different jobs. When families are crowded, rooms may have more than one function, and children learn that the same space is used differently. For example, we visited a crowded one-room apartment where two people were sleeping, another was cooking, and two children were playing on the floor most of the day. There appeared to be very limited adult–child interaction. Across the hall, the same limited space had for another family distinct functions at different times of the day; the room was a living room during the daytime hours, a kitchen and dining room during early morning and evening, and a bedroom at night. With the support of the entire family, household furniture was rearranged accordingly. Lots of discussion (even perhaps argument) ensued about what belonged where. The processing skills of children in these families appeared to be affected by these situations.

In their classroom, two children, one from each of the preceding homes, were asked to put household items into categories and place them in appropriate spaces. The child whose home space was haphazard did a random assignment for the items and had no explanation of why he organized the items that way. In fact, when asked to explain his strategies, he began to rearrange the items. The other child had a definite pattern to his selection of items for each category and a clear reason for putting each item where he did.

Organization of materials within a given space can also be a means of children's developing problem-solving skills.

❧

Three-year-old Jack discovered that the cookie jar could be reached by shoving a chair next to the cupboard and then climbing up. When his mother put the cookie jar onto the refrigerator farther from his reach, he had a new problem to solve. He began some experimentation, first with a chair and then with different-sized boxes. Finally, he discovered that if he piled the boxes one on top of another, he could reach the forbidden cookies.

Such learning is usually not planned by parents. In the preceding situation, the mother was none too pleased with the child's cleverness at the moment she discovered him teetering on the piled-up boxes. Still, when homes are organized so that items for children's use are within easy grasp and other items are stored out of reach for various reasons, curious and determined children will try out their ideas if allowed enough freedom to explore safely.

Children learn concentration skills because of space available to them in the home. Children who have lots of private space and quiet time for activities often develop good study habits. Some of these skills will carry over to school, and these children may have an easy time coping with school. Others will have more difficulty sharing space or engaging in a quiet activity if there are people around them. They have learned to focus on a particular task in quiet and solitude, and a noisy classroom is confusing to them. Still other children learn to concentrate because they have learned to do so in a large family.

Space Influences Physical and Creative Development

Family space isn't necessarily limited to the indoor space. Outdoor space and the freedom to explore it safely will assist children in developing physical skills and creative endeavors.

❧

Although Kenisha always shared a bedroom with her sisters wherever they lived, as the family moved from farm to farm, the family always shared their meal together at the end of the day, no matter how crowded the space. Outside, on most of the farms, there was a large barn and a field where Kenisha and her siblings could play. There were trees nearby and beams in the barn where she and her friends could climb when not expected in the fields. Cardboard boxes, old blankets, boards, nails, and hammers enabled them to create their own fantasy worlds. Kenisha and her siblings made creative use of the strong ropes that the family used to tie up their goods. They tied the ropes to the barn beams and to strong limbs on the trees and then developed skill in climbing and swinging on ropes.

Children thrive in whatever space they live in when adults provide consistent care, nurturing, and support while guiding their behavior and prizing their creations. Children learn important self-concepts as they are supported in their endeavors by being praised for successes and by being helped to overcome frustrations at times of failure. When children do not experience such nurturance, the home curriculum is more limited. In our media-saturated society, we find too many overly committed parents relinquishing a clear view of values that would help their children make wise choices in conflicting situations. Children in the end pay the price for disengaged and confused parents (Hymowitz, 2002).

HOME LEARNING

In Chapter 4, we defined the areas of home responsibility for children's learning as: early socialization skills; language learning; beginning experiments with natural phenomena; interaction and negotiation skills; values and attitudes, including aesthetic appreciation; and health and sex education. It should be clear that the home's responsibility is to develop basic skills for preparing children to function successfully in society. Fulfilling these responsibilities is accomplished to differing degrees.

Ethnographers (Clark, 1983; Heath, 1983; Stinnett & DeFrain, 1986) have found ways in which all families provide home learning experiences. Important skills are taught through daily routines. For example, significant adults transmit the rituals and traditions to the next generation as they share special interests, skills, and aspirations with their children and as they reach into the community to extend their children's learning. Gardner (1999), in *The Disciplined Mind,* discussed the learning absorbed in **peripheral participation**, where the child observes a skilled adult at work and is gradually drawn into the work.

In the many experiences of the home, the impact on children depends to some degree on the child-rearing practices that parents evidence (Baumrind, 1968). In Chapter 4, we explicated the different styles and suggested that the authoritative parent rears children better able to cope in mainstream American society. However, a simple examination of a "successful" child-rearing style does not account for the variations in children's growth toward becoming productive adults. Other qualities and the total ecological processes of family context and interaction patterns determine the competent family (Fine, 1993).

Daily Routines

A broad definition of curriculum includes all the experiences children have from the moment of waking to the moment of falling asleep (Doll, 1995). This implies that the home must provide a great deal of children's learning experiences.

Though modern family lifestyles appear to be hurried or harried because of job requirements, child care, children's sports, and other recreational activities, all families establish some sort of routine, though it varies from day to day. It is during the routine events that children learn to assume certain roles and responsibilities within changing family structures.

When events happen in the home in a timed sequence, children develop a better sense of society's meaning of time. First is the process of getting up and getting ready for school or work. When mealtimes are regular, the second routine involves preparation and a specified mealtime. A further set of routines revolves around bathing and other toileting procedures. The family reuniting at the end of the day is often another routine event. Bedtime is the final routine, as family members prepare for the night. During these daily events, parents support and encourage or

It is during routine events that children learn to assume responsibilities in the home

negate and suppress children's physical, emotional, social, and intellectual development.

Preparing for the Day.   Children who arise, dress, eat breakfast, and then brush their teeth as a routine morning activity establish a pattern whereby they learn through habit about a sequence of events. Parent–child discussion about these events reinforce parental values and attitudes toward the activities, assist in children's language development, assist in children learning a sense of time, and support children's memory and recall. Varying the routines is often necessary in any household. When parents can give explanations or answer children's questions, they often lessen the stress and help children learn to reason, question, and adapt to new situations. Establishing

routine times and expectations for family events gives children a keener sense of time and a view of rules and role expectations. Children develop a sense of well-being and security when limits are clear and deviations to routines are dealt with in a caring and supportive environment.

Even in homeless families, the risk factors diminish for children when the parents are able to maintain some daily routines and rituals and are able to strengthen their positive interaction patterns by playing with their children and caring for their emotional needs (Letiecq, Anderson, & Koblinsky, 1998).

Mealtime.   Mealtime in families offers many educational opportunities. How events are handled determines the amount and type of learning that take place. Two examples will serve to support the idea and suggest the degree of variation in family habits.

&

In Bonita's family, mealtimes had established routines and consistent hours. There were expectations for shared responsibilities and behaviors. On one particular day, Bonita came home from ballet lessons at 5:30 to find her father and brother starting dinner. They asked her to set the table and NO TV, since mother was late and Joe needed to leave for tae kwon do at 7:00 p.m. When mother arrived at 6:00, the family sat down and after a blessing began to eat. When Bonita started to protest that she didn't like peas, her father quietly said, "Don't eat them then, but don't fuss." Joe was going for his red belt that evening, so the family discussed how he was progressing. Then Bonita wanted to choose a word for her word bank. When her father said that the dinner was scrumptious, she wanted to use that word but didn't know how to spell it. Her mother suggested that she get the dictionary and the family would help her find the word and then practice it on the way to Joe's red-belt test. The entire family cleared the table and put the dishes in the sink for later washing.

Though Casey's family was equally supportive, their mealtimes reflected a different ambiance.

&

Casey's father picked her up at child care center and then had to get ready for an evening meeting. On his way home, he had picked up a couple of pizzas. He then engaged Casey in getting plates, and he helped her count the silverware for everyone. Casey read the instructions on the pizza package with her father as they warmed enough for each of them. Casey then went to the den to watch TV while she

ate. Her father watched the news on the small kitchen TV. Her two older brothers arrived home, greeted their father and Casey. They got themselves some pizza, milk, and ice cream, and then sat at the kitchen bar, discussing their soccer practice with each other. Ready for his meeting, the father indicated that their mother would be home soon, so the boys were to help Casey if she needed something. When the mother arrived, she, too, had some pizza, watched some TV with Casey, and reminded the boys about homework.

When it was Casey's bedtime, the mother asked the boys to clean up the counter and then do their homework. Casey, with her mother supervising, followed her routine of getting undressed, brushing her teeth, kissing her brothers goodnight, reading a story with her mother, and then climbing into bed. The mother then went downstairs and supervised her sons' homework while preparing some materials for her own job. The father arrived home from his meeting just in time to share the day's events with them before bedtime.

&

In both families, mealtime is an end-of-the-day event with all family members sharing a meal. However, the purpose of the meal is very different in each family. In Bonita's family, mealtime is not only a time for feeding the family, but also one of sharing responsibilities and learning about each person's day. A special effort is made to keep the family a single unit during that time. Evening events are often also shared by the entire family. There is not much freedom of choice, as adults make most of the decisions.

In Casey's home mealtime is not that significant. The members eat as they come in. But all members are united in greeting each other and assuming responsibilities, usually dictated by one of the adults. No attempt is made to keep the family as a unit. Though adults are definitely in charge, there are more choices and freedom allowed.

The entire process of food preparation and mealtime provides children with many learning opportunities that are available, no matter the circumstances and whenever families share in the process:

- Fine-motor skills are developed as children help in food preparation, such as when cutting up vegetables.
- Quantity measurement is learned as children help to bake cookies or a cake.
- Following along as the adult reads the recipe or the packaged directions develops sequencing skills and other prereading skills.
- Helping to make a grocery list supports writing and spelling skills and language development.
- Observing the change that takes place as liquid gelatin becomes solid in the refrigerator or as runny cake batter becomes a solid mass in the oven provides basic scientific understanding of a change process.
- The kinds and varieties of foods children eat during mealtime communicate the family's values regarding nutrition.
- Preparing or securing meals in a variety of settings extends children's knowledge of how foods are prepared (e.g., in the kitchen, cooking with the microwave, while camping, or when ordering in a deli and watching how the order is processed).

Different parental or sibling involvement in preparation and cleanup after meals teaches children the family attitude toward gender-role responsibilities. In some families, the mother is expected to get meals and clean up afterward, especially if she stays at home caring for the children. In other families, we find a sense of shared responsibility, particularly in homes where the mother works outside the home. A growing sense of maturity and responsibility develops as children assume some of the tasks in the mealtime process.

Bathing and Toileting. Bathing and toileting in some families is a time when children learn attitudes about their bodies and begin sex education.

Stacey, 3 years old, was watching her mother bathing and diapering her 4-month-old brother, Jared. She watched with great fascination as her mother sang and splashed water playfully on the baby's arms and tummy, and she joined in as her mother sang, "This is the way we wash your arms . . ." The final stage of dressing and diapering Jared was a great revelation to Stacey as Jared shot urine into the air. "Whoops, there's one less diaper needed," Mrs. B. exclaimed, and then quickly began to put on a fresh diaper.

Suddenly, Stacey asked, "When will he lose that?"

Her mother replied, "Lose what, Stacey?"

"That!" emphasized Stacey, pointing.

"Oh, his penis," Mrs. B. said. "Why, he won't lose it, Stacey. He's a boy, and boys have penises, and girls have vaginas."

Even as young as 4 months, Jared is beginning to learn about his own body in a positive and enjoyable way. As his mother and sister sing about the parts of his body, he hears terms used in a sensual and pleasing manner. Stacey is beginning to gain new knowledge about basic sexual differences in positive ways as her mother encourages her to be a part of Jared's daily bath time. Stacey's mother answers Stacey's question directly using correct terminology matter of factly.

Lifelong habits and attitudes toward health are developed in the home by the ways parents emphasize cleanliness and proceed with toilet training. Children are naturally great imitators.

They enjoy watching their parents do such mundane and routine actions as washing up, shaving, or powdering themselves, and they will imitate these actions. When such modeling is accompanied by occasional explanations for the action, children learn new language and begin to see relationships among actions.

Family Reuniting at the End of the Day. When the family's routine is such that each member goes off to work or to school, there is often a homecoming routine. The end of the day can be a stressful time, and both positive and negative lessons are learned.

Members of the family are usually tired and hungry and anxious at day's end, particularly when both parents are wage earners or if a single parent must do more in meal preparation or if where one spends the night is uncertain. Often this will be a time when children begin to learn how to cope in difficult situations. When partners argue and disagree, children are often frightened of the anger, and their sense of security is threatened. Nurturing partners resolve their differences and provide models of negotiating behaviors. Partners who lash out, demean each other, or even strike each other are modeling ways to diminish another's self-concept. When parents or partners are able to resolve differences through discussion, apologizing, and coming to agreements, they provide lessons in how to negotiate a peaceful settlement.

Many end-of-the-day routines are pleasant experiences. In some families, children and adults at home share what happened to them during their absence from each other. Even in homeless situations, some parents are better able to cope and share their daily experiences with their children (Lindsey, 1998). In such sharing, children learn important **socialization skills**, such as how to listen, how to take turns talking, and how to explain so that someone else can understand, and, in some instances, they learn the skills of sticking to the topic be-

ing discussed. How much understanding and skill children develop in the routine situations of the home depends on a combination of factors, such as the age and genders of the children, **socioeconomic factors**, the children's interest, the level of previous understanding, and adult–children interactions (Fine, 1993).

Bedtime. As children prepare for bed, one finds many procedures that assist children's development. As in all routines, regularity and consistency help children develop a sense of time and order of events and a sense of security.

Four-year-old Kevin's parents went out for the evening, and Kevin had a new babysitter, whom he appeared to like very much. The sitter played games with him and read him his very favorite stories. At his regular bedtime, she helped him get undressed and brush his teeth. After one last story, she tucked him in, turned out the light, and went downstairs. A little later, she heard Kevin crying and went up to see what was the matter. As she calmed Kevin down, she finally heard him whimper, "I want Mommy. She says my prayers, and you didn't."

Kevin derived a great deal of security from a series of routine bedtime activities. Though he apparently forgot a part of the routine, he sensed something was wrong, and when he remembered, he became upset. Besides attending to Kevin's sense of security, the episode also demonstrates activities, whereby Kevin's parents (or babysitter in their absence) fulfill their educational responsibilities. As Kevin washes and brushes his teeth before retiring, he is learning good health habits. Saying prayers at night or at mealtime can be the beginning of religious training.

Rituals and Traditions

According to Bossard and Boll (1949), family ritual is a formal procedure for defining patterns of behavior. Rituals and traditions are important to any society, for it is by such behaviors that individuals show respect for the value system within a family or clan (Goffman, 1967). Certainly, children learn many social, cognitive, and affective skills that are also learned in other families. Perhaps the most important learnings children gain from rituals are the importance of family structure and the commitment that an individual makes to the solidarity of the group (Levy, 1992). In rituals and traditions, behavior patterns are neither questioned nor examined; the behavior is continued because it is important to the family. As children learn the expected behaviors of the rituals, they learn a sense of identity and self-concept.

Religious ceremonies involve many rituals from which children extend their understanding about the world and their connection to family.

❧

At 9 years of age, Jess observed his second brother's bar mitzvah ceremony. At one point, he leaned toward his grandmother to whisper, "When will he get the shawl?"

"Soon now, just watch," replied his grandmother.

When the moment arrived, Jess's face lighted. "Oh!" he exclaimed. Afterward he asked his mother whether he'd also receive the shawl.

"Certainly, when your turn comes."

"But I'm the only one who hasn't had it!"

"Yes, but that, too, is important, for now you have your two brothers to help you understand our faith."

For Jess, the ritual of the shawl had special meaning. Later, when he was 13, he asked the rabbi if his two brothers could place the

shawl on his shoulders. At the end of the ceremony, he announced to his mother, "There are three of us now, and we're all alike!" The ritual provided Jess with a special connection with his family and religion.

❧

Customs and folklore are often part of rituals and family traditions. Bettelheim (1976) stressed the importance of folklore to children's psychological and emotional development. He maintained that as children hear the old tales, they sense deeper meanings and thus find emotional security and comfort. Such stories serve as moral lessons as well. Oladele (1999) related how the rituals in her family of memorizing Bible verses, singing spirituals, and reading created a sense of connection to her heritage.

In addition to providing emotional or moral support, rituals provide intellectual stimulus. Traditional rhymes, chants, and incantations have a language pattern and a story structure that support **literacy development**. In many families, adults chant or read the rhymes they learned as children, often in the course of playing with children. "This Is the Way the Lady Rides," "One, Two, Buckle My Shoe," or "Shoe the Old Horse" provides rhythms and language patterns that form the foundation of children's developing language. Opie and Opie (1969) pointed out how older children teach younger ones the special games, rituals, and chants of childhood that parents do not attend to. Whether singing traditional songs, writing a letter to Santa Claus, helping count candles on the cake, or learning to read their part for the seder, parents and older siblings are engaging children in literacy events.

Sharing Interests and Skills

The amount of knowledge that parents transmit to their children varies widely from family

When computer enthusiasts involve young children in learning rudimentary computer skills, their children become adept at using computers

to family. The greatest differences in children's special knowledge occur between families who explore their interests together and those who ignore each other. For example, when computer enthusiasts involve their young children in learning rudimentary computer skills, their children often enter kindergarten very adept at using computers. Saul and Newman (1986) pointed out how important parents are in interesting their children in science. When researchers asked winners of Westinghouse's Science Talent Search how they became interested in science, most claimed it was their parents who got them interested.

Families may also share interest in the arts, as the following vignette shows.

When Mrs. Jacobs placed a Seurat print in her third-grade classroom, Roberto explained to the class that Seurat used a special technique called pointillism. He and his artist father had experimented with the technique after a visit to their nearby museum. Roberto had been fascinated with the Seurat paintings, and his dad had extended that interest as the two explored the technique together through art books and in the studio.

Children's curiosity leads them to ask many questions. Parents respond differently, depending on their own interests, knowledge, and style of interaction. Children's learning and continued interest depend greatly on the response they elicit.

Eager adults can turn off children's interest as well as expand it. For example, children may learn different things from the simple question, "Where does the wind come from?" One parent may reply, "Gee, I don't know!" Given that answer too many times, children learn that their questions are not important or that they shouldn't bother trying to find answers. Another parent may respond, "From the east," and point in the direction the wind is now blowing from. If that is the end of the conversation, children may learn where east is, that the wind's origin is east, and that adults know things and you can get information from them. Another parent may expand on this answer by pointing and then adding, "See, you can tell by how the trees are swaying." Children's knowledge is expanded to finding out something about how one determines the direction of the wind. Another parent, whose own knowledge about wind and directionality is limited, may answer, "I'm not sure exactly. Let's see if we can find out." When parents and children together pursue an answer, children learn about the importance of questioning and new ways of knowing.

Besides learning the rules of the game, children learn many academic skills from children's games. For example, a game like Monopoly, Jr., reinforces the skills of following directions, planning strategies, counting, reading pictures, and basic economic concepts.

Watching television together provides opportunities for parents and children to develop a sense of shared enjoyment. Parents who watch programs with their children, in addition to deciding with their children what to watch and discussing the programs afterward, enable their children to extend their knowledge. Children's appreciation of different types of programs, their ability to select an appropriate program, and even their ability to argue for their point of view are all good skills.

Reading to children and listening to children read is the strongest home factor relating to children's reading achievement in school (Adams, 1994; Sulzby & Teale, 2003). When children have favorite stories and parents respond to their requests to read and reread them, children develop an appreciation of language; the sounds and patterns for language are reinforced. When stories and pictures are discussed, children learn much about the framework of stories and how words and text go together (Applebee, 1989).

Gardner (1983, 1999) discussed various intelligences that result because of children's different learning styles. These styles may be innate, but parents also support, reinforce, or even squelch their children's natural learning style by their ways of responding. Linguistically oriented parents tend to teach their children through explanations and expressive use of language. Parents with strong logical–mathematical orientations enjoy math and strategy games and encourage orderly and logical thinking in arriving at solutions. Spatially and kinesthetically oriented parents help their children move through space and use their bodies as they figure out how the world functions. Artistic parents expand their children's knowledge through imagining and creating. Naturalist-oriented parents discriminate among living things and are very sensitive to features of the natural world, such as cloud, rock, and land formations and configurations. These responses not only reflect the parents' orientations but also communicate different ways of knowing.

Children whose parents reinforce their ways of knowing succeed better in school, but when learning styles of home and school are too disparate, children are at a disadvantage. However, teachers who try to understand what and how children have learned at home can create classroom opportunities for supporting and expanding children's skills and knowledge.

As a teacher–researcher, Voss (1993) pointed out how she discovered a student's learning style by visiting his home and watching as his father taught him how to build. Eric could never explain in class how he did something other than by using his hands and saying, "I first did this and then this and then this." No amount of questioning and attempts at expanding his language worked. Expressing himself orally and reading were painful for Eric. Eric enjoyed school only when the class worked on projects, and he spent hours figuring out how something went together. Upon visiting the home and getting to know the parents, Voss discovered that Eric had a special relationship with his father and was allowed to work on the projects his father did as a business or around the house. Eric's father rarely explained what he was doing, but when asked by the child how he was doing something, he would slow down his activity to demonstrate. Realizing how kinesthetically oriented the child was, the teacher was able to adjust the classroom learning to accommodate Eric's way of knowing and to expand his ability in other areas.

Family Outreach

The home curriculum is enriched or limited in the ways families engage in various activities in and out of the home. The amount of learning varies as a result of many factors, including economics and personal preferences. Even though parents living on a limited income can provide their children with many and varied learning opportunities, poverty does have a debilitating effect and reduces family choices and energies for learning opportunities. Extreme poverty limits even more families' ability and energy to interact with their children, often communicating a sense of hopelessness and cynicism (Sugrue, 1999).

Affluent parents have the means to provide a rich array of toys and reading materials in the home. Their children often have their own television sets and computers. These parents arrange trips for their children as well as a variety of entertainment events, cultural activities, and recreational opportunities. Other families can't afford any of these opportunities, but the children learn important coping skills as their parents try to overcome economic deprivation. They learn to develop kinship relations with family and neighbors as they all share material goods, share responsibility for children's safety, and help each other cope in a sometimes hostile environment (Sugrue, 1999). Although poverty is limiting, it does not mean that poor families are not committed to their children's education. We find that many do make wise choices, enriching their children's experiences with appropriate toys, books, family outings, and even scheduled home lessons.

Parental opinions of the importance of different activities and the time they have to commit to their children vary considerably, and commitments change depending on children's ages. For example, in one study regarding parents' involvement with children's reading, art activities, sports, and educational television viewing (National Center for Educational Statistics, 1992), the percentage of parents involved with their children decreased as children entered school and continued to decline as children progressed through third grade. This is understandable as children become more involved with peers. However, in spite of this decline, at the end of third grade, a larger percentage of parents were still involved with their children in sports and games than in any other activity. In all families, parents who find time in their lives to enjoy and engage their children in activities together, whether it be in the home, out for a walk, or on the drive home from work, provide a rich context for their children on which further learning is built (Newman, 1998).

Learning opportunities for children vary not only with parental involvement but also with the way that parents interact with their children during these activities. The vignette in Chapter 1 about Steven's riding lessons demonstrated that curriculum provided by structured lessons is not limited to the skills being taught. In that example, Steven, encouraged by suggestions from his mother, was also learning important social interaction skills with adults.

Two other examples of the family outreach curriculum are toys and games, and travel.

Toys and Games.   The types of toys parents provide reflect the parents' value structure and extend development in different ways.

⌒

On the birth of her daughter Delaney, Mrs. Babbitt bought a complete set of unit blocks. When Delaney was old enough to sit and stack things, Mrs. Babbitt would take out a few blocks for the child to play with. The blocks were always stored on shelves according to their unit size, and gradually Delaney became involved in restoring them to their correct place on the shelf as she expanded her use of the blocks. Over time, other materials were added, such as play animals, toy trucks and cars, pieces of cloth, and paper and crayons for signs. At times, Delaney's father would join her in playing blocks and building towers or complicated structures.

Ashley's father, delighting in his new daughter, bought her a huge toy panda. He would sit on the floor beside the panda holding his infant as he fed her or played with her. As Ashley grew older, the panda became an important source of comfort and a wonderful companion to sit with while hearing a story or watching television. Ashley had many small toys that entertained her, and she punched them, turned them over, and examined them when playing.

*Zena, a staff member at the locally **subsidized child care** center, often took home toys discarded by the center. Zena had an understanding with her apartment neighbors, where all helped and shared responsibilities with one another. Often the toys could be fixed by someone in the group, and the cuddly toys provided a means of comforting a younger child by an older one. One day she brought several sets of playing cards that had been discarded because there were cards missing. At home she and the children made up several games using the numbers and the pictures for games of naming, sorting, matching, and trading. The cards were shared by all the children in the apartment complex.*

⌒

All children experience a curriculum provided through the toys they receive, and all three sets of parents previously described play with their children as they use various types of materials. In selecting blocks as the most important toy for her daughter, Mrs. Babbitt established a highly cognitive curriculum that expanded with Delaney's growth and development. Ashley's father's first gift reflected his wish to provide a warm, cozy support system to be supplemented with random selections of fun toys. Zena provided her children with what she could find but recognized that these toys gave both nurturance and some academic support. All the children are prized and cherished, and their caretakers are teaching important self-concept and academic skills that will help them as they enter school.

Travel.   Most families take trips together, some to the grocery store or to visit local relatives, others on lengthy vacations traveling throughout the United States or abroad. Local trips provide rich learning experiences when parents extend the experience with observations about the scenery and what has changed in the familiar environment or with discussions about

Local trips, even to a nearby playground can provide rich learning experiences for children

what is to be bought, why, and where to find it. Such involvement helps children learn about their natural environment and become keen observers of change. Among other things, they learn the give-and-take of discussion, reasons for doing things, and classification skills. Parents provide valuable emotional support and express values as they demonstrate pleasure in sharing these times with their children.

Ricardo, living in a housing unit in a small community, was the caregiver for his two children and often for other children in the unit. Ricardo would take his charges to help him pick up collectibles along the roadside. He did insist that older children oversee the younger ones as they gathered bottles and cans and brought them back to the truck. Here the children sorted the materials according to amount of refund they would produce, and then counted the number. At times children would find some interesting but "worthless" materials, and if they could justify how they might be

used, they could keep the items. Ricardo would also point out things along the route they drove and as they picked up items. Different birds, new blooms, and interesting rocks were often commented on and sometimes counted.

A more affluent family can provide extended travel. Parents usually make plans, buy travel guides and maps, and make reservations. If travel is to a foreign country, passports are procured and currency is exchanged. The curriculum of such trips is extensive, and the learning depends on how much children are interested in and involved with the plans. Social studies, science, math, language, literature, the arts, cultural differences, social relationships, and problem-solving skills are integrated into such trips. In the following vignette, we find parents without specific cognitive goals in mind for their trip, but through their interactions and involvement, the children had many opportunities to gain new skills and knowledge.

❧

Camping across the country, the Hi family discovered that temperatures varied considerably when they awoke in the morning. Mai Lin never seemed to dress right for the day. She was either too hot or too cold as they hiked or drove. Without saying anything to anyone, she began to solve her problem by sticking her hand out of the tent each morning to "test" the weather. As the trip progressed, she began to get better at sensing what the day's weather would be like and became a much happier traveler. She also learned how to dress by observing her parents and hearing their discussions on what they were going to wear that day. She discovered how to adapt to the abrupt changes in temperatures that sometimes occurred within a few hours as the family traveled through snow in the mountains to a hot desert valley below. In addition to learning about geography and its effect on changes in climate, Mai Lin learned during the trip to figure out how to make herself more comfortable.

❧

When school programs build on children's travel experiences and teachers encourage experimentation in class projects, all children benefit. The following two vignettes portray productive outcomes in a multiage group of children.

❧

Eight-year-old Manny and his classmates were creating a story that included a volcanic eruption. The children interrupted their story to build a pretend volcano in their classroom sandbox. As Manny watched the simulated lava roll down the sides of the "volcano," he shared his experiences of visiting a live volcano in Hawaii. Struggling to explain what he had seen, he remembered a book his teacher had added to the classroom collection that contained pictures of an erupting volcano. Manny's limited explanations of the hot lava, the students'

experiments in building a volcano, and the pictures in the book helped the other students give a more vivid description of an erupting volcano when they continued their story.

At another time, Pablo wanted to share the special rock he had picked up on a trip with Ricardo. When some children started to say that that wasn't a trip, the teacher quickly assured all the children it was indeed. Pablo was able to tell his teacher where he had found the rock, and she recognized that it came from a quartz outcropping in the area. As with Manny, she found a way to bring this rock into a discussion of local geography.

❧

When classroom teachers provide an environment whereby children can share family experiences, usually all children in the classroom benefit.

All families educate their children to some level of functioning in society. Although we have **dysfunctional families** where children's learning is hampered or even distorted, most families provide varied educational opportunities for their children through daily routines and ongoing family activities. The best outcomes occur when families assume their share of responsibility for the education of their children and work with schools and communities to assist in the process. In Chapter 10, we discuss more aspects of family functioning and delineate the characteristics of competent families where positive learning takes place.

GRANDPARENTS PROVIDE A CURRICULUM

In this section the authors present some features of grandparent influence on home curriculum. The selections and examples are chosen from the authors' experiences working with grandparents from varying cultures and from some qualitative research studies (Barbour, Barbour, & Hildebrand, 2001). The

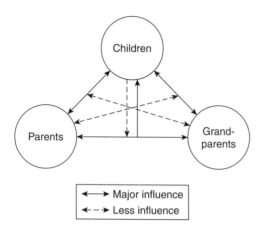

Major influence
Less influence

Figure 7–2   Grandparent connection to nuclear family members
Note: For most families, there is substantial engagement between child and parents, parents and grandparents, and also between child and grandparents. The extent of engagement is related to living arrangements, marital situation and condition, and family history. The diagram assumes a typical nuclear family with grandparents living nearby and no estrangement. Note the lessened influence of grandparents on the parent–child connection and a similar lessened influence of parents on the grandparent–child interaction. Child influence on parent–grandparent interaction is different still.
Sources: Barbour, Barbour, and Hildebrand (2001); Tomlin (1998).

ages of grandparents studied were from 40 to 85, and the ages of the grandchildren were from 3 to 8 years. Only as we observed the children's reactions or later recollections did we make assumptions about the impact of the events. In all the following situations, influences reflect the authors' assumptions that all interactions have a reciprocal affect on another's behavior. No attempt is made to assess the amount of influence in the examples (see Figure 7–2).

Grandparents Influence Children's Development

Like other providers of home curriculum, grandparents' influence on children is di-

verse. Though there has been research for 50 years on this question, the results of each study depends so much on ecological, historical, and cultural variabilities that it is hard to tease out generalizable results (Tomlin, 1998). Age of grandparents, age of grandchildren, geographical differences, relationships of grandparents with the nuclear family, plus factors of family structure and processes have an impact that ranges from minimum to substantial (Berns, 2001). Studies indicate four different categories of grandparenthood: the custodial grandparent, the nearby grandparent, the distant grandparent, and the emotionally remote grandparent.

The custodial grandparent influences the child's development in a manner much the same as a parent, so there is significant influence. The emotionally remote grandparent has little contact with the child, so there is probably little influence. It is the caring and supporting grandparents, living nearby or in a distant area, who keeps close contact with their families, that will have considerable influence on the home curriculum.

Directly or indirectly, grandparents express to their grandchildren a value system and philosophy of how children are to be instructed, whether morally, religiously, culturally, or intellectually. Elizabeth, in the following vignette, is learning two ways of writing and expressing herself because of her grandmothers. Since both grandparents live at some distance, they keep contact with her through letters, e-mail, and telephone calls.

Elizabeth was an active 6-year-old who had discovered the rhythms of language early. Her grandmother Dailey, a former English teacher, firmly believed that children should learn to speak correctly and not use "silly phrases" or "special invented terms." But her grandmother Denato delighted in the "discovered" terms

Elizabeth used and would often repeat the terms, thus reinforcing that language can be created. At Christmas, Elizabeth received a collection of rocks from Grandmother Denato and books from Grandmother Dailey. Her thank you letters to both grandmothers consisted of a drawing of the gift plus a statement. Before sending the letter to Grandmother Dailey, Elizabeth asked her mother about Babar, one of the book characters, and with her mother's help carefully copied on her drawing the words "I liked the elephant book best." On the picture she sent to Grandmother Denato, she wrote by herself, "Rnd redrks spkls lgblk rks wjshin ilvu Dne" ("Round red rocks with sparkles long black rocks which shine. I love you, Donny"—her pet name for her grandmother).

At age 6, Elizabeth has already learned what each grandmother values. In wanting to please each grandmother, she is learning valuable things. For the grandmother who is precise, she learns about story characters, and she has learned to copy a few short words with her mother's help. With her other grandmother, she has learned the fun of playing with words and sounds and is willing to experiment and try out her knowledge of letters and sounds. Elizabeth's mother supports the values of both grandparents by supporting Elizabeth's efforts without judgment.

In some situations, children receive mixed messages concerning their competence, their sense of safety, or the importance of taking risks. David, in the following vignette, receives two different messages about the same situation from his grandparents. Of course, other cultural and sociological factors will determine how he interprets these messages, especially since he sees his grandmother Hu, who lives nearby, more often. Visits to grandmother Williams are each summer for 3 or 4 weeks, plus other holidays.

David Hu, now 4 years old, was born with a partly developed left hand. He has only stubs for fingers, though his thumb appears to be well developed. His father is Chinese and his mother is European American. David, his mother, father, and grandmother Hu are visiting at the summer home of his maternal grandmother in a small seashore community. The grandmothers are supervising David at a summer playgroup program, and he has gone outside to play on the slide. Grandmother Hu immediately goes with him. His grandmother Williams finished her reading with a group of 4-year-olds and followed later. When she arrives David has begun climbing up the front of slide. He is firmly grasping the side of slide. His thumb wraps around the left inside edge. Occasionally he slips, but catches himself. Grandmother Hu is trying to stop him from climbing, but David ignores her. Grandmother Williams speaks to Mrs. Hu rather sharply. "Oh, leave him alone, he's doing a great job."

Mrs. Hu in a shrill voice and rather pleadingly: "But he get hurt" and then points to his left hand.

Mrs. Williams: "We don't know that. Let's just watch and see how he handles it".

David continues to climb two or three times, sliding gleefully down the slide. On his last slide he jerks back, loses his grip, hits his head on the slide, and begins to howl. Both grandparents rush to him and try to comfort him. Suddenly, he breaks away from them both and begins climbing and sliding again. While the two grandmothers argue over his "safety," he happily continues his activity until one of the helpers indicates that the rest of the class is doing an art project. David rushes inside with the other children.

The two grandmothers have different views of how David should be treated. Mrs. Hu feels great responsibility and anxiety about

Grandparents tend to have more fun with their grandchildren than they did with their own children. They can be more relaxed and enjoy the pleasures at hand

his safety and according to Mrs. Williams is overprotective. Mrs. Hu even hovers over him while he is doing his artwork. She is always ready to help him do the project "correctly." Mrs. Williams is happy with a sloppy approach, feeling the art project is uniquely "his."

David is developing his physical skills in a "mixed message" environment. He already knows that he can "do" more around Mrs. Williams and less around Mrs. Hu. He knows Mrs. Hu will protect him more and make sure he doesn't overextend himself. Mrs. Williams will allow him to experiment more, but he is likely to hurt himself more.

Perhaps David will learn a middle course, where he is willing to take risks, but experiment more to test out his skill level before totally plunging in.

Within the framework of "nearby" grandparents and "distant" grandparents, there is much in common regarding potency of influ-

ence. In general, the nearby grandparent has shorter but more frequent contacts, but the distant grandparent's visit involves longer sustained contact, but fewer in number. Grandparents tend to have more fun with their grandchildren than they had time for with their own children, and they tend not to feel as responsible for the well-being of their grandchildren. Cultural differences become blurred when living in the United States, but we often find differences in how families view their kin relationships (Tomlin, 1998). European Americans, though often geographically close, believe in developing independence in their children and grandchildren. They encourage their children to move away, especially for college and work, and to become financially and socially independent. Though there are often "family gatherings," one's social network in European American families tends to include one's own age group. In other cultures, family

Table 7–1   Advantages of a grandparent curriculum

Goals	Activities
Sharing values and adapting to different value systems	Elizabeth's adaptation to cultural influences was on her developing literacy skills, while David's focus was developing physical skills.
Child gaining knowledge from grandparents	The Williamses are sailors, and at age four David was allowed to help steer the boat. Later he learned to sail by himself.
Grandparents learning from grandchildren	Elizabeth's grandmother Denato learned many computer skills from 8-year-old Elizabeth, as Mrs. Denato was learning to use e-mail. David's Grandmother Hu was timid when climbing, and 4-year-old David showed her where to put her feet and where to hold on as they climbed ledges together.
Learning the skills of interaction with older people and grand- parents of different cultures	David learned to speak directly to his grandfather Williams (a bit deaf) by looking him in the eye and "speaking up." With Grandpa Hu he spoke softly and was deferent. As he learned expressions of greeting, politeness, and questioning in both languages, he learned different inflections and different body language for each grandparent.
Understanding the geography and history of family members	Elizabeth's Grandmother Denato frequently traveled and sent post cards to Elizabeth. Later she and her grandmother played games finding these places on maps, recalling who lived where, and who they were.
Understanding the different house- hold tasks and responsibilities	At one grandmother's house, Elizabeth learned that she was to make her bed, take her dishes off the table, and help with the sweeping before play or watching TV. At Grandmother Denato's, her responsibility was to get her grandmother up, and then the two would figure out the day and who would do each task.
Building healthy self-esteem	Elizabeth and David's grandparents both helped build self-esteem, as they praised them, expressed their love, attended their grand- children's sporting events and reward ceremonies, and expressed pride in their grandchild's art, music, or school papers. These grandparents listened to their grandchildren's successes and em- pathized with their struggles. Self-confidence was supported as the grandparents accepted help from the grandchildren, respected their opinions, and reinforced the parents' child-rearing practices.

relationships normally extend into their chil- dren's lives. In the families shown in the vignettes, the children experienced connec- tions to their grandparents through the rituals of their heritage: Chinese New Year, Jewish bar mitzvah, Muslims observation of Ramadan.

Advantages of Grandparent Curriculum

Though they have neither curriculum goals nor activities to achieve them, grandparents do realize that to establish a relationship with a grandchild they need to make an effort to know them as they mature and change. An im- portant aspect of grandparenthood is "having fun with them" or finding satisfaction in their encounters whether one visits a zoo, reads a story, plays games, listens to them, or attends their activities. (Cherlin & Furstenberg, 1992).

Some advantages of grandparent influence are shown in Table 7–1. These examples of specific events are adapted from Strom and

Strom (1997), Cherlin and Furstenberg (1992), and Barbour, Barbour, and Hildebrand (2001).

HOME SCHOOLING

Families that assume total responsibility for their children's education often opt to educate their children at home, at least for part of their schooling years. The term is used to define academic learning that occurs as a result of activities provided in the home (or extensions of the home), with the parents acting as teachers–facilitators.

Home schooling is not a new concept but has gained popularity in recent years, and we find enrollment figures ranging from 850,000 (U.S. Bureau of the Census, 2002) to 2 million (Kochenderfer, Kanna, & Kiyosaki, 2002). Home schooling is a flexible and diverse system of teaching and learning due to the fact that there is no set way to educate children. Just as there are various philosophies guiding curriculum in schools, so parents also approach teaching and learning from a traditional approach to a constructive approach. Because of the tutorlike environment, the home school curriculum, activities are more likely to be geared to children's interests (Kochenderfer et al., 2002; Ray, 2002). The definition is made more clear by Kerman's (1990) description of a typical day of home schooling, summarized here:

Their day starts with the family eating breakfast. Then the 9-year-old daughter leaves with her father for the library, where she will engage in some preplanned library study, and then will carry out some errands for the family. At home, the mother provides unscheduled activities for the two preschoolers that relate to the children's interests, to household needs, and to events that happen in the neighborhood. They read several stories, wash dishes, make play dough, do "dress-up" and dramatic play, and then walk down the road to watch when they notice a fire truck putting out a fire.

History of Home Schooling

Home schooling was the norm for most families during the early years of the republic. In the late 19th and early 20th centuries, with the advent of compulsory education, home schooling diminished. In the late 1970s, John Holt became a strong advocate of home schooling, and parents, disenchanted with their local schools, found support for their efforts in his writings, and especially from his newsletter *Growing Without Schooling* (Gorder, 1996). Since the 1980s, interest in home schooling, driven by differing motivations, has increased dramatically.

Mayberry, Knowles, Ray, and Marlow (1995) contended that in the past 3 decades we can identify four chronological phases for home schooling. The first phase, in the late 1960s was a period of contention, fueled by school reformers such as Jonathan Kozol, John Holt, Herbert Kohl, and Ivan Illich. This reform movement persuaded some parents that "the public school experience would harm their children in some way, or that the parents could provide a superior learning environment" (Knowles, 1989, p. 400).

The second phase, peaking in the 1970s, was marked by confrontations with the courts (Guterson, 1992; Knowles, 1989). School officials, concerned about the quality of education that homes could provide and alarmed by the loss of state funds when children were home schooled, began litigation over parental rights to home school their children. A number of landmark cases in the 1970s and 1980s defined the present guidelines for home schooling and gave parents in all states the right to home school their children (Mayberry et al., 1995). In many states, as litigation costs have risen, educators have become more reluctant to prosecute home schoolers.

Cooperation, which defines the third phase for home schoolers, is a result of changes in attitudes and legal decisions. Most state officials have changed regulations regarding education policies, especially as home school parents become more open in seeking cooperation with local schools.

As more parents select home schooling and schools become more receptive in giving support, the fourth phase is becoming apparent. Increased networking among home schoolers has provided such benefits as organizational support, publications, workshops for parents, and improvement of materials and curriculum programs (Lines, 1995). This demand for publications has become a large industry. Walsh (2002) estimated that Americans spend $700 million per year, or from $400 to $1,200 per student, for these materials. Consolidation of gains in influence and support systems, plus easy access to a variety of material, is now accompanied by greater public acceptance of home schooling as a viable alternative to public education. In some school districts, educators are joining parents in a team effort and allowing children dual enrollment—attending some classes, participating in extracurricular activities, and using schools' special services (Eley, 2002). In other areas, there are organized education centers, and school districts share their special resources and allow students to take what special classes they desire (Deckard, 1996; Duffey, 1998). Schools can also support home schoolers by being sure that notices, announcements of school events, and newsletters are mailed to their homes. Teachers can also keep in touch with home schoolers through telephone calls, e-mails, newsletters, and home visits.

Motives for Home Schooling

The reasons why parents home school their children are probably as varied as the number of parents who have decided on this option. Presently, two distinct groups—the ideologues and the pedagogues—appear in home schooling decisions, and both groups disagree with what is happening in schools today (Gorder, 1996; Kochenderfer et al., 2002). Ideologues disagree with the values and belief systems presented by teachers or by children's peers. Since schools do not permit any religious education, these parents choose to home school so that the family's religious values are what their children learn (Lines, 2001; Reich, 2002).

The growing group of pedagogues, troubled by their perceptions of school curricula, feel their children can receive a more personalized and better education if taught at home. Some parents choose to home school because they fear their children's exposure to problems such as violence, drugs, teenage pregnancy, and disruptive behavior. Others disagree with the instructional and managerial styles of teachers and school administrators. Some are concerned with the inability of teachers to meet all the individual needs, interests, and learning styles of their children and are concerned that school will turn their children off to the excitement of learning (Ray, 2000a; Stevens, 2001). Some had unpleasant experiences in their own schooling and wish to prevent that for their children. Still other parents decide to home school because their children experience difficulty in school, and they find school personnel unresponsive and or even punitive when addressing problems (Gorder, 1996; Jeub, 1994; Ray, 2000b).

Who Does Home Schooling?

Getting accurate statistics on parents who home school is difficult, partially because some parents fear litigation if their practices are revealed. Lines (1991) estimated that 250,000 to 350,000 children in the United States were home schooled at the beginning of the 1990s. Since then, numbers quoted for home schoolers has risen drastically. The 2000 census (Lines, 2001) gave a number of 850,000, but some believe the real number is as high as 2 million and will rise to 5 million by 2010 (Kochenderfer et al., 2002). These estimates are based on information from state departments of education, home school leaders, and curriculum suppliers for home schoolers.

If the reasons for home schooling are varied, the largest number of home schoolers is amazingly alike demographically. The typical home schooling family has two parents, an income near the U.S. median, and is Caucasian and Protestant. Parents tend to have some college education, are professional or skilled workers, and come mostly from rural areas, although some are suburban. Home schoolers appear to be conservative and law abiding but also individualistic and very child centered (Gorder, 1996; Lines, 2001; Stevens, 2001). Most authorities now agree that home schooling has become a forceful social movement, with effective lobbies in state and national government circles (Carper, 2000; Reich, 2002).

Teaching Methods in Home Schooling

Curriculum and methods for home schooling depend on the home, but most methods fall into three categories: **fixed curriculum, units of study**, and **unstructured learning** events (Rupp, 1998; Wade, 1998). The fixed curriculum consists of guides with specific lessons, suggestions on how to teach, and evaluation techniques. This satisfies parents who are unsure of what to teach and who find comfort in a fixed schedule and prescribed curriculum. Some parents, especially those who view home schooling as a temporary solution to their children's educational needs, use the same texts used in the local schools. Correspondence schools, in which some parents enroll their children, meet this need and provide a structure and routine for home schooling.

More and more home schooling parents are using the various resources of the Internet to provide learning opportunities for their children.

Home school organizations, such as Calvert School (Baltimore, MD; *www.jhu.edu-calvert*) and Oak Meadows (Putney, VT; *www.oakmeadow.com*), as well as regular publishing companies, have curriculum guides and suggestions for units of study. In these materials, the teaching and learning is more flexible, and children move through specific units at their own pace and as their interests dictate. Home schoolers themselves encourage others to use various teaching strategies that customize learning for their particular child (The Teaching Home, 2002).

The instructional learning events consist of the things children are interested in, and development of skills takes place as children experience various aspects of adult life. Each child's curriculum will be very different when parents follow this outlook. Parents using the "unschooled method" often write about the many ways they enable their children to be successfully schooled. Some read to their children a great deal and provide a range of quality materials. For these families, books of all sorts, including reference materials, are always available, and computers provide these home schoolers with many more learning opportunities for their children. Access to the Internet for searches on current events or other topics, use of e-mail for communicating with friends or relatives in distant places, and the multitude of computer games are but examples that knowledgeable families use.

Children schooled at home are normally included in all family work activities, such as washing dishes, doing laundry, or building the extra room on the house, as well as family recreational and educational activities, such as visiting libraries and museums. Some families write plays and poems together, and some

Home schooled children
and their parents explore
their natural environment
together

share their musical talents. Math skills are developed as parents involve children in building, using money, and figuring out family finances. Many children and parents explore their natural environment together, learning science concepts as they follow their interests.

As children grow older and their interests expand beyond their parents' expertise, some parents apprentice their children to artists, naturalists, and even sheepherders. One parent said that she had made a list of people she met who had special interests or hobbies so that when her child showed an interest, she found she had resources to draw on (Barker, 1990). Even within a single family, the routine and methods followed by home schoolers will vary from year to year as children develop skills, new interests, and the ability to pursue their own learning. The common element is that children's interests are always paramount, and drill or practice is done at the pace the children set. In most home schooled families,

projects become a major motivating factor, and parents encourage their children's pursuit of such activities (Stevens, 2001). Barfield (2002) in *Real Life Homeschooling*, demonstrated a variety of ways that parents and their children pursue education that better fits the family and their children's interests and needs.

As children grow older, some parents allow them to select whether to continue home schooling or to go to a public school. In some states, home schoolers are permitted to take part in certain school activities and even attend school for specific courses or for a part of the day (Priesnitz, 1990). Some families even alternate between sending their children to school one year and keeping them home the next, depending on which avenue they feel provides the best education (Lines, 2001). The CASA Vida program in Kyrene, Arizona (Eley, 2002), arranges for home schooled children to attend public schools for one day per week.

Legal Aspects of Home Schooling

The laws concerning home schooling vary, and as home schooling has gained momentum, many states are changing statutes. All 50 states have compulsory attendance laws, and home schoolers encounter legal problems depending on how states interpret these laws. Court and state offices use the following four issues in deciding the legality of home schooling:

1. Parental rights of choice regarding their children's welfare
2. Equivalency of education
3. Home schools defined as a viable way to educate children
4. Home schools considered as private, religious, or charter schools
5. Need for qualified teachers.

Specific state laws for each range from a most rigorous approach to parent-friendly support for homeschooling. The National Home Education Network and the National Challenged Homeschools Associates network (an international association that helps in educating children with special needs) are both excellent sources for information on laws and regulations regarding home schooling.

More rigorous states, such as Iowa, New York, and Tennessee, mandate that home schooling must provide an equivalent education to what the public school provides. Determined home schoolers in these states must provide required curriculum outlines and teach the specific courses offered in the schools. Parents are required to show proof of their children's competencies through required tests or by use of portfolios. Tests and portfolios must be evaluated by a certified teacher.

Other states are more supportive of home schoolers and even cooperate with parents in their efforts to provide what they consider the best possible education for their children. For example, Wisconsin, Missouri, and Wyoming

are favorable to home schooling requests. They do require submission of a curriculum plan, but testing, certification, and **proof of equivalency** are not required. More liberal states, like Alaska and North Dakota, maintain that home schooled children do meet the state compulsory attendance law. The remaining states fall between these extremes in terms of their openness to home schooling (Kochenderfer et al., 2002; Lines, 2001).

Criticisms and Successes of Home Schools

As the home schooling movement has grown, some states have registered concern. A California superintendent maintained that in her opinion, home schooling was illegal in California, and she claimed that home schoolers were truants (Leslie, 2003), but many legislators rushed to support parents rights in that case. Some observers maintain that the alarm means that officials are concerned about the loss of tax monies because of lower enrollments and because they view home schooling as strong criticism of public school systems (Stevens, 2001). Publicized successes of some home schoolers can, of course, be taken as a refutation of public education efforts. The following criticisms are often leveled at home schoolers:

1. Children will not develop important socialization skills or be able to function in the real world.
2. Parents do not have the knowledge and skills to teach a broad curriculum.
3. Parents are unable to provide sufficient equipment to study different subjects, especially science.
4. Parents often ignore the drill and practice necessary to acquire basic skills.

Few data have been collected to support or to refute these criticisms of home schooling, but in those states requiring standardized tests, home schoolers on average score 15% above their public school peers (Ray, 2000a). Studies also indicate that no significant relationship exists between home schoolers' achievements and parental education level (Ray, 1997; Stevens, 2001). This appears to counter the argument that parents lack the skills to teach a variety of subjects.

The criticism that home schoolers are not being as well socialized to society is harder to support or refute because we lack studies examining the differences. However, home school parents maintain that their children are being socialized by a greater diversity of people than are children in schools. Home schoolers often interact regularly with children and adults ranging in age from very young children to older persons, whereas children in schools are limited to a classroom of their peers. The limited testing that has been done on the social and psychological development indicates that home schoolers are above average in this area (Lines, 1995; Ray, 2002).

Examining the individual success stories of home schooled children, we find evidence that some home schoolers do well academically and socially when they return to public school, find jobs in the community, or gain acceptance to college (Barfield, 2002; Colfax & Colfax, 1992). But communities and authorities do have an obligation to all children under their jurisdiction, and educators recognize that home schooling is not for all parents or for all children. The reported successes are probably due to parents who wish to be an integral part of their children's learning and are willing to devote the hard work and commitment it requires. Certainly not all parents have the time, inclination, patience, or ability to sustain such nourishment on a long-term basis. We must keep in mind that teachers are key personnel in many phases of children's education, including those children being home schooled. Therefore, communication with homes where children are home schooled is vital. As a teacher, you need to give support and keep communi-

cation lines open. The situation must be analogous to the home–school–community partnership.

IMPLICATIONS FOR PROFESSIONALS

Understanding how rich the home curriculum is, whether through regular routines, family events, or the total home schooling process, will help you assess your own curriculum for children. If you follow this advice, you will be better equipped to extend all children's learning rather than follow a narrow curriculum limited to texts.

As you think of your students, you need to consider how you and your students' families reinforce each other's teaching strategies. For example, consider the vignettes in this chapter:

- The Martinez family reinforced with their own child the school's policy of inclusion of the child with Down syndrome by encouraging him to tutor the child with special needs.
- Manny's teacher was aware of Manny's trip to Hawaii and provided an environment that supported his sharing his experiences.
- A teacher aware of the types of trips children take reinforces children's memories of what they had seen, drawn, and written down on such trips.
- All children can participate when such trips as visiting a relative, going to the grocery store, helping the family clean up the highway, or walking in the woods are valued by the teacher as important learning opportunities.

Careful observation, interested listening, and learning about children's home environments provide you with a base on which to build children's learning and enrich your own curriculum.

SUMMARY AND REVIEW

Children receive a great deal of education outside the classroom walls. Whether intentionally or accidentally, parents provide a rich and varied curriculum in the home. Although great differences appear in quantity and quality of home curricula, all parents, as well as other family members, provide emotional, social, physical, and intellectual stimuli for children's development. Children learn role expectations and responsibilities as the family carries out routines and rituals. Parental interaction styles as well as the physical environment in which children are raised affect children's learning.

Children's home curriculum is an accumulation of all the experiences the children have in their home environment. Thus, each child's curriculum is different, but similarities occur as a result of the daily routines that exist in most families. Both skills and knowledge about the world are acquired as children participate in preparing for the day, meal preparation, and bathing and bedtime rituals. From family traditions and rituals, children gain an understanding of their ethnic and cultural identity and of their place in the world. As parents share their own special interests and talents, children expand their concepts of the world around them.

Extended family members will also provide stimulus for children's development. There is a "grandparent curriculum" that reinforces and supplements—or differs from—the nuclear family practices. The amount of influence depends a great deal on the relationships between the nuclear and extended families and the caring and involvement of grandparents.

Although a small group has always believed in education at home, the home schooling movement has grown rapidly since the 1960s. While numerous reasons are given, most parents choose this route for religious reasons or because of philosophical differences with schools regarding education. Home schooling is not for everybody, and all agree that this process requires lots of hard work and a strong commitment to sustain positive outcomes.

SUGGESTED ACTIVITIES AND QUESTIONS

1. Visit a suburban house and a city apartment and compare the amount of living space. What are some of the things you think children living in each space would learn about themselves? What opportunities for physical development exist in the two homes?

2. Interview two parents and ask about their routines of the day. What learning do you think their children might gain from what they indicated?

3. List the kinds of trips that you took with your family when you were growing up. Include items such as shopping, visiting relatives, and recreation outings, as well as vacation trips. From your memory of the experiences, what do you think you learned (physically, emotionally, socially, and intellectually) from these trips?

4. Check with your state's department of education to find out about the legal aspects for home schooling in your state. Discuss with classmates your feelings about parents who choose this route for their children.

5. Find a fellow student or colleague who was home schooled and discuss with him or her the feelings about the educational experience.

6. Make a list of things you did with your grandparents and share with classmates some of the learning that came from those interactions.

RESOURCES

Books

1. Applebee, A. N. (1996). *Curriculum as conversation.* Chicago: University of Chicago Press.

2. Bigner, J. J. (2002). *Parent and child relations: An Introduction to Parenting.* Upper Saddle River, NJ: Merrill/Prentice Hall.
3. Farenga, P. (2000). *The beginner's guide to home-schooling.* Cambridge, MA: Holt.
4. Thomas, A. (1998). *Educating children at home.* Herndon, VA: Cassell Academic.
5. Wasserman, S. (2001). *The long distance grand-mother* (4th ed.). Point Roberts, WA: Hartley & Marks.

Films and Videos

1. *Growing minds: Cognitive development in early childhood.* (1996). San Luis Obispo, CA: David-son Films.
2. *In our midst: Exploring the long-term impact of neonatal intensive care* [Video, 56 min]. (2002). Examines four families who were saved by neonatal intensive care and its meaning for those families. Boston: Fanlight Productions.
3. *Infant curriculum: Great explorations; Toddler curriculum: Making connections.* [Videos, 20 min each]. (1997). South Carolina Educational Television with National Association for the Education of Young Children.
4. *Nourishing language development in early childhood* [Video, 31 min]. (1998). San Luis Obispo, CA: Davidson Films, with National Association for the Education of Young Children.

Organizations

Family Service Association of America
44 East 23rd Street
New York, NY 10010

Holt Associates/Growing Without Schooling
2380 Massachusetts Ave
Cambridge, MA 02140
www.holtgws.com

National Association for the Education of Young Children
1509 16th Street, NW
Washington, DC 20036
www.naeyc.org
National Homeschool Association
P. O. Box 157290
Cincinnati, OH 45215
www.jayi.com/sbi/aagc/homesch.htm

Websites

1. www.concentric.net/-skiplac
   This Website provides information on home schooling, links to educational sites, and information on multimedia impact on education.
2. www.edexcellence.net
   Education Excellence Network site for promotion of educational reforms: vouchers, charter schools, and privatization.
3. www.ehow.com
   A new Website called eHow, with thousands of files offering step-by-step instructions for all sorts of home tasks and projects.
4. www.nauticom.net/www/cokids/index.html
   This Website is designed for educators but contains a family pages category providing useful material for parents of young children and links to other sites.
5. www.npr.org/programs
   National Public Radio's Website now has a "Library for Kids Online." Books are scanned into the library collection for children who enjoy reading from computer screens.
6. www.zerotothree.org
   An easy-to-use Website on early-learning activities.

Chapter 8

Curriculum of the School

Public schools are intended, at minimum, for a social purpose, to pass on to the next generation values and to generate new ideas that might benefit future generations.

(Meier, 2003, p. 16)

Following the first several years of life with their families and other caregivers, young children enter school, another major institution in their young lives. At this point, a different world emerges for children as well as for parents. This chapter, discusses curriculum experiences in different types of schools and how practices reflect underlying philosophical beliefs. In reading this chapter, you will learn the following:

1. School programs, including many child care facilities, enhance the cognitive and socialization processes that begin in the home and expand into the community.

2. Staffing, administration, and the location of school facilities all affect the atmosphere and the quality of school programs.

3. Some school environments support children's learning and development better than others.

4. Formal public and private schools as well as out-of-home care facilities differ in their programs because educators have differing philosophical orientations and differing work styles.

5. All school programs are enhanced when homes, schools, and communities collaborate and have common and complementary goals for youth.

Since schooling extends the cognitive and socialization processes children have begun with their families, naturally, the relationships between home and school are of major importance for children's growth. In addition to providing skills and content, the school affects children's self-concept, molds aspirations, lays the foundation for community participation and future employment, and provides a good deal of preteen socialization. Schools, where the atmosphere is warm and accepting of all children, are particularly important for integrating and including minority and immigrant at-risk children as well as children with special needs.

The success of children in school is heavily dependent on the relations that exist between home and school. Conflicts over skills and values, differing views about content, or confusion about roles erodes the effectiveness of schoolwork, confuses the objectives that both homes and schools subscribe to, and detracts from children's functioning (Liston & Zeichner, 1996a). Cooperation and compatibility between home and school enable both institutions to provide stability for children and engender progress toward healthy development.

Since schools are more impersonal than homes, children in school are required to function in a different way. Most schools have a distinct chain of command. Rules and regulations abound, and authority figures are seen everywhere. Children are expected to act in a specific way, learning according to time constraints, and teachers are expected to cover the same amount of material (National Education Commission on Time and Learning, 1994). The following vignette dramatizes the situation of a 7-year-old entering a conventional school after being home schooled.

"Jessica, please return to your seat. You shouldn't be wandering out to the hall."

The second grader turned and blurted, "I . . . saw my brother, and he needed some help."

"I understand Jessica, but there is a school rule—no leaving the classroom without permission," Ms. Strong said firmly.

When Jessica was 7, she entered school for the first time. Her mother had rejoined the family lumber business after home schooling Jessica and her 5-year-old brother. Now in second grade, Jessica was just getting used to things that her neighborhood friends had been doing for the past 2 years. "We get lots of books," Margo had said, and that was true, but they were a lot different from the library books and magazines Jessica's mom had used in teaching Jessica. "I really liked the number blocks we used last year," Cicely had mentioned. "I hope we get 'em again." Jessica enjoyed most school activities, but she yearned for the casual pace with her mother. She was reprimanded twice in one day for chatting with two boys in her cluster and then for reading a book from home instead of doing her math assignment. Ms. Strong didn't like to have social conversations going on, and visiting anyone else in class was forbidden. She expected all children to do the task assigned. "Mom, she gives us directions all the time. I can't keep track of the things she says. It's a good thing Harry showed me where to put the date on my spelling paper."

Curriculum for any child involves what happens to the child each day from the time he or she wakes until he or she goes to sleep. For children 5 years old and older, the school will have a significant impact on that total life curriculum. For an increasing number of preschool children (over 60% now), the nursery school and child care experiences affect that life curriculum.

Schooling involves a **formal curriculum** of skills and content, an **informal curriculum** (which starts at home) of habits, practices, and attitudes that all school personnel seek to implement, and a **hidden curriculum** that unfolds in an unintended way but nonetheless

permeates children's consciousness. Each curriculum will be affected by educators' philosophical orientations, which in turn influence the organizational arrangements and patterns we find in individual school buildings and classrooms. The following sections discuss the typical school curriculum and its impact on children.

OVERALL PROGRAM OF THE SCHOOL

In general, schools are seen as places where kids "grow up," learn to interact more skillfully with other children and adults, and assume new responsibilities. However, classrooms are not insulated environments: What goes on inside schools is influenced greatly by what occurs outside of schools on a daily basis (Liston & Zeichner, 1996a). While still nurturers, early childhood and elementary educators play a role different from that of parents; their attitudes, goals, and procedures also are usually quite different. Everyone knows that a teacher's association with a group of students will be short-lived (usually less than a year), and most parents and teachers thus feel that more formality in relationships is normal. Children, of course, must adjust as they move between home and school, from one teacher to another, and from one group of children to others.

In most schools, children find themselves in a rule- and ritual-bound environment. Teachers frequently compare children to one another and regularly evaluate their performance. Jessica, in the preceding vignette, was used to more independence, and it was hard for her to learn the school culture and to operate in a manner where rules and time constraints did not always make sense to her.

Consideration or allowances for what happened prior to a particular grade are no longer relevant in most school situations. It is what you know now, what you look like now, and what is going on now that are important for the agenda of most schools. Children in school are expected to be more conforming and less assertive, to accept responsibility for behaviors and achievement, and to be part of a group that they know little about. For most young children, school is very different than their prior experiences and life is starting over.

During the 20th century, school represented one major link to adulthood, and in recent years school experiences seem even more necessary for children to adjust to a postmodern, technological, and multicultural society. And though success is sometimes limited, school aims and objectives are still focused on preparing children for later roles in a bureaucratic, industrialized, high-tech society. The advantages or disadvantages that children bring to school and the school's ability to adapt to these features will naturally influence their progress in the formal learning environment. In addition, experiences in nursery school, child care, religious programs, summer camp, or libraries will help children make adjustments and transitions more easily.

But what of children in the danger zone— the child in poverty and the disenfranchised child whose home and culture is so very different from the middle-class patterns seen in the schools? It is especially imperative for these at-risk children to have healthy school experiences. Schools that find the necessary resources to assist at-risk children are frequently the only safe, stable, or consistent environments in these children's lives. Numerous accounts show that endangered children linger at their schools as long as possible to avoid neighborhood conflicts and abuse (Garbarino, Dubrow, Kostelny, & Pardo, 1998; Werner & Smith, 2001). The rise in numbers of at-risk children in the United States is sobering—one fifth of our young are in danger (Garbarino, Kostelny, & Dubrow, 1998; Urban Institute, 2002).

The case is clear for dramatically increased collaboration by all human service institutions to produce more inclusive environments and provide better transition experiences between home and school. Educators, communities, and health care providers also need to incorporate services and programs for even the youngest children (birth to age 3) in plans for 21st-century schools. These plans must recognize the strengths and advantages that all families can contribute to society. At the same time, we must find ways to overcome the disadvantages that poverty, nonacceptance, immigration, and very different cultural backgrounds can have on children.

PRESCHOOL AND CHILD CARE PROGRAMS

Before moving to components of formal school programs, we should point out how various programs for 3- and 4-year-olds fit into the overall curriculum picture. As noted in Chapters 4 and 5, over 60% of American preschool-age children are in some type of care facility for at least part of each week. Situations vary from **mother's-day-out programs,** to goal-oriented Montessori preschools, to preschool programs in elementary schools.

Is there a curriculum in these preschool and child care facilities? Most assuredly there is. Some will have a structured scope and sequence chart of particular objectives, and teaching personnel will have philosophical orientations not unlike those noted in the discussion of curriculum orientations in the following section. Others will consider their free-flowing activities as learning experiences and participation. Many out-of-home care programs will resemble in form and substance the at-home experience where, as we maintained in Chapter 7, a curriculum of some sort exists. There will also be that informal and incidental curriculum that undergirds so much of children's later attitude and outlook.

In many programs for 3- and 4-year-olds (Head Start centers, nursery schools, the preschool rooms of large child care centers, and 4-year-old programs in public schools), you will find definite planned activities with expectations identified for the enrolled children. In many ways, these resemble the kindergarten curriculum in regular public schools. One would hope that preschool teaching personnel are considerate of young children's developmental levels and have means for adjusting expectations to the learning styles and backgrounds of individual children (Bredekamp & Rosegrant, 1995; Trawick-Smith, 2003).

CURRICULUM ORIENTATIONS

As an educator, you will develop expectations for children's conduct and accomplishments, and these expectations will reflect your philosophical orientation. Since one character or disposition normally dominates in a particular

school building, we usually find the educators there similar in orientation and outlook. Of course, teachers and administrators attempt to accomplish school expectations using different teaching styles, and frequently it is with varying degrees of success.

We find a number of learning theorists with varying philosophical orientations, and the different perspectives lead them to recommend specific but different school practices (Marsh & Willis, 1999). For this text, the continuum discussed ranges from a traditionalist, teacher-dominated stance at one end to a progressive, child-centered stance at the other. All curriculum orientations focus on developing children's potential, but how to best do that and with what tools define the different perspectives. As shown in Table 8–1, we can section the continuum into several parts and ascribe to each a philosophical base, authorities, significant features, and teacher roles.

Table 8–1   Typical Curriculum Orientations

Labels	Academic rationalism; humanism.	Technologist	Cognitive process; constructivist.	Social meliorist; reconstructionist.	Personal relevance; individual fulfillment.
Philosophical bases	Idealism	Realism	Pragmatism, experimentalism	Experimentalism	Existentialism
Proponents	Adler, Hirsch, Hutchins, Bennett	Bobbitt, Tyler, Hunter, Bloom	Bloom, Bruner, Piaget, Vygotsky, Dewey	Counts Apple, Freire	Rousseau, Neill, Holt
Features	Classic studies; wisdom of the ages; focus on arts.	High order and discipline; back to basics; mastery of here and now.	Learning to learn; experiencing world and accepting changes; problem solving.	Study of world and improving one's surroundings. Social experiences.	Freedom to choose; student assisted in exploring personal learning journey.
Teacher role	Teacher mastery and enthusiasm required; models the ideal; lectures and discusses.	Well-planned and detailed objectives; lectures and demonstrates; interprets and informs.	Develops projects, stimulates study; directs attention to levels of analysis and progress.	Suggests explorations supporting learners; resource person.	Assists learners in explorations; minimal teacher agenda.

Five categories or positions that appear consistently in the literature and are supported by curriculum authorities (Doll, 1995; Eisner, 2002; McNeil, 1996) are academic, technologist, cognitive process, social reconstructionist, and personal relevance. Webb, Metha, and Jordan (2003) noted that all these positions have evolved historically as a protest against some of the prevailing ideas and practices of the times. Table 8–1 provides a summary of these orientations. You will note that borderlines are ambiguous, categories overlap, and authorities use different terms to describe each perspective. Other texts have somewhat different names for these general categories.

In the last decade, scientists have examined vigorously how genetics influences human development. Several studies explain in great detail how genes and environment interact from the moment of conception (Pinker, 2002; Ridley, 2003a). This research advances the notion that learning is not a result of either genetic endowment or environmental experiences, but a combination of factors that affect and produce changes on each other. It also suggests that individuals are unique in their development. We must acknowledge that learning is so person specific that no one set of outcomes can be dictated for a given time period. If American schools are to keep abreast of the changes in the 21st century, then how teachers, parents, and community members (including politicians) interpret high-stakes testing as the means to improve schools is very important (Wagner, 2003).

We describe here a three-section continuum of curriculum orientations condensed from the perspectives in Table 8–1. These three areas represent situations observed in many early-childhood classes today:

1. Traditional—combines aspects of **academic rationalism** and the **technologist**.

2. **Constructivist**—combines aspects of **cognitive process** and **social reconstructionist**.

3. Personal relevance—follows the **personal relevance** orientation for individual exploration.

We find the first two orientations in most U.S. schools today. Though aspects of the third orientation may occur within the first two, curricula based solely on this perspective are found only in a few private or experimental schools and in some home schooling environments.

Traditional

Traditional academic and teacher-dominated programs expect children to be conforming, respectful of authority, and anxious to learn and to look to their teachers for guidance and stimulation. Intellectual growth in "worthy subjects" is the agenda, and programs of this kind will be as structured and efficiently organized as the teacher is capable. Classrooms are replete with **behavioral objectives**, and standardized tests are most often used for assessing because the goal is to develop a particular core of knowledge that all children are expected to attain at a given age.

This orientation is known as **traditional schooling,** and it has held sway for generations. It has become the preferred disposition, since our Congress has recently enacted legislation (No Child Left Behind, for example) that take the traditional position on how children learn. Schools are now held accountable and are ranked as to quality; rankings are based on the results of standardized tests. All of this assumes that states can agree on specific standards and can develop fair tests for all children (Meier, 2002a).

Given the right circumstances—well-focused and humane teachers working with interested and organized children—this traditional didactic curriculum can be extremely successful in promoting basic skills and cultural literacy. The following vignette illustrates a well-functioning traditional classroom.

Traditional programs are replete with behavioral objectives and standardized tests

Ms. Washington is noticeable and vibrant in her second-grade classroom. The room purrs with efficiency, and Ms. Washington covers every part of the room dozens of times each day in maintaining control and helping children. The class has won the PTA banner for 5 months running now, and the 7-year-olds eagerly inform visitors that theirs is the best room.

The class is arranged as three reading and two math groups, using textbooks that Ms. Washington occasionally supplements with her own material. Assignments are neatly and clearly presented on a side chalkboard, which children consult periodically. Every student is busy at 9:15—two groups work quietly on skill sheets while Ms. W. conducts a directed reading activity with the third group. While working with the group, she beckons two children from the seated groups to check their progress. She gives frequent signals to class members in response to their raised hands; her eyes sweep across the class like a lighthouse beam on a recurring pattern.

A change in groups is handled like clockwork. In less than 2 minutes, groups have rotated and are at work once more. Ms. W.'s pleasant voice distributes accolades: "Wonderful work in Jawon's group!" "All papers are completed here, too. Super!"

Ms. W. carefully plans all activities and is ready to go at 9:00 every morning. Even such activities as science projects, which the curriculum guide called for children to do at home, Ms. W. has decided to have at school, where she can monitor and supervise. Her movements are quick and energetic, and the class emulates her.

Ms. Washington is the classic traditional teacher; she has everything down pat. She does all the planning, demonstrating, and guided practice and anticipates almost every problem. "I work hard at what I do, and I get good results," she noted, and this is demonstrated in her students' yearly achievement test scores.

Teachers in traditionally oriented schools think of themselves as in a means-to-an-end situation, as Ms. Washington does. They see themselves working diligently to overcome obstacles—whether ignorance, missing skills, or lack of interest—and devise strategies that will entice learners and build skills to support later education. The curriculum is didactic and teacher centered in nature, focused on structure; such teachers are businesslike, and their can-do aura permeates the traditional classroom.

In keeping with the **industrial model,** contract learning, programmed learning, and mastery learning all fit with this design. Time-on-task studies, goal-analysis plans, scope and sequence charts, critical paths for learning, and management by objectives all fit here very well, too. Since accountability is foremost, **norm-referenced testing** is appropriate. The expectation is development of literacy, computational, scientific, and social skills. The traditional orientation makes for a socially efficient, skills–outcome-based educational system, which is easy to rationalize. A clear goal is in sight, and teachers pursue ways to get there.

No Child Left Behind (NCLB) legislation adheres to this type of curriculum. Standardized tests mark the success or failure of a student's education. In order to graduate from high school, a child must pass selected exams. Since selected skills and knowledge are required for everyone, it is relatively easy to give report cards to the nation regarding the standing of each state's schools.

Traditionalists accept new objectives as they become relevant for contemporary living. Personal living skills, health education, and computer literacy all make sense for primary-school-age children in today's world, so schools with the traditionalist orientation assume responsibility for these areas to produce students tuned to today's needs.

The traditional program has a long line of advocates. Franklin Bobbitt was an early pro-

ponent when, in the early 20th century, he made the case for a curriculum responsive to the time. Since then, advocates such as Benjamin Bloom, Hilda Taba, Ralph Tyler, and Madeline Hunter have propounded the idea. William Bennett, a one-time secretary of education, supports the bases of traditional education, as does John Silber (1989) in his book *Straight Shooting.*

A school with traditional outlook and academic goals does not always have a successful program. Some schools have evolved this way because that is the heritage for the community. Even when a program has questionable objectives for the population served and garners unenthusiastic responses, school boards often perpetuate it. Many low-achieving schools are of this type; they cling to inappropriate goals and teaching methods seen by their communities as irrelevant. Critics of this type of teaching and testing suggest that teaching practices will become subservient to the tests (Meier, 2002b). Teachers are encouraged to find out about the content of tests and then teach to the test. It disallows that the material might be developmentally or culturally inappropriate (Wagner, 2003).

The ongoing popularity of the **traditional curriculum** assures its continued existence, but the lockstep approach seems deadly for some learners. In addition, teacher-centered programs in preschools seem to hold some risk for increasing the later antisocial behavior of disadvantaged children (Schweinhart & Weikart, 1997).

Certainly, the traditionalist plan does not accommodate different learning levels in the flexible way that constructivist and personal relevance orientations do. However, traditional education appeals to many educators working with **marginalized learners**. Because the programs are carefully structured and are developed in steps, dedicated teachers can provide consistency, predictability, and stability for children who would otherwise not find this pattern in their lives.

Constructivist

Constructivist curricula have social efficiency goals similar to the traditional orientation but employ quite different strategies, permitting individualized instruction, and varied content.

Instead of employing the traditionalist emphasis on skill sequence, the constructivist works to develop children's thinking skills. Valuing the process rather than the product, the constructivist's objective is for children to learn how to learn so that they can adapt knowledge and skill to new situations. Teacher behaviors differ from those of the manager–director stance of the traditionalist, but constructivists maintain a strong teacher presence in their classrooms to arbitrate when needed, direct projects, anticipate next steps, and coordinate activities with a general school curriculum.

Rather than use carefully designed **skill ladders, scope and sequence charts**, and behavioral objectives, constructivists favor problem-centered work. **Theme-focused programs**, units of study, project approaches, and similar programs belong in this camp. Since content is often serendipitous and subject to change, teachers with a constructivist orientation must be very secure in knowledge of content and perspectives on child development. They must keep programs relevant to the age levels of students and move the students in the direction of social and cognitive competence.

The constructivist orientation stems from educational theorist Dewey's (1913–1975) writing, and the progressive education movement of the 1930s and 1940s was based here. It is supported by Piagetian and Vygotskian theories of development. In the late 20th century we found the team-teaching, cooperative learning, and **whole-language program** strategies based on constructivism, and in some ways the 21st century findings in brain function research correlates with this orientation (Bruer, 2002; Ridley, 2003b).

Constructivist teacher styles encourage free pupil participation. The school program will be heavily project centered, and teachers think of themselves not as founts of knowledge but as helpers and guides. We do not find a predetermined knowledge base or a set of learnings such as is found in traditional schools; teachers and students enter into investigations and develop or refine skills as they proceed. Curriculum content often focuses on what is interesting and important to children. For example, since social consciousness begins in the primary grades, a focus on environment and care for the earth may be appealing for second- or third-grade children. Constructivist teachers would move in that direction.

Some teachers will retreat to specific tasks at times, and some do have drills and lectures, but group work dominates, and teachers easily move from whole-class to small-group to individual instruction. As in traditional rooms, children in constructivist classrooms are expected to be cooperative, good helpers, willing to share, and anxious to learn. In the following vignette, Mr. Perez conducts his primary program quite differently than what we would find in a traditional classroom.

❧

Mr. Perez's third grade is relaxed. Two large rugs cover most of the floor, and well-worn sofas occupy the center of the room. Mr. P. has no desk at all and uses almost the entire day in conferences with small groups and individuals. Children are at different stages in their writings about people living in their neighborhoods. Mr. P. suggested the activity more than a week ago, and students approached it in different ways—interviewing people, observing folks at home, and just recalling recent events. Youngsters are working this morning all over the room trying to get their final drafts ready for presenting to one of the response groups. Two children are sitting with Mr. P. on one sofa discussing their impressions of the custodian. They read each other's papers and nod. One asks about the word codruy.

"Maybe it's corduroy?" Mr. P. wonders. "That right, Jason?"

"Yup," comes the answer.

"Do you want the dictionary spelling, Tyrone?" Mr. P. smiles. Both say, "Yeah, OK," and Mr. P. spells it for them. "These papers both make good sense to me," he states several minutes later. "Where do you want to go from here?"

Mr. Perez teaches from a constructivist philosophy. He is casual and relaxed and corrects indirectly. All children seem happy with the slightly noisy room, and students seldom interfere with each other's projects. One of Mr. P.'s few rules is that everyone sit on the rug near the end of the day to listen to those who have decided to share their projects. Today, Andrea does not wish any reactions to or comments on the model neighborhood street she is building; she just wants to talk about it. The other presenter, Shana, does ask for comments on her description of the school principal.

Mr. Perez says, "It's easy to get this group to plow ahead on things like this. I think we're keeping up with reading skills, and I know we're way ahead on writing skills. We'll do fine at the end of the year."

Evaluation in constructivist programs is more likely to be **criterion referenced** and to involve teacher-developed instruments. Because a common core of knowledge is not the issue, standardized tests are less relevant. Teachers will favor **holistic evaluation** to determine group progress, and assessment is frequently based on presentations or portfolios (for a thorough discussion of this type of assessment, see Stiggins, 2001; Rinaldi, 1998). In addition, Kyle, McIntyre, Miller, and Moore

(2002) presented a detailed description of how this type of curriculum works.

Programs following a cognitive process orientation can be mishandled, of course, by persons with a limited grasp of curriculum. Generally, constructivist teaching is not undertaken unless personnel are confident about their background, committed to flexibility, and earnest in developing an experimental design. In its true form, it exists in less than 10% of all classrooms in the United States.

Personal Relevance

In the personal relevance, or completely child-centered, program, teachers assume a counseling or resource role. Some would say that the child-centered orientation is rooted in Rousseauian philosophy, but it is more than that. The orientation's basic premise is that children possess natural motivations for learning, and adults help best by making things available, interacting to guide and stimulate, and being supportive. The Summerhill program (Cassebaum, 2003; Neill, 1960) is the prototype for the totally child-centered program. Presently, this orientation is found in a few laboratory schools, some **alternative schools** (the Pathfinder Learning Center in Amherst, Massachusetts, is an example), and a number of preschool programs. Many home schooling situations also are very much of this order.

Responsibility for all educational progress and work is shifted to the student in these liberal programs, and learners must be proactive to make progress. Children must be interested in exploring, setting their own agendas, and working individually. Students are likely to challenge authority and abandon their projects on occasion, and often they come up with very different results. These behaviors can be disconcerting for parents and teachers who have firm ideas about what children should learn.

Since motivation and incentive are expected to rise from within, students with teacher guidance in personal relevance programs determine where, when, and how to go. These learners are often aggressive and highly individualistic, often going on "work binges." Since no published curriculum exists, teachers are responsible for displaying a smorgasbord of materials, ideas, and projects to encourage interests. Children make choices and follow their interests with all that they can muster. Typically, children work by themselves for several weeks exclusively on one study, perhaps of insects, airplanes, or computers.

Some stunning examples of success for the personal relevance orientation are evident when we view programs such as the Sudbury (Vermont) School (Gray & Chanoff, 1984) and those at some alternative schools. Many aspects of the Italian Reggio Emilia programs (see Chapter 12) might be considered personal relevance—type curriculum too. At the same time, we can find situations that are disastrous because students were not oriented to the programs or because teachers lacked commitment to this pattern.

Completely child-centered programs represent a tiny proportion of all school plans because they depend on highly committed staff members with dispositions for guiding and nurturing and require a community favoring this type of education. These conditions are quite foreign to the general American public.

We find combinations and variations for these three curriculum orientations, and different degrees of "purity" exist for all types. How do these orientations relate to marginalized children, inner-city programs, and multiethnic situations? The traditional schooling orientation is based on European American, middle-class values, which do not always make sense to poor and disadvantaged populations. Yet many would argue that the most structured plan allows marginalized children to learn basic skills, which some maintain must be attained before further learning can occur (Doll, 1995).

On the other hand, the project focus of the constructivist orientation, especially when its programs include social investigation and social relevance aspects, seems logical for improving understanding among culturally and ethnically diverse groups. However, we find that such plans are rare in schools for children from such communities. The constructivist orientation requires children to acquire patterns of self-control and to assume responsibility for classroom learning. When children are raised with little or no structure or security in their lives, many teachers find their classroom exploration difficult to manage.

Programs with minimal structure, such as the personal relevance program, which depend on individual incentive, also may be difficult to manage with some at-risk populations. If children lack experiences in work and study habits and if their world is a confusing one, programs based on personal relevance will likely render minimal value even though they are based on the premise that children's needs are foremost. On the other hand, a personal relevance program may work to an advantage in an ethnically diverse community. A positive aspect could develop when children are motivated to learn about **cross-cultural** experiences in order to operate in different cultures. New immigrants might find such a program comfortable also, since these programs are not so time or goal oriented. When schools provide after-school activities and summer programs for at-risk children, conducting a program using a personal relevance curriculum could extend children's enthusiasm for learning.

ORGANIZING SCHOOLS

All schools have their own culture and circumstances. The orientations discussed in this chapter, the student body, the adults who staff programs, the school's physical arrangement, neighborhood priorities and politics, and funding sources all contribute significantly to a school's culture and its characteristics.

Constructivist programs provide greater understanding among cultural, ethnic, and diverse groups

Staffing Plans

Staffing involves administrators, teaching personnel of all types (regular teachers, specialists, aides, and volunteers), and the service personnel (secretaries, nurses, custodians, food service personnel, bus drivers, social workers, school psychologists, and others) who come to school each day. All individuals affect the school program, and the character a school possesses comes largely from the personalities, attitudes, and styles of the people who work there.

Administration. Principals and, to a lesser extent, supervisors set the programmatic, social, and emotional tone for schools with which they are associated. We find several administrative styles commonly observed in U.S. schools.

Businesslike administrators who place a premium on efficiency, organization, and dis-

cipline inject those qualities into a school building's life. This style fits well for the school with a technologist or academic orientation. Managed with skill and tenacity, these schools show a no-nonsense air of business and urgency. While not always the most friendly or open communities, they are predictable, clean, and usually efficient. Rules and regulations are in evidence, things happen on time, all people know what is expected, and most feel secure. There are no surprises. It is the industrial model brought to school. Opinions vary on the appropriateness of the business or bureaucratic model. Many teachers, parents, and students enjoy the comfort of the organization, discipline, and high expectations. Others do not enjoy it, labeling the program as patronizing, stifling of creativity, and not conducive for teachers exercising professional judgment or for students learning decision-making skills.

Inner-city schools with the right mix of personnel have often followed the businesslike style profitably. The combination of rigorous discipline and personal power and charismatic enthusiasm has produced highly touted success stories, such as those of Joe Clark at Eastside High in Patterson, New Jersey, in the late 1980s, and more recently Thaddeus Lott's work at Wesley School in Texas (Brouillette, 2002). Other schools are run on a more democratic, less stringent, basis. Democracy is the objective in many schools, and one finds a partnership tone and an agenda for cooperative action. Principals in these buildings are normally exuberant and accepting, and people thrive in their own way. Naturally, the characteristics of these schools are considerable movement, activities that are encouraged (and that can bring about a high noise level), lots of experimentation, and even friction. The school is the playground energy and spirit brought indoors.

Many people find the less directive stance and the accepting tone of the democratic administrative position to be conducive to working at one's pace and own agenda. Teachers with charisma, dramatic flair, and outgoing personalities find this climate suitable; they can do what they enjoy doing, and incursions on their turf are not demands but collaborations. On the other hand, low-key persons often will not respond to this type of school atmosphere. They feel lost in the busy shuffle and cannot tolerate the high energy levels, noise, or distractions. However, a democratic principal, who should be a quiet consensus builder, will take time to nurture, listen, and build support for programs and policies. Many of these consensus-seeking persons are highly valued in many American communities. For example, Mr. Rider made all persons entering School 6 in Baltimore feel welcomed and valued. He arrived early in the morning and spent the hour before classes complimenting custodians, welcoming faculty, and asking children how the day was starting. This value produced an emotional environment that supported the esteem of all persons associated with the school.

Another good example is Mr. Irons, who has been at Farragut Elementary School in St. Louis for 30 years and has helped teachers and community members form strong intergenerational bonds. He built on the historically stabilizing effect of the segregated schools where African American communities claimed ownership of the black schools. He belongs to the community and is a part of the culture. His caring manner serves as a model for his staff and for community members. Students in the school have one of the highest attendance rates in St. Louis and consistently outperform other city students on standardized tests (Morris, 2002).

Children always sense the administrative tenor in buildings and adapt to it. They know what they can expect of principals and how far they can go in approaching them. This is all part of the informal curriculum discussed later in this chapter.

In the final analysis, it is the public served that determines the patterns and style for a school. A community gradually asserts its wishes for an organizational plan and a climate that fit it best. Administrators must accommodate the community served if programs are to go forward.

Teachers. In keeping with administrative styles, teachers bring a presence to schools. Much of the teacher's style is a function of their philosophical orientation or belief about how children learn and how schools should work. Just as there are parenting styles (refer to Chapter 4), we find comparable teaching styles, which are merged with personal outlooks and ways of presenting. In general, these form a four-part grid on two axes (Table 8–2): warmth (responsive vs. nonresponsive) and control (demanding vs. undemanding). Note that categories in Table 8–2 are similar to Baumrind's (1968) categories for parenting. In the following vignette, the teacher's style works well in her school, where teachers

Table 8–2   Matrix of Different Teaching Styles

	Responsive	Nonresponsive
Demanding manner	Businesslike teacher: demanding but responsive	Autocratic teacher: demanding and nonresponsive
Undemanding manner	Permissive teacher: undemanding but responsive	Indifferent teacher: undemanding and nonresponsive

Source: Adapted from Cruickshank (1990); Good and Brophy (1986); Joyce and Weil (1996).

collaborate in a team spirit to ensure inclusion of students with disabilities.

❧

Mrs. Larkin is seated in her multiage primary classroom with children who are sharing their morning work before heading for their gym activity. Eric, a child with special needs and an abusive family background, enters the room accompanied by Mrs. Stanford, his counselor, who nods to Mrs. Larkin and then leaves. "Good morning, Eric. We're ready for gym. You're just in time," says Mrs. Larkin. Eric doesn't respond, but walks behind the circle to the class folders and picks up his folder. Then he bops the child nearest him on the head. Mrs. Larkin says quietly but firmly, "Eric, that is not acceptable. Sit at your table there and work on your folder. I'm sorry, but you'll need to miss part of gym class." Eric responds by sitting and opening his folder. From time to time he looks at Mrs. Larkin, who sort of smiles but gently shakes her head.

After 5 minutes, the class lines up to wait for the gym instructor. As the instructor appears at the door, he looks questioningly at Mrs. Larkin and at a seated Eric. "Yes, Eric will be a bit late for class. I'll bring him shortly." As the class leaves, Eric's counselor returns and says she'll take Eric to gym. "He did so well with me this morning." Yesterday had been a difficult day, and the two had struck a deal about Eric's behavior and rewards for the next day. As Mrs. Larkin explains the new

situation to Mrs. Stanford, she says to Eric, "I was so pleased to see you come in and go right to your folder, but I'm sorry you weren't able to do the next step. But since your day has been so good otherwise and since you have worked well for these past 5 minutes, I think Mrs. Stanford will agree that you may go to gym." Eric's face lights up, and he hurries to put his folder back.

Eric is a child with attention deficit–hyperactivity disorder, and his individualized education plan provides for an increasing length of time in the regular classroom. Though his teachers dislike keeping children from needed physical activity, it is the one thing they have found that Eric considers worth "behaving" for. Though other strategies are used and though Eric's teachers all have somewhat different styles, they all agree on certain rules and procedures that Eric is expected to follow. With warmth but firmness, they consistently maintain this emotional environment. The other children in the classroom are friendly with one another and with Eric.

Though Eric has some difficult days, improvement is growing in how he manages his behavior. At the beginning of the year, Eric spent most of his time with the counselor and a special-needs instructor. He now receives over half of his instruction in the regular classroom setting with other students and participates in special activities with his classmates.

❧

The demanding but responsive teacher, similar to the authoritative parent, is normally popular because this person pursues plans aggressively but in a humane and friendly fashion. Mrs. Larkin, in the preceding vignette, exemplifies this style. The style coordinates well with all curriculum orientations except personal relevance, where an undemanding but responsive teacher is more likely valued. The demanding and nonresponsive, or authoritarian, style can exist in traditional programs but seems out of place in constructivist programs, where human dynamics play such an important part. The undemanding and nonresponsive profile produces an indifferent demeanor, which has little chance of succeeding in any program.

Teaching styles relate to all levels of teaching, since volunteers, aides, and specialists all project a teaching style. Various styles can be successful in different venues, and teachers are aware of this; however, all must be able to match children's learning modalities with different circumstances and different materials (Dunn, 1999; Dunn & Frazier, 1990). Good and Brophy (1996) stated that "different situations and goals call for different methods [and] a given method may have different effects on different students" (p. 375).

Service Personnel.
While teaching and administrative staff dominate the adult interaction time with schoolchildren, other members of the school community do project social and emotional qualities. Custodians, nurses, lunchroom workers, and secretaries all play a part in a school atmosphere. While teaching style is not an issue, the responsiveness that these adults show toward children and the manner in which they cooperate with teachers add to or detract from the overall school environment.

Service personnel are important in communicating and maintaining the climate of the school. A kind custodian who keeps the building clean and yet welcomes a confused parent creates a positive effect on the parent. A secretary who ignores parents entering the office can terrify newly arrived, inexperienced, or culturally different parents. A confused or fearful parent will leave with a distaste for schools and may well become one of the "difficult to reach" parents.

Volunteers. Partnerships for education means that parents and interested community members will be in schools in various capacities. See Chapter 12 for Epstein's six levels of parent involvement. They, too, are important in helping create a caring and positive learning atmosphere for children.

These volunteers will also have different styles and ways of interacting, just as teachers do. However, volunteers may be less aware of how their behavior is affecting children. As children become more comfortable interacting with different adults, they grow in their ability to communicate in different ways. Volunteers offer a wide range of talents and resources to teachers as they develop and carry out the curriculum. Adults attending school events hopefully model the desired behavior at these events, reaching out and praising different student efforts. These interactions often help to increase children's self-concept and pride of accomplishment.

When adult volunteers and teachers work together amicably, children discover how teamwork results in greater opportunities for learning. It is important for teachers to reinforce this adult involvement. At the end of a very successful unit of study, one teacher invited the aides, the volunteers, and the children to share their learning. She listed the activities they had done and what they had accomplished. The teacher exclaimed at the end, "Wow, look at all that has been done! I couldn't have done it alone." Some teachers, at meetings or elsewhere when they meet the volunteers, take a moment to share with them individual anecdotes of ways children have responded to their help.

A series of meetings or workshops help teachers and adults to find mutual satisfaction. When teachers can match parents' skills with children's needs, and when adults are able to blend into classroom routines and style of teacher interactions, all projects are more successful. Calfee, Wittwer, and Meredith (1998) have many suggestions for volunteers, teachers, and other staff working together.

Physical Organization

The physical aspects and space associated with schools differ with age and location, but these elements always suggest what can happen in particular educational environments. A large majority of U.S. children of primary school age attend schools in classrooms containing 20 to 25 students and one teacher per group. The physical plant for most school programs is still the **"egg box" type** of construction, with a central hallway and branching individual classrooms. Variations exist for the basic plan and also may exist within the egg box, including learning stations and highly flexible constructions and equipment.

One can see that physical organization of schools and classrooms relates to the program (Figure 8–1). A traditionally organized room is likely to have a traditional orientation. This message communicates itself quickly to children and others who enter a school. Some older schools built for traditional programs have been reorganized into settings containing open spaces, work stations, and resource areas. Space, including hallways and out-of-doors areas, can be used in an entirely different way to support a program where teachers want experiments and freedom in movement. Ironically, some **open-space buildings** built for more innovative programming have been reorganized as traditional. Teachers who push to reorganize their space give new life to the adage "Form follows function."

Open-space schools were developed in the 1970s in many U.S. communities. In general, they were large buildings planned around pods, or divisions that housed various grade levels or "families." The large spaces, or pods, were generally allotted to specific grade levels, and the teachers for each space developed the area as they saw fit. This often meant that one group of 25 second graders was within sight and hearing of two or more other groups.

With this plan, many activities in open-space schools are total group events, and subgroups move between the designated sections in the pod. Noise levels tend to be higher in open-space schools, but with carefully scheduled activities, study, and transition time, the interruptions are minimized. The open space permits the flexibility to move to other groups within or outside the pod for specific activities or for partnerships, and then to move back when the home group is called to session. The plan fits well with the cognitive process (constructivist) orientation and other, more individualized orientations. It does not jibe with academic or traditionalist patterns and has for this reason lost popularity in many school districts.

CURRICULUM FORMS

Schools were established originally to teach areas of skill and knowledge more efficiently and with better results than could be achieved at home. Even though the nature of this task has changed and expanded over the years, the need for skills and knowledge is still the basis for school curricula.

In the 19th century, the overarching objectives were to ensure reasonable competence in the ability to read, compose written work, and master computation skills and general problem solving. Schools were arranged exclusively on the traditional or teacher-dominated

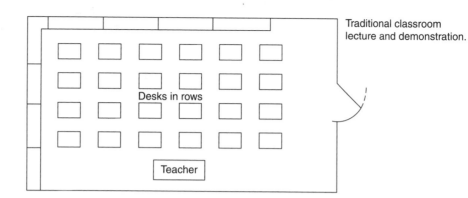

Traditional classroom
lecture and demonstration.

Desks in rows

Teacher

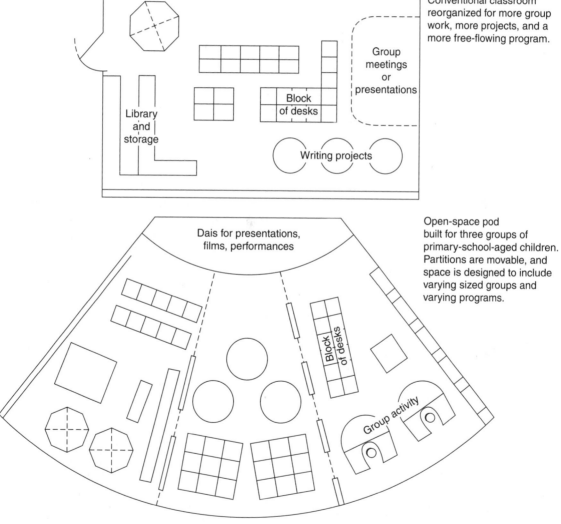

Conventional classroom
reorganized for more group
work, more projects, and a
more free-flowing program.

Group
meetings
or
presentations

Block
of desks

Library
and
storage

Writing projects

Open-space pod
built for three groups of
primary-school-aged children.
Partitions are movable, and
space is designed to include
varying sized groups and
varying programs.

Dais for presentations,
films, performances

Block
of desks

Group activity

Figure 8–1   Different classroom organization patterns

plan. Schools assumed an extensive role in providing more and new content for children as time went by. At present, U.S. schools have curricula that include not only language arts and mathematics but also social studies, science, health and recreation, and fine arts. As noted at the beginning of this chapter, the school curriculum has three distinct forms or zones—formal, informal, and hidden. All are evident each day that children attend school.

The formal, or explicit, curriculum includes the established content, concepts, and skills found in curriculum guides and teacher plan books. It is the material included in textbooks or in the projects that teachers and students decide to pursue.

The informal curriculum zone includes the social learnings, work and study habits, and protocols that learners must master to fit into school life. Students learn these through modeling by school adults, by persuasion and advisement, and sometimes simply by having a buddy to associate with and thereby to "learn the rules" from. This process compares to the etiquette practices of homes and with the social organization rules found in any subculture.

The hidden, or covert, curriculum consists of unintentional learnings accruing to children from their school experiences. Informants in this case are frequently peers; children also absorb messages from adults by observation. Through the hidden curriculum, children learn such things as whether it is a good time to make a request, which teachers get the things they want from the school office, or that third-grade boys "do not play" with girls. They also learn how school personnel and peers view their habits, dress, and home life experiences.

Formal Curriculum

The formal, explicit, or intended curriculum of a school is the plan of action or experiences delivered to attending children. Curricula are promoted in different ways and, as noted, can differ considerably from one school to another, depending on staff, district philosophy, materials and equipment involved, type of community, and acceptance level of teachers.

Often the curriculum is a detailed, written document produced through the work of teacher study groups and disseminated from a central office. The content fits neatly into a scope and sequence chart, and material often correlates closely with published textbooks. Many state offices of education publish curriculum guides for particular grade levels or subject matter guides for all grade levels, developing them in a manner similar to that of local school districts.

In each of the curriculum orientations discussed in this chapter, educators have different ways to organize and schedule curriculum content. The following sections present examples of how a formal curriculum is developed for each orientation in contemporary schools.

Formal Curriculum in Traditional Schools. Predetermined curricula fit academic or traditionally oriented schools because the philosophy of such schools holds that a common core of knowledge exists. Then the facts, concepts, and skills of that core can be written down, turned into objectives, which are developed with children, and then children's learning is evaluated by standardized or teacher-made tests.

Schedule and Structure. Grade levels for elementary schools established in the early 19th century have remained much the same to the present day. While somewhat arbitrary and contributing to many lockstep curriculum designs, the practice arranges a considerable amount of content into grade-specific levels. Teachers in traditionally oriented classrooms organize a day primarily through various routines, then schedule lessons and practice, followed by evaluation of some type. A typical day in a traditional school is shown in Table 8–3. This is a minimal

Table 8–3   A Traditional Classroom Day for Grade 2

9:00–9:15	Opening activities
9:15–11:15	Reading and other language arts
11:15–12:00	Mathematics
12:00–12:45	Lunch/recess
12:45–1:15	"Specials": art, music, or physical education
1:15–1:45	Science or social studies
1:45–2:15	Computer or media work
2:15–3:00	Language arts
3:15	Closing

plan, showing only the highlights, but it suggests the extent of schoolwork for 6- to 8-year-olds in a traditional program.

Organization. An exception to the self-contained classroom with children of specific ages is the **departmentalized program,** where children move from room to room for instruction in particular subjects. Departmentalized plans, normally associated with upper elementary grades, also have been developed in primary areas. Teachers specialize in one or more areas; for example, one teacher develops reading,

writing, and spelling (language arts) and handles those areas for two or more classrooms. Team teaching is another model that combines departmentalized features with group planning, support, and evaluation.

Cooperative learning models replace many individual assignments with a small-group focus and responsibility. Teachers may combine this strategy with most staffing arrangements and classroom organization patterns. However, the strategy blends most successfully with constructivist classrooms.

Formal Curriculum in Constructivist Classrooms. A constructivist curriculum is carefully thought out. The teacher's plans are developed in conjunction with school and community expectations; children's developmental stages and individual patterns of growth are accounted for. A constructivist teacher may use a curriculum guide but will freely interpret it as needed. Content covers all disciplines—reading, writing, math, social studies, science, fine arts, and physical education. Rather than following a sequenced listing of content and concepts, classes pursue investigations of differing topics,

Constructivist teachers recognize that arts and crafts projects support language arts and math

projects, or themes. The curriculum is integrated and involves children in active learning. Through involvement with different issues in the units studied, children develop the same set of basic skills encountered in a traditional school plan. Teachers are responsible for content and for providing continuity of experience and opportunities for learners. Classroom social interactions, which are important to curriculum development, are provided through shared experiences, flexible groupings, interactions with the teacher, and opportunities for children to reflect on their learning.

A constructivist at work is presented in the following vignette, as one teacher tells visitors about her Grade 3 unit on trees (adapted from Scully, Seefeldt, & Barbour, 2003).

I operate my third grade by establishing a flexible schedule so that I can reorganize if interests and projects require more time. I have a framework of the subject area skills that children should acquire that I pulled, along with themes and unit suggestions, from the curriculum guides. Beyond that, I try to be flexible enough to respond to children's interests and needs.

Planning for our tree unit went something like this: Children were just finishing explorations on different birds when one child brought in an apple tree branch about to blossom. Children had all sorts of questions, so I suggested that our next unit could be on trees. I encouraged children to bring some books about trees, and I gathered several as well. The next day I read Parnall's Apple Tree, and we discussed some of the things in the book that interested the students. Some of the concepts were that trees provide food for us and for other animals, trees change during the seasons, trees provide joy and delight, and trees provide shelter for some creatures.

Then I thought of some activities we could do that connected to our reading, social stud-

ies, and science curricula. In reading, we're looking at settings for stories; in social studies, we're doing mapping skills; and in science, we're studying the environment. I began to devise some projects that would engage the class in learning more about trees and their importance to the environment, but that would still be linked to subject area skills.

In reading, children are studying story settings, and from reading Apple Tree and other books, they'll examine settings and thus learn about the environments that trees need.

In social studies, children are studying mapping skills. On global maps, children will locate places where our "tree stories" take place. Children will then make topographical maps and place models of their trees appropriately. In art, they'll portray different houses that animals develop in trees.

In writing, children will reflect in journals what they're learning about trees and what is of particular interest to them. Since children are always encouraged to list new and interesting words, as they attempt creative writing, they'll have a list of new words to use.

In science, we'll examine the different foods that trees provide. We will collect some of these foods for snacks on different days.

Some of the presentations or projects will be total class, and others will require children to work in groups or individually. As a total group, we'll discuss the findings and plan out the different projects: topography, reading discussion groups, snack preparations, creative stories or reports, and house-building projects. Four basic work areas will be prepared: maps area, house-building area, food-preparation area, and arts and creative writing area. Depending on children's discoveries and their interests, they can elect to be part of two, three, or all four activities. There will be a formal independent reading time, when children read from their selected books, and then the children will meet in a discussion group to share information from the stories. Discussions during snack time and after reading time, children's journals, their creative stories, and their art projects will provide me with information on what students have learned. At the end of all our units, I will ask children to reflect on what new information or skills they've acquired. You see, I'm trying to get them to become aware of their own learning.

⤴

The typical day in a constructivist class is organized through various routines, projects, meetings, and skill sessions. Activities are usually followed by evaluations, sharing, and exhibiting. A typical schedule for a constructivist school day is shown in Table 8–4.

The advantage of doing projects in the cognitive process and constructivist programs is that such work is more informal and lends itself to experimentation and collaboration. Assignments tend to hold children's interest longer, especially when they get to help choose the topics and how to extend their study. Some sessions will seem disorganized, with children searching for materials or collaborating with others, but the advantage is that the approach to mastering material is self-selected. In these programs, children feel empowered for much of their own learning and grasp concepts and skills far beyond traditional grade expectations.

Table 8–4   Constructivist Classroom Day—Grade 2

9:00	Meeting time, greeting friends, checking and discussing day's schedule
9:30	Reading and writing workshop
10:30	Class meeting
10:45	Recess
11:00	Skill session on subtraction
12:00	Lunch
12:45	Class meeting
1:00	Independent work time for projects
2:00	Art and music sessions
2:30	Presentations, publishing, and wrap-up
3:15	Closing time

A major disadvantage to constructivist plans is that projects can become trivial or repetitive. In addition, some teachers have difficulty incorporating or inserting reasonable skill development sessions in the investigations that classes propose.

Formal Curriculum in Personal Relevance Programs. A truly child-centered program is difficult to describe, since all content emerges from the interests of the children involved. As an illustration, however, imagine that a small group of children has elected to consider frogs for a week, while other groups or individuals are focused on different topics. The classroom teacher and aides would provide as much help, guidance, and support as possible for their study, and a scenario such as the following might develop:

• Teachers accompany children on a visit to a nearby wetland after they decide to observe frog habitats.

• Discussions about materials collected follow the visit, and children ponder ways they wish to continue.

• Teachers, children, and helpers assemble books, magazines, films, and other resources, while students explore what they wish to concentrate on.

• The group shares with the entire class, and children brainstorm, or at least discuss, how they could learn more. They consider books, museum exhibits, presentations by persons in ecology departments, and interactions with local specialists and with other classrooms or schools nearby. New members might join the group at this point.

• Students incorporate writing and mathematics into their study by keeping journals on experiences and planning experiments, such as hatching frog eggs in different media. Teachers help and provide information or instruction when needed.

- The project evolves into a larger study of swamp ecology as it serves the interests of students and continues to be a stimulating topic.
- Evaluation is through documentation: children's journals and other writing, art and music compositions, skill mastery list, and other expressions of children's work. See *The Hundred Languages of Children* (Edwards, Gandini, & Forman, 1998) for an extensive listing of assessment modes.

Certain home schooling programs are conducted along this line, and evidence shows that children's interest blooms when they are given chances to investigate their surroundings. One fascinating example is the plan the Colfax family used with their four sons (Colfax & Colfax, 1992).

The content examples presented here are all explicit or intended curriculum activities of a school program. This means that teachers feel a responsibility to plan for and to steer children toward some substance or experience. As we have stated, other forms of curricula also are associated with all schools. The informal curriculum is acknowledged by most educators and parents as part of what we come to school for. The hidden curriculum is rarely apparent to teachers and parents, but its effects often outlast those of the explicit curriculum. These curricula are discussed in the following sections.

Informal Curriculum

Much of the informal curriculum is implied and unplanned; it consists of those learnings teachers and parents expect to come about but rarely bother to state, plan for, or present to children. The informal curriculum has to do with socialization into school and community life, and it is similar to the etiquette of other institutions in children's lives.

This curriculum includes events such as teachers' expecting their new students to discover procedures for lining up, passing in pa-

pers, getting recognition in class, or responding. No one plans the activities, but all are expected to follow the rules. Recall the vignette in Chapter 4, where Greg helped Philip understand their teacher's request. Informal curriculum was at work when Greg instructed the younger child. The teacher expected Philip to know the practices, but since he did not, the older child interpreted.

All teachers expect children to internalize a number of general school procedures and protocols. Some teachers, particularly primary school teachers, are more cognizant of this area of informal curriculum than others. For instance, they are aware of a need to remind children of appropriate responses and helpful communication. They often discuss possibilities for team efforts and list things to consider. We find the following items of informal curriculum in typical U.S. schools:

- School activities are organized and differ from spontaneous situations at home. Children are expected to differentiate, adapt, and fit in without any focused instruction.
- Competition is a fact of life in U.S. schools. Teachers employ notions of being first, being best, and achieving more in all areas of classwork and sports. Children are expected to absorb this value.
- Time and schedules are paramount in school life. Children are expected to work on command, change quickly to new ventures, and meet deadlines many times per day.
- Group activities are common in all schools. Children are expected to learn group roles and participate in groups cooperatively and smoothly.

The home curriculum is basically an informal curriculum (refer to Chapter 7), and learning accrues there in a haphazard but reasonable way. Few formal or organized experiences are associated with the home—exceptions are music lessons, homework, and the like—unless parents have developed a home schooling program. Language skill is a good example of the informal home curriculum. Families have no planned times for language instruction. However, by the time children enter kindergarten, they have almost complete control of their native language, and this has all come through interaction with family, caregivers, and peers.

Language development begins early and, though subject to direct instruction in school, is mainly the result of the informal curriculum. The results from family to family can be tremendous. For example, Hart and Risley (2003) pointed out the wide gap between different children's vocabulary development by age 3. The differences relate to the vocabulary, quality of language, and amount of "encouraging words," as opposed to "prohibitions" in the child's parental and community social class. Simply put, children in welfare homes hear one half as many words as children in the average working-class family and less than one third of those in a professional family. The differences are found to exist as late as ages 9 and 10. Language development is only one part of the informal curriculum, but it certainly affects many other areas of learning.

Hidden Curriculum in Homes, Schools, and Communities

We have defined *curriculum* as those experiences that make up children's waking hours, and when you consider carefully, you can see that the thousands of impressions, interactions, and experiences children have each day do amount to a curriculum. Children constantly receive stimuli that contribute to learning. Some stimuli are intentional; adults plan things that children are "supposed" to learn through school, home, or community instruction. But some learning is unintended; it comes about in accidental ways as children observe phenomena, experience situations, and associate with others. This is often called the hidden, or covert, curriculum, and makes a considerable impression on the growing child.

Unintended learning relates to a child's gender, social class, race, and ethnicity, although its extent and effects are frequently ignored. Examples of this are the nonverbal language features

Some learning is unintended or accidental, coming about informally as children observe phenomena

of tone, facial expressions, and gestures, as well as the patterns found in the family's **social network**. Recall Jana's drawings from the vignette in Chapter 4 about her family configurations at different periods in her life. These drawings indicate Jana's evolving hidden curriculum.

Children continue to encounter the hidden curriculum after entering school. When we examine it closely, we find that the hidden curriculum occupies a large part of the school day. For example, first-grade teachers plan about 5 hours of in-class time per day, but when we calculate the time actually spent on planned activities, we often find that less than one half is spent on task work. In fact, some **time-on-task** studies reveal that primary classrooms in some cases were on task less than 1 hour of the total day (Stallings, 1980). This leaves a large amount of in-class and out-of-class time, in addition to time spent going to and from school, given over to the hidden curriculum. Whether beneficial or negative, the hidden curriculum is a potent force in any child's learning.

❧

Ryan only shrugged when, during dinner, his father asked him about his school day, but later when they were reading the comics in the newspaper, some things came up about a new child in Ryan's class.

"I think Charlie takes money," Ryan said.

"Oh, really," said his dad.

"Yeah, he had three quarters that he spent on candy at Ed's Variety today . . . said he found 'em."

"Maybe he did," his dad replied.

"Yeah, but he didn't know where. . . . I think he stole 'em."

"Has Charlie been here visiting?" Ryan's father asked.

"Nope. I asked him over last week, but his dad don't let him go places. It's funny, 'cause he knows a lot."

"Oh, that so?"

Ryan nodded and volunteered, "He told me all those dirty words on the fence back of the variety store."

"Hmmm, well . . . when . . . ," his dad began.

But Ryan continued as he picked up the comics again. "There's those funny red marks on Charlie's arms. I'm gonna ask him tomorrow if we walk home from school."

❧

Ryan is a 7-year-old doing well in his traditional second-grade class, but you will note a host of items he is learning that are unrelated to school objectives. In his walk home with the new boy, Ryan is encountering a hidden curriculum. Its features are unrelated to his formal school curriculum, but the stimuli–scatological language, questions about theft, and hints of abuse all have an impact on Ryan.

The covert or hidden curriculum for at-risk children can, of course, have a negative impact and may have heartrending consequences. Aspects of these experiences surface in media reports describing particularly poignant family situations. The distressing accounts of children's lives given in Chapter 4 present all too graphically a savage curriculum that cries out for redress.

Gender, social class, race, and ethnicity, plus previous learnings, determine what children learn about themselves. For example, children may be encouraged by the words "You can be anything you want to be." But the negative effects of a bombardment of statements such as "Girls can't climb trees, but boys can," "Mommies can't be doctors," or "Blacks aren't allowed" influence a child's perception about life.

Children are always learning about others, and this learning can affect their treatment of other children. For example, a White middle-class male can get an exaggerated message about his superiority in a physical accomplishment. Girls may feel less qualified than boys due to remarks or assignments, and a black child feels chastened when she senses intolerance. As the vignette below shows, teachers often, if unwittingly, reinforce these notions.

❧

A poorly dressed Pauline sat down at a first-grade table to work with two other children on a learning center. She is told by Andrea and another well-dressed child that she can't sit there because she smells. Feisty Pauline began to battle for her rights, but her teacher intervened and said, "Pauline, you'll have to sit elsewhere today. Andrea was here first and doesn't want to work with you now."

❧

When a number of events such as this occur, Andrea acquires the feeling that she has more rights, while Pauline will take away negative feelings about herself and her ability to participate.

Adult attitudes, values, and interests are communicated not only through language but through the organization of the classroom, structure of the day, and which children are called on most often (Webb, Metha, & Jordan, 2003). Some features of the **covert curriculum** for at-risk children can have a very negative impact, and too often we find a savage curriculum unfolding for children in America's underclass.

Special Education and Curriculum

As we noted earlier, 12% of American school-children have special needs, and you will encounter some children in almost all schools who do require special services or some adaptation of instruction. The range of special needs is great, ranging from learning disabilities (about one half of the total) through mental retardation to specific physical impairments (a small proportion). If you work in urban areas where poverty and minority representation is considerable, you will find even larger proportions of children with special needs. As we have noted before, poverty is always linked to

more problems in health, social situation, and learning difficulties.

In Chapter 2 we alerted the reader to the beginnings of federal legislation that ushered in a new era for recognizing and ensuring educational opportunities for children with disabilities. In the succeeding 25 years, America has undergone considerable adjustment (not without difficulty, certainly) in providing special education facilities, restructuring buildings, reorganizing staff, and modifying curricula. Perhaps most of all, more educators have a new outlook, appreciation, and interest in accommodating children with special needs in regular classrooms.

As Table 2.2 in Chapter 2 indicates, several legislative endeavors since 1975 have expanded and clarified the provisions for special education. In 1986, legislation expanded school programs to cover preschoolers (ages 3–5) with disabilities. The notion driving this move was that early identification of disabilities meant that additional time and instruction would enhance the child's later schooling. It was only a matter of time until the first 3 years of a child's life were also considered for special services when needed. Therefore, in 1992, legislation brought services (though not through schools) to infants and toddlers. In this cohort, specialists meet with parents to help establish a better foundation for their children's later schooling.

Text limitations preclude our discussing the details for implementing good special-education programs, but we refer you to the considerable number of texts published in this area. Examples are Turnbull, Turnbull, Shank, Smith, and Leal (2002); *Exceptional Lives: Special Education in Today's Schools*; Culatta and Tompkins (1999), *Fundamentals of Special Education*; and Gollnick and Chinn (2002), *Multicultural Education in a Pluralistic Society*.

Readers anticipating a career in early-childhood education or related human services professions must be cognizant of the following provisions in the IDEA statutes that reflect the heart and intention of the legislation. The following seven principles undergirding special education reform (summarized from Culatta & Tompkins, 1999; and Turnbull et al., 2002) have become the specialized language of special education.

1. *Zero rejection.*   Rule against excluding any student.

2. *Nondiscriminatory evaluations.*   Rule requiring schools to evaluate children in their own language to determine a disability and how extensive it is.

3. *Appropriate education.*   Rule requiring educators to plan individually tailored education for each student with a disability.

4. *Least-restrictive environment.*   Rule requiring schools to merge exceptional children with regular classrooms to the maximum extent appropriate for the child.

5. *Due process.*   Rule to safeguard all students' rights for privacy and rights for legal redress.

6. *Parent and student participation.*   Rules requiring schools to collaborate with parents in designing and carrying out programs.

7. *Preschool programs.*   Rule requiring school districts to develop early-intervention programs for children with disabilities from birth through primary grades.

You will hear and read about several other fundamental terms identified with special educational practice: *mainstreaming, inclusion,* and *individualized education program.* We refer you again to the specialized texts already mentioned for in-depth discussions of how these terms undergird a lot about the field of special education, but the following descriptions will aid you in considering other content:

Mainstreaming has been used since the 1975 legislation was enacted. Though the concept brought children with special-needs into regular schools and classrooms, it provided for only limited connections in most schools. Special-education students were included in art, music, and other areas with their nondisabled peers but frequently were relocated for instruction in academic areas.

Inclusion emerged in the 1990s as a concept meaning that students with special needs are part of a regular class and participate fully in that class for almost the complete day. Inclusion practice has generated more controversy among regular and special-education teachers, but in its true sense, it calls for teachers (regular or special) to modify content, adjust material, secure more support services, and take other measures to enable the learner with special needs to enjoy the full life of a classroom. The most practical way to accommodate these children in the regular classroom is by using a team approach in planning for all children in the classroom. Such an approach would require more small group and individualized instruction. This requires a huge leap for the typical traditional educator and would move instruction toward a constructivist approach.

Almost all educators subscribe to the principle of including a large majority of children with special needs in regular schools and regular classrooms. Over a period of a generation (and numerous defining court cases), this adjustment has come to pass. A debate continues on how best to accommodate students with severe disabilities. Full inclusion for this last group involves restructuring classrooms, adding extra services, and adding more personnel as well as seriously modifying curriculum content and delivery of that content. You will meet educators and specialists with differing opinions about whether full inclusion is workable.

An **individualized education program (IEP)** is a contract for carrying out instruction for a special-needs student between

IEP means that an individualized program is worked out to serve the particular needs of a student

ages 3 and 21. The term has been in education practice for the past 25 years, and it means basically what the phrase implies, that is, a program worked out by regular teachers, specialists, parents, and sometimes the learner as well to serve the learner's needs. A modified form of this is the **individualized family services plan (IFSP),** which came with the 1992 legislation expanding services to infants and toddlers. The IFSP concept is similar, except that services are usually at the child's home or in a child care facility.

RESULTS OF SCHOOL EDUCATIVE PROCESSES

Millions of children attend schools in the United States each year. Also each year, more than 4 million young Americans (this includes dropouts) move beyond school to the workforce, to college, to homemaking, or to unemployment

(U.S. Bureau of the Census, 2002). It is common knowledge that a vast difference exists in outcomes for differing educational environments, ranging from the sublime to the pathetic.

Some schools have an easy time. Schools accepting highly motivated, advantaged students with few deficits in background and experience frequently produce quality results. With skilled administrators and energetic and focused staff members, students from these schools measure up against all expectations that communities could have. Selective private schools and well-endowed suburban schools in affluent areas show these results.

Other schools are far different and need extraordinary energy from all sources to produce even modest gains. This problem escapes the attention of much of America's middle-class community agencies. Schools in disadvantaged areas frequently enroll children with problems in nutrition, health, and socialization, and even in emotional stability. The background of deprivation has taken a toll on interest and outlook and all things of an educational nature, for day-to-day survival is the paramount consideration in the American underclass (Bradley, 2002; Schorr, 1988). The comprehensive nurturing from community families needed to engender children's self-esteem and a positive self-concept or readiness is often lacking. These schools need outstanding teachers and skilled administrators, but they often get neither, as staff assignments are often determined by length of tenure. How can schools like this compete? The answer is that they cannot. Most will continue to struggle unless or until they receive massive investments of support and supplements from outside and well-organized cooperative action with the community served. (In Chapter 12, we identify productive models for school–community partnerships.)

IMPLICATIONS FOR PROFESSIONALS

Schools differ in structure, view of curriculum, equipment, and space. School leadership varies, as does the skill of staff members in charge of day-to-day activities. The background, support, and preparation that enrolled children possess will differ. All these factors will produce different educational outcomes and will affect your professional involvement when you are affiliated.

Of course, changes are possible in all educational situations; the poor can be made better, the good can become outstanding. You can make a difference if you affiliate with schools that have a vision for improvement.

Differing curriculum orientations and various teaching strategies and techniques will all fit into the teaching equation. Keep in mind that all can be successful. The traditional teacher who demonstrates, explains, and then pursues application may be rewarded with

inquisitive, enthusiastic students. The indirect teacher, with goals firmly in mind, also can stimulate and guide students toward achievement using the same basic equipment.

As you approach work with schools, give thought to the informal and hidden curricula engulfing the children you will work with. These curricula are a fact of life for all and come with all environments. You will be powerless as an individual to change much, but you must consider them as you incorporate activities into your school day. For instance, you can take time to model modes of greeting, general rules of etiquette, or particular social language skills that will help young children's maturity.

In the final analysis, teachers must know who they are, where they are going, and the best ways to get there. If you plan to teach, this means that you must have a clear grasp of your skills and your preferred work style and then be able to see how that style matches children's interests and work habits. Teachers who are not self-aware in this way must depend on circumstances to place them in comfortable situations with eager students.

SUMMARY AND REVIEW

In this chapter, we have discussed the dimensions of school curricula, the philosophical orientations associated with curricula, and the variation in practices and structure found in U.S. schools. Philosophical orientations differ from school to school and from teacher to teacher, and orientation makes a great difference about what content teachers consider for classrooms as well as how teachers approach instruction. The physical organization of a school also reflects the school's philosophical orientation.

Formal, informal, and hidden curricula exist in all types of schools. The results of school educative processes can be positive or negative, and all results have implications for the

Chapter 9

Curriculum of the Community

The child is an ever-attentive witness of grown-up morality—or lack thereof; the child looks for cues as to how one ought to behave, and finds them galore as we parents and teachers go about our lives, making choices, addressing people, showing in action our rock-bottom assumptions, desires, values, and thereby telling those young observers much more than we may realize.

(Coles, 1997, p. 5)

The purpose of this chapter is to examine the rich but often overlooked features of the community for children's learning. Just as we have a curriculum of the school and of the home, we also have a curriculum of the community. In reading this chapter, you will learn the following:

1. Organizations and agencies within a community provide many and varied learning opportunities for children.

2. Some community education is purposeful and planned by members of community organizations and agencies.

3. Much of children's learning within the community results from their observations of how things work and how people interact with materials and other people.

4. The physical, emotional, and moral attributes of a community will either support and extend or hinder children's opportunities.

5. Social networks, involving both adults and peers, will affect the amount and quality of learning children derive from their community.

Whether or not educators extend the school curriculum, children's development, knowledge, and understanding come from various sources. The community, an amorphous mass surrounding us all, is one of these sources. As in the family and school curricula examined in Chapters 7 and 8, community curriculum is affected by the type, location, cultural aspects, and physical makeup of the region, plus the social networks established by its inhabitants.

In the 21st century, the gap between the rich and poor grows wider, and many adults and communities try new strategies to overcome the social, economics, and physical environment that hinder some children's positive learning. Most investigators know that children growing up in affluent communities or with strong parental support have a greater chance of school success than those in poor communities with high crime rates, transient family life, and poverty where parents have trouble just providing shelter and food (Adelman & Taylor, 2002). Under poor and depressed conditions, the school is the social setting that is typically stretched to assure that all students succeed. But all of society needs to examine the structures that produce inequality for learning and develop integrated approaches to support children's development. Community social agencies, entertainment outlets, and business organizations have an obligation to work with schools to find new solutions. We have some evidence that this effort works.

Chapter 1 presented the many influences on children's learning, and we found that all curricula are affected by these influences. Although we find great differences among communities, we also find many commonalities that suggest similar educational experiences.

Every community is composed of interconnected social systems, and how the people of these systems relate to one another greatly affects children's learning and development (Bradley, 2002; Bronfenbrenner, 1979). Various organizations within the community offer different aspects of curriculum, and children learn just by being exposed to these organizations. In addition, the physical, moral, and emotional environments children encounter in their immediate neighborhoods enhance or hinder intellectual development. Some communities deliberately plan additional opportunities for children's growth, while others seem oblivious to how their organizational structure affects children's learning and make no attempt at removing barriers to it.

In this chapter, we examine the context of the wider community and its potential for helping children grow. We examine community organizational structure and suggest how some of the diverse agencies "educate" children. The physical and social–emotional environments in a community together constitute a basic support system for all families, one that enables parents and child care staff to stimulate children in different ways. There are, however, communities where the physical and social–emotional environment is so destructive that children are placed at great developmental and educational risk (Randolph, Koblinsky, & Roberts, 1998). The supportive interaction of community agencies with families and schools is the key. The level of children's positive participation in the community and the social networks that they establish depend on that interaction.

COMMUNITY STRUCTURE AFFECTS CURRICULUM

Although every community varies in structure and the kinds of services available to its citizens, we find similar human, natural, and material resources. Table 9–1 presents a partial listing of these resources. A child's neighborhood may be in a city, small town, suburb, or rural area. The resources available in each

of these settings will vary, but all provide the bases for a community curriculum. Whether in a rural area or in a city, children observe different aspects of nature. Trees, birds, animals, and stars at night are more available to rural children, but city children also witness the warmth of the sun, wetness of rain, scrubby grass and small plants pushing up between concrete slabs, and ants carrying away crumbs. Southern children know palm trees; northern children, deciduous or fir trees; and southwestern children, juniper and cacti. Weather provides learning experiences also. Some children experience tornado conditions and the haphazardness of destruction. Others may enjoy long spells of soothing hot weather, but then learn the distress of drought.

Children constantly learn from persons in their neighborhoods. How much learning children gain from others besides kin in the home depends on how much association they have, how safe their neighborhood is, and how many community services and agencies their parents use. In safe neighborhoods, children have more freedom to move beyond their homes and to observe and interact with people involved in various activities and occupations. How people dress, what distinguishes young people from old, how adults treat each other and children in passing, and many other qualities and interactions teach children about life. In violent neighborhoods, children also learn important lessons from observation of community activities, but too often out of fear parents must confine their children or closely supervise them. This limits children's opportunities for physical exploration and thus limits their intellectual and social experimentation in favor of simple survival skills (Magnuson & Duncan, 2002).

Children learn from various materials generated by people in society. Some materials, such as a brochure about good eating habits for primary-school-age children, are prepared with educational intentions. Toy companies

Table 9–1 Community Resources That Educate Children

Natural Resources

Plants, animals, insects, fish, minerals, bodies of water, beaches, parks, nature preserves, farmland

Services

Education: zoos, museums, libraries, schools, parks

Communication: telephones, radio and TV stations, post offices, newspaper offices, computer networks

Entertainment: theaters, music halls, movies, fairs, festivals, circuses, restaurants, TV and radio stations

Recreation: playgrounds, church or community clubs, athletic facilities, ballparks, tennis courts, parks

Transportation: airports, train and bus stations, taxis, gas stations, car rental agencies

Commercial: department stores, grocery stores, pharmacies, different types of farms (orchards, fish farms, dairy farms), special shops (toy stores, ice cream shops, beauticians, pet stores, craft shops), factories, other business enterprises

Professional: offices of physicians, dentists, lawyers, and other professionals, fire and police departments, funeral homes, courts, clinics and hospitals, political offices, university campuses, school department headquarters

Service agencies: employment offices, social services and public assistance offices, counseling centers, food co-ops, mayor's office

Living environments: children's and teachers' homes, apartment complexes, mobile homes, new home sites, real estate offices, retirement communities, nursing homes

Materials and Media

Print: books, pamphlets, brochures, magazines and newspapers, advertisements

Audiovisual: films, TV, radio, audio-and videocassettes, computer programs, Internet sites, exhibits

Recyclables: scraps of fabric or wood or carpet samples, buttons, ribbon, wallpaper samples, bottles, cans, boxes, wire, spools, cartons, used paper

Social Networks

Adult: friends, neighbors, colleagues and coworkers, social clubs, religious groups, sports groups, family members, community theater groups

Peer: young relatives, school and neighborhood friends, club and team partners

Ethnic Associations

Contacts: different languages, festivals, area religious activities, artistic expressions

induce adults to buy various items for children, and often advertisements will suggest a device's educational value. Children also learn from many other materials, including those adults consider junk. From observing, touching, smelling, and manipulating wood scraps, earth and sand, Styrofoam, bottles, shells, cans, and the like, children learn variations in texture, size, shape, and smell. Without adult support, the learning may be minimal, or the result could put children in harm's way. Even so, children left on their own do gain considerable knowledge about materials around them.

Every community has **service agencies**, political establishments, **social–cultural agencies**, and business enterprises. Just as schools and homes provide a curriculum, so do community establishments and agencies. The efforts, products, and resources of each agency will provide formal, informal, and hidden curricula, similar to the school environment.

Children acquire knowledge, values, and social skills (positive as well as negative) from their experiences within their communities and interactions with community workers. We will find, of course, no single established curriculum for a community, any more than we find a common curriculum for all families. Resources vary, and how these resources are made available, plus the family's and children's ability to make use of them, determine learning potential.

Service Agencies

Service agencies provide families with health, transportation, protection, communication, and professional services. These agencies provide experiences from which children gain knowledge, both through the formal presentation of materials and in informal ways. Formal educational experiences from most agencies have been carefully thought through, and prepared materials are directed toward parents or teachers to assist in instruction. Other materials or experiences are directed toward children. A child's first experience with the family dentist is one example of a community professional's "educating" young clients.

Since Rodrigo was 3 years old, he accompanied his mother to the dentist for her semiannual checkup. While his mother was in the chair, he would sit nearby with a few toys. One day Dr. Garcelon asked him if he wouldn't like to sit up in the big chair where his mother had sat. As Rodrigo climbed up, the dentist allowed him to touch the instruments and told him what they were for. He encouraged him to press the water tap and to rinse his mouth from the paper cup nearby. Gradually, over two or three visits, he introduced all the cleaning instruments and even turned on the polishing brush so Rodrigo could see how it vibrated. At first Rodrigo refused to have the brush in his mouth, but gradually he became so intrigued with the instruments that he wanted to see what would happen. One day a small squirrel came to the dentist's window and chattered away. Dr. Garcelon and the young child took a moment to feed the squirrel before the dentist gave Rodrigo a toothbrush and toothpaste with verbal and written "picture" instructions on how to use the brush at home.

This dentist had a planned program for introducing dental hygiene to young patients. At first children observed parents' experiences—a rather informal learning experience. Parental comfort and the dentist's reassuring ways provided a safe and secure environment for the next phase. The formal instruction of what happens in a dentist's chair was designed to build children's trust as well as to start children on the road to good dental hygiene. The pamphlet Rodrigo received had simple instructions with pictures so that even at age 4 he could see how to brush his teeth. The squirrel's appearance was an accidental event, during which Rodrigo observed an animal close-up, discovered something about feeding animals, and experienced an adult's gentle treatment of a particular animal.

Just as teachers and homes vary in how they instruct children, so do people in various agencies and professions. Some dentists are not as thorough as Dr. Garcelon in giving information to parents whom they expect to instruct children. Many medical professionals work with schools, child care centers, and health fairs to provide free initial health checkups. In some communities, free health clinics (many are mobile units) are regularly available for needy families. It is through these avenues that materials and curricula on health care are provided by medical professionals.

Most community agencies provide materials that schools and parents can use to feature the functions of the agencies. Police and fire departments, for example, normally provide speakers for schools or encourage field trips to their stations. Some police officers and firefighters get special training in how to work with young children, and children who visit are allowed to climb, under supervision, onto fire trucks or into police cars. Department

Police officers will provide speakers for school affairs, wear uniforms and describe their equipment

representatives wear their uniforms and explain the equipment they carry and use. They also explain what children are to do when a police officer or firefighter is trying to assist them.

Transportation Services

In a mobile society, transportation facilities provide children with many enriching, as well as hostile, experiences, depending on the political, societal, or physical ambiance. There is an airport depot to explore freely in a small airport, but at large terminals children must be under close supervision. On some planes children are able to visit the cockpit and watch a pilot prepare for the flight.

In tight national security times, young children's needs are often disregarded due to official's nervousness. After 9/11, the authors witnessed a 3-year-old child pulled from her father's protective arms and made to walk through the metal detector while in hysterics. Yet, at a less tense time, the official invited a child to watch what others did and then politely asked the child to remove her shoes and together they watched them go through the scanner. She then skipped happily through the machine, smiled at the guard, and retrieved her shoes. The few adults around her smiled as they observed the interactions.

Transportation agencies provide many formal learning experiences for children, as they collaborate with schools in planning trips to airports, train stations, or bus stops. Much of the learning about modes of travel comes from schools studying such a unit or from parents as children accompany them, or from materials (maps, brochures, schedules) that adults collect. Informal learning as children use different modes of travel is enormous. One 6 year-old's explanation of how she got from her home in Minnesota to visit her grand-mother in Russia is a small example of the range of learning.

❧

In answer to her grandmother's question about her trip, an eager Galina replied in one breath. "It took a l-o-o-ng time, grandma, and I slept on the plane and I watched a movie. It was dark when Daddy put our luggage in the car and we drove to the airport. Daddy had to park our car, right Daddy, and Mommy and I took our luggage inside the station. I remember go-ing through this machine and the man asked me to take off my shoes. We were in lots of lines and there were sooo many people. There was a man with a gun, and I sat close to mommy until he went, but mommy said he was just making sure we were safe. On the plane I fell asleep after we got some food on a little tray. Here in Moscow, we took a long es-calator, and then I think some kind of train. Anyway, after we got our luggage, we had to wait in a long line until someone looked at the little book with our pictures in it. I think it's a passport. Right, Mommy? I am so glad to see you, grandma! Just look at my red suitcase!! Uncle Vanya sent it to me—see, it has wheels, and it sure helped, 'cause mommy said I had to carry my own luggage.

❧

Galina's parents capitalized on her experi-ences and discovered many other aspects of transportation that she was aware of. Her cards to her friends, her journal writing, her draw-ings, and her conversations with her relatives not only revealed what she had assimilated, but also reinforced her understanding of a new environment.

Political Agencies

All communities have government agencies, school boards, and task forces or committees empaneled by the community government to provide different types of community curric-ula. The management decisions these agencies make will affect—directly and indirectly—the social, intellectual, and physical development of children in that community. As with social agencies, political agencies often provide writ-ten materials, films, or audiotapes designed to educate the public about their functions or the community. Such agencies make use of news-papers, magazines, radio, television, and the Internet to carry their message to the public, and the assumption is that families and schools will then "educate" children.

In some communities, the formal curric-ulum is more apparent, especially during elec-tion years, and is usually handled through the schools. Mock elections are held in some schools, using local political campaign mate-rials. Students sometimes visit local and state political offices, where teachers and political workers attempt to explain the functions and responsibilities of the resident officials. Chil-dren whose parents are active politically may begin to comprehend how the system works. However, the political implications of mes-sages are usually beyond the comprehension of primary-school-age children. Children whose parents use social services managed by political officials can acquire confusing no-tions, especially when their parents have dif-ficulty obtaining services. The political knowledge that children gain from such expe-riences tends to be serendipitous.

In the United States, we have no national policy that supports children and families. Thus, families benefit from such community resources only in relationship to the personal networks they establish within the community (Pardeck, 1990). Social policies established by community leaders affect the options and de-termine the resources that any family has for establishing networks and making use of avail-able resources (Cochran & Niegro, 2002). For in-stance, people living in wealthier communities often are able to negotiate with political figures for funding well-equipped and well-maintained parks or recreational areas. They see that libraries and museums have appropriate materials and outreach programs. Citizens in affluent areas have better access to child care support services, community-based activities, and protective and health services. They tend to be better educated and so have developed better **networking** skills, which enable them to access these services (Cochran & Niegro, 2002). Children reared in poor communities are often discriminated against and have fewer opportunities for learning. Parents in these neighborhoods appear to have less clout with governmental and management agencies, and with less education have fewer skills enabling them to access fully the benefits of community learning. The following vignette illustrates different potentials for social, intellectual, and physical learning as a result of two different policies for park maintenance.

⟡

In Wexton, the recreation department has provided a park with grassy areas and paths. There are two swings, one piece of climbing equipment, and a basketball court. Maintenance of the park is poor. Swings are always in disrepair; garbage and debris litter the ground. Parents bringing children to the area will briefly exchange a smile or a word with the ever present "bag man" and occasionally with adults rushing through on their way to work or with those bringing dogs for an outing. Parents appear to use the park for children to play in, but they display little sense of coming here to meet other people. Parents are likely to discourage their children from interacting with others in the park.

In Overton, situated near a small shopping area, the community has provided a small park with lots of climbing equipment, paths for tricycles, a basketball court, bicycle paths leading off into an open grove area, and benches

where parents sit and supervise their children's play. The park is well maintained, with little debris. Paths are well cared for, as is all equipment. Park maintenance people are seen frequently cleaning up the area and have been known to remind the older, unsupervised children to watch out for others as they play. In this park, parents chat with each other, watch their children interact with one another, and often begin to develop friendships. There is a sense of bringing children for outings, but one that expands parental contacts with others in the neighborhood.

⟡

Children in these situations will learn many things in both parks, but the park in Overton, where more people, materials, and natural resources exist, has greater potential for positive learning opportunities. In both parks, one observes children gaining physical skills as they climb on equipment or play ball. Children use various strategies to engage other children in their play, and some appear to be skilled in interacting with other adults, such as when they crouch to pet a visitor's dog. However, there are differences.

In Wexton, there are fewer chances for personal interactions, since most parents discourage such interchanges, especially with "disreputable-looking characters." Since maintenance is poor, children receive different messages about the value of a clean environment. Some adults passing through the park are seen picking up trash and throwing it in available receptacles, but children witness others carelessly dropping litter. More potentially dangerous spots exist in Wexton, and children learn to be chary of their environment and aware of the danger signals.

In Overton, a different learning potential exists. Safe paths for children riding bicycles and tricycles from their homes to the park provide more opportunities for expanded physical development. Adults feel more comfortable with each other. The ambiance is welcoming, and the sense of trust among adults provides a stronger sense of trust in children. The park is kept free of debris, and maintenance personnel do not hesitate to remind children about respect for their environment. On the other hand, opportunities for learning danger signals may be more limited.

The community policy of providing and maintaining a park varies in these two communities. These policies are management choices, which in turn are influenced by the residents' pressure (or lack of such pressure) for maintaining a safe environment. Certainly, adults' abilities to use the resources available in the parks either enhance or limit what is learned in both situations.

It is not just with parks that communities provide options for adults to develop the social networks that enable them to use their community more advantageously. Governmental policy is inextricably interwoven with a community's social fabric. In some communities, policies regarding social service agencies make it much easier for adults to get the services they need (Cochran & Niegro, 2002).

Darlene, a shy mother, had moved to a new community with her new baby and 4-year-old son. She needed help but dreaded applying for food stamps at the **Women, Infants, and Children (WIC)** *program because of unpleasant experiences she had had before. However, when in desperation she finally went, she was pleasantly surprised at the quality of support. A community health organization had pressured the mayor's office into allowing food stamps to be distributed at their* **well-baby clinic.** *Also, a group of volunteers had begun a program of reading with the babies and older children at the clinic while the parents waited for appointments or discussed their children's health and nutritional needs. Darlene and the nurse discussed ways to entice children into*

good eating habits, and during her first visit, one of the volunteers invited Darlene to attend a parent support group for mothers with new babies. At these meetings, Darlene gained new confidence in herself and new skills in raising her children.

Political decisions can affect the community curriculum presented to children. Not only is Darlene gaining help in feeding her children, but she is also learning how to educate them about good eating habits and learning to make social contacts with others. Now she joins a group of mothers where children play together while the adults visit and exchange ideas of child rearing. In a more subtle way, parents at the WIC office and in the parent support group are exposed to models of adults reading to and interacting with children, and thus they may in turn provide expanded language experiences and positive social interactions for their own offspring.

Social and Cultural Agencies

The more skilled parents become at securing community services, the more opportunities they have to use other community resources, as illustrated in the following vignette.

Louisa's husband abandoned her and their two small children after they moved to a new state. Louisa was left with little money and no extended family support. After a few weeks she swallowed her pride and went to a church soup kitchen so that she and her children could have one nutritious meal a day. A series of contacts with people at the center led her to the social agencies in her community, where she learned how to tap resources for herself and her children. It wasn't always easy, for some of the policies seemed to hinder Louisa's progress. The support systems she began to establish for herself, however, enabled her to continue. Louisa eventually was able to finish high school and find a part-time job, and she now has a federally funded scholarship to college. In the process, she expanded her network of friends in the service areas so that she could use community programs to enrich her children's experiences, of which library and museum programs and a 2-week summer recreational program were recent highlights.

⤶

Churches, libraries, theaters, and recreational facilities are community agencies that supplement children's education. As with all situations, some children experience a richer curriculum than others. How well families are able to use available resources and how well agencies are able to reach all families in the community account for some of the disparity. These social and cultural agencies do not exist apart from one another, as the vignette illustrates. A church agency providing physical and social nurturance helped Louisa work through the governmental policies, which in turn helped her find other community resources for her children.

Governmental policies, concerned with so-called separation of church and state, can limit the resources that a church provides a community. Church leaders, concerned with developing memberships, often wish to provide religious activities for young people within schools, but community policies normally exclude such events. However, under the recent "No Child Left Behind" legislation, such restrictions are beginning to change so that "faith-based" organizations, as well as nonprofit organizations, can receive funding to provide supplemental educational services such as after-school programs and summer programs for economically deprived children (Community Update, 2002).

Librarians, theater personnel, and museum directors often try to develop programs with schools whereby children are invited to cultural offerings in their centers. But too often communities will not financially support such programs, or they believe that children are missing "schoolwork" and so must not be permitted to go. Those children whose parents have financial and social capital are able to profit by such community curriculum offerings while other children are left out. Some cultural agencies locate financial resources other than political agencies to help community programs expand their curriculum to include more children and families. In one New Hampshire community, when schools eliminated art programs because of cutbacks in funding, the local artists' association extended art lessons to all children in the community with help from a local community foundation.

Many social and cultural agencies provide a rich formal curriculum to children. Such settings have a strong impact on children's information-processing skills as well as on their physical, emotional, and moral development (Grumbine, 1988; Miles, 1986/1987).

Art museums offer both art instruction and art appreciation. Science museums and zoos often have formal presentations for young children. National and state parks have various educational programs that emphasize education relating both to the park theme and to conservation and environmental protection (Jacobson & Padua, 1992). Often theaters have acting lessons, summer camp experiences, children's performances, and lectures about plays and playwrights. Most libraries have educational lectures, storytelling events, and book talks. Hurst (1993) described a library program in which she uses poetry to enhance knowledge and feelings about the weather. She extends the language of poems by having children use computer graphics to create the effects of storms. The theme expands as children use reference books to find facts about storms and storybooks for descriptions of storms. Children who participate in these **literacy events**

Parks offer educational programs relating to conservation and land protection

expand their language, reading, writing, and computer skills as well as personal interaction skills and knowledge about where to find information.

Churches offer religious education classes, and many of these classes integrate art, drama, and music as a part of the instruction. Recreational facilities offer instruction in different sports, such as gymnastics, basketball, golf, or archery, as well as health-related classes such as aerobics, nutrition, and physical fitness.

As with curriculum in any context, children acquire a great deal of knowledge through the informal and hidden curricula of these social and cultural agencies. For example, posters announcing coming events and programs inform adults, but in indirect ways, they inform children as well.

In a local theater while awaiting a performance, a 5-year-old observed an adult commenting and pointing to an announcement of the next play. "Oh, look, Bill Braunhof will be playing in Cats! *I wonder what the dates are?" Running her finger under the date, she exclaimed, "Oh, too bad. It's Wednesday the 22nd, and we won't be here."*

With no intention of teaching young children, theater personnel have provided materials that can and do instruct. The adult, in seeking information for herself, unwittingly demonstrated to the child that such a poster offers information and that pieces of that information are found in different places on the poster. The child may even have discovered that "C-a-t-s" spells *cats* and recognized it when seeing it again, or that "22" can mean 22nd.

Sometimes such informal teaching is intentional. In Overton, the community librarian discovered that children would pick up, look at, and often take home books that were displayed attractively. He began to more carefully select for display outstanding books that had heretofore sat unused on the shelves. The quality of books selected by young readers took a quantum leap. The librarian then began to coordinate his efforts with units of study done by local teachers. The teachers were pleased to find children bringing into class these extra resources from the local library for current topics.

Community clubs are another means of educating children. Scout organizations, trail clubs, outing clubs, ski and skimobile clubs, and so on often have projects in which students participate with adults. Some take trips into the community and surrounding areas where children cook outdoors, practice trail maintenance, clean up litter on roadsides, observe different natural phenomena, and learn lessons in getting along with others. Some lessons are intentional, and some are unexpected. On one such trip, three 8-year-old boys came upon a family of skunks in a meadow. Wondering what the skunks would do if startled, the children gently tossed some pebbles toward the nest. To their and the other campers' dismay, the boys learned how startled skunks respond.

Business and Commercial Enterprises

All communities have business and commercial enterprises, many of which are located in large malls or along highways, though some communities still have main streets and neighborhood shops. Wherever they are, these establishments have identifying marks to advertise what they sell or what service they perform. Intentionally and unintentionally, adults and older children help younger ones sort out information regarding such businesses. Drive or walk through any of these commercial areas and observe carefully what the buildings or shops look like, the signs in and about the community, the types of vehicles in the parking areas, and the displays in the windows to get a feeling for what children learning about their world must sort out.

Children hear comments from adults, note certain identifying characteristics of buildings, and learn without specific instruction where to buy ice cream, get stamps, find interesting books, or buy a desired toy. Children begin to recognize similar and different shapes. The stop sign is always red and octagonal. Children may question why their parents are stopping or may even figure out from adult conversations what *stop* means. They learn to recognize their own car and eventually are able to find it in a large parking area.

Business enterprises distribute advertising circulars as well as put signs in shop windows. Such materials provide information about prices and the kinds of items a store sells. Window signs, especially in smaller communities, may also present information about events in the community. Children who become adept at using such resources acquire many skills about how to get information. They may also become skilled in using adults as resources for achieving certain purposes. As with other curricula, how and what children learn depend on many factors, including the kind of community in which they live, their developmental stage, and how significant adults share such information with them.

Parents, of course, are major influences, and how much parents talk and interact with their children as they are involved in the community also influences children's learning. Sometimes an important community person compensates for parental neglect or disinterest. Comer (1988) told about a shopkeeper in his community who taught a child, whom everyone believed couldn't speak, to talk. The shop was a candy store, and the child would only point to candy when he entered the shop. By refusing to acknowledge the child pointing out candy, the owner gradually got the child to tell her what he wanted and then eventually to talk to her. In the large and impersonal malls, the lessons taught may not always be so positive, but many clerks will take the time to answer children's questions and assist parents as they support children's learning. In Chapter 12 (p. 344) a vignette regarding Victoria in Tuscany is instructive. The salesperson in the leather goods shop was interested in finding a "satisfied" customer, so she focused on the child interacting with her, not the parents, regarding her needs (or wants). Many business enterprises have special programs or relationships that support children's learning. Chapter 11 discusses examples of these.

Media Forms and Configurations

Extensive learning opportunities for children are offered through various forms of media. Some children's learning takes place serendipitously, but adults extend and enhance it. We have a number of educational television and radio programs as well as Internet sites for young children. The Public Broadcasting System has for years provided educational programs, such as *Sesame Street, Mr. Rogers' Neighborhood,* the ever popular *Barney,* and *Teletubbies,* which in spirited ways introduce children to the alphabet, new words and concepts, and interesting stories and facts about everyday events. Early research on *Sesame Street* indicated that children watching such programs were learning the alphabet, numbers, and vocabulary faster than children not exposed (Ball & Bogatz, 1970; Rice, Huston, Truglio, & Wright, 1990).

Subsequent analysis of *Sesame Street* indicated, however, that rather than being a boon to disadvantaged children, the show was more likely to be watched by middle-class children, and the gains children maintained were dependent on adult reinforcement of concepts (Cook, Appleton, Comer, Shaffer, Tavekin, & Weber, 1975). Some learning from these programs may have an unintentional and perhaps undesirable effect. Children become accustomed to fast-paced materials and do not develop longer attention spans or the ability to

sustain interest in events that aren't moving rapidly. Gutrel (2003) discussed the vast changes to children's use of new media and highlighted new concerns about attention span and brain processing that were noted 30 years earlier.

On both educational and commercial radio and television stations, science and social studies programs, story reading, and reenactments of children's literature offer rich educational opportunities. In addition, network educational offices often provide teacher or parent guides for assisting children in gaining more from these programs.

Printed materials in the form of books, pamphlets, magazines, and newspapers also educate children through pictures and printed words. Printed language is different from oral language. Oral language and life experiences assist children in learning to read, but printed materials to which they are exposed also facilitate intellectual growth. In nearly all families we find some form of printed materials. Children learn early that pictures relate to real objects and have names. They are always learning the different forms that particular objects take and how the real object can differ from the picture. As stories are shared, children learn more about their world. For example, when children read Parnell's *Apple Tree,* their knowledge and concepts expand as they view an artist's interpretation and hear language describing the different ways the familiar features of apple trees are used. Children have experienced apples, if not apple trees, but may never have realized that ants and other insects feed from the trees, as do birds, who feed on the insects.

Children grow emotionally and intellectually when they can find, through books, security in loving and being loved, even while learning academic content. In Bang's *Ten, Nine, Eight,* a loving father hugs and tucks in his child as the two count objects in the room. Such a book conveys, besides the knowledge of rational counting, many and different messages to children. One child may have his understanding of a caring parent reaffirmed, while another child may realize that males as well as females can be nurturing. An Anglo child sees that African American children do things just like she does.

Feelings of security come as children see that book characters like themselves can be angry, frightened, frustrated, hateful, sad, or lonely. Models for resolving conflict, as well as lessons, can be learned. In Zolotow's *The Hating Book,* children learn how misunderstandings come about when one listens to gossip and doesn't trust a friend.

Most newspapers have a special children's section, and some offer guidance on how to use the newspaper with children. Comics have always been a source for nudging children towards reading. Comer (1988) told how his mother always read the comics from three different newspapers to him and his siblings each Sunday. This undereducated mother instinctively realized the importance of rereading the parts that especially interested each child and how this would assist her children in learning to read.

Not all influence from printed materials is necessarily positive from an adult point of view. The excitement of Max chasing his dog with a fork in Sendak's *Where the Wild Things Are* may be so attractive that a mother of a 4-year-old finds her child imitating the action with another child. Stories and other printed materials, as with television programs, also can reinforce prejudice and bias when characters of different ethnic origin are interpreted as having the characteristics of a certain cultural group. Fairy tales have been cited as reinforcing male and female stereotypes. It is possible to interpret such female characters as Cinderella, Snow White, and Rapunzel as passive women in need of rescue by active and handsome Prince Charmings. Many comic strips portray stereotyped characters and advocate violence

for solving problems. Even mainstream print has its effect, and one wonders what messages children derive from them. For example, the cover of a national news magazine portrayed strong men and women dressed in black, wearing dark sunglasses and carrying exotic weapons. The caption, in large print, read "Secrets of the new *Matrix.* We're the first to see the movie and play the video game! If we told you everything they'd have to kill us."

The various forms of media—television, computer games, Internet sources and movies—have also been criticized for their violence. When stories, other printed materials, television, computer programs, and Internet information are not comprehensible or not within children's range of experience, then, without support from an adult, the influence may be harmful to a child's self-concept and to the child's emotional, social, or intellectual development. Cornell (1993) maintained that this may be especially true for children coming from particular cultural heritages. For example, many European tales present witches as old, ugly, mean, and to be feared, but in Asian cultures, the old are wise, kind, and to be revered. The clash of cultures may be confusing, especially to new immigrants, whose understanding of and adaptation to their new country can be deterred. In the 21st century, the globalization of technology is subsuming cultural and ethnic interests, priorities, and expectations across the planet (Dickey, 2003) in a way earlier media did not.

Not all books and printed materials are well written, and the language in some is stilted and uninteresting. Well-written materials have integrity, whereas poorly written books have "flagrant repetitiveness, stiff dialogue, a gross exaggeration of humor or fantasy, conflict between realism and fantasy, didacticism, superciliousness, or a use of language that is poorly chosen for the genre of the book or for the characters in it" (Sutherland, 1996, pp. 49–50). Children acquire language

Children acquire language and richness of expression from hearing stories

and richness of expression from books. Hackneyed, mundane expressions do nothing to enrich a child's vocabulary or imagination.

A rich curriculum provided through printed materials requires adults (a) to be sensitive to children's acceptance or confusion about these materials and (b) to help children interpret printed matter in light of their own experiences.

The Internet is now a part of many young children's learning environment. No longer is the computer a part of children's lives only through programs and games. With access to the Internet, a child's world expands tremendously. Children have access to Web sites, chat groups, bulletin boards, and connections to individuals through e-mail. In some ways, this larger networking is very positive, but as with all media, it has risks. Not all material is appropriate for the children using it; adult-oriented entertainment, plus vicious hate-group

materials and video images, is easily downloaded by young children. (Lin, 2002). In addition, some children become so involved with their cyber journeys that they become addicted and have difficulty reconnecting to their regular peers.

Many professionals argue that computers will change, for the better, the way we educate young children. Some investigators see teachers moving into a constructivist model of learning with their computers, with project learning and more individualized instruction tailored to children's learning styles and preferences (Papert, 1996; Tapscott, 1999).

With all their benefits, the media also have an intentional curriculum that seeks to educate children through advertising. Some altruistic advertisements are aimed at drug or sex education, but most are directed at enticing children to be lifelong consumers (Meier, 2003). The media also have their informal and hidden curricula. Much of television, radio programming, and Internet sources are for adult consumption, but many children are exposed to programs that confuse, frighten, or misinform them when there is little or no adult guidance. The vast amount of programs and information that children can connect to makes it difficult, even with adult supervision, to be assured that children will not be exposed to inappropriate materials. Technology has developed several filtering systems to determine the appropriateness of materials, rated by a computer-based program, human judgment alone, or computer-based and human judgment. Adults can access these ratings and determine if they want certain materials to be inaccessible to the child user or if they want the child to be able to access only certain selected materials (Thornburg & Lin, 2002).

In order for children and thus society to benefit from this huge amount of community curriculum, parents, schools, and community members must work together to teach children how to make wise choices as they use the media tools and to learn important Internet behaviors, as they use e-mail, chat rooms, and other means of communication. Community members have a responsibility to engage schools and parents in forming healthy policies regarding media. Chapter 1 and Chapter 10 contain more detailed discussions of media influence on children and illustrates the importance of adult intervention.

PHYSICAL, SOCIAL, AND EMOTIONAL ENVIRONMENTS IN A COMMUNITY

The physical and social–emotional environment in a community provide a curriculum that both positively and negatively affects children's development. Children look to adults in the larger community and model their behavior on these adults. Usually, children look to

parents as role models and will identify with their positive qualities, such as caring, loving, and protecting. Depending on their age, children often find attractive models in their peer group, from adults they know and from media personalities (Anderson & Cavallaro, 2002).

Children's chances of becoming healthy, confident, and competent adults are greater when they have both a safe home environment and a safe neighborhood where they are able to play, explore, and form relationships (Garbarino, Dubrow, Kostelny, & Pardo, 1998). Regrettably, today many children are exposed to dangers both within family situations, in their communities, and from unhealthy media programs. When too many risk factors exist (see Chapter 4), children's total development is affected. Emergent intellectual capacity, motor development, coping strategies, social–emotional development of trust, autonomy, a sense of self-worth, and the ability to benefit from the environmental curriculum can be hampered (Gouvis, 1995; Randolph, Koblinsky, & Roberts, 1998).

Social Networks

Children's ability to benefit from their neighborhood is influenced extensively by the social networks their parents have established. As children mature, they develop additional social networks within their peer groups. In earlier generations, family structures tended to be stable, and community members formed bonds that enabled them to look after each other's children and to some degree control children's peer groups. But nowadays, children and their families need community support more than ever because parental supervision is far less in **dual-income** and single-parent homes (Adelman & Taylor, 2002; Kagan, 1993).

Adults Connections and Support.   In today's society, adults are likely to move often during children's growing years, and children's development is affected by adults' ability to adapt to change (Lichter & Crowley, 2002). Some parents establish new relationships easily, thus helping their children profit by participating in neighborhood activities, but in general high mobility is a risk factor.

The ambiance of a particular neighborhood may be welcoming or threatening, making it easier or riskier to initiate social contact. For example, in one part of Eastern City, homes, streets, and sidewalks are well maintained. One residential street is a dead-end street with little traffic, so residents sit outside on doorsteps and watch their children play close to the street. Families moving into this community feel secure in reaching out to others. Children come to know the adults in the neighborhood easily and are able to interact with them.

In another part of Eastern City, broken bottles litter sidewalks, poorly maintained buildings restrict families from venturing out, and illicit activities are common. Adults and neighborhood gangs are in such conflict with each other that children feel unsafe, even in their own homes. The street violence causes such trauma for families that children have difficulty learning anything positive from any community source.

Rural and suburban neighborhoods also vary in providing physical and mental safety for inhabitants, thus influencing learning. Poverty is perhaps the greatest deficit, as it limits families in making the diverse social ties that enable children to participate in a neighborhood's growth opportunities (Cochran & Niegro, 2002; Lichter & Crowley, 2002). When children are able to move comfortably throughout their neighborhoods, socialization becomes more available, and children benefit.

❧

Janice and Peter lived on the same street in look-alike houses in a large suburban neighborhood.

Although the yards were all fenced, children felt free to visit from one house to the other, stopping to watch and ask endless questions of kindly neighbors. One day, Janice and Peter roamed and stopped to watch while one neighbor trimmed roses in her front yard and another washed his car. They even got to spray some water on the soapy car, getting a bit wet themselves. After a while they wandered onto a muddy area in another neighbor's backyard. Making a few mud balls, they proceeded to toss the balls at the neighbor's garage. When Janice's mother caught up with them, she obtained buckets and water from the neighbors and insisted that the children clean up the mess they had made. With help from some of the older neighbor children, Janice and Peter managed to get the garage quite clean.

❧

That day, among other lessons, Janice and Peter learned a bit about the why and how of gardening, how cars are cleaned, and what makes water spray. They also discovered they would be held accountable for any mess they created. They learned about helping others when they received help from the older children. Of course, children's everyday lessons from the neighborhood are not always the ones adults might wish. Still, Cochran and Niegro (2002) pointed out that when children have more adults and older children with whom they do a variety of activities, they tend to do better in school. Children who have caring adults beyond family members to assist them in mastering skills and attitudes in a gradual way have greater **metacognitive** and problem-solving strategies. Children learn how to cope with their environment differently depending on their circumstances.

Not all children have extended support, and many can have regrettable experiences which create serious barriers to their cognitive accomplishments. Kumove (1966) found that when children under age 7 were able to move freely in their immediate environment, they became more independent than children whose parents found it necessary to keep them homebound. Children unable to move about in their community because of pervasive community violence often are unable to develop coping skills and thus are more likely to become aggressive or violent themselves (Slaby, Roedell, Arezzo, & Hendrix, 1995). If reforms are to take place in neighborhoods that are unsafe, these require help and support from schools. Some authorities contend that community-type schools are needed in this case. Neighborhood schools would be places "where people from the neighborhood come to learn and play together; share experiences and wisdom; nurture each other; and strengthen young people, families, and the fabric of community life. . . . It becomes a home away from home" (Adelman & Taylor, 2002).

Peer Group Settings.   Peers become strong socializing agents. Both in school and in the community, children learn more about who they are and how to behave in society from their peers. When the cultural milieu is diverse and inclusive, children can learn different interactions and expand their repertoire of social and language skills (Trawick-Smith, 2003). Parents teach children moral and ethical values, but the peer group is powerful in setting the social tone and imposing behavioral patterns.

Even as young as 18 months, children learn how their actions affect others and thus begin the process of learning behavioral codes (Hartup, 1983). A toddler who tries to take a desired toy away from another child soon learns the consequences of the behavior. It may be an indignant yell; it may be a slap; it may be acquiescence and subsequent loss of a playmate. As children begin to form peer groups and play with each other, they begin to form rules of conduct so that they can continue to operate as a group. It is in peer groups that children learn to negotiate, problem solve, and compromise in order to continue to play and work together. Some children will be more dominant than others and will learn the rules for domination and acquiescence. Children are often rewarded by **significant others** in the group for conforming, or they are ostracized (Elkin & Handel, 1989).

Children experiment with various roles (leader, compromiser, follower, negotiator, etc.) and discover from their peers how to act to fulfill roles as well as how their peers respond to them. Children also learn about their own abilities from their peers. They learn that they can run faster, jump higher, or read better as they compare their skills with others. But the group also dictates what skills are prized.

Although parents teach children about gender roles, by preschool, peers begin to segregate into boy and girl groups that dictate what roles each group is permitted to play. A physician's daughter, after beginning preschool, insisted that her doctor mother was really a nurse. At school, she had learned in her play group that doctors are boys and nurses are girls, even though her teacher and parents insisted differently. In addition, children learn cultural and social differences as they interact with their peers. They compare notes about their own family's customs, values, and ways of doing things. Peer group acceptance or rejection can influence how individual children change their own behaviors (Bigner, 2002).

Sexual understandings and misunderstandings are learned from family, extensive media exposure, and peers. Many young children learn the physical difference between boys and girls by examining each other. They often learn about birth, when some "wiser" child informs them of their knowledge or misunderstanding. It is through such discussions, along with other teachings, that children figure out for themselves the confusing information they receive (Sadker & Sadker, 2003).

Children experiment with various roles and learn from peers how to fulfill these roles

Cognitive information and development of numerous skills come from children's interactions with peers. Children have rituals and routines, just as adults do. Older peers teach younger ones the chants and rhymes of childhood. Memory skills and counting, as well as physical endurance, are enhanced as children jump rope to such rhymes as "One Potato, Two Potato" or "First Comes Love, Then Comes Marriage." As they play together, children learn from more skilled peers how to climb higher, catch a ball, read a story, or add up their money for ice cream. Learning may result from a desire to compete with a peer or because the peer has more information and passes it on. Learning may also come because a new idea has been introduced and children need to test out the new concept.

~

Billy was watching Ahmed copy words from a book he was reading. "Whatcha doing?" asked Billy.

"I'm making an "r" for red," replied Ahmed. "Nunh, nunh, that's not an R. I'll show you how to make an R." Billy wrote a capital R. Ahmed retorted, "Oh! That's a big R, and I'm making a little r!" After much discussion, Ahmed in disgust turned to his book. "Look," he pointed, "that says 'Red' and that says 'red.' See, that's a big R and that's a little r."

~

Ahmed has challenged Billy's thinking, so now Billy will examine writing in a new way. New learning has been opened up to him by a friend. Ahmed's scorn for his not knowing seemed to spur Billy on, for later he got a book and paper and came to sit beside Ahmed and tried to make the little r, asking his friend for help.

Not all learning from peer groups is positive. Gangs can be a destructive force in any society, as children seek approval and find that they must develop antisocial codes of behavior to be accepted. Some children can be targets for peer victimization, but when these at-risk children have a "best friend," this friendship acts as a strong buffer against such attacks (Hodges, Boivin, Vitaro, & Bukowski, 1999). When a community provides opportunities for children to develop social networks among different adult and peer groups, children have more options. When this happens, the lure of destructive peer groups is lessened, and children are helped to find more positive peer associations.

Ethnic Community Contributions

As we noted in Chapter 3, most American communities are becoming ethnically diverse. In recent decades, immigration to the United States (both sanctioned and illegal) has intensified to such a degree that immigration is one fourth of population growth in any one year (United States Census Bureau, 2002). In addition, ethnic minority groups are dispersing throughout the United States. When observing the *American Demographics* minority population maps, we find only a handful of the neutral areas showing no integration in 2002.

All of this means that our country is rapidly becoming a highly multiethnic nation, and schools need to take advantage of the dynamic aspects linked to ethnic differences in their communities. In almost all communities today, there is a rich mixture of culture and races from which children learn about differences and how to accept and learn about each other. But often children do not understand their own culture, and in order to be enriched by another culture it is important that children first understand their own culture and its variations. This understanding should be the start of multicultural education.

Schools can profit from the various ethnic cultures in learning about the richness of community life, and students learn to be analytical thinkers as they discover the cultural orientations of other persons in their school and community. Schools in the past have focused more on the outward manifestations of culture—clothing and celebrations—not recognizing variations of behavior. It is important to get beyond the stereotypic images that schools often have used in the past to present different cultures—Japanese women appearing with kimono, obi, and parasol, or a Hawaiian appearing barefoot with a grass skirt and leis.

Attainment in the arts, the special festivals and entertainment performances, plus business and commercial successes of ethnically different individuals in a community are highly visible areas for enhancing a multicultural curriculum. Comparing similarities and differences in the daily events of children in one community offers insights to another culture as well as variations within a culture.

We have to remember that the unique behaviors, language, learning patterns, and values of different ethnic groups are acquired for a reason. The fact that they differ from mainstream society means that these have a particular purpose in another cultural milieu, and when we seek to learn about and from the differences, we come closer to an appreciation of the rich cultural history we all have around us. If we have different cultures in our community, we should want to understand and appreciate their talents and traditions. Everyone is proud of his or her culture and background, and if given a chance to present it, will do something that enriches our knowledge. Some teachers have used the following objectives in seeking to acknowledge a community's various cultural groups:

1. Solicit the stories behind the food choices that different ethnic groups prize.

2. Get the history of the dances and music that each ethnic group possesses.

3. Feature different family schedules, the rewards that different cultures use in rearing children, and ways different families praise individual successes.

4. Solicit and record the stories behind the immigration journeys people undertook to reach where they are now.

❧

In one ethnically diverse classroom, a teacher extended the "homework" project designed for parent–child reading to promote different viewpoints. While reading In Monet's Garden *to her class, Mrs. McCloud introduced a doll of Linnea, the story's main character, and talked about Linnea's interest in Monet's house and garden. From there the children became intrigued with taking the Linnea doll home and introducing her to their families. With their parents' help, each child pretended to be Linnea and wrote in her journal the food they were eating that day, what games they played, the TV they watched, and stories they read. At school they developed charts to list experiences Linnea had in each of their homes. The journal always went with Linnea, so the parents could read about the different adventures in other homes. Parents and children started to see commonalities they all shared, and they noted differences. This led to curiosity about the different ethnic families in their community and opened up an appreciation of the differences and the challenges of other's lives.*

In literature class, the teacher introduced stories with different ethnic protagonists, and children took these books home to share with parents. The librarian noticed that children started to select more books on different cultures, so she began displaying different aspects of life in a single ethnic culture. Children's artwork and projects brought out diverse cultural elements. PTA meetings became quite lively, and Mrs. McCloud even introduced to parents Mary Pipher's (2002) The Middle of Everywhere: The World's Refugees Come to Our Town. *Parents discussed the book and then began to share their own family's arrival in the United States and how they adapted. Mrs. McCloud had each child develop a personal book of "Who am I and where did I come from?" This meant that all children began to research their own family's history and arrival in this country.*

During this unit the teachers, students, and families witnessed the many cultural variations. Thanks to the student's projects, parents and community members could appreciate differences in diets, clothing, living conditions, communication styles, celebrations, choice of music, literary interests, and skills in crafts, as well as the everyday vocations.

❧

The changing demographics in our society means that our children must be learning about and accepting differences. No longer are schools a "melting pot" for immigrants in this country, but places where a rich fabric of cultures exist and where we learn from each other's experiences (Futrell, Gomez, & Bedden, 2003).

Natural Environments

As children move about their neighborhood, the outdoor environment offers a rich curriculum from which they gain understanding about their world. This curriculum is, of course, all of nature. Learning differs depending on the combination of children's ability, social interactions regarding the environment, and children's freedom of movement to explore. Louv (1990) discovered that many U.S. children spend very little time outdoors. Although they do learn about nature in various ways, their understanding and appreciation of nature are limited.

Studies on children's play activity indicate that the quality of children's outdoor and indoor play differs, and thus different learning opportunities emerge. Children engage in more dramatic and **constructive play** outdoors (Moore, 1985; Perry, 2003) and in more **exploratory play** (Anderson, 1972; N. J. Wagner,

Children may climb indoors, but viewing the world from a tree branch gives them a broader perspective

1995) when they feel, touch, examine, crunch, and test materials, such as when learning the sounds different rocks make when dropped into the water. Balancing while walking on uneven rocks in a dry riverbed develops different skills than balancing on the smooth surface of a gymnasium balance beam. Children may climb indoors, but viewing the world from a tree branch gives them broader perspectives. "Twigs, soil, mud, stones, leaves, and grass are materials of sensory pleasure, play, and learning" (Dighe, 1993, p. 58).

Good children's books capture the many wonders of nature and can extend children's appreciation of what they experience, but without experiencing the reality of the world, their knowledge is limited. In the following vignette, Davon has book knowledge about snow, but it is the real experience that enriches his understanding.

☙

Davon lived all of his 5 years in Florida. He had heard lots about snow and was especially fond of Ezra Jack Keats's The Snowy Day, *but he had never seen real snow. While visiting his cousin in Boston that winter, he awoke to white flakes outside his window. He had never imagined snow to look like that. As the week wore on and more snow fell, Davon learned much*

*more about the feel of snow on his face and
the taste of snow as he and his cousin held out
their tongues to catch it. He learned how snow
could limit and enhance activity and how it
felt to walk through drifts.*

Not all of nature's lessons are pleasant. The
first snow can be an exciting and beautiful
time, but a blizzard followed by power outages
and snarled traffic teaches a different lesson.
Learning to observe the outdoor environment
enhances children's cognitive learning as well
as their social and emotional understanding.
Joshua learned many things about his surroundings one late-winter day while watching
the waterfront.

*Joshua lived near the St. Lawrence River and
with his mother loved to watch the seals bob
up and down in the harbor. One winter day, a
small, and undoubtedly ill, seal crawled out
on the ice floe and collapsed. While watching
and wondering about the seal, Joshua noted two
eagles swoop down on the seal and begin tear-
ing at the carcass. Alarmed, Joshua ran to get
his mother, who tried to explain about the natural process of creatures in the wild. Then she
remembered Cherie Mason's book,* Everybody's
Somebody's Lunch. *Together they read how a
young girl whose cat was devoured by a fox
discovers that there are predators and prey in
our world and that all are part of nature's food
chain. Joshua then became quite fascinated
with the eagles and their 3-day venture of cleaning up the dead seal. He watched as several
crows tried to claim their share but were chased
away. A neighbor farther along the shore telephoned and asked Joshua's mother whether
she knew what was agitating the crows. An excited Joshua took the phone to explain to the
neighbor about the eagles.*

Joshua's nature lessons didn't all happen
in one day, but he gradually became a more interested and astute student of the world
around him, discovering other fascinating avenues for learning.

INTERACTIONS AMONG COMMUNITY AGENCIES, FAMILIES, AND SCHOOLS

The learning that took place in the vignettes in
this chapter did not happen in isolation within
these communities, for the community curriculum was affected by how the families and
schools linked children to community resources and agencies (see Figure 9–1). Stronger
links heighten the potential for children's
learning.

Many community agencies welcome children's visits, either with their families or with
schools. Some agencies actively attempt to

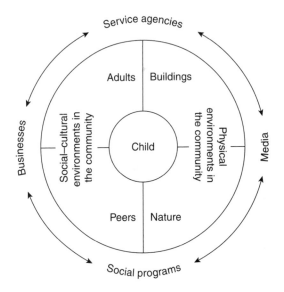

Figure 9–1 Community impact on children
through the environment, social networks,
cultural events, and from interactions among
agencies

reach families of differing cultural and economic backgrounds. Other agencies limit their support to those families who can afford their services, or to those families who reach out. Louisa, in the earlier vignette, was able to use more community resources because church members aggressively presented programs to assist her in her dilemma. As she became more confident of her ability to help her children, she more actively sought those recreational programs that provided richer learning experiences.

All families at some time use the business enterprises of a community. In today's society, many families patronize large, impersonal organizations for purchases, banking, and communicating, and the education that children receive is more limited than what happens in a small neighborhood, such as Joshua's, with supportive parents and neighbors.

Many community agencies that offer programs to children depend on family or Big Brother and Big Sister types of support. A Scout-sponsored camping trip, for example, may include one or both parents or another adult accompanying children. Trailblazing and fire-building lessons may be a planned part of the trip, but how the learning is extended depends on parental involvement with the organization. Some churches have family nights where leaders invite entire families to be involved in extended learning situations.

Communities and schools can collaborate to provide concrete experiences to extend children's learning, but this is not done as much as is possible. Trips into the community are enriched when the agencies have materials, people, and specific events appropriate for the learning level of the children visiting. When teachers make visits and discuss the trip with community agencies beforehand, learning is more likely to be enhanced. Some school trips within a community are not done collaboratively, however, and children's learning is thus limited and may even be negative.

One child care center decided to make a trip to McDonald's without checking first with the establishment. It was noon, and McDonald's was crowded. Children, when let off the bus, ran to the play area and began to play noisily. Teachers' attempts to find a place for children to eat together and to give them experience in selecting and ordering food were disastrous. The bus driver had left, and the harassed teachers had to keep track of the children as they rushed to the playground, roamed the restaurant, and visited other children waiting for lunch. Another distraction was a family watching a miniature TV, which attracted children from the child care center. The teachers struggled to get children to order their food, and they pushed and jostled the adults waiting to order. Some children finally received their food, but then the bus returned and teachers hurried everyone onto it, some carrying uneaten food while others protested they hadn't gotten anything. The children, the teachers, and the McDonald's personnel were all unhappy with the experience.

Many restaurants welcome children's visits and provide opportunities for children to visit the kitchen and to experience ordering and eating food in a relaxed manner. In the preceding episode, lack of planning resulted in an unpleasant experience for both adults and children. It would be wrong to assume that no learning took place from this trip; however, with more care, the trip could have been more valuable and pleasant for everyone.

In community programs, where children interact with materials, observe events, or see animals acting in a natural situation, youngsters usually learn more than in those programs where adults lecture, expecting children to be enraptured with what they say. The community, through natural phenomena and by the nature of the community's organization, offers a rich curriculum for all children. Children learn from this curriculum in direct relationship to the social networks available to them.

IMPLICATIONS FOR PROFESSIONALS

The curriculum of the community is a vast resource for teachers. Information from this chapter can be used to start your **resource file** (or a computer file) that will assist you in classroom instruction, working with families, and making use of community resources. There are many ways to organize and build such a file. The following steps are suggestions for proceeding:

- List the four major categories from Table 9–1.
- Under each category, select one subcategory that is likely to be part of your professional assignment (e.g., you think you will teach in the inner city, so you select animals).
- Be specific on items: What animals are children in a city environment likely to observe? As you choose items, keep in mind what children may be familiar with but could learn more about.
- Expand by selecting one animal and begin a list of resources (e.g., places animals can be found, persons who might bring animals to classroom, books about animals, films about animals and their owners or trainers, Internet sources appropriate for the age group).
- Examine the other categories to ascertain if at this time you might wish to cross-list (e.g., pet shops for free materials regarding animals).
- Move on to another category. Consider what general information at this point you think will be helpful in your teaching (e.g., select Services, then the subcategory Recreation, then Parks).

- Expand by listing different types of parks and what learning opportunities would be available to children. Include any materials or resources that you could bring into the classroom.
- At a later point, consider what resources would be helpful for working with children and which are better for parents.
- An important category in your file will be the service agencies. List them separately with addresses and the services they render for parents. Collect brochures from these agencies.

Beginning a resource file before teaching helps you to organize so that you are able to add specific addresses and resources later as you discover what works for your classroom.

SUMMARY AND REVIEW

Most community curricula can be made rich and varied, depending on how adults in society structure the environment and how they develop supportive educational policies in various service agencies. Political, social, cultural, and business agencies offer, both intentionally and unintentionally, a learning environment for children in a community. Political agencies, for the most part, focus their formal education on political endeavors toward adults or older children, expecting the teaching to be done by adults important to children. However, political decisions in different communities regarding management of a community and its social agencies can result in children learning from totally different curricula.

Service agencies, transportation services, social and cultural agencies, and business and commercial enterprises usually produce materials aimed at educating the public about their services. What children learn from these formal materials depends largely on the use parents and teachers make of them.

Like schools, all agencies provide informal and hidden curricula whereby children learn about their world. The natural and manufactured resources found within communities provide learning experiences even when there is little adult intervention. Children see signs, notice buildings, observe nature, note adult actions, and learn something from all their encounters. The ways that important adults use the resources, explain things to children, and interact with each other all enhance children's learning.

Children who live in communities providing safe physical, emotional, and moral environments have more educational opportunities, for in these areas families are better able to establish social networks that enable them to tap community resources. For children outside such safe environments, schools, parents, and other agencies must work especially hard to compensate and must strive to build a solid curriculum so that these children, too, will thrive in tomorrow's world.

SUGGESTED ACTIVITIES AND QUESTIONS

1. Take a 1- to 2-mile hike around your neighborhood. List all the natural resources, human resources, and materials that you observe. Rate the learning potential linked to them for children living here and start a resource file from information gathered.

2. Visit a business establishment in your community. Interview the owner or manager to learn whether they have materials aimed at educating children and how they distribute such materials. While there, ask yourself what children might learn just from being in the building.

3. From the list of community resources in this chapter, identify those your family was connected with as you grew up. List three things you think you learned from involvement with these resources.

4. Observe two or more children playing together. What learning do you think is taking place in this interaction? What community resources could support or hinder what these children are learning?

5. Reread the Galina vignette (or select your own story). Discuss social, physical, and cognitive learning as evidenced by her own words.

RESOURCES

Books

1. Carter, M. & Curtis, D. (2003). *Designs for living and learning: Transforming early childhood environments.* St. Paul, MN: Redleaf.
2. Cornell, J. B. (1998). *Sharing nature with children* (2nd ed.). Nevada City, CA: Dawn.
3. Harlan, J. D., & Rivkin, M. S. (2003). *Science experiences for the early childhood years: An integrative, affective approach* (8th ed.). Upper Saddle River, NJ: Merrill/Prentice Hall.
4. Prasuraman, S., & Greenhaus, J. H. (1997). *Integrating work and family: Challenges and choices for a changing world.* Westport, CT: Quorum.
5. Rivkin, M. C. (1995). *The great outdoors: Restoring children's right to play outside.* Washington, DC: National Association for the Education of Young Children.

Films and Videos

1. *The adventure begins: Preschool and technology* [Video, 10 min]. (1997). Demonstrates how computers enhance learning. Produced by the National Association for the Education of Young Children, with Apple Computer, Inc.
2. *Early intervention: Natural environments for children* [Video, 28 min]. (1998). All children grow in special ways when learning environments such as schools, homes, parks, and restaurants provide for the special-needs child. Washington, DC: National Association for the Education of Young Children.
3. *Exploring science and nature* [Video, 28 min]. (1995). Washington, DC: National Association for the Education of Young Children.

4. Kids Express Field Trip videos. Examples for primary-school ages are *Happy Campers* (1997; on exploring nature) and *Kids Can Cook* (1997) [45 min each]. Springfield, MO: Kids Express.

5. School Works videos supplement field trips. Examples for primary-school ages are *To the Zoo* (1996) and *To the Glassmaking Studio* (1997) [30 min each]. Alameda, CA: School Works.

Organizations

Community Relations Service
U.S. Department of Justice
5550 Friendship Boulevard, Suite 330
Chevy Chase, MD 20815
www.usdoj.gov/office/crs.html

National Legal Resource Center for Child Advocacy and Protection
1800 M Street, NW
Washington, DC 20036
http://nccanch.acf.hhs.gov

Smithsonian Institution
Washington, DC 20560
www.si.edu

Websites

1. www.c-zone.net/fisher/wn
   An on-line service for nutritional news and articles.
2. www.2.childrensoftware.com
   Website for Children's Software Revue, a publication helping teachers and parents examine software programs for children.
3. www.clueintosafety.com
   A collection of valuable safety information points about neighborhoods. Focus is to educate the public about safety.
4. http://lcweb.loc.gov
   Library of Congress home page with links to all congressional sites. Useful for accessing library services.
5. www.wri.org
   World Resources Institute. Focus is on the environment, with sites on health, marine resources and global trends.

Chapter 10

Effective Social and Cultural Settings for Learning

What goes on inside schools is greatly influenced by what occurs outside of schools.
(Liston & Zeichner, 1996a, p. xi)

After looking at the various curricula found in homes, schools, and communities, we now identify settings that will provide the best possible educational experiences. Of course, the model programs we describe in Chapter 12 will thrive in settings that include the features associated with effective homes, schools, and communities. In reading this chapter, you will learn the following:

1. Particular characteristics identify effective homes, schools, and communities.

2. Educators, parents, and community workers have a number of tools to use for evaluating the different social settings.

3. Connections are needed among the three social settings to produce the best educational environments for children.

4. The school is the most capable force, both to begin and then to nurture partnerships, for uniting the three social settings.

Well-functioning homes, effective schools, plus dynamic and prosperous neighborhoods are goals to which all cultural groups and political units aspire. These goals are being reached in some areas across the United States, and those areas are heralded in media reports under such banners as "most desirable location in America." Investigators inform us, however, that many towns and cities in the United States are suffering and have damaged neighborhoods (Coles, Testa, & Coles, 2001, Garbarino, Dubrow, Kostelny, & Pardo, 1998; Kotlowitz, 1998). Consider the following descriptions of two very different U.S. communities:

1. This southwestern city has the most sought-after climate in the United States. Days are sunny, atmosphere is clear, and the demeanor on city streets is uplifting. Careful development from the area's small-town origins produced wide streets, inviting parks, and pleasantly designed neighborhoods. The multiethnic population flows in harmonious ways and appears truly integrated. Electronics production provides a strong economic base, and poverty seems completely absent. Crime statistics are the lowest in the United States for small cities, and a pleasant ambience in the city is felt by even short-term visitors. All schools are new, spacious, and well-equipped. The curriculum for students is conservative but apparently in keeping with community wishes. It seems an almost utopian setting (adapted from A. B. Prescott, 1994, personal communication).

2. The public housing project is an impoverished community with rat-infested apartments, where plumbing often does not work and there is almost no maintenance. Buildings and grounds are in constant disrepair—windows are boarded up, and the effects of vandalism are seen everywhere. The project is also dangerous. Crime has increased 400% in recent years, and death is so frequent that young children play funeral in the after-school program. Gangs and drug lords dominate the community, instilling fear in all residents. Conditions have made families into internal refugees, and rules that parents give their children reflect the sobering conditions: "Don't go out in the hallway. Stay away from windows. Stay together all the time. When you hear shots, hit the floor" (adapted from Garbarino, Kostelny, & Dubrow, 1998, pp. 130–142).

The two settings described result from the overarching social, political, and economic forces at work in their respective communities. Certain favorable circumstances produced one venue; a series of misfortunes and miscalculations produced the other. It is beyond the scope of our text to define or explain even part of the dynamics producing quality and distressed areas in any city. However, we can identify characteristics of effective social settings and recommend ways to make our own workplaces effective examples.

All three social settings in children's lives naturally affect children's learning and experience. Also, for good or ill, one setting will affect the other two. Problems in one setting make functioning in the others more difficult, although the positive effects of two settings often counterbalance an inferior third. For instance, effective homes can and do offset negative community influences (Clark, 1983; Comer, 1988, 1997), and effective school programs can make a difference for struggling families and communities (Meier, 1995, 2002a; Quint, 1994). In Chapter 12, we highlight some model programs that illustrate the better opportunities for children when more cohesion develops among the major social settings. So, how do we start?

We must first assess what exists in children's lives. Then, establishing goals for improvement and creating plans for action become relevant. One underlying thesis of this text is that schools are best situated to assess the social settings of an area, make plans for remediation, and begin the process of drawing institutions together for the betterment of children.

Collaborative efforts are easily instituted in vigorous and healthy social settings; when deficits and problems exist in the settings, the challenge is, of course, far greater. In problem settings, agents of change must be more engaged, work harder, and experiment aggressively to bring about improvements.

In this chapter, we examine the features of competent families, effective schools, and effective communities. We also include the converse of some features when they illuminate explanations. We conclude by examining the role of the school as a broker for linking social settings.

COMPETENT FAMILIES

As we noted in Chapters 3 and 4, U.S. families have different cultural heritages, values, and socioeconomic bases, plus different approaches to health care, nutrition, recreation, and social experiences. No family is perfect, yet most families have their particular strengths. Families function in the context of a community and in association with a school, and the quality of this interaction determines to a large extent the success or failure of children attending a school.

Most readers are familiar with the hundreds of self–help books, articles, and programs about advice on parenting. New tips and survival guides appear each year, and we find of course valuable items spread out in many of these. The writers recommend one basic approach, labeled RPMS (for responding, preventing, monitoring, mentoring, and modeling) and developed from research on "What Works" by the **National Institute of Child Health and Human Development (NICHD)**. The material is available from the NICHD (see the Resources section) and lends itself to community parent education classes, school in-service education sessions, and individual study.

Areas of home and family competence that we explore in this section are organization and management, beliefs and value structures, intellectual stimuli, parental knowledge of child development, health and nutrition practices, social and emotional environments, and social networking. Since all these areas have a serious impact on children's growth and learning, what if problems exist in one or more? As stated, all families probably have some deficits, but the issue is the number and extent of those deficiencies. The Sameroff, Seifer, Barocas, Zax, and Greenspan (1987) research and the Werner and Smith (1992) studies inform us that at-risk children with one or two risk factors seem to manage well when compensating help is available from other social settings.

Organization and Management

As we discussed in Chapter 3, the United States contains numerous cultures, each of which represents a somewhat different pattern of child rearing. But, across cultures, we find strands undergirding the competent home and differentiating it from less effective ones.

Since the Bernstein (1972) and Baumrind (1966) studies, social scientists have continued to recognize the several general management styles found in U.S. homes. The styles overlap and combinations exist, but most families seemingly tend toward one style or another. Baumrind (1966, 1968) labeled three basic parenting styles: authoritarian, authoritative, and permissive. Others refined Baumrind's terms somewhat and added different labels, but in essence all investigators focus on similar major categories. The authoritative, democratic, or **sponsored-independence** style is the one we associate with the effective family. Family members managing according to the authoritative style are democratic and controlling but warm and receptive. These attributes contrast with the authoritarian's detached control and the noncontrolling and nondemanding approach of the permissive style. The styles are discussed more fully in Chapter 4.

Some follow-up studies, by Maccoby and Martin (1983) for example, failed to find, in selected ethnic families, all the relationships that Baumrind's European American population revealed between style and schoolwork. However, Clark's (1983) team looked at Caucasian, Mexican American, and African American homes to identify effective families in difficult living conditions. He found that particular attitudes and behaviors—generally the authoritative style—made the difference

between success and failure in school and life for children. The Baumrind and Clark findings were reinforced by more recent research (e.g., Hart, DeWolf, & Burts, 1993; Hrabowski, Maton, Greeve, & Greif, 2002).

A significant finding in Clark's (1983) work is that "these [effective] families believe they can make a difference in a child's life, and they are not overwhelmed by circumstances" (p. 198). Clark identified a number of characteristics of effective families, irrespective of socioeconomic conditions and these highlighted—control over life events, high expectations, mutual support, consistent rules, and spiritual investment.

Frequently, we associate the preceding as characteristics of the Protestant ethic—a hallmark of prospering U.S. families—although Clark found these same characteristics in poor homes having many economic and social disadvantages. Specialists in all professions working with children can value the Clark characteristics as benchmarks for identifying successful families.

So what can we do about the families that lack many of these features? It is useless to wring our hands and write off 20% or more of U.S. homes as unsalvageable. Changed circumstances for families with children are key. Governmental policies (federal, state, and municipal) must aim to improve health conditions, stimulate economic opportunities, and attempt to redirect the living conditions of those in poverty. The welfare reform efforts by federal and state agencies have indicated these as goals, but results are mixed. Some reporters note that the successes in the late 1990s are largely due to overall economic gains in the United States since reform was instituted (Children's Defense Fund, 1998); the early years of the 21st century again find us with increasing numbers of poor families (Webb, Metha, & Jordan, 2003). Even without government intervention, school and community groups working together can bring about changes in the perceptions families have of themselves. Good schools and humane communities do make a difference in the pressures affecting families and can provide incentives for families to grow in effectiveness. Model programs show this (see particularly the Comer plan in described in Chapter 12).

In some instances, parents are so remote and out of touch that the best teachers can do is to give constant support, believe in children, and hope that some success unfolds in the classroom. Some hard-to-reach parents can be included through persistent communication and emphasis on their strengths and their successes with their children. Effective parent education means seeking ways to support parents to gradually accept responsibility for their children's education—and at the parents' level of ability. It means trying out different approaches, such as listening to parent responses, and building on what works.

Beliefs and Value Structures

A number of writers point out that children's attitudes, beliefs, and values resemble those of their parents (Coles, 1997; Goleman, 1995; Scarf, 1999), but all allow that schools and

communities extend these considerably. Parenting practices and parent values do become critical in children's lives.

Educating about stealing, lying, and disorderly conduct is normal for most families, although the instruction can take different forms. Some parents teach morals and values through intimidation and punishment, while others approach the challenge by explaining children's problems and the impact of one's actions on others. The latter approach, called induction, results in stronger development of conscience and **internal control** (Sadker & Sadker, 2003). The effective family will focus on values, morals, and attitudes by modeling behaviors and discussing them with their children, reasoning through solutions, and labeling the behavior when seen in public (see Table 10–1). Children very much need a sense of purpose and direction in their lives, and this begins with values established by the home.

Literary and Intellectual Stimuli

Competent families provide children with life-long learning interests as they go about their daily lives. Families that provide intellectual challenges stimulate children's interest in

Table 10–1   Helping Children Develop Internal Locus of Control

1. When caregivers are responsive, affectionate, and comforting, children know their actions count.
2. Allow children to accept consequences for their actions; for example, they can manage cleanup after some water play.
3. Avoid performing tasks children can do for themselves. Caregivers encourage effort and experiments so children learn to do for themselves.
4. Give children responsibilities that fit their age and skill levels.
5. Let children know if and when they perform well.
6. Model behaviors and attitudes that show you are proactive; for example, communicate to children that persons can make things happen.
7. Encourage and support children's particular interests and show respect for their accomplishments.
8. Explain the reasons for needed rules and limits, but establish reasonable standards for behavior.
9. Allow children to make age appropriate decisions as often as possible. Start with minor choices and graduate to consequence-bearing actions.

Source: Adapted from Berns, 2001, Lefcourt, 1984; Sadker & Sadker, 2003.

natural phenomena and sharpen skills used in acquiring knowledge from different media (Bruer, 1998, 2002). Parents encourage these practices by conversing, questioning, demonstrating, and modeling the use of literary, problem-solving, and investigative skills.

Language Patterns. Children's vocabulary and grammatical abilities are patterned almost totally after caregiver modeling in the course of family interactions (Heath, 1983; Sigel, Dreyer, & McGillicuddy-DeLisi, 1984). Competent homes provide a rich language environment where conversations, active listening, and interactions with all members are valued and demonstrated. Bernstein (1972) noted the elaborate codes that middle-class families use that prepare children for interaction and communication within schools and the greater community.

In homes where multiple languages or dialects are used, competent parents, through their demonstrations, ensure that children learn **code-switching** to deal with different social venues (Tabors & Snow, 2001). Language expands and develops for all children as they are exposed to literacy experiences in different forms, dialects, or cultures. Hearing the language patterns of stories, dramatizing these stories, and discussing them with others so the patterns become familiar contributes to children's expanding understanding of language (Pinnell, 1996).

Published Materials. Competent families have books, read, and often refer to other publications in the home. Numerous studies confirm that the amount of reading in homes is directly related to children's success in reading as well as other school subjects (McGee & Richgels, 2004). Quality child care arrangements and Head Start programs contribute to literacy, and their efforts can compensate somewhat for deprived circumstances, but the major influence still comes from the family (Edelsky, 1996; Hart & Risley, 1995). Some school–community collaborations, as in the following vignette, are purposely intended to increase the amount of reading in homes.

The Growing Up Reading program in a small New England community is a community–school–home collaboration directed at improving literacy. New books are delivered to homes of new babies born in the community,

Studies confirm that the amount of reading in homes is directly related to children's success in reading at school

and then each preschool birthday is celebrated with another good, age-appropriate book. "Grandparent" volunteers deliver the books to homes and interact with parents and children. The program also has a follow-up scheme to bring young parents and their children together. In this, parents and their preschool children meet at least once a month with childhood specialists and grandparent volunteers. At these meetings, parents, teachers, and volunteers exchange stories, demonstrate techniques of book sharing, and discuss how to use other materials while children engage in play activities.

Illiteracy is a lingering problem afflicting many marginal homes. The United States has a surprising number of functionally illiterate young parents who have few printed materials in their homes and therefore meager ways of stimulating the prereading skills and interests of their children. Collaborations and networks, as in the preceding vignette, to involve these parents are critical. School early-intervention plans are backup strategies when collaborations are not available.

Use of Television and the Internet.   As is not the case with published materials, almost every home in the United States has one or more television sets. How each family uses television is, of course, the salient factor. Sitcoms, game shows, and soap operas, while providing some stimulation, give children few readiness skills for reading. Children's shows are aired in all areas of the country, but unless parents and children both watch and discuss them, the shows appear to have little cognitive benefit (Singer & Singer, 2001; Van Evra, 1998).

Television watching and its association with aggression and violence has been a concern for decades. Readers will recall the startling statistics on the number of violent acts viewed every hour by elementary school children (McChesney, 1999) . These are sobering and seem not to be diminished in spite of the V-chip for controlling access to particular programs and the increase in children's programming.

Positive links to achievement have been found when children viewed television programs such as *Sesame Street, Blue's Clues*, and *Mr. Rogers' Neighborhood*. In addition, some researchers have found benefits when parents watched television with their children and then discussed the programs (Alexander, 2001; Gunter & McAleer, 1997). Here again, it is the effective family that pursues the objective of tapping the educational dimensions of television or Internet sources (see Table 10–2). Community and school programs can have a similar positive effect on "education via media" for at-risk children if advocates can influence the home behaviors through parent education.

Similar recommendations go with children's use of the Internet. Parents can seek to control children's access to Web sites through CyperPatrol or NetNanny, but family agreements and sharing on positive sites is far better. Nationally, more concern about distasteful on-line material has appeared, and media manufacturers now distribute software to limit children's on-line travel (Thornburgh & Lin, 2002)

One new Web site, Kidfu.com, developed in 2002 by former organizers of FreeZone.com, shows the latest in a protected virtual community for youngsters (Hafner, 2002). Its chat rooms are constantly monitored by "chat jockeys" who can even provide homework help. However, it is not free, and this limits participation in a quality venue. Other quality sites that have subscription fees are JuniorNet.com and iKnowthat.com. But Lin (2002), a longtime researcher in child use of the Internet, is not encouraging when he states that presently there is little stimulating and compelling material designed for children. Therefore, it is not

Table 10–2   Sensible Television Use

Controlling TV Use at Home

Pediatricians, media specialists, and teachers advocate TV controls as well as "media literacy" for children. But parents are in the best position to shape any media effects into positive influences for their children. Below are strategies for parents to use in setting regulations, making wise TV choices, and performing follow-through.

1. Keep children under 2 away from TV programs. Avoid using TV as an emergency babysitter.
2. Ration older children to 2 hours of screen time daily, i.e., TV and computers.
3. Monitor what children watch, and coview the programs with your youngsters.
4. Encourage child interaction with beneficial TV shows and then talk about the program after the set is off.
5. Place the TV set apart from family areas so it doesn't intrude on meals and other family times together.
6. Keep TV out of children's bedrooms. This leads to TV overdose.
7. Exploit the TV and book connection. Children's programming for shows such as *Arthur* and *Book of Pooh* comes from well-known books. After watching, children are often enthused about reading the "real story."
8. Parents must watch their own TV behavior. Predetermine programs for everyone to watch, watch those, and then turn the set off. Surfing through programs encourages children to do the same.

Source: Adapted from Andreason, (2001); Singer & Singer (2001); Van Evra (1998).

surprising that children, after moving around the Net for awhile, are tempted to move to other "not so nice" sites. The following items in Table 10–3 are some general rules for families to follow regarding children's on-line connections.

Parental Knowledge of Child Development

In effective family situations, caregivers are aware that children move through developmental stages and that instruction and expectations depend on where children are in their growth.

Some young parents have extended families and a social network of neighbors to inform them about normal and reasonable stages of children's growth. Others have books, such as the guides published by Dr. Spock, Penelope Leach, or T. Berry Brazelton from which to view their children's progress. Others will depend on services gained through clinics, such as Women, Infants, and Children (WIC) programs, well-baby clinics, and family

health centers. Still others remain quite ignorant of the basics of child development and depend on intuition and even folklore.

When communities address child development needs, results can be haphazard. Adult education programs on child care and community outreach programs are available in some areas, but historically they attract few parents. Some high schools provide a basic course on home management and child development for students. Such opportunities (e.g., the Dunbar [Baltimore] High School program for pregnant teens and young mothers) provide some knowledge and experience about developmental concepts and nurturing.

Health and Nutrition

Health implies attention to complete personal well-being, not just the absence of disease or infirmities. Competent parents provide safe and healthy environments in which children develop and prosper. Most health and safety concepts derive from parents and caregivers

Table 10–3   Internet Safety for Children

Basic Rules for Internet Safety

Parents, caregivers, and community social workers need to be cognizant of the dangerous potential of Internet use as well as its many advantages and educational opportunities.

1. Adults must know about the features of the Children's Online Privacy Protection Act of 2002.
2. Adults must have a procedure for monitoring, and blocking if necessary, young children's use of the Internet. Software programs available from AOL and Microsoft Network will do this.
3. Caregivers should know their children's on-line visits and the amount of time spent on-line.
4. Adults must know the safe Web sites and how to steer children toward them. Parents should discuss with the child the Web site content and their chat room participation.
5. All learners agree there will be no rudeness on-line and that they will not impersonate another.
6. Adults and children should agree that learners need to be as wary of persons met on-line as those met off-line.
7. All learners should agree with their parents and instructors about not posting any personal data on on-line diaries, Web logs, or in chat rooms.
8. All learners should agree that children will not share names, e-mail addresses, phone numbers, or street addresses with a general audience.
9. Parents and instructors should know that on-line accounts, diaries, and chat rooms all can be "password protected."
10. Adults should know that controlled Web sites now exist (e.g., Kidfu) that users pay a monthly fee for using. These are carefully monitored, have no pop-up advertising, and are password controlled. When using these Web sites, families need not worry about dangerous encounters occurring.

Source: Adapted from Hafner, 2002; Singer & Singer, 2001; Thornburgh & Lin, 2002.

and grow out of situations associated with everyday living. As a result of poverty and depressed living conditions, marginalized families frequently suffer from chronic health problems, accidents, and inadequate nutrition. A surprising 33% of Americans have little or no health care plans, and children are often in that group (Children's Defense Fund, 1997; U.S. Bureau of the Census, 2001). Illness and health problems become all too often a function of income.

Health problems affect all poor families. Inadequate housing, high population densities, poor sanitation, poor diets, smoking, and poor habits in managing resources engender unhealthy homes. Some problems stem from ignorance about basic home maintenance; some come from poor habits and substance abuse; and many come from the inability of persons to secure and follow through on available care and help from social agencies. Clearly, one way to address these problems is through parent education.

Competent families, on the other hand, know about health practices, the basics of nutrition, and how to secure medical attention. When health and nutrition standards are preserved, we observe the following in competent homes:

Nutrition

- Meals with food from major food groups
- Reduced use of prepackaged, treated foods containing high fat, salt, and chemical additives
- Reduced use of sweets, soft drinks, and fatty products
- Regular eating habits and sensible snacks

Hygiene and Physical Health

- Immunizations
- Annual checkups and evaluations
- Adequate lighting, ventilation, and heat in homes
- Smoke-free buildings

Sanitation

- Avoidance of toxic substances
- Washing before meals and food preparation
- Regular bathing
- Keeping rubbish cleared away
- Sensible, maintained home space

Most of these practices can be extended to all homes when good social networks exist, when parent education programs are given a priority, and when wholesome community collaborations emerge.

Consistent Social and Emotional Environments

Effective homes develop environments that nurture children's social and emotional well-being. The overriding dimension is one of care and interest. Too often children state that they are not watched over, that no one cares. This situation worsens when we encounter families in stress—7% of poor children state that no one cares about them (Noddings, 2002b). Children's range of perceptions about self, from confidence to spiritual growth, will be affected by this feeling.

Parents' workplaces affect their perceptions of life and the way they interact with children and other family members (Bronfenbrenner & Crouter, 1982; Wohl, 1997). In turn, these perceptions foster parenting styles that conform to parents' experiences and how they see themselves in the world. On the positive side, we have the effective-family investigations (Clark, 1983; Scarf, 1997;

Noddings, 2002b), showing that the functioning family views itself as a problem-solving unit with a mutual support system and that valuing spiritual life is important.

How can we encourage parents in guiding and nurturing their children and at the same time establish contacts outside the home? Workshops and discussions that parents attend are only part of the answer. Supporting families through family–school–community collaborations and involving parents in extended networks will do the most to enhance social and emotional health in homes. Benson (1997), Hammer and Turner (2000), and Gonzales-Mena (2002) all have nicely developed collaboration schemes.

Child-rearing patterns certainly affect children's level of moral development. Children's attitudes are formed early, and parents and peers have a significant impact through instruction, modeling, rewards, and punishments (Bronfenbrenner et al., 1984). Children's values tend to reflect those of their family. Other experiences also affect this development; individuals exposed to many socializing agents are more likely to achieve a higher level of moral reasoning than those exposed to only a few (Coles, 1997; Damon, 1988).

Locus of control is directly related to parenting (refer to Table 10–1). Whether children see themselves or others in control determines the way they look toward the future.

Developing Interactive Skills. Competent families engender interactive skills that permit children to interact with the world with their values and moral notions in place. Modeling, discussions in the home, and being a part of the larger community, that is, extending children's social contacts so that they use more than one interactive style (Salzstein, 1976; Walker & Taylor, 1991), all help children develop these skills. Children's growth will reflect their participation and experience.

Developing Problem-Solving Skills. Homes foster problem-solving skills through participation and experimentation. By modeling problem-solving skills and exploring problems and solutions with children, parents steer their children toward competence (Leach, 1997). Homes where highly directive and punitive behaviors are the norm actually discourage interest and skill for analyzing tasks, and some even produce a sense of helplessness (Bronfenbrenner, Moen, & Garbarino, 1984).

Teaching Coping Skills. Children able to confront adversity and seek ways to approach difficulties usually have had guided experiences in approaching tasks. These are **resilient children**, and they have schemes for processing impacts (Werner, 1999). Competent families entertain questions about solving problems. This means that caregivers verbally or kinesthetically lead children through a series of tasks and also frame questions leading to a reasonable conclusion (Dyson, 1986; Hammer & Turner, 2000). Children with experiences in considering alternatives and choices have a background for confronting challenges and even adversity. The classic studies of resilient children by Emmy Werner and associates give helpful cues on the "turning points" in children's lives and the protective factors that guide children to healthy lives (Werner & Smith, 2001). All of this fits in the arsenal of coping skills that all youth need. Alert adults will promote these and look for ways to enhance them. Domineering, prejudiced, or autocratic adults engender thinking for one "correct" set of rules or format. This does little to help children develop coping skills.

Recreational Pursuits. Competent homes value recreation, gaming sessions, and play. Children normally select their own levels of participation in play, sports, and creative work, but parents and other family members can always encourage and support their interest.

Children require time, space, and equipment to pursue recreation, and effective parents will plan for this, support it, and even participate. Few things solidify families better than recreational pursuits. Benefits that children derive from recreation and play include the following (Seefeldt & Barbour, 1998):

• Working with others
• Small and large muscle exercise
• Establishing an interest in fitness
• Lifelong interests and attitudes about recreation
• Guided exploration of challenges and new ventures
• Sensible and accurate use of equipment
• Release from tension
• Experiencing pleasure, gratification, and satisfaction.

Figure 10–1 provides questions that professionals may wish to use when evaluating whether a family is effective. An effective family will display a high percentage, though not necessarily all, of the features.

EFFECTIVE SCHOOLS

Numerous publications discuss the programs and character of "effective schools," and we frequently see such items as student achievement, inclusive programs, or values and beliefs highlighted. Of course, these areas are important, but other school features also are factors in school success. On the other hand, some program traits have a defeating effect when we carefully analyze situations.

Student Achievement

Often we assume that standardized achievement test results are proof of what happens in schools. When related to aptitude scores, program resources, or support, these tests may

In evaluating effective families, assessors will answer yes for most of the following questions:

1. Is an authoritative parenting style evident?

2. Is there consistency in home management, family routines (bedtime, meals, and relaxation), and household regulations?

3. Are rules and codes of conduct understood and consistently enforced?

4. Are discussions, conversations, and interactions noticeable and frequent?

5. Do children have responsibilities in the home?

6. Are expectations of children in keeping with the children's stages of development?

7. Do parents have high hopes for their children's success?

8. Do family members evince a sense of success and pride?

9. Are good nutrition practices observed?

10. Are sanitary practices in evidence?

11. Do family members know where others work, play, and socialize?

12. Is there warmth in the home—do members accept others?

13. Do family members encourage and praise each other?

14. Does the family have a social network of friends?

15. Are values and moral codes apparent in the family?

16. Are literary and other intellectual stimuli present in the home?

17. Do members read to each other?

18. Does the family show skill in using the social and welfare services available to them?

19. Are health checkups done regularly and immunizations scheduled?

20. Can parents verbally and kinesthetically lead children through tasks and problems with appropriate questions, comments, and demonstrations?

Figure 10–1   Evaluating family effectiveness
Source: Adapted from Berger, 2000; Berns, 2001; Curran, 1983; Galinsky, 1987; Rich, 1992.

indicate statistically whether particular school programs have realized expected gains. But the results of norm-referenced tests cannot be used in guiding individual children.

If overall success rates are high when comparing achievements among schools, educators and citizens alike often assume that all is right at their school and that programs must be appropriate. However, group tests often hide areas of deficiency and often fail to assess specific children's skills (Stiggins, 2001). Frequently a test may be inappropriate for a particular subgroup in the school. For example, gifted children, while performing adequately in school, sometimes receive lower than anticipated scores on tests.

When problems appear in effective schools—for example, if scores are well below an area norm—educators, parents, and other community citizens demand explanations. Are community problems or area demographics confounding parts of the program and school curriculum? Are scores lower because schools are reserving time for nonacademic areas, such as developing esteem and readiness or expanding cultural background, before returning to achievement-tested basic skills? Again, standardized tests measure particular academic skill levels and do not assess achievements in all the curriculum areas schools work with today (refer to Chapter 8). Schools can, however, determine children's achievement using tools other than batteries of norm-referenced tests. In effective schools, teachers incorporate other assessment forms, such as diagnostic instruments, portfolios of children's work, or observation devices to diagnose needs for remediation or program changes. (For a thorough discussion of the relative strengths and weaknesses of the different types of assessment available to teachers, see Stiggins, 2001.)

Values and Beliefs

Anna Freud once observed that the early elementary years are "times when a child's character and conscience is built—or isn't!" With school comes the beginning of a child's community participation, and of course there is much to wonder about and to learn about the rights and wrongs of life.

Just as parents model values and beliefs, so do teachers and other school personnel (Coles, 1997). Getting along with others, sharing with others, and helping others are areas that successful schools expand on after these basics are started at home or child care centers. It is one thing to post rules for courtesies or sharing, but another to inculcate these valuable

Successful schools model values and beliefs of home and child care centers–such as getting along with others, sharing, and helping as part of the curriculum

features in an effective school. First, teachers, like parents, must model these behaviors. In effective schools, primary teachers develop units on social communication and ways of getting along with others. A variety of successful techniques have been used. Challenges can be taken from everyday life or even from newspapers, and the students have an opportunity to analyze and discuss ways to work through the problems.

Many teachers find that some of the best ways to address values is to use a story narrative. (The children's book section in Appendix 1 includes many suitable titles.) Others have used film or video clips focusing on a social situation.

Effective schools also promote the values related to appreciation of diverse cultures in their community and making positive connections with persons with special needs.

Provision for Individual Differences and Inclusion

Many American schools at the beginning of the 21st century are administered under the principles of diversity, or inclusion. We have used a generation to move to this place, but at present, all schools are obligated to provide educational experiences for children at all learning levels and in the "least restrictive environment." We discussed inclusion from a historical perspective in Chapter 2, and we present a curriculum viewpoint in Chapter 8. Effective schools have an inclusion model that provides services for children with special needs from birth through high school.

Though you may find some schools in America with more traditional orientations and techniques, in large part you will find that effective schools will be working toward the concept of inclusion. Full inclusion indicates that every child belongs in a regular classroom and that support services are used so that appropriate instruction is carried out by the classroom teacher and others. Inclusion means that instruction for each child will be provided by whichever personnel or setting is most appropriate for that part of the child's curriculum. In this manner, children with special needs are in contact and associate with typically developing children for a large part of their school day. Of course, as schools and child care facilities have moved to incorporate the legislation, schools have needed to alter some parts of their programs.

More than restructured buildings and more specialized personnel, the thing you will notice most in a school practicing inclusion is the attitude and demeanor toward the abilities of all children. Remember that typically developing children of a generation back rarely encountered diversity in their classrooms. Most schools up through the 1960s were monolingual and monoracial and showed little evidence of special needs. In effective schools today, the mix is truly comprehensive, and most educators agree that living and learning with diversity makes all individuals more tolerant, more accepting, and more eager to use the skills and talents of persons they heretofore did not come to know or value.

Education in an inclusive school situation means that teachers work and interact with different personnel, for example, specialists for different disabilities, diagnosticians, and aides trained to work with particular needs. They adjust content and mode of instruction to fit the needs of particular individuals—not just those identified with "special needs" but also able-bodied children who have different learning modalities or even gaps in experience (Culatta & Tompkins, 1999). Teachers involve parents and other specialists in planning the educational program. Effective schools are thus already involved in supporting one main thrust of this text.

In effective schools, teachers have particular knowledge and skills regarding children of varying abilities and from diverse cultures. The following undergird the effective teacher's work:

1. An open mind and a humane disposition.

2. The ability to recognize disabling conditions, knowledge about the general characteristics and general needs of children with frequently observed disabilities, and an openness to seek diagnostic services to help merge the needs of particular children into the classroom.

3. Knowledge regarding the homes from which children with special needs come and willingness to work with the parents for the benefit of the child.

4. Knowledge regarding the support services in the school and how the services support teachers and their ability to present anecdotal information, hunches, and other experiences to persons making evaluations.

5. The ability to adapt the classroom environment to address any special needs that particular children have.

6. Familiarity with the child's and the child's family rights in regard to service.

7. Knowledge regarding responsibilities as a part of an IEP team.

8. The ability to enlist help from aides and volunteers and the ability to work with those persons for children's benefit.

9. The ability to merge students with disabilities into the classroom in a productive and healthy fashion.

10. Self-reflection on one's feelings about working with language minority students and children with disabilities.

Positive School Features

School effectiveness researchers have identified several characteristics that are observed consistently in schools demonstrating good achievement gains (Cruickshank, Jenkins, & Metcalf,

2002; Good & Brophy, 1986, 1996). In addition to the previously listed qualities, the following items appear consistently on most lists:

1. Strong leadership that produces consensus

2. A safe, orderly school climate

3. Positive teacher attitudes toward students

4. High expectations regarding children's abilities

5. Efficient use of instructional time

6. Careful monitoring of progress

7. Strong parental involvement programs

8. Emphasis on the importance of skills and achievement

9. Meaningful use of praise and encouragement

10. Support for different learning modalities and abilities.

The preceding are general school practices and will fit with almost any program, goal, or strategy. The curriculum content, teaching strategies, equipment used, and level of instruction to develop a program can, of course, vary greatly among classrooms and schools. For example, two effective teachers can develop a topic in very different ways and still have successful outcomes. One may use direct instruction (showing and telling) to establish ideas of growing plants or writing poems, while the other uses inductive thinking (discovery) with several experiments so that children arrive at the same understandings. Successful classrooms use a variety of models, and successful teachers understand how to use different instructional models, techniques, and strategies when appropriate.

Children attending our schools today will work in a different world tomorrow, and that world means increased diversity of interests, cultures, abilities, and ways of working. Effective schools will prepare children to live productively and contentedly in that new world.

Barriers for Effective Schools

Some schools do less well than others in supporting educational opportunity. Problems may exist only in certain areas, or they may range throughout the curriculum, administration, and school life. Impediments to learning come from such things as inappropriate curriculum, negative teacher attributes, bias, problems in physical facilities, and community forces such as special interest groups, defensive attitudes, and dangerous streets.

Inappropriate Curriculum. Educators occasionally miscalculate when selecting and implementing curricula. For example, when content doesn't relate to the developmental stages of children served or when material is redundant or too simplistic, a program falters. Some material may also be inappropriate because of social or cultural mores in a community.

Some teachers lack motivation and a sense of urgency about education. They excessively repeat material or resurrect old material and keep students "busy" with worksheets unrelated to the day's activities. Large segments of time can be absorbed in mindless tasks that go nowhere. Children quickly tire of repetition and make excuses for avoiding work. The myth of "boring" school thus becomes reality (Kralovec, 2002).

Negative Teacher Attributes. While it is difficult to accept the notion that teachers can be less than helpful, from time to time it is true. Some individuals come to teaching for the wrong reasons, perhaps because they wish to dominate situations, have children look up to them, or enjoy expounding. Such individuals rarely fulfill the requirements of guide, director, or supporter of learning and may overlook children's needs or misunderstand children's perceptions of the concepts being addressed.

At times, a teacher's personality does not support learning situations. Brittle and demanding personalities logically do not serve children, nor do indifferent, sarcastic, or introverted temperaments. It is paradoxical that persons with these characteristics wish to be in a helping profession, but we do meet them once in a while.

Bias and Prejudice. Our society still struggles to shed the problems associated with racism, ethnocentrism, elitism, sexism, **homophobia**, and discrimination against certain disabilities; these qualities regrettably still affect some schools. Perpetuating stereotypes in monocultural schools is a problem; stereotyping restricts everyone's social competence. The situation becomes intensified in ethnically integrated schools if hints of bias and careless use of ethnocentric language appear. The same can be said of coed schools when sexist language is used. When demeaning language surfaces, minority persons are affronted, their aspirations suffer, and children's growth in social competence is diminished (Comer, 1988; Sadker & Sadker, 2003). For all persons involved, bias is costly.

Problems with Physical Facilities. Limited physical facilities, while sometimes adaptable by creative people, become burdensome for inexperienced teachers. Poorly lighted buildings, poorly ventilated areas, and a badly maintained school become difficult to work in and are dangerous and depressing. Rooms too large or too small for instructional activity are a problem; poorly arranged materials contribute to confusion.

Lobbyists and Policy Advocates. Volunteer groups often come together to be advocates and sources of support for schools. A group formed to lobby for a new school building project can be positive in impact. However, some lobbying groups are formed, as in the following vignette, to counteract school projects or to prevent curricula from being implemented.

Minority children's social competence is diminished when unwelcome messages are given to minority parents

A group of parents and two clergymen in one Texas community organized themselves as a self-appointed school review committee. When they reviewed the reproduction-of-creatures unit for the second-grade classrooms, the books and charts used became a highly charged topic. The group's complaints about the material became intense, and the committee visits to the school caused confrontations and wild charges. One teacher resigned because of accusations, and negative publicity dragged on for weeks before the administration abandoned the unit. Even though the unit had been developed in previous years and had been accepted by the health education committee, a militant anti-sex-education group spread dissension and won their case. Community and school working relations were set back considerably for more than a year.

Censorship of books is still a common occurrence in school districts throughout the United States (Sutherland, 1996). Too often schools acquiesce to pressure from lobbying groups to abandon certain publications and other resources; then programs can suffer in scope and purpose.

Other Challenges.   Community violence can spill over into schools. Weapons are carried to school by too many children who seek to protect themselves, prey on others, or maintain status in a peer group (Garbarino, 1999; Jenkins & Bell, 1997). Whereas some schools have been considered safe havens from distressful conditions in a neighborhood, too often this haven is savaged by intrusions, bullets, and intimidation from gang activities. Weapons have an unsettling effect on any school climate, but in the hands of secure teachers, the trauma resulting from witnessing

violence can become a part of the school curriculum. One teacher, trying to resolve fears in
a Baltimore neighborhood experiencing periodic violence, used story writing and sharing
to deal with children's anxieties and to help
the children understand precautions and
safety measures (Notar, 1992).

Changes in Schools

Schools in the United States are always evolving. New building plans, new procedures, new
equipment, and curriculum innovations appear on a regular basis. Adjustments appear
that seem serious or far-reaching at times, but
in fact schools change very slowly (Demarris &
LeCompte, 1998; Webb et al., 2003).

It takes time for a school staff to adopt a
new method of teaching: New materials are
needed, in-service education must be arranged,
and teachers need to be convinced of the
method's efficacy. Even though a few teachers
implement a new plan, the school as a whole
often lags behind. Consider the phased-in
"**writing to read**" program in the following
vignette.

 ❧

*In the fall of 1994, a New Jersey school system
set up a "writing to read" workshop. Two second-grade teachers from Elwood Elementary
(in the school district) were interested in trying the new plan immediately, and their experiment encouraged them. The two gave
glowing reports at faculty meetings the following spring, but only one third-grade and one
first-grade teacher agreed to try the plan the
next year. Halfway through the year, the first-
grade teacher supplemented her program with
basal readers, and her evaluation of the experiment was iffy. With heavy urging, two more
teachers agreed to experiment later that year.
At the end of 3 years, only half of the primary-
school teachers in the building were involved.*

*Although most evaluations were positive, the
principal still wondered how she could increase participation. It took 5 years and repeated reports of success before most of
Elwood's primary-school teachers made a serious commitment to the program.*

 ❧

Schools change faster socially than they
do academically. Neighborhoods can change
quickly in urban and suburban areas, and the
cultural and socioeconomic mix can alter demographics in a school within a few years.
Many U.S. schools have experienced this phenomenon in recent years (refer to the demographic changes discussed in Chapter 3). For
many reasons, a large number of schools are
less successful today than in previous decades.
Achievement results, SAT scores, school
attendance, the rising amount of school-
identified disabilities, plus crime and other
social problems have alarmed many. The result has been a host of studies and evaluations
to assess what is happening in U.S. education.

National Goals and Standards

A number of task forces representing various
interests have conducted national studies to
identify problems in U.S. education. Some offer recommendations to correct the problems
they find. Some results have to do with school
practices and curriculum, but many have implications for vast changes in society at large
regarding health care, the prevention of substance abuse, correcting violence, changing
U.S. attitudes, and so on. Some studies also include new plans for teacher preparation.

Educational Assessments. About 20 years
ago, the warning *A Nation at Risk* (National
Commission on Excellence in Education
[NCEE], 1983) was published, and it identified
higher illiteracy and decreasing achievement

in American schools. The report succeeded in energizing discussion of the issues, but 20 years later, only marginal improvement in achievement, teacher preparation, or time in school has been documented (Goertz, 2001; Webb et al., 2003).

The Carnegie Forum on Education and the Economy (CFEE, 1986) produced a report focused on changing the preparation of teachers. The report, *A Nation Prepared: Teachers for the 21st Century,* quickly affected programs in the United States and inspired the American Association of Colleges for Teacher Education (AACTE) and individual state certification offices to recast accreditation standards. Using an economic rationale, the Carnegie Forum concluded that a constructivist curriculum directed by more intellectually skilled and empowered teachers was the only way the United States could retain its competitive edge in a global economy. Most states have followed through with higher standards for teacher preparation and also for "Learning Results" for enrolled teacher candidates.

Government Action. The accumulation of education reports has prompted the last three administrations to address issues and concerns identified in U.S. schools. Their initiatives grew out of several annual conferences of governors plus greater interest in accountability, school choice, and the place of religion in schools.

The Bush administration in 1990 advanced *America 2000: An Education Strategy* (U.S. Department of Education, 1991), a formula for addressing the large problems in the country's education. The objectives were sound and desirable (refer to the listing in Chapter 2), and authorities asked for the time, money, and training to bring about the goals. At the end of the Bush administration, the plan remained as it had started—a desirable goal statement.

The Clinton administration followed in the footsteps of the previous plan, and the Goals 2000: Educate America Act in 1993 extended the America 2000 plan to add family involvement (U.S. Department of Education, 1993). Even though the administration steadily emphasized social reconstruction, implementation of the principles to achieve Goals 2000, except in a few states, remained in the beginning stages. The new Bush administration has started a vigorous set of proposals to support education and increase the federal role in schoolwork. The No Child Left Behind statute has received considerable press attention and professional scrutiny.

The awareness of difficulties and needs in poor and minority groups in the United States has reached high levels. Continuing problems with the higher standards, testing requirements, student achievement, and voucher plans continue to worry many (Goertz, 2001; Webb, et al., 2003). On a positive note, some communities have started experimental programs, which do provide models for use. See chapter 12 for several examples.

Evaluating Schools

Nationwide, the present state of U.S. schools appears fairly stable (Rose & Gallup, 2002). Phi Delta Kappa's annual survey even shows some gains in public attitudes about America's schools. In regard to particular areas and projects, we find amazing success stories. In others, particularly in many urban areas, polls show conditions, services, and outlooks deteriorating badly (Garbarino, Kostelny, & Dubrow, 1998; Kotlowitz, 1998).

Figure 10–2 presents questions that professionals will wish to use when evaluating the effectiveness of a particular school. The questions will reveal much about a school's effectiveness, adequacy, and chances for

For effective schools, assessors will answer yes for most of the following questions:

1. Is consonance of philosophy found among board of education members, administrators, and teaching staff members, as well as aides and volunteers?

2. Are school facilities adequate?

3. Is the school facility maintained and serviced well?

4. Is space used appropriately and efficiently?

5. Does continuity of content and concepts exist between grade levels and from home experiences?

6. Are collaborations between home and school evident?

7. Do children evidence achievement in social and academic skills through their practices and activities?

8. Do teachers show a command of various teaching strategies and techniques?

9. Are teaching techniques varied for different children?

10. Are children constructively engaged in projects, follow-up activities, or the application of ideas? Or are they nonfocused, disruptive, glancing about, or wandering from place to place?

11. Is time off task kept to a minimum?

12. Do children evince various levels of thinking as they work and investigate?

13. Is a pleasant climate for learning and enthusiasm noticeable?

14. Are children allowed opportunities to interact with others and grow in social relationships?

15. Do teachers display command of several teaching models (direct instruction, discovery learning, roundtable discussion)?

16. Are teaching approaches sensible and realistic for the particular classrooms?

17. Do teachers praise and encourage learners and value different contributions to classwork?

18. Do all children succeed from time to time?

Figure 10–2   Assessing schools for effectiveness
Source: Adapted from Doll, 1995; Good and Brophy, 1996; Joyce and Weil, 1996; Rich, 1992.

success. An effective school will display positives for most features indicated.

The quality future school will emerge from secure connections among homes, schools, and communities as they become complementary and supplement all school objectives. But educational change and enhancement affect more than academic achievement. Also linked to school success are changes in health care, improved living conditions, improved interethnic relations, and diminished crime in neighborhoods. Liston and Zeichner (1996b) remind us that "what goes on inside schools is greatly influenced by what occurs outside of schools" (p. xi).

EFFECTIVE COMMUNITIES

Because communities are made up of sets of subsystems, research on competent communities is problematic. It is difficult to determine cause-and-effect relationships within a community, especially those that affect children. While some change has been effected through the National Association for the Education of Young Children (NAEYC) and the Interstate New Teacher Assessment and Support Consortium (INTASC), standards relating to communities are seldom perceived as important referents by authorities in child development (Bronfenbrenner, 1995; Garbarino & Abramowitz, 1992). This means that we continue to find less attention paid to this important third social setting.

Substantial research, however, is available on the effects of community on family health and school attainment (Bronfenbrenner, 1995; Quint, 1994). For instance, communities with consolidated health services support prenatal and **perinatal** situations better than those without such consolidation. Researchers have identified a number of features visible in promising communities, irrespective of economic base, that can be linked with children's educational achievements (Noddings, 2002b).

Community Organization

Formal community organizations that we find almost everywhere are health services, welfare and social services, religious institutions, civic services, businesses, and media. Informal organizations that develop but are far less obvious are (a) **special-interest groups** and (b) the social networks that individuals and families form.

Health Services. Children must remain healthy to develop properly, yet access to a health care system depends on the community

that children live in and on the economic status of the family. It is well documented that poor families have greater health problems, including chronic health conditions, more infectious diseases, higher incidence of low-birth-weight babies, and higher infant mortality rates (Children's Defense Fund, 1998).

The effective community will have comprehensive care systems striving to serve citizens impartially. Many communities have both neighborhood health centers (such as those funded through the Office of Economic Opportunity) and a private health care system. By uniting family care offices in one setting, officials diminish the expense, frustration, and transportation problems that poor families experience when seeking services.

In addition to offering health care, all medical facilities have an educational function. Important features of health services include distributing materials about disease prevention and counseling by personnel who are positively oriented to their clients.

Welfare and Social Services. While directed primarily at those in poverty, welfare and social services are relevant to the larger community. Employment offices, legal aid offices, and counseling centers cut across socioeconomic levels and are needed to address concerns for most U.S. communities. Regrettably, welfare services in the United States have always carried a stigma, and only in recent years have programs such as Head Start led to changed attitudes and the welcome involvement of middle-class citizens.

As with health care, accessibility of social services is a key to their use. Media, local directories, and interagency referrals are the normal channels for distributing information on services, and word of mouth is of considerable importance. One Florida community established a family services office in its new elementary school. An active director and proximity of services led to teachers' reevaluating the types of services available for families and children. Increased accessibility brought more parent visitors to school, and all persons involved showed a greater acceptance of the need for and benefits of the programs.

Religious Institutions. Churches, synagogues, and mosques are central facets of many communities. While less so in recent decades, religious associations have dominated large portions of community life in the United States. In fact, they represented the largest part of the out-of-home activity for pre-20th-century Americans.

National surveys reveal a drop in religious participation in recent decades (Lindner, 2003), but still, more individuals belong to church-related groups than to any other voluntary grouping. Religious institutions continue to influence many segments of U.S. communities, promoting ethnic as well as theological identity. With outreach programs and social action objectives, many places of worship now provide social, cultural, and other support for their communities as well as spiritual nurturance for their membership groups. Food pantries, soup kitchens, and drug abuse and family counseling services are all operated by or through religious organizations in thousands of communities. Many care programs are not-for-profit arrangements developed and maintained by local religious organizations, even in the smallest communities. This service has received more attention since the Bush proposals for "faith based" group funding for community welfare. It is controversial in political as well as educational circles.

Civic Services. All communities require fire departments, sanitation programs, and public safety offices. Supported by tax revenues, these services provide for the general stability and safety of the community.

Community services provide an educational function for children. What goes on in those departments, how the jobs are done, and the problems workers encounter are of interest to all children. Most offices publish materials and have personnel who head information programs for schools and other local groups. Elementary school children, when directed by their teachers, learn to understand the meaning of organized communities and the interdependence of community residents. They learn how community services affect their lives and perform for them as individuals.

Businesses. Most communities contain private commercial enterprises linked to daily life in those venues, such as filling stations, newsstands, and mom-and-pop grocery stores that we find in nonindustrialized suburbs. (The so-called hypermarts are both replacing these businesses in many communities and retaining their function as informal links in the lives of community residents.) Other communities contain factories, wharves and piers, large merchandise outlets, plus financial and information-processing establishments that employ residents and give flavor to a community. As children become acquainted with local businesses, they become knowledgeable about the economics of their town—where people work, what they produce, and where products go. They also learn of the need for many specialties as they become attuned to the world of work and the effects each institution has on community life and interaction.

In effective communities, commercial establishments cooperate with schools and families. Such cooperation demonstrates commitment to the interdependence of community settings and to the need for mutual support. (Refer to Chapters 11 and 12 for discussion of techniques and models for such collaboration.)

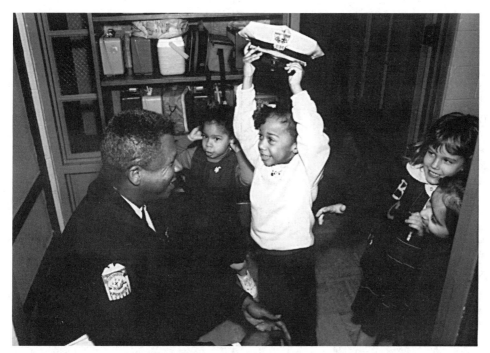

Children understand the meaning of organized community and the interdependence of community residents when they encounter friendly civic officers

Media. With the explosion and transmission of knowledge in the information age, communities are engulfed with media of all kinds. From standard newspapers through television programs to the Internet, visual and aural messages descend in increasing amounts across the United States. Whether in an isolated prairie town or an urban neighborhood, the impact of media is all encompassing.

Media affect all other institutions of a community. The type, quality, and amount of information an area receives produce responses from individuals, families, and schools. Effects can be positive or negative, but they are rarely neutral. Since most media are protected under First Amendment provisions, media outlets are largely self-policing, and public accept-ance of the products determines the boundaries for individual distributors.

Appropriateness of media products is a significant issue when we consider children's education. Many publications and recordings are adult oriented in topic, format, and relevance, but children are nonetheless exposed to large amounts of them. The V-chip for television, and Internet filters such as KidWatch, will block only a fraction of adult material. Media products that fall outside a community's standard invite thoughts of censorship, and problems always surface when that issue is raised. It is therefore desirable for communities, through public forums, to reach consensus on acceptable quality and then to work for that standard through educational programs and lobbying efforts when required.

Strictly speaking, community agents and teachers can withhold from children only those materials prohibited by law. This means that all adults working with children must educate them about appropriate and inappropriate materials. Reasonable objectives for media can evolve through the work of churches, civic associations, schools, and neighborhood groups. The effective community is knowledgeable about its media, the effect the media have on residents, and the sentiments of its citizens.

Special-Interest Groups. In the late 20th century, the United States witnessed the formation of numerous special-interest groups, from the small group of citizens seeking to pressure schools to include or exclude something to the highly organized lobbying groups seeking changes in legislation. As we noted in Chapter 1, a special-interest group has a particular cause and stance (e.g., antinuclear energy, save the whales, antipornography, prochoice or prolife regarding abortion). Many groups disappear after accomplishing a mission; others become entrenched because their cause is ongoing.

Special-interest groups are grassroots associations and are very American in concept. Taking as their basis the constitutional amendment protecting association and assembly, citizens come together to work for or against something. In this way, altruistic groups have formed to gain privileges for disenfranchised persons, such as the education for persons with disabilities legislation started in the 1970s, or to highlight a public problem, such as cleaning up the Nashua River (Cherry, 1982). Other groups form to oppose regulations or practices. A nonsmoking lobby is one example; a group censoring local library materials is another.

How do communities respond to special interest groups? If partnerships are in good

working order, we normally find that special-interest-group pressure can be accommodated and processed in a healthy fashion. All too often this is not the case, and a part of the community bows to the pressure of the campaigning group. For example, one Pennsylvania library contained several volumes on cults and pagan rituals. When a member of a PTA subgroup saw these volumes, the group started a search through the library to identify and condemn all volumes containing information about the occult. Having no agency and little organization to counter the arguments of the group, library staff quickly acquiesced to the demands and removed all offending materials. This established a dangerous precedent for library materials in this community. The campaign ultimately removed even children's fantasy books featuring ghosts and goblins.

Social Networks

The informal, everyday contacts of relatives, neighbors, friends, and colleagues produce social networks for adults and children in almost all neighborhoods. These groupings, which can cross gender, age, and socioeconomic status lines, provide enormous support for individuals. Werner (1999) showed in *Through the Eyes of Innocents* the strong impact of healthy behavior in a community on children caught up in war.

Positive Adult Groups. Social science research shows the importance of friends and relatives in providing exchanges of goods and services as well as psychological support (Coleman, 1991). Werner and Smith (1992) and Cochran and Davila (1992) indicated that support groups are especially important for at-risk families when kin and colleagues provide emotional support for child raising, on confronting adversity, or even on integration into

Peer groups are essential for adequate socialization and maturation

the community—the targeted family benefits. Healthier adult groups mean healthier environments for children. Information about social services, work opportunities, or new resources in a community is often delivered through the social networks of adults, and this benefits children.

Children's Peer Groups. Children's social networks, often called peer groups, are natural and can have desirable results, although at times certain combinations may become destructive (Berndt & Ladd, 1989; Harris, 1998). The effect on a community may be extensive when children associate in groups. Loosely affiliated groups of children often tour malls and parks, visit businesses, and play games with pleasant and positive results. Other groups may harass citizens and damage property.

Children's contacts beyond the home are necessary as children mature, and the emotional support and exchange of information within networks are powerful influences for all children (Cochran & Davila, 1992). When conducted in supervised and constructive ways, peer groups are essential for adequate socialization and maturation and offer opportunity for many educational insights. Through networks, children learn physical skills for games, such as baseball, hopscotch, or jump rope, and develop negotiating skills when settling disputes.

Healthy communities recognize the presence of social networks and endorse the formation and continuation of groups of individuals. Effective communities also have ways to monitor children's social networks and to steer them in constructive ways (see Figure 10–3).

Assessors will find most of the following characteristics in effective communities:

1. A workable health care system available to all income levels

2. Social programs, health facilities, and health offices clustered to maximize usage and cut logistics

3. Community programs designed to educate as well as serve

4. Religious institutions participating in community life and demonstrating concern through social-action programs

5. Religious associations that nurture children's ethnic and spiritual identities

6. Municipal service departments that are stable, well maintained, and available for educational visits

7. Commercial enterprises that welcome visits and conduct information sessions

8. Commercial establishments that see adopt-a-school plans as an enhancement to the business

9. Media producers who realize the effects of mass communication and who responsibly produce material appropriate for young children

10. Communication between media outlets, schools, and community agencies regarding available media

11. Special-interest groups responsive to community questions about their objectives and policies

12. Positive social networks in evidence (social gatherings, block parties, community clubs)

13. Social clubs for children (sports programs, scout programs, 4-H clubs, seasonal recreational facilities)

14. Citizens interested in community schools, neighborhoods, and individual children.

Figure 10–3   Assessing the competent community

EFFECTIVE PARTNERSHIPS

Schools as Brokers for Social Settings

When viewing the three major social settings in children's lives, we can see the overlap and interlocking nature of curricula for any one child. One sees areas of effectiveness in each setting and their relation to outcomes for children's lives. These connections, however, do not necessarily form the three settings into a partnership or any type of collaborative venture. No requirement exists in any community for collaboration, and institutions do not collaborate unless an agent appears and serves as catalyst.

Groups and communities should not wait for the fortuitous appearance of persons who will engineer **collaborations**. We have one institution now that can provide the incentive and stimulus, and that has the position and requisite skills to best solicit effective social settings in which children prosper. That institution is the school.

Occupying this position means that schools must prepare themselves with information, establish a plan for making connections among the social settings, and implement that plan. It is hard and extensive work. It involves the commitment of instructional staff and administrators who must redefine their own roles and work piecemeal to get consensus among all forces in the community.

One required change is in thinking about what schools are for. The traditional view of teaching has been remediative, that is, filling in the knowledge gaps and developing skills. For too long, schools have thought of the communities and the families with which they work as possessing "deficits" that must be overcome or accommodated. But schools can no longer consider themselves as compensating for inherited faults and inabilities. Schools must now articulate the roles that communities and families can and should bear and devise ways to steer, guide, and collaborate with them to best accomplish these roles.

What would it take to effect such a plan? First, school personnel must be educated in the ways of collaboration, and teachers must work hard at "figuring out" the community served to discern steps and approaches necessary to accomplish the job. Schools may then use their broker position to farm out responsibilities and then address the findings that concern the in-school lives of children served. To start a true collaborative plan is a major effort for most communities. Leadership is essential, and the steps will most likely be taken slowly. But involving families and the community must begin somewhere (see the Implications for Professionals section for a beginning step).

Programs for Teacher Preparation

Empowered school staffs are needed for any plan based on partnerships and collaborations, but we find too many unprepared for the challenges. To establish collaborations, present staff members in most schools need to rethink their role. New teacher programs must include work in the sociology of education, work with volunteers, work with adult learners, collaboration as a skill, and internships with social agencies or community organizations. A focus of this type implies a very different teacher preparation program and emphasis, and universities must attract talented candidates for these roles. Collaborating schools of the future will require fewer teachers, but the core staff must be skilled assessment people who are able to change programs and unite efforts. Few courses exist for this particular focus. One effort was started a few years ago at Wayne State University (Kaplan, 1992); another initiative is the "reflective practices" proposals on teacher preparation, initiated for teacher education projects in Wisconsin (Liston & Zeichner, 1996b).

IMPLICATIONS FOR PROFESSIONALS

Think of yourself filling a new niche in the home–school–community matrix. Then think about how it would unfold.

When approaching the classroom, newly empowered teachers will think of themselves as "at-home" Peace Corps workers who analyze situations and then figure out how best to serve the population with which they find themselves. For example, starting with the literacy skills, teachers will ask themselves, "Where are students in their reading and writing development?" When that assessment, or diagnosis, is accomplished, they will meet with parents or others, conduct demonstration lessons, and confer with others on objectives and ways to attain them. They will use suggestions and ideas that people present about resources in the community that can be used beneficially to enhance or illuminate any subject matter, project, or skill area. For instance, a teacher's class might accept an invitation to the area water treatment plant to learn about its operation and effect on the community. The group of helpers would plan the trip and study the site as a place for learning. Then, later, the teacher would use

cooperative learning and coaching skills to help students reason out the benefits of the treatment plant. Finally, the teacher would use literacy skills to describe the treatment plant for parents, other school students, and community members.

This is one simple collaboration on a social science project, but this partnership activity would be followed by others as the school becomes a refocused institution with new teaching strategies. The partnership notion replaces the school where teachers welcome groups of children and teach by distributing books, conducting a reading lesson, assigning a writing lesson, and then proceeding to the next subject. As we point out in Chapter 8, students and teachers in traditional schools consume large amounts of time in classroom protocols, for example, lining up, moving to and fro, collecting papers, and distributing and collecting books while focusing on one item. Ritual-filled classrooms exist all over and produce little beyond what each child is motivated to seek. The time has arrived to move beyond these time-consuming, tightly structured schools.

SUMMARY AND REVIEW

We have defined effective families, schools, and communities as those entities in which children have maximum opportunities to grow, develop, and prosper. We have discussed effective social settings and provided examples of effective settings working well.

General guidelines exist by which you may examine families, schools, and communities, assess the social settings you encounter, and ascertain how each measures up to standards of effectiveness. Imperfect settings exist for different reasons, and finding a resolution lies beyond the reach of educators acting alone. Providing individual support in areas where deficits exist is an option, and some professionals have at times been able to

give that support. However, the best resolution for most deficiencies lies in linking the strengths of all the social settings.

The road to stronger relationships is made easier when each social setting is effective in itself. When this is not the case, professionals look for ways to pull together to help children. Each setting affects the others, and the strength of one always bolsters another. The school must be the place where such interactions are coordinated. Schools need to become the brokers for new learning communities, which can thrive with the contributions of all homes, schools, and communities.

SUGGESTED ACTIVITIES AND QUESTIONS

1. Relate the assessment lists in Figures 10–1, 10–2, and 10–3 to (a) a home you are acquainted with, (b) a school you know well, and (c) the community in which you now live. What profiles do you find? Which setting seems strongest?

2. Assume that you are to be the director of a new collaboration involving the three settings. As the school administrator, what will be your three greatest challenges in establishing a collaborative effort?

3. Describe the hypothetical competent family of a 6-year-old child. Describe a less competent family for another 6-year-old. Speculate on how you could use your knowledge of the competent family to assist the less competent one.

4. Imagine that you are working on a new home–school–community collaboration. An official from your state board of education is visiting to view your district's new plan. Develop an outline of your working partnership to show the visitor how the three social settings support each other.

RESOURCES

Books

1. Curtis, D., & Carter, M. (2002). *The art of awareness: How observation can transform your teaching.* St. Paul, MN: Red Leaf.
2. Hart, B., & Risley, T. R. (1995). *Meaningful differences in the everyday experiences of young American children.* Baltimore: Brookes.
3. Liston, D., & Zeichner, K. (1996). *Culture and teaching.* Mahwah, NJ: Erlbaum.
4. Polly, J. A. (2002). *Net-moms' Internet kids and family yellow pages* (4th ed.). New York: McGraw-Hill/Osborne.
5. Reynolds, D., Creemers, B., Stringfield, S., Teddlie, C., & Schaffer, G. (Eds.). (2002). *World class schools: International perspectives on school effectiveness.* New York: Routledge-Falmer.

Films and Videos

1. *Emotional Intelligence* [Video, 29 min]. (1997). Examines methods of teaching emotional intelligence and related social skills. Princeton, NJ: Princeton University, Films for Humanities and Science.
2. *Nutrition for infants and children under six* [Video, 30 min]. (1994). A program on nutritional needs for three specific stages of development. Cambridge, MA: Cambridge Educational.
3. *Raising healthy kids: Families talk about sexual health* [Video, 30 min]. (1997). For parents of young children. Shows importance of parent–child communication and deals with the issue of the parent as the child's primary sexuality educator. New York: Media Works.

Organizations

Children's Defense Fund
122 C Street, NW
Washington, DC 20001
www.childrensdefense.org

Council for Exceptional Children
1920 Association Drive
Reston, VA 21091
www.cec.sped.org

Federal Interagency Forum on Child and Family Statistics
2070 Chain Bridge Road
Vienna, VA 22182
www.childstats.gov

Websites

1. www.davidsonfilms.com
   The site identifies good films on early childhood education.
2. www.kidfu.com
   A carefully monitored site for children developed by the managers of the former FreeZone.com site. The Pickle Syndicate, Inc., 3540 N. Southgate Avenue, Chicago, IL 60657.
3. www.ncrel.org/sdrs/areas/teOcont.htm
   The Pathways to School Improvement site gives articles, forums, and links for using up-to-date information on schooling.
4. www.nea.org
   The site presents an overview of the major U.S. teacher association, plus publications, reports, and statistics on U.S. schools.
5. www.responsiveeducation.org
   The site has links to effective school, family, and community partnerships.

Chapter 11

Traditional and Innovative Strategies for Working Together

In partnerships, educators, families and community members work together to share information, guide students, solve problems, and celebrate successes. Partnerships recognize the shared responsibilities of home, school and community for children's learning and development.

(Epstein, 2001, p. 4)

Someone must start **collaborations,** and the beginning steps may be small ones. If **partnerships** are to flourish, teachers need a wide range of approaches for building relationships and establishing communication with parents and community agencies as the first steps toward increased involvement in children's learning. This chapter examines traditional and innovative practices for collaborative action and discusses things to consider when using these strategies. In reading the chapter, you will learn the following:

1. Teachers have long used traditional practices to develop rapport with parents, communicate with them about their children, and encourage their involvement in the classroom and school.

2. Teachers have also developed a variety of innovative strategies to involve parents and community members in children's schooling.

3. There are many effective strategies for communicating with parents about children's progress and involving parents in classroom events.

4. Parent involvement in schools occurs along a continuum that moves from basic to **participatory** levels to **advocacy levels.** Teachers must offer many choices for parents to participate in their children's schooling.

5. Many strategies for working with parents of children with special needs or with different family lifestyles are similar to those for working with all parents, but teachers must consider particular factors as they work with different parent groups.

Our changing society, even with the advantages of mass communication systems, has evolved to a point where at the beginning of the 21st century, school programs alone are not sufficient for the task of formally educating children. The collaboration of parents and community agencies is essential if schools are to succeed in educating young children for a different society. Over 30 years ago, Evans (1975) pointed out that the ultimate goal of active parent involvement is "enhancing the family's ability to respond to its children" (p. 11). This goal is as vital today as it was then.

Parental and community involvement have always been a part of U.S. education. As we discussed earlier in this text, most parents historically were totally responsible for their children's education, but beginning in the 1800s, schools accepted more responsibility for academic learning. Later, professional educators also assumed responsibility for educating parents about children's growth and development, instructing them on ways of preparing their children for school, and advising them on how to support their children's education once they began formal schooling.

By and large, parental cooperation in educational matters during the 20th century meant parental acquiescence to school suggestions, but this has begun to change. Parental and community involvement in some districts has moved gradually from teacher-dominated procedures to collaborations with parents and community agencies. The authors contend that successful schools need to become **embedded partners** with parents and community members to cope with increasing challenges in the educative process. In this chapter, we discuss traditional but still useful strategies that schools and teachers use for involving parents and then we note helpful variations and innovative practices.

Most teachers' established ways of communicating with parents and community members have proven to work well, but many parents are not reached by these methods. Teachers must be open to new means of establishing communication, because parents and teachers, like children, have different communication and work styles. If children are to benefit, teachers must provide the impetus to break down communication barriers resulting from different cultural expectations and habits of interacting. Of course, to be successful, both teachers and parents need to adapt and respond to each other's interests, concerns, and needs. But keep in mind that, it is the school's responsibility to lead, and teachers need to be prepared to go more than halfway in reaching out to parents.

As schools develop more welcoming strategies toward all families, parents and community members feel more comfortable in visiting classrooms, becoming aides or volunteers in schools, and contributing special expertise to children's learning. These individuals learn about the schools and about school culture, which enables them to help their children and to communicate to the larger community their sense of the importance of school programs.

The community is also an important educating force. Schools and families have always made excursions into their communities for educational purposes or have invited community members into the classroom. This involvement becomes even more important as schools include community and local environmental issues as part of the curriculum and as community agencies become partners with their neighborhood schools.

ESTABLISHING RELATIONSHIPS WITH FAMILIES

Establishing good relationships with children's families early in the school year is important. Many teachers have found that reaching out to children even before school begins can be a useful way to get to know families.

Tools for Early Contacts

Home visits, telephone calls, letters, post cards, or invitations to school for brief, informal meetings are all tools teachers use to set a welcoming tone and lay the foundation for an effective working relationship.

Letters, PostCards, and E-mail.   During the summer, some teachers send children a short note or post card to introduce themselves and to welcome the child to the class. The following vignette demonstrates how one kindergarten teacher created enthusiasm and excitement for a child and established a sense of security and trust with the parents even before school began.

Jack's eyes shone as he tore open the envelope that had come for him in the mail. As he reached into the letter, he found a small plastic dinosaur that he clutched eagerly, as he handed the letter to his mother to read.

Dear Jack,

Welcome to the Dinosaur Kindergarten Class! We are so excited about your coming to our class. You can bring a favorite toy or book from home for your first day of school. We have lots of places ready for you to keep your things and each place will have your name and special sticker. Your sticker looks like this:

♥♥♥

We sent you something special from the Dinosaur teachers. You can bring it to school, too. We will see you at school on Tuesday, August, 26th!

Your teachers,

Ms. Howell and Ms. Moll

Jack's excitement over receiving mail and the family's satisfaction in this individual welcome to their child created an immediate bond between them and his new teachers. Carrying his dinosaur to school on the first day and knowing that there was a place waiting for him marked with some hearts eased Jack's transition into school.

Telephone Contact.   In the past, parents and teachers telephoned each other only when concerned about a child's progress. Today, the telephone is a tool for collaborating on all aspects of a child's education. Teachers can begin this process with a brief telephone conversation before or soon after school begins for the year. In this first call, introduce yourself to the family and express pleasure in having their child in your class (Olsen & Fuller, 2003). Inform parents that unless they wish otherwise, you'd like to call or e-mail them on a regular (once a week or month) basis just to keep in contact, inform them of their child's progress and school events, and answer any questions or concerns they might have (Gustafson, 1998). Establishing positive communication early in the school year enables parents and teachers to be comfortable about contacting each other when later confusion or misunderstanding arises, as the following vignette demonstrates.

Melissa Jacobs was entering a new school for third grade. She knew no one and was terrified, especially since she "didn't read so good." Mrs. Jacobs was relieved when Ms. Thomas called to welcome Melissa to school and to invite the mother to visit. As the year wore on, Mrs. Jacobs was delighted in Melissa's

successful adaptation to school. So she called Ms. Thomas one November morning to see how Melissa's reading was going.

*The next day, Melissa came home very angry, not wanting to go to school. "I don't see why I have to go to that dumb teacher and do **phonics**. I hate phonics!"*

Distressed, Mrs. Jacobs immediately called the teacher to ask what was happening. Before Mrs. Jacobs could say much more than hello, Ms. Thomas said, "I am so glad you called. I was about to call you. You know, I really don't think it's a good idea for Melissa to go to the reading teacher. I know you are concerned about her reading, but she was just miserable today. Her reading is coming along well, and she doesn't need this extra pressure."

In the course of the conversation, it became clear that there had been a misunderstanding during the last telephone conversation. Mrs. Jacobs had intended to just maintain contact, and Ms. Thomas had interpreted it as concern. Since good communication had been established early, both teacher and parent could resolve the misunderstanding in good faith and do what was best for Melissa.

Formal and Informal Classroom Visits

Traditionally, parents are invited to children's classrooms on special occasions, such as during National Education Week, or as audiences for special events. Increasingly, schools are establishing an open-door policy, and one recent innovation is an invitation to parents and children to drop in during one of the days before school begins to meet the teacher and see the classroom. These short, 10- to 15-minute visits are especially helpful for younger children or children transferring into the school and can help ease some of the anxiety parents and children feel about entering a new classroom.

Another traditional practice has been a Back-to-School Night early in the school year.

This event, held in the evening and generally for adult family members only, gives teachers the opportunity to meet children's parents or caregivers. This is also a time for teachers to introduce themselves and help parents get to know them and why they became a teacher. Families meet other parents at Back-to-School Night and learn about the curriculum, classroom procedures, discipline policies, and ways the teacher plans to communicate with parents.

The following vignette demonstrates an innovative twist that one classroom teacher instigated, that invited parents to participate in some of the classroom activities on Back-to-School Night. While people participated, the teacher gave information about the value of the different activities and an overview of their child's day.

☙

During the day before Back-to-School Night, Jack's teacher asked each child to tell what area of the classroom they thought their parent might want to explore. As a result, when Jack's mother arrived for the Open House, she was instructed to start her evening at the snack table. Later she had a chance to make something for him in the art area that he would find in his cubby when he arrived at school the next day.

☙

Recognizing the needs of families, some schools are also offering child care during the Back-to-School Night so that single parents or both parents can attend the event. Many schools use this event to introduce the many ways that families can contribute to the success of the classroom.

Home Visits

Visiting the homes of preschool-age children prior to the start of school has been common practice for many years. This is particularly true for early childhood programs like Head

During Back-to-School Night teachers encourage students to participate and explain the value of their activities to the parents

Start, where such visits are required several times a year. Many public school prekindergarten classes, child care programs, and private nursery schools also require teachers to visit children in their homes. These visits can be aimed at assisting parents in providing better health care and obtaining needed social services, as well as in becoming more knowledgeable teachers.

Other home visiting programs are designed to establish home–school relationships early by helping children become acquainted with the teacher and helping the teacher to understand the home situation. The responsibility for such visits always rests with the classroom teacher, but most will have an assistant teacher or other adult accompany them on the home visit. Besides meeting needs for safety, this allows one of the visitors to talk to the parent while the other can play with the child.

Traditional Practices. Traditional practices for making the home visit comfortable for both teachers and parents abound in early childhood literature. Recommendations include the following:

1. Clarify the purpose of the visit with an initial telephone call.

2. Arrange a convenient time so that children will be part of the process.

3. Set a specific time for the visit. Arrive and depart on time and leave earlier if events warrant it.

4. As a guest in the home, respect the cultural and ethnic values the family exhibits.

5. If other family members are present, include them in your conversation.

6. Be an attentive listener, but don't oversocialize or get drawn into family controversies.

7. Be prepared to suggest agencies and types of services that parents might pursue in getting help if the family asks.

8. Invite the parents to become active participants in the school program, suggesting several levels of involvement.

9. Follow up the visit with a thank you note and indicate action for what was agreed on during the visit.

Innovative Practices. In the traditional home visiting arrangement, the teacher was the resource person assisting parents in some way, especially by helping parents understand how they could support their children's education. Innovative programs change this relationship, making home visits collaborative efforts. The teacher acknowledges the parent as the expert on that particular child and seeks to get to know the child better through the visit. Parents can also initiate visits, plan an agenda, and discuss educational aspirations for their children. Parents and teachers may then become equal partners in developing good educational programs for children (Powell, 1990).

Successful home visits depend on a teacher's ability to develop a trusting relationship with parents. Home visits can provide teachers with new insights into the social, cultural, and cognitive functioning of children and their parents. By working cooperatively, parents and teachers can more easily support children's development and learning. Keep in mind, however, that some parents may decline a home visit for various reasons, and their refusal must be respected and an alternate plan for meeting should be arranged (Hanhan, 2003).

ESTABLISHING ONGOING COMMUNICATION WITH PARENTS

Almost all parents are keenly interested in their children and what happens to them at school. Teachers, knowing of this concern, have developed various ways to communicate to parents about their children's school experiences. Parent–teacher conferences, newsletters, telephone contacts, e-mail, Web sites, and written communiques inform parents about children's progress, school programs and curricula, and ways parents can help their children. Most techniques have proved very successful, and many innovative ideas are variations on these basic strategies.

Informal Contacts

Parents with children in preschool normally accompany their children to school, and this gives both parents and teachers a chance to talk informally. Teachers can allow time at the beginning and end of the day for brief conversations with parents. Parents like to hear what their children have been doing, and a brief statement, such as "Phil climbed to the top of the jungle gym for the first time today; he'll be excited to tell you about it," communicates to parents that you are aware of what is happening with each child.

Parents also must share in the communication process. Parents who comment about how their child is at home or note their child's enjoyment of a school activity communicate their involvement in their child's learning. Teachers who write a short synopsis of the day and post it on the parent bulletin board by saying, "Ask your child or me about . . . " help to foster communication between parent and child. By asking questions and being attentive, you can help parents feel more comfortable talking with you.

Lengthy conversations, however, are a problem at the beginning or end of the day. Busy parents are anxious to get to work or home, and busy teachers need to prepare for the day or clean up after a long day. Brief statements at this time are important, and if a parent needs more time, you should suggest either a scheduled conference or telephone call. When parents linger in the classroom, skilled teachers suggest that they observe something

special or help their children in some constructive way.

Parents usually do not accompany their older children to school but are often present in welcoming schools where partnerships have been formed with parents and communities. These parents still anticipate brief words of welcome or an exchange about what is going on with their children. Such exchanges communicate to all parties, including children, that responsibility for educating the young is shared by the entire community.

All school personnel can assist or hinder parents' reactions to schools. School custodians, secretaries, and classroom aides are especially important members of the school team. They often live in the neighborhood and can offer a bridge into the school community when they are friendly and open. Principals and teachers who look up from their work and smile at, greet, or offer assistance to persons entering give parents the feeling that the school community cares about them.

Written Communication

Teachers have traditionally given assignments with the hope that parents would oversee the homework and help their children as needed. Such homework provides children with practice on skills and concepts taught at school, and parents who review the work with their children get information about what they are expected to learn. In addition to assigning homework, some schools have devised other interesting ways for communicating with parents about their children's school involvement, including bulletin boards, newsletters, and informal notes.

Homework.   With research indicating the importance of parents' involvement in their children's education, schools are increasingly looking for ways to reach parents at home. Homework has traditionally been the device teachers have used to increase children's skills, and teachers assume that parents will supervise the work and thus come to know what school expectations are. Homework assignments are often seen by teachers as a parent's obligation and by parents as a great nuisance (Kralovec & Buell, 2000).

All too often, traditional homework consists of worksheets to complete or drill work on specific skills. Changing the emphasis of homework, however, can help parents see that they are indeed a contributing member of their child's classroom success. Assignments can be given that develop certain skills but are also part of the family's life (Trahan & Lawler-Prince, 1999). For example, children and parents might cook something together to share in the classroom. One teacher had children and parents look at the moon each night and mark the time of observation and the spot on the horizon where it was seen. Another teacher devised a Love Note Project whereby children selected a book to read with a parent or special person each evening. The parent wrote a simple love note about the interaction, and the child (or teacher) read it to the class next morning. In all the preceding examples, the teacher created a follow-up system that informed parents of the success of their work with their children.

Parents also appreciate having advance notice of upcoming homework projects and adequate time to complete them during the busy school week. Some teachers now provide a homework packet that has a week's worth of assignments that children and parents can work on at their own pace. Some schools have also established a homework hot line to help parents help their children. Community libraries are increasingly partnering with schools to support children and parents with homework (Mediavilla, 2001).

Bulletin Boards.   All classrooms have bulletin boards, and most schools have boards in the halls. Traditionally, teachers place on these boards children's work, information about special events, and material for a particular unit. Parents visiting the school gain information about the school by looking at these boards. They see their children's artwork, their written or retold stories, reports on books they have read, and information on units they have studied. They read the teacher's explanation of the work and what it shows about the children's learning. Photos with captions are especially appealing to parents, as they show children's involvement in classroom activities. The increasing use of digital cameras allows teachers to easily share such photos with parents through e-mail.

Innovative schools have special bulletin boards just for parents, and the interests of parents dictate what is posted. If teachers regularly change postings, parents will learn to look to the board for information. Teachers may post special articles regarding children's growth and development, information regarding meetings and availability of social services, and health and nutritional information.

Parent volunteers often arrange the board or assist teachers in highlighting information, such as bibliographies of children's books, educational toy suggestions for birthdays or holidays, and recipes for nutritional snacks. Sometimes teachers photocopy materials and put them in a wall pocket for parents to take home. Parents are also invited to post materials of interest for other parents, and one school even added a wipe board for parents to write notes to other parents.

Newsletters and Websites.   Classroom and school newsletters, while varying in purpose, are traditional methods for schools to communicate with parents. Most newsletters communicate school news, including notices of school events, parent–teacher conferences, and other important meetings. Traditionally, most newsletters have included tips for helping children at home and for parents seeking resources. All information can go on a school Web site, too, with paper copies sent home to those families without a computer.

Innovative teachers find extended purposes for newsletters or Websites. One teacher gives out the first newsletter at Back-to-School Night and uses it to communicate much of the information she shares verbally. Another teacher includes in her newsletters artwork by children, photos of classroom activities, thank you notes for parental and community support, examples of how children use materials parents contribute, and extracts of classroom discussions children had because of parental support. Such a complete newsletter provides parents with many examples of what and how children learn from various resources.

Informal Notes and E-mail. Traditionally, teachers have used informal notes to inform parents of their concerns regarding their students' work. Now, more teachers recognize the value of notes that reflect students' special accomplishments in developing social, cognitive, or physical skills, thus giving both parents and children a sense of well-being. Of course, all notes can go to parents via e-mail for homes so equipped. Most notes don't require a response, but you may occasionally wish to query how parents see their child's skill development at home. You also want to invite two-way communication through notes for parents who find this a helpful way to keep in touch.

Like the first telephone call home, the first note should be a positive communication designed to build a collaborative relationship. Some teachers like to send home some kind of weekly report for all children (see Figure 11–1) and ask parents to sign and return the report. Informal notes or weekly reports can also express concern about a change in a child's behavior.

When notes are positive in tone, even if you have some concern, parents come to understand the importance of working cooperatively to provide the best for their children. Most teachers believe it is wise to let children know about communications with their parents and, in general, what the notes contain. Children's involvement is essential, for children need to know that parents and teachers are working together to help them learn. In classrooms where children's parents speak a language other than English at home, teachers have elicited the aid of bilingual parents in translating notes sent home.

Interactive Portfolios.   In many classrooms now, teachers have children assemble their work in a portfolio. Over time, the work accumulated here provides materials for children, teachers, and parents to assess the child's learning. Technology expands possibilities for communicating with parents via these portfolios. For example, digital cameras allow teachers to record classroom events and share these with parents on a regular basis. Some teachers print these photos and include some in individual, **interactive portfolio** notebooks that are shared between the home and school (Gronlund & Engel, 1999). Periodically, the teacher will write a short entry about a special event, accomplishment, or issue in each child's portfolio and send it home with the child to share. The family is invited to write a response or to share information, photos, and news from home and add to the portfolio.

Electronic mail and telephone answering machines are other ways that teachers provide more information to parents. Some teachers use an e-mail address or an answering machine to record brief messages for parents concerning children's home assignments, events of the day, upcoming meetings, or things that children are asked to bring to school. Parents can call in at their leisure and have easy access to information or leave messages for the teacher.

Parent–Teacher Conferences

Conferences are one of the most frequently used methods of parent–teacher communication and

WEEKLY REPORT

NAME: _____   DATE: _____

_____

In general, your child's behavior was:

(G) GOOD   (F) FAIR   (N) IN NEED OF IMPROVEMENT

_____ Listening skills   _____ Behaves in specials

_____ Works quietly   _____ Behaves in hallways

_____ Stays on task   _____ Shows respect

_____ Completes class work   _____ Completes homework

_____ Interacts appropriately with peers

TEACHER COMMENTS

_____

_____

_____

_____

PARENT/GUARDIAN SIGNATURE _____

PARENT/GUARDIAN COMMENTS:

_____

_____

_____

_____

Figure 11–1   Weekly progress report

**Interactive portfolios
provide children, teachers
and parents an opportunity
together to assess the
child's learning**

have been a successful way to discuss a child's progress. As schools begin to develop a sense of partnership, conferences, although not different on the surface, become forums for mutual exchange. Partnership conferences mean that both partners share examples of children's development, show respect for each other's responsibility, and propose ideas for continuing a program or changing direction. In successful conferences, parents and teachers are able to communicate the child's strengths, progress, and possible areas for improvement in more detail than in any other format (Henniger, 2002).

Establishing Collaboration Through Conferences. Teachers work from a sound traditional base when creating an environment for successful collaboration. Current strategies reflect changes in attitudes of teachers and parents. Figure 11–2 presents a general scheme that you as a teacher may use to ensure that your parent–teacher conferences result in effective collaboration (adapted from Coleman, 1991; Seefeldt & Barbour, 1998).

Innovative Practices for Conferences. Although initiating conferences has traditionally been the teacher's responsibility, innovative schools encourage parents or other involved adults to suggest meetings and to come to conferences prepared. Student involvement in conferences also has proven to be successful for all concerned.

Parental Involvement. To enhance parent involvement, some teachers have been successful in recommending ways parents can prepare for the conference. Innovative schools will make sure that parents know about the following strategies and will clarify that teachers recognize different family lifestyles:

- If children have more than one adult responsible for them, both adults should plan to attend, if possible. A single parent may

bring a grandparent or another significant adult.

- Since the conference is an important part of the child's education and evaluation, adults should make the appointment a priority and get it on the calendar early.
- Children's understanding of the purpose of the conference is important, and parents or surrogates should talk with children about the conference and ask for their input about school and how they view their progress.
- Any materials that parents and children want to share with the teacher should be brought to the conference.
- Adults attending the conference should make note of any questions or concerns that either they or their children wish to share with the teachers.
- Because of busy schedules, teachers and parents may need to work out special arrangements so that all can attend the conference. Early morning, late afternoon, and evening appointments should be available for parents who need them.
- Afterward, parents need to talk about the conference as positively as possible to help the children see the relationship of the home environment to school life.
- A follow-up letter or e-mail to the school clarifies for the teacher the parents' or surrogate's view of the conference.

Parents and teachers all develop a sense of partnership in children's learning when they recognize the significant impact these meetings have on learning.

Student Involvement. Traditionally, students have had little say or involvement in parent–teacher conferences. As parents assume some responsibilities for conferences, both teachers and parents seek input from children regarding questions they would like the adults to discuss. Another facet of innovative

PREPARATION FOR THE CONFERENCE

1. Develop mutual respect by scheduling conferences at convenient times for both teachers and parents.

2. Establish a sense of equality with seating arrangements. Avoid physical barriers by sitting beside parents at a table where everyone can view all materials.

3. Prepare an agenda and send it to the parents. Include a statement of purpose and allow times for parent input, your input, and questions from both you and parents.

4. Assemble materials from areas of the curriculum that demonstrate children's classroom work over time.

5. To demonstrate the value you place on parental teaching, invite parents to bring items their children have produced at home, such as charts of children's home responsibilities, craft projects children have made, food they have prepared, letters they have written, any collections, or sets of favorite books.

THE CONFERENCE

1. Begin the conference on a positive note by sharing children's accomplishments at school with parents.

2. Invite parents to share their children's meaningful achievements at home.

3. Share your mutual academic and personal concerns.

4. Discuss ideas for resolving these concerns.

5. Allow time for parental questions. If parents appear reluctant to ask questions, assist them by suggesting what other parents often ask: codes of behavior for the classroom, academic questions not attended to in this particular conference, parent involvement in schools or in children's learning.

6. Keep the conference to the allotted time. If you need more time, schedule a new conference.

ENDING THE CONFERENCE

1. End the conference on a positive note, be complimentary to the children involved.

2. Review conference highlights.

3. Restate your understanding of any decisions mutually made.

4. Indicate how information or material parents have shared has helped you understand their children better.

5. Thank the parents for coming and inform them of the next conference period, next school event for parents, or next PTA meeting.

6. Indicate your anticipation at seeing the parents again.

CONFERENCE FOLLOW-UP

1. Write a brief summary for your records. Include any and all parental suggestions or questions.

2. Follow through on your promises and inform the parents of your efforts.

Figure 11–2 Making parent–teacher conference work

conferences is including students themselves. When students are included in the conferences, steps need to be taken to prepare them:

- Determine the reason for including the children; for example, students have been working on a new project, and evaluation of the project will be enhanced with student input.
- Review with the class the purpose of the conference, and help the children as a class to develop some possible questions and ideas to discuss in upcoming conferences. Students may want to consider their strengths as learners, how they have changed during this time period, any difficulties they may be having, and how they might improve (Weldin & Tumarkin, 1999).
- Help students gather materials they wish to bring, to demonstrate the ideas brought up and questions asked.
- During the conference, have students describe their materials and how they see their progress. Have them ask questions of both teachers and parents.
- Have parents discuss their observations, and then discuss yours, being sure that children's are addressed too.
- Review the conference highlights and recommendations made.
- Understand the importance for all parties to follow up conferences with notes to one another.

While there are advantages to including children in the conference, there are drawbacks as well. Some information that the adults wish to share may not always be appropriate for the child to hear.

In nearly all classrooms, teachers and children often have individual conferences without the parents. It is important that children understand that parents and teachers will also have some conferences without the children.

Keys to Effective Communication

Whether communication is verbal, written, or electronic, there are certain key elements to consider for effective communication and for avoiding misunderstandings:

- Work at understanding the other's point of view. It is important to listen carefully to parents without interrupting. When responding to parent messages, try to consider their perspective without getting defensive. Repeat what you think you are hearing, seek clarification, and try to be empathetic in responding to concerns.
- Language differences can cause misunderstandings when care is not taken. Avoid seeming to model or correct another's speech pattern. When terms are used that either party is unfamiliar with, ask for or give an explanation in a nonjudgmental way.
- Traditionally, the teacher has been seen as the expert. Good collaboration requires a partnership in which teachers and parents acknowledge the contributions each makes to the child's development. Body language, such as pursed lips, folded arms, and hands on hips, can undermine positive communication by conveying a different message than the words expressed. Try to be aware of your own body language and respect the communication styles of various families.
- Voice pitch and tonal qualities are used to convey different meanings. Cultural and family differences exist, and they can cause misunderstandings. Learning about these differences in a reciprocal exchange can ease potential conflicts. In chapter 4, Greg helps Philip learn "the school way." In the same way, it is incumbent on the teacher to lessen the gap by recognizing that parents may not have "the school way." Being honest in how you have been affected by differences will open communication and will help parents recognize and even accept differences.

Thoughtful, ongoing communication with parents is an important component of parent–teacher cooperation. It involves parents at a basic level in their children's education. Table 11.1 summarizes the traditional and innovative communication strategies discussed in this section of the chapter.

PARENTS IN THE SCHOOLS

Many teachers invite parents to special events throughout the year, knowing that getting families in the classroom can be the first step toward further involvement. When parents are in classrooms, they see firsthand how their children respond to the school learning environment. Though we find exceptions, involved parents usually become strong supporters of their children's schools. They come to appreciate what teachers are doing and what is involved in educating their children. Besides basic participation as visitors or observers, some parents make a commitment as volunteers, classroom resource persons, or even paid aides. Teachers need to help parents understand that there are different levels of involvement (see Chapter 12, Figure 12–1) and encourage them to contribute where they can on the continuum.

School Visitation

Traditionally, parents are invited into children's classrooms on special occasions, such as during National Education Week, or as audiences for special events. Innovative schools have established open-door policies, welcoming parents whenever they wish to visit. One school in Baltimore County, Maryland, makes a point of inviting all parents to come to the first day of school each year. A celebratory atmosphere is created as families accompany their child to the classroom and stay for awhile. The level of parent involvement has

increased dramatically in this school since this policy was established several years ago.

When parents are free to drop in on their child's classroom at any time, certain guidelines must be developed so the visits are productive. Back-to-School Night provides an ideal forum for introducing parents to routines of the day and how children are involved. Parents will know that when they visit the teacher may suggest where they should sit to get the most out of their observation. If there is activity that parents can observe better moving about the room, the teacher suggests the best time to do so.

In some classrooms, children are accustomed to adults and are comfortable asking them for help. In such cases, parents are advised that children will approach them. If parents are visiting to observe general classroom activities and how children interact with one another, the teacher provides a list of things parents can watch for. If a parent is visiting for a particular reason, the parent and the teacher confer regarding what to look for and how.

In some families, grandparents, uncles, and aunts are closely involved in a child's life. Teachers should make it clear that these other important people are welcome in the school. At the Kensington/Forest Glen Children's Center, one of classes has an "I Love You" dinner each February. The children cook and serve a simple meal to all their loved ones, including siblings, parents, extended family, and other important people in their lives.

Most classrooms have special events to which teachers invite parents. Such occasions give children experiences in writing invitations, planning for the event, demonstrating some skill or talent, and even preparing special snacks. Increasingly, teachers are planning family breakfasts once a month or several times a year. Parents all bring some simple breakfast foods to share and join with their children, the teachers and other families in an informal gathering that can fit easily into the

Table 11–1 Parent and Teacher Communication Strategies: Traditional and Innovative

Conferences	
Traditional	**Innovative**
Teacher schedules and direct conference. Teacher prepares materials, provides input, and strives for cordial and productive exchanges.	Parents as well as teachers prepare for conferences. Parents schedule appointment. Child contributes ideas to the conference and/or attends.

Home Visits	
Traditional	**Innovative**
Teacher attempts to understand the home and establish positive relations.	Collaboration is sought. Parents become partners in planning visits and sharing ideas. Parent empowerment is sought.

Telephone Contact	
Traditional	**Innovative**
Teacher initiates calls when concerned.	E-mail allows either parent or teacher to initiate calls or leave messages.
Teacher uses phone as substitute for conference.	Answering machines with messages on schedules, homework, etc. permit exchange of information.

Informal Contact	
Traditional	**Innovative**
Beginning and ending of the school day are times for brief exchanges between parent and teacher. Demonstrating interest is the goal.	Parents can accept more responsibility for communication.

Written Communication	
Traditional	**Innovative**
Teachers develop bulletin boards.	Parents can help arrange bulletin boards or collaborate with school personnel in developing one.
Newsletters include school news, dates to remember, and tips for helping children at home.	New items are included: photos of schoolwork, artwork, notes on parents' contributions, and how kids learn. Web sites highlight school news.
Informal notes are ways to keep in contact with and inform parents.	Notes reflect children's special accomplishments. Notes and e-mail are designed to give both parents and children a sense of well-being.

1. *Stone Soup Day*. As part of their folktale study, a third-grade class invited their parents to celebrate the end of the unit. Children performed their version of "Stone Soup" and then had parents join them in eating a nutritious meal of "stone" soup and corn muffins, which they had prepared the day before.

2. *Celebrating Mrs. Jones*. Once a month, the second-grade class celebrated a special person in the school and invited her or him in for snack time. Besides preparing the snack, children always made a special gift reflecting some aspect of their current study unit. Different parents joined to help with preparations and to express their appreciation for the person's services.

3. *Circus Day*. A kindergarten class invited parents to the culminating session of their circus unit. Their circus had only one ring, but all contributed special skills as acrobats, lions, and dogs, or trainers, clowns, and a ringmaster. One parent, a skilled pianist, accompanied the acts with appropriate music.

4. *Father's Day Breakfast*. A first-grade class invited their fathers, grandfathers, or special adult males to join them monthly for a special breakfast they helped prepare. As a variation, the class had unrelated adults from the school and community join parents and students for breakfast. The price for breakfast was $1.00; however, if a student found an unrelated adult to join her or him, the student saved the $1.00 charge. At first teachers helped engage students and adults in conversations regarding school events. As the idea caught on, students began to seek out volunteers other than their parents to join them. Not only did community volunteers get a better understanding of what happens in schools, but students also began to appreciate the diversity of interests within their community.

5. *Coffee Hour*. At one school, the principal, staff members, and teachers, on a rotating basis, were freed from responsibilities each Friday morning. Parents were invited in to have coffee and chat with them about school in general and to get to know one another. As the year progressed, sharing "things that were working well" and "things that could work better" became part of the agenda. Gradually, the evolving good fellowship and trust led to both parents and school personnel taking responsibility for seeking solutions for expressed concerns.

Figure 11–3   Special events for classrooms

daily routine. The list of events for such visits is almost endless. Some interesting examples are noted in Figure 11–3.

Child's Role in Visitations.   Children need to be prepared for adults visiting their classroom. Teachers usually have explained to their classes that parents and other adults enjoy coming in to see what they are doing. Traditionally, teachers introduce visitors, explaining to children the purpose of the visit. An innovative approach to these visits is to help children take responsibility for welcoming visitors.

Mrs. Horton has many visitors to her class at school near Atlanta, and she established the role of greeter to be filled as one of the weekly classroom duties. Children practice the role so they will feel comfortable with adults. When adults come into the room, the greeter quietly welcomes them, takes their coat, and suggests where to sit. The child points out the daily schedule, which is always posted, and tells the visitors what is currently happening.

Parents as Aides or Volunteers

Most teachers realize that having volunteers to regularly assist children in the classroom pays off in a richer curriculum for students. To be most effective, classroom volunteers need orientation and training in order to participate in ongoing classroom activities. Teachers are legally responsible for the children in their classroom, and if parents don't understand the rules and procedures, conflicts can arise. Misunderstandings can result, and neither children, parents, nor teachers are well served.

Since most parents are employed, teachers have become more flexible in their expectations of parent volunteers so that even working parents may be able to participate at some level. Schools are also turning to grandparents, active retirees, high school students, and other community members as volunteers. While some schools have money allotted to hire one or more parents to work as aides in the classroom, volunteers are still needed to serve a variety of roles in schools.

Skillful teachers make good, creative use of volunteers. Although methods vary for orienting and training volunteers, the following procedures have proven successful for many teachers.

Back-to-School Night can provide a forum for teachers to acquaint parents with the vol-unteer opportunities in the classroom. At this point, some parents may be able to commit to a regular schedule of classroom participation. A later meeting, sometimes led by the reading specialist or guidance counselor along with the classroom teacher, introduces these parents to the classroom routines and provides guidelines for their participation. As classroom volunteers, they will be able to help individual children with projects, listen to them read, and assist them in practicing certain skills. They may also read to individual children and, when it is comfortable, may read to small groups or to the class. Volunteers can also help the teacher prepare materials or set up activities.

Schedules for regular classroom volunteers work more smoothly if teachers make a monthly calendar and send parents reminders of the volunteer days. Each morning before the children arrive, the teacher and volunteers spend a few minutes discussing the events of the day. At the end of the day, they meet again briefly to discuss how the day went. For the experience to be successful, both teachers and

A specialist works with parent-volunteers guiding them in ways to assist children in reading or in practicing certain skills

volunteers need to recognize that the teacher is the major decision maker and authority figure in the classroom. Teachers must respect the skills volunteers bring, but they must establish and communicate the classroom rules to volunteers so that children do not receive mixed messages.

To involve other parents who can only participate occasionally, one creative teacher has an open policy on volunteers and invites working parents to observe and help whenever they have time off. He keeps a list of special activities that need extra classroom help. When parent volunteers arrive, the teacher is then ready to use them productively to assist children. This policy has been especially helpful in securing more male volunteers.

Parents and Community Members as School Resources

Teachers and schools are finding other ways that parents and community members can assist them. Some programs use volunteers as tutors or **mentors**. Some tutors work with students having particular difficulties, while others work with gifted children who need enrichment programs. Other mentors work with children who have a special interest in their area of expertise.

Traditional Practices.   Many programs use parents to help children with reading. Volunteers come regularly, take children to a quiet area, and read with and to them. Some programs even have special work sessions for volunteers, helping them to develop skills for involving children in reading (Lilly & Green, 2004).

When parents do not have time for regular classroom volunteer work, they can help on special occasions in ways that parents have been traditionally involved. When children go on field trips, parents often accompany children or help in organizing the trip. Classrooms have materials that can be prepared or repaired at home such as making play dough or sewing smocks. And all schools have nonclass functions in which parents can render support services, such as helping organize for National Education Week, helping with fund-raising activities, or supporting the Read a Book Club.

Innovative Programs.   Some educators have devised plans whereby volunteers offer an enriched program for children in their school. In one Maryland program, on Wednesday afternoons, community members present a variety of programs that reflect particular volunteers' skills and interests. An expert quilter provided quilting lessons for 6 weeks. A bird carver introduced the beginning steps of carving. There were flower-growing and -arranging classes, bird and rock identification classes, and discussions on topics from Caldecott and Newbery Award–winning children's books. At the beginning, volunteers wrote a brief description of their "course," indicating the number of lessons and appropriate age range. Children then signed up, but as the program developed, some adults began to join their children in taking the classes. Both children and adults found that they enjoyed learning in such multiage groupings.

Expressions of Appreciation.   Volunteers receive rewards for their efforts in different ways. Seeing children's progress is very satisfying, and children have their unique ways of showing delight in having someone read to them or help them with a project. Reaching to take the adult's hand, offering a hug, expressing, "I read this entire book to my mom after you helped me yesterday," or making a special drawing of "us reading together" expresses better than anything how much children benefit. Letters of appreciation can come from children, teachers, the parent coordinator, or the school principal. Many schools have special dinners or events to formally thank volunteers.

Parents and community members regularly involved in classrooms or school events find themselves at a committed level of involvement from which they gain knowledge about their schools. Children's education is further enhanced when the entire community arrives at this level of cooperation and participation.

Parents as Advocates

In general, teachers expect parents to be involved with their children's education at the basic or minimum level. This means communicating with the school about the child's progress and participating in major events like conferences and special occasions. Many teachers are willing to take responsibility for trying to get more parents involved as more committed participants in the classroom since they find that it produces better results for their students (Berger, 2000). However, there is a third level of involvement that teachers and school administrators are not always comfortable with—that of advocacy.

When parents or community members become advocates for children, they become decision makers, serving as equal partners on school policy boards, curriculum committees, steering committees, and school councils (Moriarty & Fine, 2001). Some parents in this role work within the framework of committees and the administrative structure. Parents who feel that the school policy is adversely affecting their children may initiate action. In such cases, they meet with teachers, principals, school board members, and even local and state legislators to advocate a change in policy. Recall that it was a single parent, and then a group of parents on a grassroots level, who eventually succeeded in securing appropriate education for children with disabilities through PL 94-142, the Individuals With Disabilities Education Act (IDEA).

Other parents become strong advocates for change within an entire school system. Parents may seek election to school board positions because they wish to see change and feel that this is a way for their voices to be heard. Federal legislation also has resulted in some parents having a policy-making role. Head Start programs, Chapter I programs, and programs under IDEA are required to have parents on their policy-level councils. These parents then have a voice in program development, hiring teachers, the kinds of training offered to teachers, and other policies that affect the programs.

Not all school systems or teachers embrace parent advocacy enthusiastically, nor can all parents operate at an oversight level of involvement. Such advocacy and involvement work well only when both parties—parents and teachers—have a voice in the decisions and work cooperatively together. Some parents have served on curriculum committees, steering committees, or school improvement teams and have advocated or demanded change, only to find that nothing changes. This means frustration. Only when parents, teachers, and school administrators are able to recognize each other's expertise and are willing to assume responsibility for pulling together can change occur. Building coalitions of parents and teachers working for the best interests of their children is the most powerful advocacy role any person can undertake (Bloom, 1992).

Parent Education

Chapter 2 discussed the trends of parent education during the past century. As noted, in the early history of the United States, parents learned about educating their children from their own parents or relatives. Then, as psychology moved to the fore, professionals became the experts, and parent education regarding child development and wise parenting practices became a part of the school's responsibility.

Presently, we again find recognition of parents' skills and expertise. In some innovative programs, parent education means that teachers are learning new skills for interacting with parents. Teachers value parents' ideas, help parents understand their own skills, and more effectively integrate home and community knowledge with classroom learning. In addition, innovative practices in parent education reflect efforts to include parents from all economic and ethnic groups within a community (Fine & Lee, 2001).

Some schools attempt to involve their parent group in those education programs that parents themselves see as particularly needed. Seefeldt and Barbour (1998) described a program of outreach in which a principal succeeded in getting parents involved by allowing parents to choose and plan their own topics. Many hard-to-reach parents became intrigued and began coming to these informal but educational sessions.

Some schools find that developing a **parent center** within the school gives parents a sense of belonging. Sessions in parent centers run the gamut from good child-rearing practices to dealing with behavioral problems and drugs in the community to language instruction for non-English speakers. The meetings often are unstructured, led by laypersons, and involve a great deal of discussion and idea exchange among the participants. Some schools provide a collection of materials, including books, videos, and articles, related to child development, health and safety, managing behavior, and other topics of interest in their parent centers and encourage parents to check them out. The center may also have listings of local resources and social services for parents.

Several specially designed programs exist for training parents to develop skills in working with their children. Three popular program models used during the past 25 years are: Gordon's (2000) Parent Effectiveness Training; Popin's (1990) Active Parenting Discussion Group; and the Dinkmeyer, McKay, and Dinkmeyer (1997) Systemic Training for Effective Parenting.

Children's Resources International (Daniels, 2002) in partnership with Montgomery County, Maryland, Early Childhood Services, developed a unique series of workshops designed to assist parents in helping their children develop the skills needed to learn to read and write. Each literacy-learning party, as these workshops are called, introduces a specific literacy component and offers parents practical and useful activity suggestions for home use. Like most effective parent education, these workshops include lecture and discussion, practical suggestions, and lots of opportunities for interaction among the participants.

Education Through Materials. Learning packets and family theme bags are two innovative practices that teachers have devised for helping parents of at-risk children. In these, parents receive a packet of information and ideas for how to interact in a way that increases children's early literacy development (Spewock, 1991).

In one Maine program, learning packets are sent to parents of newborns and each succeeding year until age 5. The packet contains information about child development, ideas for fostering growth, and tips on good parenting. Ideas include ways to use books, simple games to play at each age level, and artworks or crafts to create using inexpensive materials.

Family theme bags are cloth bags sent home with preschoolers that contain a stuffed animal, a journal, a file-folder game, "What if . . . ?" cards, songs–finger plays, a storybook, and art supplies. An introductory letter outlines the purpose of the bag and the value of the activities suggested. The stuffed animal or puppet provides a theme, and games, songs, and activities relate to that theme. For example, the zoo bag contains ideas for making zoo sandwiches, a song about an elephant, and a simple board game with a zoo pattern. The journal is provided so that parents can write their comments on how children respond to the materials and games. When children return the bags, the teacher reads the journals to the class (Helm, 1994).

COMMUNITY INVOLVEMENT

All children have experience with their community and have learned many different concepts from these encounters. Traditionally, preschool and primary schools take field trips that focus on specific aspects of community life and provide children with new and extended insights.

Trips into the Community

Carefully planned field trips enhance and make more meaningful the objectives of a unit of study. Students studying economics, for example, can set up a bank and a store in their classroom and practice using the bank and store in ways they learned from their parents or from books they have read. But a trip to an actual bank and store, where they can ask specific questions, allows them to view how adults behave in such places. It gives students behind-the-scenes experience.

When children have particular questions to ask or things to see or do, they gain skills in observing, collecting information, making inferences, comparing information with others, and drawing conclusions. Also, trips produce new ideas, which children transfer to their dramatic play, reading, writing, and other classroom instruction. A trip provides motivation for further interests and learning, as it did for the first graders in the following vignette.

Field trips focusing on specific aspects of community life provide children new and extended insights

❧

Nigel's class, accompanied by several parents, took a walking trip to the pet store to get food for the lizard they had found in the play yard and were now studying in class. While at the store, they were fascinated by a hermit crab and convinced their teacher to buy one for further study. Nigel became so interested that with his parents he visited the local aquarium. A naturalist at the aquarium told him more about hermit crabs and where they lived. With this information, the family took a trip to the seashore, and all were able to observe hermit crabs in their natural habitat. Nigel's stepfather videotaped the family's excursion, and Nigel showed the tape to the class and described his experience to his classmates.

꩜

Innovative Trips. Trips into the community are not restricted to gaining understanding of the neighborhood. Children can make trips intended to contribute in some way to the community, such as enhancing the local environment. Trips around the school can focus on cleaning up the area or planting flowers or shrubs. Some organizations "adopt" a highway, assuming the responsibility to clean up litter along a specific section of the road. Classrooms can adopt a neighborhood park, a playground, or a street and keep it attractive.

A visit to a nursing home or hospital presents opportunities for children to show older or ill people their artwork, sing or play some special songs, or present a dramatic presentation. When child care centers are located in adult day care centers or nursing homes, older persons often regularly read to children or engage in activities, such as cooking or making collages, with the children.

A related idea became a project for older children, who followed the Foxfire concept of visiting and interviewing older residents to hear their stories of yesteryear. The class collected and published the stories in book form

and sold them at school functions. In this case, the intent was not to help other people, but was to help children interact, appreciate, and be involved with an older generation.

Good ideas for collaboration aren't always between school and community agencies. The Chicago Public Library and the Chicago Police Department teamed up to provide a number of interactive programs. One program was a Mystery Beat Book Club, where students read mysteries and met various police officers who explained how mysteries are solved in real life. Another was a Get Hooked on Fishing, Not on Drugs program. Police personnel spent time with youngsters, both in the library and at special fishing spots, examining the art of fishing. All agreed that the programs helped the police reach youngsters in positive ways, the library maximized its resources, and children had fun, associated with good role models, and became involved in interactive activities that enhanced their reading skills (Burnette, 1998).

Community as Resource for Materials

Children can travel in their community for educational purposes, but it is also possible to include community members in the classroom. Traditionally, teachers have invited doctors, firefighters, or police officers to share their services with children, but imaginative teachers have found other ways to involve community members. One kindergarten teacher instituted a "Royal Reader" program and each week invited a person from the community to read aloud to the class. Using some regal music as background, the teacher introduced the reader, who entered the room wearing a crown and cape. Over the course of the year, employees of the power plant, water company, community college, retail stores, and various other local business and services came to the classroom to read and tell a little bit about their work.

Teachers also invite specific community members to the classroom to extend or enhance taking part of his collection of rare butterflies to a second-grade classroom each year during their "butterfly unit." In the spring, he walked in nearby fields with children hunting out cocoons or newly hatched butterflies.

As in planning for field trips, teachers need to plan for special guests. They tell children about the guest, encourage them to think of things they want to know, and help them understand how they are expected to act during the visit. It is important that teachers remind visitors of children's interest level, attention span, and need for hands-on experience.

Some resources from the outdoor environment can be brought into the classroom for closer examination, but teachers must carefully choose these resources. Endangered plants must not be disturbed, and certain animals are unsafe to bring into classrooms. But colorful leaves, nuts, and fruit, twigs fallen from trees, rocks and seashells, minerals embedded in bits of rock, insects in aerated jars, and pond creatures for classroom aquariums are specimens that children can examine and study in the classroom. See Figure 9–1 for a listing of community resources.

Involving the Business Community

Businesses have provided support for schools in various ways for many years, most often in the form of contributions of goods or funds. Restaurants have contributed gift certificates but may also contribute a percentage of their profits on a particular night that has been designated for a school. Parents are encouraged to patronize the restaurant on that evening. Other restaurants have established a "Dine Out for Charity" month and will donate a percentage of each order to the local school or agency. Still other business will contribute funds for some particular project or materials. Band uniforms or costumes for a school production are items that local businesspeople take pride in providing for community junior and senior high schools.

Other businesses have contributed classroom equipment such as calculators and computers. Some businesses will sponsor special programs such as "Read to a Parent and Get a Pizza." A school-supplies store agreed to provide one enterprising kindergarten teacher with a year's supply of fingerpaints when her classroom budget was reduced. In return, children's work, demonstrating the creative potential of finger paint, was exhibited in the store.

Businesses also cooperate with schools by providing release time for employees to volunteer in the schools. In some instances, it is parents and employees who wish to be a part of their children's classroom, but in other instances, time is allowed for unrelated employees to become volunteer readers or mentors or to relate their special expertise with children.

Collaborating with business for better schools requires a spirit of mutual respect and reciprocity of benefit. For partnerships to be effective, teachers must visit the business establishment to determine its educational possibilities, and business personnel should visit schools to become acquainted with their function, goals, and daily operation. Each partner needs to know the other's resources, ideas, and commitments. Committees for each organization need to make decisions affecting the support and purpose of the collaboration. Teachers must be represented on the appropriate business committee, and involved business personnel should be a part of the school planning committee. Through such collaborations, teachers, parents, and community members gain new understanding of the importance of good schools to a community and of how the community can contribute to the school's excellence.

WORKING WITH SELECTED FAMILIES

The strategies used for collaborating with parents of all children in your classroom can be effective, no matter what the circumstances are. However, some groups need special consideration, especially when traditional methods are not working.

Parents of children with disabilities, members of ethnic minorities, **homeless** and migrant **families,** and gay and lesbian parents often find that schools do not reach out to them as easily as they do to other parents. It is imperative that schools find ways to reach all families. The first step is for teachers to examine their own feelings toward parents who are outside the mainstream and who may be more difficult to reach. It is natural for teachers to feel angry, guilty, frustrated, exhausted, and even disapproving when no communication seems to work or when others exhibit different priorities or a different lifestyle. Being honest about your feelings and discussing them with others will help you to avoid using terms or making statements that hurt or anger parents who may have been rejected in other situations (Olsen & Fuller, 2003).

Children with Disabilities

All professionals must know the legal rights and the responsibilities parents have with regard to their children's education. Public Law 94-142 requires that parents of children with disabilities participate in planning and implementing educational programs for their children. Parents also have the right, if they deem it necessary, to challenge an educational plan. Regulations regarding educational planning include the following requirements, intended to establish positive communication between home and school (Gearheart, Weishahn, & Gearheart, 1996):

1. In discussions, the parents' native language must be used, with an interpreter if needed, so that good communication can be established.

2. Parents must give permission for assessments to be done on their children and

must be informed about conferences whenever results are being considered.

3. Parents should attend the meeting when the child's individualized education program (IEP) is confirmed. The law requires the time and place to be convenient for the parents.

4. Parents have a right to review their children's school records and ask for amendments if they feel records are inaccurate. If they disagree with the records or the evaluation, they have the right to an independent evaluation.

Parents of children with disabilities may be working through the grief that can accompany the realization that a child is going to require special care and services (Lerner, Lowenthal, & Egan, 2003). Many need to be treated more sensitively than do parents of typically developing children. Therefore, all educators and community workers must make a special effort to be knowledgeable about disabilities and their implications for families.

With the increased amount of communication between teachers and parents of children with disabilities, we must be especially clear and precise about procedures and objectives. It is important that parents understand the continuum of services available within the school system and what the 1997 mandate regarding "inclusion" means. While there is a preference for including children with disabilities in the regular education classroom, a number of factors, including the child's needs, parental preference, required related services, and progress, helped to determine the level of inclusion appropriate for each child (Howard, Williams, Port, & Lepper, 2001).

Parents and educators must work closely and listen to each other's perspectives in order to develop the most effective placement for the child (O'Shea et al., 2001): Workshops in which parents of children with disabilities and teachers participate together are particularly valuable in facilitating cooperation. Parents and teachers need these workshops to share information, deal with everyday situations, help all parties cope with stress, and cement bonds with others.

Ethnic Diversity

When working with ethnically diverse families, teachers must understand the differences that exist between the language of the school and that of the home (Neito, 2002). Keep in mind that over 13 million residents of the United States do not speak English well, and another 4 million have almost no English language facility. If parents speak limited English, it is essential to find someone who can translate. When teachers work with different linguistic groups, learning some words and expressions in the other language communicates to parents that the teacher values their language and accepts the two-way responsibility for communicating. Even when working with families whose native language is English, teachers must refrain from using educational jargon or other language patterns that may inhibit communication.

Educational activities designed to respect all cultures in the classroom enhance communication between home and school. By making a special effort to involve families from ethnic minority groups, teachers can strengthen understanding. Most parents have special knowledge of their heritage and culture that they will share with a class when approached in a positive way.

In one California school, parents of different ethnic backgrounds contributed in several ways. A Mexican American parent helped children prepare tacos, and a Japanese American mother showed children how to make origami birds. A Native American father invited a second-grade class to his workshop and demonstrated basic skills in silver work. A

Children draw upon their ethnic background as they label pictures or materials from their home experiences

recent German immigrant brought her collection of dolls to the school and explained the regional costumes the dolls wore.

Prop boxes have been used in many early childhood classrooms as a means of providing enrichment for children's dramatic play, and this idea can be extended to include the home. The teacher can send theme prop boxes home with children to be used as stimuli for reading, writing, and play. For example, a grocery prop box would contain empty food boxes, play money in a box, signs for the items, and a pad for writing a grocery list. Inviting parents to add special items to the prop boxes from their family's cultural experience gives a multicultural aspect to the play and also connects children's home experiences to the school (Neuman & Roskos, 1993).

Homeless and Migrant Families

Working with homeless and migrant families is one of the most challenging tasks a teacher faces. In spite of the McKinney Homeless Assistance Act of 1987 (PL 100-77) and subsequent amendments, which require states to guarantee access to education for homeless children, many homeless children are not in school. The requirements for registration, such as proof of residency, age, immunizations, and health records, are too much for many homeless families to cope with, and often these families find it easier to keep their children out of school (Eddowes & Hranitz, 1989). When children do have access to schooling, they often are not in the school for long, as parents are forced to move again.

Often migrant and homeless families are struggling with other problems, such as illness, spouse abuse, depression, and poverty. Most need assistance in securing social services, and if asked to help a school educate their children, the request will be beyond the skill of most homeless parents. It is important to remember, however, that the lack of a permanent home and financial resources doesn't mean that parents don't love their children and want them to succeed.

When homeless and migrant children are in a school, personnel need to unite their efforts to find support services that will enable parents to support their children's education. The following list contains several suggestions for teachers to assist parents in homeless situations (Quint, 1994; Yamaguchi, Strawser, & Higgins, 1997):

1. Provide information about the availability of various services and funding options and how to qualify for mental health services, child care, after-school care, and transportation arrangements.

2. Suggest options for parent involvement in the school. Although regular commitment to volunteering in classrooms is beyond most homeless parents, it is wrong to assume that the parents are unable or unwilling to help. They may be able to spend a day tutoring or supervising recess. When they give comfort to another child, they receive the joys of assisting someone else.

3. Be sensitive to parents' ability to provide baked goods, pay for special class events, or have children bring materials for classroom projects. Children whose families cannot provide such materials are often discriminated against by other children and even by teachers. Consider asking homeless parents to assist in a cooking experience in the classroom.

4. Keep in mind that homeless parents, too, need parent workshops and opportunities to share their concerns and "stories." It often takes special handling to get these parents to trust enough to be a part of such sessions.

5. Coordinate efforts with local shelters. Some school programs or workshops can be started at shelters. If parents gain confidence in shelter personnel, those parents often are willing to participate in school

programs with support for transportation and even child care for younger children. We must try not to segregate the homeless, denying children and parents opportunities for interaction with diverse groups.

Children of Gay and Lesbian Parents

Most teachers today are sensitive to different family structures and are trained to support children when families are in the process of change due to death, divorce, remarriage, or adoption. Less attention has been given to working with gay and lesbian parents or with families who have relatives who are gay or lesbian. Although relatively small in number, this group is increasingly visible, and these parents need to be supported as partners in their children's education. Teachers may need workshops to enable them to come to grips with their feelings about this family configuration and to find ways to support children whose parents or other important family members are gay or lesbian.

In a diverse society, parents expect that all family structures presented in the classroom will be treated with dignity and respect. Beyond this, it is important for educators to be sensitive to the needs of children from gay and lesbian households. Such parents may fear discrimination against themselves or their children and in some states may face custody difficulties if their sexual orientation is known. Teachers must help these parents support their children's learning as they do all others. Respect for all persons is a key ingredient, and using appropriate terminology for diverse groups should always be that which is currently acceptable—in this case, gay and lesbian (Clay, 1990). Teachers should also learn what the child calls each parent and use those terms when referring to the parent.

When children of gay and lesbian parents experience difficulty in school, teachers must approach the parents to discuss their

problems. By noting harassment, as well as by noting special friendships, teachers and parents can work together to help children deal with negative experiences. It is important to note and reinforce positive interactions among the children, for all children need to form networks of friends, family, and community relationships (Williams, 1998). In classrooms where some parents oppose books or discussions related to this topic, special handling is required. Janosik and Green (1992) have substantial recommendations for working with families that include gay members. Also, some communities have gay and lesbian groups specially trained to work with adults whose strong beliefs reject this lifestyle. Inviting parents to join you in one of these sessions can open the door for discussion and for better understanding and tolerance.

HANDLING COLLABORATIVE RELATIONSHIPS

Conditions for Positive Relationships

As noted in earlier chapters, we have a long history of parental involvement in U.S. schools. Some relationships have been very positive for particular parents, teachers, and community members. But good relationships do not just happen. Both internal and external conditions and factors help establish better relationships.

One important human factor for developing positive collaborations is mutual respect. Each party in a collaborative effort needs the concern of the others as well as the expertise, viewpoints, and experiences others possess.

Recognizing and supporting the expertise of others is not always easy. Comer (1980), in developing his collaboration model, maintains that the project nearly failed several times. It took 3 years to develop the trust and respect necessary for the school to begin a change process that would offer equal access and opportunity for all students. Commenting on this, Comer stated, "In order to provide good learning experiences for students, trust and respect must exist so that behavior, teaching and learning issues can be addressed. Such a climate cannot be imposed: it must grow out of governance and management arrangements and ways of working based on knowledge of social conditions and human and system behaviors" (p. 230).

Developing such respect requires compassion, a willingness to listen to others' points of view, and a willingness to compromise. Often it is school personnel who must take the initiative in establishing a sense of respect. However, for the relationship between teachers and parents to develop its fullest potential, both must consider each other as equals and share a commitment to open, two-way communication (Hanhan, 2003). No one right way exists to accomplish this, but concerned teachers and administrators devise ways that establish relationships with their students' parents through face-to-face, electronic, and written communication.

There are two very simple and immediate techniques that teachers can use to improve communication with parents. One is to *ask* instead of *tell*. The other is to *listen* instead of *talk*. A key component in establishing good partnerships is people's ability to really listen to each other. Regrettably, although professional adults are involved in communication activities about 70% of the time, less than half of that is spent listening, and even at that, the listening is not done well (Studer, 1993/1994). When teachers listen well, they do not interrupt to move on to their own agenda. When they reply to parents, they reflect back what they have heard and seek to validate, empathize, and problem solve with the parent. When both teachers and parents are willing to learn about and practice communication skills, student success increases (Miller, 1991).

Beyond the willingness to establish respect and develop good communication, external factors help collaborative efforts to function. It is important to establish support systems such as workshops to assist people in developing better communication skills. Time must be provided for meetings to discuss needs and objectives. To meet parent, teacher, and community members' time constraints, schedules must remain as flexible as possible. Teachers may need to be released from classes or compensated for evening meetings. Businesses need to examine the possibility of flexible hours of operation or flexible working hours for their parent employees. Having options for parent and community member involvement establishes a good basis for collaborative efforts, allowing all who are or wish to be involved to select a comfortable participation level.

A welcoming physical and social environment is an essential first step in creating a school climate that encourages parent and community involvement (Lim, 2003). Schools must place a priority on image. Sometimes a simple change in what visitors see when entering a building makes a great difference. Student artwork and other projects brighten up an entrance. A welcome sign directing visitors to the school office helps, as does a smile and positive attitude from the office staff once a visitor arrives. Space where parents can comfortably wait, perhaps with a coffee pot and some interesting literature about schools, gives visitors a sense of being welcome.

The process of collaboration is one of identifying, establishing, and cultivating positive factors to support interactions. Many ideas make sense for cooperative arrangements—the strategies of most any helping profession can be adapted appropriately. If schools are to become engaged in true partnerships, all concerned must expand and refine their communication, negotiation, and cooperation skills.

Barriers to Good Relationships

No matter how well intentioned people are, some barriers surface that will result in breakdowns of communication and good relationships. One basic hurdle revolves around the different philosophical positions and perspectives people have regarding how children learn and what they should be taught. For example, if a school attempts a constructivist approach to learning and parents do not understand how their children are being taught to read, write, and learn number facts, a barrier can develop. Parents could well become angry and accuse the school of ignoring discipline and not teaching the basics.

Different beliefs about how and who should teach sex education can create misunderstandings. Or, parents may consider discipline measures as either too harsh or too lenient, and these different perceptions will cause friction between home, school, and community. Issues such as these can spark problems, and they will fester and add to existing subsurface distrust if no mechanism is present to address them.

Attitudes can also present barriers to good relationships. Parents and community members have feelings and attitudes about school that date back to their own childhoods. Parents who had unpleasant school experiences are often reluctant to become involved with their children's schools. A diminished self-concept is often present in such cases, and the isolation breeds more fear. Such parents resist contact with schools out of fear of criticism of themselves and their children. This circumstance helps no one, least of all the children. Schools need to work gently but with determination to overcome negativism and encourage positive contact.

Nonverbal interactions often cause barriers to good relationships. Teachers or parents may state one thing while their nonverbal stance communicates another. For example, during a conference, one parent crossed her arms, saying, in what seemed an annoyed tone, "I thought Janey did well on that project." The teacher interpreted this to mean, "I don't agree

with what you said." The teacher then paused, moved slightly away, and murmured, "Well, it was an interesting project." When both moved on to another topic, the real significance of Janey's effort was lost. Both left the situation feeling defensive because the nonverbal behavior of both parties cut off further communication.

Fear affects teachers as well as parents, and teachers may do little to encourage parental or community involvement. When teachers are uncertain or insecure about their own teaching skills, they fear criticism of how they do their job and discourage parent participation in their classrooms. When we have local criticism of schools, teachers become tired of being scapegoats for all the wrongs of society, and they often express a desire to be left alone to teach. When such attitudes permeate the school, parents are made to feel unwelcome in many different ways.

When wide socioeconomic and cultural differences exist between school personnel and local families, misunderstandings can cause friction and often anger. Barriers are created when value systems differ and neither party is willing or able to examine differences and find common ground.

External features may also become barriers. Entering a school for the first time can be daunting even for the experienced. In some instances, doors are locked for safety reasons, and one must ring to enter. Sometimes the first thing one sees on entering a school is the notice, "All Visitors Must Report to the Principal's Office." Parents who were often sent to the principal's office during their school years will not feel very welcome. When the office is difficult to find and no one is around to assist, schools again communicate that visitors are unwelcome. Office personnel are sometimes too busy to assist or may appear annoyed at the interruption, or they may ask in an intimidating way, "Do you have an appointment?"

Admonishments and other external features can become barriers to positive home/school relationships

Unwelcoming signals are easily discerned and too often found.

Teachers and administrators are busy people struggling to maintain a productive environment for student learning. That is their most important task, and many think the time and energy needed to add parental and community involvement to their workloads just isn't available. Such school personnel communicate the unimportance of parental involvement.

Parents also find external barriers as they try to maintain a commitment to schools (Swap, 1993). Many have busy schedules, and families who live a distance from the school may have a problem with transportation. When involvement means going to the school in the evenings, child care may be difficult to arrange. Few businesses have flexible hours that allow parents to meet teachers during daytime hours. Hot lines and help lines can resolve some time and schedule conflicts when schools have a priority for maintaining communication.

IMPLICATIONS FOR PROFESSIONALS

We have described some strategies that schools around the country have found helpful. The important concept to draw from this information is that you have a number of ways to involve families and communities in children's education. Not all families or agencies can participate fully, nor is it even desirable to do so. But it is incumbent on you to help parents and others understand the continuum of involvement that will assist their children:

- *Basic or minimal level.* Assisting children at home is an important basic level of involvement and doesn't require any time off from work. It requires involvement such as reading to or with children, supervising TV viewing, playing games that require special cognitive skills, and assisting with homework and projects.

- *Participatory or associative level.* Visiting in the classrooms and attending parent–

teacher conferences and special school events require parents to participate in the educational process. These visits are more doable for working parents than classroom volunteer work. Parents may also be resources for working on occasional projects. Volunteering regularly as an aide or helping with special projects or tutoring requires a fair commitment of time during the day.

- *Advocacy or decision level.* The advocacy or decision-making level requires the most involvement from parents and other citizens. This means serving on boards and committees and rallying others to support schools.

SUMMARY AND REVIEW

Forming special relationships with parents and communities to enhance the education of children is not a new concept in the United States. As educators have gained more responsibility and authority over children's education, they have realized that parental education and parent involvement become part of the equation. Although educators have normally considered themselves experts in teaching children, they acknowledge that without parental and community support their job is more difficult.

Teachers over the years have developed many effective strategies for involving parents in their children's education. Many traditional strategies still work very well, but when these strategies are not sufficient or are outmoded, creative teachers and administrators test innovative means for reaching parents.

Frequent communication between home and school is important. Parent–teacher conferences, newsletters, phone calls, home visits, e-mail, and Web sites as well as parents' participation in classroom and school activities are more effective when teachers experiment with different strategies so that each family is reached at some level.

Teachers have developed many effective traditional and innovative strategies for parent education, for involving the community, and for working with parents of children with special needs. Most traditional strategies can be extended in innovative ways.

Many educators now recognize that when teachers, parents, and community members form a relationship of equality and shared responsibility, schools become strong and children acquire greater cognitive and social skills.

SUGGESTED ACTIVITIES AND QUESTIONS

1. Ask your parents (or someone you know well) about parent–teacher conferences or home visits in which they were involved when you were a child. Determine how useful they felt such activity was. If you know a parent of a primary-school-aged child, ask the same questions and compare strategies and parental reactions then and now.

2. Interview parents who volunteer in their children's classroom. Solicit their opinion of this involvement, asking how often they volunteer, how they became involved, why they think it is important, and what they are learning from the experience.

3. Locate a commercial establishment that displays children's work and ask how the school became involved. Compare notes with classmates who have interviewed other establishments to determine what kinds of involvement your community appears to have with schools.

4. Obtain from a school administrator (or parents of a school-age child) copies of newsletters sent home to parents. In your class, compare the kinds of information they contain. Discuss whether some are more "parent friendly" than others, and why.

RESOURCES

Books

1. Epstein, J. L., Sanders, M., Salinas, K. C., Jansorn, N. R., & Van Voorhis, F. (2002). *School, family, and community partnerships: Your handbook for action* (2nd ed.). Thousand Oaks, CA: Corwin.
2. Lilly, E., & Green, C. (2004). *Developing partnerships with families through children's literature.* Upper Saddle River, NJ: Merrill/Prentice Hall.

Films and Videos

1. *Building bridges between teachers and families* [Video, 21 min]. (2003). Seattle, WA: Harvest Resources.
2. *A children's journey: Investigating the fire truck* [Video, 45 min]. (2000). New York: Teachers College Press.
3. *Conducting effective conferences with parents* [Video, 22 min]. (1998). New York: Insight Media.
4. *Partnerships with parents* [Video, 28 min]. (1996). Columbia: South Carolina Educational Television with the National Association for Education of Young Children.

Organizations

Alliance for Parental Involvement in Education
P.O. Box 59
Chatham, NY 12060
www.croton.com/allpiex

Association for Childhood Education International 17904
Georgia Avenue Olney, MD 20832
(http://www.udel.edu/bateman/acei)

Center for Media Education
2120 L Street, NW, Suite 200
Washington, DC 20036
(http://www.cme.org)

Learning First Alliance
1001 Connecticut Avenue, NW, Suite 335
Washington, DC 20016
(http://www.learningfirst.org)

Websites

1. http://www.education-world.com This search engine for education Websites also includes original articles on various topics, including parent involvement in the schools.
2. http://ncela.gwu.edu/library/parent.htm The on-line library of the National Clearinghouse for English Language Acquisition provides materials on different ways schools can encourage parents and the community to take an active role in the education of linguistically and culturally diverse students.
3. http://projectappleseed.org The National Campaign for Public School Improvement provides information and resources necessary to become committed to school improvement.

Chapter 12

Models for Parent–School–Community Partnerships

The nation's schools must do more to improve the education of all children, but schools can't do it alone. More will be accomplished if families and communities work with children, with each other, and with schools to promote successful students.

(Davies, Palanki, & Burch, 1993, p. 22)

Much is right with U.S. educational experiences in spite of some glaring and well-publicized problems. Education planners and policy makers in most communities have a suitable base to build on, and they have numerous models to draw from to bring about improvements and viable partnerships. This final chapter addresses the issues for working together, and it highlights several of the worthy collaborations we find in American school districts. In reading this chapter, you will learn the following:

1. Collaborations among families, schools, and communities evolve, and we find one or more levels of involvement by the area adults at any one point.

2. Certain conditions enhance the growth of partnerships, and other factors can present barriers to forming good working relationships and collaborations.

3. Six particular criteria demonstrate the status of partnerships, and we can use them to design new collaborative ventures.

4. Major partnerships work because of thoughtful planning, careful implementation, straightforward accountability, and honest communication.

5. Partnership models vary, but quality programs have many common features.

While seldom using the term *collaboration*, residents in rural and urban communities have always had ways of influencing the upbringing of their youngest citizens. In the following vignette, a teacher recalls her childhood years in a poor rural community of the 1930s and indi-cates directions that would serve us well as we begin a new century.

A minister, the school principal, and our town fathers frequently discussed school problems, recommended solutions, and showed great concern for the children in our little town. Their efforts were supported by local parents, and our party-line telephone system, where most families could listen in, aided their communication. For example, one child, returning late from school on a spring day, was easily found, reprimanded by a passerby, and sent on his way with knowledge that his parents would follow through on the reprimand. Children who needed clothes were identified at school, and with the support of "town fathers," teachers and sometimes others visited the homes. Food, clothing, and other resources were found and delivered, and at times, negligent parents were counseled. Teachers taught formal lessons in the schoolrooms, but they often walked home with us, continuing our education as they discussed the natural world all around us. The community was our playground, and adults who were present supervised the children. Older children educated younger ones in many skills and safety rules. One could feel that this was a cohesive community and one marked by caring. It was, of course, not an ideal system: A few children didn't reach their potential. But an overarching support system enhanced our opportunities, and of 13 children in my first-grade class, all completed high school, and 7 went on to college in the 1940s.

The narrator of the preceding vignette demonstrates how parents, schools, and community members all assumed responsibility for children's development. Times were simpler then, and many communities were closely knit, but the lesson of communal caring and the need for shared expectations are still valid today. Author James Comer lived in a close-knit urban community during his childhood, and he tells of a similar collaboration of the social institutions that cared for him. In *Maggie's American Dream: The Life and Times of a Black Family,* Comer (1988) recalled his parents, neighbors, and teachers reinforcing each other's goals for children's engagement in learning. The process in Comer's case wasn't formal, either, but individuals in each social setting seemed to understand each other's roles. In both stories, these neighborhood children whose parents were sympathetic to the school's and community's goals were more successful than were children whose parents were out of touch.

Society at the beginning of the 21st century is different from that of several decades earlier. It is harder to establish common objectives where social institutions can work effectively together. Families have new worries and heavier burdens, and children have fewer advocates. In many situations, schools have assumed more of the educative, counseling, and social oversight for children (Good & Early, 2000; Kearney, 1999), but from many accounts, it is apparent that schools cannot effectively do the job alone (Meier, 2002a; Partnership for Family Involvement in Education [PFIE], 1999b). The most disturbing fact in the United States is that our society seems to annually write off as dispensable a large fraction of its youth, condemning them to lives of dysfunction and nonproductiveness (Kotlowitz, 1998; Osofsky, 1998).

Some accounts show that different outlooks have appeared in our nation's communities in recent years. A significant number of professionals and laypersons speak convincingly that education is much more than school buildings, books, and daily schedules. We find a growing recognition that lifestyle diversity and multiculturalism are here to stay and that it makes sense for all residents to pull together in making communities more liveable and schools more productive (Goodlad, 2002; PFIE, 1999b).

Amid the high hopes and vision for redoing the educational landscape, practical considerations sober us; we know that change comes slowly. Some workers in the helping professions will have to settle for small victories. But small steps can be beneficial; they represent building blocks. For example, getting cooperation and involving parents and community associations in building playground equipment for a North Carolina school helped hundreds of citizens in that community become familiar with and interested in school functions. Getting local businesses involved in science and math projects for third graders in a rural Michigan town pulled education very close to the lives of many citizens. Small steps do provide a base.

In this chapter, we detail five particular program models that have shown success in improving schools and children's education through family, school, and community collaborations. We examine the components that led to the success of these models and remark on some of the changes made as a result of implementing them on a larger scale. But first, we discuss some basic principles and distinctive features that one sees with collaborative efforts.

LEVELS OF INVOLVEMENT IN COLLABORATIONS

Good collaborative efforts mean that individuals in any group must recognize different levels or a hierarchy of involvement (Epstein, Sanders, Simon, Salinas, Jansorn, & Van Voorhis, 2002; Rubin 2002). Some individuals will participate at a **minimum level**, others at an **associative level**, and still others at a **decision-making** level. Though educators are in the best position for encouraging and establishing partnerships, some parents and community members will also assume stronger leadership roles in a collaborative effort.

Understanding Involvement

Laypeople interpret parental and community involvement in school affairs in different ways. Some citizens are proactive and feel naturally connected to their schools. A larger group views teachers as having total control of children's education and either do not seek involvement or feel shut out of the process. This latter group tends to view schools from afar, but its members are often critical when their children don't progress well. This view, of course, contributes very little of substance and generates even more isolation. All educators and community workers have a duty to work on attracting this part of the constituency and seeking more participation.

So, how much involvement is productive? Different programs will call for differing amounts of involvement by parents and community members, and generally, participatory intensity varies with level. The key to successful collaboration is for almost all community citizens to be involved at one level or another, with a few individuals contributing at all levels.

Minimum Level. School personnel reach out to parents and community members in various ways, seeking support for school programs. This has been the case for several generations. For example, children have homework that teachers request parents to supervise. The homework might involve finding information about different community businesses. Teach-

ers expect that parents and other community members will respond to these requests and help with the projects.

The community at large is normally invited to school-sponsored events for which teachers often seek assistance. For example, parents and community members help make costumes for school plays or props for exhibits. Schools have various fund-raising events, such as bake sales and fairs. Again, school personnel seek cooperation from parents and others to attend, contribute items to, and help with the events. Calls go out for such items as egg cartons, juice cans, and carpet samples to use in school projects.

The preceding are all examples of minimal involvement, and most readers will recognize and recall similar events from their own childhood. Such minimal involvement is commonplace; it serves a definite purpose; and it is a good foundation from which to start working for more complete participation.

Associative Level. Some parents and schools seek more than minimal participation. Many teachers request parents and community members to become classroom volunteers on a regular basis. Volunteers assist teachers in various ways—from copying materials to reading with children and assisting them in activities. Still others become room mothers (or fathers), organizing other community members, helping to supervise children on school trips, or making calls to solicit classroom support. Some volunteers become involved in enrichment programs where they offer their special expertise with children in a classroom. Another example is the advocacy work of parents of children with disabilities. These parents frequently become knowledgeable about their child's special needs and also about school processes, so they can go on to become local leaders and advocates for teachers working with children with disabilities.

At the associative level, community members also participate in local organizations that support schools. Parent–Teacher Association (PTA) chapters have traditionally supported schools as parents and teachers cooperated in school improvement ventures. At times, PTAs center on fund-raising events; at other times, they may become a political force in the community to improve conditions for children.

Children benefit from involvement of adults at the associative level; due to their school experience and intensified role, school expectations are much clearer to these parents, and all communication is facilitated. Stronger ties mean stronger programs, and divisiveness is far less likely when schools and communities enjoy this level of interaction. At any point in time, fewer parents will be involved at the associative level than at the minimal level. Comer (1980) noted that if 5% to 10% of parents become actively involved at this associative level, that number makes up an adequate group as long as it represents a cross-section of the community.

Decision-Making Level. The third level of parent and community involvement in schools is the decision-making level. At this level, individual parents, businesspersons, professionals, and community leaders participate actively in decision making for the education of children.

Parent participation produces little controversy at the minimum and associative levels of involvement. Teachers and school administrators are still in charge of all educational decision making, and parents and community members assist and support the decisions. However, when parents and others become involved in decision making, friction can emerge (Rubin, 2002). Controversy that paralyzes is, of course, not in the best interests of children. Therefore, successful collaboration of parents, teachers, administrators, and community members at this level requires mutual respect and a new definition of shared responsibility and accountability (Bloom, 1992; Comer, Ben-Avie, Haynes, & Joyner, 1999). Acting at this level requires hard work.

Parents at the decision-making level move beyond being committed advocates for their children into sharing responsibility for providing quality (school) education for their own and other children. They serve on curriculum committees, identifying goals and objectives and deciding how to achieve them. At this level, parents are expected to serve on committees that hire school staff. They also might assist in forming advocacy groups to secure necessary local, state, or federal funding. Again the parents of children with special needs, are often able to take leadership roles due to prior experience working with school personnel, in making decisions for appropriate placement of their children, and in development of their children's individualized education programs (IEPs).

Usually, parent and community involvement at this level requires only a small percentage of parents, but these representatives must represent the different constituencies within the community. Such involvement dictates changes within the school hierarchy, and such changes can be detrimental unless teachers, administrators, parents, and community members work carefully and with genuine mutual respect to bring gradual change (Comer, Haynes, & Joyner, 1996). Figure 12–1 illustrates the collaborative relations of each level of involvement.

Thus, having community adults functioning at the decision-making level marks a true collaborative venture—and that is the goal. To get there, let's follow the ideas in the following section and then look at some examplar programs in the United States today.

Figure 12–1   Three levels of involvement

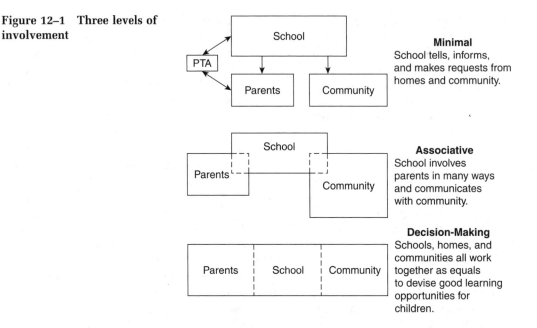

Minimal
School tells, informs, and makes requests from homes and community.

Associative
School involves parents in many ways and communicates with community.

Decision-Making
Schools, homes, and communities all work together as equals to devise good learning opportunities for children.

COMPONENTS OF SUCCESSFUL CHANGE

Research shows that children improve academically when schools work for better school and community involvement (Epstein, 1999; U.S. Department of Education, 1994). Because of this finding, and because of extensive federal interest in partnerships, a number of school districts are now caught up in the rhetoric of "collaboration." Some have taken serious steps to establish links with social service agencies, arranging for more parental involvement, providing integrated services for their total school plan, and becoming full-service schools. Others have struggled and had little success beyond goal statements and committee assignments (Epstein, 2001; O'Neil, 1997).

As more businesses and community agencies become involved with schools, there always exists a danger that leaders in these agencies start to usurp the rights and responsibilities that classroom teachers owe to their students. In any collaboration, parents and

teachers must assume the ethical responsibility for ensuring that everyone involved understands children's developmental levels and vulnerability. Most school personnel want parents and community members to share in the responsibility of educating children, and they seek outside support for resolving nonacademic problems. In academic matters, however, educators are more hesitant to involve parents and community members. Nonetheless, successful partnerships mean shared responsibilities, and successful schools mean that parents, school personnel, and community groups share responsibilities for educational decision making.

Successful programs have different strategies for achieving collaboration, but all have certain elements in common, which Gardner (1993) called "the hooks and glue of joint ventures" (p. 15). All good programs have a planning process, an implementation process, and an accountability process (Carter, 1993). Equally important is that in each process, all involved pay constant attention to establishing good communication and nurturing trust plus

Collaboration requires a community-wide team

developing familiarity and understanding (Epstein, 2001; Smrekar, 1993).

Planning

Collaboration requires a communitywide team. Members of social agencies, businesses, and government agencies, plus teachers, administrators, and parents, come together, and all make a commitment to work for the benefit of the community's children. The community team needs a strong leader, and all participants must be willing to work out differences when necessary. Key people in the community are crucial for the project. Trust and respect for other viewpoints are even more vital.

During planning, the team determines the needs of children in the community, develops goals, and designs procedures for accomplishing these goals. The team identifies children's particular needs within the various commu-

nity contexts, then assesses the community to identify resources to meet these needs. Communication, collaboration, and cooperation among the various team members mean that all agencies will surrender some autonomy in seeking solutions, but in so doing, all recognize their mutual benefits.

Implementation

As the collaboration team develops procedures for implementing strategies, members ascertain which agencies can provide personnel and financial resources. Implementation is guaranteed greater success when a team provides orienting and training sessions, ensuring that parents, teachers, and community people have collaborative skills.

A major step in beginning collaboration is providing workshops that reduce the social distance among participants and that also improve relationships among parents, community workers, school staff, and students. Another involves understanding the interests and expertise of teachers, parents, and other volunteers so that all can contribute their best. All contributions must be respected, and ideally, all gain an understanding of how their service contributes to the goals and objectives.

After the team sets the priorities for the community's needs, it begins to plan and collaborate on such activities as providing families with needed services, improving school and home discipline, adapting curriculum to particular community needs, establishing appropriate social activities, and developing program evaluation strategies.

Assessment

People working with collaborative programs must have ways to determine how well their goals are being met. Most projects will review students' classroom work, and many programs develop questionnaires to get feedback from the community about the success of their activities. Data are collected and interpreted regularly, and then strategies are altered or continued accordingly. Parents, school staff, and community members are kept informed about progress and the changes being made to improve conditions. Project members normally summarize progress once a year for the community at large.

Communication

The success of all collaborative programs depends on good communication and careful monitoring of activities. Parents must feel welcome to visit schools and to participate, and teachers must feel they are able to visit homes as needs arise. Community persons must also be part of the communication loop. All must feel welcome in schools and free to offer suggestions.

Many avenues provide parents and community members with information about school activities and what is happening with the collaboration. Routine notices, telephone messages, personal notes, newsletters, articles in local papers, a Web site, and the direct approach, which volunteers employ in contacting hard-to-reach parents, are all used. Parents are encouraged to write notes, use e-mail, or call teachers when concerns arise and are encouraged to express appreciation.

Features of Successful Collaboration

New partnerships are rapidly emerging across the United States, and though the stimulus varies, projects often start in response to educational problems at the local and state levels. Irrespective of the motivation, we find that collaborative efforts do result in greater opportunities for students when the "whole child, whole community" concept is adopted (Davies, 1993). Each successful partnership will be unique, but all seem to include the following features (Comer et al., 1996; Rubin, 2002):

- Programs integrate educational and social services for all children, but especially for needy families.
- Parents, school personnel, and community members are empowered to make decisions about, plan for, and implement changes for their community's children.
- School bureaucracy is reduced, and involvement of community and home in school management increases.
- Schools become family centers to promote better interactions among teachers, parents, and community members.
- Programs include strong volunteer programs, with parents, grandparents, and community members contributing expertise to support children's learning and to assist in school operations.
- Community and home are viewed as important children's learning environments and are integrated into school learning.

- University programs provide training for the establishment of successful partnerships.
- Faculty and staff have time for training and develop skills needed to build and maintain relationships of trust and respect with children and families.
- Researchers, teachers, and parents work together in assessing the successes of school programs.

PROGRAM MODELS

In this section, we examine the characteristics that five program models exhibit. Though changes have been made in each, the basic underlying concepts tend to remain. As you read about and compare these models, you should get a feeling for how the process unfolds.

Head Start

Head Start is one of the best-known educational programs in the United States and enrolls approximately 1 million 4- and 5-year-olds each year. Though it precedes our current focus on family, school, and community collaborations by many years, it fits all the "conditions" of a true partnership.

When Project Head Start was conceived in 1965, authorities acknowledged that children were not only family members but also community members. Thus, if Head Start was to succeed in changing the lives of children, parental involvement and community commitment to the program's goals were paramount. Through this involvement and commitment, Head Start began to provide, in holistic rather than fragmented ways, comprehensive services in health, nutrition, and economic counseling for individuals, as well as school readiness for children and their families. Today, Project Head Start is referred to as an integrated service program for low-income families. A caseworker is assigned each child, and that person

monitors the health, education, and social services provided for the child and his or her family (Hurd, Lerner, & Barton, 1999).

Purpose. The purpose for involving communities in Head Start was to make the community aware of the importance of providing adequate health, educational, and nutritional services for children's development. If skills developed in the Head Start programs were to be sustained, parents and community had to reinforce the learning. Parent involvement reached even further, since the programs created avenues for parents to gain skills themselves for participating in different social contexts and thereby gain greater confidence and sense of self-esteem.

Types of Parental Involvement. Parents assist in a variety of ways at Head Start centers or in classrooms. The Head Start Manual of Policies and Instruction, still in force today, outlines the types of parental involvement available.

Parents as Partners. Parents are partners with professionals in the decision-making process, and we find two levels open to parents of Head Start children. At the informal level, parents work with center staff in determining program content and how their children will participate. At a more formal level, parents serve on a parent policy committee or council. Fifty percent of council membership must be parents of Head Start children and be elected by other parents. Council parents are involved in program improvements, parent activities, recruiting volunteers, and planning and developing a budget for the parent activity fund. They are also involved in decisions about program goals, criteria for the selection of children, hiring of Head Start staff, and major changes in budget and work programs.

Parents as Observers. Parents participate in Head Start classrooms as visitors, volunteers, and paid aides to see different ways of working with their children. They gain a better understanding of what their children are learning and what they can do to assist them at home. Children seeing their parents in the classroom know that their parents are interested in their learning and witness the cooperation and support between parents and teachers. When parents become more involved as volunteers or as paid aides, they gain skills and confidence, which in turn help them qualify for employment elsewhere.

Parents as Learners.   Head Start parents become involved in their own learning by planning and identifying opportunities that correspond to their own interests and aspirations. Workshops and other learning experiences for a center are often requested and designed by parents, who in this fashion increase their own education. Career ladders have been developed where parents are able to progress through workshops to obtain their general equivalency diploma (GED). Some parents in Head Start programs have continued their education at technical schools and colleges, increasing their opportunities for employment.

Supporting Children's Learning.   Parents work at home with their children to support and reinforce children's Head Start experiences. Center personnel create and distribute ideas and suggestions for home activities and often visit homes to observe and suggest ways family members can support children's education. As parents become aware of their impact on children's learning, they become confident about helping their children grow and develop (Greenberg, 1990; Head Start Bureau, 1980).

Research.   Since Project Head Start's inception, the effects of early intervention on children's development have been a subject of much research and public concern. Initial research by Westinghouse Learning Corporation—Ohio University (1969) indicated cognitive gains for Head Start children after the first year, but by the third year, these gains had nearly disappeared.

The study had many critics who pointed to several limitations of the study, including viewing all Head Start programs as if they were of equal quality, examining only one aspect of potential benefits, not recognizing the importance of medical and nutritional benefits, and ignoring the questionable validity of some evaluation instruments (Evans, 1975). The study did alert the public that a basic assumption of the War on Poverty was unrealistic: A single summer or 1-year program could not produce rapid academic results for economically disadvantaged children. This led to some federally supported outgrowths of Head Start, for example, Even Start and Follow Through plus some private foundation programs.

Long-term studies of the initial Head Start programs (Schweinhart & Weikart, 1997), reveal that the programs have been both cost-effective and beneficial to society. Both the Consortium for Longitudinal Studies and the Perry School Project indicated that children of poverty had profited from Head Start experiences. Though initial achievement gains tended to disappear and Head Start children never "caught up" cognitively with their middle-class peers: By high school, these children demonstrated significant differences from those disadvantaged children who had not attended Head Start. Head Start children did better in school, repeated fewer grades, had fewer emotional problems, and were less often placed in remedial classes. As adults, they were less likely to end up in jail, more likely to attend college, more active volunteers in their communities, and more likely to marry than their peers who had not attended Head Start (Schweinhart & Weikart, 1997).

Studies also revealed that Head Start children's social development improved to equal their middle-class peers. Children became more task oriented, sustained attention to task longer, and developed curiosity about learning. Children with disabilities appeared to benefit the most after involvement in Head Start programs. Collins's (1984) synthesis of over 1,500 Head Start studies confirmed the positive impacts on children's cognitive, social, and health development, as well as improvements in parenting.

Many Head Start programs successfully coordinated health and social services for children, and a large percentage of participants thus maintained their immunizations as well as medical and dental exam schedules. As a result of this medical attention and the sound nutritional school programs, Head Start participants are found healthier today than other disadvantaged children. This feature has been emulated by other programs as they attempt to include medical and social services within the school program.

As noted, parental involvement is a requirement of Head Start programs and was really the first large-scale involvement of parents in children's formal education. Parents have served as policy makers, teachers, aides, and volunteers, and two of every three students in Head Start have parents involved in one of

these capacities. An additional payoff exists for that connection: Studies indicate that children of involved Head Start parents had higher academic achievement, were more likely to graduate from high school or college, and were more apt to have full-time employment.

Communities that established and maintained Head Start programs have benefited as well. A number of poor and minority parents in these communities have moved into the workforce, and area public schools have changed programs because of the models that Head Start provided. Advantages include providing strategies for parental participation, implementing developmentally appropriate curricula, mainstreaming children with special needs, modifying health services, and implementing practices accommodating the needs of poor children and minorities.

Certainly, Head Start has not succeeded in fulfilling the dream of diminishing poverty in

Parents of Head Start children serve on a parent policy committee

Figure 12–2   Relationship of federally funded compensatory programs to the typical elementary school. (Ages may vary at each level.)

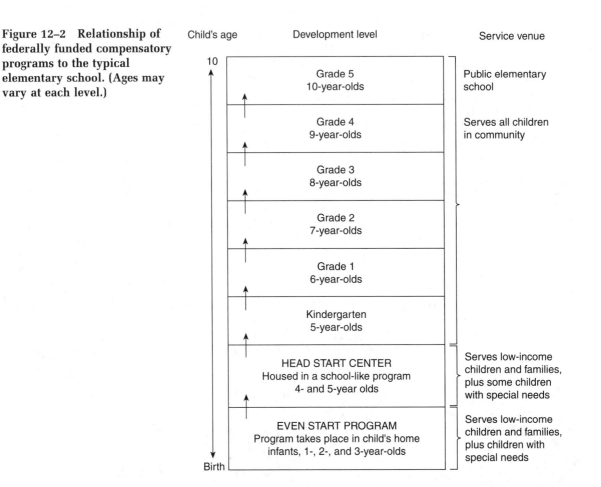

Child's age   Development level   Service venue

10

Grade 5
10-year-olds

Public elementary
school

Grade 4
9-year-olds

Serves all children
in community

Grade 3
8-year-olds

Grade 2
7-year-olds

Grade 1
6-year-olds

Kindergarten
5-year-olds

HEAD START CENTER
Housed in a school-like program
4- and 5-year olds

Serves low-income
children and families,
plus some children
with special needs

EVEN START PROGRAM
Program takes place in child's home
infants, 1-, 2-, and 3-year-olds

Serves low-income
children and families,
plus children with
special needs

Birth

the United States or in eliminating all learning gaps, but its impact has been positive, and its benefits for helping poor and minority families become partners in their children's education outweigh the costs. More recent collaborative efforts have profited from the procedures and experiences of this model program.

Outgrowths of Head Start. Head Start results showed that poor children from birth to age 4 needed help, too, if they were to overcome the debilitating effects of poverty. This notion led to ideas for developing home-based programs in the late 1960s and 1970s that would serve as precursors of Head Start. Figure 12–2 presents the relationship of the

federally funded programs to the typical elementary school programs. One of the important continuing programs is Even Start.

Even Start. Many communities adapted one or another of the pre–Head Start model programs developed by Gordon, Weikart, and others in the late 1960s and 1970s. These continue on a modest level up to the present, and they provided the background and base for the federally funded Even Start, begun in the late 1980s. Success in all of these is dependent on the quality of the program.

Even Start and other home-based programs use the home as a beginning point in children's education. The concept recognizes that parents are children's first teachers and that it is important to help parents to become more effective teachers. The emphasis since the early 1990s for many home-based programs has been family literacy. In the late 1980s, Even Start, a family literacy program, was initiated under Title I, Part B, of the Elementary and Secondary School Act. The funding for this program, administered through the states, was to provide all-encompassing support to enlist parents as full partners in their children's education with the hope that they could then help their children reach their full potential as learners (Even Start, 1999). The parent educator, with help from local Head Start teachers, works directly with parents in the home. This person, a sort of educational social worker, plans activities to be carried out in the home.

Gordon's Program. In Gordon's (1969) original model, the parent educator, a person from the community served, was the key component of home visiting. These parent educators spent half of their time in homes demonstrating prepared lessons and the other half in classrooms working with teachers and children. In homes, they engaged parents in role-playing lesson activities as well as in discussions of the intent and purpose of the teaching. In the classroom, they became better acquainted with the children and learned techniques for the school curriculum.

Today, programs of this type are often referred to as family literacy programs, and directors continue to seek involvement with other agencies serving these children: professional social workers, early childhood specialists, psychologists, and nurses. Ideally, some team members have specialized training in the development of infants and toddlers and in the specific needs of parents with very young children. Many programs are adapted from these early models, but currently, educators focus more on collaboration as they seek to build on skills parents already possess. Programs

differ, but for many, the home curriculum emphasizes the role of play in children's development, the importance of reading to young children from infancy, and the value of quality interaction between parent and child. Nutritional, health, and safety information continues to be a feature of most programs (An Ounce of Prevention Fund, 1994).

Research on Even Start programs, often encouraging on a single program basis, is also difficult to assess because of variations in programs and the difficulty in maintaining consistency for participation. Still, we have some very encouraging results. When participation is high and there is intensity of services, children gain significantly in tests of school readiness and language development (Tao, Khan, Gamse, St. Pierre, & Tarr, 1996).

Comer's School Development Program

In 1968, James Comer and his colleagues at the Yale Child Study Center began the School Development Program, a collaboration with two New Haven elementary schools to increase parental involvement in children's education. Both schools were located in low-income areas, all children were African American, and parent participation in school activities was very low. When examining parent interest and involvement, the team discovered three levels or patterns that revealed home–school connections:

1. Most parents expressed interest in the activities their children participated in at school.

2. Some parents were also interested in volunteering for particular activities in the school.

3. A few parents were interested in curriculum and how teachers instructed their children. (Comer & Haynes, 1991).

With this knowledge, Comer and his team began a series of experiments and adjustments that used parents' interests to bring about collaboration. Now, over two decades after the conclusion of the project, the experiment has become a highly touted model for involving parents.

Major Goals. The initial School Development Program evolved over a 5-year period, and participants gradually adjusted the structure as programs evolved and needs changed. A steering committee, formed of administrators, teachers, parents, aides, professional and nonprofessional support staff, and the Yale Child Center mental health team, established the following major goals for the project (Comer, 1980):

- Modify the social and psychological climate of the school to facilitate greater student learning.
- Improve students' basic skills.
- Raise students' motivation for learning and their academic and occupational aspiration level.
- Create a sense of shared responsibility and decision making among parents and staff.
- Connect child development and clinical services to the educational program of the schools.

Structure of the Program. The program consisted of three teams: the school planning and management team (SPMT); (originally called the steering committee), a Yale Child Study Center mental health team, and the pupil personnel team, plus four major features: a parent program, a focus program, workshops, and an extended-day program.

School Planning and Management Team. This committee, composed of **stakeholders** in the school, developed and implemented academic and social programs, designed staff development, evaluated the program, and made necessary adjustments. After various experiments,

three important guidelines evolved for the SPMT: (1) solving problems with a no-fault approach, (2) using principles of child development for decision making, and (3) ensuring that collaborative management did not paralyze the school principal (Comer & Haynes, 1991).

Mental Health Team. The mental health team consisted of a child psychiatrist, two social workers, an educator with early childhood education training, an educator involved in teacher training, and a psychologist–program evaluator. Its main purpose was to assist school staff in understanding and applying principles of social and behavioral science to school problems and opportunities. The mental health team at first helped parents and school staff develop skills of cooperation and assisted teachers in managing behavior problems and in changing or creating school rules. After behavior problems decreased at the school, the team began to help with curriculum planning and facilitating communication between school personnel and families, between teachers and students, and among teachers, administrators, and nonprofessional staff.

Pupil Personnel Team. A pupil personnel team initially cooperated with the principal, community social service personnel, and special teachers by giving services directly to students who needed such support. As conditions in the school changed and behavioral problems lessened, this service then became more educational in nature and less behavioral.

Parent Program. A parent program started, with a small group of parents receiving a stipend for assisting teachers. This core group formed the nucleus of the parent group and served on governance bodies and subcommittees that helped plan social and educational programs. Their function was to "bring attitudes, values, ways, and needs of the community to these committees and activities" (Comer, 1980, p. 65). As the program changed to meet school and community needs, the parent program evolved to include parent involvement at three different levels.

At the first level, five or six parents were elected to serve on the school planning and management team, where decisions about programs and operations were made. These parents enlisted other community residents for other levels of participation and helped overcome the barriers inhibiting hard-to-reach parents. They also brought a community perspective to the planning process by assisting teachers in planning culturally appropriate programs.

At the second level, parents were involved in helping in classrooms or in sponsoring and supporting school programs. The strength of this involvement was that parents and teachers worked together to motivate students to achieve academically and socially.

At the modest third level, parents became involved in activities in which their children were engaged. They attended student performances and other teacher–parent activities, where "good news" was shared, and generally supported the program from a distance.

Focus Program. At the start of the project, a focus program was established to help children one or more years behind in reading and math skills. Three times a week, these children were taught in small groups to supplement classroom teaching of reading and mathematics. The focus groups changed as children's learning needs were identified.

Workshops. At the beginning, 2-week summer workshops allowed parents and teachers to get to know each other and share their perspective on the academic and social experiences they felt children needed. Workshops became ongoing and were offered when teachers or parents indicated a need.

Extended-Day Programs. Initially, teachers were required but were paid to attend after-school programs. This program included workshops for teachers to learn more about

child development and behavior, teaching and curriculum development, and the use of arts in promoting academic skills. In addition, teachers developed skills in meeting with parents and planning parent participation projects.

Social Skills Curriculum. In establishing community involvement, Comer's team found that many distinctions between low-income and middle-income children involved differences in social skills that middle-income children acquired in their homes. As a result, the team devised a social skills curriculum for inner-city children consisting of four units: politics and government, business and economics, health and nutrition, and spiritual and leisure time. Field trips, visits by community members, and lots of hands-on activities enabled low-income children to enhance their interpersonal skills, writing skills, and interactive skills with adults. A banking unit provided experiences in receiving a "bank check" for work done and then spending the check or learning to save it for a specific purpose. A gospel choir helped students learn group responsibility on how to plan, organize, and select programs, as well as learn rehearsal procedures and performance demeanor. In the government unit, students learned to write and give speeches, and then hold a miniconvention and election.

School Development Program. Many aspects of the original implementation serve as guidance for schools associated with Comer's School Development Program. Figure 12–3 illustrates the current "Comer process." To implement a model that offers respect to all and sustains learning, Comer et al. (1996) maintained that there are three guiding principles, three teams, and three operations:

- Three principles—consensus (planning requires that all parties come to agreement on the plans), collaboration (all work in tandem with each other), and no-fault (no one party

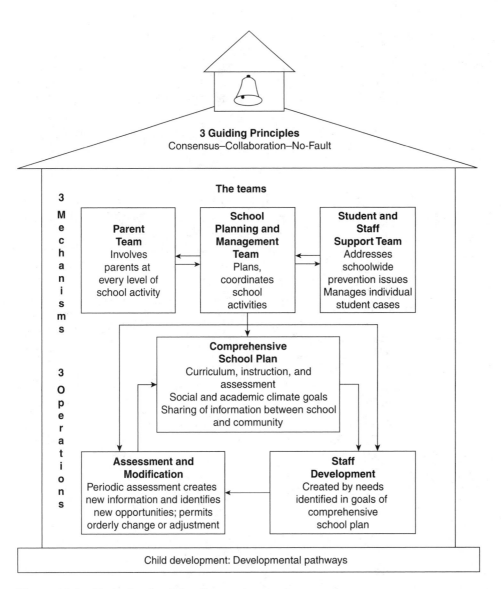

Figure 12–3   Comer's school development program
Source: From *Rallying the Whole Village: The Comer Process for Reforming Education* (p. 10),
J. P. Comer et al. (Eds.), 1996. New York: Teacher's College Press. Reprinted with permission.

is at fault for any lack of success, but all
share in the responsibility to improve).

• Three teams—the school planning and management team, which plans and coordinates
all school activities; the student and staff
support team (SSST), which addresses stu-

dent and staff problems and manages individual situations; and the parent team (PT),
which involves parents at all levels.

• Three operations—comprehensive school
plan, developed to meet academic and social
goals; assessment and modification, for

Comer's program emphasizes how field trips whether to a hardware store or a bank enhance interpersonal skills, computing skills, and interactive skills

periodic assessments and provision for change when necessary; and staff development, as needed to achieve goals.

Comer, Haynes, and Joyner (1996) believed that this model permits communities to transform and change their programs by involving school personnel and families in a participatory approach. To sustain change, they emphasized that all adults must feel respected and all children must feel valued and be motivated to learn and achieve.

Research on Comer's Model.   After 5 years of working through problems and modifying procedures, rules, teaching strategies, and programs, the School Development Program showed remarkable success. The two participating schools progressed from having the worst attendance records in New Haven to having the best. Overall academic achievement went from third from the bottom to

among the top schools in the city. Behavior problems were greatly reduced, and parent–teacher misunderstandings lessened as parental participation in school activities increased. The consensus is that home, school, and community links growing from the School Development Program in New Haven have provided essential ingredients for children's healthy development (Comer & Haynes, 1991).

Outgrowths of the Model.   The Comer model has been replicated in over 650 schools across the nation. In Washington, D.C., several neighborhoods have successfully changed their schools from places where violence, drugs, and crime were paramount to schools with "high expectations and where everyone working together . . . has become an attitude, a way of learning and an education for life" (Ramirez-Smith, 1995, p. 19). Further success of the Comer process is explicated in the publication by Comer, Ben-Avie, Haynes, and

Joyner (1999), in which readers find firsthand accounts of communities working through the model. Comer's 1996 book, *Rallying the Whole Village,* is the publication that best describes the Comer process.

Reggio Emilia

The Reggio Emilia program was developed in northern Italy by a group of parents soon after World War II. The first school, in Villa Celia, was built with revenues from sales of abandoned vehicles and scrap materials in the war-torn countryside. It was built and staffed by parents and community members deeply steeped in their Italian heritage, who held to a profound belief and respect for children's natural learning. Under the leadership of Loris Malaguzzi and the community's strong commitment to be decision makers for their children's education, Reggio Emilia was born.

The curriculum in these municipal prepri-mary schools has evolved as teachers, children, and parents worked together, learned about each other, and valued each others' ways of processing information. The Reggio Emilia philosophical and educational precepts have also matured over the years, though never straying from the basic premises: Children are active participants in their own learning, and schooling should reflect community values, beliefs, and a wealth of materials (Edwards, Gandini & Forman, 1998). In the past decade, American educators have attempted to emulate the practices of the Reggio Emilia approach, as it epitomizes a significant success for parent–school–community collaborations.

Goals. The purpose of Reggio Emilia is to develop a school where children are at the center of the curriculum, where they develop a sense of belonging by participating in the school community. Leaders find that children's self-concepts are strengthened over their 3 years of belonging to the same group of

children and adults (Gandini, 1993). From the beginning, the founders recognized that parents, teachers, and community members were partners in planning and executing any curriculum, and they felt that a curriculum should be reflective of the community's values and distinct qualities, including all of nature. Young children in Reggio programs are viewed as informants to adults regarding their current interests, unique learning styles, and prior knowledge. Therefore, the children are active participants and decision makers in what, when, and how to study.

Philosophical Perspective. One basic principle of Reggio Emilia is that a program for children must be dynamic, vibrant, and evolving (Gandini, 1997). As new theories of children's development emerge, new political orders occur, and new social events unfold, the directors expect that the program's philosophical and psychological underpinnings will change and programs will reflect these changes. New (1998) pointed out that fidelity to a single theory is unnecessary in Reggio Emilia, and that as theory informs practice, so practice and documentation of children's learning informs theory.

The ever evolving philosophical views found in Reggio schools have reflected for some time the perspectives of Dewey, Piaget, Vygotsky, and other developmentalists. In recent years, New (2003) found substantial incorporation of Comer's partnership ideas and Gardner's views on multiple intelligences. Quite logically, decision makers in these schools also subscribe to Bronfenbrenner's social–cultural perspective. The expectation is that teachers, children, and other adults learn from each other and are both facilitators and constructors of new knowledge.

Programs. We do not find a set of procedures in Reggio schools, as we can in Montessori or Waldorf schools, because situation and context is considered first. We do find, however, common practices and modes that help describe the everyday school endeavors.

Organization.   A beginning objective for a Reggio school is to provide an amicable environment for children, families, and teachers. The classrooms are organized so that projects or themes are pursued according to children's and adults' interests. When people make arrangements, they need to consider that collaborative problem solving among children and children with adults is important. Spaces for individual study, as well as small group and total group activities, are provided. Teachers and other adults are considered guides for children in exploring and investigating. To abet this, the Reggio schools have areas, called ateliers, for storage, displays, and reflective study.

Children demonstrate their growth through many different "languages," or modes of communication: words, movement, artistic expression, play, music, and the like. Analysis of these communication activities by adults is the documentation of what is being learned (Gandini, 1997). Since learning is viewed as spiral, rather than linear, children continually examine their own development through this documentation. They observe what they have accomplished, consider what else they might learn, and then reconsider their objectives (Gandini, 1997). Space for displays, documentation of children's individual and communal projects, and analyses are accommodated in the ateliers.

Scheduling.   Since the notion of Reggio is that children learn by continual active involvement in their environment and by doing

In the Reggio Emilia philosophy, children review their projects, determine what they have learned and decide what their next step should be

projects, the daily routine is related more to scheduling the staff time rather than children's. Teachers spend most of their 36 hours per week with children in observing their activities, talking with them about what they are doing, and planning for children's additional study. Each week, staff spend 4½ hrs in meetings, planning, and in-service training, plus 1½ hours in documenting and analyzing children's work. They keep records (*diarios*) of the children's work, communications, and their own analyses for parental and administrator preview (Giovanni, 2001).

Implementation Is Evolving. Society has changed since 1945, and the notion of schooling and who is responsible for schools has also changed in Italy. For example, in the 1960s, national and regional policies dictated guidelines and new goals for all Italy. However, Reggio Emilia programs maintained their credibility by insisting on local decision making—a process approach by all participants would have a say in what was to be studied. Learning, they maintain, is not dictated from "above," but "negotiated" with those who will benefit. Content and sequence in any project is determined by the particular group, and it takes responsibility for maintaining connections among all the parties (Terzi & Cantarelli, 2001). This is similar to many **charter school** programs in the United States today.

Developing the various programs that exist today has a long historical story. Back in 1945, the group formed to "invent" a school free from government control but instead run by school personnel, parents, and other community members. Their goal was to defend the rights of children. Validation for the evolution and process culminated in the 1970s, as national laws in Italy were passed to formalize community-based management for schools similar to that advocated at Reggio Emilia. At present, the national government provides public funding, regional government is re-sponsible for overall planning for the region, and the municipal authorities oversee the community-based boards (Spaggiari, 1998).

Parents and community members are also a very important part of the network. They serve on the community advisory councils, attend various school meetings for planning, and work in classrooms on specific tasks and projects. Teachers do not assign tasks to these other adults, but since they are part of the planning, they become part of the execution (Gandini, 1997). In a dinosaur project, for example, a parent typed up the conversations of children discussing and arguing about what they knew. Later, when the children seemed to lose interest, the parent was part of the discussion on whether the project should be dropped. The parent helped in reviewing children's discussions and found areas that everyone was excited about. So, the group decided to go on with the project, but because of new interests, it decided on a different direction (Rankin, 1998).

The network of educational services has evolved over the years (see Figure 12–4). The line of authority proceeds upward, from the Community Advisory Council (parents, all school staff, and townspeople) planning, making decisions, and supporting the educational process. Every 2 years the community elects representatives to the Municipal Advisory Council Board. With members experienced in communicating and planning, this board forms strong subcommittees, each with specific objectives that take on different concerns related to children. Because of such involvement, families have learned that fully educating a child requires solidarity and support. Working in groups, compromising, and seeking solutions collectively has given parents many skills and provided psychological support. Not only do children gain from such programs, but so do the families and municipalities (Spaggiari, 1998).

Research and Evaluation. Unlike our American penchant for assessment, there has been

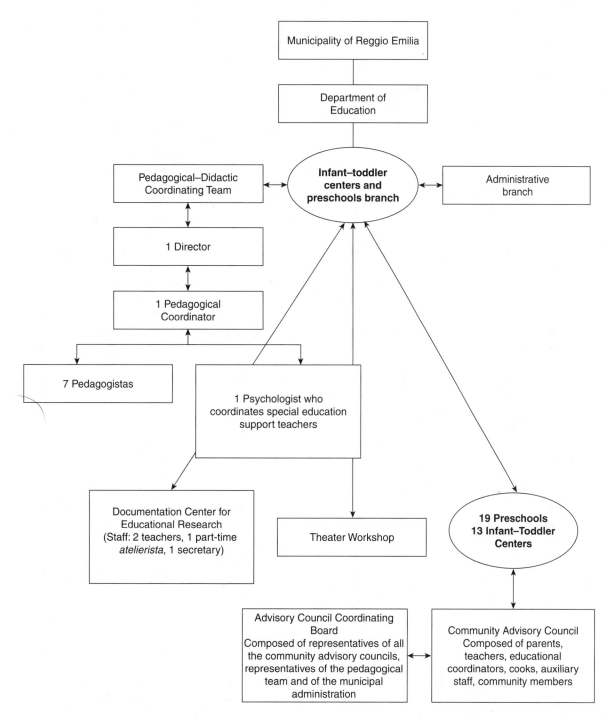

Figure 12–4 The network of educational services of the Reggio Emilia Municipal Administration
Source: From *First Steps Toward Teaching the Reggio Way.* (p. 12), J. Hendrick (Ed.), 1997. Upper Saddle River, NJ: Merrill/Prentice Hall. Reprinted by permission.

no attempt in Italy to validate by empirical research the practices of Reggio Emilia, nor has children's learning been measured by tests that compare children's learning to predetermined scales. Children's learning is viewed as spiral. Italian leaders believe that all children have unique styles of learning, and that evaluation procedures must be compatible with this type of growth. The mode of evaluation used in Reggio programs is similar to qualitative research in the United States.

The components of evaluation in Reggio schools are the same both for the children and for a program. The "researchers" are the teachers and other adults who record children's dialogues or monologues and reflect on children's other modes of expression. Children's work is collected, stored, and filed in spaces (*ateliers*) to which everyone has access.

Adults working in the school record anecdotes and reflections on children's activity in a notebook for "two voices" (the child's and the adult's). When children first enter school, they receive a personal calendar on which, in brief notations, is a record of each child's particular activities. From these materials, a diary is developed reflecting the child's development from beginning to end.

These two sets of materials form the basis of information for any qualitative research. In 1996 and again in 1998, the Spencer Foundation supported Rebecca New as principal investigator in examining the role of culture on adult beliefs and decision making regarding the quality of children's care and education in Reggio Emilia. New (2001b) found varying interpretations of high-quality early education in Italy, though there was a shared cultural view regarding the importance of social relationships and shared responsibilities. She concluded that a society that has a commitment to high standards with multiple interpretations of quality, and a sense of shared responsibility for children's well-being, does foster healthy child development, enhances

adult lives, and contributes to a vital community.

Outgrowths of Reggio Emilia. With the interest in the Reggio Emilia schools now, and with attempts for implementing such a procedure in American schools, Malaguzzi and his colleagues devised a production that demonstrates the Reggio Emilia process. The exhibit helps explain the process, but at the same time these leaders tried hard to emphasize the importance of cultural context when someone modifies and adapts a program for a different cultural context.

The exchange of ideas and the traveling Hundred Languages Exhibit by Malaguzzi has created a burgeoning interest in the **child-centered**, developmentally appropriate early childhood **programs** of Reggio Emilia. Americans, impressed and idealistic, see Reggio Emilia as an "idyllic place in which all members of society support each other and where children never throw tantrums." But to implement a Reggio Emilia program, Americans must first come to grips with significant differences in American and Italian culture. The following example will illustrate.

The writers on a recent visit to Italy with a 6-year-old granddaughter began to understand why implementing a healthy concept of home, school, and community collaboration is often difficult in America. The grandparents witnessed how mainstream Italians value children and trust the children to know what their interests and needs are. In restaurants, waiters acknowledged granddaughter Victoria's hunger and charmingly brought her a plate of spaghetti before taking adult orders.

On a shopping trip, Victoria could not find the pink purse she longed for. Finally in one shop, the shopkeeper listened to her, showed her several purses, and then gave her options for some blue purses matching her blouse. The woman engaged the adults only after Victoria, and she had found the "perfect" purse.

Daily, Victoria made drawings and sketches of places she visited, wrote in her journal, kept accounts of her purchases, planned her route each day, and noted Italian words she had learned.

Back in the United States, Victoria's rich experience was not acknowledged by her classroom teacher or the school, nor was any of the documentation reviewed. Instead, the school cited her mother for absenteeism and neglect, which could lead to a court summons. Tests and established rules were more in line with America's view of schooling. In comparison, Italian teachers use documentation like that described to demonstrate to a child, the parents, and other adults the extent of children's learning.

A number of American teachers experiment with aspects of the Reggio Emilia philosophy by using projects that are suggested by children. They then listen and document how children learn to read, write, or count, and increase language skills while learning science concepts.

The Grant Early Childhood Center in Cedar Rapids, Iowa (Edmiaston & Fitzgerald, 2000), with 350 children, is a designated site for inclusion of children with disabilities. Ten percent of the children attending the program have special needs, and the directors have combined the local and national requirements for special education with Reggio Emilia's approach of collaborative relationships. Children learn to develop a project working with a typically developing peer or a friend with disabilities who is also interested. Project groups learn how to be inclusive as they work with children with particular talents as well as children with disabilities. They build a caring and effective environment guided by all staff members in the classroom and by parents who become involved. They use a Reggio Emilia–style documentation: a process that examines student growth in a variety of ways and facilitates successful inclusion.

As American educators, charmed with the results of Reggio Emilia in Italy, attempt to incorporate the principles into their programs, many realize that before transferring the Reggio Emilia model into American education they must first examine their own societal values and their views about children (Linn, 2001). Many have hope that a **bottom-up approach** to curriculum building will convince others of the value of trusting children in their desire to learn.

National Network of Partnership Schools

Joyce Epstein, with colleagues at Johns Hopkins University, has worked for more than 20 years conducting studies and establishing programs to enhance educational opportunity for children and to demonstrate values of partnerships. In 1995, Epstein established the National Network Partnership Schools at Johns Hopkins to demonstrate the important intersections of research, policy, and practice for school improvement. To date, over 1,700 schools in 150 school districts across the United States have been involved to some degree in this network, which features partnerships.

As in other partnership models, the framework of Epstein's program is centered in the notion of the shared responsibilities of home, school, and community for children's learning and development. She referred to this as the "overlapping spheres of influence" in a student's schooling (see Figure 12–5), and she articulates this in her writings (Epstein, 2001; Epstein et al., 2002), which present the important structures and processes needed to develop effective partnership programs. We should note that Epstein places the school in the center of her paradigm and promotes the idea of school as a broker for starting and facilitating the partnership.

Epstein has a firm belief that the concept of a community school is reemerging in American society. She noted that we now find it in more

Figure 12–5 Overlapping spheres of influence of family, school, and community on children's learning

Source: From *School, Family and Community Partnerships: Your Handbook for Action* (2nd ed., p. 163) by J. L. Epstein et al., 2002. Thousand Oaks, CA: Corwin. Reprinted by permission.

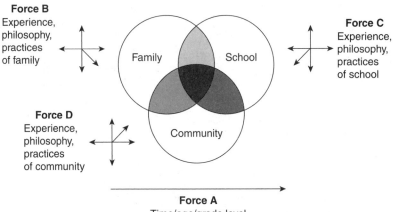

Force B
Experience, philosophy, practices of family

Force C
Experience, philosophy, practices of school

Force D
Experience, philosophy, practices of community

Force A
Time/age/grade level

schools, programs and services for student and parents, and also in before school, during school, and after the regular school-day activities everywhere. She feels confident that the education enterprise can work toward creating more "familylike" schools and more "schoollike" families when the full power of partnership is employed. A familylike school makes each child feel special and included; a schoollike family reinforces the importance of schooling and provides activities that build student skills and a feeling of success. Communities also create familylike settings, services, and events to enable families to better support their children.

Basic Assumptions and Objectives. The underpinnings and necessary ingredients, attitudes, and work ways that maximize the endeavors of National Network programs are the following:

1. "Caring for the children we share." Epstein feels that if this condition is present, then schools, parents, and communities recognize their shared interests in and their responsibilities for children.

2. Help children succeed in school and in life. She points to the "overlapping spheres of

influences" of the three social contexts as the key for harnessing their united power.

3. Students are central to a successful partnership and must be part of decision making. She shows several items and qualities that we often overlook when planning programs: The student determines learning, and we should not think of him or her as something to do things for or to; and the student interprets school activities to parents, interprets home activities to schools, and interprets the community for both teachers and parents.

4. The student is the stakeholder and has the most to gain or lose in schoolwork.

5. Effective partnerships have an accumulation of support. Whether our team is "raising a barn, playing tug of war, or building materials for learning units," the enthusiasm and commitment from the group effort is far more than what individuals can accomplish singly.

6. Healthy partnerships tolerate changes, challenges, and disagreements because there is a base of trust and respect. Basic ground rules on communication and expression will develop the base of trust required for any cooperative endeavor. This validates the reason to aim for a multiyear cycle of long-term im-

provement rather than a "fix-it" blitz of action for one year.

7. Partnerships will differ in size, particular focus, and arrangement but will have many common elements (see Figure 12–5).

8. Establishing an action team is key. All collaborations require some type of steering group if the program is to involve more than a handful of workers.

9. Collaboration focuses on curriculum areas. Participants must keep in mind that their work and energy is directed to enhanced educational opportunity. Public relations, community celebrations, and the like all have a cohesive quality but mean less if the student is not gaining in schooling.

Considerable research supports the need for these underlying qualities in programs using National Networks designs.

Guiding Principles

Framework. In the Network programs, we find six levels of involvement that have evolved. These provide a basic structure for the National Network designs, and they help educators and other leaders develop a comprehensive schedule for any particular partnership. Each level of involvement (see Figure 12–6) will have many different practices that schools can select from to help them achieve a goal they have identified. Thus, any partnership will make a commitment for the six types of involvement as a framework; then each venue will select practices that will produce results for their particular area of involvement. For example, if a partnership selects "Parenting" to focus on, they might select practices such as (a) set up parent education courses, (b) develop support groups on child rearing, or (c) develop home visiting teams to help needy families.

Challenges. In addition to refining the types of involvement and identifying the best practices to carry them out, the researchers at the National Network have encountered many challenges as the widespread partnerships have attempted to implement programs over the years. For example, in the "Volunteering"

Home visitor programs stress the importance of building on family strengths and family involvement in the neighborhood

The Keys to Successful School, Family, and Community Partnerships

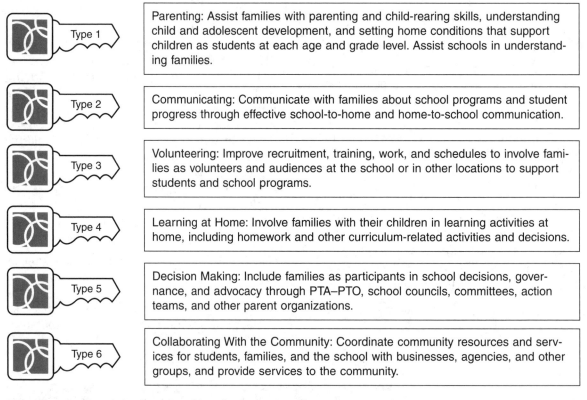

Figure 12–6   Epstein's six types of involvement
Source: From *School, Family and Community Partnerships: Your Handbook for Action* (2nd ed., p. 165),
by J. L. Epstein et al., 2002, Thousand Oaks, CA: Corwin. Reprinted by permission.

goal, challenges are often encountered in providing basic training for volunteers, or providing opportunity for all volunteers to do something, or having too many volunteers at one time. Another example is the challenges found in "Collaborating With the Community." For instance, professional turf problems frequently develop when leaders decide where to locate activities and how to staff those.

All challenges must be addressed, and in many cases a "redefinition" made for the goal or practice that seemed promising. Epstein teams have provided a listing of protocols that groups work through in settling their differences (Epstein et al., 2002).

Action Team. The most essential component of the programs will revolve around the decision-making part. For this, Epstein advised the establishment of an action team, or general steering committee to guide the partnership effort and to act as the direction-setting team. The group membership is, of course, important, and the partnership that evolves will want to follow a reasonable arrangement of delegates from the several constituencies:

1. A few teachers from different grade levels

2. A few parents

3. The school principal

4. At least one community delegate

5. A student delegate if at junior high level or above.

The job of the action team is to assess the partnership practices, arrange for the implementation of the agreed-on activities, and to improve and coordinate all practices for the types of involvement. The action team leads in these responsibilities but is assisted by other teachers, parents, students, administrators, and community members.

Organizing. In organizing a National Network design, Davies, Burch, and Palanki (1993) have found the following to be most beneficial:

- *Create an action team.* Give it responsibility for assessing practices, implementing selected activities, and coordinating types of involvement.

- *Obtain funds and support.* A modest budget is needed to support any general steering commitee.

- *Identify starting points.* Check out present strengths and needed changes. Researchers find that in most schools, some people are involved in good current practices. These people should be studied and perhaps selected for schoolwide mentoring or demonstration work.

- *Take inventory.* Find out what families we now reach and which ones are not reached. What are our expectations for families? What information do students expect the school to share with their families? How might family and community connections assist the school in helping more students achieve more success?

- *Develop plans.* Construct a 3-year outline and also a 1-year action plan. After the inventorying is done, the action team develops an outline of steps that will help the school progress to where it wants to be after several years. The 1-year action plan is the first step in that journey. This will include the specific activities that will be implemented, improved, or maintained for each type of involvement. This is shared with school personnel, the parent organization, and all teachers, parents, and students.

- *Continue planning and working.* Each year there is an annual celebration of progress so that all persons know about the work finished. Displays of accomplishments on all the types of involvement are done. Problems are discussed and ideas shared about improvements and additions needed.

Each year the team updates its 3-year outline and develops a detailed 1-year action plan to start each year. In other words, the team continues to find out how it can improve its structure and practices to increase the families as partners.

Research. Research on the success rate of programs in the National Network is ongoing. Each year an annual survey is returned to the Headquarters from the numerous schools that are participating. These are helpful in giving data about the successes, problems, and changes in the various programs. Research on individual experiments is also proceeding. These findings all result in new recommendations to practitioners who are in the Network programs.

Most of the current recommendations on levels of involvement, practices, and recommendations have come about from the 20 years of research on particular parts of the Network's activities. In addition, considerable research efforts continue at the headquarters for the Network. For instance, the TIPS program has carried out research on the efficacy of homework and developed criteria for home activities as a result of its study on family practices. Research on discipline and student behavior is another area currently investigated. (See Sheldon & Epstein, 2002, for a description of improved student behaviors in programs with family and community involvement.)

Outgrowths of the Network.   As noted previously, the National Network has expanded over the years and is now located in 20 different states. Formal links with the League of Schools Reaching Out was accomplished more than 10 years ago, and a number of partnership plans and collaborative efforts across the country have adopted parts of Epstein's recommendations for National Network programs.

Charter Schools

Featuring Charter Schools as a good model, for family–school–community cooperation is risky, because in the 13 years of their existence, the variety in these school programs has surged by leaps and bounds. We find charter schools with traditional and highly directive programs that come nowhere close to the cooperative models espoused by the writers. And there are others with a structure so relaxed that they resemble an alternative school of the 1970s. However, in the mix there are schools that truly reflect the best practices of the partnerships highlighted in this text. We discuss the features of one school to show that investigators can find a high-quality model for partnership under the charter school label. Indeed, some programs resemble the structure found in a Comer program or in one of the National Network schools.

The charter school movement began in the early 1990s, when Minnesota developed the first charter school statute. For various reasons, the movement grew rapidly, and by the end of the 20th century, 36 states had enacted legislation to permit formation of a variety of charter schools (Brouillette, 2002). In 2002 we found 2,700 charter schools in existence, serving over a half million students (Center for Education Reform, 2003). But as noted before, the reasons for establishing charter schools

falls all along the education continuum, and proponents make strange bedfellows. For example, the legislation is supported by traditionalists seeking a return to classic study, by parent's rights advocates annoyed by school bureaucracy, and by progressives seeking a **project-oriented curriculum**.

Objectives.   The basic concept of the charter school movement is to free individual public schools from large-district bureaucracy and grant them autonomy to make decisions regarding structure, personnel, curriculum, and educational emphasis while holding them accountable for academic achievement. This stems from the somewhat revolutionary idea of "decentralization," where parents, teachers, and local citizens are the decision makers, as opposed to the idea of centralization and use of "best practices" as determined at the state or district levels (Wang & Walberg, 2001).

As in many reform movements, charter schools show a wide range of philosophical orientations. They demonstrate the entire spectrum shown in Figure 2–1 in Chapter 2 of this text. One other significant objective for the charter schools in many states is to stimulate competition with nearby district schools regarding efficiencies in administration, curriculum process, and use of personnel.

Structure of Programs.   As with regulations on home schooling, laws vary from state to state on the definition of a charter school. In some, the local school authority grants the charter; in other states, it is the state education department, and a few states allow the boards of universities to grant charters (Good & Braden, 2000). But all charter schools are publicly supported institutions and must be nonsectarian, cannot violate federal and state regulations or violate students' civil rights, may not charge tuition, and in most cases are not allowed to use admissions requirements. In addition, they must conform to either a district or a state's learning outcomes and have clearly defined goals, a solid administrative structure, a comprehensive curriculum plan, and an assessment and evaluation plan. To promote accountability, most states plan not to renew the charters of those schools that fail to meet their required standards (Murphy & Shiffman, 2002). This has happened already in several states.

Charter schools vary widely in their concept of "good schooling" and in establishing partnerships with parents or the community. Some of these schools have received and maintained strong local support: others have succeeded only after long debate. Some schools are controlled by a central decision maker who works closely with parents, teachers, and strong community leaders (Brouillette, 2002). Others have a team of parents, teachers, and community leaders who are the decision makers.

One charter school in the southwest United States adheres to an academic curriculum that uses Hirsch's **cultural literacy** outline and has a principal making all decisions. Another school in that same district has a shared leadership approach, that is, instead of a designated administrator, a group of parents, teachers, and community members have formed a partnership to provide for the learning needs of the students (Raywid, 1995).

Some schools have sought charter school status when there have been clashes between a strong school leader and central administration. The Wesley School in Texas is an example. Thaddeus Lott in the 1970s and 1980s assumed leadership of the minority-heavy Wesley School when it had the worst reading scores in the state. He changed the curriculum of the school following a **DISTAR** model, training teachers in its philosophy and techniques. He also provided strong discipline and strong teacher support. Students showed great improvement in their standardized test

scores, even outscoring wealthier schools in the area. When the pendulum swung in the 1980s for a less-structured curriculum, Lott was labeled a maverick as he struggled to maintain a traditional curriculum. Because of these differences, the school and community leaders sought and were granted charter status. Wesley continued the very conservative curriculum, and students continued to succeed. As Lott and his immediate successor have moved into other positions, the question will be whether the school can survive under different leadership (Brouillette, 2002).

A similar situation occurred in California, where a principal and a team of teachers realized that their inability to improve the school was due to a domineering bureaucracy. As a team, they decided to seek charter school status. With complete freedom from the Los Angeles district, the students did indeed show some academic improvement. However, the team felt their greatest success was in having happily working students, contented and hardworking teachers, healthy parent volunteers, and parents strongly supporting the school (Manno, 2001).

These two instances support the belief that without the encumbrances of regulations, charter schools are able to work more closely with parents, respond better to children's needs, and reflect the aspirations of families served. This reform means that schools will be more accountable, have greater **autonomy**, present greater choices to families, infuse competition, and hopefully be models for innovation (Wells, 1998). Research on charter schools does show that some charter schools show promise of fulfilling some of these goals in spite of overwhelming odds. Many parents, teachers, and community persons who work in or send their children to charter schools are committed to and pleased with their schools. Students feel challenged and respected in a school community that prizes learning and innovation (Weiss, 1997).

Research.   Despite the many challenges for the charter school movement, vast differences exist regarding their effectiveness, and there is only small evidence that charter schools, especially in urban systems, produce any better academic results than the large system as a whole (Fuller, 2003). Yet other studies have found that, especially after the 2nd and 3rd years of operation, parents and children are better satisfied with their new school experiences and approve of the new policies (Walberg, 2001).

Findings show that almost all charter schools are smaller, friendlier, and more open. Students get more personal attention, and though in many instances the teachers are less experienced and have minimal credentials, they show students that they care, are knowledgeable in content areas, and are excited about teaching. Most of these schools are places where parents have some decision-making power and develop a sense of community. Thus, teachers and students feel more comfortable in examining values and a sense of morality (Naisknov, 2002; Schorr, 2002).

The charters are also effective in bringing changes to the professional cultures where new "ideas" in teaching are integrated with other ideas and result in a more cohesive program (Murphy & Shiffman, 2002). In districts where there are enough charters to affect the traditional schools financially, investigators find that a number of regular school personnel have started to make changes in their public schools. They reach out more to the community and parents, make schools more attractive, expect more of students, and offer more challenging courses (Center for Education Reform, 2003; Schorr, 2002). This is satisfying to those proponents who expect the competitive effect of charters to enhance all education.

Fenton Avenue Charter School: An Example.
The Fenton Avenue School in San Fernando Valley was established as a charter in 1994. In 1992, an innovative principal and his staff, frustrated with the bureaucracy, began the process of forming a charter school. This was finally granted in 1994 and gave them full autonomy from the Los Angeles district. They

On the whole charter schools are small friendly places where new ideas of teaching are integrated with other ideas

now feel successful in programs serving 1,300 students: 78% Hispanic and 17% African American (Manno, 2001). The school has developed as a true community school. The school operates the entire year, has strong bilingual programs, after-school enrichment classes and study halls. Parents are an integral part of the program and develop strong bonds with teachers. The Fenton Avenue School has developed clear guidelines with help from representatives of all interested parties. These guidelines focus on school and home responsibilities (including homework policies, student responsibility codes, rules of behavior, and school discipline procedures). On Saturdays there are workshops for parents, led by the Fenton Avenue teachers, on techniques for working with their children at home. Community representatives offer other classes open to all, such as citizenship, computer, and English classes (Manno, 2001).

Presently, the school is staffed by an executive director plus a director of instruction, 65 teachers, 20 full-time classified staff, and 50 part-time aides. Class size is 20 in K–3, and 24 in Grades 4 to 6. The school is open 6 days a week and provides after-school care.

This school has reduced costs for maintenance, since directors negotiate for work outside the system bureaucracy. Their school governance structure consists of four councils, each consisting of parents, teachers, staff, and community members: (1) budget, facilities, and safety; (2) curriculum and assessment, (3) human resources and personnel; and (4) school–community relations. These groups are coordinated by the executive director and the director of instruction and meet at 7 a.m. to enable greater attendance (Manno, 2001).

Charter schools are not free from political battles, and it takes strong leadership and community will to sustain them (Schorr, 2002). The previously described charter school programs have provided needed services to some of our neediest families, but long-term commitment and dedication to the idea that collaboration can make a difference in children's education is required. Maintaining that commitment is hard work and often difficult.

Investigators find that schools that use one or two years of study and start-up time to develop a charter program have greater chances of success. The instigators of the model schools discussed in this chapter have discovered that lesson.

With the differences in state regulations, results from the various state studies on charter schools are likely to reflect differences. For example, research thus far indicates that in many of the states, accountability, greater choices for all students (not just the vocal or wealthier), models for innovations, and even greater efficiency are not happening (Garn, 1998; Wells, 1998). Nevertheless, from our studies and review of research, we believe that some of these programs are likely to fulfill the notions of this text, that is, the importance of harnessing more and greater family and community resources than has been the case historically. The experiments bear watching, for some will become exemplars, showing what happens when we ask more of the adults involved in a school endeavor.

Outgrowths of Charter Schools. As we noted earlier, charter schools have proliferated in unprecedented fashion during the last decade as most states have granted authority. Even though significant amounts of literature exist to guide groups, some have borrowed models from existing pilot schools in the Comer model, a National Network school, or even the Reggio Emilia plan.

Comer has sage advice on the degree of success in school reform efforts. He notes that one third of the projects maintain change, one third achieve limited change until the initiators depart, and one third do not have any success (O'Neil, 1997).

Critical Features of Partnerships

Partnership models and collaborative arrangements are all different, whether they are established under the centralized control of schools using the state-required curriculum, or under local control where each school determines the curriculum. But there are commonalities, and we find most of the following features appearing in quality programs. These ideas may be helpful as evaluation tools when you have an opportunity to become involved in a partnership program.

1. Collaboration requires strong leadership, committed coordinators, and partners able to gain the support of the **power brokers** in their social setting.

2. Each participant knows that he or she must surrender some decision-making power so as to find common ground for collaborating. To keep communication channels open, each partner must express feelings and reactions while respecting skills, knowledge, ideas, culture, and values of other partnership members.

3. Partners know that it is imperative to establish with the group some long-range goals at the beginning yet be able to redirect their objectives when necessary to overcome barriers.

4. Leaders realize that all program steps require careful planning, that these steps must include learning experiences from all social settings, and that all partners are to participate in educational decision making.

5. Continuous assessment is needed to determine progress or to determine change so that participants can recognize and reward each other's efforts.

6. Because change in educational structures is slow, partners recognize that alterations cannot be rushed.

7. The entire community must be kept informed of progress in a partnership.

ACHIEVING PARTNERSHIPS

As we have discussed program models, we have demonstrated that true collaboration does emerge when properly nurtured. These model collaborations take time to build, and as each continues, even more time is required to monitor and fine-tune in it for it to stay healthy. Successful models may be in systems with schools of choice, such as charter schools, or in systems where there is centralized control for education but where teachers form a succesfull collaboration with parents and the community.

As such models show, the effort is worthwhile, and the reported educational benefits to children and communities are inspirational. Anyone interested in achieving partnerships for their schools should carefully examine the literature on established programs. Information about the sustainability of these programs is helpful for beginners developing their own particular plans.

Individual Responsibility

Even strong leaders cannot accomplish all tasks alone. They require the participation and cooperation of many people. All parents, teachers, and community members have a responsibility to become involved at the different levels of participation if the best rewards are to emerge. At a minimum level, just as some parents are active only in helping children with homework, there will be teachers who will limit their involvement to the traditional ways described in Chapter 11. They will take advantage of the community programs that serve children's educational needs. Then some other teachers will seek more involvement as they plan their curriculum for parent and other volunteer support in the classroom. They will participate in workshops with parents and serve on committees with them as equal partners. And a few teachers will campaign hard for parents and the community to be involved in decision making and will relish serving with them on partnership teams.

Realizing the dream of partnerships requires more than the effort exhibited in most U.S. school districts today. A spirit for undertaking change has germinated in many areas but seems slow to blossom fully. We all know that change takes time. The recent surge of interest at state and federal levels for partnerships must be viewed positively. Publications, funding, and legislation all provide a fertile base for more collaboration.

When reading about model programs, we can certify that those programs that included a research and assessment dimension have shown great strides in reaching a new level of participation. We also find from those model programs that exciting things happen when new ideas are introduced, nurtured carefully, and built as change mechanisms. The results certainly reinforce the desirability of bringing more collaborative work to our nation's schools.

IMPLICATIONS FOR PROFESSIONALS

Partnerships can begin with a single teacher and parent collaborating in a classroom, although possibilities exist for enthusiastic colleagues and parents to expand all sorts of desirable educational programs in any school. When you affiliate with a program that is launching a collaborative venture, you will want to consider the following important steps.

When your team considers collaborations, first define your objectives and agree on what changes are necessary. It's also wise to find out how collaboration has worked for others. Your team will need to locate resources and decide how to assess the progress it makes. Bringing in new helpers and involving them in collaborative ventures always requires finesse. Communication is often a problem as more people

become involved in collaborations. You and your teammates must be alert to how you are communicating and how your messages are being interpreted. Finally, you will want to first try out ideas on a small scale and then expand the experiment.

As you continue planning for moving a larger school unit toward collaboration, other requirements appear. You'll want to keep the following requirements in mind for planning and implementing any larger scale home–school–community partnership:

1. Community spirit for welcoming new ideas is primary. Success comes naturally when dedicated and committed people are working together to make a difference.

2. Proactive planners, leaders, and researchers must initiate, guide, and polish emerging plans for collaboration.

3. Financial resources, such as grants, must be available to subsidize pilot programs.

4. Interested citizens and community officials must commit to enacting and supporting partnerships. (Such people are often present, for most homes and communities wish for better connections to their schools.)

5. Educators must appreciate public input and want better communication with homes and community agencies.

6. Training and development programs must be available to nourish beginners and provide a background for new leaders. Too many programs erode when a strong leader leaves.

SUMMARY AND REVIEW

When schools are brokers for new learning communities and invest time and energy in forming links with homes and communities, exciting and productive results materialize. We have much evidence that this is true. The

work of James Comer in New Haven, Connecticut, and the expansion of Epstein's
National Network of Schools, to name but a
few, show that we have both reason and compelling need for communities to reach further
to obtain better functioning school operations.

New collaborations can mean reaching objectives by somewhat different routes and different rates. These different routes might take
more energy, more careful planning, and more
financial commitment, but a successful result
means a far better and richer product. Even implementing the principles of partnerships in
part of a school district eventually enriches the
experiences of all district students.

Schools are still the catalysts in most new
endeavors. No other social institution in the
United States has the oversight or the trained
personnel to serve in this capacity. Partnership
programs may start with a few small projects
or may grow from a well-conceived and well-
directed program. However it grows, a plan
must call for teachers and administrators to be
committed to the new practice. Being committed, gaining knowledge about other programs,
devising a plan, establishing means for communicating the plan, and involving others are
necessary to the success of any project.

If we are to achieve the type of social and
educational change we advocate, we must find
and nourish ways to make the practices behind
partnerships real. This means setting aside
some of the highly competitive stances that
our society sponsors and working for the common good. Everyone will benefit, and the least
fortunate will win a larger share of respect and
educational opportunity.

SUGGESTED ACTIVITIES AND QUESTIONS

1. Talk with three teachers about parent involvement in their programs. Have them
describe the things parents do when they
come to school. To determine the stage of
collaboration, relate their statements to the
three levels of involvement discussed in
this chapter.
2. Interview three parents to learn how they
have participated in their children's school
programs within the past year. What levels
of involvement do you find?
3. Examine a school district with which you
are acquainted to ascertain its stage of evolution in collaborative efforts. How does
your district compare to the programs featured in Chapter 12?

RESOURCES

Books

1. Benson, P. L. (1997). *All kids are our kids: What communities must do to raise caring and responsible children and adolescents.* San Francisco: Jossey-Bass.
2. Cadwell, L. B. (2003*). Bringing learning to life: The Reggio approach to early childhood educa-tion.* New York: Teachers College Press.
3. Comer, J. P., Haynes, N. M., Joyner, E., & Ben-Avie, M. (1996). *Rallying the whole village: The Comer process for reforming education.* New York: Teachers College Press.
4. Epstein, J., Sanders, M., Simon, B., Salinas, K., Jansorn, N., & Van Voorhis F. (2002). *School, fam-ily and community partnerships: Your handbook for action* (2nd ed.). Thousand Oaks, CA: Corwin.

Films and Videos

1. *Cultivating Roots—Home/school/partnerships* (1997). [Video, 30 min] Washington, DC: Na-tional Association for the Education of Young Children.
2. *Not just any place—Reggio Emilia: An education experience as told by the protagonists* [Video, 72 min]. (2003). The video highlights the unique-ness of the program. Burlington, VT: Learning Materials Workshop.
3. *Parentmaking Educators Training Program: A comprehensive skills development course to train early childhood parent educators* [3 videos,

2 hr each, plus manual]. (1996). Focus is on parent educator training. Palo Alto, CA: Children's Health Council.

4. *Rethinking school organization* [3 audiocassettes, 1 hr each]. (1996). Six authorities on schooling processes, parent involvement, and other educational developments. Bloomington, IN: Agency for Instructional Technology.

Organizations

Children's Rights Council
300 I Street, NE, Suite 401
Washington, DC 20002
www.vix.com/crcl

Council of the Great City Schools
1301 Pennsylvania Avenue, NW
Washington, DC 20004

www.cgcs.org

Phi Delta Kappa
408 N. Union Street
Bloomington, IN 47402

www.pdkintl.org

Websites

1. www.cgcs.org.
   Council of Great City Schools Online. Presents information on the nation's large public school systems and their interschool projects.
2. www.classroom.net
   Classroom Connect has an on-line magazine for all levels of teachers and features on-line education programs.
3. www.dac.neu.edu/ire
   Institute for Responsive Education Website. Contains extensive reports and publications on partnerships and collaborations.
4. http://ericeec.org/reggio.html
   The ERIC Website for information on Reggio Emilia.
5. www.pfie.ed.gov
   Features a database for Partnership for Family Involvement in Education and gives examples of successful collaborations.

Appendix I

Bibliography of Children's Books

If we are fortunate, we . . . belong to a small, more particular community, defined by ethnicity or kinship, belief system or geography. It is in this intimate circle that we are most "ourselves," where our jokes are best appreciated, our special dishes most enjoyed. These are the people to whom we go first when we need comfort or empathy, for they speak our own brand of cultural shorthand, and always know the correct things to say, the proper things to do.

(Dorris, 1993, p. 1)

The following selected bibliography of children's books portrays a variety of American family structures where individuals are learning together in the home, the school, and the community:

H Indicates that the book reveals children learning through the home environment

S Indicates that children from different family structures are learning together at school

C Indicates that different family members are sharing and learning from their community environment

Different Cultures

Anacona, G. (1998). *El barrio, Jose's neighborhood.* New York: Harcourt. **C**

Ashley, B. (1991). *Cleversticks* (D. Brazell, Illus.). New York: Crown. **S**

Bartoletti, S. (1999). *Polish dancing with Dziadziu.* (A. Nelson, Illus.). New York: Harcourt. **H**

Breckler, R. K. (1992). *Hoang breaks the lucky teapot.* (A. Frankel, Illus.). Boston: Houghton Mifflin. **H**

Bunting, E. (1996). *Going home* (D. Diaz, Illus.). New York: HarperCollins. **H, C**

Bunting, E. (1997). *Moonstick, the seasons of the Sioux.* (J. Sanford, Paintings.). New York: HarperCollins. **C**

Calhoun, M. (1996). *Tonio's cat* (D. Stanley, Illus.). New York: Morrow Junior. **C**

Carling, A. L. (1998). *Mama and papa have a store.* New York: Dial. **H, C**

Clifton, L. (1974, 1992). *Three wishes* (M. Hays, Illus., 1992). New York: Dell. **C**

Cohen, M. (1989). *See you in second grade.* New York: Greenwillow. **S**

Cross, V. (1992). *Great grandma tells of threshing day* (G. Owens, Illus.). Morton Grove, IL: Whitman. **H, C**

Crowley, J. (1998). *Big moon tortilla* (D. Strongbow, Illus.). Honesdale, PA: Boyd's Mills. **H**

Cummings, P. (1991). *Clean your room, Harvey Moon!* New York: Macmillan. **H**

Diouf, S. (2001). *Bintou's braids* (S. W. Evans, Illus.). San Francisco: Chronicle. **H, C**

Dooley, N. (1991). *Everybody cooks rice* (P. J. Thornton, Illus.). Minneapolis, MN: Carolrhoda. **H, C**

Fazio, B. L. (1996). *Grandfather's story.* Seattle, WA: Sasquatch. **H**

Franklin, K. L. (1994). *The shepherd boy* (J. Kastner, Illus.). New York: Atheneum. **C**

Good, M. (1993). *Reuben and the fire* (P. B. Moss, Illus.). Intercourse, PA: Good Books. **C**

Hamm, D. J. (1991). *Laney's lost mama* (S. G. Ward, Illus.). Morton Grove, IL: Whitman. **C**

Hartman, W. (1993). *All the magic in the world* (N. Daly, Illus.). New York: Dutton. **C**

Heide, F. P., & Gilliland, J. H. (1990). *The day of Ahmed's secret* (T. Lewin, Illus.). New York: Mulberry. **H, C**

Hooks, B. (1999). *Happy to be nappy* (C. Raschka, Illus.). New York: Jump at the Sun/Hyperion for Children. **H**

Hoyt-Goldsmith, D (1990). *Totem pole* (L. Migdale, Photographs). New York: Holiday House. **H**

Hu, D. (1993). *Joshua's Masai mask.* (A. Rich, Illus.). New York: Lee & Low. **S**

Johnson, A. (1990). *Do like Kyla* (J. E. Ransome, Illus.). New York: Orchard. **H**

Johnson, A. (1991). *One of three* (D. Soman, Illus.). New York: Orchard. **H**

Katz, K. (1999). *The color of us.* New York: Holt. **H, C**

Kendall, R. (1992). *Eskimo boy: Life in an Inupiaq Eskimo village.* New York: Scholastic. **C**

Ketterman, H. (1992). *Not yet, Yvette* (I. Trivas, Illus.). Morton Grove, IL: Whitman. **H**

Kimmelman, L. (2000). *Hooray! It's Passover!* (J. Himmelman, Illus.). New York: Harper Festival. **H**

Kroll, V. (1994). *Masai and I* (N. Carpenter, Illus.). New York: Four Winds. **C**

Levy, J. (1995). *The spirit of Tio Fernando* (M. Fuenmayor, Illus.; T. Mlawa, Trans.). Morton Grove, IL: Whitman. **C**

London, J. (1997). *Ali, child of the desert* (T. Lewin, Illus.). Shepard, NY: Lothrop, Lee & Shepard. **C**

MacDonald, S. (1995). *Nanta's lion: A search-and-find adventure.* New York: Morrow. **C**

Mandelbaum, P. (1990). *You be me, I'll be you.* New York: Kane-Miller. **H**

Markhun, P. M. (1993). *The little painter of Sabana Grande* (R. Casilla, Illus.). New York: Bradbury/Macmillan. **C**

McCloskey, R. (1952). *One morning in Maine.* New York: Viking. **H, C**

Mora, P. (2003). *The rainbow tulip.* New York: Puffin. **S**

Onyefulu, I. (1995). *E Meka's gift: An African counting book.* New York: Cobblehill. **C**

Ormerod, J. (1991). *When we went to the zoo.* New York: Lothrop. **C**

Partridge, E. (2003). *Oranges on Golden Mountain.* New York: Puffin. **H, C**

Pinkney, A. (2001). *Mim's Christmas jam* (B. Pinkney, Illus.). New York: Harcourt. **H, C**

Pinkney, B. (1994). *Max found two sticks.* New York: Simon & Schuster. **C**

Polacco, P. (1990). *Just plain fancy.* New York: Simon & Schuster. **C**

Pomerana, M. (1998). *The American Wei* (A. Di Salvo-Ryan, Illus.). Morton Grove, IL: Whitman. **C**

Pryor, B. (1996). *The dream jar* (M. Graham, Illus.). New York: Morrow. **H**

St. James, S. (1996). *Sunday.* New York: Whitman. **H**

Say, A. (1991). *Tree of cranes.* New York: Scholastic. **H**

Smalls, I. (1994). *Dawn and the round to-it* (T. Geter, Illus.). New York: Simon & Schuster. **H**

Sonneborn, R. A. (1970, 1987). *Friday night is papa night* (E. A. McCully, Illus.). New York: Puffin. **H**

Soto, G. (1993). *Too many tamales* (E. Martinez, Illus.). New York: Putnam's. **H**

Stroud, V. A. (1994). *Doesn't fall off his horse.* New York: Dial. **C**

Surat, M. M. (1993). *Angel child, dragon child* (V.-D. Mai, Illus.). New York: Carnival. **S**

Villanueva, M. (1993). *Nene and the horrible math monster* (R. Unson, Illus.). Chicago: Polychrome. **S**

Waboose, J. (2000). *Sky sisters.* (B. Deines, Illus.). Niagara Falls, NY: Kids Can Press. **C**

Watkins, S. (1994). *White bead ceremony* (K. Doner, Illus.). Tulsa, OK: Council Oak. **C**

Weiss, N (1992). *On a hot, hot day.* New York: Putnam. **C**

White Deer of Autumn. (1992). *The great change* (C. Grigg, Illus.). Hillsboro, OR: Beyond Words. **C**

Williams, K. L. (1998). *Painted dreams* (C. Stock, Illus.). New York: Lothrop, Lee & Shepard. **H, C**

Williams, V. (1997). *"More, more, more," said the baby.* New York: Greenwillow. **H**

Woodson, J. (2001). *The other side.* New York: Putnam's Sons. **C**

Wright, C. C. (1994). *Jumping the broom* (G. Griffith, Illus.). New York: Holiday. **C**

Yamate, S. (1991). *Char Siu Bao boy.* Chicago: Polychrome. **S**

Yashima, T. (1955). *Crow boy.* New York: Viking. **S**

Divorced Families

Abercrombie, B. (1995, 1990). *Charlie Anderson.* Upper Saddle River, NJ: Simon & Schuster. **H**

Baum, L. (1986). *One more time* (P. Bouma, Illus.). New York: Morrow. **H**

Binch, C. (1998). *Since Dad left.* Brookfield, CT: Millbrook. **H**

Boegehold, B. (1985). *Daddy doesn't live here anymore* (D. Borgo, Illus.). New York: Western. **H**

Bunting, E. (2001). *The days of summer* (W. Low, Illus.). New York: Harcourt. **H**

Girard, L. W. (1987). *At Daddy's on Saturdays* (J. Friedman, Illus.). Morton Grove, IL: Whitman. **H**

Hazen, B. S. (1983). *Two homes to live in: A child's view of divorce* (P. Luks, Illus.). New York: Human Sciences. **H**

Mayle, P. (1988). *Why are we getting a divorce?* (A. Robins, Illus.). New York: Harmony. **H**

Rotner, S., & Sheila K. (2002). *Something's different.* Brookfield, CT: Millbrook. **H**

Rush, K. (1994). *Friday's journey.* New York: Orchard. **C**

Schotter, R. (2003). *Room for Rabbit* (C. Moore, Illus.). New York: Clarion. **H**

Vigna, J. (1984). *Grandma without me.* Morton Grove, IL: Whitman. **H**

Watson, J. W., Switzer, R. E., & Hirschberg, J. C. (1988). *Sometimes a family has to split up* (C. B. Smith, Illus.). New York: Crown. **H**

Weinger, B. (1995). *Good-bye, Daddy* (A. Mark, Illus.). New York: North–South. **H**

Blended Families

Boyd, L. (1990). *Sam is my half-brother.* New York: Viking Penguin. **H**

Delton, J. (1989). *Angel's mother's baby* (J. Weber, Illus.). Boston: Houghton Mifflin. **H**

Gibbons, F. (1996). *Mountain wedding* (T. Rand, Illus.). New York: Morrow Junior. **H, C**

Hines, A. G. (1996). *When we married Gary.* New York: Greenwillow. **H**

Hoffman, M. (1995). *Boundless grace* (C. Binch, Illus.). New York: Scholastic. **H, C**

MacLachlan, P. (1985). *Sarah, plain and tall.* New York: Harper & Row. **H, C**

Ransom, C. F. (1993). *We're growing together* (V. W. Frierson, Illus.). New York: Bradbury. **H, C**

Vigna, J. (1980). *She's not my real mother.* Chicago: Whitman. **H, C**

Willner-Pardo, G. (1994). *What I'll remember when I am a grownup* (W. L. Krudop, Illus.). New York: Clarion. **H**

Single-Parent Household and Special Relationship with One Parent or with Grandparents

Ackerman, K. (1988). *Song and dance man* (S. Gammell, Illus.). New York: Scholastic. **H**

Ackerman, K. (1994). *By the dawn's early light* (C. Stock, Illus.). New York: Atheneum. **H**

Atwell, D. (2003). *The Thanksgiving door.* Boston: Houghton Mifflin. **C**

Bunting, E. (1994). *Smoky night* (D. Diaz, Illus.). San Diego, CA: Harcourt Brace Jovanovich. **C**

Chaconas, D. (2003). *On a wintry morning* (S. T. Johnson, Illus.). New York: Puffin. **H, C**

Clifton, L. (2001). *One of the problems of Everett Anderson* (A. Grifalconi, Illus.). New York: Holt. **H, S**

Cohen, C. Lee. (2003). *Everything is different at Nonna's house* (H. Nakata, Illus.). New York: Clarion. **H**

Cooper, S. (1993). *Danny and the kings* (J. A. Smith, Illus.). New York: McElderry. **C**

Greenfield, E. (1988). *Nathaniel talking* (J. S. Gilchrist, Illus.). New York: Black Butterfly. **H, S, C**

Haggerty, M. E. (1993). *A crack in the wall* (R. de Anda, Illus.). New York: Lee & Low. **H**

Harrison, Troon. (1994). *The long weekend.* New York: Harcourt Brace. **C**

Joosse, B. M. (1991). *Mama, do you love me?* (B. Lavallee, Illus.). New York: Scholastic. **H**

Lindsay, J. W. (1982, 1991). *Do I have a daddy? A story about a single-parent child* (2nd ed.; C. Boeller, Illus.). Buena Park, CA: Morning Glory. **H**

Moon, N. (1994). *Lucy's picture* (A. Ayliffe, Illus.). New York: Scholastic. **S**

Parr, T. (2002). *The daddy book.* Boston: Little, Brown. **H**

Peterson, J. W. (1994). *My mama sings* (S. Speidel, Illus.). New York: HarperCollins. **H**

Plourde, L. (2003). *Thank you, Grandpa* (J. Cockcroft, Illus.). New York: Dutton. **H, C**

Saller, C. (1991). *The bridge dancers.* Minneapolis, MN: Carolrhoda. **H**

Sharp, N. L. (1993). *Today I'm going fishing with my dad* (C. Demarest, Illus.). Honesdale, PA: Boyd's Mill. **C**

Sisulu, E. B. (1996). *The day Gogo went to vote* (S. Wilson, Illus.). Boston: Little, Brown. **H, C**

Smalls, I. (1992). *Jonathan and his mommy* (M. Hays, Illus.). Boston: Little, Brown. **C**

Smalls, I. (1999). *Kevin and his dad* (M. Hays, Illus.). Boston: Little, Brown. **H, C**

Testa, M. (1996). *Nine candles* (A. Schaffer, Illus.). Minneapolis, MN: Carolrhoda. **C**

Tran, K.-L. (1994). *Tet: The new year* (M. Vo-Dinh, Illus.). New York: Simon & Schuster. **C**

Vigna, J. (1987). *Mommy and me by ourselves again.* Morton Grove, IL: Whitman. **H**

Waddell, M. (1994). *The big, big Sea* (J. Eachus, Illus.). Cambridge, MA: Candlewick. **C**

Ziefert, H. (2003). *Home for Navidad* (S. Cohen, Illus.). Boston: Houghton Mifflin. **H**

Ziefert, H. (2003). *31 Uses for a mom* (R. Doughty, Illus.). New York: Putnam. **C**

Adoptive Families

Bloom, S. (1991). *A family for Jamie: An adoption story.* New York: Potter. **H**

Brodzinsky, A. B. (1996). *The mulberry bird: An adoption story* (D. Stanley, Illus.). Indianapolis, IN: Perspective. **H**

Cais, S. (1998). *Why so sad, Brown Rabbit?* New York: Dutton. **H**

Cole, J. (1995). *How I was adopted: Samantha's story* (M. Chambliss, Illus.). New York: Morrow. **H**

Curtis, J. L. (1996). *Tell me again about the night I was born* (L. Cornell, Illus.). New York: Harper-Collins. **H, C**

D'Antonio, N. (1997). *Our baby from China: An adoption story.* Morton Grove, IL: Whitman. **H, C**

Girard, L. W. (1986). *Adoption is for always* (J. Friedman, Illus.). Morton Grove, IL: Whitman. **H**

Girard, L. W. (1989). *We adopted you, Benjamin Koo* (L. Shute, Illus.). Morton Grove, IL: Whitman. **H, S**

Kasza, K. (1992). *A mother for Choco.* New York: Putnam. **H**

Katz, K. (1997). *Over the moon: An adoption tale.* New York: Holt. **H, C**

Koehler, P. (1990, 1997). *The day we met you.* Old Tappen, NJ: Simon & Schuster. **H**

Lamperti, N. (1999). *Brown like me.* Johnstown, NY: New Victoria. **H, C**

Lifton, B. J. (1993). *Tell me a real adoption story* (C. Nivola, Illus.). New York: Knopf. **H**

McCully, E. A. (1994). *My real family.* San Diego, CA: Harcourt. **H, C**

Miller, K. A. (1994). *Did my first mother love me? A story for an adopted child* (J. Moffett, Illus.). Buena Park, CA: Morning Glory. **H**

Okimoto, J. D., & Aoki, E. M. (2002). *White swan express* (M. So, Illus.). New York: Clarion. **C**

Rogers, F. (1995, 1998). *Let's talk about it: Adoption* (J. Judkins, Illus.). New York: Putnam. **H**

Turner, A. (1990). *Through moon and stars and night skies* (J. Graham Hale, Illus.). New York: Harper & Row. **H, C**

Foster Care, Orphanages, and Shelters

Blomquist, G., & P. Blomquist. (1993, 1990). *Zachary's new home: A story for foster and adoptive children.* Milwaukee, WI: Stevens. **H**

Bunting, E. (1996). *Train to Somewhere* (R. Himler, Illus.). New York: Clarion. **C**

Cannon, J. (1994). *Stellaluna.* San Diego, CA: Harcourt. **H, C**

Chalofsky, M., Finland, G., Wallace, J. (1992). *Changing places. A kid's view of shelter living.* Mt. Rainier, MD: Gryphon. **H, C**

Herbert, S. (1991). *I miss my foster parents.* Washington, DC: Child Welfare League of America. **H, C**

MacLachlan, P. (1982). *Mama one, mama two* (R. L. Bornstein, Illus.). New York: Harper. **H**

Steptoe, J. (1969). *Stevie.* New York: Harper. **H**

Multigenerational Households and Extended Families

Bauer, M. D. (1995). *When I go camping with gramma* (A. Garns, Illus.). New York: Bridgewater. **C**

Bunting, E. (1991). *Sunshine home* (D. DeGroat, Illus.). New York: Clarion. **H**

Burden–Patman, D., with K. D. Jones. (1992). *Carnival* (R. Ruffins, Illus.). New York: Simon & Schuster. **H, C**

Chiemruom, S. (1994). *Dara's Cambodian new year* (D. N. Pin, Illus.). New York: Simon & Schuster. **H**

Choi, S. N. (1993). *Halmoni and the picnic* (K. M. Dugan, Illus.). Boston: Houghton Mifflin. **S**

Coleman, E. (1996). *White socks only* (T. Geter, Illus.). Morton Grove, IL: Whitman. **H, C**

Crews, D. (1991). *Bigmama's.* New York: Greenwillow. **H, C**

Dorros, A. (1991). *Abuela* (E. Kleven, Illus.). New York: Dutton. **C**

Falwell, C. (1995). *Feast for 10.* New York: Clarion. **H, C**

Flournoy, V. (1985). *The patchwork quilt* (J. Pinkney, Illus.). New York: Dial. **H**

Fox, M. (1989, 1994). *Sophie* (A. Robinson, Illus.). New York: Harcourt. **H**

Guback, G. (1994). *Luka's quilt.* New York: Greenwillow. **H**

Heide, F. P., & Pierce, R. H. (1998). *Tio Armolo.* New York: Lothrop & Shepard. **H**

Hoffman, M. (1991). *Amazing grace* (C. Binch, Illus.). New York: Dial. **H, S**

Howard, E. F. (1988). *The train to Lulu's* (R. Casilla, Illus.). New York: Bradbury. **H, C**

Howard, E. F. (1991). *Aunt Flossie's hats (and) crab cakes later.* New York: Clarion. **H, C**

Jones, R. (1995). *Great Aunt Martha.* New York: Dutton. **H**

Levine, A. (1995). *Bono and Nonno* (J. Lanfredi, Illus.). New York: Tambourine. **C**

Lewin, T. (1998). *The story tellers.* New York: Lothrop, Lee & Shepard. **C**

Mathis, S. B. (1975). *The hundred penny box* (L. Dillon & D. Dillon, Illus.). New York: Viking. **H**

Matthews, M. (2000). *Magid fasts for Ramadan* (E. B. Lewis, Illus.). Boston: Houghton Mifflin. **H**

McCully, E. A. (1993). *Grandmas at bat.* New York: HarperCollins. **C**

McFarlane, S. (1991, 1993). *Waiting for the whales* (R. Lightburn, Illus.). New York: Philomel. **H, C**

Miles, M. (1971). *Annie and the old one* (P. Parnall, Illus.). Boston: Little, Brown. **H**

Moore, E. (1995). *Grandma's smile* (D. Andreasen, Illus.). New York: Lothrop, Lee & Shepard. **H**

Nomura, T. (1991). *Grandpa's town* (A. M. Stinchecum, Trans.). New York: Kane/Miller. **H, C**

Polacco, P. (1990). *Thunder cake.* New York: Philomel. **H**

Polacco, P. (1992). *Mrs. Katz and Tush.* New York: Bantam (Little Rooster). **C**

Poydar, N. (1994). *Busy Bea.* New York: Macmillan. **H**

Reiser, L. (1998). *Cherry pies and lullabies.* New York: Greenwillow. **H**

Simon, F. (1998). *Where are you?* (D. Melling, Illus.). Atlanta, GA: Peachtree. **C**

Swartz, L. (1992, 1994). *A first Passover* (J. Chwast, Illus.). New York: Simon & Schuster. **H**

Swentzell, R. (1992). *Children of clay: A family of pueblo potters* (B. Steen, Photographs). Minneapolis, MN: Lerner. **C**

Wells, R. (1996). *The language of doves* (G. Shed, Illus.). New York: Dial. **H**

Wild, M. (1994). *Our granny* (J. Vivas, Illus.). New York: Ticknor & Fields. **H**

Wild, M. (1996). *Old pig.* New York: Ticknor & Fields. **H, C**

Williams, V. (1997). *Lucky song.* New York: Greenwillow. **H**

Woodruff, E. (1998). *Can you guess where we're going?* (C. Fisher, Illus.). New York: Holiday House. **C**

Zalben, J. B. (1996). *Papa's latkes.* New York: Holt. **H**

Zamorano, A. (1997). *Let's eat* (J. Vivas, Illus.). New York: Scholastic. **H**

Homeless Families

Barbour, K. (1991). *Mr. Bowtie.* San Diego, CA: Harcourt. **C**

Bunting, E. (1991). *Fly away home* (R. Himler, Illus.). New York: Clarion. **C**

Bunting, E. (1999). *December* (D. Diaz, Illus.). New York: Harcourt. **H, C**

DiSalvo-Ryan, D. (1991). *Uncle Willie and the soup kitchen.* New York: Morrow Junior. **C**

Guthrie, D. (2000, 1988). *A rose for Abby.* Nashville, TN: Abington Press. **C**

Hathorn, L. (1994). *Way home* (G. Rogers, Illus.). New York: Crown. **C**

Weninger, B. (1997). *Lumina* (A. Bell, Trans; J. Wintz-Litty, Illus.). New York: North–South. **C**

Wolf, B. (1995). *Homeless.* New York: Orchard. **H, C**

Migrant Workers and Immigrants

Bunting, E. (1988). *How many days to America? A Thanksgiving story* (B. Peck, Illus.). New York: Clarion. **C**

Bunting, E. (1994). *A day's work.* New York: Clarion. **H, C**

Isadora, R. (1991). *At the crossroads.* New York: Greenwillow. **C**

Krall, K. (2003). *Harvesting hope* (Y. Morales, Illus.). New York: Harcourt. **H, C, S**

Rosenberg, M. (1986). *Making a new home in America* (G. Ancona, Photographs). New York: Lothrop. **H**

Williams, S. A. (1992). *Working cotton* (C. Byard, Illus.). San Diego, CA: Harcourt. **C**

Gay and Lesbian Families

Bosche, S. (1983). *Jenny lives with Eric and Martin.* London: Gay Men's Press. **H**

Brown, F. (1991). *Generous Jefferson Bartleby* (L. Trawin, Illus.). Boston: Alyson Wonderland. **H, C**

Elwin, R. & Paulie, M. (1990). *Asha's mums* (D. Lee, Illus.). Toronto, Ontario, Canada: Women's Press. **S**

Greenberg, K. E. (1996). *Zack's story.* Minneapolis MN: Lerner. **H, S, C**

Heron, A. & Maran, M. (1991). *How would you feel if your dad was gay?* (K. Kovick, Illus.). Boston: Alyson Wonderland. **H**

Newman, L. (1991). *Belinda's bouquet* (M. Willhoite, Illus.). Boston: Alyson Wonderland. **H, C**

Newman, L. (1991). *Gloria goes to gay pride* (R. Crocker, Illus.). Boston: Alyson Wonderland. **H, C**

Newman, L. (1993). *Saturday is pattyday* (A. Hegel, Illus.). Norwich, CT: New Victoria. **C**

Newman, L. (2000). *Heather has two mommies, 10th anniversary* (D. Souza, Illus.). Boston: Alyson Wonderland. **H, S**

Quinlan, P. (1994). *Tiger flowers* (J. Wilson, Illus.). New York: Dial. **H**

Vigna, J. (1995). *My two uncles.* Morton Grove, IL: Whitman. **H**

Wickens, E. (1994). *Anna Day and the O-ring.* Los Angeles: Alyson. **H**

Willhoite, M. (1990). *Daddy's roommate.* Boston: Alyson Wonderland. **H**

Willhoite, M. (1993). *Uncle what-is-it is coming to visit!* Boston: Alyson Wonderland. **H**

Children, Family Members, and Friends with Special Needs

Alexander, S. H. (1990). *Mom can't see me.* (G. Ancona, Photographs). New York: Macmillan. **H**

Cowen-Fletcher, J. (1993). *Mama zooms.* New York: Scholastic. **H**

Day, S. (1995). *Luna and the big blur: A story for children who wear glasses* (D. Morris, Illus.). New York: Brunner/Mazel. **H**

Dugan, B. (1992). *Loop the loop* (J. Stevenson, Illus.). New York: Greenwillow. **C**

Dwight, L. (1998). *We can do it.* New York: Starbright. **C**

Hines, A. G. (1993). *Gramma's walk.* New York: Greenwillow. **C**

Karim, R. (1994). *Mandy Sue day.* New York: Clarion. **H, S**

Kroll, V. (1993). *Naomi knows it's springtime* (J. Kastner, Illus.). Honesdale, PA: Boyd's Mill. **C**

Lakin, P. (1994). *Dad and me in the morning* (R. O. Steele, Illus.). Morton Grove, IL: Whitman. **C**

Martin, B., Jr., & Archambault, J. (1966, 1987). *Knots on a counting rope* (T. Rand, Illus.). New York: Holt. **C**

Miller, M. B. & Ancona, G. (1991). *Handtalk school.* (G. Ancona, Illus.). New York: Four Winds. **S**

Mohr, N. (1995). *Old Lativia and the Mountain of Sorrows* (R. Gutierrez, Illus.). New York: Greenwillow. **H, C**

Muldoon, K. M. (1989). *Princess Pooh* (L. Shute, Illus.). Morton Grove, IL: Whitman. **H**

Osofsky, A. (1992). *My buddy* (T. Rand, Illus.). New York: Holt. **H, C**

Rabe, B. (1988). *Where's Chimpy?* (D. Schmidt, Photographs). Morton Grove, IL: A. Whitman. **H**

Stuve-Bodeen, St. (1998). *We'll paint the octopus red* (P. DeVito, Illus.). Bethesda, MD: Woodbine. **H**

Thompson, M. (1992). *My brother Matthew.* Rockville, MD: Woodbine House. **H**

Waddell, M. (1990). *My great grandpa* (D. Mansell, Illus.). New York: Putnam. **C**

Defining Families

Abramchik, L. (1993). *Is your family like mine?* (A. Bradshaw, Illus.). New York: Open Heart, Open Mind. **H, S**

Adoff, A. (2002). *Black is brown is tan* (E. A. McCully, Illus.). New York: HarperCollins. **H**

Jenness, A. (1990). *Families: A celebration of diversity, commitment, and love.* Boston: Houghton Mifflin. **H**

Kroll, V. (1994). *Beginnings: How families come to be.* Morton Grove, IL: Whitman. **H**

Leedy, L. F. (1995, 1999). *Who's who in my family?* New York: Holiday House. **H**

Morris, A. (1990). *Loving* (K. Heyman, Photographs). New York: Mulberry. **H, C**

Skutch, R. (1995). *Who's in a family* (L. Nienhaus, Illus.). Berkeley, CA: Tricycle. **H, C**

Strickland, D. S., & Strickland, M. S. (Eds.). (1994). *Families: Poems celebrating the African American experience* (J. Ward, Illus.). Honesdale, PA: Boyd's Mill. (Wordsong). **H**

Thomas, M. (1987). *Free to be a family: A book about all kinds of belonging.* New York: Bantam. **H**

Valentine, J. (1994). *One dad, two dads, brown dad, blue dads* (M. Sarecky, Illus.). Boston: Alyson Wonderland. **H**

Appendix II

NAEYC Code of Ethical Conduct
Guidelines for Responsible Behavior in Early Childhood Education

NAEYC recognizes that many daily decisions required of those who work with young children are of a moral and ethical nature. The NAEYC Code of Ethical Conduct offers guidelines for responsible behavior and sets forth a common basis for resolving the principal ethical dilemmas encountered in early childhood care and education. The primary focus is on daily practice with children and their families in programs for children from birth through 8 years of age, such as infant/toddler programs, preschools, child care centers, family child care homes, kindergartens, and primary classrooms. Many of the provisions also apply to specialists who do not work directly with children, including program administrators, parent and vocational educators, college professors, and child care licensing specialists.

Core Values

Standards of ethical behavior in early childhood care and education are based on commitment to core values that are deeply rooted in the history of our field. We have committed ourselves to:

- Appreciating childhood as a unique and valuable stage of the human life cycle
- Basing our work with children on knowledge of child development

- Appreciating and supporting the close ties between child and family
- Recognizing that children are best understood and supported in the context of family, culture, community, and society
- Respecting the dignity, worth, and uniqueness of each individual (child, family member, and colleague)
- Helping children and adults achieve their full potential in the context of relationships that are based on trust, respect, and positive regard

Conceptual Framework

The Code sets forth a conception of our professional responsibilities in four sections, each addressing an arena of professional relationships: (1) children, (2) families, (3) colleagues, and (4) society. Each section includes an introduction to the primary responsibilities of the early childhood practitioner in that arena, a set of ideals, and a set of principles defining practices that are required, prohibited, and permitted.

The ideals reflect the aspirations of practitioners. The principles are intended to guide conduct and assist practitioners in resolving ethical dilemmas encountered in the field. There is not necessarily a corresponding principle for each ideal. Both ideals and principles are intended to direct practitioners to those questions which, when responsibly answered, will provide the basis for conscientious decision making. While the Code provides specific direction and suggestions for addressing some ethical dilemmas, many others will require the practitioner to combine the guidance of the Code with sound professional judgment.

The ideals and principles in this Code present a shared conception of professional responsibility that affirms our commitment to the core values of our field. The Code publicly acknowledges the responsibilities that we in the field have assumed and in so doing supports ethical behavior in our work. Practitioners who face ethical dilemmas are urged to seek guidance in the applicable parts of this Code and in the spirit that informs the whole.

Ethical Dilemmas Always Exist

Often, the right answer—the best ethical course of action to take—is not obvious. There may be no readily apparent, positive way to handle a situation. One important value may contradict another. When we are caught "on the horns of a dilemma," it is our professional responsibility to consult with all relevant parties in seeking the most ethical course of action to take.

Section I:

Ethical Responsibilities to Children

Childhood is a unique and valuable stage in the life cycle. Our paramount responsibility is to provide safe, healthy, nurturing, and responsive settings for children. We are committed to supporting children's development, respecting individual differences, helping children learn to live and work cooperatively, and promoting health, self-awareness, competency, self-worth, and resiliency.

Ideals

I.1.1—To be familiar with the knowledge base of early childhood care and education and to keep current through continuing education and in-service training.

I.1.2—To base program practices upon current knowledge in the field of child development and related disciplines and upon particular knowledge of each child.

I.1.3—To recognize and respect the uniqueness and the potential of each child.

I.1.4—To appreciate the special vulnerability of children.

I.1.5—To create and maintain safe and healthy settings that foster children's social, emotional, intellectual, and physical development and that respect their dignity and their contributions.

I.1.6—To support the right of each child to play and learn in inclusive early childhood programs to the fullest extent consistent with the best interests of all involved. As with adults who are disabled in the larger community, children with disabilities are ideally served in the same settings in which they would participate if they did not have a disability.

I.1.7—To ensure that children with disabilities have access to appropriate and convenient support services and to advocate for the resources necessary to provide the most appropriate settings for all children.

Principles

P-1.1—Above all, we shall not harm children. We shall not participate in practices that are disrespectful, degrading, dangerous, exploitative, intimidating, emotionally damaging or physically harmful to children. *This principle has precedence over all others in this Code.*

P-1.2—We shall not participate in practices that discriminate against children by denying benefits, giving special advantages, or excluding them from programs or activities on the basis of their race, ethnicity, religion, sex, national origin, language, ability, or the status, behavior, or beliefs of their parents. (This principle does not apply to programs that have a lawful mandate to provide services to a particular population of children.)

P-1.3—We shall involve all of those with relevant knowledge (including staff and parents) in decisions concerning a child.

P-1.4—For every child we shall implement adaptations in teaching strategies, learning environment, and curricula, consult with the family, and seek recommendations from appropriate specialists to maximize the potential of the child to benefit from the program. If, after these efforts have been made to work with a child and family, the child does not appear to be benefiting from a program, or the child is seriously jeopardizing the ability of other children to benefit from the program, we shall communicate with the family and appropriate specialists to determine the child's current needs, identify the setting and services most suited to meeting these needs, and assist the family in placing the child in an appropriate setting.

P-1.5—We shall be familiar with the symptoms of child abuse, including physical, sexual, verbal, emotional abuse, and neglect. We shall know and follow state laws and community procedures that protect children against abuse and neglect.

P-1.6—When we have reasonable cause to suspect child abuse or neglect, we shall report it to the appropriate community agency and follow up to ensure that appropriate action has been taken. When appropriate, parents or guardians will be informed that the referral has been made.

P-1.7—When another person tells us of a suspicion that a child is being abused or neglected, we shall assist that person in taking appropriate action to protect the child.

P-1.8—When a child protective agency fails to provide adequate protection for abused or neglected children, we acknowledge a collective ethical responsibility to work toward improvement of these services.

P-1.9—When we become aware of a practice or situation that endangers the health or safety of children, but has not been previously known to do so, we have an ethical responsibility to inform those who can remedy the situation and who can protect children from similar danger.

Section II:

Ethical Responsibilities to Families

Families are of primary importance in children's development (The term *family* may include others, besides parents, who are responsibly involved with the child). Because the family and the early childhood practitioner have a common interest in the child's welfare, we acknowledge a primary responsibility to bring about collaboration between the home and school in ways that enhance the child's development.

Ideals

I.2.1—To develop relationships of mutual trust with families we serve.

I.2.2—To acknowledge and build upon strengths and competencies we support families in their task of nurturing children.

I.2.3—To respect the dignity of each family and its culture, language, customs, and beliefs.

I.2.4—To respect families' childrearing values and their right to make decisions for their children.

I.2.5—To interpret each child's progress to parents within the framework of a developmental perspective and to help families understand and appreciate the value of developmentally appropriate early childhood practices.

I.2.6—To help family members improve their understanding of their children and to enhance their skills as parents.

I.2.7—To participate in building support networks for families by providing them with opportunities to interact with program staff, other families, community resources, and professional services.

Principles

P-2.1—We shall not deny members access to their child's classroom or program setting.

P-2.2—We shall inform families of program philosophy, policies, and personnel qualifications, and explain why we teach as we do—which should be in accordance with our ethical responsibilities to children (see Section I).

P-2.3—We shall inform families of and, when appropriate, involve them in policy decisions.

P-2.4—We shall involve families in significant decisions affecting their child.

P-2.5—We shall inform the family of accidents involving their child, of risks such as exposures to contagious disease that may result in infection, and of occurrences that might result in emotional stress.

P-2.6—To improve the quality of early childhood care and education, we shall cooperate with qualified child development researchers. Families shall be fully informed of any proposed research projects involving their children and shall have the opportunity to give or withhold consent without penalty. We shall not permit or participate in research that could in any way hinder the education, development, or well-being of children.

P-2.7—We shall not engage in or support exploitation of families. We shall not use our relationship with a family for private advantage or personal gain, or enter into relationships with family members that might impair our effectiveness in working with children.

P-2.8—We shall develop written policies for the protection of confidentiality and the disclosure of children's records. These policy documents shall be made available to all program personnel and families. Disclosure of children's records beyond family members, program personnel, and consultants having an obligation of confidentiality shall require familial consent (except in cases of abuse or neglect).

P-2.9—We shall maintain confidentiality and shall respect the family's right to privacy, refraining from disclosure of confidential information and intrusion into family life. However, when we have reason to believe that a child's welfare is at risk, it is permissible to share confidential information with agencies and individuals who may be able to intervene in the child's interest.

P-2.10—In cases where family members are in conflict, we shall work openly, sharing our observations of the child, to help all parties involved make informed decisions. We shall refrain from becoming an advocate for one party.

P-2.11—We shall be familiar with and appropriately use community resources and professional services that support families. After a referral has been made, we shall follow up to ensure that services have been appropriately provided.

Section III:

Ethical Responsibilities to Colleagues
A—Responsibilities to co-workers

Ideals

I-3A.1—To establish and maintain relationships of respect, trust, and cooperation with co-workers.

I-3A.2—To share resources and information with co-workers.

I-3A.3—To support co-workers in meeting their professional needs and in their professional development.

I-3A.4—To accord co-workers due recognition of professional achievement.

Principles

P-3A.1—When we have a concern about the professional behavior of a co-worker, we shall first let that person know of our concern, in a way that shows respect for personal dignity and for the diversity to be found among staff members, and then attempt to resolve the matter collegially.

P-3A.2—We shall exercise care in expressing views regarding the personal attributes or professional conduct of co-workers. Statements should be based on firsthand knowledge and relevant to the interests of children and programs.

B—Responsibilities to employers

Ideals

I-3B.1—To assist the program in providing the highest quality of service.

I-3B.2—To do nothing that diminishes the reputation of the program in which we work unless it is violating laws and regulations designed to protect children or the provisions of this Code.

Principles

P-3B.1—When we do not agree with program policies, we shall first attempt to effect change through constructive action within the organization.

P-3B.2—We shall speak or act on behalf of an organization only when authorized. We shall take care to acknowledge when we are speaking for the organization and when we are expressing a personal judgment.

P-3B.3—We shall not violate laws or regulations designed to protect children and shall take appropriate action consistent with this Code when aware of such violations.

C—Responsibilities to employees

Ideals

I-3C.1—To promote policies and working conditions that foster mutual respect, competence,

well-being, and positive self-esteem in staff members.

I-3C.2—To create a climate of trust and candor that will enable staff to speak and act in the best interests of children, families, and the field of early childhood care and education.

I-3C.3—To strive to secure equitable compensation (salary and benefits) for those who work with or on behalf of young children.

Principles

P-3C.1—In decisions concerning children and programs, we shall appropriately utilize the education, training, experience, and expertise of staff members.

P-3C.2—We shall provide staff members with safe and supportive working conditions that permit them to carry out their responsibilities, timely and non-threatening evaluation procedures, written grievance procedures, constructive feedback, and opportunities for continuing professional development and advancement.

P-3C.3—We shall develop and maintain comprehensive written personnel policies that define program standards, and when applicable, that specify the extent to which employees are accountable for their conduct outside the workplace. These policies shall be given to new staff members and shall be available for review by all staff members.

P-3C.4—Employees who do not meet program standards shall be informed of areas of concern and, when possible, assisted in improving their performance.

P-3C.5—Employees who are dismissed shall be informed of the reasons for their termination. When a dismissal is for cause, justification must be based on evidence of inadequate or inappropriate behavior that is accurately documented, current, and available for the employee to review.

P-3C.6—In making evaluations and recommendations, judgments shall be based on fact and relevant to the interests of children and programs.

P-3C.7—Hiring and promotion shall be based solely on a person's record of accomplishment and ability to carry out the responsibilities of the position.

P-3C.8—In hiring, promotion, and provision of training, we shall not participate in any form of discrimination based on race, ethnicity, religion, gender, national origin, culture, disability, age, or sexual preference. We shall be familiar with and observe laws and regulations that pertain to employment discrimination.

Section IV:

Ethical Responsibilities to Community and Society

Early childhood programs operate within a context of an immediate community made up of families and other institutions concerned with children's welfare. Our responsibilities to the community are to provide programs that meet its needs, to cooperate with agencies and professions that share responsibilities for children, and to develop needed programs that are not currently available. Because the larger society has a measure of responsibility for the welfare and protection of children, and because of our specialized expertise in child development, we acknowledge an obligation to serve as a voice for children everywhere.

Ideals

I-4.1—To provide the community with high-quality (age and individually appropriate, and culturally and socially sensitive) education/care programs and services.

I-4.2—To promote cooperation among agencies and interdisciplinary collaboration among professions concerned with the welfare of young children, their families, and their teachers.

I-4.3—To work, through education, research, and advocacy, toward an environmentally safe world in which all children receive adequate health care, food, and shelter, are nurtured, and live free from violence.

I-4.4—To work through education, research and advocacy toward a society in which all young children have access to high-quality education/care programs.

I-4.5—To promote knowledge and understanding of young children and their needs. To work toward greater social acknowledgement of children's rights and greater social acceptance of responsibility for their well-being.

I-4.6—To support policies and laws that promote the well-being of children and families, and to oppose those that impair their well-being. To participate in developing policies and laws that are needed, and to cooperate with other individuals and groups in these efforts.

I-4.7—To further the professional development of the field of early childhood care and education and to strengthen its commitment to realizing its core values as reflected in this Code.

Principles

P-4.1—We shall communicate openly and truthfully about the nature and extent of services that we provide.

P-4.2—We shall not accept or continue to work in positions for which we are personally unsuited or professionally unqualified. We shall not offer services that we do not have the competence, qualifications, or resources to provide.

P-4.3—We shall be objective and accurate in reporting the knowledge upon which we base our program practices.

P-4.4—We shall cooperate with other professionals who work with children and their families.

P-4.5—We shall not hire or recommend for employment any person whose competence, qualifications, or character makes him or her unsuited for the position.

P-4.6—We shall report the unethical or incompetent behavior of a colleague to a supervisor when informal resolution is not effective.

P-4.7—We shall be familiar with laws and regulations that serve to protect the children in our programs.

P-4.8—We shall not participate in practices which are in violation of laws and regulations that protect the children in our programs.

P-4.9—When we have evidence that an early childhood program is violating laws or regulations protecting children, we shall report it to persons responsible for the program. If compliance is not accomplished within a reasonable time, we will report the violation to appropriate authorities who can be expected to remedy the situation.

P-4.10—When we have evidence that an agency or a professional charged with providing services to children, families, or teachers is failing to meet its obligations, we acknowledge a collective ethical responsibility to report the problem to appropriate authorities or to the public.

P-4.11—When a program violates or requires its employees to violate this Code, it is permissible, after fair assessment of the evidence, to disclose the identity of that program.

Statement of Commitment

As an individual who works with young children, I commit myself to furthering the values of early childhood education as they are reflected in the NAEYC Code of Ethical Conduct.

To the best of my ability I will

- Ensure that programs for young children are based on current knowledge of child development and early childhood education.

- Respect and support families in their task of nurturing children.

- Respect colleagues in early childhood education and support them in maintaining the NAEYC Code of Ethical Conduct.

- Serve as an advocate for children, their families, and their teachers in community and society.

- Maintain high standards of professional conduct.

- Recognize how personal values, opinions, and biases can affect professional judgment.

- Be open to new ideas and be willing to learn from the suggestions of others.

- Continue to learn, grow, and contribute as a professional.

- Honor the ideals and principles of the NAEYC Code of Ethical Conduct.

Reprint of the NAEYC's brochure Code of Ethical Conduct and Statement of Commitment. *Washington, DC: National Association for the Education of Young Children, 1998.* Reprinted with permission.

Glossary

academic curriculum The objectives, procedures, and materials schools use to ensure children's acquisition of the knowledge and skills affirmed by the community.

academic learning The acquisition of knowledge and skills relating to subject-matter disciplines and organized fields of study.

academic rationalism Curriculum focused on education as the pursuit of knowledge in specified study fields and subject-matter disciplines to develop the rational mind.

acculturation Modification of an individual's cultural behavior patterns by another cultural group (usually the dominant group).

adoptive family A family unit with at least one legally adopted child.

advocacy The process of publicly supporting a group, person, or cause.

after-school care Care provided for working parents' children (usually 5–10 years of age) during after-school hours.

alternative insemination A method of conception by inserting gathered sperm into a woman's uterus to fertilize an egg. Also known as artificial or donor insemination.

alternative schools Schools organized with curricula different from and usually in reaction to conventional public school curricula.

assessment Evaluation or determination of the extent of learning or change in behavior.

associative level When parents and community members accept some responsibility for helping in a school program. (See **participatory level.**)

at-risk children (families) Children or families in danger of experiencing developmental gaps and problems due to poverty, abuse, illness, or social disturbance.

authentic assessment An assessment strategy based on group or individual needs and the kinds of activities undertaken.

authoritarian parenting style Baumrind's term for an autocratic, controlling, and somewhat detached method of raising children.

authoritative parenting style Baumrind's term for a receptive and somewhat democratic, though firm and in control, manner of raising children.

autonomy The ability of persons to regulate and determine their own behavior.

backup care Child care provided on an occasional basis when regular arrangements are not available (e.g., school is closed) or inappropriate (e.g., child is ill).

behavioral objectives Intentions of education stated in terms of observable actions.

behaviorism The belief that learning occurs because of a system of rewards, punishments, and reinforcements.

bidirectional process Process whereby the influence of genetics and environmental factors have equal importance for development.

bilingual education Teaching practices designed to encourage fluency in two languages.

bioecological theory Theory of development espoused by Bronfenbrenner that recognizes both biological (genetic) and ecological (environmental) factors as important aspects for explaining development.

biracial family Family in which the racial makeup of the parents is different. Some U.S families claim multiracial makeup because of past generations' biracial marriages.

blended family Two basic family units with children that join together to form a single family unit; often a remarriage, although some partners choose to forego wedlock.

bottom-up Practices and procedures designed to bring about changes or learning through local efforts or individuals' wishes.

center-based care (See **child care center.**)

charter school An authorized school designed to improve educational opportunities and supported but not regulated by a local or state authority.

child care   Programs provided for children whose parents work outside the home.

child care center   A facility providing care and educational programs for children from infancy to 5 years old.

child care providers   Adults who care for a group of children in family child care or a child care center.

child-centered curriculum   Teaching practices and materials focusing on children's interests, needs, and desires, with teachers responding to these interests by providing materials and guidance.

child-centered parenting   Practices focused on responding to the child's interests, needs, and desires.

code switching   The ability to move easily from one language or dialect to another.

cognitive process   A series of actions producing changes in learners' methods of thinking, organization of perceptions, and problem solving.

collaboration   Two or more persons or groups working together on joint endeavors for mutually determined objectives.

concrete operational thinking   The third stage of the Piagetian developmental theory (ages 7–11), characterized by the child's use of logical thought processes applied to real objects or events. At this stage, the child does not yet apply logic to abstract or hypothetical problems.

constructive play   Stage of play whereby children begin to build and create things.

constructivist curriculum   Curriculum based on the premise that the goal of education is for children to learn how to learn; when the individual is active in the learning process and is internally responding to outer stimuli.

cooperative learning   Group work and projects in which all members of the group share responsibility and rewards for the group's effort.

covert curriculum   The curriculum parents and teachers are unaware of. (See **hidden curriculum.**)

criterion-referenced test   Test designed to examine how well students have mastered a set of materials based on specified instructional goals and predetermined criteria.

critical periods of development   Erikson's label for periods of human development when positive

aspects of behavior need to be satisfied if development is to proceed in a positive manner.

cross-cultural   Involving features and objectives of more than on cultural group.

cultural background   The traditions, customs, knowledge, beliefs, art, mores, and regulations adhered to by a given group of people.

cultural deprivation   Formerly used to describe the problems of certain families and groups. The notion that individuals lacked certain skills for productive school learning as a result of gaps in cultural background.

cultural literacy   The corpus of knowledge of major historical and literary events that all literate persons should know to be considered "educated" by their culture.

cultural pluralism   The concept that all cultures have value and contribute to society.

cultural-context theories   Theories that include the cultural and social dimensions of children's lives, in addition to genetics and environment, as factors in development. Also referred to as social–cultural context.

custodial parent   The parent to whom a court assigns the primary responsibility of a child's care and upbringing.

day care   An older term for child care.

decision-making level   Parents, community members, and educators sharing equally in making decisions regarding school policy.

departmentalized program   School practices in which students are taught different academic subjects by specialists in these academic fields.

DISTAR   A curriculum designed by Bereiter and Englemann based on behavioral principles of instruction and learning.

drop-in child care   A place where parents may find child care services for brief periods of time and with flexible schedules.

dual-income family   A family where both parents or resident adults have income.

dysfunctional family situation   Abnormal, impaired, or incomplete functioning of the family unit.

Early Head Start   A component of the federal Head Start program that focuses on children younger than three and assists parents in improving their nurturing skills.

early-intervention service Service provided in natural environments to infants and toddlers at risk for developmental delays.

egg-box construction A popular school design of the 1950s and 1960s. The building resembled an egg box, with a central corridor and classrooms on either side.

elaborated language code Syntactically complex speech that requires persons one communicates with to use judgment, imagination, and reason to interpret ambiguities and abstractions.

embedded partner Person who is an integral part of a home, school, or community partnership.

employer-sponsored child care Child care that is provided for children of employees, generally at or nearby their workplace.

enculturation The process by which one learns the mores and habits of a particular cultural group.

ethnic orientation Relating to the complex set of characteristics and values, including national origin and linguistic, physical, and religious traits, by which a social group identifies itself.

ethnocentrism The process by which one concentrates and specializes in the values of one's own cultural milieu.

Even Start Federally funded home-based family literacy program requiring established links to the Head Start program.

exploratory play A type of play where children begin to expand their horizons and experiment.

extended community The area and population beyond the immediate neighborhood or local environment.

extended family The kin of the basic family unit who are economically dependent on and/or emotionally attached to the household.

faith-based organization Religious agency (usually a church) that includes educational and social help programs.

family Two or more persons living together and linked for emotional and economic support.

family child care Care provided to children in a home setting but outside of the child's own home.

family literacy program Approach to helping children learn to read and write by assisting parents in improving their skills so that they can help their children and improve their own prospects.

fixed curriculum The curriculum, often perceived to be mandated by local, state, and national education boards, that has been determined for a particular grade level.

formal community structure The organizations and agencies within a community that support services for that community.

formal curriculum The curriculum authorized by state and local education boards that is public, usually printed, and indicates the objectives, procedures, and materials for student learning.

foster children Children in the legal custody of a state office placed in an arranged living situation for a period of time.

foster family A family unit wherein adults offer support to children who are not related by blood or adoption.

gay and lesbian Persons with a sexual preference for some of their own sex. Gay is a generic term; lesbian refers specifically to women.

gender-appropriate behavior Qualities and behaviors a community or culture consider appropriate for female and male roles and actions.

general equivalency diploma (GED) Certification equal to a high school diploma but not granted by an accredited high school.

group norm Way in which most people in a group respond.

Head Start Comprehensive federally funded program for poor preschool children and their families. It is designed to provide health, nutritional, social, and educational experiences to compensate for the negative effects of poverty.

hidden curriculum Instructive events in a child's life that influence learning and attitude, often seen as hindering the stated goals of the school.

holistic evaluation Assessment based on examination of a child's total accomplishments and then synthesizing the judgments.

home care Care of children by someone other than the parents but provided in the child's home setting.

home curriculum   Learning that children acquire while under the influence of family members.

home schooling   The education of children undertaken completely by parents and done in the home environment.

homeless family   A family that chronically has no permanent place of residence and thus constantly moves from one place to another.

homophobia   Fear and rejection of same-sex partners and their lifestyles.

hyperactivity   Behavior characterized by excessive or abnormal body movements and high expenditure of energy.

immersion program   Program for language minority students whose education is basically in English but with some follow-up work in students' native language.

inclusion   Instruction for each child provided, preferably in a regular classroom, with support services from personnel most appropriate at that moment in the child's schedule.

individualized education program (IEP)   A program, mandated by law, developed by those responsible for the education of a child with special needs.

individualized family service plan (IFSP)   A written plan, mandated by law, that provides appropriate services for at-risk infants and toddlers and their families.

Individuals with Disabilities Education Act (IDEA)   Reauthorization and amendment of the 1975 Education for All Handicapped Students Act, which governs how students with disabilities are to be educated in today's schools.

industrial model   A model for educational practice based on the manner in which industry operates.

infant–toddler program   Program that offers a combination of play activities for infants and toddlers and parent education for the adults.

informal community structure   The personal relationships that families establish with members outside the home or extended family.

informal curriculum   The events, stimuli, and activities that children undertake outside classrooms and from which learning occurs.

in-home care   (See **home care**.)

interactionist–constructivist theory   Theory of learning (development) that maintains that through interacting with their environment, children begin to acquire a body of knowledge and understanding.

interactive portfolio   A student's work and materials collected in a folder or portfolio and that are shared with and commented on by parents and teachers.

interethnic family   A family unit that has more than one ethnic group represented in the unit. Blood parents may be of different groups, but children of different groups may be adopted by parents of a single group.

internal control   Self-determination guided by one's own behavior and actions. (See **locus of control**.)

interracial   A relationship where racial groups are combined, for example, interracial marriages.

itinerant family   A family unit that moves regularly, often following crop harvests or is engaged in other temporary work.

kinesthetic orientation   A manner of human functioning that best produces learning through the sensations of touch or body movement.

kinship adoption   Child adopted into a family related by blood or marriage.

kinship care   Care of children provided by close relatives.

latchkey child   Child of school age who returns after school to an empty house because all resident adults are at work.

learning modality   Consistent set of behaviors and performances by which an individual approaches tasks to be learned.

least restricted environment   Environment that suits the particular learning needs of children without constraining them.

linguistically diverse family   Family that speaks a language other than English.

literacy development   The process of acquiring meaning from signs and symbols and of transferring meaning to signs and symbols.

literacy event   Activity related to reading and writing that supports literacy development.

local educational authority (LEA) The agency with the obligation and right to oversee the education of children in its jurisdiction.

locus of control The perception one has of where responsibility for one's actions lie. May be internal or external.

lower working class That part of the population, usually consisting of unskilled laborers, which is less secure financially, at risk of unemployment, and at times receiving government assistance with basic living needs.

magnet school School organized around a particular focus, such as math or drama, and drawing students from a large area (metropolitan center or state).

mainstream Integrate special-needs children into the regular classroom. (See **inclusion**.)

marginalized family (children) Persons responsible for the welfare of families and children who are unable or unwilling to provide for basic needs and nurturance.

marginalized learner Child denied educational benefits due to environmental difficulties or problems in school, home, or community.

matriarchal A form of family organization in which the mother or eldest female is recognized as head of the family.

melting pot thesis Concept that a single culture will emerge if children are educated for one set of behavior patterns and beliefs.

mentor Person serving as guide or teacher to others on a one-to-one basis.

mesosystem Bronfenbrenner's label for the area of secondary importance in a child's life space—usually home and neighborhood.

metacognitive The process used in understanding how one gains knowledge.

microsystem Bronfenbrenner's label for the area of primary importance in a child's life space, such as the nuclear and extended family.

middle class That part of the population whose income falls within the median range for the whole. Professionals and businesspersons are often in this class.

migrant worker (See **itinerant family**.)

minimum level The minimal participation of parents and community members in school programs, for example, holding a bake sale.

monocultural Reflecting the beliefs, behavior patterns, and characteristics of a single cultural group.

mores Those rituals, traditions, customs, and behavior patterns seen as essential for a social group's survival and well-being.

mothers'-day-out programs Programs that offer children a few hours of supervised care so that their mothers may take time for themselves.

multicultural Association with and appreciation of the practices of different cultures, religions, and ethnic groups.

multicultural education Curriculum that is based on the inclusion and appreciation of the practices of different cultures, religions, and ethnic groups.

nanny care Care provided by a specially trained person to care for children in their homes. Au pair care is similar but refers to foreign students who care for young children in exchange for room and board.

National Council for the Accreditation of Teacher Education (NCATE) National organization that sets standards for and evaluates teacher education programs.

networking A system of making connections with individuals and groups that allows communication and involvement as a unit.

NICHH Acronym for the National Institute for Child Health and Human Development.

No Child Left Behind (NCLB) Congressional legislation adopted in 2001 to stimulate school performance.

norm-referenced testing Assessment whereby evaluation is based on comparison to a predetermined control group, often peers of the individual being tested.

nuclear family A family unit consisting of two parents and their biological and/or adopted children.

nursery school A program, usually private, designed for 2- to 5-year-olds. Often a half-day program, but may have a full-day schedule.

nurturance (See **nurturing practice**.)

nurturing practice The process of raising and promoting the development of children.

open door policy A school policy that suggests to parents that they are always welcome in the school and classroom.

open-space buildings School buildings with large open spaces, or "pods," in which several teachers organize the space to fit the needs of their particular students.

out-of-home care Regular care provided to young children outside of the home setting.

paradigm A pattern, example, or model.

parent center A specific location, usually within a school, where parents can work and socialize and feel they are a part of the school.

parent cooperative Private nursery school or preschool program where parents share both the teaching and administrative decision making.

parent cooperative nursery school (See **parent cooperative**.)

parent education Courses, workshops, and reading materials designed to assist parents in improving their nurturing skills.

parent empowerment A process whereby parents become decision makers, often in collaboration with school personnel, for the education of their children.

participatory level The second level of involvement for parents in school partnerships whereby they cooperate and work as volunteers and helpers. (See **associative level**.)

partnerships Relationship among different groups in which each group has equal influence on decision making.

patriarchal A form of family organization in which the father or eldest male is recognized as head of the family.

peer group People of similar race, ethnicity, age, social status, or other trait.

perceptual field The human range of recognition and organization of sensory input.

perinatal The period of life just before and shortly after birth.

peripheral participation Observation of an activity without active participation in it.

permissive parenting style Baumrind's term for a manner of raising children that is nondemanding and noncontrolling and that allows children to develop according to their natural instincts.

personal relevance curriculum Curriculum based on the belief that the goal of education is to support personally satisfying experiences for each student.

person-oriented family A family unit focused on the development of individual children.

phonics The letter–sound relationships of a language.

play-oriented curriculum Curriculum for children that emphasizes the belief that children learn as they play with materials and others.

play school or group Program designed, usually for toddlers, to focus on the importance of children engaging in play as a means of enhancing development.

position-oriented family Manner of family functioning that is present oriented and object oriented and that assigns roles according to position in the family.

postmodern family Family of today that views parenting as a shared responsibility of father, mother, and care provider.

postnuclear family units Family units that vary from the traditional mother–father–child units.

power brokers Members of a community or group with enough influence and power to become major decision makers for that community or group.

preoperational thinking The second stage of Piagetian developmental theory (ages 2–7), characterized by symbolic functions. The child moves from functioning as a result of sensorimotor stimuli to developing the ability to internally represent events and act on this memory.

Project Follow Through U.S.-government-sponsored program that supports students after Head Start programs through kindergarten and the primary grades. (See **Head Start**.)

project-oriented curriculum A curriculum of study that uses themes or projects as a means of presenting content and concepts.

proof of equivalency A requirement that home schoolers have proof that the education they provide for their children is equivalent to what children would receive in the formal school.

resilient child   Child demonstrating the ability to cope and manage in spite of debilitating environmental circumstances.

resources and referral programs   Community agencies that support the development and improvement of child care and assist parents in finding appropriate and affordable care for their children.

resource file   A professional's organized collection of plans, materials, and equipment to supplement units, projects, and daily activities.

restricted language code   A manner of speaking that is syntactically simple and direct and that has concrete meanings.

role expectation   Behavioral expectation for an individual depending on status or function within the family, peer group, school, or community.

Scholastic Aptitude Test (SAT)   Norm-referenced exam for high school students. Often used by colleges and scholarship boards to determine the ability for advanced study.

school-identified disability   Learning difficulty or problem identified after a child enters school.

scope and sequence chart   List of important skills for children's achievement, arranged on two dimensions: (1) the broad extent of the skill, (2) the order in which a skill or set of related skills is learned.

secular education   Education in which there is no religious or spiritual training.

secular humanism   Belief that the goals of education are to develop children's sense of personal growth, integrity, and autonomy but should not encompass the religious or spiritual part of the person.

self-fulfilling prophecy   The concept that expectations of others shape and reinforce one's behavior such that the expectations are eventually met. Also known as the Pygmalion effect.

sensory mode   The manner of receiving information through the five senses.

service agency   Organization within a community that provide the health, educational, transportation, protection, and communication services necessary to the community's citizens.

SES   Acronym for socioeconomic status.

sexism   Prejudice based on gender.

sexual energy   Freudian concept that human behavior and energy is derived from the primal sex drive.

significant other (adult)   The person in a child's life who is particularly important to the child. This relationship exists independently of any biological or formal social relationship between child and adult.

single-parent family   A family unit consisting of one parent, either mother or father, and children, and no other adults.

site-based management   A procedure for managing schools in which organizational and educational decisions for children at a particular school should be made by persons at that school.

skill ladder   Child's systematic and sequential steps in acquiring a level of proficiency in an area of study.

social agencies   Broad grouping of community offices and institutions that administer human services, governmental benefits, or counseling. (See **service agencies.**)

social capital   The amount of human connections and relationships resulting in learning.

social climate   The attitudes, feelings, and relationships that people within a community maintain toward one another.

social network   Parallel relationships developed among individuals in a community that foster communication and a sense of belonging.

social reconstructionist curriculum   Curriculum based on the thesis that the goals of education are to effect social change. Students learn social needs and values and how to use these concepts in critical thought processes.

social setting   A place, such as a home, a school, or a community, where interactive events between or among individuals happen naturally.

socialization skill   The acquired ability to interact within the norms, values, and mores of a social group.

socioeconomic factors   The social relationships and financial developments that exist in a family or community.

socioeconomic status (SES) The economic and social level to which one belongs because of wealth, occupation, and educational background.

special-interest group Group with a narrow purpose or agenda organized to influence others to accept their point of view.

sponsored independence parenting style Clark's term, similar to Baumrind's *authoritative style,* describing a manner of raising children. Indicates a rational, receptive, and warm but demanding style.

stage of development Distinct step in the growth process that individuals pass through from infancy through adulthood.

stakeholder Person who stands to gain or profit from selected activities and programs in a school or community.

standardized test Test with scientifically chosen items, given under similar conditions, that enable persons to be compared to a group standard. Tests may be either criterion referenced or norm referenced.

Structural English Immersion (SEI) Program where bilingual children are taught all subjects in English, receiving special English-language assistance as needed and using their own language only to clarify concepts.

subfamily A family cluster living with other adults or families in which the parent in the cluster is not the central figure in the household.

subsidized child care Care supported by government funding for families with financial need.

surrogate parent program Informal or formal arrangement that places children in the care of relatives, agencies, or organizations, for example, big brother/big sister programs, foster care.

technological intelligence Those parts of human intelligence related to literacy and numeracy skills.

technologist curriculum A curriculum based on the notion that the primary goal of education is for students to master the basic skills of reading and computing in order to function in present society.

theme-focused program A phase of curriculum, based on a particular theme, wherein important objectives are identified and activities are prepared so that students acquire knowledge and skills relating to that theme.

three-group rotation A technique for schooling that organizes a class of children into three groups and then rotates groups throughout the day into different learning centers or events.

time on task The actual amount of time a student is engaged in or attending to a particular assigned task.

Title I school School where students meet the poverty guidelines developed under Title I legislation.

top-down practice Procedure designed to didactically bring about changes or learning. Typically, changes are initiated at the administrative or supervisory level and imposed on groups, classrooms, or schools.

traditional curriculum Curriculum based on the notion that the objective of education is for students to acquire knowledge in subject-matter disciplines and specified fields of study. Similar to **academic curriculum.**

transactional process of development The process whereby multiple facets of the environment (people, objects, symbols) unleash the child's genetic potential to produce varied behaviors. Children's reactions and behaviors in turn affect new actions or movements from the environment.

transcultural Extending across cultures or involving more than one culture.

transracial Encompassing the physical features or interests of two or more races.

underclass The part of the population limited in opportunity and resources and locked into a cycle of poverty and despair.

unit of study Part of a curriculum based on a particular theme, around which learning activities are organized. Similar to **theme-focused program.**

unstructured learning Learning resulting from incidental and self-selected experiences in which children become interested and involved.

upper class The most economically advantaged group of a population; often wealth is inherited.

upper working class The population group represented by skilled laborers who are financially able to cope but severely affected by economic depressions.

voucher plan   Plan whereby parents receive certificates indicating the financial support for their children's education. Parents have the right to select a school and use the certificate to pay the cost of education.

War on Poverty   President Lyndon B. Johnson's War on Poverty became the by-word for legislation aimed at helping disadvantaged populations overcome the effects of poverty.

welfare reform measures   (See **welfare to work program.**)

welfare to work program   Welfare Reform Act of 1996 requiring welfare parents to seek education and employment or lose benefits.

well-baby clinic   Health clinic or hospital program where parents can, without cost, bring their children for regular checkups and discussions regarding ways to provide a healthy environment.

whole-language program   Curriculum practice emphasizing the totality of language, presuming that children should learn to read the same way they learn to speak, that is, holistically with respect to their environment. Reading, writing, speaking, and listening are all aspects of language learned in conjunction with all experiences.

Woman, Infants, and Children (WIC)   Federally funded program to supply nutritional and health support for lower income families or families on welfare.

writing-to-read   A strategy for teaching reading in combination with teaching writing.

zone of proximal development   Vygotsky's label for the distance between a child's ability to perform a task independently and his or her ability to perform it under guidance.

References

Adams, D. B. (2001). The quest for quality child care. In J. C. Westman (Ed.), *Parenthood in America: Undervalued, underpaid, under siege* (pp. 150–157). Madison: University of Wisconsin Press.

Adams, M. J. (1994). *Beginning to read: Thinking and learning about print.* Cambridge, MA: MIT Press.

Adelman, H. S., & Taylor, L. (2002). Building comprehensive multifaceted and integrated approaches to address barriers to student learning. *Childhood Education, 78*(5), 261–273.

Afterschool Alliance. (2002). *Afterschool alliance poll.* Retrieved August 10, 2003, from www.afterschoolalliance.org

Alexander. A. (2001). The meaning of television in the American family. In J. Bryant & J. A. Bryant (Eds.), *Television and the American family* (2nd ed., pp. 273–287). Mahwah, NJ: Erlbaum.

Allen, K. R., Fine, M. A., & Demo, D. H. (2000). An overview of family diversity: Controversies, questions and values. In D. Demo, K. Allen, & M. Fine (Eds.), *Handbook of family diversity* (pp. 1–14). New York: Oxford University Press.

Althouse, R., Johnson, M. H., & Mitchell, S. T. (2003). *The colors of learning: Integrating the visual arts into the early childhood curriculum.* Washington, DC: National Association for the Education of Young Children.

American Academy of Pediatrics, Task Force on Children and Television. (1990). *Children, adolescents and television.* Elk Grove Village, IL: Author.

American Anthropological Association. (2002). *AAA statement on race.* Retrieved August 30, 2003, from http://www.aaanet.org/stmts/racepp.htm

American Association of School Administrators. (1986). *Religion in the public schools.* Arlington, VA: Author.

American Civil Liberties Union. (1995). *Religion in the public schools: A joint statement of current laws.* New York: Author.

AmeriStat. (2003). *Bilingual instruction.* Retrieved August 30, 2003, from www.ameristat.org

An Ounce of Prevention Fund. (1994). *Head start on Head Start: An Ounce of Prevention Fund paper.* Chicago: Author. (ERIC Document Reproduction Service No. ED368475)

Anderson, C. (2003). The diversity, strength, and challenges of single-parent households. In F. Walsh (Ed.), *Normal family processes: Growing diversity and complexity* (3rd ed., pp. 121–152). New York: Guilford Press.

Anderson, J. W. (1972). Attachment behavior out of doors. In N. Blurton Jones (Ed.), *Ethological studies of child behavior* (pp. 199–225). New York: Cambridge University Press.

Anderson, K. J., & Cavallaro, K. (2002). Parents or pop culture? Children's heroes and role models. *Childhood Education, 78*(3), 161–168.

Anderson, M. T. (2002). *Feed.* Cambridge, MA: Candlewick Press.

Andreasen, M. (2001). Evolution in the family's use of television: An Overview. In J. Bryant & J. A. Bryant (Eds.), *Television and the American family* (2nd ed., pp. 3–30). Mahwah, NJ: Erlbaum.

Annie E. Casey Foundation. (2002). *Kids Count data book: State profiles of child well-being.* Baltimore: Author. Also retrieved September 2003 from http://www.Kidscount.org

Apple, M. W. (1995). *Education and power* (2nd ed.). New York: Routledge.

Applebee, A. N. (1989). *Child's concept of story. Ages 2–17.* Chicago: University of Chicago Press.

Applebee, A. N. (1996). *Curriculum as conversation.* Chicago: University of Chicago Press.

Arce, E. (1999). Family-centered communities benefit young children: What policies enhance the developing child? In E. Arce (Ed.), *Perspectives: Early childhood education* (pp. 136–137). Boulder, CO: Coursewise.

Arendell, T. (1997). A social constructionist approach to parenting. In T. Arendell (Ed.),

Contemporary parenting: Challenges and issues: Vol. 9. Understanding families (pp. 1–45). Thousand Oaks, CA: Sage.

Aronson, S. (2002). *Healthy young children: A manual for programs.* Washington, DC: National Association for the Education of Young Children.

Bailyn, B., Dalleck, R., Davis, D., Donald, D., Thomas, J., & Wood, G. S. (2000). *The great republic: A history of the American people* (6th ed.). Lexington, MA: Heath.

Baker, K. (1998). Structural English immersion: Breakthrough in teaching limited English proficient students. *Phi Delta Kappan, 80,* 199–204.

Ball, S., & Bogatz, G. (1970). *The first year of Sesame Street: An evaluation.* Princeton, NJ: Educational Testing Service.

Banks, J. A. (1996). *Multicultural education, transformative knowledge, and action: Historical and contemporary perspectives.* New York: Teachers College Press.

Banks, J. A. (1998). *An introduction to multicultural education* (2nd ed.). Boston: Allyn & Bacon.

Banks, J. A. (2002). *Teaching strategies for ethnic studies* (7th ed.). Boston: Allyn & Bacon.

Barbour, C., Barbour, N., & Hildebrand, J. (2001, April). *Building a grandparent curriculum.* Paper presented at the conference of the Association for Childhood Education International, Toronto, Ontario, Canada.

Barbour, N. H., & Seefeldt, C. (1993). *Developmental continuity across preschool and primary grades.* Wheaton, MD: Association for Childhood Education International.

Barfield, R. (2002). *Real-life homeschooling.* New York: Fireside.

Barker, P. (1990). The home schooled teenager grows up. In A. Pedersen & P. O'Mara (Eds.), *Schooling at home: Parents, kids, and learning* (pp. 203–208). Santa Fe, NM: Muir.

Bartolome, L. I., & Macedo, D. P. (1997). Dancing with bigotry: The poisoning of racial and ethnic identities. *Harvard Educational Review, 67*(2), 222–246.

Baumrind, D. (1966). Effects of authoritative parental control on child behavior. *Child Development, 37,* 387–407.

Baumrind, D. (1968). Authoritarian vs. authoritative parental control. *Adolescence, 3,* 255–272.

Baumrind, D. (1971). Current patterns of parental authority. *Developmental Psychology Monograph, 75,* 43–88.

Baumrind, D. (1995). *Child maltreatment and optimal caregiving in social contexts.* New York: Garland.

Beaty, J. J. (2002). *Observing development of the young child.* Upper Saddle River, NJ: Merrill/Prentice Hall.

Bennett, W. (1998). *A nation still at risk* (Policy Review No. 90, pp. 23–29). Washington, DC: U.S. Department of Education.

Benson, P. (1997). *All kids are our kids.* San Francisco: Jossey-Bass.

Bergen, D., Reid, R., & Torelli, L. (2001). *Educating and caring for very young children: The infant/toddler curriculum.* New York: Teachers College Press.

Berger, E. H. (2000). *Parents as partners in education: Families and schools working together* (4th ed.). Englewood Cliffs, NJ: Merrill/Prentice Hall.

Berlin, I. (1998). *Many thousands gone: The first two centuries of slavery in North America.* Cambridge, MA: Belknap/Harvard University Press.

Berndt, T. J., & Ladd, G. W. (1989). *Peer relationships in child development.* New York: Wiley.

Berndt, T. J., & Murphy, L. M. (2002). Influences of friends and friendships: Myths, truths, and research recommendations. *Advances in Child Development and Behavior, 30,* 275–310.

Berns, R. M. (2001). *Child, family, school, community: Socialization and support* (5th ed.). Fort Worth, TX: Harcourt.

Bernstein, B. (1972). A sociolinguistic approach to socialization with some reference to educability. In J. Gumperz & D. Hymes (Eds.), *Directions in sociolinguistics* (pp. 465–497). New York: Holt, Rinehart & Winston.

Bettelheim, B. (1976). *The uses of enchantment.* New York: Knopf.

Bianchi, S. M., & Casper, L. M. (2000). American families. *Population Bulletin, 55*(4), 3–43.

Bianchi, S. M., & Spain, D. (1996). Women, work and family in America. *Population Bulletin, 47*(2), 2–47.

Bigner, J. J. (2002). *Parent–child relations: An introduction to parenting* (6th ed.). Upper Saddle River, NJ: Merrill/Prentice Hall.

Bjork, C. (1987). *Linnea in Monet's garden.* New York: Farrar, Straus & Giroux.

Black, J. K., & Puckett, M. B. (2001). *The young child: Development from prebirth through age eight* (3rd ed.). Upper Saddle River, NJ: Merrill/Prentice Hall.

Blank, H. (1997). Child care in the context of welfare reform. In S. B. Kamerman & A. J. Kahn (Eds.), *Child care in the context of welfare "reform"* (pp. 1–44). New York: Columbia University School of Social Work, Cross-National Studies Research Program.

Bloom, B. S., Englehart, M. D., Furst, E. J., Hill, W. H., & Krathwohl, D. R. (1956). *Taxonomy of educational objectives: Handbook I. Cognitive domain.* New York: McKay.

Bloom, J. (1992). *Parenting our schools: A hands-on guide to education reform.* Boston: Little, Brown.

Bond, J. T., Galinsky, E., & Swanberg, J. (1997). *The 1997 national study of the changing workforce.* New York: Families and Work Institute.

Borkowski, J. G., Ramey, S. L., & Stile, C. (2002). Parenting research: Translations to parenting practices. In J. G. Borkowski, S. L. Ramey, & M. Bristol-Power (Eds.), *Parenting and the child's world* (pp. 365–386). Mahwah, NJ: Erlbaum.

Bornstein, M. H. (2001). Refocusing on parenthood. In J. C. Westman (Ed.), *Parenthood in America: Undervalued, underpaid, under siege* (pp. 5–20). Madison: University of Wisconsin Press.

Bornstein, M. H. (2002). Parenting infants. In M. H. Bornstein (Ed.), *Handbook of parenting: Vol. 1. Children and parenting* (2nd ed., pp. 3–43). Mahwah, NJ: Erlbaum.

Bossard, J., & Boll, E. (1949). Ritual in family living. *American Sociological Review, 14,* 526–530.

Boyd-Franklin, N. (2003). Race, class, and poverty. In F. Walsh (Ed.), *Normal family processes: Growing diversity and complexity* (3rd ed., pp. 260–279). New York: Guilford.

Bradley, R. H. (2002). Environments and parenting. In M. H. Bornstein (Ed.), *Handbook of parenting: Vol. 2. Biology and ecology of parenting* (2nd ed., pp. 281–314). Mahwah, NJ: Erlbaum.

Brazelton, T. B., & Greenspan, S. I. (2000). *The irreducible needs of children: What every child must have to grow, learn, and flourish.* Cambridge, MA: Perseus.

Bredekamp, S., & Copple, C. (Eds.). (1997). *Developmentally appropriate practice in early childhood programs* (Rev. ed). Washington, DC: National Association for the Education of Young Children.

Bredekamp, S., & Rosegrant, T. (1995). *Reaching potential: Appropriate curriculum and assessment for young children* (Vol. 2). Washington, DC: National Association of the Education for Young Children.

Bronfenbrenner, U. (1979). *The ecology of human development: Experiment by nature and design.* Cambridge, MA: Harvard University Press.

Bronfenbrenner, U. (1986). Ecology of the family as a context of human development: Research perspectives. *Developmental Psychology, 22,* 723–742.

Bronfenbrenner, U. (1993). The ecology of cognitive development: Research models and fugitive findings. In R. H. Wozniak & K. W. Fisher (Eds.), *Development in context: Activity and thinking in specific environments* (pp. 3–24). Hillsdale, NJ: Erlbaum.

Bronfenbrenner, U. (1995). Developmental ecology through space and time: A future perspective. In P. Moen, G. H. Elder, & K. Luscher (Eds.), *Examining lives in context* (pp. 619–648). Washington, DC: American Psychological Association.

Bronfenbrenner, U. (2001). Growing chaos in the lives of children, youth and families: How can we turn it around? In J. Westman (Ed.), *Parenthood in America: Undervalued, underpaid, under siege* (pp. 197—210). Madison: University of Wisconsin Press.

Bronfenbrenner, U., & Crouter, A. (1982). Work and family through time and space. In S. B. Kammerman & C. D. Hayes (Eds.), *Families that work: Children in a changing world* (pp. 39–83). Washington, DC: National Academy Press.

Bronfenbrenner, U., Moen, P., & Garbarino, J. (1984). Child, family, and community. In R. D. Parke (Ed.), *Review of child development research: Vol. 7. The family* (pp. 283–328). Chicago: University of Chicago Press.

Bronfenbrenner, U., & Weiss, H. (1983). *Beyond policies without people: An ecological perspective on child and family policy.* New York: Cambridge University Press.

Brooks, S. (2003). *Invisible children in the society and its schools* (2nd ed.). Mahwah, NJ: Erlbaum.

Brouillette, L. (2002). *Charter schools: Lessons in school reform.* Mahwah, NJ: Erlbaum.

Bruer, J. T. (1998). Brain science: Brain fiction. *Educational Leadership, 56*(3), 8–18.

Bruer, J. T. (1999). *The myth of the first three years: A new understanding of early brain development and life-long learning.* New York: Free Press.

Bruer, J. T. (2002, October). *A rational approach to education: Integrating behavioral, cognitive, and brain science.* Address at Oxford University, Oxford, England.

Buchwald, A. (1994). *Leaving home: A memoir.* New York: Putnam.

Bullivant, B. M. (1993). Culture: Its nature and meaning for educators. In J. A. Banks & C. A. McGee-Banks (Eds.), *Multicultural education: Issues and perspectives* (2nd ed., pp. 29–47). Boston: Allyn & Bacon.

Bullock, H. A. (1967). *A history of Negro education in the South from 1619 to the present.* Cambridge, MA: Harvard University Press.

Burnette, S. (1998). Book'em! Cops and librarians working together. *American Libraries, 29*(2), 48–50.

Burtless, G., & Smeeding, T. M. (2001). The level, trend and composition of poverty. In S. H. Danziger & R. H. Haverman (Eds.), *Understanding poverty* (pp. 27–68). New York: Russell Sage Foundation.

Bus, A. G., & Van Ijzendoorn, M. H. (1995). Mothers reading to their 3-year-olds. The role of mother–child attachment security in becoming literate. *Reading Research Journal Quarterly, 30*, 998–1014.

Bushman, B. J., & Huesman, L. R. (2001). Effects of televised violence on aggression. In D. G. Singer & J. L. Singer (Eds.), *Handbook of children and the media* (pp. 255–268). Thousand Oaks, CA: Sage.

Butler, R. D. (1976). Black children's racial preference: A selected review of literature. *Journal of Afro-American Issues, 4*(2), 168–171.

Cadwell, L. (2003). *Bringing learning to life: The Reggio approach to early childhood education.* New York: Teachers College Press.

Calfee, C., Wittwer, F., & Meredith, M. (1998). *Building full-service schools.* San Francisco: Jossey-Bass.

Campbell, F. A., & Ramey, C. T. (1995) Cognitive and school outcomes for high-risk African American students in middle adolescence: Positive effects of early intervention. *American Educational Research Journal, 32*, 743–772.

Carnegie Corporation. (1994). *Starting points. Meeting the needs of our youngest.* New York: Author. Also retrieved August 10, 2003, from http://www.carnegie.org/starting_points/startpt1.html

Carnegie Forum on Education and the Economy. (1986). *A nation prepared: Teachers for the 21st century.* New York: Carnegie Corporation.

Carper, J. C. (2000). Pluralism to establishment to dissent: The religious and educational context of home schooling. *Peabody Journal of Education, 75*(1), 8–19.

Carter, D. A. (1993). Community and parent involvement: A road to school improvement. *ERS Spectrum, 11*(1), 39–45.

Casper, L. M., & Bianchi, S. M. (2002). *Continuity and change in the American family.* Thousand Oaks, CA: Sage.

Cassebaum, A. (2003). Revisiting Summerhill. *Phi Delta Kappan, 84*, 575–578.

Ceci, S. J., & Hembrooke, H. A. (1995). A bioecological model of intellectual development. In P. Moen, G. Elder, & K. Luscher (Eds.), *Examining lives in context. Perspective on the ecology of human development* (pp. 303–306). Washington, DC: American Psychological Association.

Center for Education Reform. (2003a). *Charter report flawed: California Research Group offers baseless criticism* [Press release]. Retrieved August 12, 2003, from http://edreform.com/press/2003/pace.htm

Center for Education Reform. (2003b). *National charter school directory* (3rd ed.). Washington, DC: Author. Also retrieved August 12, 2003, from www.edreform.com

Cherlin, A. J., & Furstenberg, F. (1992). *The new American grandparent: A place in the family, a place apart.* Cambridge, MA: Harvard University Press.

Cherry, L. (1982). *A river ran wild.* San Diego, CA: Harcourt Brace.

Child Welfare League of America. (2003). *Family foster care fact sheet.* Retrieved June 11, 2003, from www.cwla.org.

Children's Defense Fund. (1997). *Key facts about child care and early education: A briefing book.* Washington, DC: Author.

Children's Defense Fund. (1998). *The state of America's children: A report from the Children's Defense Fund.* Boston: Beacon Press.

Children's Defense Fund. (2001). *The state of America's children: A report from the Children's Defense Fund.* Washington, DC: Author.

Children's Foundation. (2003). *2003 family child care licensing study.* Washington, DC: Author.

Children's Online Privacy Act (2000). Washington, DC: U.S. Government Printing Office.

Chrisman, K., & Couchenour, D. (2002). *Healthy sexuality development: A guide for early childhood educators and families.* Washington, DC: National Association for the Education of Young Children.

Christie, J., Enz, B., & Vukelich, C. (2003). *Teaching language and literacy: Preschool through the elementary grades* (2nd ed.). Boston: Allyn & Bacon.

Clark, R. M. (1983). *Family life and school achievement: Why poor Black children succeed or fail.* Chicago: University of Chicago Press.

Clarke-Stewart, K. A. (1993). *Daycare* (Rev. ed.). Cambridge, MA: Harvard University Press.

Clarke-Stewart, K. A., Allhusen, V. D., & Clements, D. C. (1995). Nonparenting caregiving. In M. H. Bornstein (Ed.), *Handbook of parenting: Vol. 3. Status and social conditions of parenting* (pp. 141–175). Mahwah, NJ: Erlbaum.

Clawson, B. (1992). Preparing for successful children. In L. Kaplan (Ed.), *Education and the family* (pp. xix–xxii). Boston: Allyn & Bacon.

Clay, J. W. (1990). Working with lesbian and gay parents and their children. *Young Children, 45*(3), 31–35.

Clay, M. M. (1991). *Becoming literate: The construction of inner control.* Portsmouth, NH: Heinemann.

Cleveland, G., & Krashinsky, M. (1998). *The benefits and costs of good child care: The economic rationale for public investment in young children.* Toronto, Ontario, Canada: University of Toronto, Centre for Urban and Community Studies, Child Care Resource and Research Unit.

Cloud, N., Landurand, P., & Wu, S. T. (1989). *Multisystems systematic instructional planning for exceptional bilingual students* (Gov. Doc. 1:310–2:396–485). Washington, DC: U.S. Department of Education, Office of Educational Research and Improvement.

Cochran, M., & Davila, V. (1992). Societal influences on children's peer relationships. In R. D. Parke & G. W. Ladd (Eds.), *Family-peer relationships: Modes of linkage* (pp. 191–214) Hillsdale, NJ: Erlbaum.

Cochran, M., & Niegro, S. (2002). Parenting and social networks. In M. H. Bornstein (Ed.), *Handbook of parenting: Vol. 4. Social conditions and applied parenting* (2nd ed., pp. 123–148). Mahwah, NJ: Erlbaum.

Cochran, M., & Riley, D. (1990). The social networks of six-year-olds: Context, content, and consequence. In M. Cochran, M. Larner, D. Riley, L. Gunnarsson, & C. R. Henderson, Jr. (Eds.), *Extending families: The social networks of parents and their children* (pp. 154–179). New York: Cambridge University Press.

Cohen, S. (1974). *A history of colonial education, 1607–1776.* New York: Wiley.

Cohen, S. (2001). *Championing child care.* New York: Columbia University Press.

Coleman, J. S. (1966). *Equality of educational opportunity.* Washington, DC: U.S. Government Printing Office.

Coleman, J. S. (1990). *Foundations of social theory.* Cambridge, MA: Harvard University Press.

Coleman, J. S. (1991). *Policy perspectives: Parental involvement in education.* Washington, DC: U.S. Department of Education, Office of Educational Research and Improvement.

Coleman, J. S. (1996). *Parents, their children and schools.* Boulder, CO: Westview.

Coles, R. (1997). *The moral intelligence of children.* New York: Random House.

Coles, R. (2003). *Children of crisis.* Boston: Back Bay Books/Little, Brown.

Coles, R., Testa, R., & Coles, M. (Eds). (2001). *Growing up poor.* New York: New Press.

Colfax, J. D., & Colfax, M. (1992). *Hard times in paradise.* New York: Warren.

Collins, R. C. (1984, April). *Head Start: A review of research with implications for practice in early childhood education.* Paper presented at the annual meeting of the American Educational Research Association, New Orleans, LA. (ERIC Document Reproduction Service No. ED245833)

Comer, J. P. (1980). *School power: Implications of an intervention project.* New York: Free Press.

Comer, J. P. (1988). *Maggie's American dream: The life and times of a Black family.* New York: New American Library.

Comer, J. P. (1997). *Waiting for a miracle: Why schools can't solve our problems and how we can.* New York: Penguin Putnam.

Comer, J. P., Ben-Avie, M., Haynes, N., & Joyner, E. T. (Eds.). (1999). *Child by child: The Comer process for change in education.* New York: Teachers College Press.

Comer, J. P., & Haynes, N. M. (1991). Parent involvement in schools: An ecological approach. *Elementary School Journal, 91,* 271–277.

Comer, J. P., Haynes, N. M., & Joyner, E. T. (1996). The School Development Program. In J. P. Comer, N. M. Haynes, E. T. Joyner, & M. Ben-Avie (Eds.), *Rallying the whole village: The Comer process for reforming education* (pp. 1–27). New York: Teachers College Press.

Community Update. (2002, July/August). *Secretary Paige focuses on supplemental services.* Retrieved August 16, 2003, from www.NoChildLeftBehind.gov

Cook, T., Appleton, H., Conner, R., Shaffer, A., Tamkin, G., & Weber, S. (1975). *"Sesame Street" revisited.* New York: Russell Sage Foundation.

Coontz, S. (1997). *The way we really are: Coming to terms with America's changing families.* New York: Basic Books.

Coontz, S. (1999). Introduction. In S. Coontz (Ed.), *American families: A multicultural reader* (pp. ix–xxxii). New York: Routledge.

Corliss, J. C. (1998). *Crossing borders with literature of diversity.* Norwood, MA: Gordon.

Cornell, C. E. (1993). Language and culture monsters that lurk in our traditional rhymes and folktales. *Young Children, 48*(6), 40–46.

Cowan, P. A., & Cowan, C. P. (2003). Normative family transitions, normal family process, and healthy child development. In F. Walsh (Ed.), *Normal family processes: Growing diversity and complexity* (pp. 424–459). New York: Guilford.

Cremin, L. A. (1961). *The transformation of the school: Progressivism in American education, 1876–1957.* New York: Knopf.

Cremin, L. A. (1982). *American education: The national experience, 1783–1876.* New York: Harper & Row.

Cross, W. E. (1987). Black identity: Rediscovering the distinction between personal identity and reference group orientation. In M. B. Spencer, G. Brookins, & W. Allen (Eds.), *Beginnings: The social and affective development of Black children* (pp. 155–171). Mahwah, NJ: Erlbaum.

Cruickshank, D. (1990). *Research that informs teachers and teacher educators.* Bloomington, IN: Phi Delta Kappa Educational Foundation.

Cruickshank, D. R., Jenkins, D. B., & Metcalf, K. K. (2002). *The act of teaching* (3rd ed.). New York: McGraw-Hill.

Cryer, D., & Clifford, R. M. (Eds.). (2003). *Early childhood education and care in the USA.* Baltimore: Brookes.

Culatta, R. A., & Tompkins, J. R. (1999). *Fundamentals of special education.* Upper Saddle River, NJ: Merrill.

Curran, D. (1983). *Traits of a healthy family.* Minneapolis, MN: Winston.

Curry, J. 1999. *The initial impact of Proposition 227.* Davis, CA: University of Linguistic Minority Institute.

Cutler, W. W. (2000). *Parents and schools: The 150-year struggle for control in American education.* Chicago: University of Chicago Press.

Dahlberg, G., Moss, P., & Pence, A. (1999). *Beyond quality in early childhood and care: Postmodern perspectives.* London: Falmer.

Damon, W. (1988). *The moral child: Nurturing children's natural moral growth.* New York: Free Press.

Daniels, E. (2002). *Family literacy parties.* Washington, DC: Children's Resources International.

Danzberger, J. P., & Gruskin, S. J. (1993). *Project abstracts: Educational Partnerships Program. Programs for the improvement of practice.* Washington, DC: Office of Educational Research and Improvement.

D'Arcangelo, M. (2003). On the mind of a child: A conversation with Sally Shaywitz. *Educational Leadership, 60*(7) 6–10.

Dash, J. (1992). *Daughters of the dust*. New York: New Press.

Dash, L. (1996). *Rosa Lee: A mother and her family in urban America*. New York: Basic Books.

Davies, D. (1993). Looking backward. In S. Thompson (Ed.), *Whole child, whole community* (pp. 67–72). Boston: Institute for Responsive Education.

Davies, D., Burch, P., & Palanki, A. (1993). *Fitting policy to family needs: Delivering comprehensive services through collaboration and family empowerment*. Boston: Center on Families, Communities, Schools, and Children's Learning.

Davies, D., Palanki, A., & Burch, P. (1993). The whole school for the whole child. In S. Thompson (Ed.), *Whole child, whole community* (pp. 18–23). Boston: Institute for Responsive Education.

De Carvalho, M. E. P. (2001). *Rethinking family–school relations: A critique of parental involvement in schooling*. Mahwah, NJ: Erlbaum.

Deckard, S. (1996). *Home schooling laws and resource guide for all fifty states* (9th ed). Ramona, CA: Vision.

Deiner, P. L. (1997). *Infants and toddlers: Development and program planning*. New York: Harcourt Brace.

Demarris, K. P., & LeCompte, M. D. (1998). *How schools work: A sociological analysis of education*. New York: Longman.

Desmond. R. (2001). Free reading. In D. G. Singer & J. L. Singer (Eds.), *Handbook of children and the media* (2nd ed., pp. 29–45). Thousand Oaks, CA: Sage.

Desouze, J. M. S., & Jereb, J. (2000). Gravitating toward Reggio: Let the children learn about the concepts of force and motion. *Science and Children 37*(7), 26–29.

DeVita, C. J. (1995). The United States at mid-decade. *Population Bulletin, 50*(4), 2–42.

DeVita, C. J., & Mosher-Williams, R. (2001). *Who speaks for America's children?* Washington, DC: Urban Institute.

Dewey, J. (1975). *Interest and effort in education*. Edwardsville: Southern Illinois University Press. (Original work published 1913)

Dickey, C. (2003, September 8). Not silly kid stuff. *Newsweek, 162*(10), E22–E24.

Dighe, J. (1993). Children and the earth. *Young Children, 48*(3), 58–63.

Dilworth, M. E., & Brown, C. E. (2001). Consider the difference: Teaching and learning in culturally rich schools. In V. Richardson (Ed.), *Handbook of research on teaching* (4th ed., pp. 643–667). Washington DC: American Educational Research Association.

Dimidijian, V. J. (2001). Helping vulnerable families give their children an even start toward school success. *Childhood Education, 77,* 379–395.

Dinkmeyer, D., & McKay, G. D., & Dinkmeyer, J. (1997). *Parenting young children: Systematic training for effective parenting (STEP) of children under six*. Circle Pines, MN: American Guidance Service.

Doll, R. C. (1995). *Curriculum improvement: Decision making and process* (9th ed.). Boston: Allyn & Bacon.

Dorris, M. (1993). Foreword. In M. Roesell (Ed.), *Kinaalda: A Navajo girl grows up* (pp. 1–2). Minneapolis, MN: Lerner.

Douville-Watson, L., & Watson, M. A. (2002). *Infants and toddlers: Curriculum and teaching* (5th ed.). Albany, NY: Delmar.

Dreeben, R. (1970). Schooling and authority: Comments on the unstudied curriculum. In N. V. Overly (Ed.), *The unstudied curriculum: Its impact on children* (pp. 85–103). Washington, DC: Association of Supervision and Curriculum Development.

Duffey, J. (1998). Home schooling: A controversial alternative. *Principal 77*(5), 23–26.

Dunn, K., & Frazier, E. R. (1990). *Teaching styles*. Reston, VA: National Association of Secondary School Principals.

Dunn, R., & Dunn, K. (1999). *Complete guide to the Learning Styles Inservice Program*. Upper Saddle River, NJ: Prentice Hall.

Durkin, D. D. (1966). *Children who read early*. New York: Teachers College Press.

Dyson, A. H. (1986). Transitions and tensions: Interrelationships between the drawing, talking and dictating of young children. *Research in the Teaching of English, 20,* 379–409.

Eccles, J., Wigfield, A., Harold, R., & Blumenfeld, P. (1993). Age and gender differences in children's self and task perceptions during elementary school. *Child Development, 64,* 830–847.

Ecksel, I. B. (1992). Schools as socializing agents in children's lives. In L. Kaplan (Ed.), *Education and the family* (pp. 86–99). Boston: Allyn & Bacon.

Eddowes, E. A., & Hranitz, J. R. (1989). Educating children of the homeless. *Childhood Education, 65*(4), 197–200.

Edelsky, C. (1996). *With literacy and justice for all: Rethinking the social in language and education* (2nd ed.). Bristol, PA: Taylor & Francis.

Edin K., & Lein, L. (1997). *Making ends meet: How single mothers survive welfare and low wages.* New York: Russell Sage Foundation.

Edmiaston, R. K., & Fitzgerald, L. (2000). How Reggio Emilia encourages inclusion. *Educational Leadership, 58*(1), 66–69.

Education Commission of the States. (1996). *Bridging the gap between neuroscience and education. Summary of the workshop cosponsored by Education Commission of the States and the Charles A. Dana Foundation.* Denver, CO: Author.

Edwards, C. P., Gandini, L., & Forman, G. (1998a). *The hundred languages of children: The Reggio Emilia approach* (2nd ed.). Greenwich, CT: Ablex.

Edwards, C. P., Gandini, L., & Forman, G. (1998b). Introduction, background and starting points. In C. Edwards, L. Gandini, & G. Forman (Eds.), *The hundred languages of children: The Reggio Emilia approach—Advanced reflections* (2nd ed., pp. 5–25). Greenwich, CT: Ablex.

Eisner, E. W. (2002). *The educational imagination: On the design and evaluation of school programs* (3rd ed.). Englewood Cliffs, NJ: Merrill/Prentice Hall.

Eley, M. A. (2002). Making the homeschooling connection. *Educational Leadership, 59*(7), 54–56.

Elgin, C. Z. (1990). Representation, comprehension and competence. In V. A. Howard (Ed.), *Varieties of thinking* (pp. 62–75). New York: Routledge, Chapman & Hall.

Elkin, F., & Handel, G. (1989). *The child and society* (5th ed.). New York: Random House.

Elkind, D. (1988). *The hurried child* (Rev. ed.). Reading, MA: Addison-Wesley.

Elkind, D. (1994). *Ties that stress: The new family imbalance.* Cambridge, MA: Harvard University Press.

Elkind, D. (1995). School and family in the postmodern world. *Phi Delta Kappan, 77,* 8–14.

English First (2003). *English First news and notes.* Retrieved July 2, 2003, from www.englishfirst.org

Epstein, J. (1999). *School and family partnerships: Preparing educators and improving schools.* Boulder, CO: Westview Press.

Epstein, J. L. (2001). *School, family and community partnerships: Preparing educators and improving schools.* Boulder, CO: Westview Press.

Epstein, J. L., & Sanders, M. G. (2002). Family, school, and community partnerships, In M. Bornstein (Ed.), *Handbook of parenting: Vol. 5. Parents and social institutions* (2nd ed., pp. 407–438). Mahwah, NJ: Erlbaum.

Epstein, J. L., Sanders, M. G., Simon, B., Salina, K., Jansorn, N., & Van Voorhis, F. (2002). *Schools, family and community partnerships: Your handbook for action* (2nd ed.). Thousand Oaks, CA: Corwin Press.

Erikson, E. (1963). *Childhood and society.* New York: Norton.

Essa, E. L., & Murray, C. I. (1999). Sexual play: When should you be concerned? *Childhood Education, 75*(4), 231–234.

Evans, E. (1975). *Contemporary influences in early childhood education* (2nd ed.). New York: Holt, Rinehart & Winston.

Even Start. (1999). *Even Start.* Retrieved August 2, 2003, from http://www.ed.gov/legislation/ESEA/sec1201.html

Federal Interagency Forum on Child and Family Statistics. (2002). *America's Children 2002.* Washington, DC: Author.

Fine, M. J. (1993). Current approaches to understanding family diversity. *Family Relations, 43*(3), 235–237.

Fine, M. J., & Lee, S. W. (2001). *Handbook of diversity in parent education: The changing faces of parenting and parent education.* San Diego, CA: Academic Press.

Flood, J., Lapp, D., Squire, J., & Jensen, J. (Eds.). (2003). *Handbook of research on teaching the English-language arts* (2nd ed.). Mahwah, NJ: Erlbaum.

Fox, R. A., Anderson, R. C., Fox, T. A., & Rodriguez, M. A. (1991). STAR parenting: A model for helping parents effectively deal with behavioral difficulties. *Young Children, 46*(4), 54–61.

Fraenkel, P. (2003). Contemporary two-parent families: Navigating work and family challenges. In

F. Walsh (Ed.), *Normal family processes: Growing diversity and complexity* (3rd ed., pp. 61–95). New York: Guilford.

Fu, V. R., Stremmel, A. J., & Hill, L. T. (2002). *Teaching and learning: Collaborative exploration of the Reggio Emilia approach.* Upper Saddle River, NJ: Prentice Hall.

Fuchs, D., & Fuchs, L. S. (1998). Inclusion versus full inclusion. *Childhood Education, 74,* 309–320.

Fuller, B. (2003). *Policy analysis for California education (PACE). Charter schools and inequality: National disparities in funding, teacher quality and student support.* Retrieved August 21, 2003, from www.edreform.com/press/2003/pace.htm

Fuller, M. L., & Olsen, G. (1998). *Home–school relations: Working successfully with parents and families.* Boston: Allyn & Bacon.

Futrell, M. H., Gomez, J., & Bedden, D. (2003). Teaching the children of a new America: The challenge of diversity. *Phi Delta Kappan, 84,* 381–385.

Gadsden, V. L. (1998). Family cultures and literacy learning. In J. Osborn & F. Lehr (Eds.), *Literacy for all: Issues in teaching and learning* (pp. 32–51). New York: Guilford.

Galinsky, E. (1987). *The six stages of parenthood.* Reading, MA: Addison-Wesley.

Galinsky, E., Howes, C., & Kontos, S. (1995). *The family child care training study: Highlights of the findings.* New York: Families and Work Institute.

Galinsky, E., Howes, C., Kontos, S., & Shinn, M. (1994). *The study of children in family child care and relative care: Highlights of the findings.* New York: Families and Work Institute.

Galle, O., Gove, W., & McPherson, J. (1972). Population density and pathology: What are the relationships for men? *Science, 176,* 23–30.

Gallego, M. A., & Cole, M. (2001). Classroom cultures and cultures in the classroom. In V. Richardson (Ed.), *Handbook of research on teaching* (4th ed., pp. 951–997). Washington, DC: American Educational Research Association.

Gandini, L. (1993). Fundamentals of the Reggio Emilia approach to early childhood education. *Young Children, 49*(1), 4–8.

Gandini, L. (1997). Foundations of the Reggio Emilia approach. In J. Hendrick (Ed.), *First steps toward teaching the Reggio way* (pp. 14–25). Upper Saddle River, NJ: Merrill/Prentice Hall.

Gandara, P., Maxwell J. J., Garcia, E., Asato, J., & Gutierez, K., Stritikus, T., et al. (1999). *The initial impact of Proposition 227.* Davis, CA: University of Linguistic Minority Institute.

Garbarino, J. (1999). *Lost boys: Why our sons turn violent and how we can save them.* New York: Free Press.

Garbarino, J., & Abramowitz, R. H. (1992). The family as a social system. In J. Garbarino (Ed.), *Children and families in the social environment* (2nd ed., pp. 71–98). New York: De Gruyter.

Garbarino, J., & Bedard, C. (2001). *Parents under seige: Why you are the solution not the problem in your child's life.* New York: Free Press.

Garbarino, J., Dubrow, N., Kostelny, K., & Pardo, C. (1998). *Children in danger: Coping with the consequences of community violence* (2nd ed.). San Francisco: Jossey-Bass.

Garbarino, J., Kostelny, K., & Dubrow, N. (1998). *No place to be a child: Growing up in a war zone* (2nd ed.). Lexington, MA: Heath.

Gardner, H. (1983). *Frames of mind. The theory of multiple intelligences.* New York: Basic Books.

Gardner, H. (1999). *The disciplined mind: What all students should understand.* Upper Saddle River, NJ: Simon & Schuster.

Gardner, S. (1993). Failure by fragmentation. In S. Thompson (Ed.), *Whole child, whole community* (pp. 11–17). Boston: Institute for Responsive Education.

Garn, G. (1998). The thinking behind Arizona's charter movement. *Educational Leadership, 56*(2), 48–50.

Gearheart, B. R., Weishahn, M., & Gearheart, C. J. (1996). *The exceptional student in the regular classroom* (6th ed.). Upper Saddle River, NJ: Merrill/Prentice Hall.

Gelfer, J. I. (1991). Teacher–parent partnerships: Enhancing communications. *Childhood Education, 67*(3), 164–167.

Gersten, J. C. (1992). Families in poverty. In M. E. Procidano & C. B. Fisher (Eds.), *Contemporary families: A handbook for school professionals* (pp. 137–158). New York: Teachers College Press.

Giovanni, D. (2001). Traces of childhood: A child's diary. In L. Gandini & C. Edwards (Eds.), *The Italian approach to infant/toddler care* (pp. 146–152). New York: Teachers College Press.

Giroux, H. A. (1978). Developing educational programs: Overcoming the hidden curriculum. *The Clearing House, 52*(4), 148–152.

Goertz, M. E. (2001). Redefining government roles in an era of standards-based reform. *Phi Delta Kappan, 83*(1) 62–66.

Goetz, E. (2003). *Clearing the way: Deconcentrating the poor in urban America.* Washington, DC: Urban Institute.

Goffin, S. G. (2003). NAEYC commission seeks comments on early childhood program standards. *Young Children, 58*(2) 78–80.

Goffman, E. (1967). *Interaction ritual: Essays on face-to-face behavior.* New York: Harper & Row.

Goleman, D. (1995). *Emotional intelligence.* New York: Bantam Books.

Gollnick, D. M., & Chinn, P. C. (2002). *Multicultural education in a pluralistic society* (6th ed.). Upper Saddle River, NJ: Merrill/Prentice Hall.

Gonzalez-Mena, J. (2002). *The child in the family and the community* (3rd ed.). Upper Saddle River NJ: Merrill/Prentice Hall.

Good, T. L., & Braden, J. S. 2000. *The great school debate: Choice, vouchers and charters.* Mahwah, NJ: Erlbaum.

Good, T. L., & Brophy, J. E. (1986). School effects. In M. C. Wittrock (Ed.), *Handbook of research on teaching* (3rd ed., pp. 570–604). Upper Saddle River, NJ: Merrill/Prentice Hall.

Good, T. L., & Brophy, J. E. (1996). *Looking in classrooms* (7th ed.). Boston: Addison-Wesley.

Good, T. L., & Brophy, J. E. (2002). *Looking in classrooms* (9th ed.). Boston: Allyn & Bacon.

Good, T. L., & Early, M. (Eds). (2000). *American education: Yesterday, today and tomorrow: 99th yearbook of the National Society for the Study of Education. Part II.* Chicago: University of Chicago Press.

Goodlad, J. (2002). Kudzu, rabbits, and school reform. *Phi Delta Kappan, 84,* 16–23.

Gorder, C. (1996). *Home schools: An alternative. You do have a choice!* (4th ed.). Tempe, AZ: Blue Bird.

Gordon, I. J. (1969). *Reaching the child through parent education: The Florida approach.* Gainsville, FL: Gainesville Institute for the Development of Human Resources. (ERIC Document Reproduction Service No. ED057880)

Gordon, I. J., Guinagh, B. J., & Jester, R. F. (1977). The Florida Parent Education Infant and Toddler Program. In M. C. Day & R. K. Parker (Eds.), *The preschool in action* (2nd ed., pp. 95–127). Boston: Allyn & Bacon.

Gordon, T. (2000). *Parent effectiveness training: The proven approach for raising responsible children.* New York: Crown.

Gorsuch, R. L. (1976). Religion as a major prediction of significant human behavior. In W. J. Donaldson, Jr. (Ed.), *Research in mental health and religious behavior* (pp. 206–221). Atlanta, GA: Psychological Studies Institute.

Gorter-Reu, M. S., & Anderson, J. M. (1998). Home kits, home visits, and more! *Young Children, 53*(3), 71–75.

Gouvis, C. (1995). *Special report on children and violence: Maryland KIDS COUNT.* Baltimore: Urban Institute.

Graue, M. E., Weinstein, T., & Walberg, H. J. (1983). School-based home instruction and learning: A quantitative analysis. *Journal of Educational Research, 76,* 351–360.

Gray, P., & Chanoff, D. (1984). When play is learning: A school for self-directed education. *Phi Delta Kappan, 65,* 608–611.

Greenberg, P. (1990). Head Start—Part of a multi-pronged antipoverty effort for children and their families. Before the beginning: A participant's view. *Young Children, 45*(6), 40–73.

Greene, S. M., Anderson, E., Hetherington, E. M., Forgatch, M. S., & DeGarmo, D. S. (2003). Risk and resilience after divorce. In F. Walsh (Ed.), *Normal family processes: Growing diversity and complexity* (3rd ed., pp. 96–120). New York: Guilford Press.

Greenfield, P. M., & Suzuki, L. K. (2001). Culture and parenthood. In J. C. Westman (Ed.), *Parenthood in America: Undervalued, underpaid, under siege* (pp. 20–33). Madison: University of Wisconsin Press.

Greenspan, S., & Salmon, J. (2001). *The four-thirds solution: Solving the child-care crisis in America.* Cambridge, MA: Perseus Press.

Groebel, J. (2001). Media violence in cross-cultural perspective. In D. G. Singer & J. L. Singer (Eds.),

Handbook of children and the media (pp. 255–268). Thousand Oaks, CA: Sage.

Gronlund, G., & Engel, B. (1999). *Focused portfolios: A complete assessment for the young child.* St. Paul, MN: Redleaf Press.

Groves, B., Zuckerman, B., & Marans, S. (1993). Silent victims: Children who witness violence. *Journal of American Medical Association, 269*(2), 262–265.

Grumbine, E. (1988). The university of the wilderness. *Journal of Environmental Education, 19*(4), 3–7.

Gunter, B., & McAleer, J. (1997). *Children and television* (2nd ed.). New York: Routledge

Gustafson, C. (1998). Phone home. *Educational Leadership, 56*(2), 31–33.

Gutek, G. L. (2000). *Historical and philosophical foundations: A biographical introduction* (3rd ed.). Upper Saddle River, NJ: Prentice Hall.

Guterson, D. (1992). *Family matters: Why homeschooling makes sense.* New York: Harcourt.

Gutrel, F. (2003, September 8). Overloaded? Today's kids are tech addicts. *Newsweek, 162*(10), E4–E8.

Haberman, M. (1992). Creating community contexts that educate: An agenda for improving education in inner cities. In L. Kaplan (Ed.), *Education and the family* (pp. 27–40). Boston: Allyn & Bacon.

Haddock, S. A., Zimmerman, T. S., & Lyness, K. P. (2003). Changing gender norms: Transitional dilemmas. In F. Walsh (Ed.), *Normal family processes: Growing diversity and complexity* (3rd ed., pp. 301–336). New York: Guilford.

Hafner, K. (2002, October 31). Making the Web child-safe. *The New York Times,* p. E4.

Hagan, J. L. (1998). The new welfare law is tough on work. *Families in Society, 79,* 596–605.

Haley, A. (1976). *Roots.* Garden City, NY: Doubleday.

Hammer, T. J., & Turner, P. H. (2000). *Parenting in contemporary society* (4th ed). Boston: Allyn & Bacon.

Hanhan, S. F. (2003). Parent–teacher communication: Who's talking. In G. Olsen & M. L. Fuller (Eds.), *Home–school relations: Working successfully with parents and families* (pp. 111–133). Boston: Pearson.

Harrington, M. (2000). *Care and equality: Inventing a new family politics.* New York: Routledge.

Harris, J. (2002). Beyond the nurture assumption. Testing hypotheses about the child's environment. In J. G. Borkowski, S. L. Ramey, & M. Bristol-Power (Eds.), *Parenting and the child's world* (pp. 3–20). Mahwah, NJ: Erlbaum.

Harris, J. R. (1998). *The nurture assumption.* New York: Free Press.

Hart, B., & Risley, T. R. (1995). *Meaningful differences in the everyday experience of young American children.* Baltimore: Brookes.

Hart, B., & Risley, T. R. (1999). *The social world of children learning to talk.* Baltimore: Brookes.

Hart, B., & Risley, T. R. (2003). The early catastrophe: The 30 million word gap by age 3. *American Educator, 27*(1), 5–9.

Hart, C. H., DeWolf, M., & Burts, D. C. (1993). Parental disciplinary strategies and preschool behavior in playground settings. In C. H. Hart (Ed.), *Children on playgrounds: Research perspectives and applications* (pp. 271–340). Albany: State University of New York Press.

Hartman, A. (2003). Family policy: Dilemmas, controversies, and opportunities. In F. Walsh (Ed.), *Normal family processes: Growing diversity and complexity* (3rd ed., pp. 635–662). New York: Guilford.

Hartup, W. W. (1983). Peer relations. In P. H. Mussen (Ed.), *Handbook of child psychology: Vol. 4. Socialization, personality, and social development* (pp. 103–196). New York: Wiley.

Head Start Bureau. (1980). *A handbook for involving parents in Head Start* (DHHS Publication No. OHDS 88–331187). Washington, DC: U.S. Government Printing Office.

Heath, S. D. (1983). *Ways with words: Language, life, and work in communities and classrooms.* New York: Cambridge University Press.

Heath, S. D., & MacLaughlin, M. W. (1989). A child resource policy. Moving beyond dependence on school and family. *Phi Delta Kappan, 68,* 576–581.

Heaverside, S., & Farris, E. (1989). *Educational partnership in public elementary and secondary schools.* Washington, DC: Office of Educational Research and Improvement.

Helburn, S. (1995). *Cost, quality and child outcomes in child care centers: Technical Report.* Denver: University of Colorado, Center for Research in Economic and Social Policy.

Helburn, S., & Bergmann, B. (2002). *America's child care problem: The way out.* New York: Palgrave/St. Martin's.

Heleen, O. (1990). Schools reaching out: An introduction. *Equity and Choice, 6*(3), 5–9.

Helm, J. (1994). Family theme bags: An innovative approach to family involvement in the school. *Young Children, 49*(4), 48–52.

Henderson, A. T., Marburger, C. L., & Ooms, T. (1986). *Beyond the bake sale: An educator's guide to working with parents.* Columbia, MD: National Committee for Citizens in Education.

Hendrick, J. (Ed.). (1997). *First steps toward teaching the Reggio way.* Upper Saddle River, NJ: Merrill/Prentice Hall.

Henniger, M. L. (2002). *Teaching young children: An introduction* (2nd ed.). Columbus, OH: Merrill/Prentice Hall.

Hess. A. (2001). *Concepts of social stratification: European and American models.* New York: Palgrave.

Hess, R. D., & Holloway, S. D. (1999). Family and school as educational institutions. In R. D. Parke (Ed.), *Review of child development research: Vol 7. The family* (pp. 174–222). Chicago: University of Chicago Press.

Hetherington, E. M. (1988). Parents, children and siblings six years after divorce. In R. A. Hinde & J. Stevenson-Hinde (Eds.), *Relationships within families* (pp. 311–331). Oxford, England: Oxford University Press.

Hetherington, E. M., & Kelly, J. (2002). *For better or worse: Divorce reconsidered.* New York: Norton.

Hetherington, E. M., & Stanley-Hagan, M. M. (2002). Parenting in divorced and remarried families. In M. Bornstein (Ed.), *Handbook of parenting: Vol 3. Being and becoming a parent* (pp. 287–316). Mahwah, NJ: Erlbaum.

Hiatt-Michael, D. B. (1999). Promising practices for family involvement in schools [whole volume]. In D. Hiatt-Mitchell (Ed.), *Family, school, community partnership issues: Vol 1. Partnership for family involvement in education (PFIE).* Washington, DC: Information Age.

Hildebrand, V., Phenice, L. A., Gray, M. M., & Hines, R. P. (1996). *Knowing and serving diverse families.* Columbus, OH: Merrill/Prentice Hall.

Hill, E. (1967). *Evan's corner.* New York: Holt.

Hillis, M. R. (1996). Allison Davis and the study of race, social class, and schooling. In J. A. Banks (Ed.), *Multicultural education, transformative knowledge and action: Historical and contemporary perspectives* (pp. 115–128). New York: Teachers College Press.

Hodges, E. V. E., Boivin, M., Vitaro, F., & Bukowski, W. M. (1999). The power of friendship: Protection against an escalating cycle of peer victimization. *Developmental Psychology, 35*(1), 94–101.

Hoffer, T. B., & Coleman, J. S. (1990). Changing families and communities: Implications for schools. In B. Mitchell & L. L. Cunningham (Eds.), *Educational leadership and changing contexts of families, communities and schools: 89th yearbook of the NSSE, Part II* (pp. 118–134). Chicago: National Society for the Study of Education.

Hofferth, S. L. (1991). *National child care survey, 1990.* Washington, DC: Urban Institute.

Hoge, D. R. (1996). Religion in America: The demographics of belief and affiliation. In E. P. Shafranske (Ed.), *Religion and the clinical practice of psychology* (pp. 21–41). Washington, DC: American Psychological Association.

Holmbeck, G. N., Paikoff, R., & Brooks-Gunn, J. (1995). Parenting adolescents. In M. Bornstein (Ed.), *Handbook of parenting Vol: 1. Children and parenting* (pp. 91–118). Mahwah, NJ: Erlbaum.

Holt, J. C. (1964). *How children fail.* New York: Pitman.

Honig, A. S. (1993). Mental health for babies: What do theory and research teach us? *Young Children, 48*(3), 69–76.

Howard, V. F, Williams, B. F., Port, P., & Lepper, C. (2001). *Very young children with special needs: A formative approach for the 21st century.* Upper Saddle River, NJ: Merrill/Prentice Hall.

Hrabowski, F. A., Maton, K. I., Greene, M., & Greif, G. L. (2002). *Overcoming the odds: Raising academically successful African American young women.* New York: Oxford University Press.

Hrabowski, F. A., Maton, K. I., & Greif, G. L. (1998). *Beating the odds: Raising academically successful African American males.* New York: Oxford University Press.

Hughes, E. (2002). Planning meaningful curriculum: A mini story of children and teachers working together. *Childhood education, 78*(3), 134–139.

Hurd, T. L., Lerner, R. M., & Barton, C. E. (1999). Integrated services: Expanding partnerships to meet the needs of today's children and families. *Young Children, 54*(2), 74–81.

Hurst, C. O. (1993). Teaching in the library: Dark and stormy reading. *Teaching Pre-K–8, 23*(5), 92–94.

Huston, P. (2001). *Families as we are: Conversations from around the world.* New York: Feminist Press.

Hymowitz, K. S. (2002). Parenting: The lost art. *American Educator 25*(1), 4–9.

Jacobson, S. K., & Padua, S. M. (1992). Pupils and parks: Environmental education in national parks of developing countries. *Childhood Education, 68*(5), 290–294.

Janosik, E., & Green, E. (1992). *Family life: Process and practice.* Boston: Jones & Bartlett.

Jencks, C., Smith, M. S., Acland, H., Bane, M. J., Cohen, I., Gintis, H., et al. (1972). *Inequality: A reassessment of family and schooling in America.* New York: Harper & Row.

Jenkins, E. J., & Bell, C. C. (1997). Exposure and response to community violence among children and adolescents. In J. Osofsky (Ed.), *Children in a violent society* (pp. 9–31). New York: Guilford.

Jeub, C. (1994). Why parents choose home schooling. *Educational Leadership, 52*(1), 50–52.

Johnson, V. R. (1990). Schools reaching out: Changing the message to "good news." *Equity and Choice, 6*(3), 20–24.

Jones, K. (1988). *Interactive learning events: A guide for facilitators.* New York: Nichols.

Jones, S. (2000). *Darwin's ghost: The origin of the species updated.* New York: Ballantine.

Joyce, B., & Weil, M. (1996). *Models of teaching* (5th ed.). Boston: Allyn & Bacon.

Joyce, B., Weil, M., & Calhoun, E. (2003). *Models of teaching* (7th ed.). Boston: Allyn & Bacon.

Kagan, S. L. (1993). Home–school linkages. In S. L. Kagan, D. R. Powell, B. Weisbourd, & E. F. Zigler (Eds.), *America's family support programs: Perspectives and prospects* (pp. 160–181). New Haven, CT: Yale University Press.

Kagan, S. L., & Neuman, M. J. (1997). Highlights of the quality 2000 initiative: Not by chance. *Young Children, 50*(6), 54–62.

Kaplan, L. (1992). Parent education in home, school, and society: A course description. In L. Kaplan (Ed.), *Education and the family* (pp. 273–278). Boston: Allyn & Bacon.

Karpowitz, D. H. (2001). American families in the 1990s and beyond. In M. J. Fine & S. W. Lee (Eds.), *Handbook of diversity in parent education* (pp. 3–14). San Diego, CA: Academic Press.

Katz, P. A. (1976). The acquisition of racial attitudes in children. In P. A. Katz (Ed.), *Towards the elimination of racism* (pp. 125–154). New York: Pergamon.

Kearney, M. (1999). The role of teachers in helping children of domestic violence. *Childhood Education, 75*(5), 290–296.

Kerman, K. (1990). Home schooling day by day. In A. Pedersen & P. O'Mara (Eds.), *Schooling at home: Parents, kids, and learning* (pp. 175–182). Santa Fe, NM: Muir.

Kidder, T. (1989). *Among schoolchildren.* Boston: Houghton Mifflin.

Kidwell, C. S., & Swift, D. W. (1976). Indian education. In D. W. Swift (Ed.), *American education: A sociological view* (pp. 329–390). Boston: Houghton Mifflin.

Kieff, J. E., & Casbergue, R. M. (2000). *Playful learning and teaching: Integrating play into preschool and primary programs.* Boston: Allyn & Bacon.

Kinch, A. F., & Schweinhart, L. J. (1999). Making child care work for everyone. *Young Children, 54*(1), 68–73.

Knowles, J. G. (1989). Cooperating with home school parents: A new agenda for public schools? *Urban Education, 23*, 392–411.

Kochenderfer, R., Kanna, E., & Kiyosaki, R. (2002). *Homeschooling for success: How can parents create a superior education for their child?* New York: Warner.

Kontos, S., Howes, C., Shinn, M., & Galinsky, E. (1995). *Quality in family child care and relative care.* New York: Teachers College Press.

Kotlowitz, A. (1991). *There are no children here: The story of two boys growing up in the other America.* New York: Doubleday.

Kotlowitz, A. (1998). *The other side of the river: A story of two towns, a death and America's dilemma.* New York: Talese/Doubleday.

Kozol, J. (1967). *Death at an early age.* Boston: Houghton Mifflin.

Kozol, J. (1991). *Savage inequalities: Children in America's schools.* New York: Crown.

Kozol, J. (2000). *Ordinary resurrections: Children in the years of hope.* New York: Crown.

Kralovec, E. (2002). *Schools that do too much: Wasting time and money in schools and what we can do about it.* Boston: Beacon.

Kralovec, E., & Buell, J. (2000). *The end of homework: How homework disrupts families, overburdens children and limits learning.* Boston: Beacon.

Krathwohl, D. R., Bloom, B. S., & Masia, B. B. (1984). *Taxonomy of educational objectives: The classification of educational goals: Handbook II. Affective domain.* New York: Longman.

Kumove, L. (1966). *A preliminary study of the social implications of high-density living conditions.* Toronto, Ontario, Canada: Social Planning Council of Metropolitan Toronto.

Kyle, D. W., McIntyre, E., Miller, K. B., & Moore, G. H. (2002). *Reaching out: A K–8 resource for connecting families and schools.* Thousand Oaks, CA: Corwin.

Ladd, G. W., & Pettit, G. S. (2002). Parents and children's peer relationships. In M. Bornstein (Ed.), *Handbook of parenting: Vol. 4. Applied and practical parenting* (2nd ed., pp. 377–409). Mahwah, NJ: Erlbaum.

Lancaster, P. E. (2001). Parenting children with learning disabilities. In M. J. Fine & S. W. Lee (Eds.), *Handbook of diversity in parent education* (pp. 233–253). San Diego, CA: Academic Press.

Larner, M., & Halpern, R. (1987). Lay home visiting: Strengths, tensions, and challenges. *Zero to Three, 8,* 1–7.

Larzelere, R. E. (2001). Combining love and limits in authoritative parenting. In J. C. Westman (Ed.), *Parenthood in America: Undervalued, underpaid, under siege* (pp. 81–89). Madison: University of Wisconsin Press.

Lazar, I. (1977). *The persistence of preschool effects: A long-term follow-up of fourteen infant and preschool experiments.* Washington, DC: Administration for Children, Youth, and Families.

Lazzara, K. C., & Poland, S. (2001). Managing crisis: Intervention skills for parents. In M. J. Fine & S. W. Lee (Eds.), *Handbook of diversity in parent education: The changing faces of parenting and parent education* (pp. 339–372). San Diego, CA: Academic Press.

Leach, P. (1994). *Children first: What our society must do—And is not doing—for our children today.* New York: Knopf.

Leach, P. (1997). *Children first.* New York: Random House.

Lee, S. W., & Guck, T. P. (2001). Parenting chronically ill children. In M. J. Fine & S. W. Lee (Eds.), *Handbook of diversity in parent education* (pp. 277–298). San Diego, CA: Academic Press.

Lefcourt, H. M. (1984). *Research with the locus of control construct.* New York: Academic Press.

LeFrancois, G. R. (1996). *Psychology for teachers* (9th ed). Belmont, CA: Wadsworth.

Leland, C. H., & Kasten, W. C. (2002). Literacy education for the 21st century. *Reading and Writing Quarterly, 18*(1), 5–15.

Lerner, J. W., Lowenthal, B., & Egan, R. W. (2003). *Preschool children with special needs: Children at risk and children with disabilities.* Boston: Allyn & Bacon.

Leslie, T. (2003). What's with homeschooling in California? *Homeschool World, 11*(4), 1. Also retrieved July 1, 2003, from www.home-school.com/news/wwhsca

Letiecq, B. L., Anderson, E. A., & Koblinsky, A. (1998). Social support of homeless and house mothers: A comparison of temporary and permanent housing arrangements. *Family Relations, 47,* 415–421.

Levin, D. E. (1998). *Remote control childhood? Combating the hazards of media culture.* Washington, DC: National Association for the Education of Young Children.

Levine, D. U., & Levine, R. F. (1995). *Society and education* (9th ed.). Boston: Allyn & Bacon.

Levy, D. E. (1992). Teaching family ritual: Sunday, sausage, and solidarity. *Teaching Sociology, 20,* 311–313.

Lichter, D. T., & Crowley, M. L. (2002). Poverty in America: Beyond welfare reform. *Population Bulletin, 57*(2), 3–34.

Lightfoot, S. L. (1978). *Worlds apart: Relationships between schools and families.* New York: Basic Books.

Lilly, E., & Green, C. (2004). *Developing partnerships with families through literature.* Upper Saddle River, NJ: Pearson.

Lim, S. (2003). Parent involvement in education. In G. Olsen & M. L. Fuller (Eds.). *Home school relations: Working successfully with parents and families* (2nd ed.). Boston: Allyn & Bacon.

Lin, H. (2002, November 16). Making the Net childsafe. *The New York Times*, p. 25.

Lindner, E. (2003). *Yearbook of American and Canadian churches, 2002.* Nashville, TN: Abingdon.

Lindsey, E. W. (1998). The impact of homelessness and shelter life on family relationships. *Family Relations, 47*(3), 243–252.

Lines, P. (1995). Home schooling. *ERIC Digest, 95,* 1–7. (Gov. Doc. ED 1.310/2:381849)

Lines, P. (2001, July). *Home school in the United States: 1999.* Washington DC: U.S. National Center for Educational Statistics.

Lines, P. M. (1991). *Estimating the home-schooled population* (Rep. No. OR 91-537). Washington, DC: Office of Educational Research and Improvement. (GPO ED 1.310/2:337903)

Linn, M. I. (2001). An American educator reflects on the meaning of Reggio Emilia. *Phi Delta Kappan, 83,* 332–335.

Liston, D. P., & Zeichner, K. M. (1996a). *Culture and teaching.* Mahwah, NJ: Erlbaum.

Liston, D. P., & Zeichner, K. (1996b). *Reflective teaching: An introduction.* Mahwah, NJ: Erlbaum.

Lombardi, J. (2003). *Time to care: Redesigning child care to promote education, support families, and build communities.* Philadelphia: Temple University Press.

Louv, C. (1990). *Childhood's future.* Boston: Houghton Mifflin.

Macaulay, D. (1998). *The new how things work.* Boston: Houghton Mifflin.

Maccoby, E. E., & Martin, J. (1983). Socialization in the context of family: Parent–child interaction. In P. H. Mussen (Ed.), *Handbook of child psychology: Socialization, personality and social development* (4th ed., pp. 1–102). New York: Wiley.

Maccoby. E. E. (2002). Parenting effects: Issues and controversies. In J. G. Borkowski, S. L. Raney, & M. Bristol-Power (Eds.), *Parenting and the child's world* (pp. 35–46). Mahwah, NJ: Erlbaum.

Maeroff, G. I. (1998). Altered destinies: Making life better for schoolchildren in need. *Phi Delta Kappan, 79,* 424–432.

Magnuson, K. A. & Duncan, G. J. (2002). Parents in poverty. In M. H. Bornstein (Ed.), *Handbook of parenting: Vol. 4. Social conditions and applied parenting* (2nd ed., pp. 95–122). Mahwah, NJ: Erlbaum.

Mahood, H. R. (2000). *Interest groups in American national politics.* Upper Saddle River, NJ: Prentice Hall.

Malaguzzi, L. (1998) History, ideas and basic philosophy: An interview with Lella Gandini. In C. Edwards, L. Gandini, & G. Forman (Eds.), *The hundred languages of children: The Reggio Emilia approach—Advanced reflections* (pp. 49–97). Greenwich: CT: Ablex.

Mallett, D. (1995). *Inch by inch: The garden song.* New York: HarperCollins.

Manno, B. (2003). *What research reveals about charter schools.* Washington, DC: Center for Educational Reform.

Manno, B. V. (2001). Chartered governance of urban public schools. In M. C. Wang & H. J. Walberg (Eds.), *School choice and best systems* (pp. 39–65). Mahwah, NJ: Erlbaum.

Mardell, B. (2002). *Growing up in child care: A case for quality early childhood education.* Portsmouth, NH: Heinemann.

Mares, M., & Woodward, E. H. (2001). Prosocial effects on children's social interaction. In D. G. Singer & J. L. Singer (Eds.), *Handbook of children and the media* (pp. 183–205). Thousand Oaks, CA: Sage.

Marsh, C., & Willis, G. (1999). *Curriculum: Alternative approaches, ongoing issues* (2nd ed.). Upper Saddle River, NJ: Merrill/Prentice Hall.

Maslow, A. H. (1970). *Motivation and personality* (Rev. ed.). New York: Norton.

Mason, C. (1998). *Everybody is somebody's lunch.* Gardner, ME: Tilbury House.

Mason, M. A. (1998). The modern American stepfamily: Problems and possibilities. In M. A. Mason, A. Skolnick, & S. D. Sugarman (Eds.), *All our families: New policies for a new century* (pp. 95–116). New York: Oxford University Press.

Mayberry, M., Knowles, J. G., Ray, B., & Marlow, S. (1995). *Home schooling: Parents as educators.* Thousand Oaks, CA: Corwin.

Mayer, S. (1997). *What money can't buy: Family income and children's life chances.* Cambridge, MA: Harvard University Press.

McChesney, R. W. (1999). *Rich media, poor democracy: Communication politics in dubious times.* Urbana: University of Illinois Press.

McCormick, L., & Holden, R. (1992). Homeless children: A special challenge. *Young Children, 57*(6), 61–67.

McDermott, D. (2001). Parenting and ethnicity. In M. J. Fine & S. W. Lee (Eds.), *Handbook of diversity in parent education* (pp. 73–96). San Diego, CA: Academic Press.

McFalls, J. A., Jr. (1998). Population: A lively introduction. *Population Bulletin, 53*(3), 3–47.

McGee, L. M., & Richgels, D. J. (2003). *Literacy's beginnings: Supporting young readers and writers* (4th ed.). Boston: Allyn & Bacon.

McGee-Banks, C. A. (2003). Families and teachers working together for school improvement. In J. A. Banks & C. A. McGee-Banks (Eds.), *Multicultural education: Issues and perspectives* (4th ed., pp. 402–420). New York: Wiley.

McGoldrick, M. (1993). Ethnicity, cultural diversity and normality. In F. Walsh (Ed.), *Normal family processes* (2nd ed., pp. 331–360). New York: Guilford Press.

McGoldrick, M. (2003). Culture: A challenge to concepts of normality. In F. Walsh (Ed.), *Normal family processes: Growing diversity and complexity* (3rd ed., pp. 235–259). New York: Guilford Press.

McNeil, J. D. (1996). *Curriculum: A comprehensive introduction* (5th ed.). Reading, MA: Addison-Wesley.

Meadows, S. (1996). *Understanding child development: Psychological perspectives in an interdisciplinary field of inquiry.* London: Hutchinson.

Mediavilla, C. (2001). *Creating the full-service homework center in your library.* Chicago: American Library Association.

Meier, D. (1995). *The power of their ideas: Lessons for America from a small school in Harlem.* Boston: Beacon Press.

Meier, D. (2003). Becoming educated: The power of ideas. *Principal Leadership 3*(7), 16–19.

Meier, D. (2002a). *In schools we trust: Creating communities of learning in an era of testing and standardization.* Boston: Beacon Press.

Meier, D. (2002b). Standardization versus standards. *Phi Delta Kappan, 84,* 190–198.

Melaville, A. (1998). *Learning together: The developing field of school–community initiatives.* Flint, MI: Mott Foundation.

Melton, J. G. (2000). *American religions: An illustrated history.* Santa Barbara, CA: ABC-CLIO.

Melton, J. G. (2002). *Encyclopedia of American religions* (7th ed.). Detroit, MI: Gale Research Co.

Merenda, D. W. (1989). Partners in education: An old tradition renamed. *Educational Leadership, 47*(2A), 4–7.

Meringoff, L. K. (1980). Influence of the medium on children's story apprehension. *Journal of Educational Psychology, 72*(2), 240–249.

Metz, E. G. (1993). The camouflaged at-risk student: White and wealthy. *Momentum, 24*(2), 40–44.

Miles, J. (1986/1987). Wilderness as a learning place. *Journal of Environmental Education, 18*(2), 33–40.

Miller, M. S. (1991). *The school book: Everything parents should know about their child's education, from preschool through eighth grade.* New York: St. Martin's Press.

Mitchell. C. J., & Spencer, L. M. (1997). *21st-century community learning centers program.* Washington, DC: U.S. Department of Education, Office of Educational Research and Improvement.

Monroe, L. (1997). *Nothing's impossible: Leadership lessons and stories from the front.* New York: Time Books.

Moore, G. T. (1985). State of the art in play environment. In J. L. Frost & S. Sunderlin (Eds.), *When children play* (pp. 171–192). Wheaton, MD: Association for Childhood Education International.

Moriarty, M. L., & Fine, M. J. (2001). Educating parents to be advocates for their children. In M. Fine & S. W. Lee (Eds.), *Handbook of diversity in parent education: The changing faces of parenting and parent education* (pp. 315–336). San Diego, CA: Academic Press.

Morris, J. E. (2002). A "community bonded" school for African American students, families, and community. *Phi Delta Kappan 84*(3), 230–234.

Morris, M., & Western B., (1999). Inequality in earnings at the close of the twentieth century. *Annual Review of Sociology, 25,* 623–657.

Morse, S. C. (1997). *Unschooled migrant youth: Characteristics and strategies to serve them* Washington, DC: Superintendent of Documents. (Gov. Doc. ED 1.310/2:405158)

Mukhopadhyay, C., & Henze, R. C. (May 2003). How real is race: Using anthropology to make sense of human diversity. *Phi Delta Kappan, 84,* 669–678.

Murphy, J., & Shiffman, C. D. (2002). *Understanding and assessing the charter school movement.* New York: Teachers College Press.

Murray, J. P. (1997). Media violence and youth. In J. D. Osofsky (Ed.), *Children in a violent society* (pp. 72–97). New York: Guilford Press.

Naisknov, A. (2002, June 16). Charter schools share ideas. *Boston Globe,* p. E6.

Nash, M. (1997, September 3). Fertile minds. *Time, 152,* 48–56.

National Association for Bilingual Education. (2003). *NABE examines language policies.* Retrieved July 2, 2003, from www.nabe.org

National Association for the Education for Young Children. (1990). *How to choose a good early childhood program.* Washington, DC: Author.

National Association for the Education of Young Children. (1998). *Accreditation criteria and procedures of the National Association for the Education of Young Children.* Washington, DC: Author.

National Association for Family Child Care. (2003). *The quality standard for NAFCC accreditation* (3rd ed.). Washington DC: Author.

National Center for Educational Statistics. (1992). What young children do at home: Reading and TV watching are among the most common family activities for 3- to 8-year-olds. *Principal, 72*(2), 21–24.

National Center for Educational Statistics. (1996). *National household education survey.* Washington, DC: U.S. Department of Education.

National Commission of Excellence in Education. (1983). *A nation at risk: The imperative for educational reform.* Washington, DC: U.S. Government Printing Office.

National Commission on Migrant Children. (1992). *Invisible children: A portrait of migrant educa-* tion in the United States (Supt. of Documents, Stock No. 022–003–01173–1). Washington, DC: Author.

National Education Commission on Time and Learning. (1994). *Prisoners of Time: Report of the national commission on time and learning.* Washington, DC: Author.

National Home Education Network. (2003). NHENotes online. Retrieved May 3, 2003, from www.nwhen.org

National Institute for Child Health and Human Development Early Child Care Research Network. (1997a). Characteristics of infant child care: Factors contributing to positive caregiving. *Early Childhood Research Quarterly, 11,* 269–306.

National Institute of Child Health and Human Development Early Child Care Research Network. (1997b). Child care in the first year of life. *Merrill–Palmer Quarterly, 43,* 340–360.

Neill, A. S. (1960). *Summerhill.* New York: Hart.

Neito, S. (2002). *Language, culture and teaching: Critical perspectives for a new century.* Mahwah, NJ: Erlbaum.

Nelson, E. (1986). *Home schooling* (Rep. No. R-86–0003). Washington, DC: Office of Educational Research and Improvement. (ERIC Document Reproduction Service No. ED282348)

Neuman, S. B. (1995). *Myth of the TV effect.* Norwood, NJ: Ablex.

Neuman, S. B. (1997). Television as a learning environment: A theory of synergy. In J. Flood, S. Brice-Heath, & D. Lapp (Eds.), *Handbook of research on teaching literacy through the communicative and visual arts* (pp. 15–23). New York: Simon & Schuster.

Neuman, S. B., & Dickinson, D. K. (2001). *Handbook of early literacy research.* New York: Guilford.

Neuman, S. B., & Roskos, K. (1993). Access to print for children of poverty: Differential effects of adult mediation and literacy-enriched play settings on environmental and functional print tasks. *American Educational Research Journal, 30*(1), 96–122.

Neuman, S. B., & Roskos, K. (1994). Bridging home and school with a culturally responsive approach. *Childhood Education, 70*(4), 210–214.

New, R. (1998). Theory and praxis in Reggio Emilia: They know what they are doing, and why.

In C. Edwards, L. Gandini, & G. Forman (Eds.), *The hundred languages of children: The Reggio Emilia approach—Advanced reflections* (pp. 261–285). Greenwich, CT: Ablex.

New, R. S. (2003). Reggio Emilia: New ways to think about schooling. *Educational Leadership, 60*(7), 34–39.

New, R. (2001a). *Reggio Emilia. Some lessons for U.S. educators.* Champaign, IL: ERIC Clearinghouse on Elementary and Early Childhood. (ERIC Document Reproduction Service No. ED477971)

New, R. (2001b). Quando o'e figli [Where there are children]. Observations in an Italian Early Childhood Program. In L. Gandini & C. P. Edwards (Eds.), *Bambini: The Italian approach to infant/toddler care* (pp. 210–216). New York: Teachers College Press.

Newberger, J. J. (1997). New brain development research: A wonderful window of opportunities to build public support for early childhood education. *Young Children, 52*(4), 4–10.

Newman, R. (1998). Making time for family. *Childhood Education, 74*(3), 174–175.

Noddings, N. (2002a). *Starting at home: Caring and social policy.* Berkeley, CA: University of California Press.

Noddings, N. (2002b). *Educating moral people: A caring alternative to character education.* New York: Teachers College Press.

Noddings, N. (2004). *Happiness and education.* New York: Cambridge University Press.

Notar, E. E. (1989). Children and TV commercials: Wave after wave of exploitation. *Childhood Education, 66*(2), 66–67.

Notar, E. E. (1992). They come with stories. *Childhood Education, 68*(3), 131–133.

O'Hare, W. P. (1992). America's minorities: The demographics of diversity. *Population Bulletin, 47*(4), 2–40.

O'Hare, W. P. (1996). A new look at poverty in America. *Population Bulletin, 51*(2), 1–42.

O'Neil, J. (1997). Building schools as communities: A conversation with James Comer. *Educational Leadership, 54*(8), 6–10.

O'Reilly, R. C., & Green, E. T. (1992). *School law for the 1990s: A handbook* (2nd ed.). New York: Greenwood.

Oehlberg, B. (1996). *Making it better: Activities for children living in a stressful world.* St. Paul, MN: Redleaf Press.

Ogbu, J. U. (1994). Racial stratification and education in the United States: Why inequality persists. *Teachers College Record, 96*(2), 265–298.

Oladele, F. (1999). Passing the spirit. *Educational Leadership, 56*(4), 62–65.

Olsen, G., & Fuller, M. L. (Eds.). (2003). *Home–school relations: Working successfully with parents and families* (2nd ed.). Boston: Allyn & Bacon.

Olson, M. R., & Haynes, J. A. (1993). Successful single parents. *Families in Society, 74*(5), 259–267.

Opie, I. A., & Opie, P. (1969). *Children's games in street and playgound: Chasing, catching, seeking, hunting, racing, duelling, exerting, daring, guessing, acting, pretending.* Oxford-England: Clarendon.

O'Shea, D. J., O'Shea, L., Algozzino, R. & Hammittee, D. (2001). *Families and teachers of individuals with disabilities: Collaborative orientations and responsive practices.* Boston: Allyn & Bacon.

Osofsky, J. D. (1997). Children and youth violence: An overview of the issue. In J. D. Osofsky (Ed.), *Children in a violent society* (pp. 3–8). New York: Guilford Press.

Osofsky, J. D. (1998). Children as invisible victims of domestic and community violence. In G. W. Holden, R. Geffner, & E. N. Jouriles (Eds.), *Children exposed to marital violence* (pp. 95–120). Washington, DC: American Psychological Association.

Owens, K. (1993). *The world of the child.* Englewood Cliffs, NJ: Merrill/Prentice Hall.

Paik, H. (2001). The history of children's use of electronic media. In D. G. Singer & J. L. Singer (Eds.), *Handbook of children and the media* (pp. 7–27). Thousand Oaks, CA: Sage.

Papert, S. (1996). *The connected family: Bridging the digital generation gap.* Marietta, GA: Longstreet Press.

Paratore, J. R. (2001). *Opening doors, opening opportunities: Family literacy in an urban community.* Boston: Allyn & Bacon.

Paratore, J. R., Melzi, G., & Krol-Sinclair, B. (1999). *What should we expect of family literacy? Experiences of Latino children whose parents* participate in an intergenerational literacy program. Newark, DE: International Reading Association.

Pardeck, J. T. (1990). An analysis of the deep social structure preventing the development of a national policy for children and families in the United States. *Early Child Development and Care, 57*(1), 23–30.

Parke, R. D. (1990, Fall). *Family–peer systems: In search of a linking process. Developmental Psychology, 5*, 20–29.

Partnership for Family Involvement in Education. (1999a). *Excelencia en educacion.* Washington, DC: U.S. Office of Education.

Partnership for Family Involvement in Education. (1999b). *What is the partnership for involvement in education?* Retrieved June 3, 2003, from http://www.pfie.ed.gov./about_main.htm

Pavao, J. M. (1998). *The family of adoption.* Boston: Beacon Press.

Pence, A. B., & Goelman, H. (1987). Silent partners: Parents of children in three types of day care. *Early Childhood Research Quarterly, 2,* 103–118.

Perry, D. G. (1987, Fall). How is aggression learned? *School Safety,* 23–25.

Perry, J. (2003). Making sense of outdoor pretend play. *Young Children, 58*(3), 26–30.

Piaget, J. (1952). *The origins of intelligence.* New York: International Universities Press.

Piaget, J. (1967). *Six psychological studies.* New York: Random House.

Pierce, S. H., Alfonso, E. M., & Garrison, M. E. B. (1998). Examining proximal processes in young children's home environments: A preliminary report. *Family Relations, 27*(1), 3–35.

Pinker, S. (2002). *The blank slate: The modern denial of human nature.* New York: Viking.

Pinnell, G. S. (1996). Ways to look at the foundation of children's language. In B. M. Power & R. Hubbard (Eds.), *Language development: A reader for teachers* (pp. 146–155). Upper Saddle River, NJ: Prentice Hall.

Pipher, M. (1996). *The shelter of each other: Rebuilding our families.* New York: Ballantine Books.

Pipher, M. (2002). *The middle of everywhere: The world's refugees come to our town.* New York: Harcourt.

Polakow, V. (1993). *Lives on the edge: Single mothers and their children in the other America.* Chicago: University of Chicago Press.

Polly, J. A. (2002). *Net mom's Internet kids & family yellow pages* (4th ed). New York: McGraw-Hill/Osborne Media.

Popin, M. (1990). *The active parenting discussion program.* Marietta, GA: Active Parenting.

Population Reference Bureau. (2003). *Immigration: shaping and reshaping America.* Washington, DC: Author. Retrieved August 30, 2003, from www.prb.org

Powell, D. R. (1990). Home visiting in the early years: Policy and program design decisions. *Young Children, 45*(6), 65–73.

Priesnitz, H. (1990). First day of school at thirteen. In A. Pedersen & P. O'Mara (Eds.), *Schooling at home: Parents, kids, and learning* (pp. 200–202). Santa Fe, NM: Muir.

Proctor, P. (1984). Teacher expectations: A model for school improvement. *Elementary School Journal, 84*, 469–481.

Puckett, M. B., & Black, J. K. (2001). *The young child: Development from prebirth through age eight* (3rd ed.). Upper Saddle River, NJ: Merrill/Prentice Hall.

Quint, S. (1994). *Schooling homeless children: A working model for America's public schools.* New York: Teachers College Press.

Ramirez-Smith, C. (1995). Stopping the cycle of failure: The Comer model. *Educational Leadership, 52*(5), 14–19.

Ramsey, P. G. (1987). Young children's thinking about ethnic differences. In J. S. Phinney & M. J. Rotheram (Eds.), *Children's ethnic socialization: Pluralism and development* (pp. 56–72). Newbury Park, CA: Sage.

Ramsey, P. G. (1998). *Teaching and learning in a diverse world: Multicultural education for young children* (2nd ed.). New York: Teachers College Press.

Randolph, S. M., Koblinsky, S. A., & Roberts, D. D. (1998). Studying the role of family and school in the development of African American preschoolers in violent neighborhoods. *Journal of Negro Education, 65*, 282–294.

Rankin, B. (1998). Curriculum development in Reggio Emilia: A long-term curriculum project about dinosaurs. In C. Edwards, L. Gandini, & G. Forman, (Eds.), *The hundred languages of children: The Reggio Emilia approach—Advanced reflections* (pp. 215–237). Greenwich, CT: Ablex.

Rapp, R. (1999). Family and class in contemporary America: Notes toward and understanding of ideology. In S. Coontz (Ed.), *American families: A multicultural reader* (pp. 180–197). New York: Routledge.

Ray, B. (1997, May/June). Home education across the United States. *Home School Court Report, 13*(3), 11–16.

Ray, B. D. (2002). Customization through homeschooling. *Educational Leadership, 59*(7), 50–55.

Ray, B. D. (2000a). Homeschooling for individual's gains and society's common good. *Peabody Journal of Education, 75*(1, 2), 272–293.

Ray, B. D. (2000b). Homeschooling: The amelioration of negative influence on learning? *Peabody Journal of Education, 75*(1, 2), 71–106.

Raywid, M. A. (1995). The struggles and joys of trail-blazing: A tale of two charter schools. *Phi Delta Kappan, 76*, 555–560.

Reich, R. (2002). The civic perils of homeschooling. *Educational Leadership, 59*(7), 56–59.

Report of the National Education Commission on Time and Learning. (1994, April). *Prisoners of time.* Washington, DC: National Education Commission on Time and Learning.

Reppucci, N. D., Britner, P. A., & Woolard, J. L. (1997). *Preventing child abuse and neglect through parent education.* Baltimore: Brookes.

Rice, M. L., Huston, A. C., Truglio, R., & Wright, J. C. (1990). Words from *Sesame Street:* Learning vocabulary while viewing. *Developmental Psychology, 26*, 421–428.

Rich, D. (1987). *Teachers and parents: An adult-to-adult approach.* Washington, DC: National Education Association.

Rich, D. (1992). *Megaskills: In school and life—The best gift you can give your child.* Boston: Houghton Mifflin.

Rich, J. M. (1997). *Foundations of education: Perspectives on American education.* Upper Saddle River, NJ: Merrill/Prentice Hall.

Richards, M. H., & Duckett, E. (1994). The relationship of maternal employment to early adolescent daily experience with and without parents. *Child Development, 65*(1), 225–236.

Ridley, M. (2003a). *Nature via nurture: Genes, experience and what makes us human.* New York: Random House.

Ridley, M. (2003b). What makes you who you are? *Time, 161*(22), 54–63.

Riley, R. W. (1995). Reflections on Goals 2000. *Teachers College Record, 96*, 380–389.

Rinaldi, C. (1998). Projected curriculum constructed through documentation—Progottazione: An interview with L. Gandini. In C. Edwards, L. Gandini, & G. Forman. (Eds.), *The hundred languages of children: The Reggio Emilia approach—Advanced reflections* (2nd ed). Greenwich, CT: Ablex.

Rivkin, M. (1995). *The great outdoors: Restoring children's right to play outside.* Washington, DC: National Association for the Education of Young Children.

Robinson, J. D., & Godbey, G. (1999). *Time for life: The surprising way Americans use their time* (2nd ed.). University Park: Penn State University Press.

Romanowski, M. H. (2001). Teaching migrant students: The voices of classroom teachers. *Rural Education, 23*(1), 31–38.

Root, M. P. (1999). Resolving "Other" status: Identity development of biracial individuals. In S. Coontz (Ed.), *American families: A multicultural reader* (pp. 459–454). New York: Routledge.

Rose. L. C., & Gallup, A. M. (2002). The 34th annual Phi Delta Kappa/Gallup Poll of the public's attitude toward the public schools. *Phi Delta Kappan, 84,* 41–56.

Rose, L. C., & Gallup, A. M. (2003). The 35th annual Phi Delta Kappa/Gallup Poll of the public's attitude toward the public schools. *Phi Delta Kappan, 85,* 41–66.

Rosenthal, R., & Jacobson, L. (1968). *Pygmalion in the classroom.* New York: Holt, Rinehart & Winston.

Rowe, D. C. (1994). *The limits of family influence: Genes, experience and behavior.* New York: Guilford Press.

Rubin, H. (2002). *Collaborative leadership: Developing effective partnerships in communities and schools.* Thousand Oaks, CA: Corwin.

Rupp, R. (1998). *The complete home learning resource book.* New York: Three Rivers Press.

Sadker, D. (2002). An educator's primer on the gender war. *Phi Delta Kappan, 84*(3), 225–240.

Sadker, D., & Sadker, M. (1995). *Failing at fairness: How America's schools cheat girls.* New York: Touchstone.

Sadker, M. P., & Sadker, D. M. (2003). *Teachers, schools and society* (6th ed.). New York: McGraw-Hill.

Salend, S. J. (2001). *Creating inclusive classrooms: Effective and reflective practices* (4th ed.). Upper Saddle River, NJ: Merrill/Prentice Hall.

Salzstein, H. D. (1976). Social influence and moral development: A perspective on the role of parents and peers. In T. Lickona (Ed.), *Moral development and behavior: Theory, research, and social issues* (pp. 241–252). New York: Holt, Rinehart & Winston.

Sameroff, A. J. (1993). Models of development and developmental risk. In C. H. Zeanah, Jr. (Ed.), *Handbook of infant and mental health* (pp. 3–13). New York: Guilford Press.

Sameroff, A., Seifer, R., Barocas, R., Zax, M., & Greenspan, S. (1987). Intelligence quotient scores of 4-year-old children: Social–environmental risk factors. *Pediatrics, 79,* 343–350.

Sanders, M. G. 2003. Community involvement in schools: From concept to practice. *Education and Urban Society, 35*(2), 161–180.

Sanders, M. G., & Harvey, A. (2002). Beyond the school walls: A case study of principal leadership for school–community collaboration. *Teachers College Record, 104,* 1345–1368.

Sanderson, D. R. (2003). Engaging highly transient students. *Education, 123,* 600–605.

Sanderson, S. K. (1995). *Social transformations: A general theory of historical development.* Cambridge, MA: Blackwell.

Saul, W., & Newman, A. R. (1986). *Science fare: An illustrated guide and catalog of toys, books, and activities for kids.* New York: Harper & Row.

Scarf, M. (1995). *Intimate worlds: Life inside the family.* New York: Random House.

Scarf, M. (1997). *Intimate worlds: How families thrive and why they fail.* New York: Ballantine Books.

Scarf, M. (1999). *Intimate worlds: Life inside the family.* Collingdale, NY: Diane.

Scarr, S. (1998). American child care today. *American Psychologist, 53,* 95–108.

Scarr, S., & Eisenberg, M. (1998). Child care research: Issues perspective and results. *Annual Review of Psychology, 44,* 613–644.

Schlossman, S. (1976). Before Home Start: Notes towards a history of parent education in America, 1897–1929. *Harvard Educational Review, 46,* 436–467.

Schorr, J. (2002). *Hard lessons: The promises of an inner city charter school.* New York: Ballantine Books.

Schorr, L. (1988). *Within our reach: Breaking the cycle of disadvantage.* New York: Anchor.

Schorr, L. B. (2001). Neighborhoods and communities that support parenthood. In J. C. Westman (Ed.), *Parenthood in America: Undervalued, underpaid, under siege* (pp. 257–264). Madison: University of Wisconsin Press.

Schott, J. C. (1989). Holy wars in education. *Educational Leadership, 47*(2), 61–66.

Schwartz, L. L., & Kaslow, F. W. (1997). *Painful partings: Divorce and its aftermath.* New York: Wiley.

Schwartz, P. (1995, February 16). The silent family: Together, but apart. *The New York Times,* p. C6.

Schweinhart, L. J., & Weikart, D. P. (1997). *Lasting differences: The High/Scope preschool curriculum comparison study through age 23* (Monographs of the High/Scope Educational Research Foundation, 12). Ypsilanti, MI: High/Scope.

Scully, P. (2003). Time out from tension: Teaching young children how to relax. *The Journal of Early Education and Family Review, 10*(4), 22–29.

Scully, P., Seefeldt, C., & Barbour, N. H. (2003). *Developmental continuity across the preschool and primary grades: Implications for teachers* (2nd ed). Olney, MD: Association for Childhood Education International.

Seefeldt, C., & Barbour, N. (1998). *Early childhood education: An introduction* (4th ed.). Upper Saddle River. NJ: Merrill/Prentice Hall.

Sheldon, S. B., & Epstein, J. L. (2002). Improving student behavior and school discipline with family and community involvement. *Education and Urban Society, 35*(1), 4–26.

Shoop, R. J., & Dunklee, D. R. (1992). *School law for the principal: A handbook for practitioners.* Boston: Allyn & Bacon.

Sigel, I. E., Dreyer, A. S., & McGillicuddy-DeLisi, A. V. (1984). Psychological perspectives of the family. In R. D. Parke (Ed.), *Review of child development research: Vol. 7. The family* (pp. 42–79). Chicago: University of Chicago Press.

Sigel, I. E., McGillicuddy-DeLisi, A. V., & Goodnow, J. J. (Eds.). (1992). *Parental belief systems: The psychological consequences for children* (2nd ed.). Hillsdale, NJ: Erlbaum.

Silber, J. (1989). *Straight shooting: What's wrong with America and how to fix it.* New York: Harper & Row.

Singer, D. S., & Singer, J. L. (2001). Introduction: Why a handbook on children and media. In D. S. Singer & J. L. Singer (Eds.), *Handbook of children and the media* (pp. vi–xxii). Thousand Oaks, CA: Sage.

Singer, J. L., & Singer, D. G. (1992). *The house of make believe: Children's play and the developing imagination.* Cambridge, MA: Harvard University Press.

Slaby, R. G., Roedell, W. C., Arezzo, D., & Hendrix, K. (1995). *Early violence prevention: Tools for teachers of young children.* Washington, DC: National Association for the Education of Young Children.

Sleeter, C. E., & Grant, C. A. (2003). *Making choices for multicultural education: Five approaches to race, class, and gender* (4th ed.). New York: Wiley.

Smrekar, C. E. (1993). Rethinking family–school interactions: A prologue to linking schools and social services. *Education and Urban Society, 25*(2), 175–186.

Sonenstein, F. L., Gates, G., Schmidt, S., & Bolshun, N. (2002). *Primary child care arrangements of employed parents: Findings from the 1999 national survey of America's families.* Washington, DC: Urban Institute.

Spaggiari, S. (1998). The community–teacher partnership and its expansion in the governance of the schools. In C. Edwards, L. Gandini, & G. Forman (Eds.), *The hundred languages of children: The Reggio Emilia approach—Advanced reflections* (pp. 99–113). Greenwich, CT: Ablex.

Spewock, T. S. (1991). Teaching parents of young children through learning packets. *Young Children, 47*(1), 28–30.

Spitz, R. (1945). Hospitalism: An inquiry into the genesis of psychiatric conditions in early childhood. *Psychoanalytic study of the child, 1*(1), 53–74.

Stallings, J. (1980). Allocated academic learning time revisited, or beyond time on task. *Educational Researcher, 9*(11), 11–16.

Stanford, B. H., & Yamamoto, K. (Eds.). (2001). *Children and stress: Understanding and helping.* Olney, MD: Association for Childhood Education International.

Stein, C. B., Jr. (1986). *Sink or swim: The politics of bilingual education.* Westport, CT: Greenwood.

Steinberg, L. (1991). Authoritative parenting and adolescent adjustment across various ecological niches. *Journal of Research in Adolescence, 1*, 19–36.

Stevens, M. L. (2001). *The kingdom of children: Culture and controversy in the homeschooling movement.* Princeton, NJ: Princeton University Press.

Stiggins, R. J. (2001). *Student-involved classroom assessment* (3rd ed.). Upper Saddle River, NJ: Merrill/Prentice Hall.

Stille, A. (1998, June 11). The betrayal of history. *New York Review of Books, 45*(10) pp. 8–11. Also retrieved from May 4, 2003, from www.nybooks.com

Stinnett, N., & DeFrain, J. (1986). *Secrets of strong families.* Boston: Little, Brown.

Strasburger, V. C., & Wilson, B. J. (2002). *Children, adolescents, and the media.* Thousand Oaks, CA: Sage.

Strom, R., & Strom, S. (1997). Building a theory of grandparent development. *Journal of Aging and Human Development, 9*, 255–285.

Stroud, J. E., Stroud, J. C., & Staley, L. M. (1997). Understanding and supporting adoptive families. *Early Childhood Journal, 24*(9), 229–234.

Studer, J. R. (1993/1994). Listen so that parents will speak. *Childhood Education, 70*(2), 74–76.

Sugrue, T. J. (1999). Poor families in an era of urban transformation: The underclass family in myth and reality. In S. Coontz, (Ed.), *American families: A multicultural reader* (pp. 243–258). New York: Routledge.

Sulzby, E., & Teale, W. H. (2003). The development of the young child and the emergence of literacy. In J. Flood, D. Lapp, J. Squire, & J. Jensen

(Eds.), *Handbook of research on teaching the English-language arts* (2nd ed., pp. 300–313). Mahwah, NJ: Erlbaum.

Sutherland, Z. (1996). *Children and books* (9th ed.). Boston: Allyn & Bacon.

Swap, S. M. (1993). *Developing home–school partnerships: From concepts to practice.* New York: Teachers College Press.

Swick, K. J. (1999). Empowering homeless and transient children and families: An ecological framework for early childhood teachers. *Early Childhood Education Journal, 26*(3), 195–201.

Szasz, M. C. (1977). *Education and the American Indian.* Albuquerque: University of New Mexico Press.

Szasz, M. C. (1988). *Indian education in the American colonies, 1607–1783.* Albuquerque: University of New Mexico Press.

Tabors, P. O., & Snow, C. E. (2001). Young children and early literacy development. In S. Neuman & D. K. Dickinson (Eds.), *Handbook of early literacy research* (pp. 159–178). New York: Guilford Press.

Tao, F., Khan, S., & Arriola, C. (1997). *Special analysis of migrant education: Even Start Projects 1995–1996 program year.* Washington, DC: U.S. Department of Education, Office of Educational Research and Improvement. (ERIC Document Reproduction Service No. ED417921)

Tao, F., Gamse, B., & Tarr, H. (1998). *National evaluation of the Even Start Family Literacy Program: 1994–1997* (Gov. Doc. ED 1.310/2:427889). Washington, DC: U.S. Department of Education, Office of Educational Research and Improvement.

Tapscott, D. (1999). Educating the Net generation. *Educational Leadership, 56*(5), 6–11.

Taylor, K. W. (1981). *Parents and children learn together.* New York: Teachers College Press.

Taylor, R. L. (2000). Diversity within African American families. In D. Demo, K. Allen, & M. Fine (Eds.), *Handbook of family diversity* (pp. 232–257). New York: Oxford University Press.

Teachman, J. D. (2000). Diversity of family structure: Economic and social influences. In D. Demo, K. Allen, & M. Fine (Eds.), *Handbook of family diversity* (pp. 32–58). New York: Oxford University Press.

Teale, W. H. (1986). Home background and young children's literacy development. In W. H. Teale & E. Sulzby (Eds.), *Emergent literacy: Writing and reading* (pp. 173–206). Norwood, NJ: Ablex.

Terzi, N., & Cantorelli, M. (2001). Parma: Supporting the work of teachers, through professional development, organization and administrative support. In L. Gandini & C. P. Edwards (Eds.), *Bambini: The Italian approach to infant–toddler care* (pp. 78–89). New York: Teachers College Press.

Teaching Home. (2002). *Educational approaches and methods.* Retrieved May 3, 2003, from www.teachinghome.com

Thomas, R. M. (2001). *Recent theories of human development.* Thousand Oaks, CA: Sage.

Thornburgh, D., & Lin, H. S. (Eds). (2002). *Youth, pornography and the Internet.* Washington, D.C: National Academy Press.

Tiedt, P. L., & Tiedt, I. M. (2001). *Multicultural teaching: A handbook of activities, information and resources.* Reading, MA: Allyn & Bacon.

Tittle, C. K. (1986). Gender research and education. *American Psychologist, 41*, 1161–1168.

Tomlin, A. M., (1998). Grandparents' influences on grandchildren. In M. E. Szinovacz (Ed.), *Handbook on grandparenthood* (pp. 161–171). Westport, CT: Greenwood.

Tompkins, G. E. (2003). *Literacy for the 21st century: Teaching reading and writing in prekindergarten through grade 4.* Upper Saddle River, NJ: Merrill/Prentice Hall.

Trahan, C., & Lawler-Prince, D. (1999). Parent partnerships: Transforming homework into home–school activities. *Early Childhood Education Journal, 27*(1), 65–68.

Travers, P. D., & Rebore, R. W. (2000). *Foundations of education: Becoming a teacher* (4th ed.). Boston: Allyn & Bacon.

Trawick-Smith, J. (2003). *Early childhood development: A multicultural perspective* (3rd ed.). Upper Saddle River, NJ: Merrill/Prentice Hall.

Turnbull, R., Turnbull, A., Shank, M., Smith, S., & Leal, D. (2002). *Exceptional lives: Special education in today's schools* (3rd ed.). Upper Saddle River, NJ: Merrill/Prentice Hall.

Tyson, H. (1999). A load off the teachers' backs: Coordinated school health programs. *Phi Delta Kappan, 80*, K1–K8.

U.S. Bureau of the Census. (1998a). *Current population report: P20–497–1998*. Washington, DC: Author.

U.S. Bureau of the Census. (1998b). *Statistical abstract of the United States: 1998* (118th ed.). Washington, DC: Author.

U.S. Bureau of the Census. (2002b). *Statistical abstract of the United States: 2002* (122nd ed.). Washington, DC: Author.

U.S. Bureau of the Census. (2001). *Current population report* (pp. 20–52). Washington, DC: Author.

U.S. Bureau of the Census. (2002a). *Current population report: P20-537-2000*. Washington, DC: Author.

U.S. Bureau of the Census. (2003). *Annual social and economic supplements*. (Current population survey 196C–2003). Washington, DC: Author. Also retrieved September 19, 2003, from www.census.gov/hhes/poverty

U.S. Department of Education. (1991). *America 2000: An education strategy*. Washington, DC: Author.

U.S. Department of Education. (1993a). *Goals 2000: Educate America*. Washington, DC: Author.

U.S. Department of Education. (1993b). *National Education Goals*. Gov. Doc. ED 1.2:G 53/5) Washington, DC: Author.

U.S. Department of Education. (1994). *Strong families, strong schools*. Washington, DC: Author.

U.S. Department of Education. (1999). *Twenty-first annual report to congress on the implementation of the Individuals with Disabilities Education Act*. Washington, DC: Author.

U.S. Department of Education. (2003). The nation's report card. *The Achiever, 2*(1), 2–3.

Uphoff, J. K. (1993). Religious diversity and education. In J. A. Banks & C. A. McGee-Banks (Eds.), *Multicultural education: Issues and perspectives* (2nd ed., pp. 90–107). Boston: Allyn & Bacon.

Urban Institute. (2002). *Homeless Americans*. Washington, DC: Author. Also retrieved August 10, 2003, from www.nationalhomeless.org/numbers.html

Uttal, L. (2002). *Making care work: Employed mothers in the new childcare market*. New Brunswick, NJ: Rutgers University Press.

Valente, W. D., & Valente, C. (2001). *Law in the schools* (5th ed.). Upper Saddle River, NJ: Prentice Hall.

Van Evra, J. (1998). *Television and child development* (2nd ed.). Mahwah, NJ: Erlbaum.

Vissing, Y. M. (1996). *Out of sight, out of mind: Homeless children and families in small-town America*. Lexington: University Press of Kentucky.

Vosler, N. R. (1996). *New approaches to family practice: Confronting economic stress*. Thousand Oaks, CA: Sage.

Voss, M. M. (1993). "I just watched": Family influences on one child's learning. *Language Arts, 70*, 632–641.

Vygotsky, L. S. (1978). *Mind in society*. Cambridge, MA: Harvard University Press.

Wade, T. E., Jr. (1998). *The home school manual: Plans, pointers and resources*. Bridgman, MI: Gazelle.

Wagner, M. (1995). *Contributions of poverty and ethnic background to the participation of secondary school students in special education*. Washington, DC: U.S. Department of Education.

Wagner, N. J. (1995). *Into the woods*. Unpublished master's thesis, University of Maryland, Baltimore.

Wagner, T. (2003). Reinventing American schools. *Phi Delta Kappan, 84*, 665–668.

Wagstaff, L. H., & Gallagher, K. S. (1990). Schools, families and communities: Idealized images and new realities. In B. Mitchell & L. L. Cunningham (Eds.), *Educational leadership and changing contexts of families, communities, and schools: Eighty-ninth Yearbook of the NSSE, Part II* (pp. 91–117). Chicago: National Society for the Study of Education.

Walberg, H. J. (1984). Improving the productivity of America's Schools. *Educational Leadership, 41*(8), 19–27.

Walberg, H. J. (2001). Understanding market-based school reform. In C. Wang & H. J. Walberg (Eds.), *School choice or best systems: What improves education?* (pp. 3–38). Mahwah, NJ: Erlbaum.

Walker, L. J., & Taylor, J. H. (1991). Family interaction and the development of moral reasoning. *Child Development, 62*, 264–283.

Waller, P. L., & Crawford, K. (2001). Education advocacy for the nation's invisible population—The migrant community. *Delta Kappa Gamma Bulletin, 68*(1),24–27.

Wallerstein, J., Lewis, J., & Blakeslee, S. (2000). *The unexpected legacy of divorce.* New York: Hyperion.

Wallerstein, J. S. (2001). The challenges of divorce for parents and children. In J. C. Westman (Ed.), *Parenthood in America: Undervalued, underpaid, under siege* (pp. 127–139). Madison: University of Wisconsin Press.

Walsh, F. (2002). Family resilience: Strengths forged through adversity. In F. Walsh (Ed.), *Normal family processes: Growing diversity and complexity* (pp. 399–423). New York: Guilford Press.

Walsh, M. (2002, June 5). Home school enrollment surge fuels "cottage" industry. *Education Week, 21*(39), 8.

Wang, M. C., & Walberg. H. J. (2001). Epilogue. In M. C. Wang & H. J. Walberg (Eds.), *School choice or best systems: What improves education.* Mahwah, NJ: Erlbaum.

Wardle, F. (2003). *Introduction to early childhood education: A multidimensional approach to child-centered care and learning.* Boston: Pearson.

Wassermann, S. (2000). *Serious players in the primary classroom: Empowering children through active learning experiences* (2nd ed.). New York: Teachers College Press.

Wassermann, S. (2001). *The long-distance grandmother* (4th ed.). Point Roberts, WA: Hartley & Marks.

Webb, L. D., Metha, A., & Jordan, K. F. (2003). *Foundations of American education* (4th ed.). Upper Saddle River, NJ: Merrill/Prentice Hall.

Weber, E. (1969). *The kindergarten.* New York: Teachers College Press.

Weikhart, D. P., & Schweinhart, L. J. (1991). Disadvantaged children and curriculum effects. In L. Rescorla, M. C. Hyson, & K. Hirsch-Pasek (Eds.), *Academic instruction in early childhood: Challenge or pressure?* (No. 53, pp. 57–64). San Francisco: Jossey-Bass.

Weinberg, M. (1977). *A chance to learn: A history of race and education in the United States.* New York: Cambridge University Press.

Weiss, A. R. (1997). *Going it alone: A study of Massachusetts charter schools.* Boston: Institute for Responsive Education.

Weldin, D. J., & Tumarkin, S. R. (1999). More power in the portfolio process. *Childhood Education, 75*(2), 90–96.

Wells, S. S. (1998). Charter school reform in California: Does it meet expectations? *Phi Delta Kappan, 80,* 305–312.

Werner, E. E. (1999). *Through the eyes of innocents: Children witness World War II.* Boulder, CO. Westview Press.

Werner, E. E., & Smith, R. S. (1992). *Overcoming the odds: High-risk children from birth to adulthood.* Ithaca, NY: Cornell University Press.

Werner, E. E., & Smith, R. S. (1998). *Vulnerable but invincible: A longitudinal study of resilient children and youth.* New York: McGraw-Hill.

Werner, E. E., & Smith, R. (2001). *Journeys from childhood to midlife: Risk, resilience, and recovery.* Ithaca, NY: Cornell University Press.

Westinghouse Learning Corporation–Ohio University. (1969). *The impact of Head Start.* Springfield, VA: U.S. Department of Commerce, Clearinghouse for Federal Scientific and Technical Information.

Westman, J. C. (2001). Growing together: Parenthood as a developmental experience. In J. C. Westman (Ed.), *Parenthood in America: Undervalued, underpaid, under siege* (pp. 34–46). Madison: University of Wisconsin Press.

White, B. L. (1971, October). *Fundamental early environmental influences on the development of competence.* Paper presented at the Third Western Symposium on Learning and Cognitive Learning, Washington State College, Bellingham.

White, B. L., & Watts, J. C. (1973). *Experience and environment: Major influences on the development of the young child* (Vol. 1). Upper Saddle River, NJ: Prentice Hall.

Whitman, W. (1855). *Leaves of grass.* New York: Andrew & James Rome.

Williams, M. R. (1997). *The parent centered early school.* New York: Garland.

Williams, W. L. (1998). Social acceptance of same-sex relationships in families: Models from other cultures. In C. J. Patterson & A. R. D'Augelli (Eds.), *Lesbian, gay, and bisexual identities in families: Psychological perspectives* (pp. 53–75). New York: Oxford University Press.

Winn, M. (2002). What television chases out of life *American Educator, 26*(2), 40–45.

Wohl, F. (1997). A panoramic view of work and family. In S. Parasuraman & J. H. Greenhaus (Eds.), *Integrating work and family: Challenges and choices for a changing world* (pp. 15–24). West-port, CT: Quorum Books.

Woodruff, D. W. (1999). Keeping community "real" for urban school success. In E. Arce (Ed.), *Perspectives: Early childhood education* (pp. 155–157). Boulder, CO: Coursewise.

Woolfolk, A. E. (2000). *Educational psychology* (8th ed.). Boston: Allyn & Bacon.

Wortham, S. (2002). *Early childhood curriculum: Developmental bases for learning and teaching* (3rd ed.). Upper Saddle River, NJ: Prentice Hall.

Wright, J., & Huston, A. (1995). *Effects of educational TV viewing of lower-income preschoolers on academic skills, school readiness, and school adjustment one to three years later.* Lawrence, KS: Center for Research on the Influence of Television on Children.

Wright, M. A. (1998). *I'm chocolate, you're vanilla: Raising healthy Black and biracial children in a race-conscious world.* San Francisco: Jossey-Bass.

Wynter, L. (2002). *American skin: Pop culture, big business, and the end of White America.* New York: Crown.

Yamaguchi, B. J., Strawser, S., & Higgins, K. (1997). Children who are homeless: Implications for educators. *Intervention in School and Clinic, 33*(2), 90–97.

Yell, M. L. (1998). The legal bases of inclusion. *Educational Leadership, 56*(2), 70–71.

Young, K. T., Marsland, K. W., & Zigler, E. (1997). The regulatory status of center-based infant and toddler child care. *American Journal of Orthopsychiatry, 67*, 541–560.

Zeanah, C. H., & Scheeringa, M. S. (1997). The experiences and effects of violence in infancy. In J. S. Osofsky (Ed.), *Children in a violent society* (pp. 97–123). New York: Guilford.

Zehr, M. A. (2002b). Oregon school district reaches out to our arrivals from Mexico. *Education Week, 21*(28), 16–18.

Zehr, M. A. (2002a). No end seen to flap over California home school policy. *Education Week, 22*(9), 23–26.

Zelizer, V. A. (1994). *Pricing the priceless child: The changing social value of children.* Princeton, NJ: Princeton University Press.

Index

Abramowitz, R. H., 171, 281
Abuse and neglect, of children, 112
Abusive behavior, 89
Academic contributions, girls *vs.* boys, 7
Academic curriculum, 143
Academic learning, 176–177
Academic rationalism, 207t, 208
Academic success, reading, 6
Achievement, promoting, 90–91
Acland, H., 107
Active Parenting Discussion Group, 310
Adams, D. B., 120
Adams, M. J., 186
Adelman, H. S., 234, 248, 250
Adjacency condition, parenting, 103
Administration, 160, 214–215
Adoptive families, 64
  children's books about, 362
Adult connections and support, 248–249
Adult to child ratios, child care, 131f
Adversity, 271
Advertising, 20
Advisory committees, child care quality, 135
Advocates, parents as, 309
Aesthetic education, 148
Aesthetics, appreciation for, 146
Affectionate interactions, 10
Affective impact, 150
African Americans, 49
  advancing children's education, 49–50
Age levels and influence, 9–16
Aggression
  in society, 20
  television, 267–268

Aggressive-acting behavior, 3
Aid to Families with Dependent Children (AFDC), 44, 121
Alexander, A., 267
Alfonso, E. M., 170
Algozzino, R., 314
Allen, K. R., 59
Allhusen, V. D., 13, 145
Alternative insemination, 65
Alternative schools, 212
Althouse, R., 146
America Reads Challenge, 42
America 2000: An Education Strategy, 279
American Disability Act, 44
American households
  distribution of income, 73f
  types of, 60f
Among Schoolchildren, 155
Anderson, C., 109, 110, 156
Anderson, E., 109
Anderson, E. A., 180
Anderson, J. W., 253
Anderson, K. J., 248
Andreason, M., 268
Apple, M. W., 143
Apple Tree, 245
Applebee, A. N., 186, 201
Appleton, H., 245
Appropriate education, 228
Arab Americans, 51
Arce, E., 142
Arendell, T., 20
Arezzo, D., 250
Aronson, S. S., 147, 148, 149
Arriola, C., 76
Art museums, 242
Asato, J., 51
Asian Americans, 51
Asian cultures, 246
Asking, 318
At-risk children, 72

Attitudes, 148, 270, 274–275, 319
  changing, 4
  community influence, 8
  definition, 4
  home influence, 5–6
  multicultural education, advancing children's education, 52
  parenting, 93
  school influence, 6–8
Authoritarian (autocratic) parenting, 100
Authoritative (democratic) parenting, 100
Autonomy, 351

Babies, books for, 146
Back-to-School Night, 294–295, 304, 307
Bailyn, B., 62, 81
Baker, K., 51
Ball, S., 245
Bane, M. J., 107
Banks, C. A., 94, 97
Banks, J. A., 53, 60, 84, 94
Barbour, C., 195
Barbour, N., 26, 40, 103, 120, 146, 195, 222, 271, 310
Barfield, R., 198, 200
Barnard, Henry, 38
Barney, 245
Barocas, R., 109, 114, 263
Bartolome, L. I., 8
Barton, C. E., 331
Bathing, 182–183
Baumrind, D., 100, 101, 104, 179, 215, 264
Baumrind's classification, parenting styles, 100–101
Beaty, J. J., 26
Bedard, C., 156
Bedden, D., 170, 253

Bedtime, 179, 183
Behavioral objectives, 208
Behaviorism, 29t
Beliefs, 196, 265, 273–274
  parenting, 93
Bell, C. C., 277
Ben-Avie, M., 327, 339, 356
Bender, J., 140
Benson, P. L., 72, 83, 112, 154,
  155, 156, 270, 356
Bergen, D., 128, 133, 140
Berger, E. H., 272, 309
Berlin, I., 36, 48
Berndt, T. J., 150, 285
Berns, R. M., 4, 13, 17, 92, 98,
  120, 175, 191, 265, 272
Bernstein, B., 102, 264, 266
Bettelheim, B., 184
Bianchi, S. M., 63, 64, 92, 93,
  109, 120, 136
Bias, 276
Bi-directional process, 3
Big Brother, 256
Big Sister, 256
Bigner, J. J., 92, 112, 115, 202,
  250
Bilingual education, 68
Biological-physiological and
  cultural factors advancing
  children's education, 31–32
Biracial families, 66, 69
Black, J. K., 146
Black Muslims, family
  diversity, 78
Blakeslee, S., 11, 109
Blank, H., 45
Blended families, 64
  arrangements, 64
  children's books about, 361
Bloom, Benjamin, 210
Bloom, B. S., 150
Bloom, J., 309, 327
Blue-collar workers, 81
Blue's Clues, 267
Blumenfeld, P., 7
Bobbitt, Franklin, 210
Bogatz, G., 245
Boivin, M., 252
Boll, E., 184

Bolshun, N., 122, 123
Bond, J. T., 122
Book censorship, 277, 284
Book talks, 242
Books, 245, 266
  for babies, 146
  nature, 253
Borkowski, J. G., 6
Bornstein, M. H., 4, 13, 15, 34,
  89, 92, 97
Bossard, J., 184
Bottom-up approach, 344–345
Bowman, B., 231
Boyd-Franklin, N., 91
Boys *vs.* girls, academic
  contributions, 7
Braden, J. S., 350
Bradley, R. H., 230, 235
Brain structure and activity,
  child development, 9
Brain-environment interactive
  development, 9
Brazelton, T., 114, 268
Bredekamp, S., 128, 207
Britner, P. A., 112, 143, 162
Bronfenbrenner, U., 8, 13, 14,
  31, 32, 56, 143, 145, 170,
  171, 235, 270, 271, 281
  bioecological theory, 3
Brooks, S., 158
Brooks-Gunn, J., 101
Brophy, J. E., 216, 217, 275,
  280
Brouillette, L., 215, 350, 351
Brown, C. E., 8
Bruer, J. T., 3, 10, 266
Buddhism, family diversity, 78
Buell, J., 298
Bukowski, W. M., 252
Bulletin boards, 298
Bullivant, B. M., 96
Bullock, H. A., 50
Burch, P., 324, 349
Burtless, G., 74
Burts, D. C., 264
Bus, A. G., 6
Bushman, B. J., 20
Businesses, 282
  community, 313

enterprises, 236, 244–245
Butler, R. D., 95

Cadwell, L. B., 356
Calfee, C., 218
Calvert School, 197
Campbell, F. A., 14
Camping, 190
Cantorelli, M., 342
Care, 270
Caregivers
  responsibilities of, 144–147
  understanding, 24
Carper, J. C., 197
Carter, D. A., 328
Carter, M., 258, 289
CASA Vida program, 198
Casbergue, R. M., 145
Casper, L. M., 63, 64, 92, 93,
  109, 120, 136
Cassebaum, A., 212
Catholics, family diversity, 78
Cavallaro, K., 248
Ceci, S. J., 3
Center-based care, 13, 126–127
Change, components of
  successful, 328–331
Chanoff, D., 213
Charren, P., 23
Charter school programs, 342,
  350–354
Chat groups, 247
Cherlin, A. J., 194, 195
Cherry, L., 284
Child Abuse Prevention and
  Treatment Act of 1974, 148
Child care, 40, 108f
  adult to child ratios, 131f
  affordability, 136–137
  arrangements, 124–129
    for children under 5, 123f
    parenting, 108
    for school-age children,
    123–f
  concerns, 123–124
  curriculum, 132–134
  features of quality, 130
  financial considerations,
    136–137

government funding, 120
government remedies, 120
history of, 119–121
middle-class families, 121
needs
  from infancy through
    school age, 117–140
  in United States, 121–124
options, 118
programs, 206–207
qualities of caregivers, 132
quality, 136–137
  advisory committees, 135
  characteristics, 134–136
  creation of alliances, 135
  effects of, 136
  high standards, 135
  institutional structures,
    135
  need for, 118
  staff benefits, 135
questions, about quality,
  136–137
regulations and voluntary
  accreditation, 129–130
services, market-based
  system, 121
state standards, 121
trends, 122–123
workforce, 137
Child care centers, 13, 39,
  126–127
Child Care Development Block
  Grant (CCDBG), 45, 120
Child-centered parenting, 100
Children
  attitudes, 4–9
  below poverty, by race and
    Hispanic origin, 113f
  books, bibliography of,
    359–364
  development
    brain structure and brain
      activity, 9
    grandparents influencing,
      191–194
    historical perspective
      theories, 29t
    parental knowledge of, 268

with disabilities, parenting,
  112–113
educating and protecting,
  141–166
education in school, 147–148
influence, 4f
learning affected by, 2
maltreatment, 149t
perceptions and attitudes,
  4–9
protecting, 148
rearing, 144
  patterns, 270
  range of, 88–89
Children's Defense Fund, 111,
  155
Children's Resources
  International, 310
Chinn, P. C., 47, 48, 51, 78, 79,
  81, 227
Chrisman, K., 147
Christianity, family diversity, 78
Christie, J., 146
Churches, 242, 243, 282
Civic services, 282
Civil Rights Act of 1964, 44
Civil rights movement,
  advancing children's
  education, 39
Civil War, advancing children's
  education, 49
Clark, R. M., 101, 104, 107, 177,
  179, 263, 264, 270
Clarke-Stewart, K. A., 13, 145
Classrooms
  organization patterns of, 219f
  setting, children with
    disabilities, 46f
  visits to, 294–295
Clawson, B., 170, 173
Clay, J. W., 317
Clay, M. M., 6
Clements, D. C., 13, 145
Cleveland, G., 146
Clifford, R. M., 136, 138
Cloud, N., 170
Cochran, M., 239, 240, 241,
  249, 284, 285
Codes, religious groups, 79–80

Code-switching, 266
Cognitive growth, 146
Cognitive impact, 150
Cognitive information, 251
Cognitive process, 207t, 208
Cohen, I., 107
Cohen, S., 37, 137
Cole, M., 7
Coleman, J. S., 4, 6, 8, 14, 25,
  76, 81, 96, 107, 156, 284
Coles, R., 160, 234, 262, 265,
  270, 272
Colfax, J. D., 200, 224
Colfax, M., 200, 224
Collaborations, 286–287,
  292–321
  achieving, 328
  advancing children's
    education, 43–44
  assessment of, 330
  associate level involvement,
    326–327
  communication, 330
  decision-making level
    involvement, 327
  implementation of, 329–330
  levels of involvement in,
    325–327
  minimum level involvement,
    326
  planning for, 329
  successful features, 330–331
  understanding involvement
    in, 326–327
Collaborative relationships,
  317–320
Collins, R. C., 332
Comenius, John, 37
Comer, J. P., 74, 114, 244, 245,
  246, 263, 276, 317, 325,
  327, 330, 335, 336, 337,
  338, 339, 340, 356
Comer's School Development
  Program, 335–348, 338f
  extended-day programs, 337
  focus program, 337
  goals of, 336–337
  mental health team, 336
  outgrowths of, 339–340

Comer's School Development
    Program (*continued*)
  parent program, 336–337
  pupil personnel team, 336
  research, 339
  school development program,
      337–338
  school planning and
      management team, 336
  social skills curriculum, 337
  structure of, 336–337
  workshops, 337
Comics, 246
Commercial enterprises,
    244–245
Communal living arrangements,
    81
Communication, 293
  collaborations, 330
  establishing with parents,
      296–304
  parent-teacher strategies, 305t
Communities, 143
  advancing children's
      education, 28, 36–38
  agencies, 255–257
  clubs, 244
  collaboration, 256
  curriculum, 234–258
  governance, 164
  hidden curriculum, 225–227
  influence on children
      attitudes, 8
      early age, 9–16
      perceptions, 8
      personnel affected by, 2
  involvement, 311–313
  libraries, homework, 298
  materials, 236t
  media, 236t
      influence, 4f
  members, as school resources,
      308–309
  nurturance, 159–160
  organizations, 281
  personnel affected by, 2
  resource for materials,
      312–313
  resources, 236t

responsibilities of, 148–154
services, 236t
and society, code of ethical
    conduct, 370–371
structure, impact on
    curriculum, 235–248
trips, 311–313
understanding, 24
violence, 250, 277
workers, 236
Competency, mixed messages,
    192
Competent community,
    assessing, 286t
Competent families, 263–271
  parenting, 114–115
Competent parents, 114
Compulsory education, 38, 195
Computers, 247
Conferences, 301
  innovative practices for,
      301–307
Conley, D. T., 166
Connor, R., 245
Constructive play, 253
Constructivist, 207t, 208,
    211–212
  classrooms
      day schedule, 223t
      formal curriculum, 221–222
Contemporary families, changes
    in, 80–83
Cook, T., 245
Coontz, S., 59, 61, 70, 81, 171
Cooperation, home schooling,
    196
Cooperative learning, 221
Coping skills, teaching, 271
Copple, C., 128
Corliss, J. C., 95
Cornell, C. E., 246
Cornell, J. B., 258
Corsaro, W. A., 56
Cosleeping, cultural groups, 99
Couchenour, D., 147
Counting, 251
Court confrontations, home
    schooling, 195
Covert curriculum, 227

Cowan, C. P., 143
Cowan, P. A., 143
Crawford, K., 75
Creation of alliances, child care
    quality, 135
Creative development, space
    influencing, 178–179
Creemers, B., 289
Cremin, L. A., 38
Critical periods of development,
    31
Cross, W. E., 95
Cross-cultural experiences,
    213
Crowley, M. L., 47, 48, 72, 74,
    77, 249
Cruickshank, D., 216, 275
Cryer, D., 136, 138
Culatta, R. A., 75, 228, 274
Cultural agencies, 241–244
  organization and
      management, 264–265
Cultural background, 66
Cultural deprivation, 52
Cultural differences, kin
    relationships, 193–194
Cultural expectations, family
    diversity, 69
Cultural factors, advancing
    children's education, 31–32
Cultural groups
  cosleeping, 99
  parenting, 97
  physical contact, 99
Cultural pluralism, 67
Cultural-context theories, 3
Culture, 96
  children's books about,
      359–360
  clash of, 246
  definition, 96
  values, transmitted, 98
Curran, D., 272
Curriculum, 147–148
  child care, 132–134
  community structure impact,
      235–248
  content of, 165
  forms, 218–229

grandparents providing, 190–195
guides for home schooling, 197
inappropriate, 276
orientations, 207–213
special education, 227–229
traditional schools, 220–221
Curriculum and materials, 52–53
Curtis, D., 258, 289
Custodial grandparents, 191
Customs, 184
Cutler, W. W., 163
CyperPatrol, 267

Dahlberg, G., 108
Daily routines, 179–183
Dalleck, R., 62, 81
Dame schools, 35
Damon, W., 270
Danzberger, J. P., 43
D'Arcangelo, M., 9
Darwin, Charles, 30–31
Dash, J., 95
Dash, L., 112
Davies, D., 324, 330, 349
Davila, V, 284, 285
Davis, D., 62, 81
Day, preparing for, 180
De Carvalho, M. E. P., 162, 163
Deckard, S., 196
DeFrain, J., 179
DeGormo, D. S., 109, 110
Deiner, P. L., 4
Demarrais, K. P., 231, 278
Demo, D. H., 59
Democratic, parenting, 100
Demographics, changing, 253
Dentist, 237
Desmond, R., 17, 18, 20
Development
  factors, 3
  impact on parental behaviors and attitudes, 4
Developmental stage, 143
DeVita, C. J., 47, 75, 82
Dewey, John, 211
DeWolf, M., 264

Dickey, C., 246
Dighe, J., 254
Digital cameras, 299
Dilworth, M. E., 8
Dimidijian, V. J., 76
Dinkmeyer, D., 310
Dinkmeyer, J., 310
Disabilities, children with, 45–46, 46f
Disabled, 45
  children, 314–315
Discipline, 319
Disciplined Mind, 179
Discourse function, parenting, 103
Distant grandparents, 191, 193
Diversity, 274–275. *See also* Family diversity
  ethnic, 315–316
  professional implications, 83
Divorce consequences, parenting, 109
Divorced families, children's books about, 360–361
Doll, R. C., 147, 179, 208, 213, 280
Donald, D., 62, 81
Dorris, M., 359
Douville-Watson, L., 4
Dramatic play, 316
Dreeben, R., 143
Dreyer, A. S., 5, 266
Drop-in child care, 129
Drug abuse counseling, 282
Drug lords, 262
Dual-income families, 248
  parenting, 110
Dubrow, N., 105, 112, 160, 206, 248, 262, 279
Duckett, E., 104
Due process, 228
Duffey, J., 196
Duncan, G. J., 235
Dunklee, D. R., 162
Dunn, K., 217
Durkin, D. D., 6
Dysfunctional family situations, 89, 190
Dyson, A. H., 271

Early, M., 325
Early childhood program, quality features of, 130
Early contacts with families, 293–294
Early Head Start, 147
Early infant-mother attachment, 11
Early socialization skills, 144–145
Early years, strong home influence, 9
Eastern aggregations, family diversity, 79
Eastern Orthodox, family diversity, 78
Eating habits, 147
Eccles, J., 7
Ecksel, I. B., 4, 12
Economic status, advancing children's education, 35
Economic support, 11
  family, 91
Economics
  and American families, 72–73
  effects of family diversity, 76
Eddowes, E. A., 316
Edelsky, C., 266
Edin, K., 64
Educate America Act, 42
Educating and protecting children, 141–166
Education
  equivalency of, 199
  governance of, 160–165
  philosophical swings, 39
Education for All Handicapped Children Act (PL 94–142), 45, 161
Educational assessments, 278–279
Educational opportunities, nurturing, 155–160
Educational orientation, 69f
  family diversity, 67–68
Educational toys, 144
Educational underpinnings, parenting, 95

Educators. *See also* Professionals; Teachers
advancing children's education, 43–44
Edwards, C. P., 162, 224, 340
Effective communities, 281–285
Effective partnerships, 286–287
Effective schools, 271–280
barriers for, 276–277
Effective teachers, 275
Egan, R. W., 314
Egg box construction, 218
Eisner, E., 208, 231
Electronic bulletin boards, 247
Electronic media, 20
Elementary and Secondary Act of 1965 (PL 89–10), 44
Eley, M. A., 196, 198
Elgin, C. Z., 104
Elitism, 276
Elkin, F., 250
Elkind, D., 53, 124, 145
E-mail, 247, 293, 299
Embedded partners, 292
Emotional abuse, 149t
Emotional bonds, parenting, 92
Emotional environment, 270–271
Emotional growth, space influencing, 177
Emotional neglect, 149t
Emotional support, 12–13, 90
family, 92
Emotionally remote grandparents, 191
Employer-sponsored child care centers, 126
Engel, B., 299
Englehart, M. D., 150
Entertainment facilities, 152–153
Entertainment industry, 21–22
influence on children, 17
Environmental and biological factors, 28
Environmental influences, 28
Enz, B., 146
Epstein, J., 155, 166, 292, 322, 325, 328, 329, 345, 346, 348, 349, 356

Erikson, E., 9, 11, 31
Essa, E. L., 147
Esteem, promoting, 90–91
Ethical conduct, NAEYC Academy for Early Childhood Program Accreditation, 365–371
Ethnic and cultural groups, parenting, 97
Ethnic associations, 236t
Ethnic background, definition, 96
Ethnic community contributions, 252–253
Ethnic diversity, 315–316. *See also* Family diversity
Ethnic group, percentage of population, 97t
Ethnic identification, 66
Ethnically diverse neighborhoods, 14
Ethnic orientation, 66
Ethnicity and culture, 96
Ethnocentrism, 18, 276
European tales, 246
Evans, E., 292, 332
Even Start, 76, 334–335
Exceptional Lives, 227
Expectations, 69f
Experiences, 143
Exploration, 146
Exploratory play, 253
Extended-day programs, 337
Extended families, 53, 61–62, 119
children's books about, 362–363
roles and rituals, 174–175
External barriers, 320

Faith-based organizations, 242
Faith-based social support groups, 79
Faith-specific holidays, 79
Families. *See also* Extended families
adoptive, 64
advancing children's education, 34–36

affected by, influence on children, 2
biracial, 66, 69
blended, 64
children's books about, 361
changes in functions, 96
with special needs, children, 77
code of ethical conduct, 367–368
competent, 263–271
parenting, 114–115
concepts, 59
configuration, influence on children, 10
connotation, 60
contemporary, changes in, 80–83
counseling, 282
cultural patterns and functions, 96–100
defining, 59
children's books about, 364
diverse nature of, 57–85
divorce, 109–110
children's books about, 360–361
consequences, 109
financial aspects, 109
dual-income, 248
parenting, 110
dysfunctional situations, 89, 190
early contacts, 293–294
emotional support, 92
establishing relationships with, 293–296
evaluating effectiveness, 272t
experiences of, 105–109
gay and lesbian, 65, 317
children's books about, 363–364
governance, 162–163
groupings, 65–66
health, 269
homeless, 75, 316–317
children's books about, 363
illness, 112–113
income, 248

levels, 73f
parenting, 110–111
interaction games, 106
interaction styles, 99
interethnic, 69
itinerant, 75
lesbian, 65, 80, 317
  children's books about,
    363–364
lifestyles, 63
limited-English-proficiency,
    68
linguistically diverse, 156
literacy programs, 144
low-SES, 76
middle- and lower middle-
    class, 71
middle- and upper income at-
    risk children, 72
middle-class, 71
  child care, 121
middle-income, 73
migrant, 75–76, 316–317
  children's books about,
    363
and minority populations,
    advancing children's
    education, 48
mobility, 106–107, 144–145
multigenerational family unit,
    61–62
multiracial and lesbian, 80
nontraditional, prejudices
    toward, 60
nuclear, 61, 72
nurturance, 88–91, 155–158
outreach, 187–190
postnuclear family units, 64
reconstituted, 64
reuniting at end of day, 183
role, 91–96
  parenting cultures, 100
separation, 109–110
services office, 281–282
single-parent, 62–64
  structural variations, 63
social factors relating, 66–70
socialization, 92
socioeconomic status, 70–77

status and role expectations,
    11–12
stress, parenting, 108–109
support from, 157–158
types of, 61–66
  in 2001, 62f
underclass, 74–75
upper middle-class, 71
values, 59
welfare to work, 72
working-class, 73–74
working with, 313–317
Family centers, 330
Family child care, 126
  group, 13
Family-community-school
    relationships, events
    affecting, 33t–34t
Family diversity, 57–85
  Black Muslims, 78
  Buddhism, 78
  Catholics, 78
  Christianity, 78
  cultural expectations, 69
  Eastern aggregations, 79
  Eastern Orthodox, 78
  educational orientation,
    67–68
  effects of economics, 76
  Hasidic sects, 78
  Industrial Revolution, 80
  interethnic families, 69
  Islam, 78
  Judaism, 78
  learning strategies, 67–68
  learning styles, 67–68
  minority status, 67–68
  Native American religious
    practices, 78
  postindustrial era, 81
  Protestants, 78
  race, 70
  racial, ethnic, and cultural
    factors, 66–67
  religious orientation, 77–80
  Roman Catholic, 78
  20th-century households, 81
  urbanization, 81
  women workforce, 81

World War II, 81
Family Support Act of 1988, 45
Farenga, P., 202
Farris, E., 43
Fear, of teachers, 319
Federal agencies as special-
    interest groups, 23
Federal government,
    advancing children's
    education, 41–42
Federal mandates, 23
Fenton Avenue Charter School
    (San Fernando Valley),
    352–353
Filtering systems for the
    Internet, 21
Financial aspects of divorce,
    parenting, 109
Financial capital, 14
Financial resources, child care
    quality, 135
Fine, M. A., 59
Fine, M. J., 155, 157, 179, 183,
    309, 310
Fire department, 237
Flatter, C. H., 140
Focus program, Comer's
    School Development
    Program, 337
Folklore, 98, 184
Food, 147
Food pantries, 282
Forced mobility, 107
Forgatch, M. S., 109, 110
Formal curriculum, 205,
    220–224
  constructivist classrooms,
    221–222
  personal relevance programs,
    223–224
  in traditional schools,
    220–221
Formal structures, influence
    from, 8
Forman, G., 162, 224, 340
Foster care, children's books
    about, 362
Foster children, 64–65
Foster families, 64–65

Foster roles and responsibilities, parents, 171–174
Fraenkel, P., 111, 130, 156
Frazier, E. R., 217
Freud, Sigmund, 31
Froebel, Friedrich, 37
Froebelian programs, 39
Fuller, B., 352
Fuller, M. L., 161, 162, 314
Fundamentals of Special Education, 227
Furst, EJ, 150
Furstenberg, F., 194, 195
Futrell, M. H., 170, 253

Galinsky, E., 130, 136, 272
Gallagher, K. S., 157
Galle, O., 177
Gallego, M. A., 7
Gallup, A. M., 5, 163, 279
Games, 186, 188
  family interactions, 106
Gamse, B., 335
Gandini, L., 162, 224, 340, 341, 342
Gandra, P., 51
Gangs, 251, 262, 277
Garbarino, J., 14, 105, 112, 156, 160, 171, 206, 248, 262, 270, 271, 277, 279, 281
Garcia, E., 51
Gardner, H., 179, 186
Gardner, S., 328
Garn, G., 353
Garrison, M. E. B., 170
Gates, G., 122, 123
Gay and lesbian families, 65, 317
  children's books about, 363–364
Gearheart, B. R., 314
Gearheart, C. J., 314
Gender identification, siblings aiding, 175–177
Gender roles, 250
  parenting, 93–94
  responsibilities, 183
Gender socialization process, 93

Genetic and environmental factors, 3
Gersten, J. C., 112
Gesell, Arnold, 30
Gintis, H., 107
Giovanni, D., 342
Girls *vs.* boys, academic contributions, 7
Giroux, H. A., 143
Goals 2000: Educate America Act, 42, 279
Godbey, G., 95
Goelman, D., 118
Goertz, M. E., 279
Goetz, E., 72, 75
Goffin, S. G., 130
Goffman, E., 184
Goleman, D., 265
Gollnick, D. M., 47, 48, 51, 78, 79, 81, 227
Gomez, J., 170, 253
Gonzalez-Mena, J., 67, 140, 270
Good, T. L., 216, 217, 275, 280, 325, 350
Goodlad, J., 325
Goodnow, J. J., 170
Gorder, C., 195, 196, 197
Gordon, I. J., 310, 335
Gorsuch, R. L., 79
Gouvis, C., 248
Gove, W., 177
Governance
  of education, 160–165
  legal requirements, 161–162
Government action, 279
Government funding
  child care, 120
  resource and referral programs, 120
  school-age care, 120
Government remedies, child care, 120
Grandparents
  connection to nuclear family members, 191f
  curriculum, 190–195
  advantages of, 194–195, 194t
  custodial, 191

distant/nearby, 191, 193
  emotionally remote, 191
  influencing child development, 191–194
  providing curriculum, 190–195
Grant, C. A., 95
Grant Early Childhood Center, 345
Graue, M. E., 156
Gray, P., 60, 67, 213
Green, C., 308, 322
Green, E.., 98, 317
Green, E. T., 161
Greenberg, P., 332
Greene, M., 76, 264
Greene, S. M., 109, 110
Greenfield, P. M., 98, 99
Greenhaus, J. H., 258
Greenspan, S., 108, 114, 136, 137, 263
Greif, G. L., 8, 67, 76, 264
Grief, 314–315
Gronlund, G., 299
Group norms, 16
Groups, list of, 22
Group-sanctioned modes of behavior, 16
Groves, B., 14
Growing community influence, 14–15
Growing Without Schooling, 195
Growth
  factors, 3
  role children played, 3
Grumbine, E., 242
Gruskin, S. J., 43
Guck, T. P., 112
Gunter, B., 19, 20, 153, 267
Gutek, G. L., 50, 52
Guterson, D., 195
Gutieniz, K., 51
Gutrel, F., 245

Haberman, M., 150, 158
Haddock, S. A., 91, 94
Hafner, K., 21, 267, 269
Hagan, J. L., 45

Haley, A., 95
Hall, G. Stanley, 40
Hammer, T. J., 270, 271
Hammittee, D., 314
Hand washing, 147
Handel, G., 250
Handicapped, 45
Hanhan, S. F., 318
Hard-to-reach parents, 265
Harlan, J. D., 258
Harold, R., 7
Harrington, M., 125
Harris, J., 6, 15, 16, 151, 171, 177, 285
Hart, B., 103, 104, 225, 266, 289
Hart, C. H., 264
Hart and Risley studies, parenting, 103–104
Hartman, A., 121, 138
Hartup, W. W., 16, 250
Hasidic sects, family diversity, 78
Hating Book, 246
Hayghe, H. V., 82
Haynes, N. M., 110, 327, 330, 335, 336, 337, 338, 339, 356
Head Start, 44–45, 144, 147, 295–296, 309, 331–334
  health, 333
  literacy, 266
  outgrowths of, 334–335
  parental involvement, 331–332
  research, 332–333
Health
  Head Start, 333
  marginalized families, 269
  parent education, 269
  poverty, 269
Health education, 147, 148, 268–269
Health services, 281
Heath, S. D., 6, 14, 150, 179, 266
Heaverside, S., 43
Helbum, S., 136
Helm, J., 311
Hembrooke, H. A., 3
Henderson, A. T., 163
Hendrick, J., 162, 343

Hendrix, D., 250
Henniger, M. L., 92, 301
Henze, R. C., 66
Hetherington, E. M., 11, 13, 59, 64, 109, 110, 177
Hidden curriculum, 205, 225–227
High standards, child care quality, 135
Hildebrand, V., 60, 67, 190, 195
Hill, E., 150, 177
Hillis, M. R., 97
Hines, R. P., 60, 67
Hispanic Americans, advancing children's education, 50
Historical and philosophical perspectives, 27–56
Historic class descriptions, 70–71
Hodges, E. V. E., 252
Hoffer, T. B., 8, 96
Hofferth, S. L., 136
Hoge, D. R., 78, 79
Holidays, observance, 79
Holmbeck, G. N., 101
Holt, J. C., 158
Holt, John, 195
Home. *See also* Families
  curriculum, 170–201, 172f, 225–227
  influence on children
    early age, 9–16
  physical environment, 177–179
Home governance, 162–164
Home influence
  attitudes, 5–6
  early years, 9
  influence on children, 10
  perceptions, 5–6
Home learning, 179–190
Home nurturance, inadequate, 157–158
Home responsibility, 144–147
Home schooling, 170, 195–200
  chronological phases for, 195
  cooperation, 196
  court confrontations, 195
  criticism of, 199–200

curriculum guides, 197
defined, 195
demographics of, 196–197
history of, 195–196
legal aspects of, 199
motivation for, 196
networking, 196
professional implications, 200
successes of, 199–200
teaching methods in, 197–198
Home Start, 44–45
Home *vs.* school expectations, 174
Home visits, 295–296, 305t
  innovative practices, 296
  traditional practices, 296
Homeless families, 75, 316–317
  children's books about, 363
Homework, 297–298
  community libraries, 298
  hotline, 298
Homes, schools, and communities
  historical patterns, advancing children's education, 32–34
Homogenized American ethic, 47
Homophobia, 276
Honig, A. S., 13
Household income levels, 73f
How Children Fail, 158
Howard, V. F., 314
Howes, C., 130, 136
Hrabowski, F. A., 8, 67, 76, 264
Hranitz, J, R., 316
Huesman, L. R., 20
Humanism, 207t
Hundred Languages of Children, 224
Hunter, Madeline, 210
Hurd, T. L., 331
Hurst, C. O., 242
Huston, P., 21, 84, 245
Hygienic, 270
Hymowitz, K. S., 179

Ideologues, 196
IKnowthat.com, 267
Illich, Ivan, 195

Illiteracy, 267

Illness, stressor in families,
   112–114

Immersion and submersion
   programs, 68

Immigrants
   children's books about, 363
   family diversity, 79

Immigration, advancing
   children's education, 47

Inclusion, 46, 228, 274–275

Inclusive schools, 14

Income, distribution of, 73f

Income levels of U.S.
   households, 73f

Individual differences, 274–275

Individual fulfillment, 207t

Individual responsibility,
   354–355
   professional implications,
   355

Individualized education
   program (IEP), 45, 228–229

Individualized family service
   plan (IFSP), 45, 229

Individualized instruction, 247

Individuals with Disabilities
   Education Act (IDEA), 45,
   309

Induction, 265

Industrial Revolution
   advancing children's
   education, 37
   family diversity, 80

Infant care, cultural groups, 98

Infant–toddler care programs,
   government funding, 120

Infant–toddler programs,
   127–128

Influences
   parent and child, 4
   positively and negatively, 3

Informal contacts, 297, 305t

Informal curriculum, 143, 144,
   205, 224–225

Informal notes, 299

Information age, 81

In-home child care, 118,
   125–126

Institutional structures, child
   care quality, 135

Intellectual development, 14
   print media, 18–19
   space influencing, 177–178

Intellectual stimuli, 265–266

Interaction, 146
   parent and child, 4
   patterns, 53
      multicultural education, 52
   quality, 104f
   styles within family, 100–104

Interactionism, 29t

Interactionist-constructionist
   theories, 3

Interactionist-constructivist
   view, 31

Interactive portfolios, 299

Interactive skills, developing,
   270

Interactive-constructive
   perspective, 28

Interests, 143, 270
   sharing, 184–187

Interethnic families, 69
   family diversity, 69

Interethnic marriages, 69

Internal control, 265, 265t

Internet, 21, 247, 267–268
   filters, 283
   impact on children, 16f
   rules for safety, 269t
   sites, 245

Interracial marriages, 69

Intimacy, 12–13

Intimidation, 265

Isenberg, J. P., 231

Islam, family diversity, 78

Islamic presence, 51–53

Itinerant families, 75

Jacobson, S. K., 242

Jalongo, M. R., 231

Janosik, E., 99, 317

Jansorn, N., 322, 325, 345, 346,
   348, 356

Jencks, C., 107

Jenkins, D. B., 275

Jenkins, E. J., 277

Jeub, C., 196

Johnson, M. H.., 146

Johnson, V. R., 146

Jones, G. W., 84

Jordan, K. F., 36, 46, 62, 67, 68,
   162, 208, 227, 264, 278,
   279

Joyce, B., 216, 280

Joyner, E., 327, 330, 337, 338,
   339, 340, 356

Judaism, family diversity, 78

JuniorNet.com, 267

Kagan, S. L., 39, 43, 52, 248

Kanna, E., 195, 196, 197, 199

Kaplan, L., 287

Karpowitz, D. H., 106

Kaslow, F. W., 110

Kasten, W. C., 6

Kearney, M., 325

Kelly, J., 11, 13, 59, 110

Kerman, K., 195

Khan, S., 76, 335

Kidder, T., 155

Kidfu.com, 267

KidWatch, 283

Kidwell, C. S., 48

Kieff, J. E., 145

Kinch, A. F., 134

Kindergartens, 39
   extensions of, 39

Kin relationships, cultural
   differences, 193–194

Kinship adoption, 64

Kiyosaki, R., 195, 196, 197, 199

Knowles, J. G., 195

Kochenderfer, R., 195, 196, 197,
   199

Kohl, Herbert, 195

Kontos, S., 130, 136

Kostelny, K., 105, 112, 160, 206,
   248, 262, 279

Kotlowitz, A., 112, 160, 262,
   279, 325

Kozol, J., 23, 158, 195

Kralovec, E., 276, 298

Krashinsky, M., 146

Krathwohl, D. W., 150

Krol-Sinclair, B., 156
Kumove, L., 249
Kyle, D. W., 212

Ladd, G. W., 150, 151, 285
Lancaster, P. E., 113
Landurand, P., 170
Language, 146, 148
    parenting, 101
Language development,
    parenting, 103
Language differences, 303
Language patterns, 266
Language tolerance,
    professional implications,
    83
Lawler-Prince, D., 298
Laws, advancing children's
    education, 37
Lazar, I., 44
Lazzara, I., 144
Leach, P., 12, 112, 155, 165,
    268, 271
Leal, D., 44, 45, 77, 227, 228
Learning, 143–155
    roles and responsibilities,
    171–177
    strategies, 69f
    styles, 69f, 186
Least restrictive environment,
    45, 228
LeCompte, M. D., 231, 278
Lee, S. W., 112, 310
Lefcourt, H. M., 265
LeFrancois, G. R., 90
Legal aspects, home schooling,
    199
Legal requirements, 161
Legislation advancing
    children's education, 37,
    42
Lein, L., 64
Leland, C. H., 6
Lepper, C., 314
Lerner, R. M., 314, 331
Leslie, T., 199
Letiecq, B. L., 180
Letters, 293
Levin, D. E., 26, 93

Levine, D. U., 71
Levine, R. F., 71
Levy, D. E., 184
Lewis, J., 11, 109
Libraries, 242, 243
Lichter, D. T., 47, 48, 72, 74, 77,
    249
Lifestyles, professional
    implications, 83
Lightfoot, S. L., 144
Lilly, E., 308, 322
Lim, S., 318
Limited-English-proficiency
    families, 68
Lin, H., 17, 248, 267, 269
Lindner, H., 78, 79, 282
Lindsey, E. W., 183
Lines, P., 196, 197, 198, 199,
    200
Linguistic assistance, need for,
    68
Linguistically diverse families,
    156
Linn, M. I., 345
Listening, 318
Liston, D. P., 204, 205, 262, 280,
    287, 289
Literacy
    development, 184
    events, 242–243
    Head Start, 266
    interactions, 6f, 146
    learning party, 310
    skills, 148
Literary stimuli, 265–266
Lobbyists, 276
Local schools, disenchantment
    with, 195
Local-level decisions, 161
Locke, John, 28–30
Locus of control, 270
Lombardi, J., 139, 140
Lott, Thaddeus, 351
Louv, C., 253
Love, providing, 90
Lowenthal, B., 314
Lower working class, 71
Low-SES families, 76
Lyness, K. P., 91, 94

Macaulay, D., 105
Maccoby, E. E., 3, 101, 104, 264
Macedo, D. P., 8
MacLaughlin, M. W., 14
Maeroff, G. I., 158
Magazines, 245
Maggie's American Dream, 325
Magnuson, K. A., 235
Mahood, H. R., 23
Mainstreamed, 46, 228
Mallett, L., 105
Mann, Horace, 38
Manno, B., 351, 353
Marans, S., 14
Marburger, C. L., 163
Mardell, B., 136
Mares, M., 20
Marginalized families
    health, 269
    support from, 157–158
Marginalized learners, 210
Marlow, S., 195
Marsh, C., 207
Marsland, K. W., 136
Martin, J., 101, 104, 264
Masia, B. B., 150
Maslow, Herbert, 9
Maslow, A. H., 9, 89
Maslow's hierarchy of needs,
    90f
Mason, C., 64
Materials, 310–311
    community as resource for,
    312–313
Math competencies, 148
Math development, interrelated
    in home, school, and
    community, 151f
Maton, K. L., 8, 67, 76, 264
Maxwell, J. J., 51
Mayberry, M., 195
Mayer, S., 76
McAleer, J., 19, 20, 153, 267
McDermott, D., 98
McFalls, J. A., 106
McGee, L. M., 266
McGee-Banks, C. A., 84
McGillicuddy-DeLisi, A. V., 5,
    170, 266

McGoldrick, M., 96, 98
McIntyre, E., 212
McKay, G. D., 310
McKinney Homeless Assistance
    Act of 1987 (PL 100–77),
    316
McMillan, Margaret, 40
McNeil, J. D., 148, 208
McPherson, J., 177
Meadows, S., 11
Mealtime, 179, 180–182
Media, 283
    forms
    and configurations, 245–248
    greatest impact, 17
    influence, 16–22
    on children, 19f
    vehicles, list of, 16
    violence, 20
Mediavilla, C., 298
Meier, D., 24, 204, 208, 210,
    247, 263, 325
Melting-pot thesis, 51
Melton, J. G., 78, 79
Melzi, G., 156
Memory recall, 16f
Mental health team, Corner's
    School Development
    Program, 336
Mentors, 308
Meredith, M., 218
Merenda, D. W., 43
Meringoff, L. K., 17
Mesosystem, 171
    of outer linkages, 13–14
Metacognitive strategies, 249
Metcalf, K. K., 275
Metha, A., 36, 46, 62, 67, 68,
    162, 208, 227, 264, 278, 279
Metz, E. G., 107, 155, 156
Mexican American populations,
    advancing children's
    education, 50
Microsystem of home, 13–14
Middle- and lower middle-class
    families, 71
Middle- and upper income
    families
    at-risk children, 72

Middle-class families, 71
    child care, 121
Middle-income families, 73
Migrant families, 75–76,
    316–317
    children's books about, 363
Migrant workers, 75
Miles, J., 242
Miller, K. B., 212, 318
Mills, K., 56
Minorities and the community,
    48–49
Minority populations
    advancing children's
    education, 47
    growth, 68f
Minority populations and
    families, advancing
    children's education, 48
Minority status, family
    diversity, 67–68
Mitchell, C. J., 42
Mitchell, S. T., 146
Mixed race, 69
Mobility of families, 106–107,
    144–145
Mock elections, 239
Modeling, 270
Models, parents, 5–6
Moen, P., 14, 270, 271
Monroe, L., 107
Moomaw, S., 84
Moore, G. H., 212, 253
Morals, 265, 270
Moriarty, M. L., 155, 157, 309
Morris, M., 72
Morse, S. C., 75
Mosher-Williams, R., 75, 82
Mosques, 282
Moss, P., 108
Mother's-day-out programs, 129
Motivation, home schooling,
    196
Mr. Rogers' Neighborhood, 245,
    267
Mukhopadhyay, C., 66
Multicultural classroom, 54f
Multicultural curriculum, 53
Multicultural education, 95

advancing children's
    education
    attitude, 52
    curriculum and materials,
    52
    interaction patterns, 52
staffing patterns
    advancing children's
    education, 52
Multicultural Education in a
    Pluralistic Society, 227
Multicultural ethic, 83
Multigenerational family unit,
    61–62
Multigenerational households,
    children's books about,
    362–363
Multiracial and lesbian
    families, 80
Multiracial children and adults,
    2000 census, 94f
Murphy, J., 151, 351, 352
Murray, J. P., 22, 147
Mutual respect, 317–318

Naisknov, A., 352
Nash, M., 9
National Association for the
    Education of Young
    Children's (NAEYC)
    Academy for Early
    Childhood Program
    Accreditation, 130
    code of ethical conduct,
    365–371
National Association of Family
    Child Care (NAFCC), 129
National Association of Parents
    and Teachers, 40
National Challenged
    Homeschools Associates,
    199
National goals and standards,
    278–279
National Home Education
    Network, 199
National Institute of Child
    Health and Human
    Development (NIHCD), 263

National Network of
  Partnership Schools,
  345–350
    action team, 348–349
    objectives of, 346–347
    organization, 349
    outgrowth, 350
    principles of, 347–348
    research, 349–350
National Resource Center for
  Health and Safety in Child
  Care
  and Web site, 129
Nation at Risk, 278–279
Nation Prepared, 279
Native Americans
  communities, advancing
    children's education, 48, 49
  cultural beliefs, 98f
  religious practices, family
    diversity, 78
Nativism, 29t
Natural environment, 253–255
  exploration of, 198
Natural phenomena, 266
Natural resources, 236t
Natural science competencies,
  148
Nature and nurture, 9
Nature books, 253
Nature-nurture controversy, 28
Nearby grandparents, 191, 193
Need recognition, child care
  quality, 135
Neglect of children, 112
Negotiating skills, 146, 148
Neighborhoods, 248–252
  ambiance, 249
  and community, 14
  learning from, 235
Neill, A. S., 212
Neito, S., 315
NetNanny, 267
Networking, home schooling,
  196
Networking skills, 240
Neuman, M. J., 17, 52, 316
New, R., 340, 344
New Deal programs, 44

Newberger, J. J., 10
Newman, R., 16, 185, 187
Newsletters, 298–299
Newspapers, 245
Niegro, S., 239, 240, 241, 249
No Child Left Behind (NCLB),
  23, 42–43, 208, 210, 242,
  279
Noddings, N., 270, 281
Nondiscriminatory evaluation,
  228
Nontraditional families,
  prejudices toward, 60
Nonverbal interactions, 319
Norm-referenced testing, 210
Notar, E. E., 20, 278
Nuclear families, 61, 72
Nursery schools, 40
Nurturance
  communities, 159–160
  families, 88–91, 155–158
  natural tendency to, 156–157
  schools, 158–159
Nurturing adults, characteristics
  of, 156–157
Nutrition, 268–269, 269

Oak Meadows, 197
Oehlberg, B., 108
Ogbu, J. U., 8
O'Hare, W. P., 45, 66, 74
Oladele, F., 174, 184
Olsen, G., 161, 162, 314
Olson, M. R., 110
O'Neil, J., 328, 353
Ooms, T., 163
Open space buildings, 218, 219f
Opie, I. A., 184
Opie, P., 184
O'Reilly, R. C., 161
Organizing schools, 213–218
Orphanages, children's books
  about, 362
O'Shea, D. J., 314
O'Shea, L., 314
Osofsky, J. D., 113, 325
Outdoors, 253
Out-of-home care, Out-of-
  wedlock births, 81

influence, 13
Owens, K., 11

Padua, S. M., 242
Paik, S., 22
Paikoff, R., 101
Palanki, A., 324, 349
Pamphlets, 245
Papert, S., 247
Paratore, J. R., 6, 144, 155, 156,
  157
Pardeck, J. T., 239
Pardo, C., 105, 206, 248, 262
Parent
  as advocate, 309
  attitudes and feelings,
    influence on children, 5–6
  behaviors and attitudes,
    impact on development, 4
  centers, 310
  community involvement, 244
  cooperatives, 40
  education, 40, 309–310
    child care quality, 135
    health, 269
    for increase child support,
      157
  environment, influence on
    children, 10
  establishing communication
    with, 296–304
  foster roles and
    responsibilities, 171–174
  influence on children,
    negative attitudes, 5–6
  involved in conferences, 301
  involvement
    in child care, 134
    Head Start, 331–332
    in schools, 39
  knowledge of child
    development, 268
  as learners, 332
  models, 5–6
  nursery schools, cooperative,
    162–163
  as observers, 331–332
  participation, 228
  as partners, 331

Parent (*continued*)
  responsibilities of, 144–147
  rights of choice, 199
  as school resources, 308–309
  in schools, 304–311
  support children's learning,
    332
  training, 310
  as volunteers, 306–308
Parent Effectiveness Training,
  310
Parenting
  advice on, 263
  attitudes, 93
  authoritarian, 100
  authoritative, 100
  beliefs, 93
  Bernstein's work, 101
  child care arrangements, 107
  children with disabilities,
    112–113
  competent families, 113–114
  discourse function, 103
  divorce consequences, 109
  dual-income families, 110
  educational underpinnings,
    95
  emotional bonds, 93
  ethnic and cultural groups, 97
  family role, cultures, 99
  financial aspects of divorce,
    109
  gender roles, 93
  Hart and Risley studies,
    103–104
  implications for
    professionals, 114
  influence on children, 87–116
  language, 102
    development, 103
  person-oriented family, 102
  position-oriented family, 102
  racial and ethnic identity,
    94–96
  sentence usage, 103
  separation and divorce,
    109–110
  skill levels and experience,
    105

  storytelling, 106
  stress in families, 108–109
  styles, Baumrind's
    classification, 100–101
  valence of communications,
    104
  values, 93
  various cultures, 97–98
  vocabulary, 103
Parent-school-community
  partnerships, 52, 324–356
  models for, 328f, 334f
  program models, 331–351
Parent-Teacher Association
  (PTA), 40
Parent-teacher conferences,
  299–301, 302f, 305t
Parent-teacher strategies,
  communication, 305t
Parke, R. D., 15
Parks, 240–241, 242
Partnerships, 292–321
  achieving, 354–355
  advancing children's
    education, 43–44
  features of, 354
Pathfinder Learning Center, 212
Patriarchal society, advancing
  children's education, 35
Patterns, family, 92
Pavao, J. M., 64
Peabody, Elizabeth, 39
Pedagogues, 196
  Children's, 285
  influence, 15–16
  settings, 250–252
Peer victimization, 251
Pence, A., 108, 118
Perceptions
  community influence, 8
  home influence, 5–6
  school influence, 6–8
Perinatal services, 281
Peripheral participation, 179
Permissive parenting, 100
Perry, D. G., 16
Perry, J., 253
Personal meaning, reading *vs.*
  television, 17

Personal relevance, 207t, 208,
  212–213
Personal relevance programs,
  formal curriculum,
  223–224
Personal Responsibility and
  Work Opportunity
  Reconciliation Act of 1996
  (PL 104–93), 120–121
Person-oriented family,
  parenting, 102
Pestalozzi, Johann, 37
Pettit, G. S., 150, 151
Phenice, L. A., 60, 67
Philosophical positions, 319
Physical abuse, 149t
Physical competencies, 148
Physical contact, cultural
  groups, 99
Physical development
  print media, 18
  space influencing, 178–179
Physical endurance, 251
Physical environment of home,
  177–179
Physical facilities, problems
  with, 276
Physical health, 270
Physical neglect, 149t
Physical safety, 89
Physiological needs, 89
Piaget, Jean, 9, 31
Pierce, S. H., 170
Pinker, S., 9, 39, 208
Pinnell, G. S., 266
Pipher, M., 11, 112
PL 89–10, 44
PL 94–142, 45, 161
PL 99–457, 45
PL 100–77, 316
PL 104–93, 120–121
Play activities, 253
Play-oriented curriculum, 40
Point of view, 303
Polakow, V., 112
Poland, S., 144
Police department, 237
Policy advocates, 276–277
Political agencies, 239–241

Political correctness, 53
Polly, J. A., 289
Poor communities, 240
Popin, M., 310
Port, P., 314
Position-oriented family,
    parenting, 102
Positive adult groups, 284–285
Positive and secure
    environments, influence on
    children, 10
Positive nurturance, features of,
    89–91
Positive relationships, 317–319
Postcards, 293
Postindustrial era
    family diversity, 81
Postnuclear family units, 64
Post-racial period, 70
Poverty, 11
    children, 111f
    family diversity, 74–75
    health, 269
    increasing, 264
    influence on children, 44
    parenting, 111–112
    social ties, 249
Powell, D. R., 296
Prasuraman, S., 258
Prejudice, 276
Prenatal services, 281
Preschool and Early
    Intervention Program Act
    (PL 99–457), 45
Preschool and kindergarten
    years, 13–14
Preschool day, sample schedule
    for, 128t
Preschool intelligence, risk
    factors, 109f
Preschool programs, 128,
    206–207, 228
Prescott, A. B., 262
Priesnitz, H., 198
Primary caregiver, emotional
    support, 12f
Primary years, 14–15
Print media, 16, 245
    influence on children, 18–19

intellectual development,
    18–19
    physical development, 18
Problem-solving skills,
    developing, 271
Problem-solving stage, 32
Process elements, child care,
    132
Process quality, definition,
    132
Proctor, P., 7
Professionals. *See also* Teachers
    implications for, 24–25,
    53–54
    diversity, 83
    family diversity, 83
    individual responsibility,
    355
    language tolerance, 83
    lifestyles, 83
    parenting, 115
Project Follow Through, 44–45
Project-oriented curriculum,
    350
Prop boxes, 316
Protecting children, 141–166
Protective factors, 271
Protestant ethic, 264
Protestant religious heritage,
    77–79
Protestants, family diversity, 78
Psychoanalytical
    (psychological) theory,
    29t–30t, 31
Psychological and
    socialization support, 11
Psychology, 39
Public Broadcasting System,
    245
Public schools and family
    diversity, 60–61
Published materials, 266
Puckett, M. B., 146
Punishment, 265
Pupil personnel team, Comer's
    School Development
    Program, 336
Puritans, advancing children's
    education, 36f, 37

Qualities of caregivers, child
    care, 132
Quint, S., 263, 281

Race, family diversity, 70
Race labels, 66
Racial, ethnic, and cultural
    factors
    family diversity, 66–67
Racial and ethnic identity
    parenting, 94–96
Racism, 276
Ramey, C. T., 6, 14
Ramirez-Smith, C., 339
Ramsey, S. L., 77, 94, 95, 104
Randolph, S. M., 235, 248
Rankin, B., 342
Ravitch, D., 26
Ray, B., 195, 196, 200
Raywid, M. A., 351
Reading, 186, 312–313
    academic success, 6
Reading *vs.* television, personal
    meaning, 17
Real Life Homeschooling, 198
Rebore, R. W., 36, 37
Reconstituted family, 64
Reconstructionist, 207t
Recreation skills, 148
Recreational facilities, 242,
    243
Recreational pursuits, 271
Reggio Emilia, 340–345
    goals of, 340
    implementation of, 342
    network, 343f
    organization of, 341–342
    outgrowths of, 344–345
    philosophical perspective of,
    340
    programs of, 340–341
    research and evaluation of,
    342–343
Rehabilitation Act, 44
Reich, R., 196, 197
Reid, R., 128, 133, 140
Religion, applications of, 79–80
Religious ceremonies, 184
Religious groups, codes, 79–80

Religious institutions, 153–154, 282

Religious orientation, family diversity, 77–80

Religious participation, drop in, 282

Reppucci, N. D., 112, 143, 162

Residential mobility, 106

Resilient children, 271

Resource and referral programs, government funding, 120

Responding, preventing, monitoring, mentoring, modeling (RPMS), 263

Responsibilities, 174
  linking, 153–154

Responsive environment, influence on children, 10

Restaurants, 256

Reynolds, D., 289

Rice, M. L., 245

Rich, D., 272, 280

Rich, J. M., 48, 50

Richards, M. H., 104

Richgels, D. J., 266

Ridley, M., 208

Rinaldi, C., 212

Risk factors, preschool intelligence, 109f

Risks, 192

Risley, T. R., 103, 104, 225, 266, 289

Rituals, 184

Rivkin, M. C., 146, 258

Roberts, D. D., 235, 248

Robinson, J. D., 95

Roedell, W. C., 250

Role identification, siblings aiding, 175–177

Roles and rituals, extended family, 174–175

Roman Catholic, family diversity, 78

Romanowski, M. H., 75

Root, M. P., 69

Rose, L. D., 5, 163, 279

Rosegrant, T., 207

Roskos, K., 16, 316

Rousseau, Jean-Jacques, 30, 37

Rowe, D. C., 6, 15

Rubin, H., 325, 327, 330

Rupp, R., 197

Sadker, D. M., 7, 37, 50, 53, 98, 250, 265, 276

Sadker, M. P., 7, 37, 50, 53, 98, 250, 265, 276

Safety, 192

Salend, S. J., 53

Salinas, K., 322, 325, 345, 346, 348, 356

Salmon, J., 136, 137

Salzstein, H. D., 270

Sameroff, A., 3, 108, 114, 263

Same-sex marriages, 65

Same-sex partnerships, 81

Sanders, M., 322, 325, 345, 346, 348, 356

Sanderson, S. K., 34

Sanitation, 270

Saul, W., 185

Scarf, M., 105, 112, 265, 270

Scarr, S., 119, 136

Schaffer, G., 289

Schedules, traditional, 220–221

Scheeringa, M. S., 112

Schlossman, S., 40, 41

Schmidt, S., 122, 123

School
  activities
    middle income families, 74f
    religious affiliations, 78f
  advancing children's education, 28, 38–44
  changes in, 278
  curriculum, 204–231
    professional implications, 230
  decisions, parents right to challenge, 46
  disenchanted with, 195
  educative processes, results of, 229–230
  evaluation of, 279–280, 280t
  expectations vs. home expectations, 174
  funds availability, student perception, 8

governance, 163–164, 163f
hidden curriculum, 225–227
influence, 4f, 13–14
  attitudes, 6–8
  perceptions, 6–8
influence on children, early age, 9–16
nurturance, 158–159
parents opinion, 5–6
performance, 14
personnel
  attitude toward families status, 7
  expectations of children, 7
personnel affected by, influence on children, 2
physical organization of, 218
planning and management team, Comer's School Development Program, 336
positive features of, 275
programs, 205–206
funds availability, 8
public opinion, 5–6
reinforce, 3
resources, community members for, 308–309
responsibility of, 147–148
sports funds availability student perception, 8
visitation, 304–305
voucher plans, 79

School-age care, 128–129
  government funding, 120

School-identified disabilities, 77

Schorr, J., 352, 353

Schorr, L. B., 112, 230

Schott, J. C., 23

Schwartz, L. L., 111

Schweinhart, L. J., 14, 135, 210, 332

Science museums, 242

Scope and sequence charts, 211

Scully, J. L., 84

Scully, P., 26, 109, 222

Seefeldt, C., 26, 40, 103, 119, 146, 222, 271, 310

Seifer, R., 108, 114, 263
Self-actualization, 91
Sensory play, 146
Sentence usage, parenting, 103
Separation and divorce,
  parenting, 109–110
Service agencies, 236, 237
Service personnel, 217
Sesame Street, 245, 267
Sex education, 147, 148, 319
Sexism, 276
Sexual abuse, 149t
Sexual behavior, family
  diversity, 81
Sexual energy, 31
Sexual understandings, 250
Shaffer, A., 245
Shank, M., 44, 45, 77, 227,
  228
Sheldon, S. B., 349
Shelters, children's books
  about, 362
Shiffman, C. D., 351, 352
Shinn, M., 130, 136
Shoop, R. J., 162
Shopkeepers, 244
Siblings aiding
  gender identification,
    175–177
  role identification, 175–177
Sigel, I. E., 5, 170, 266
Significant adults, emotional
  support, 12f
Significant others, 250
Silber, J., 210
Simon, B., 325, 345, 346, 348,
  356
Singer, D. S., 16, 17, 19, 20, 21,
  93, 153, 267, 268, 269
Singer, J. L., 16, 17, 19, 20, 21,
  93, 153, 267, 268, 269
Single-parent families, 62–64,
  248
  children's books about,
    361–362
  percent of families with
    children, 110f
  structural variations, 63
Skill ladders, 211

Skill levels and experience,
  parenting, 105
Skills, sharing, 184–187
Skinner, B. F., 30
Slaby, R. G., 250
Sleeter, C. E., 95
Smeeding, T. M., 74
Smith, C. A., 115
Smith, M. S., 107
Smith, R. S., 105, 206, 263, 271,
  284
Smith, S., 44, 45, 77, 227, 228
Smrekar, C. E., 329
Snow, C. E., 266
Social agencies, 241–244
Social and cultural settings,
  262–289
Social capital, 14
Social classes, 70, 71f
Social-cultural agencies, 236
Social-cultural context, 29t–30t
  theorists, 31
Social development
  Head Start, 332–333
  print media, 18
Social environment, 270–271
Social factors, 3
Social meliorist, 207t
Social networks, 226, 236t,
  248–252, 255f, 284–285
Social reconstructionist, 208
Social services, 281–282, 316
  Head Start, 333
Social setting influences,
  according to age, 4f
Social settings, 286–287
Social skills, 148, 183, 199–200
Social ties, poverty, 249
Socialization, family, 92
Society, philosophical ideas,
  28
Socioeconomic factors, 183
Socioeconomic status (SES), 70
  and children's cognitive
    development and
    achievement, 76
  of families, 70–77
Sonenstein, F. L., 122, 123
Sorrentino, J. M., 140

Soup kitchens, 282
Space, influencing
  creative development,
    178–179
  emotional growth, 177
  intellectual development,
    177–178
  physical development,
    178–179
Spaggiari, S., 342
Spain, D., 64
Special education, curriculum,
  227–229
Special events, 304–306, 306t
Special guests, 312–313
Special needs, 274–275
  children's books about, 364
  children with, 44–51
Special-interest group
  influence, 22–24, 281, 284
Spencer, L. M., 42
Spewock, T. S., 310
Spitz, R., 13
Spock, Benjamin, 41
Sports, funds availability
  student perception, 8
Staff benefits, child care
  quality, 135
Staffing patterns, 52
Staffing plans, 214–215
Stallings, J., 226
Stanford, B. H., 109
Stanley-Hagan, M. M., 64, 177
Stein, C. B., 52, 53
Steinberg, L., 101
Stereotypes, 246, 276
Stevens, M. L., 196, 197, 198,
  199, 200
Stiggins, R. J., 212, 272
Stile, C., 6
Stille, A., 53
Stimuli, 143
Stinnett, N., 179
Story narratives, values, 274
Storytelling, 242
  parenting, 106
Story writing, 278
Straight Shooting, 210
Strasburger, B. C., 152

Stress in families, parenting, 108–109
Stringfield, S., 289
Stritikus, T., 51
Strom, R., 195
Strom, S., 195
Structural elements of child care environment, 131–132
Structure, traditional, 220–221
Structured English immersion (SEI), advancing children's education, 51
Students
  achievement, 271–273
    effect of community attitudes, 8
  involved in conferences, 301
  participation, 228
Studer, J. R., 318
Subfamilies, 64
Submersion programs, 68
Success, promoting, 90–91
Sugrue, T. J., 72, 187
Sulzby, E., 186
Surrogate parent program, 65
Surroundings, messages from, 3
Sutherland, Z., 19, 246, 277
Suzuki, L. K., 98, 99
Swanberg, J., 130, 136
Swap, W. M., 320
Swick, K. J., 75
Swift, D. W., 48
Synagogues, 282
Systemic Training for Effective Parenting, 310
Szasz, M. C., 48, 49

Taba, Hilda, 210
Tabors, P. O., 266
Takin, G., 245
Tao, F., 76, 335
Tapscott, D., 247
Tarr, H., 335
Taylor, J. H., 40, 234, 248, 250, 270
Teachers, 8, 215–217. *See also* Professionals
  advancing children's education, 43–44

discrimination, 7–8
effective, 275
fear of, 319
high achievers, differential treatment, 8
negative attributes of, 276
parent–teacher conferences, 305t
parent–teacher strategies, communication, 305t
personality, 276
preparation programs for, 287
understanding, 24
Teaching styles, 216t
Teachman, J. D., 73
Teale, W. H., 6, 186
Technologist, 207t, 208
Teddlie, C., 289
Teeth brushing, 147
Telephone answering machines, 299
Telephone contacts, 294
Teletubbies, 245
Televised advertising, 20
Television, 153, 186, 267–268
  aggression, 267–268
  impact of viewing on academic achievement, 21
  impact on children, 16f
  influence on children, 19–21
  sensible use of, 268t
  violence, 267–268
Temporary Assistance for Needy Families (TANF), 121
Ten, Nine, Eight, 245
Terzi, N., 342
Testa, R., 262
Theaters, 242
Theme-focused programs, 211
Thomas, A., 202
Thomas, J., 62, 81
Thomas, R. M., 29
Thornburgh, D., 17, 248, 267, 269
Through the Eyes of Innocents, 284
Tiedt, I. M., 66
Tiedt, P. L., 66

Time-on-task studies, 226
Title I schools, 43
Title I/Chapter I, 44–45
Tittle, C. K., 7
Toileting, 182–183
Tomlin, A. M., 191, 193
Tompkins, J. R., 75, 228, 274
Torelli, L., 128, 133, 140
Toys, 188
Traditional programs, 208–209
Traditional schools, 208
  classroom day, 221t
  formal curriculum, 220–221
Traditions, 98, 184
Trahan, C., 298
Transactional process of development, 3
Transcultural events, 14
Transportation services, 238–239
Transracial effect, 18
Travel, 188–190, 238–239
Travers, P. D., 36, 37
Trawick-Smith, J., 51, 207, 250
Truglio, R., 245
Trust, 246
Turnbull, A., 44, 45, 77, 227, 228
Turnbull, R., 44, 45, 77, 227, 228
Turner, P. H., 270, 271
Turning points, 271
Tutors, 308
TV-Turnoff Network, 153
20th-century households, family diversity, 81
Two-parent home with children, 61
Tyler, Ralph, 210
Underclass, 71–72
Underclass families, 74–75
Units of study, 197
Uphoff, J. K., 79
Upper class, 70–71
Upper middle-class families, 71
Upper working-class, 71
Urban society, 41–42
Urbanization, family diversity, 81

U. S. households, income levels, 73f
U. S. Office of Education, 41
Uttal, L., 121, 132

Valence of communications, parenting, 104
Valente, C., 162
Valente, W. D., 162
Values, 148, 196, 265, 273–274, 319
 development of, 146
 parenting, 93
 story narratives, 274
Van Evra, J., 17, 20, 21, 93, 153, 267, 268
Van Ijzendoorn, M. H., 6
Van Voorhis, F., 322, 325, 345, 346, 348, 356
V-chip, 153, 267, 283
Violence, 15, 246
 television, 267–268
Violent neighborhoods, 235
Virtual communities, 267
Visitations, child's role in, 306
Vissing, Y. M., 155
Vitaro, F., 252
Vocabulary, quality and richness, 103, 103f
Vocational skills, advancing children's education, 35
Voice, pitch and tone of, 303
Volunteers, 217–218, 306–308, 330
 appreciation of, 308–309
Vosler, N. R., 82
Voss, M. M., 105, 187
Vukelich, C., 146
Vygotsky, L., 31, 32

Wade, T. E., 197
Wagner, M., 77
Wagner, N. J., 253
Wagner, T., 210
Wagstaff, L. H., 157
Walberg, H. J., 77, 156, 350, 352
Walker, L. J., 270

Waller, P. L., 75
Wallerstein, J., 11, 109, 110
Walsh, F., 145
Walsh, M., 196
Wang, M. C., 350
Wardle, F., 127
War on poverty program, 23
Wasserman, S., 202
Watson, M. A., 4
Watts, J. C., 101
Weapons, 277
Webb, L. D., 36, 46, 62, 67, 68, 162, 208, 227, 264, 278, 279
Weber, S., 39, 245
Web filters, 153
Web sites, 247, 298–299
 controlling access to, 267
 National Resource Center for Health and Safety in Child Care, 129
Weekly progress report, 300f
Weikart, D. P., 14, 210, 332
Weil, M., 216, 280
Weinberg, M., 48, 50
Weinstein, T., 156
Weishahn, M., 314
Weiss, H., 143, 352
Welfare, 281–282
Welfare to work families, 72
Wells, S. S., 351, 353
Werner, E., 105, 206, 263, 271, 284
Wesley School, 351
Western, B., 72
Westman, J., 88, 92, 115
Where the Wild Things Are, 246
White, B. L., 101, 102
White, Burton, 41
White House Conference on Care of Dependent Children, 41
White's study, parenting, 101
Whitman, W., 2
Whole-language programs, 211
Wigfield, A., 7
Williams, B. F., 314

Williams, M. R., 156
Williams, W. L., 317
Willis, G., 207
Wilson, B., 152
Winn, M., 20, 21
Wittwer, F., 218
Women joining workforce, 81
Wood, G. S., 62, 81
Woodruff, D. W., 144
Woodward, E. H., 20
Woolard, J. L., 112, 143, 162
Woolfolk, A. E., 4
Working together, 292–321
Working-class families, 73–74
Workplaces, 270
Workshops
 for collaboration, 329–330
 Comer's School Development Program, 337
Works Progress Administration (WPA), 40–41
World War II, family diversity, 81
Wortham, S., 133
Wright, J. C., 21, 95, 245
Written communication, 297–298, 305t
Wu, S. T., 170
Wynter, L., 18, 70

Yamamoto, K., 108
Yell, M. L., 46
Young, K. T., 136
Young Men's Christian Association (YMCA), 126

Zajac, Chris, 155
Zax, M., 109, 114, 263
Zeanah, C. H., 112
Zeichner, K., 204, 205, 262, 280, 287, 289
Zelizer, V. A., 35
Zero rejection, 228
Zigler, E., 136
Zimmerman, T. S., 91, 94
Zone of proximal development, 32
Zuckerman, B., 14